尾田栄一郎

I've heard that some swimmers grow webbing between their fingers in order to be able to paddle harder. That's evolution. I'm always drawing manga, so I want to evolve somehow too. Like...having my fingernail become a pen tip. Or being able to see through the clothes of women on the street. And now, on with volume 51!!!

-Eiichiro Oda, 2008

Eiichiro Oda began his manga career at the age of 17, when his one-shot cowboy manga **Wanted!** won second place in the coveted Tezuka manga awards. Oda went on to work as an assistant to some of the biggest manga artists in the industry, including Nobuhiro Watsuki, before winning the Hop Step Award for new artists. His pirate adventure **One Piece**, which debuted in Weekly Shonen Jump in 1997, quickly became one of the most popular manga in Japan.

ONE PIECE VOL. 51
SABAODY PART 2

SHONEN JUMP Manga Edition

STORY AND ART BY EIICHIRO ODA

English Adaptation/Jason Thompson
Translation/John Werry
Touch-up Art & Lettering/John Hunt
Design/Sean Lee
Supervising Editor/Alexis Kirsch
Editor/Yuki Takagaki

Printed in the U.S.A.

Published by VIZ Media, LLC
P.O. Box 77010
San Francisco, CA 94107

10 9 8
First printing, June 2010
Eighth printing, December 2016

www.viz.com

THE WORLD'S
MOST POPULAR MANGA

SHONEN JUMP

www.shonenjump.com

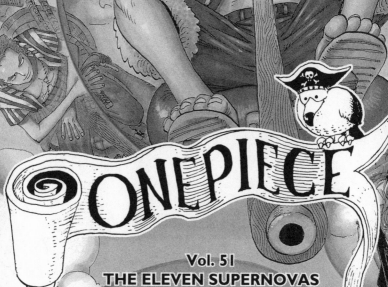

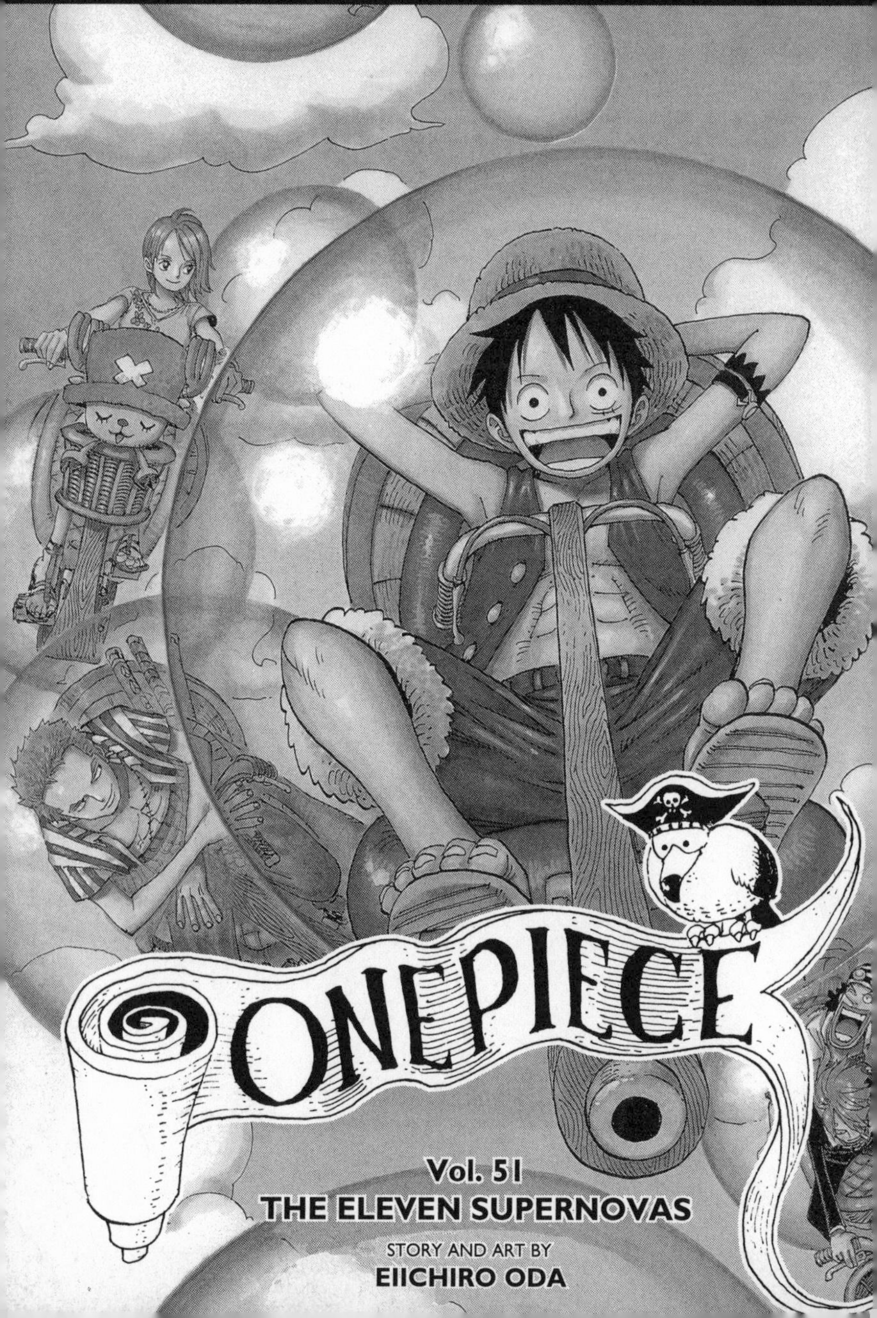

ONE PIECE

Vol. 51
THE ELEVEN SUPERNOVAS

STORY AND ART BY
EIICHIRO ODA

Designer in training and
octopus fritter store clerk
Kissing Gourami Mermaid

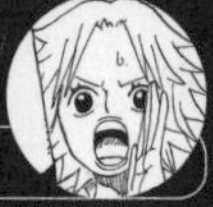

Camie

Starfish and designer of
the Criminal brand

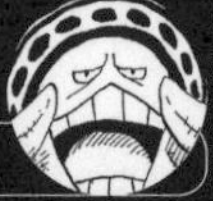

Pappagu

The Straw Hats

Total bounty:
700,000,050 berries

Boundlessly optimistic and able to
stretch like rubber, he is determined
to become King of the Pirates.
Bounty: 300 million berries

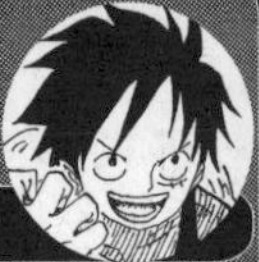

Monkey D. Luffy

A former bounty hunter and master
of the "three-sword" style. He aspires
to be the world's greatest swordsman.
Bounty: 120 million berries

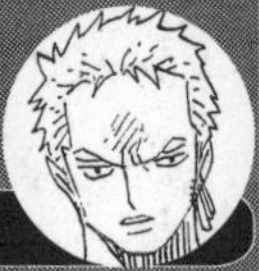

Roronoa Zolo

A thief who specializes in robbing
pirates. Nami hates pirates, but Luffy
convinced her to be his navigator.
Bounty: 16 million berries

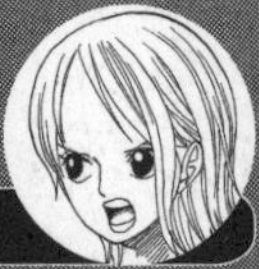

Nami

A village boy with a talent for telling
tall tales. His father, Yasopp, is a
member of Shanks's crew.
Bounty: 30 million berries (Sniper King)

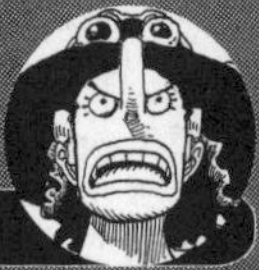

Usopp

The bighearted cook (and ladies'
man) whose dream is to find the
legendary sea, the "All Blue."
Bounty: 77 million berries

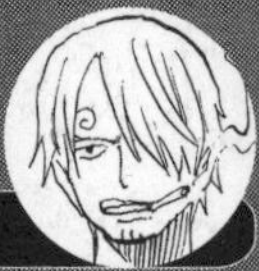

Sanji

A blue-nosed man-reindeer and
the ship's doctor.
Bounty: 50 berries

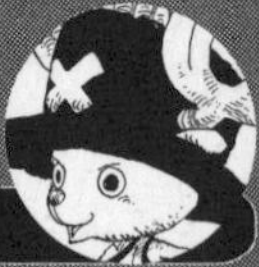

Tony Tony Chopper

A mysterious woman in search of
the Poneglyph on which true history
is recorded.
Bounty: 80 million berries

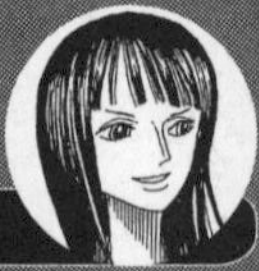

Nico Robin

A softhearted cyborg and talented
shipwright.
Bounty: 44 million berries

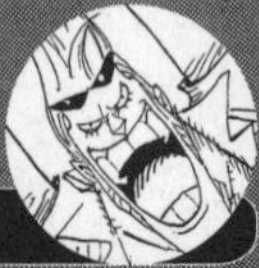

Franky

A musician swordsman whose
shadow was stolen. He's on a quest
to take it back.
Bounty: 33 million berries

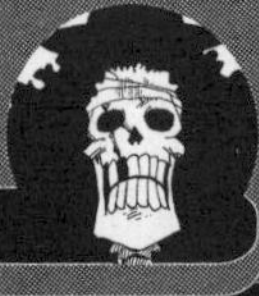

Brook

THE STORY OF ONE PIECE

Volume 51

Monkey D. Luffy started out as just a kid with a dream—to become the greatest pirate in history! Stirred by the tales of pirate "Red-Haired" Shanks, Luffy vowed to become a pirate himself. That was before the enchanted Devil Fruit gave Luffy the power to stretch like rubber, at the cost of being unable to swim—a serious handicap for an aspiring sea dog. Undeterred, Luffy set out to sea and recruited some crewmates—master swordsman Zolo; treasure-hunting thief Nami; lying sharpshooter Usopp; the high-kicking chef Sanji; Chopper, the walkin' talkin' reindeer doctor; mysterious archaeologist Robin; and cyborg shipwright Franky.

In their new ship made by Franky, the *Thousand Sunny*, Luffy and his crew head for Fish-Man Island, which lies directly along the route to the "New World." Along the way, they get lost in the dark and gloomy Florian Triangle, where they meet Brook, a living skeleton, sailing a ghost ship through the fog. Luffy invites Brook to join their crew, but Brook is unable to leave the Florian Triangle because his shadow has been stolen by Gecko Moria, one of the Seven Warlords of the Sea. The *Thousand Sunny* is ensnared by Gecko Moria's enormous pirate ship, *Thriller Bark*, and Gecko's crew attacks them with an army of ghosts and zombies. After an epic battle, the Straw Hat pirates manage to defeat the shadow-stealing Moria. But before they can recover from the fight they are confronted by another Warlord of the Sea, the incredibly strong Bartholomew Kuma! The crew is forced to flee, and in the process Zolo is badly injured.

Brook becomes an official member of the Straw Hat pirates, and the ship continues toward Fish-Man Island Along the way they encounter Camie, a mermaid, and her talking starfish. Camie's friend Hatchan has been taken by kidnappers, and Luffy and his crew agree to help rescue him. But along the way, they are attacked by the kidnappers' allies, the Flying Fish Riders, whose leader has a terrible grudge against the Straw Hats!

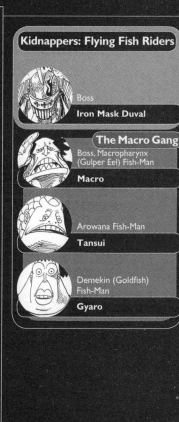

Kidnappers: Flying Fish Riders

Boss

Iron Mask Duval

The Macro Gang

Boss, Macropharynx (Gulper Eel) Fish-Man

Macro

Arowana Fish-Man

Tansui

Demekin (Goldfish) Fish-Man

Gyaro

A pirate that Luffy idolizes. Shanks gave Luffy his trademark straw hat.

"Red-Haired" Shanks

Vol. 51
The Eleven Supernovas

CONTENTS

Chapter 492: Iron Mask Duval   7

Chapter 493: You Know Me   27

Chapter 494: Duval's Tragedy   47

Chapter 495: Gaon Cannon   67

Chapter 496: Yarukiman Mangrove   87

Chapter 497: Adventure on the Archipelago of Dancing Soap Bubbles   107

Chapter 498: The Eleven Supernovas   127

Chapter 499: Sabaody Park   147

Chapter 500: The Embers of History   167

Chapter 501: The World Begins to Swell   187

Chapter 502: The Incident of the Celestial Dragons   207

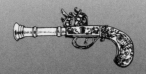

Chapter 492:
IRON MASK DUVAL

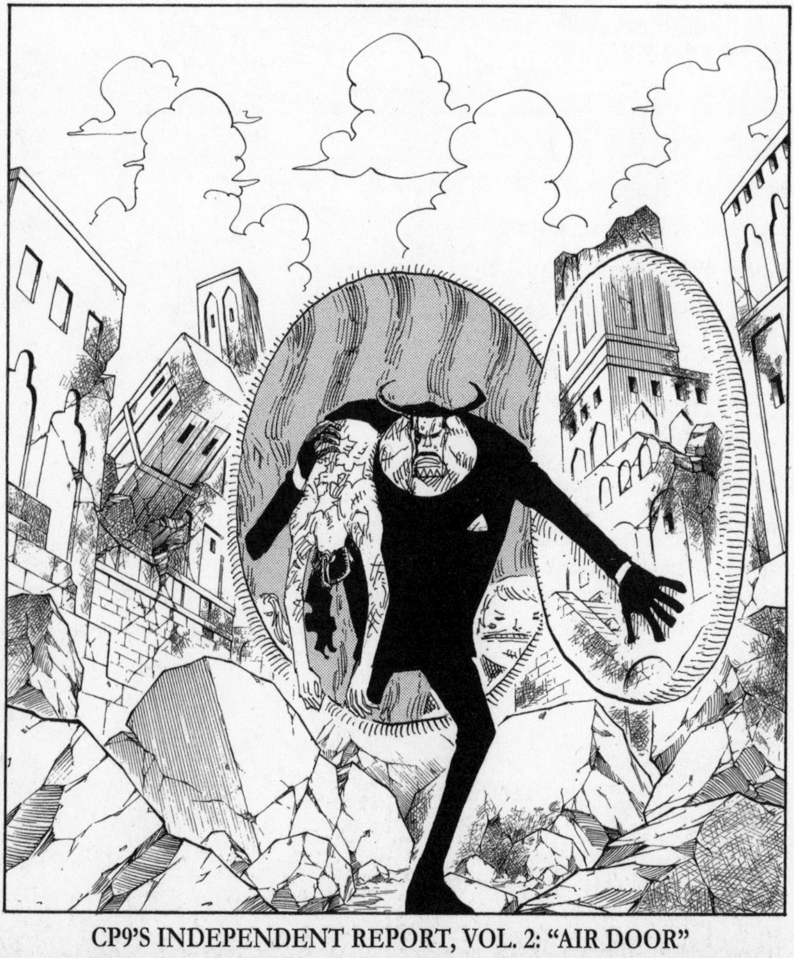

CP9'S INDEPENDENT REPORT, VOL. 2: "AIR DOOR"

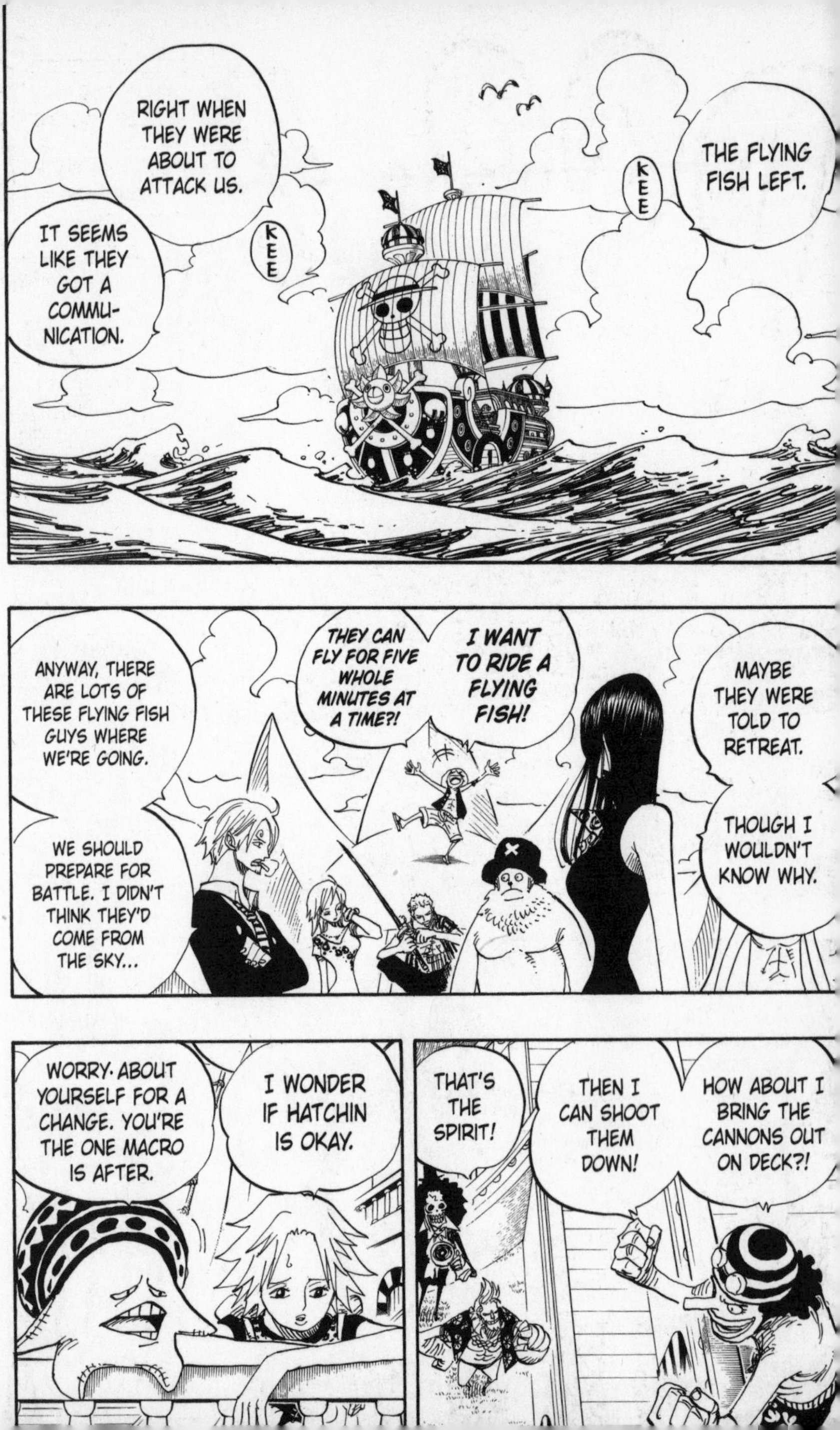
KEE
THE FLYING FISH LEFT.
KEE
RIGHT WHEN THEY WERE ABOUT TO ATTACK US.
IT SEEMS LIKE THEY GOT A COMMUNICATION.
MAYBE THEY WERE TOLD TO RETREAT.
THOUGH I WOULDN'T KNOW WHY.
I WANT TO RIDE A FLYING FISH!
THEY CAN FLY FOR FIVE WHOLE MINUTES AT A TIME?!
ANYWAY, THERE ARE LOTS OF THESE FLYING FISH GUYS WHERE WE'RE GOING.
WE SHOULD PREPARE FOR BATTLE. I DIDN'T THINK THEY'D COME FROM THE SKY...
HOW ABOUT I BRING THE CANNONS OUT ON DECK?!
THEN I CAN SHOOT THEM DOWN!
THAT'S THE SPIRIT!
I WONDER IF HATCHIN IS OKAY.
WORRY ABOUT YOURSELF FOR A CHANGE. YOU'RE THE ONE MACRO IS AFTER.

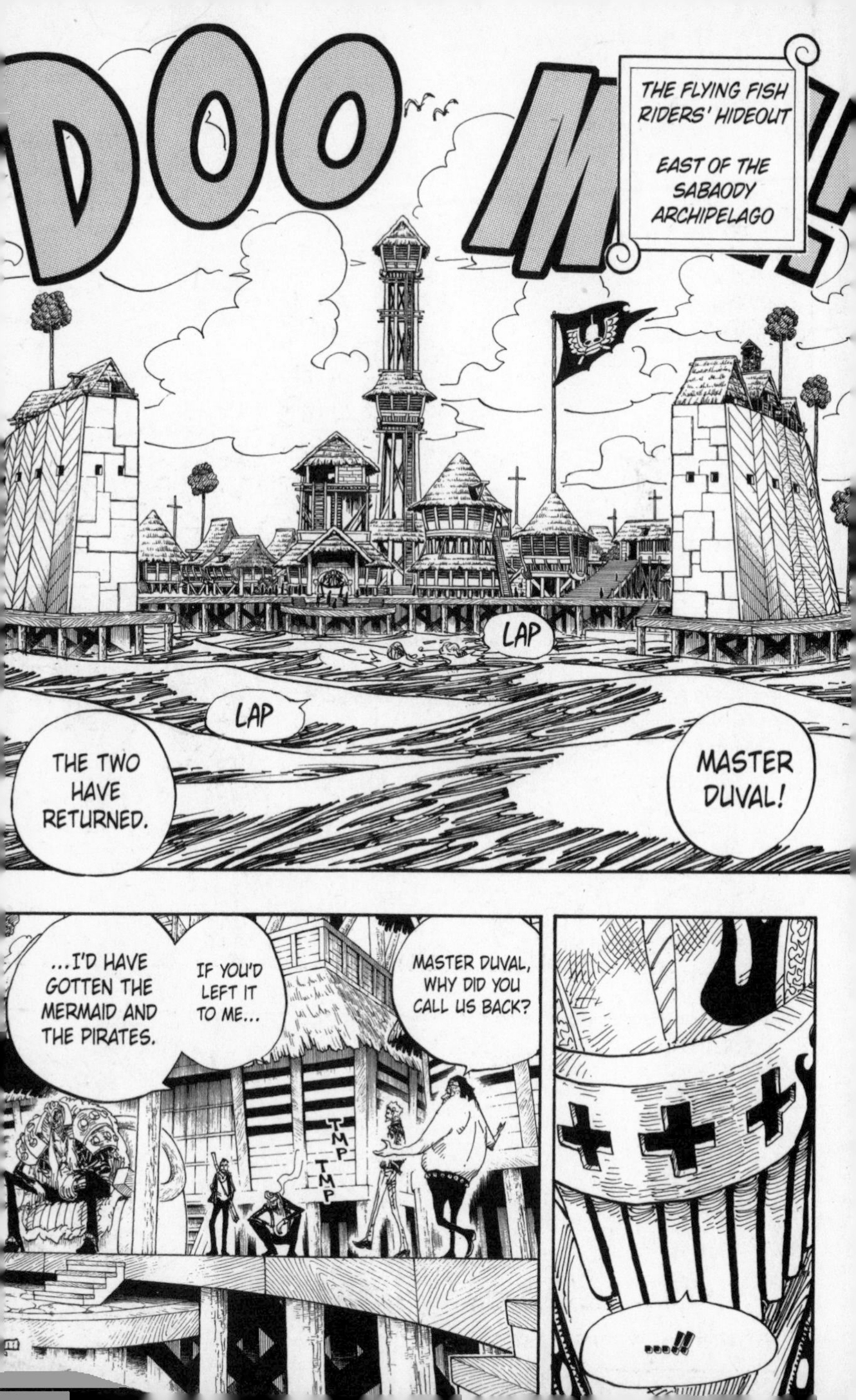
DOOM
THE FLYING FISH RIDERS' HIDEOUT
EAST OF THE SABAODY ARCHIPELAGO
LAP
LAP
MASTER DUVAL!
THE TWO HAVE RETURNED.
...!!
MASTER DUVAL, WHY DID YOU CALL US BACK?
TMP
TMP
IF YOU'D LEFT IT TO ME...
...I'D HAVE GOTTEN THE MERMAID AND THE PIRATES.

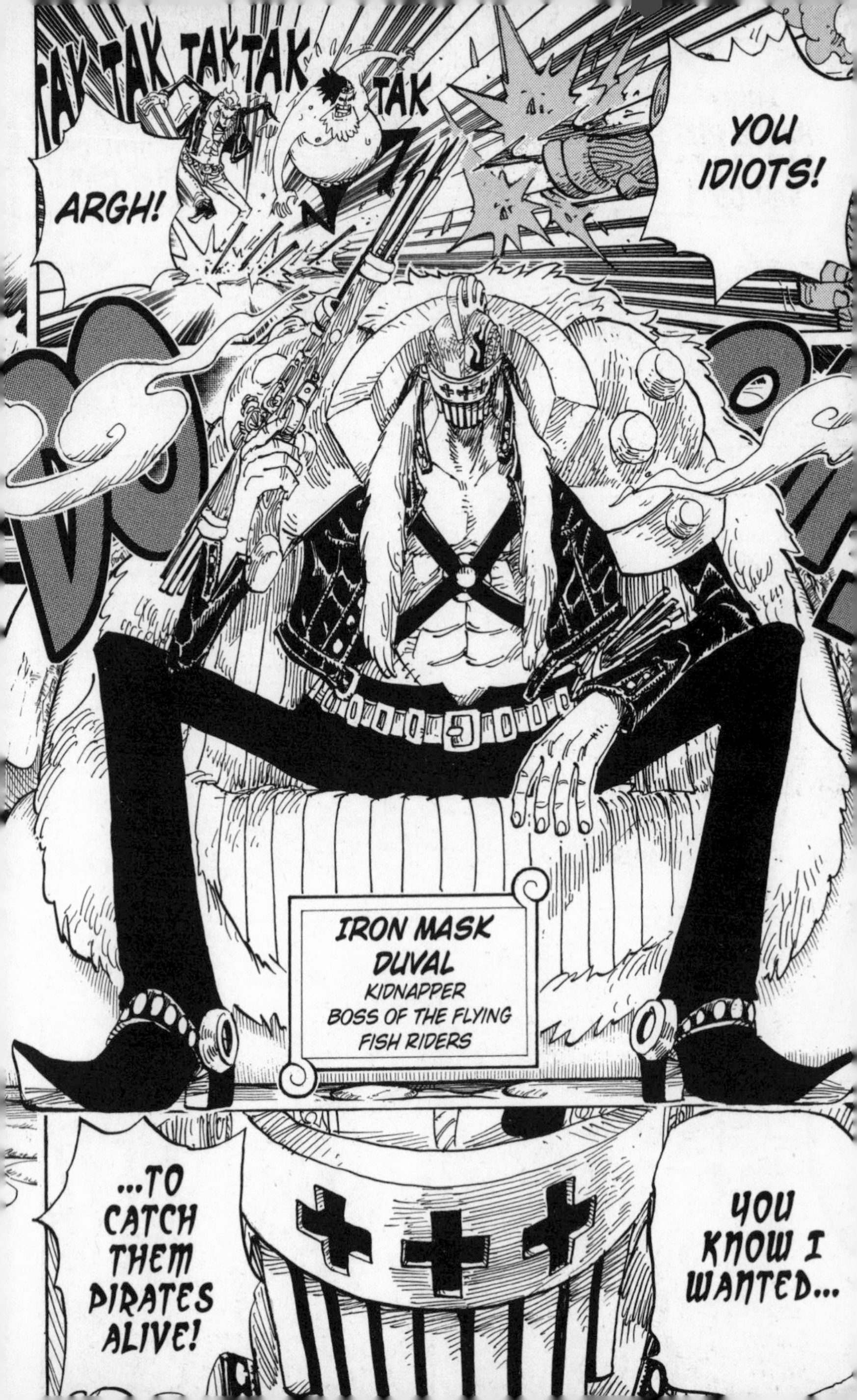
YOU IDIOTS!
TAK
TAK TAK TAK
ARGH!
IRON MASK DUVAL
KIDNAPPER
BOSS OF THE FLYING FISH RIDERS
YOU KNOW I WANTED...
...TO CATCH THEM PIRATES ALIVE!

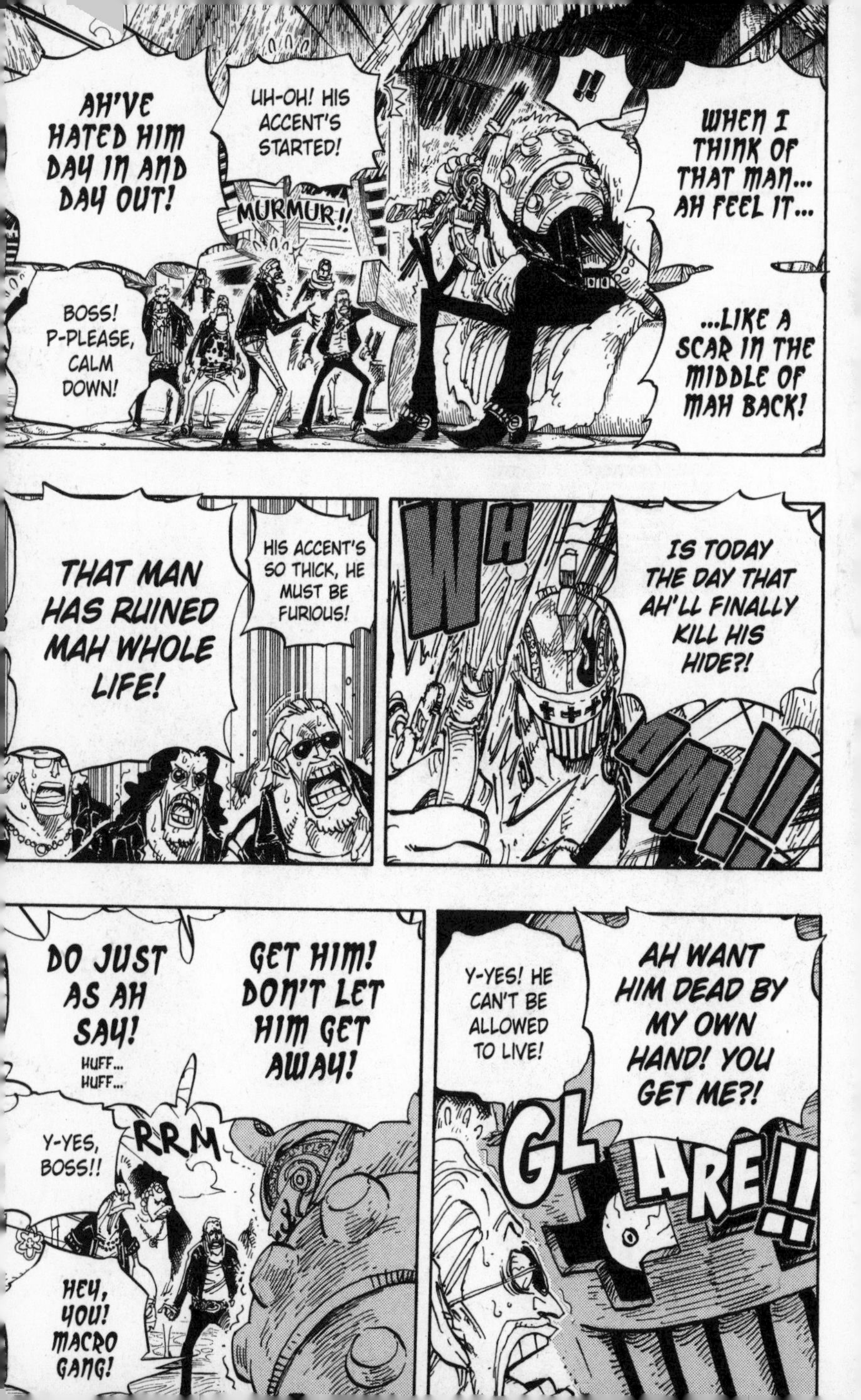
!!
WHEN I THINK OF THAT MAN... AH FEEL IT...
...LIKE A SCAR IN THE MIDDLE OF MAH BACK!
UH-OH! HIS ACCENT'S STARTED!
MURMUR!!
AH'VE HATED HIM DAY IN AND DAY OUT!
BOSS! P-PLEASE, CALM DOWN!
WH
IS TODAY THE DAY THAT AH'LL FINALLY KILL HIS HIDE?!
AM!!
HIS ACCENT'S SO THICK, HE MUST BE FURIOUS!
THAT MAN HAS RUINED MAH WHOLE LIFE!
AH WANT HIM DEAD BY MY OWN HAND! YOU GET ME?!
Y-YES! HE CAN'T BE ALLOWED TO LIVE!
GL
ARE!!
GET HIM! DON'T LET HIM GET AWAY!
DO JUST AS AH SAY!
HUFF... HUFF...
RRM
Y-YES, BOSS!!
HEY, YOU! MACRO GANG!

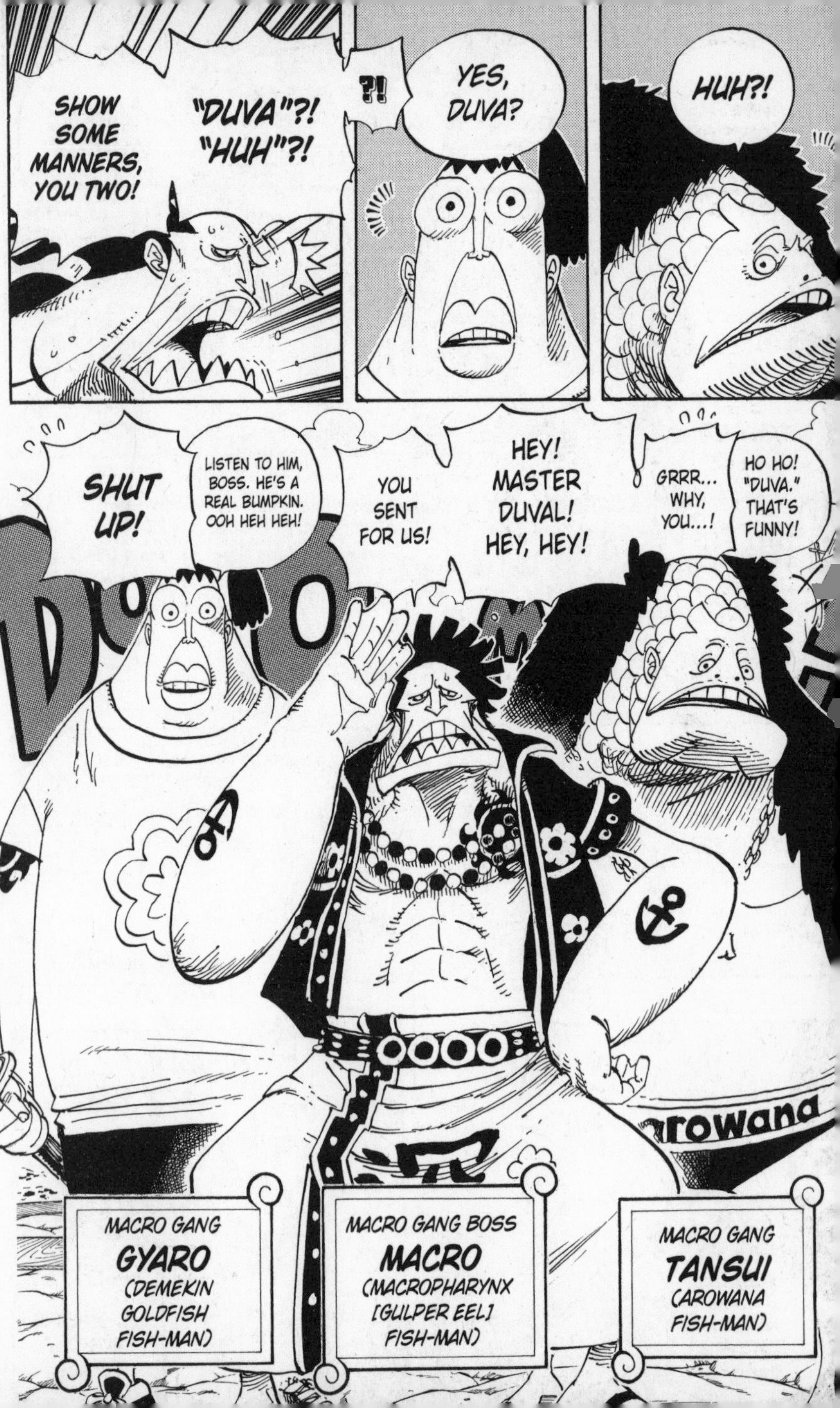
HUH?!
YES, DUVA?
?!
"DUVA"?! "HUH"?!
SHOW SOME MANNERS, YOU TWO!
HO HO! "DUVA." THAT'S FUNNY!
GRRR... WHY, YOU...!
HEY! MASTER DUVAL! HEY, HEY!
YOU SENT FOR US!
LISTEN TO HIM, BOSS. HE'S A REAL BUMPKIN. OOH HEH HEH!
SHUT UP!
MACRO GANG TANSUI (AROWANA FISH-MAN)
MACRO GANG BOSS MACRO (MACROPHARYNX [GULPER EEL] FISH-MAN)
MACRO GANG GYARO (DEMEKIN GOLDFISH FISH-MAN)

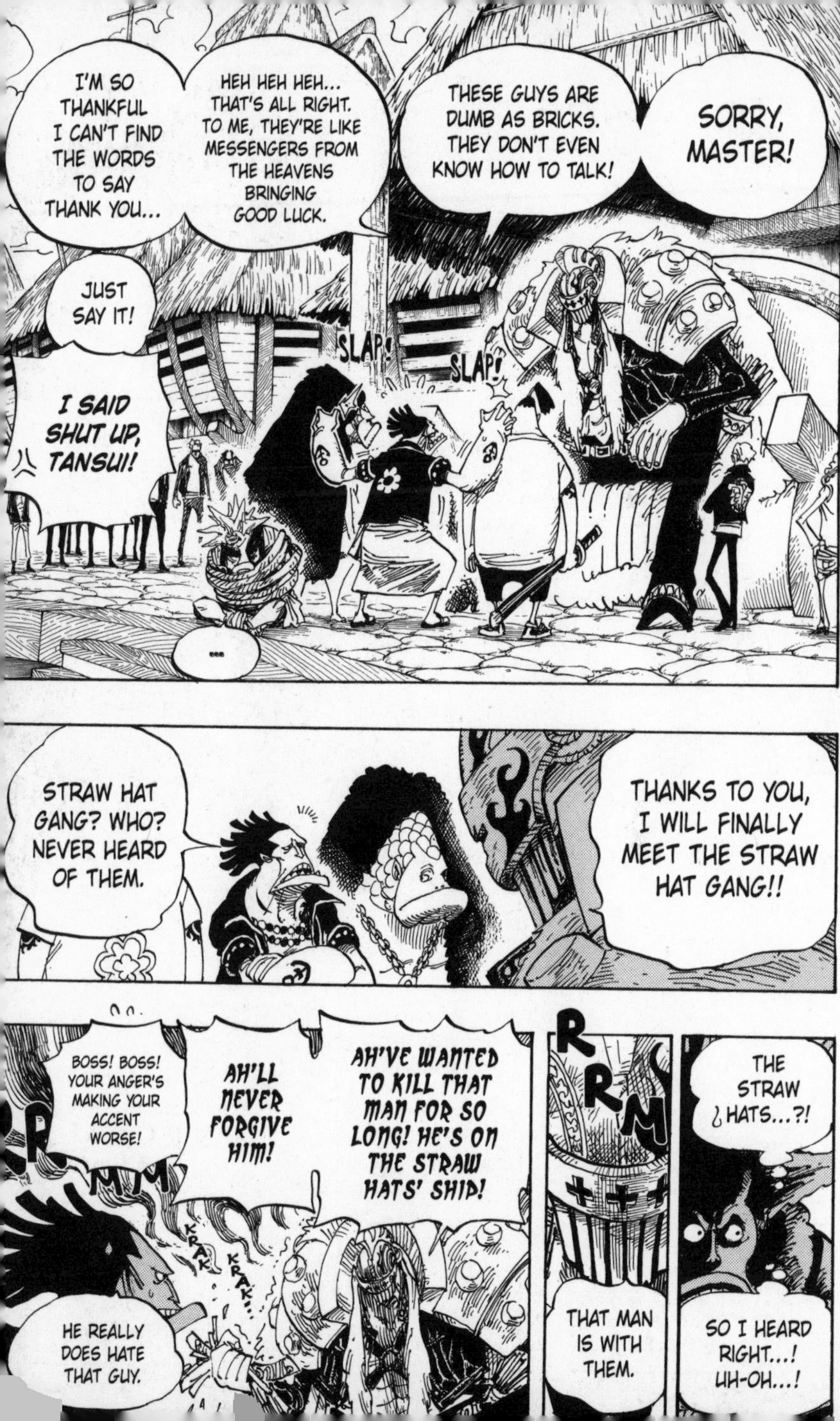
SORRY, MASTER!
THESE GUYS ARE DUMB AS BRICKS. THEY DON'T EVEN KNOW HOW TO TALK!
HEH HEH HEH... THAT'S ALL RIGHT. TO ME, THEY'RE LIKE MESSENGERS FROM THE HEAVENS BRINGING GOOD LUCK.
I'M SO THANKFUL I CAN'T FIND THE WORDS TO SAY THANK YOU...
JUST SAY IT!
SLAP!
SLAP!
I SAID SHUT UP, TANSUI!
...
THANKS TO YOU, I WILL FINALLY MEET THE STRAW HAT GANG!!
STRAW HAT GANG? WHO? NEVER HEARD OF THEM.
THE STRAW HATS...?!
SO I HEARD RIGHT...! UH-OH...!
RRRM
THAT MAN IS WITH THEM.
AH'VE WANTED TO KILL THAT MAN FOR SO LONG! HE'S ON THE STRAW HATS' SHIP!
AH'LL NEVER FORGIVE HIM!
BOSS! BOSS! YOUR ANGER'S MAKING YOUR ACCENT WORSE!
RRMM
KRAK
KRAK...
HE REALLY DOES HATE THAT GUY.

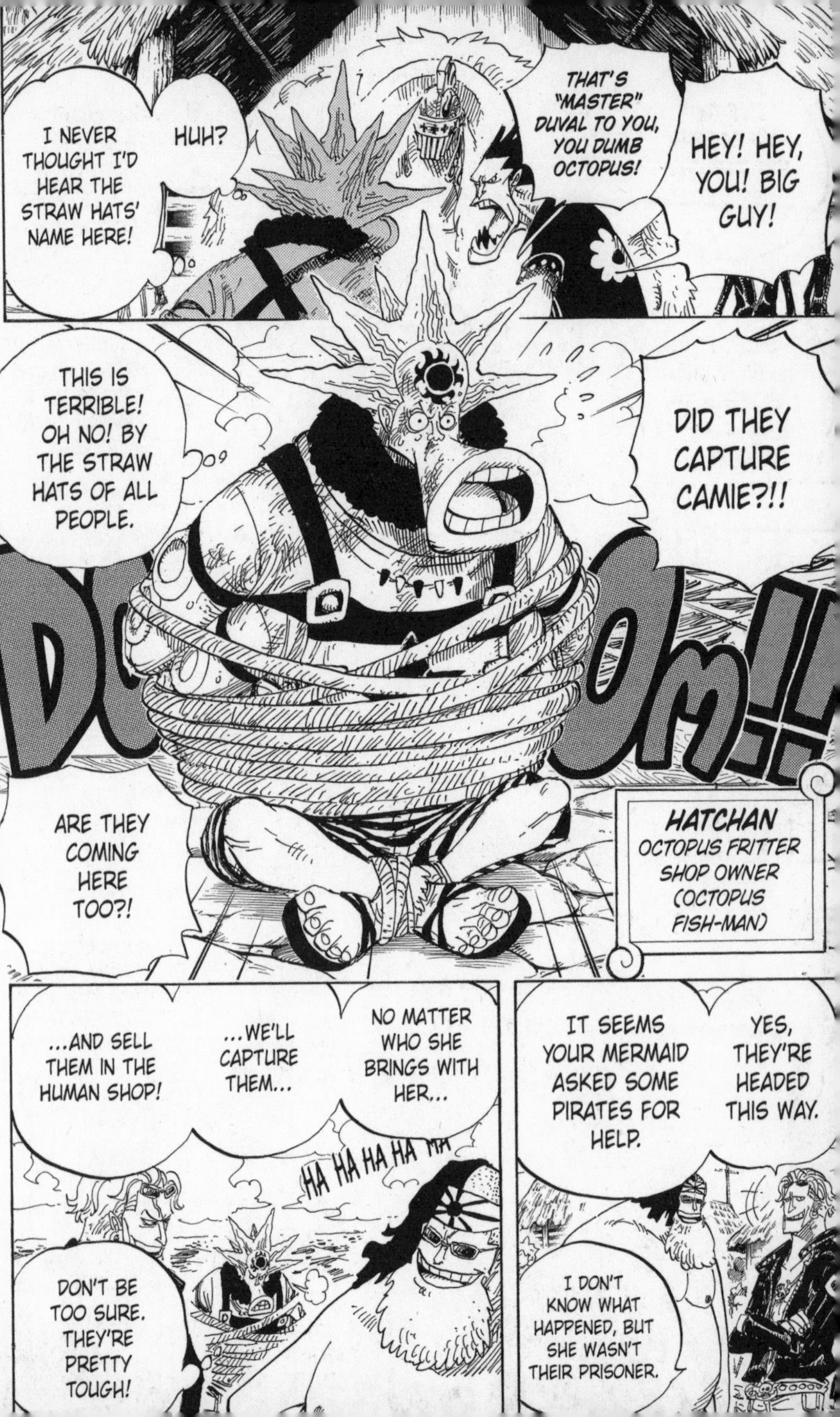
HEY! HEY, YOU! BIG GUY!
THAT'S "MASTER" DUVAL TO YOU, YOU DUMB OCTOPUS!
HUH?
I NEVER THOUGHT I'D HEAR THE STRAW HATS' NAME HERE!
DID THEY CAPTURE CAMIE?!!
THIS IS TERRIBLE! OH NO! BY THE STRAW HATS OF ALL PEOPLE.
HATCHAN OCTOPUS FRITTER SHOP OWNER (OCTOPUS FISH-MAN)
ARE THEY COMING HERE TOO?!
YES, THEY'RE HEADED THIS WAY.
IT SEEMS YOUR MERMAID ASKED SOME PIRATES FOR HELP.
I DON'T KNOW WHAT HAPPENED, BUT SHE WASN'T THEIR PRISONER.
NO MATTER WHO SHE BRINGS WITH HER...
...WE'LL CAPTURE THEM...
...AND SELL THEM IN THE HUMAN SHOP!
HA HA HA HA HA
DON'T BE TOO SURE. THEY'RE PRETTY TOUGH!

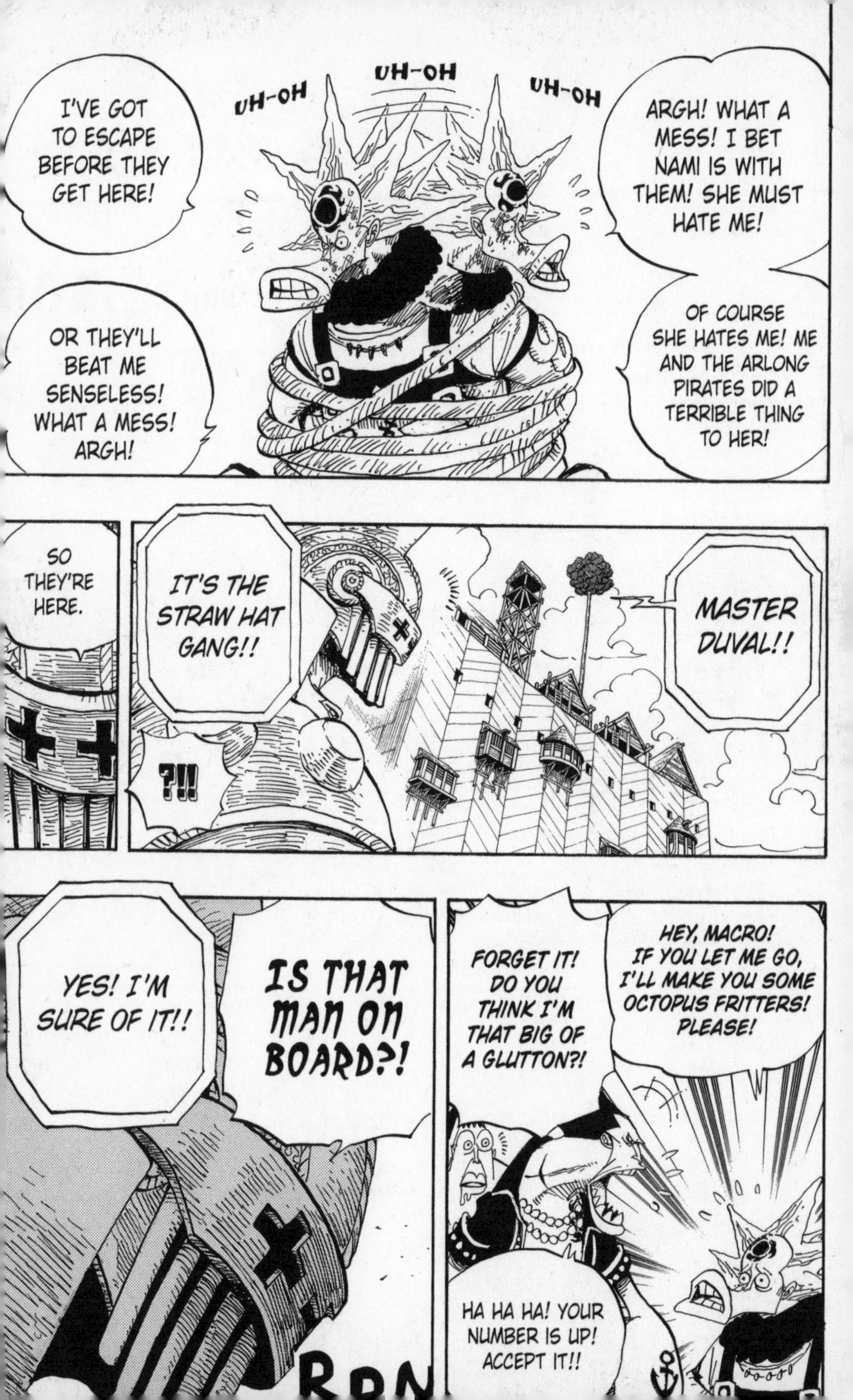
ARGH! WHAT A MESS! I BET NAMI IS WITH THEM! SHE MUST HATE ME!
OF COURSE SHE HATES ME! ME AND THE ARLONG PIRATES DID A TERRIBLE THING TO HER!
UH-OH
UH-OH
UH-OH
I'VE GOT TO ESCAPE BEFORE THEY GET HERE!
OR THEY'LL BEAT ME SENSELESS! WHAT A MESS! ARGH!
MASTER DUVAL!!
IT'S THE STRAW HAT GANG!!
?!!
SO THEY'RE HERE.
HEY, MACRO! IF YOU LET ME GO, I'LL MAKE YOU SOME OCTOPUS FRITTERS! PLEASE!
FORGET IT! DO YOU THINK I'M THAT BIG OF A GLUTTON?!
HA HA HA! YOUR NUMBER IS UP! ACCEPT IT!!
IS THAT MAN ON BOARD?!
YES! I'M SURE OF IT!!

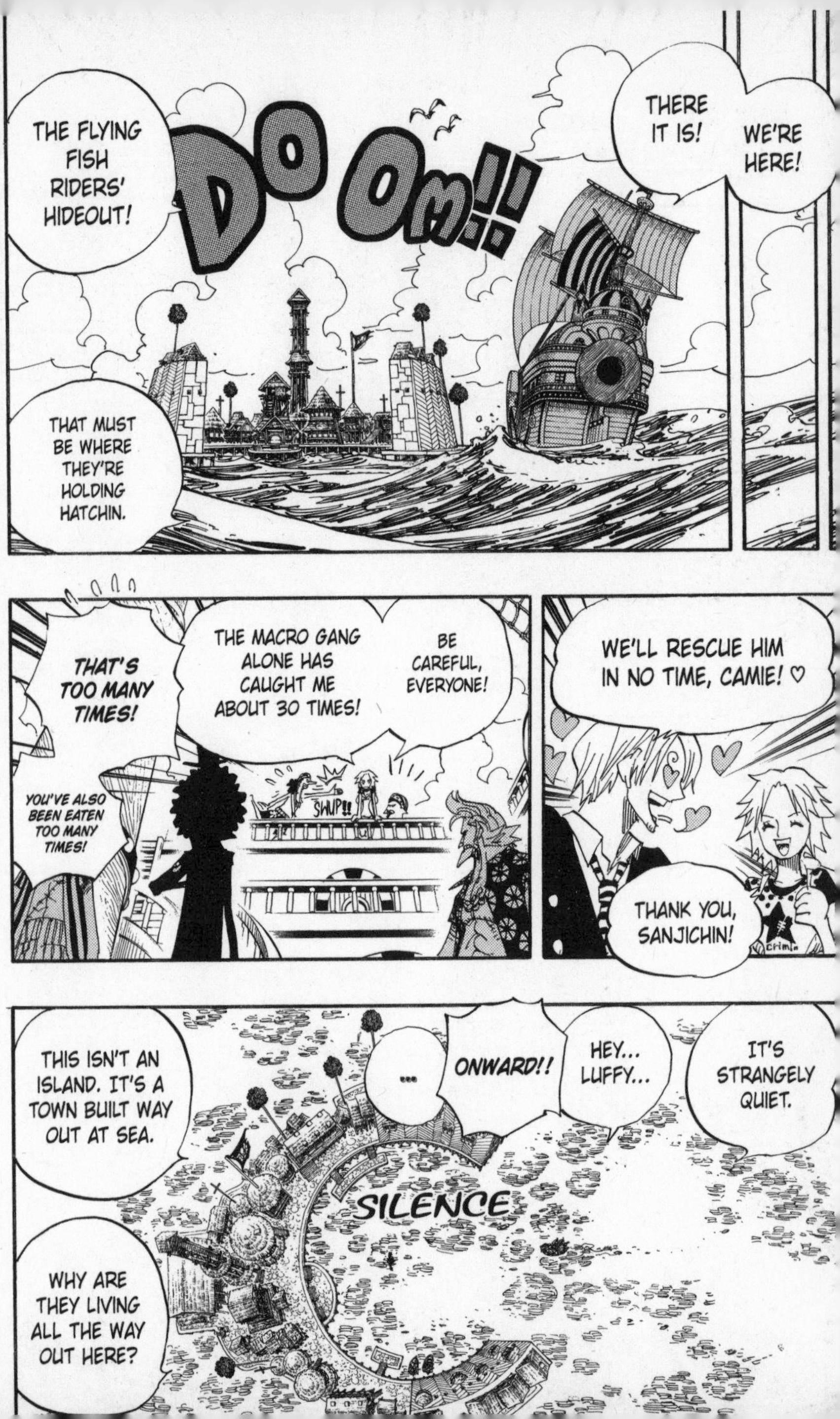
WE'RE HERE!
THERE IT IS!
DOOM!!
THE FLYING FISH RIDERS' HIDEOUT!
THAT MUST BE WHERE THEY'RE HOLDING HATCHIN.
WE'LL RESCUE HIM IN NO TIME, CAMIE! ♡
THANK YOU, SANJICHIN!
BE CAREFUL, EVERYONE!
THE MACRO GANG ALONE HAS CAUGHT ME ABOUT 30 TIMES!
SHUP!!
THAT'S TOO MANY TIMES!
YOU'VE ALSO BEEN EATEN TOO MANY TIMES!
IT'S STRANGELY QUIET.
HEY... LUFFY...
ONWARD!!
...
THIS ISN'T AN ISLAND. IT'S A TOWN BUILT WAY OUT AT SEA.
SILENCE
WHY ARE THEY LIVING ALL THE WAY OUT HERE?

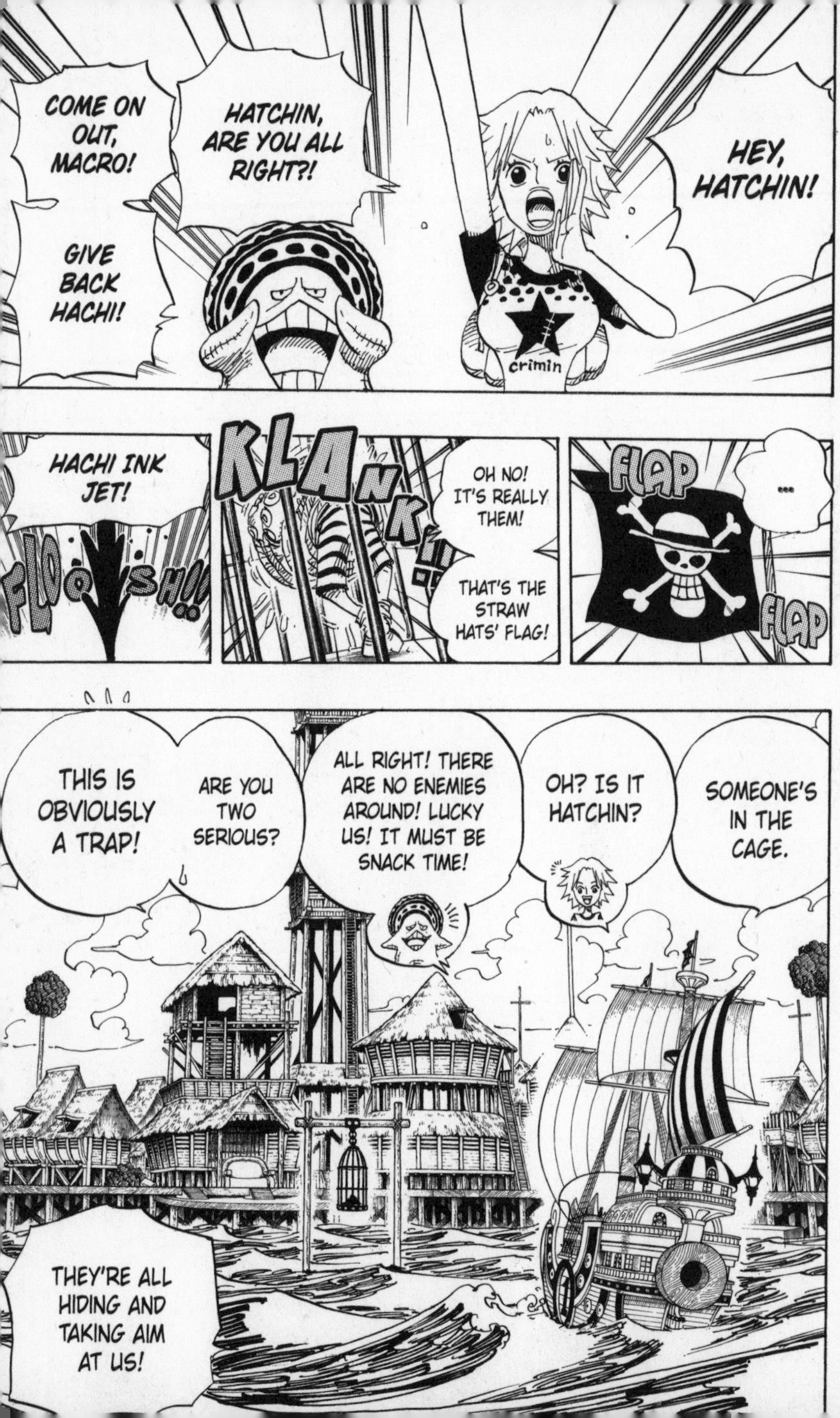
HEY, HATCHIN!
HATCHIN, ARE YOU ALL RIGHT?!
COME ON OUT, MACRO!
GIVE BACK HACHI!
crimin
FLAP
...
FLAP
OH NO! IT'S REALLY THEM!
KLANK!!
THAT'S THE STRAW HATS' FLAG!
HACHI INK JET!
FLOOSH!!
SOMEONE'S IN THE CAGE.
OH? IS IT HATCHIN?
ALL RIGHT! THERE ARE NO ENEMIES AROUND! LUCKY US! IT MUST BE SNACK TIME!
ARE YOU TWO SERIOUS?
THIS IS OBVIOUSLY A TRAP!
THEY'RE ALL HIDING AND TAKING AIM AT US!

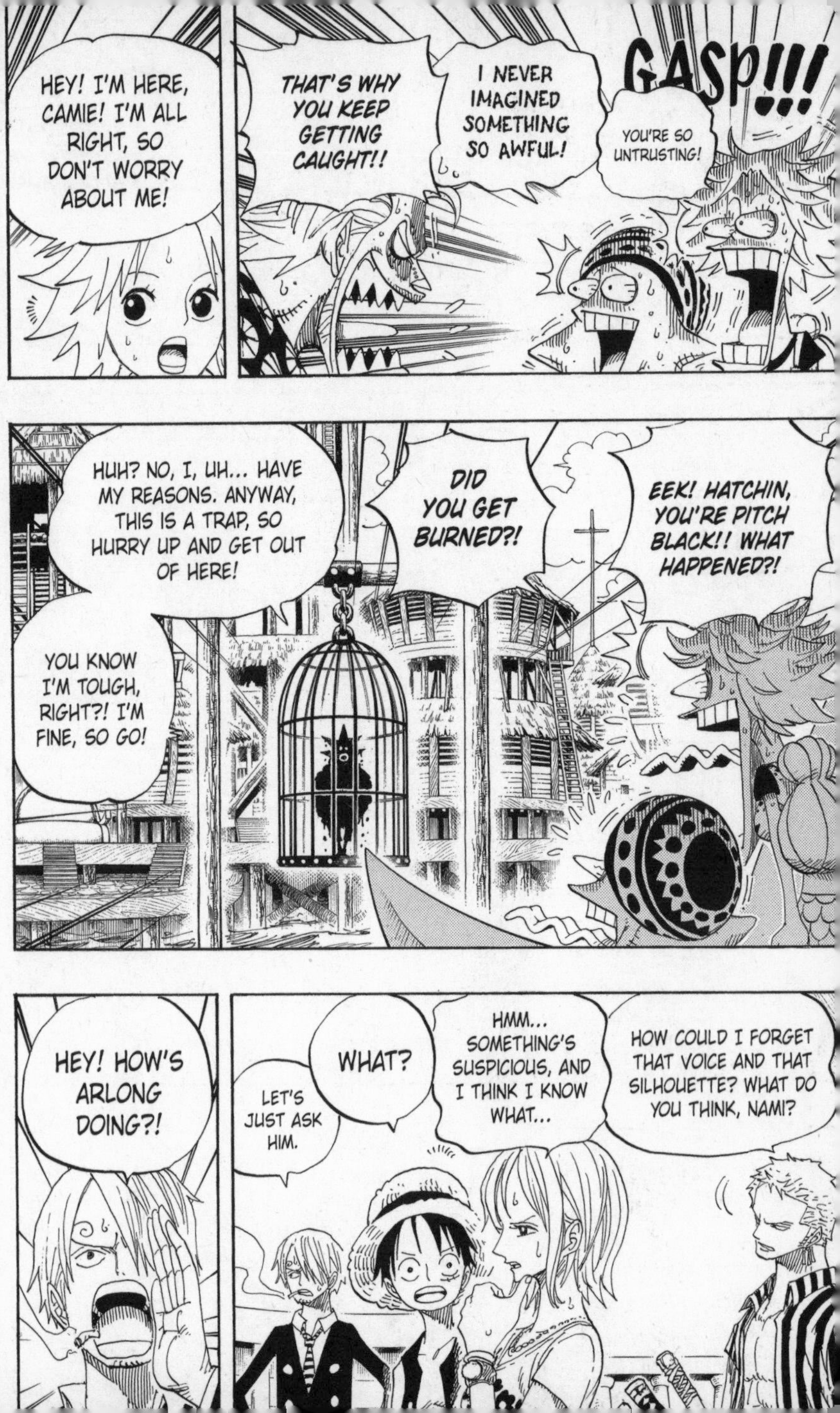
GASP!!!
YOU'RE SO UNTRUSTING!
I NEVER IMAGINED SOMETHING SO AWFUL!
THAT'S WHY YOU KEEP GETTING CAUGHT!!
HEY! I'M HERE, CAMIE! I'M ALL RIGHT, SO DON'T WORRY ABOUT ME!
EEK! HATCHIN, YOU'RE PITCH BLACK!! WHAT HAPPENED?!
DID YOU GET BURNED?!
HUH? NO, I, UH... HAVE MY REASONS. ANYWAY, THIS IS A TRAP, SO HURRY UP AND GET OUT OF HERE!
YOU KNOW I'M TOUGH, RIGHT?! I'M FINE, SO GO!
HOW COULD I FORGET THAT VOICE AND THAT SILHOUETTE? WHAT DO YOU THINK, NAMI?
HMM... SOMETHING'S SUSPICIOUS, AND I THINK I KNOW WHAT...
WHAT?
LET'S JUST ASK HIM.
HEY! HOW'S ARLONG DOING?!

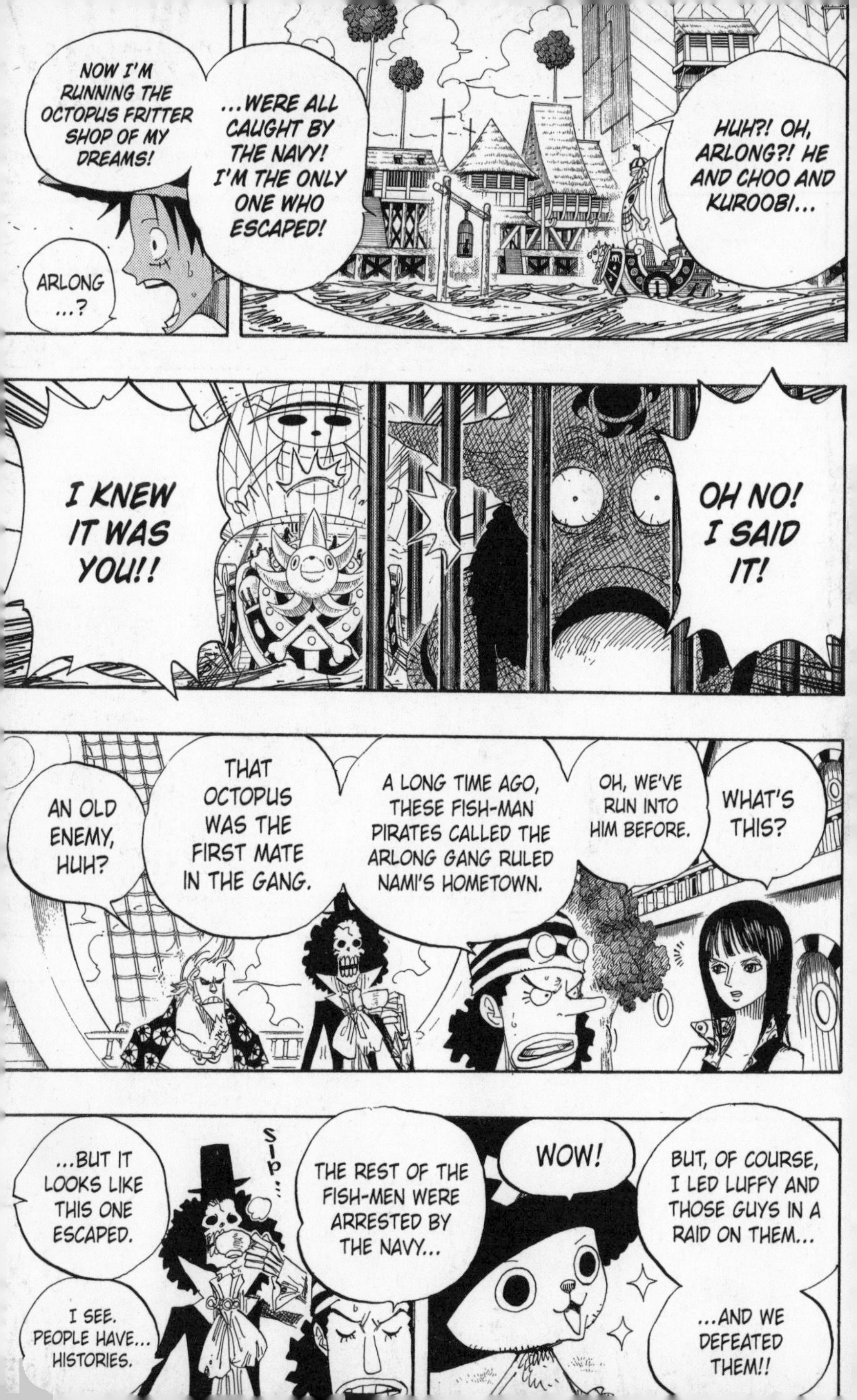
HUH?! OH, ARLONG?! HE AND CHOO AND KUROOBI...
...WERE ALL CAUGHT BY THE NAVY! I'M THE ONLY ONE WHO ESCAPED!
NOW I'M RUNNING THE OCTOPUS FRITTER SHOP OF MY DREAMS!
ARLONG ...?
OH NO! I SAID IT!
I KNEW IT WAS YOU!!
WHAT'S THIS?
OH, WE'VE RUN INTO HIM BEFORE.
A LONG TIME AGO, THESE FISH-MAN PIRATES CALLED THE ARLONG GANG RULED NAMI'S HOMETOWN.
THAT OCTOPUS WAS THE FIRST MATE IN THE GANG.
AN OLD ENEMY, HUH?
BUT, OF COURSE, I LED LUFFY AND THOSE GUYS IN A RAID ON THEM...
...AND WE DEFEATED THEM!!
WOW!
THE REST OF THE FISH-MEN WERE ARRESTED BY THE NAVY...
SIP...
...BUT IT LOOKS LIKE THIS ONE ESCAPED.
I SEE. PEOPLE HAVE... HISTORIES.

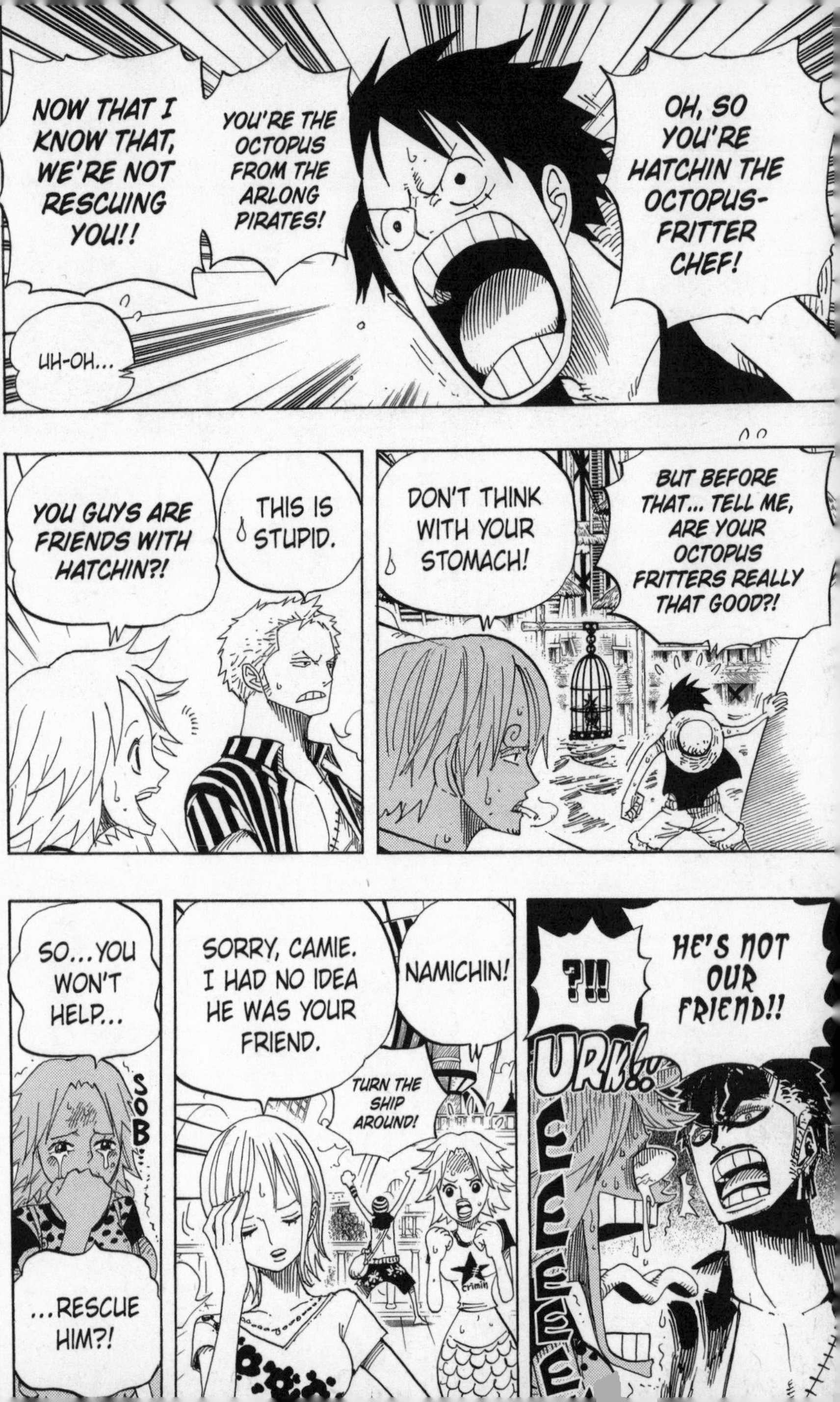
OH, SO YOU'RE HATCHIN THE OCTOPUS-FRITTER CHEF!
YOU'RE THE OCTOPUS FROM THE ARLONG PIRATES!
NOW THAT I KNOW THAT, WE'RE NOT RESCUING YOU!!
UH-OH...
BUT BEFORE THAT... TELL ME, ARE YOUR OCTOPUS FRITTERS REALLY THAT GOOD?!
DON'T THINK WITH YOUR STOMACH!
THIS IS STUPID.
YOU GUYS ARE FRIENDS WITH HATCHIN?!
HE'S NOT OUR FRIEND!!
?!!
URK!..
NAMICHIN!
SORRY, CAMIE. I HAD NO IDEA HE WAS YOUR FRIEND.
TURN THE SHIP AROUND!
SO...YOU WON'T HELP...
SOB
...RESCUE HIM?!

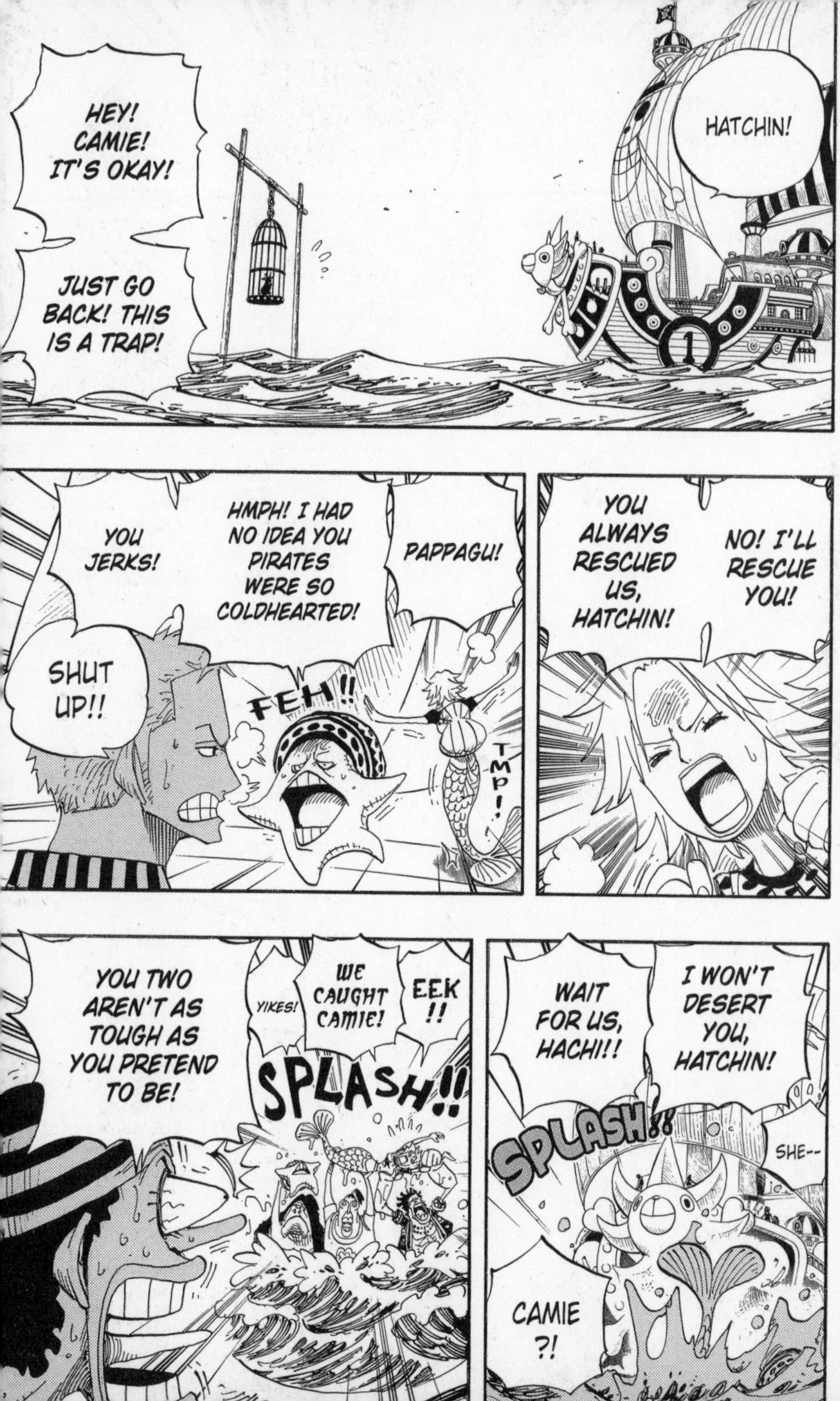
HATCHIN!
HEY! CAMIE! IT'S OKAY!
JUST GO BACK! THIS IS A TRAP!
NO! I'LL RESCUE YOU!
YOU ALWAYS RESCUED US, HATCHIN!
PAPPAGU!
HMPH! I HAD NO IDEA YOU PIRATES WERE SO COLDHEARTED!
YOU JERKS!
SHUT UP!!
FEH!!
TMP!
I WON'T DESERT YOU, HATCHIN!
WAIT FOR US, HACHI!!
SHE--
SPLASH!!
CAMIE ?!
EEK !!
WE CAUGHT CAMIE!
YIKES!
YOU TWO AREN'T AS TOUGH AS YOU PRETEND TO BE!
SPLASH!!

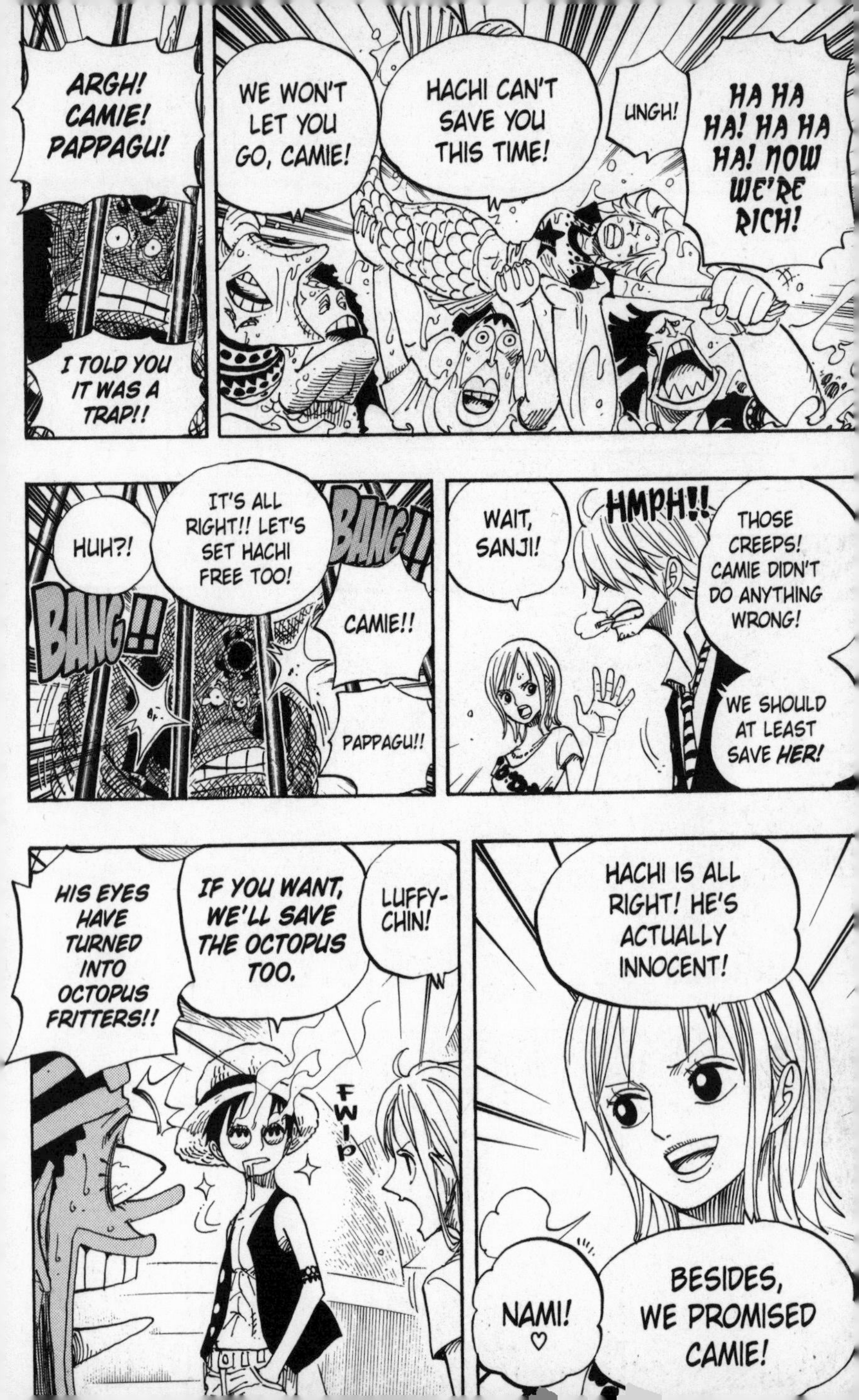
HA HA HA! HA HA HA! NOW WE'RE RICH!
UNGH!
HACHI CAN'T SAVE YOU THIS TIME!
WE WON'T LET YOU GO, CAMIE!
ARGH! CAMIE! PAPPAGU!
I TOLD YOU IT WAS A TRAP!!
THOSE CREEPS! CAMIE DIDN'T DO ANYTHING WRONG!
HMPH!!
WAIT, SANJI!
WE SHOULD AT LEAST SAVE HER!
BANG!!
IT'S ALL RIGHT!! LET'S SET HACHI FREE TOO!
HUH?!
CAMIE!!
BANG!!
PAPPAGU!!
HACHI IS ALL RIGHT! HE'S ACTUALLY INNOCENT!
BESIDES, WE PROMISED CAMIE!
NAMI! ♡
LUFFY-CHIN!
IF YOU WANT, WE'LL SAVE THE OCTOPUS TOO.
HIS EYES HAVE TURNED INTO OCTOPUS FRITTERS!!
FWIP

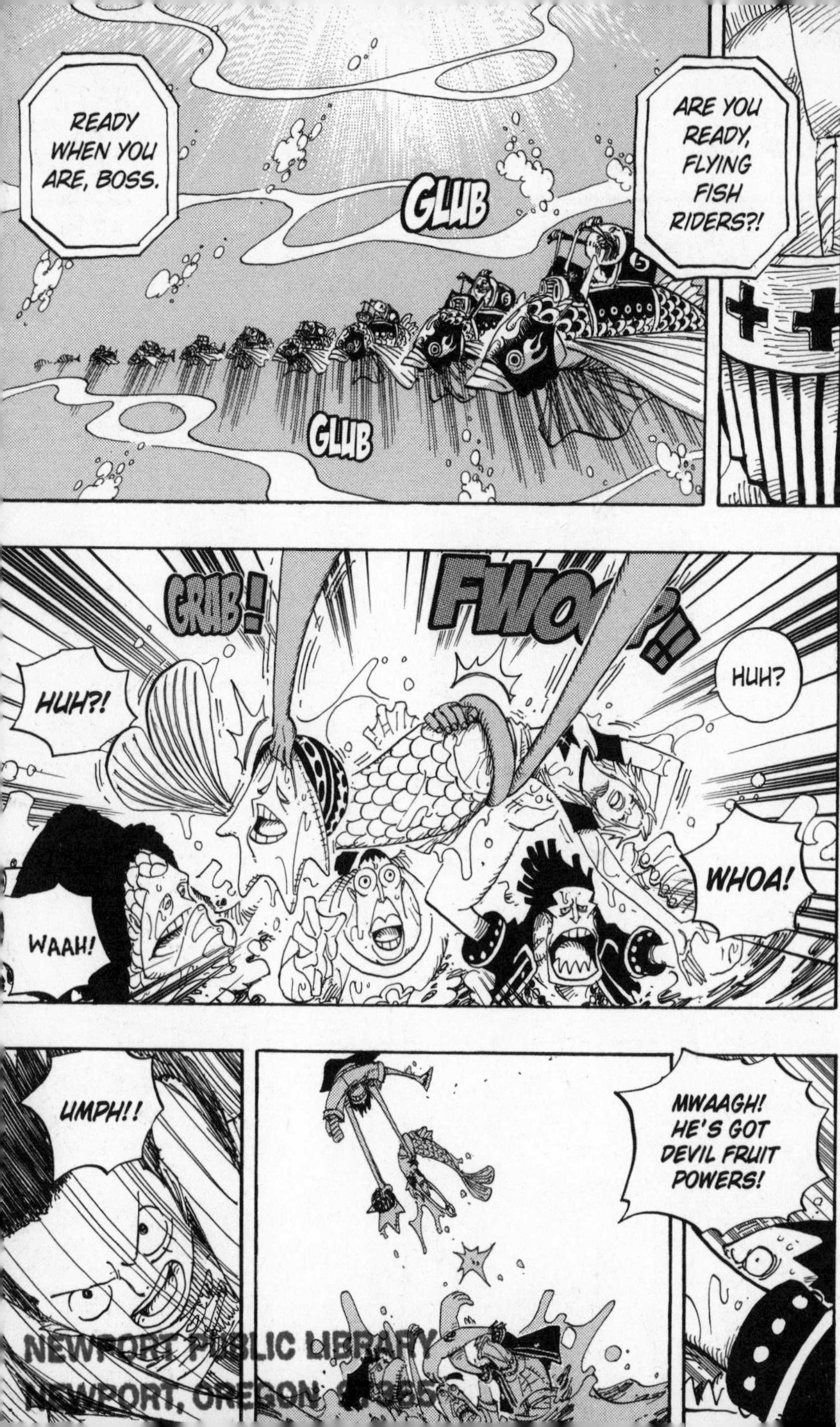
ARE YOU READY, FLYING FISH RIDERS?!
GLUB
READY WHEN YOU ARE, BOSS.
GLUB
HUH?
GRAB!
HUH?!
WHOA!
WAAH!
MWAAGH! HE'S GOT DEVIL FRUIT POWERS!
UMPH!!

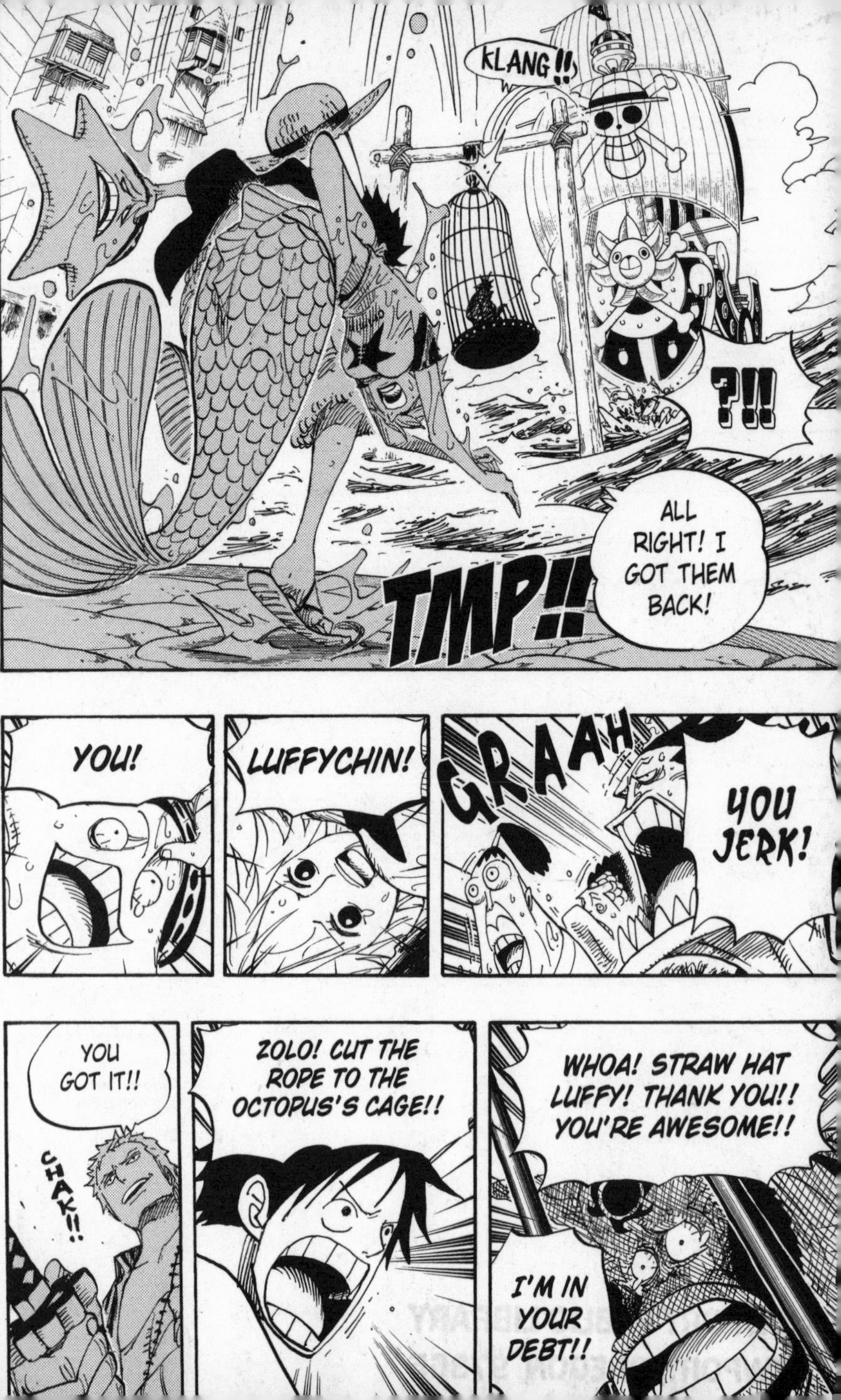
KLANG!!
?!!
ALL RIGHT! I GOT THEM BACK!
TMP!!
GRAAH
YOU JERK!
LUFFYCHIN!
YOU!
WHOA! STRAW HAT LUFFY! THANK YOU!! YOU'RE AWESOME!!
I'M IN YOUR DEBT!!
ZOLO! CUT THE ROPE TO THE OCTOPUS'S CAGE!!
YOU GOT IT!!
CHAK!!

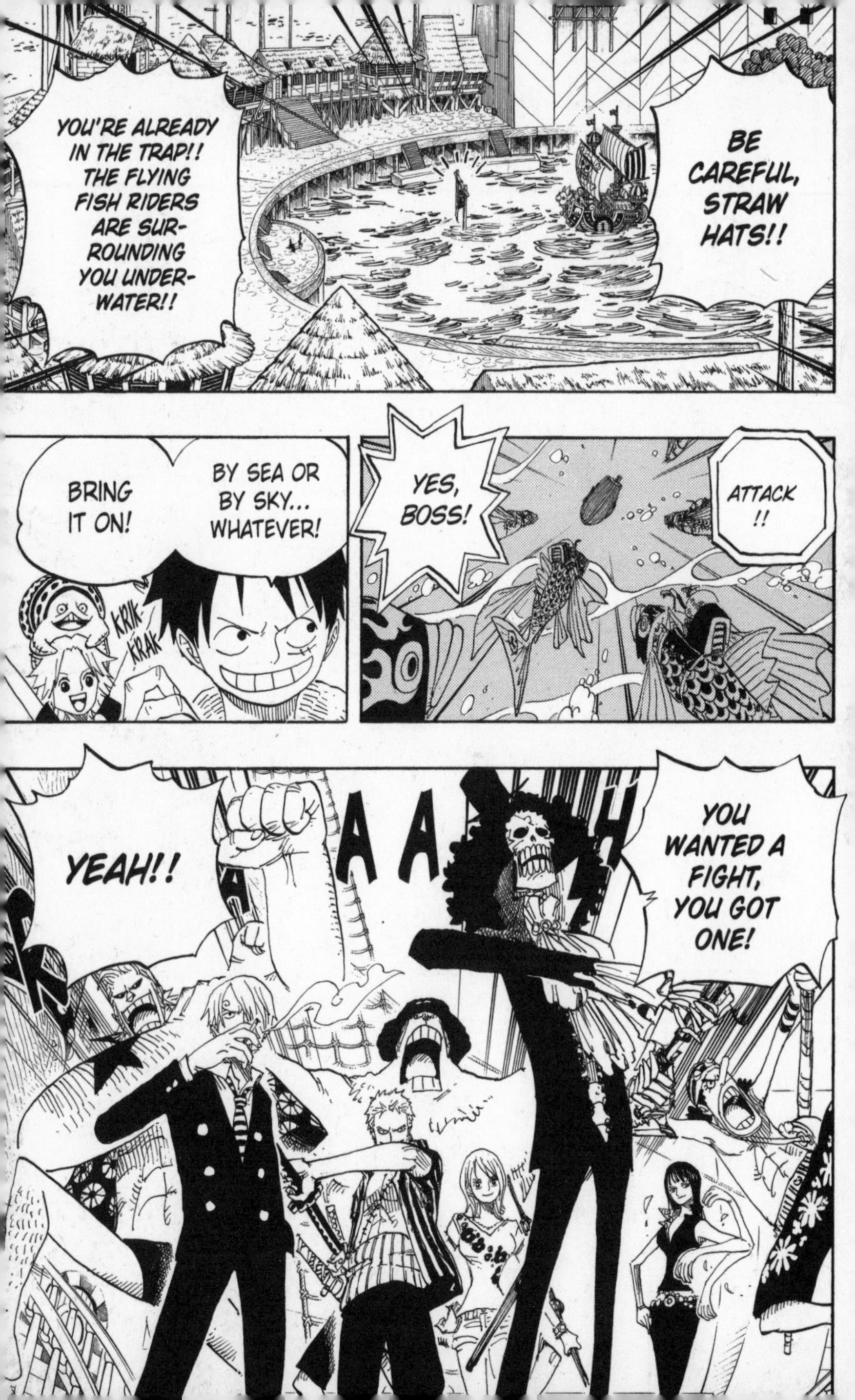
BE CAREFUL, STRAW HATS!!
YOU'RE ALREADY IN THE TRAP!! THE FLYING FISH RIDERS ARE SURROUNDING YOU UNDERWATER!!
ATTACK!!
YES, BOSS!
BY SEA OR BY SKY... WHATEVER!
BRING IT ON!
KRIK-KRAK
YOU WANTED A FIGHT, YOU GOT ONE!
YEAH!!

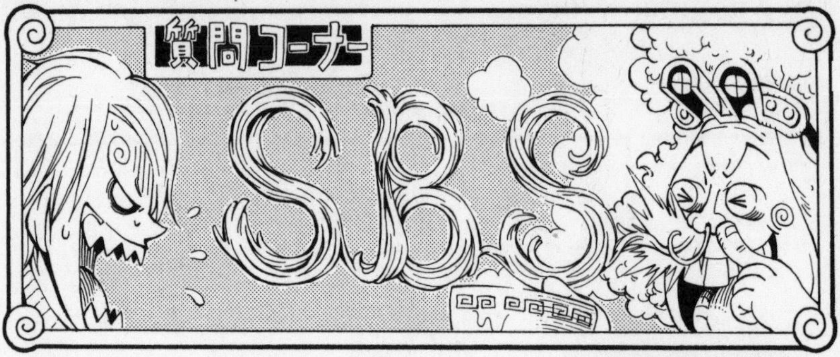
質問コーナー
SBS

(Harry Milky, Tokyo)

Reader (Q): Oda Sensei! Dos Fleurs! Grab! Squeeze! I got a good hold of you. So now, please begin the Question Corner.

--Kana-chan 2

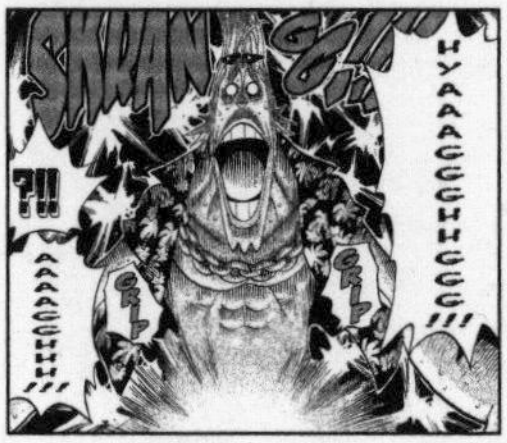
HYAAAAGGGHHGGG!!!
SKRAN
GRIP
GRIP
?!!
AAAAAGGHHH!!!

Oda (A): **HYAAAGGGHHGGG!!!**
The...Question...Corner...is...
HYAAAGGGHHGGG!!!

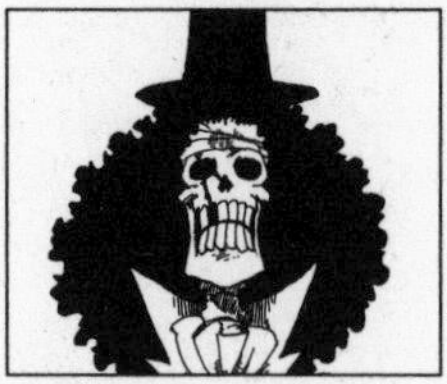

Q: Um, this is the first time I've sent in a postcard. Oda Sensei, I've been in love with Brook from the first time I laid eyes on him. Please tell me his age and height!

--A child pirate

A: Okay. Fifty years ago Brook was 38, so now he's 88. He's 8 feet 9 inches tall. He also wears a silk hat (approx. 8 inches tall). He's a BIG man.

Chapter 493:
YOU KNOW ME

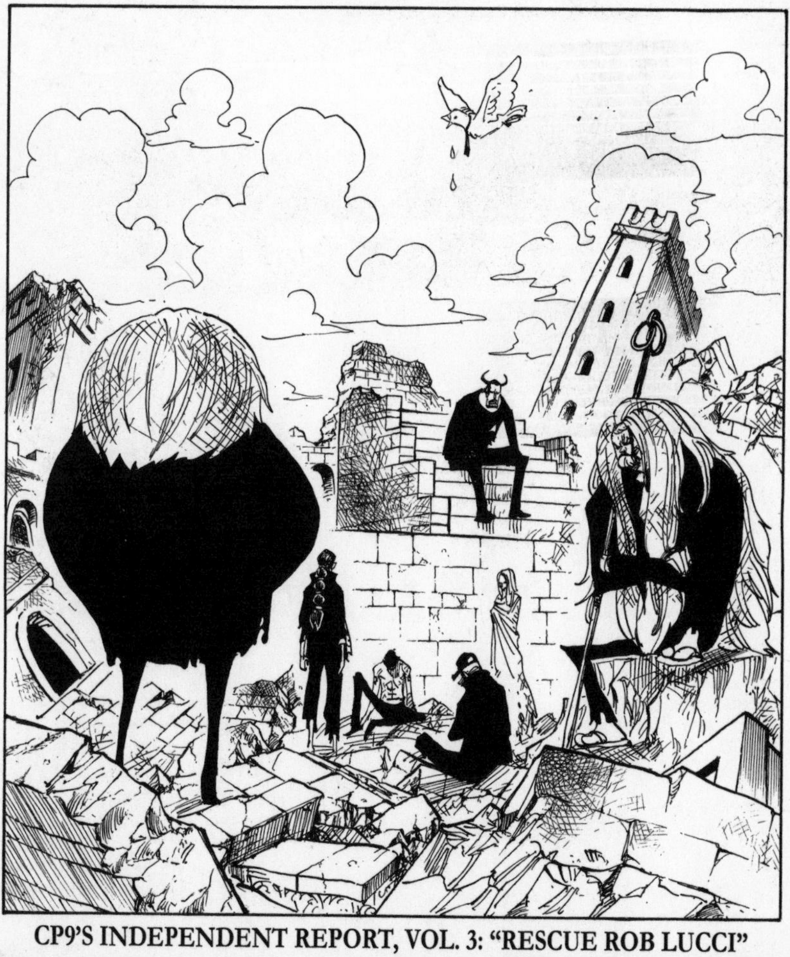

CP9'S INDEPENDENT REPORT, VOL. 3: "RESCUE ROB LUCCI"

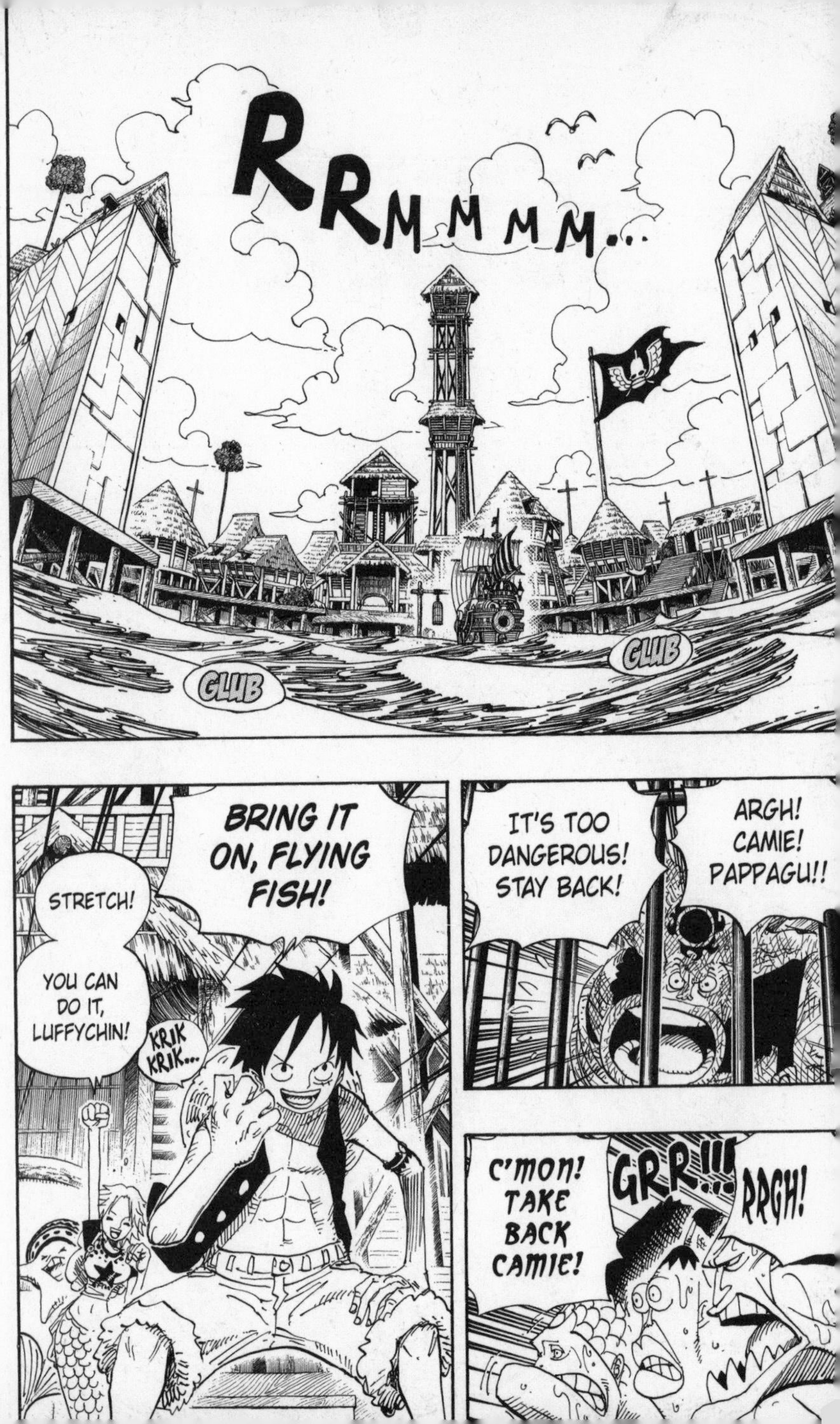
RRMMMM...
GLUB
GLUB
ARGH! CAMIE! PAPPAGU!!
IT'S TOO DANGEROUS! STAY BACK!
RRGH!
GRR!!!
C'MON! TAKE BACK CAMIE!
BRING IT ON, FLYING FISH!
STRETCH!
YOU CAN DO IT, LUFFYCHIN!
KRIK KRIK...

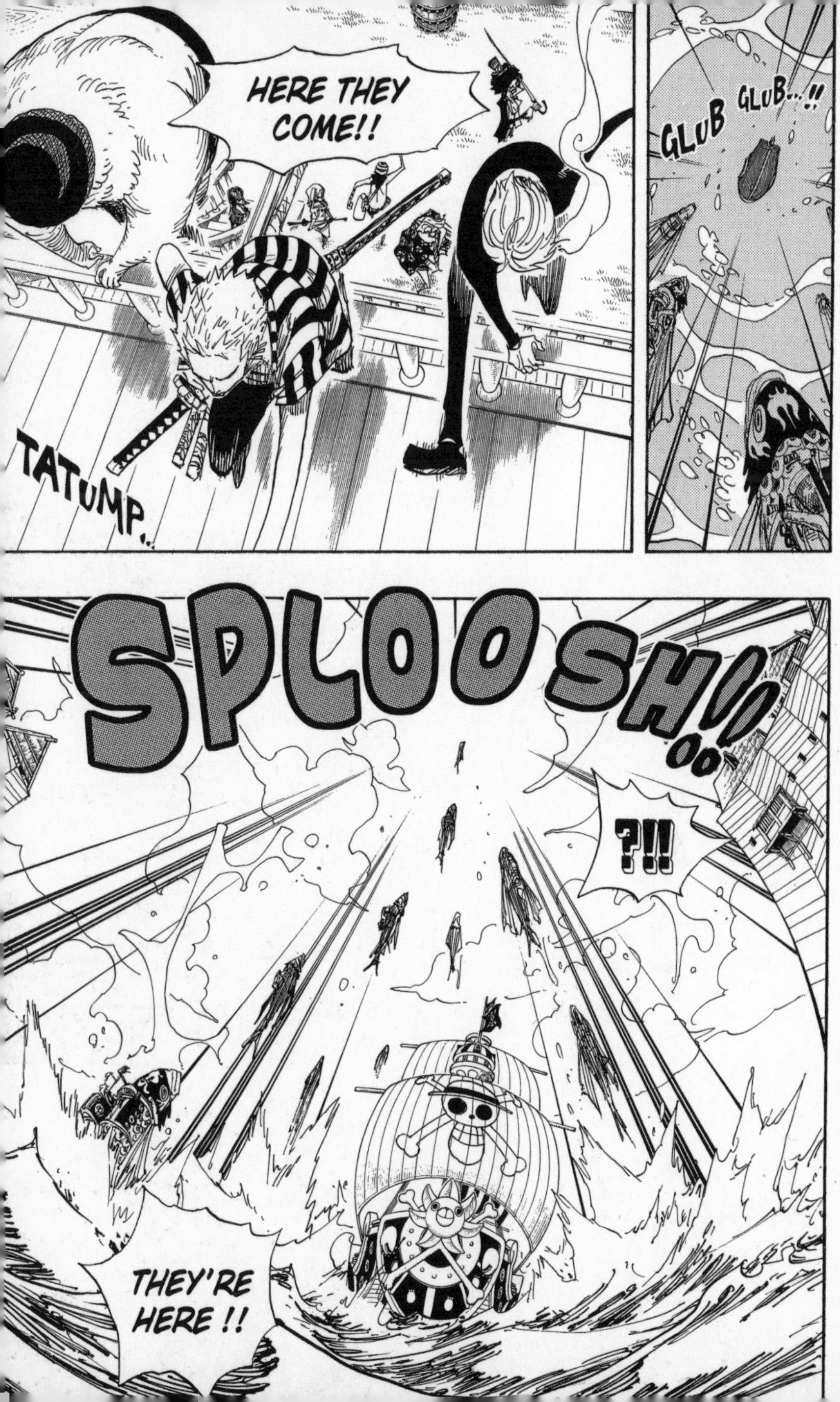
GLUB GLUB...!!
HERE THEY COME!!
TATUMP..
SPLOOSH!!
?!!
THEY'RE HERE!!

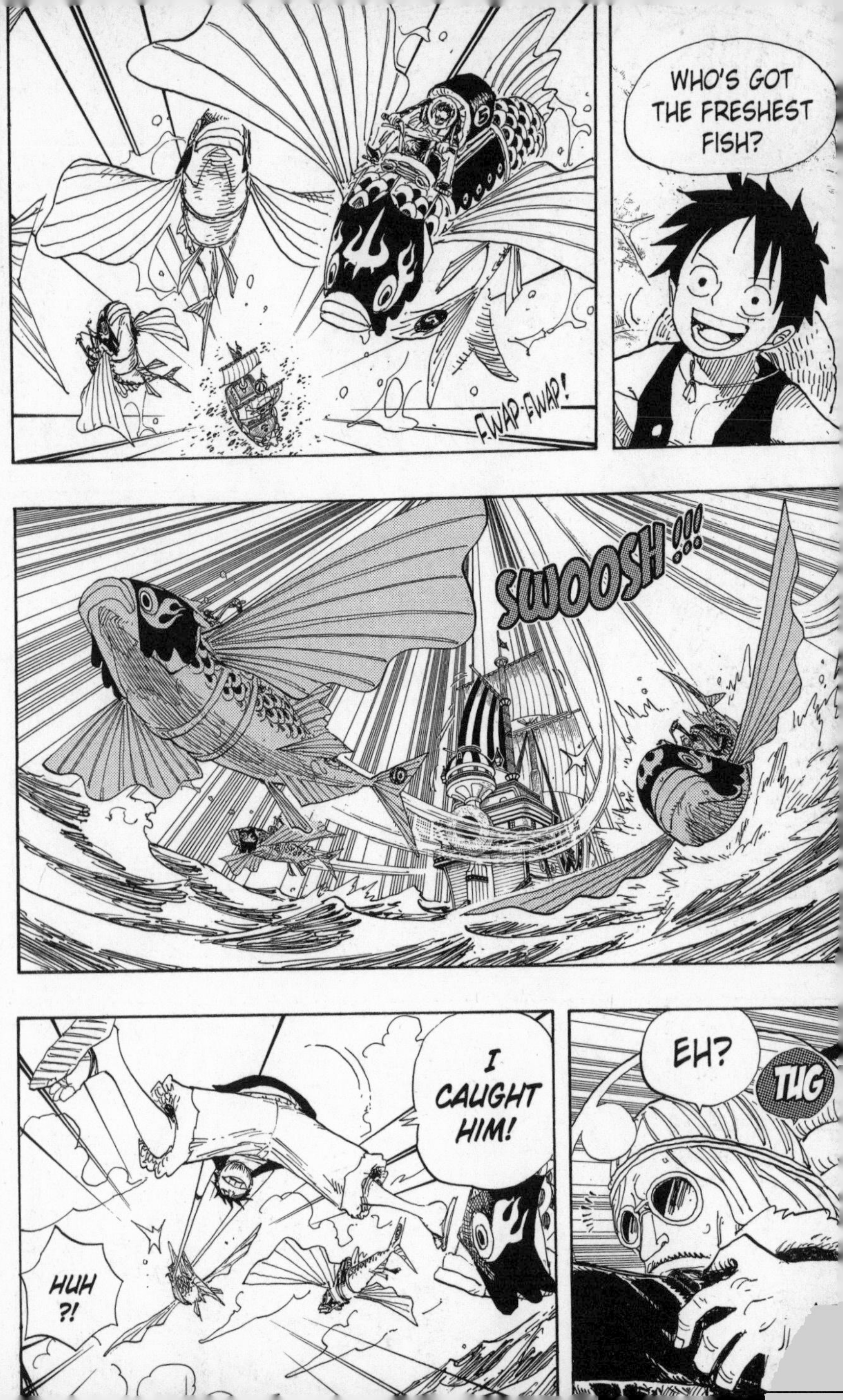
WHO'S GOT THE FRESHEST FISH?
FWAP-FWAP!
SWOOSH!!!
EH?
TUG
I CAUGHT HIM!
HUH ?!

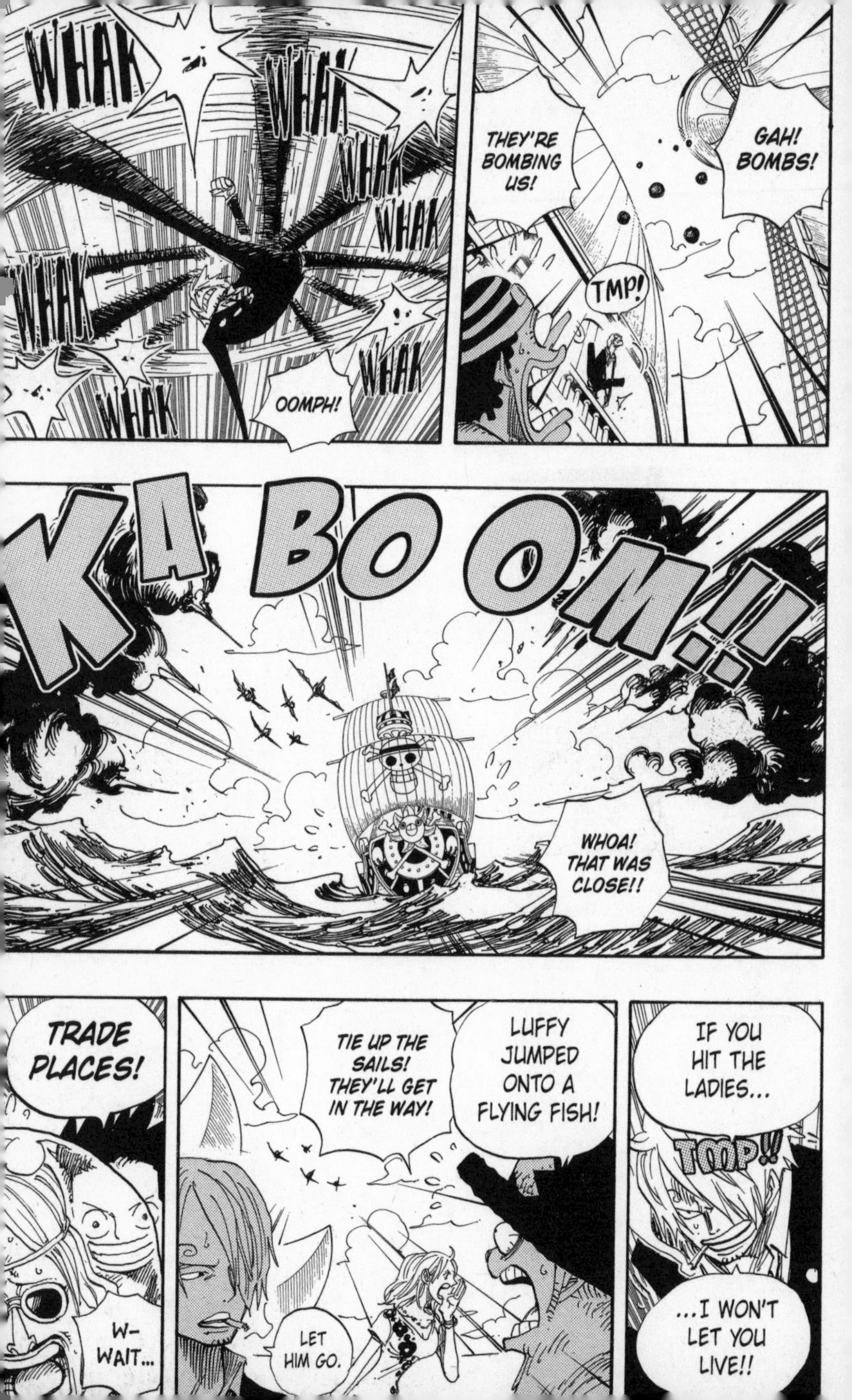
GAH! BOMBS!
THEY'RE BOMBING US!
TMP!
WHAK
WHAK
WHAK
WHAK
WHAK
WHAK
WHAK
WHAK
OOMPH!
KA BOOM!!
WHOA! THAT WAS CLOSE!!
IF YOU HIT THE LADIES...
TOOP!!
...I WON'T LET YOU LIVE!!
LUFFY JUMPED ONTO A FLYING FISH!
TIE UP THE SAILS! THEY'LL GET IN THE WAY!
LET HIM GO.
TRADE PLACES!
W- WAIT...

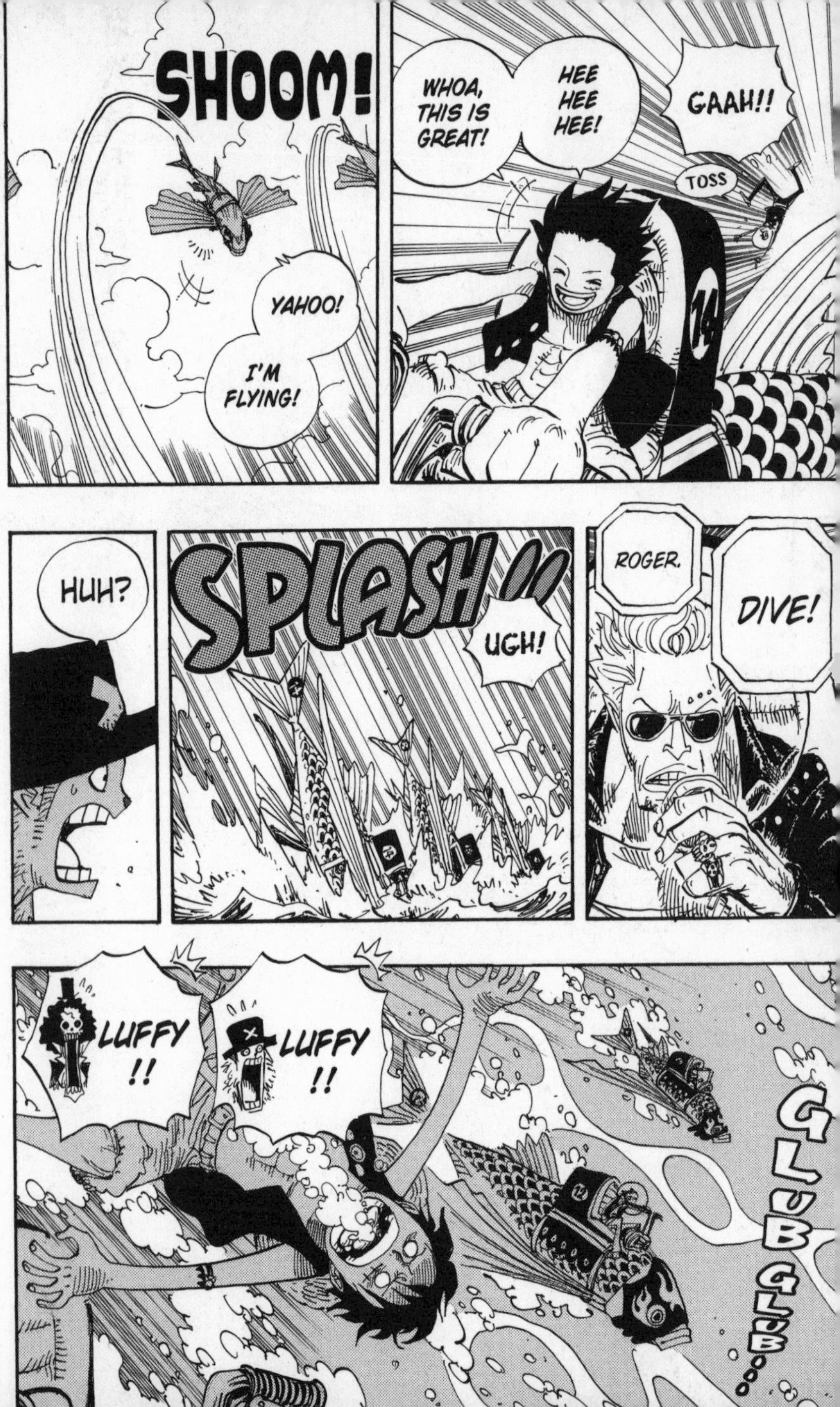
GAAH!!
HEE HEE HEE!
WHOA, THIS IS GREAT!
TOSS
SHOOM!
YAHOO!
I'M FLYING!
ROGER.
DIVE!
SPLASH!!
UGH!
HUH?
LUFFY!!
LUFFY!!
GLUB GLUB...

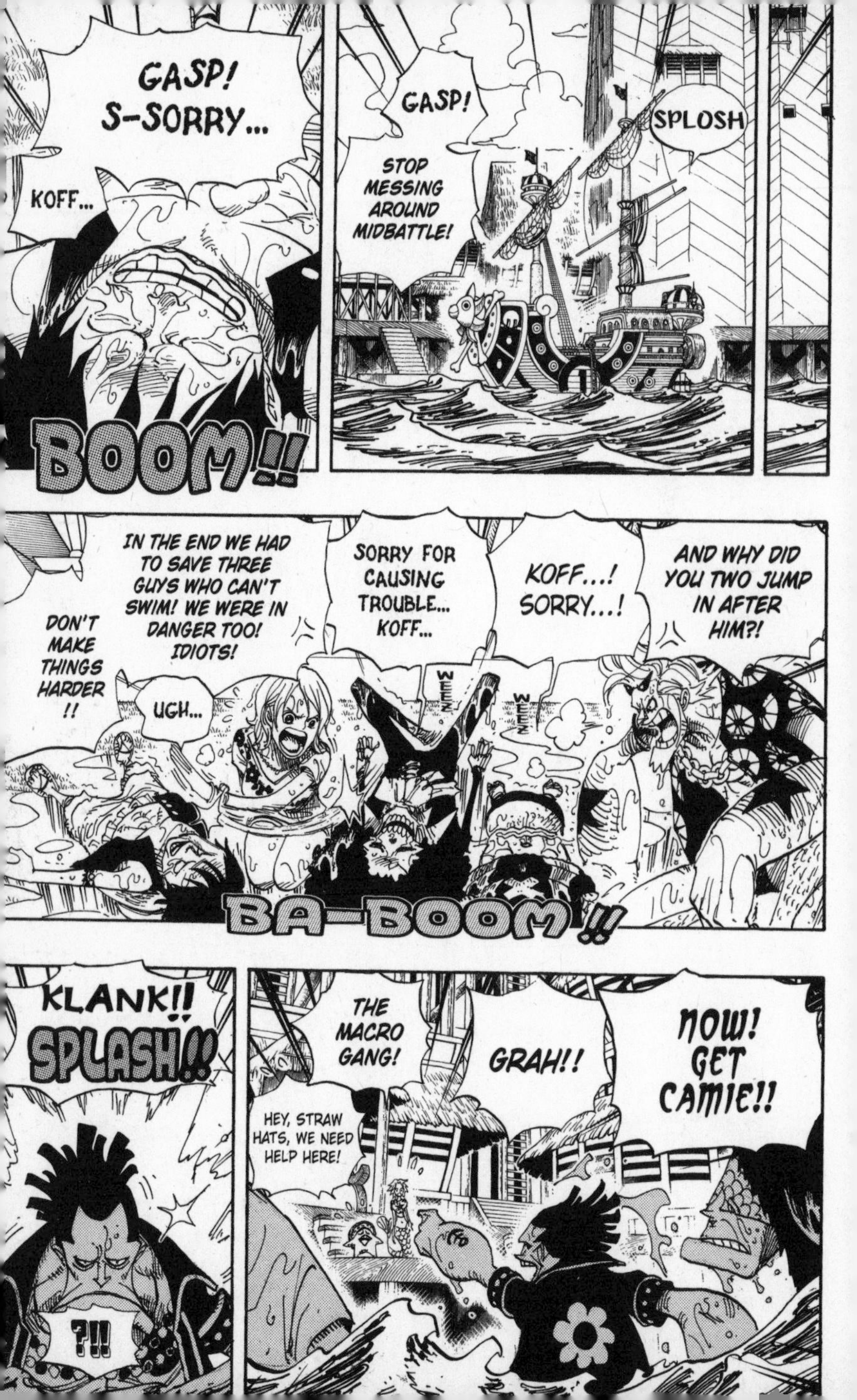
SPLOSH
GASP!
STOP MESSING AROUND MIDBATTLE!
GASP! S-SORRY...
KOFF...
BOOM!!
AND WHY DID YOU TWO JUMP IN AFTER HIM?!
KOFF...! SORRY...!
WEEZ
SORRY FOR CAUSING TROUBLE... KOFF...
WEEZ
IN THE END WE HAD TO SAVE THREE GUYS WHO CAN'T SWIM! WE WERE IN DANGER TOO! IDIOTS!
DON'T MAKE THINGS HARDER!!
UGH...
BA-BOOM!!
NOW! GET CAMIE!!
GRAH!!
THE MACRO GANG!
HEY, STRAW HATS, WE NEED HELP HERE!
KLANK!!
SPLASH!!
?!!

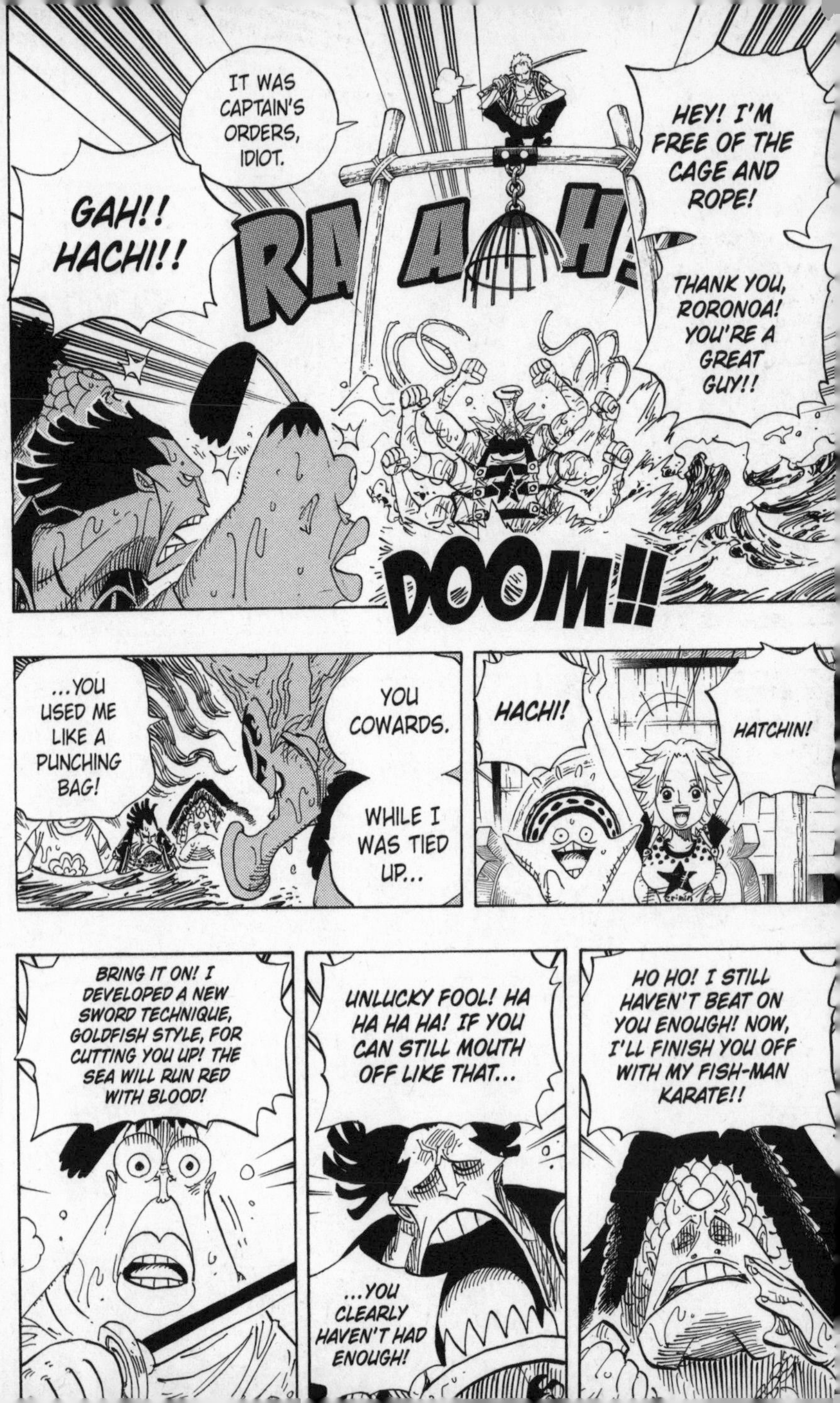
HEY! I'M FREE OF THE CAGE AND ROPE!
THANK YOU, RORONOA! YOU'RE A GREAT GUY!!
RAAH
IT WAS CAPTAIN'S ORDERS, IDIOT.
GAH!! HACHI!!
DOOM!!
HATCHIN!
HACHI!
YOU COWARDS.
WHILE I WAS TIED UP...
...YOU USED ME LIKE A PUNCHING BAG!
HO HO! I STILL HAVEN'T BEAT ON YOU ENOUGH! NOW, I'LL FINISH YOU OFF WITH MY FISH-MAN KARATE!!
UNLUCKY FOOL! HA HA HA! IF YOU CAN STILL MOUTH OFF LIKE THAT...
...YOU CLEARLY HAVEN'T HAD ENOUGH!
BRING IT ON! I DEVELOPED A NEW SWORD TECHNIQUE, GOLDFISH STYLE, FOR CUTTING YOU UP! THE SEA WILL RUN RED WITH BLOOD!

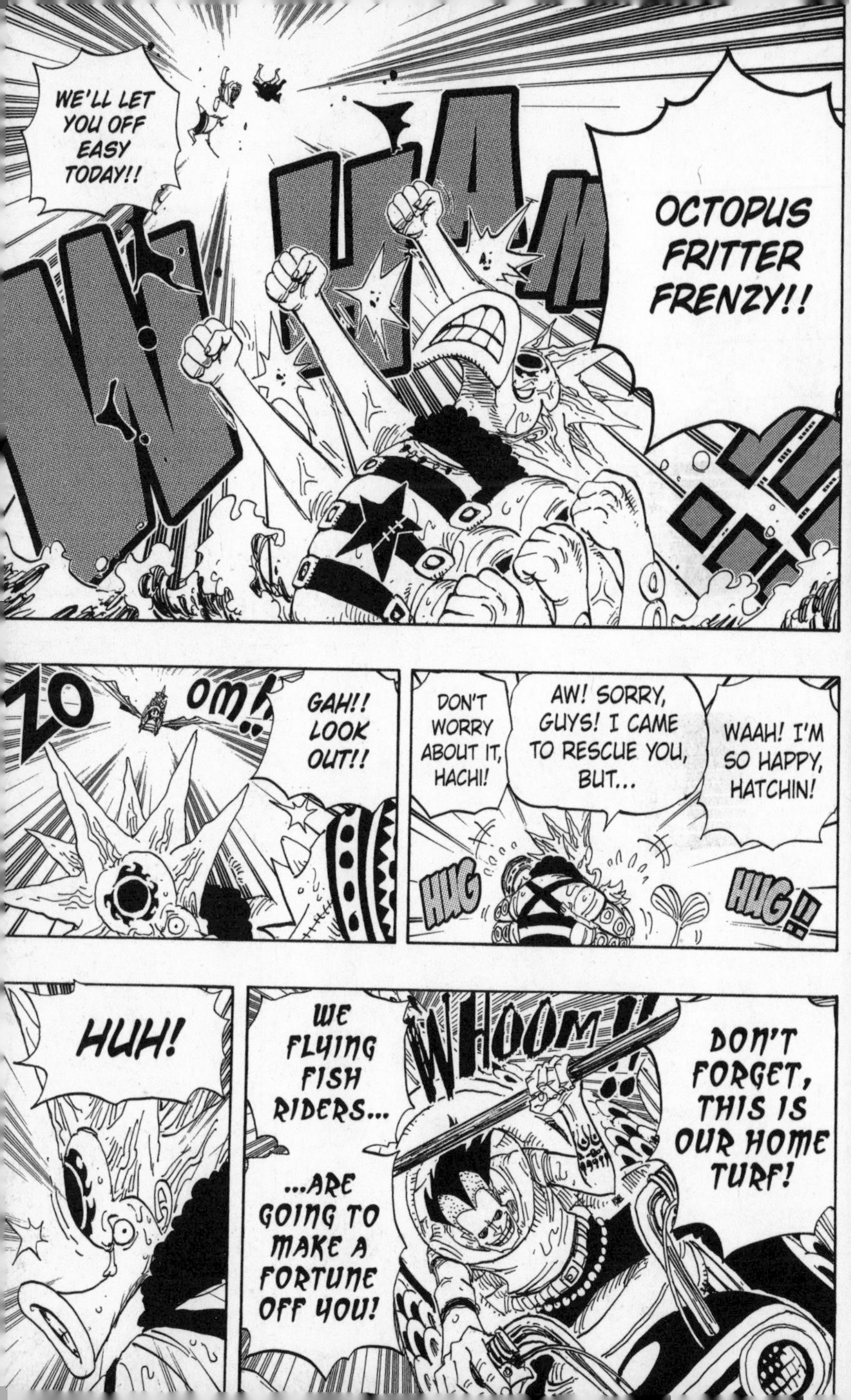
OCTOPUS FRITTER FRENZY!!
WE'LL LET YOU OFF EASY TODAY!!
WAAH! I'M SO HAPPY, HATCHIN!
AW! SORRY, GUYS! I CAME TO RESCUE YOU, BUT...
DON'T WORRY ABOUT IT, HACHI!
HUG!!
HUG
GAH!! LOOK OUT!!
ZOOM!!
DON'T FORGET, THIS IS OUR HOME TURF!
WHOOM!!
WE FLYING FISH RIDERS...
...ARE GOING TO MAKE A FORTUNE OFF YOU!
HUH!

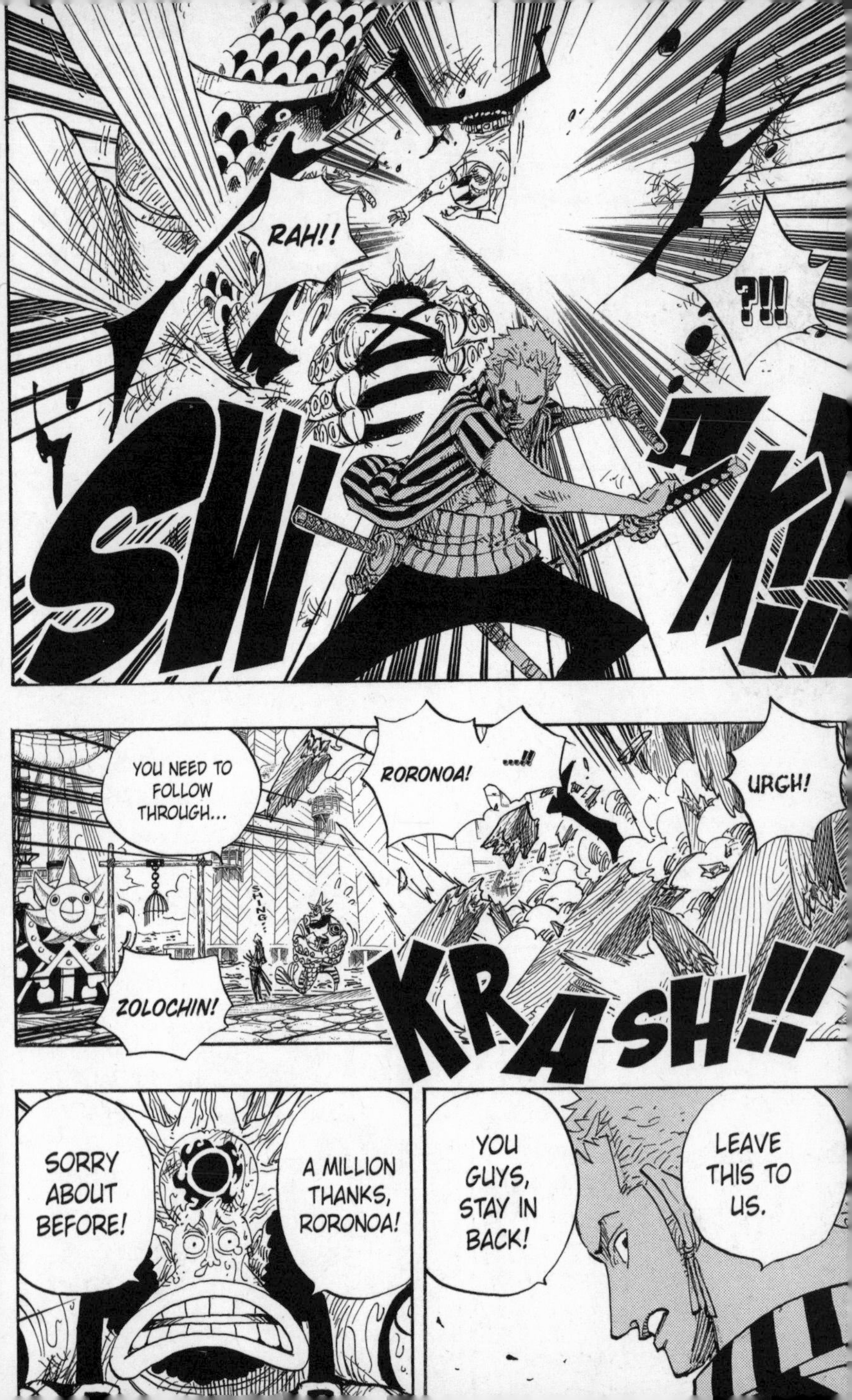
?!!
RAH!!
URGH!
RORONOA!
...!!
YOU NEED TO FOLLOW THROUGH...
SHING...
KRASH!!
ZOLOCHIN!
LEAVE THIS TO US.
YOU GUYS, STAY IN BACK!
A MILLION THANKS, RORONOA!
SORRY ABOUT BEFORE!

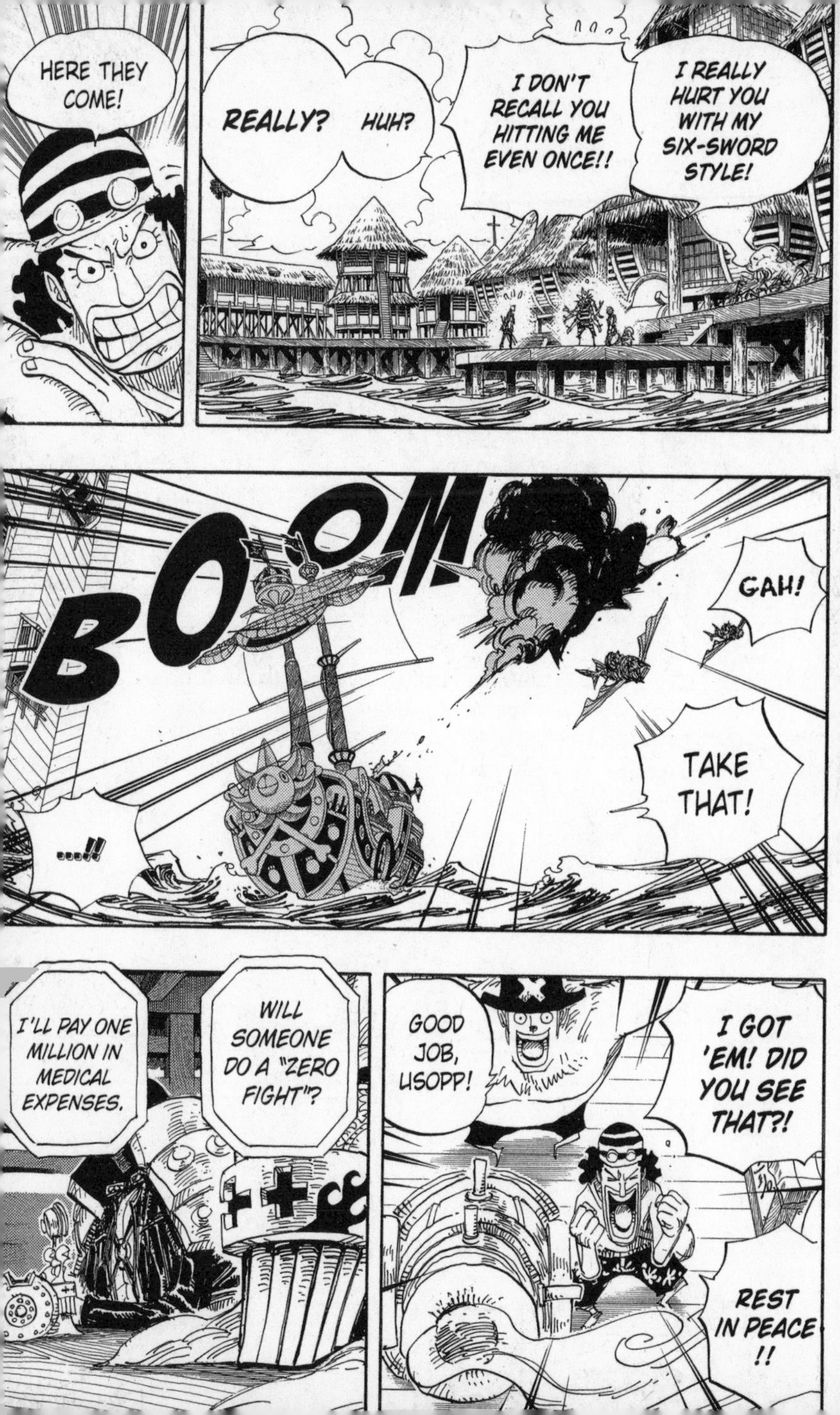
I REALLY HURT YOU WITH MY SIX-SWORD STYLE!
I DON'T RECALL YOU HITTING ME EVEN ONCE!!
HUH?
REALLY?
HERE THEY COME!
GAH!
TAKE THAT!
BOOM
...!!
I GOT 'EM! DID YOU SEE THAT?!
GOOD JOB, USOPP!
REST IN PEACE!!
WILL SOMEONE DO A "ZERO FIGHT"?
I'LL PAY ONE MILLION IN MEDICAL EXPENSES.

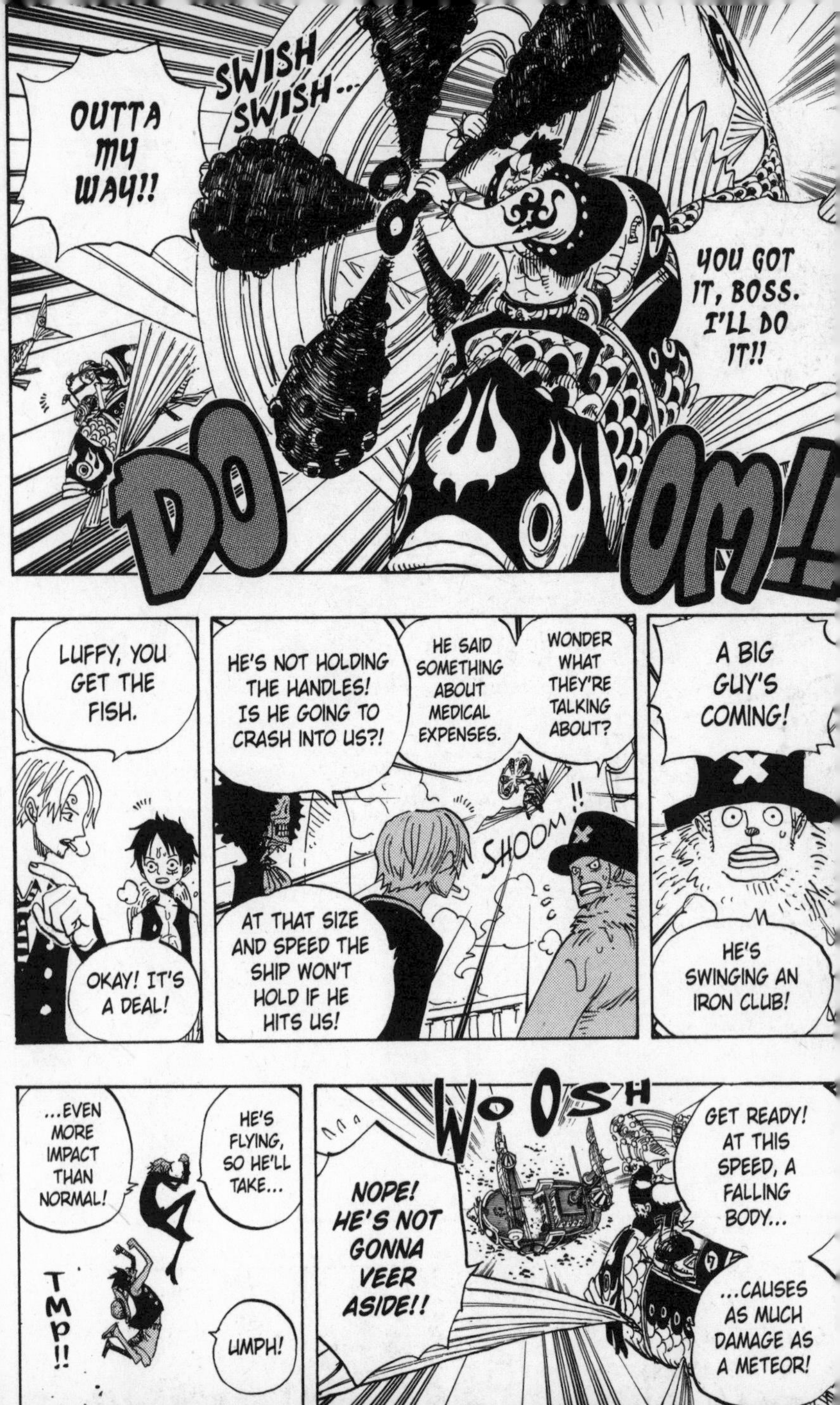
YOU GOT IT, BOSS. I'LL DO IT!!
SWISH SWISH...
OUTTA MY WAY!!
DOOM!!
A BIG GUY'S COMING!
HE'S SWINGING AN IRON CLUB!
WONDER WHAT THEY'RE TALKING ABOUT?
HE SAID SOMETHING ABOUT MEDICAL EXPENSES.
HE'S NOT HOLDING THE HANDLES! IS HE GOING TO CRASH INTO US?!
SHOOM!!
AT THAT SIZE AND SPEED THE SHIP WON'T HOLD IF HE HITS US!
LUFFY, YOU GET THE FISH.
OKAY! IT'S A DEAL!
WOOSH
GET READY! AT THIS SPEED, A FALLING BODY...
NOPE! HE'S NOT GONNA VEER ASIDE!!
...CAUSES AS MUCH DAMAGE AS A METEOR!
HE'S FLYING, SO HE'LL TAKE...
...EVEN MORE IMPACT THAN NORMAL!
UMPH!
TMP!!

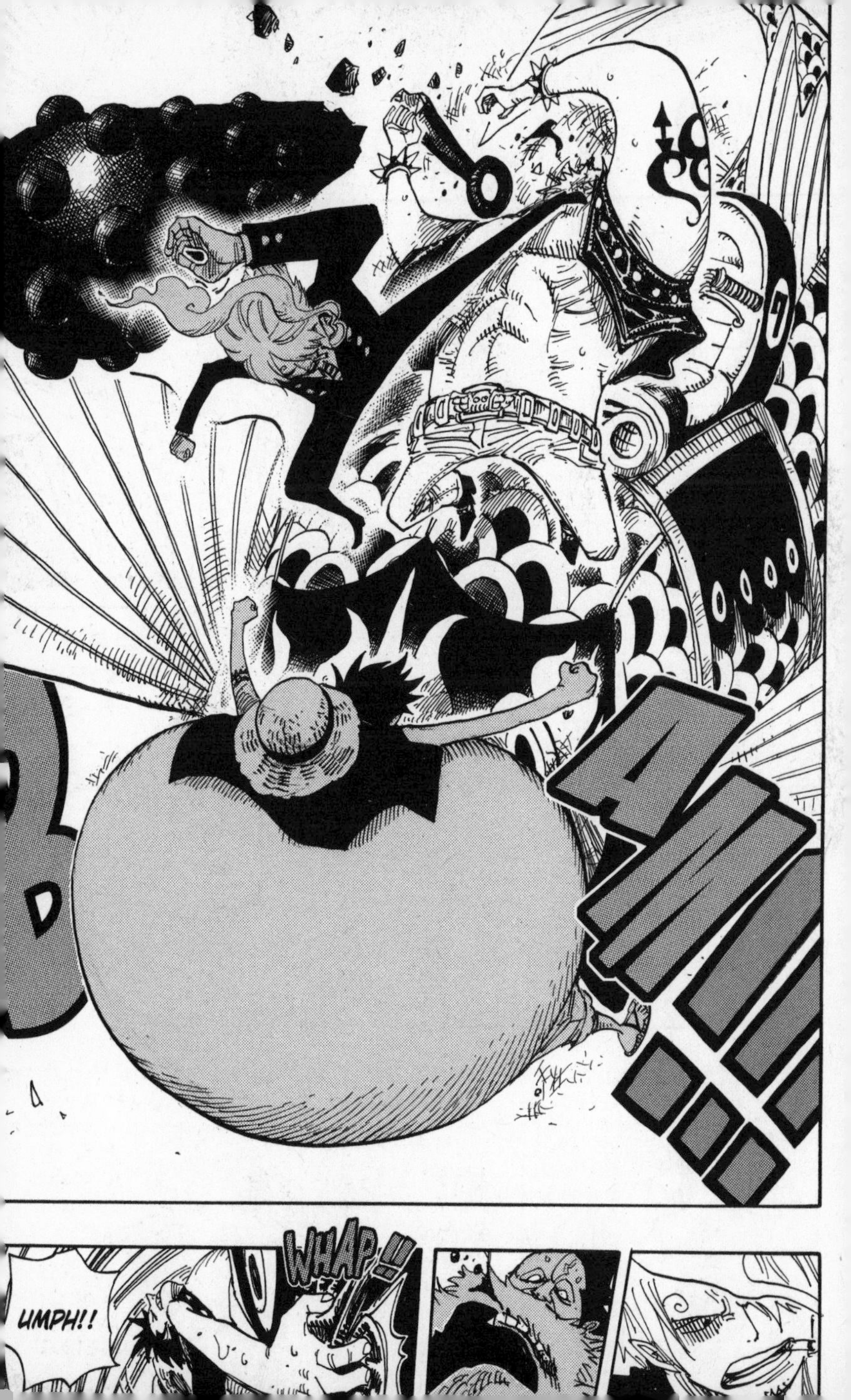
WHAP!!
UMPH!!

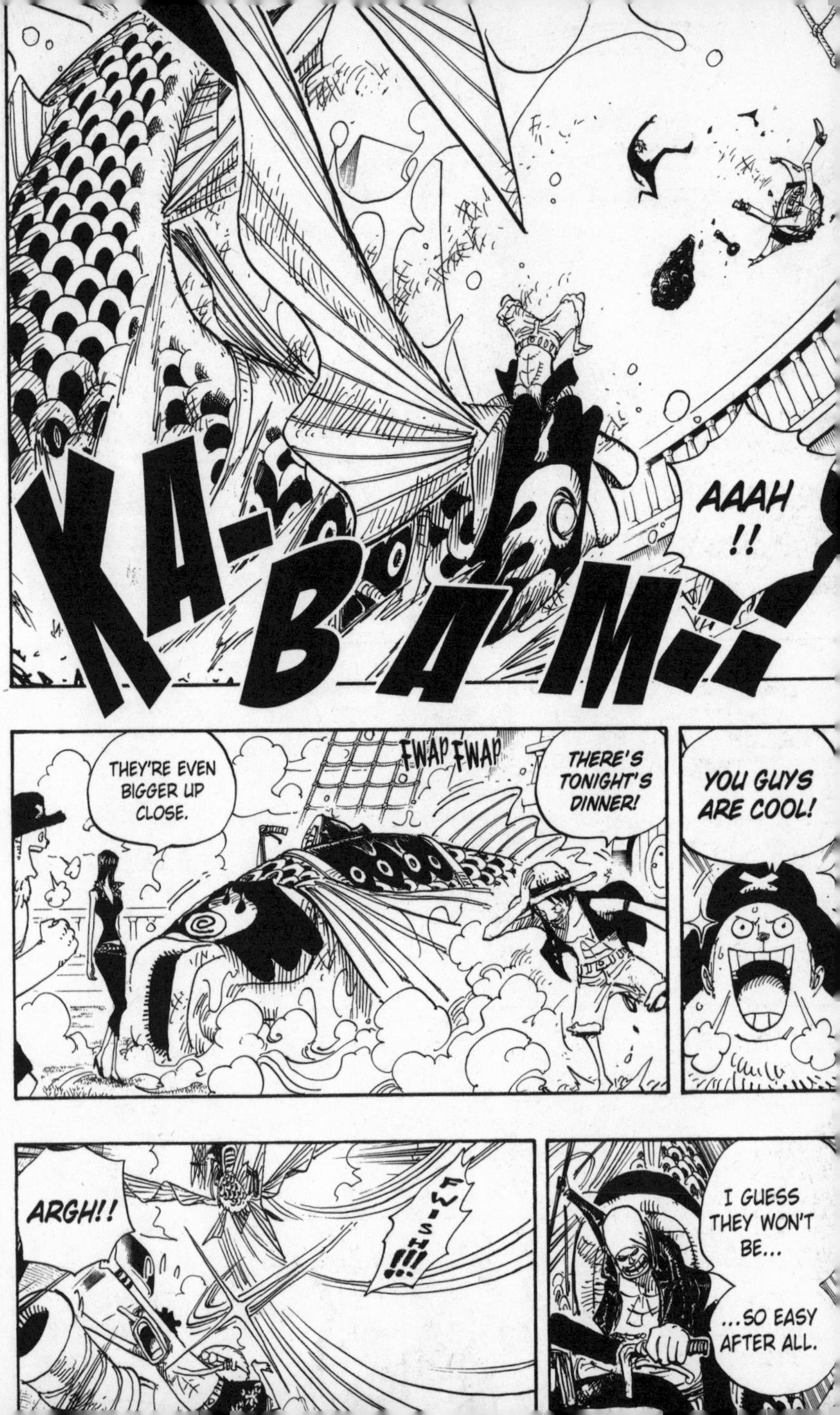
AAAH!!
KA-BAM!!
YOU GUYS ARE COOL!
THERE'S TONIGHT'S DINNER!
FWAP FWAP
THEY'RE EVEN BIGGER UP CLOSE.
I GUESS THEY WON'T BE...
...SO EASY AFTER ALL.
FWISH!!!
ARGH!!

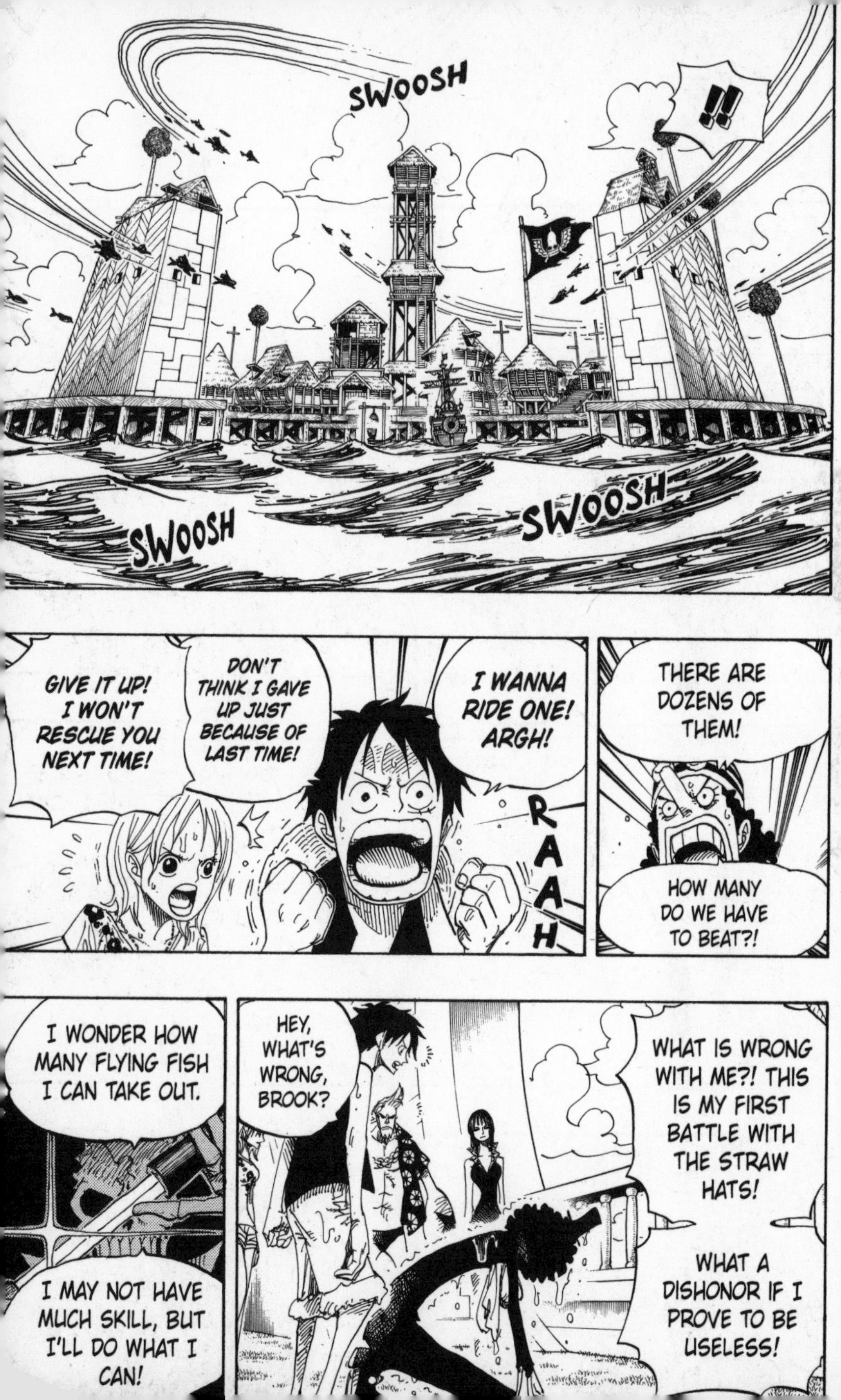
!!
SWOOSH
SWOOSH
SWOOSH
THERE ARE DOZENS OF THEM!
HOW MANY DO WE HAVE TO BEAT?!
I WANNA RIDE ONE! ARGH!
RAAH
DON'T THINK I GAVE UP JUST BECAUSE OF LAST TIME!
GIVE IT UP! I WON'T RESCUE YOU NEXT TIME!
WHAT IS WRONG WITH ME?! THIS IS MY FIRST BATTLE WITH THE STRAW HATS!
HEY, WHAT'S WRONG, BROOK?
WHAT A DISHONOR IF I PROVE TO BE USELESS!
I WONDER HOW MANY FLYING FISH I CAN TAKE OUT.
I MAY NOT HAVE MUCH SKILL, BUT I'LL DO WHAT I CAN!

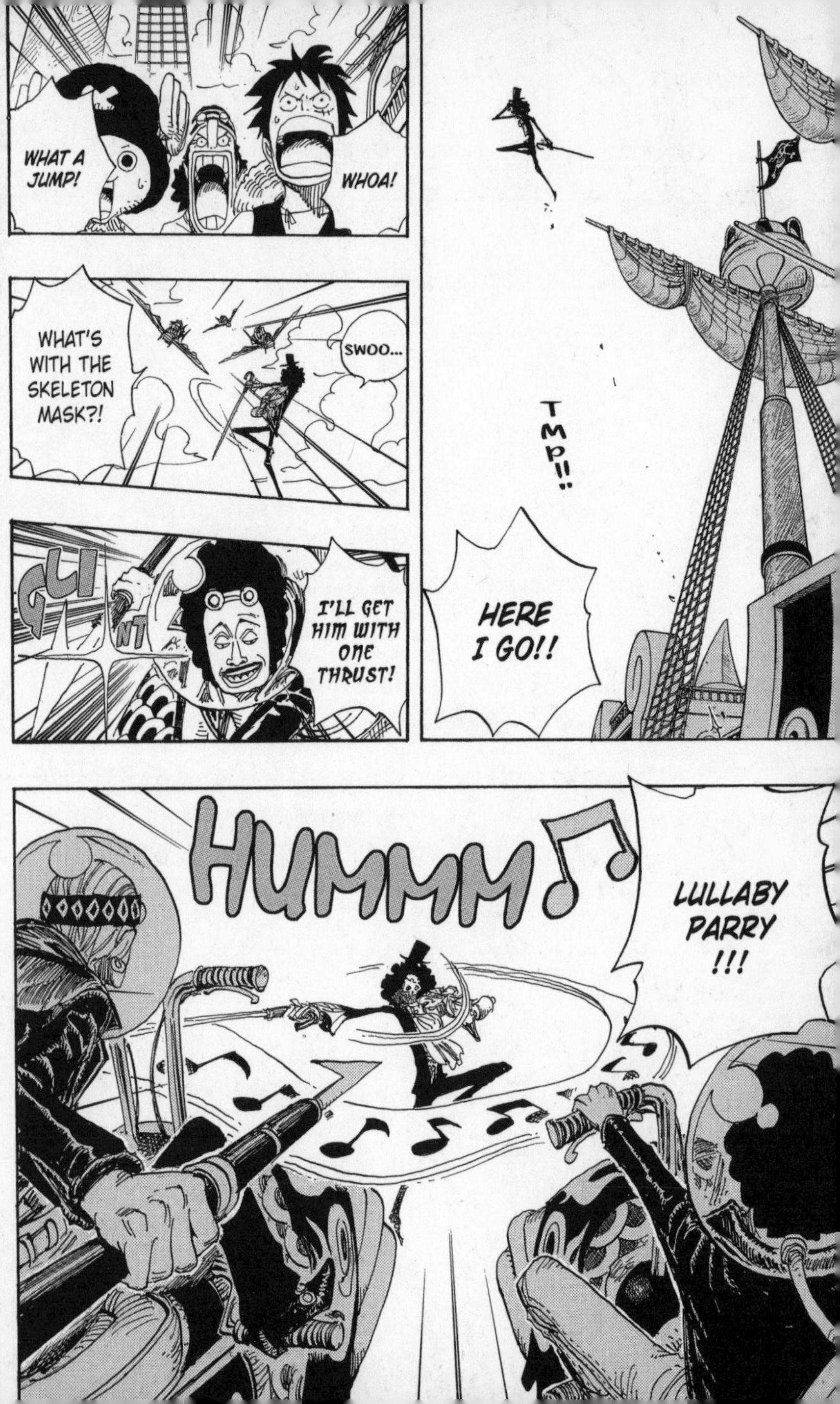
TMP!!
HERE I GO!!
WHOA!
WHAT A JUMP!
SWOO...
WHAT'S WITH THE SKELETON MASK?!
GLINT
I'LL GET HIM WITH ONE THRUST!
LULLABY PARRY !!!
HUMMM

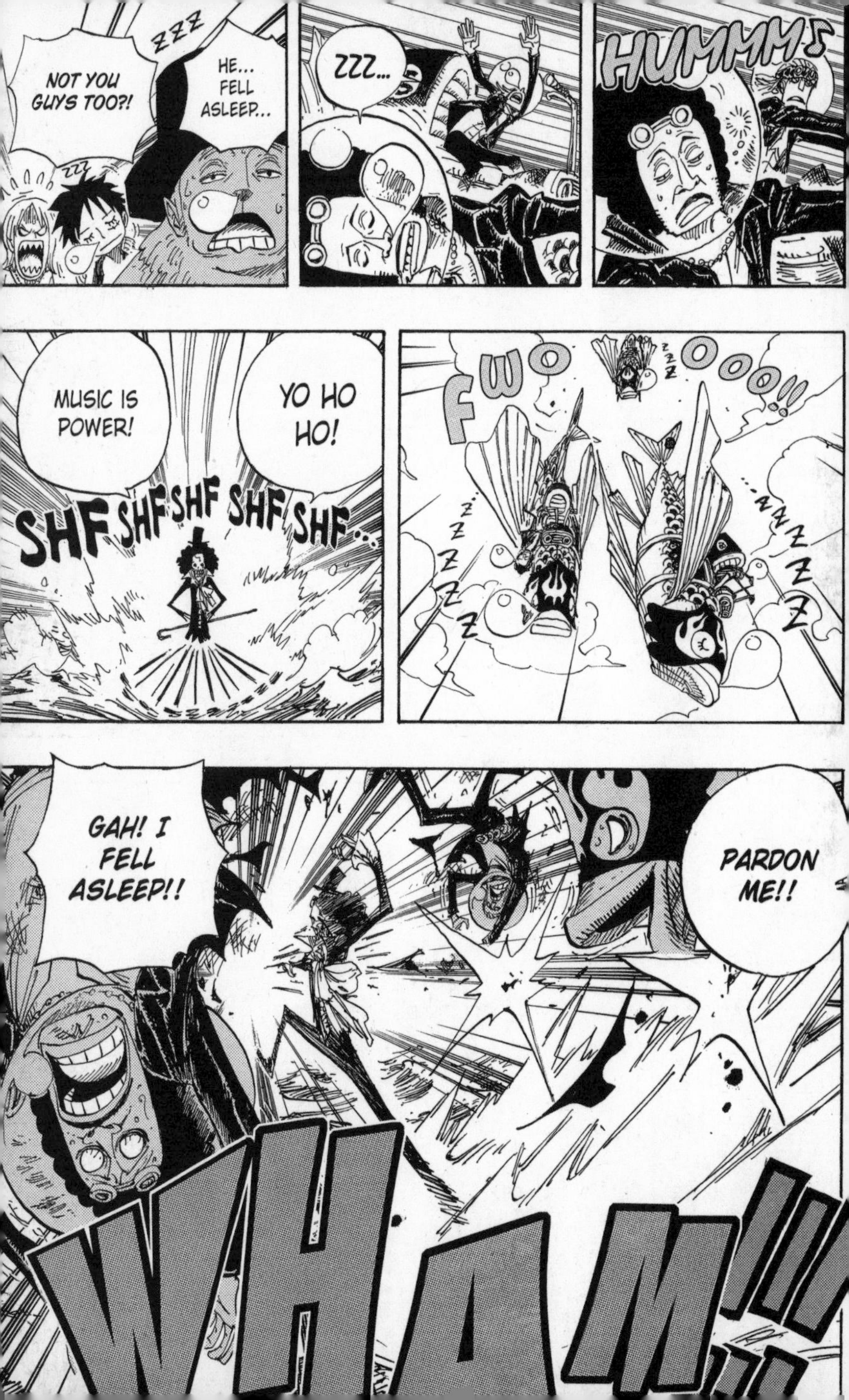
HUMMM
ZZZ...
ZZZ
HE... FELL ASLEEP...
NOT YOU GUYS TOO?!
ZZZ
FWOOOOO!!
ZZZ
ZZZZZZ
ZZZZZ
YO HO HO!
MUSIC IS POWER!
SHF SHF SHF SHF SHF...
PARDON ME!!
GAH! I FELL ASLEEP!!
WHAM!!

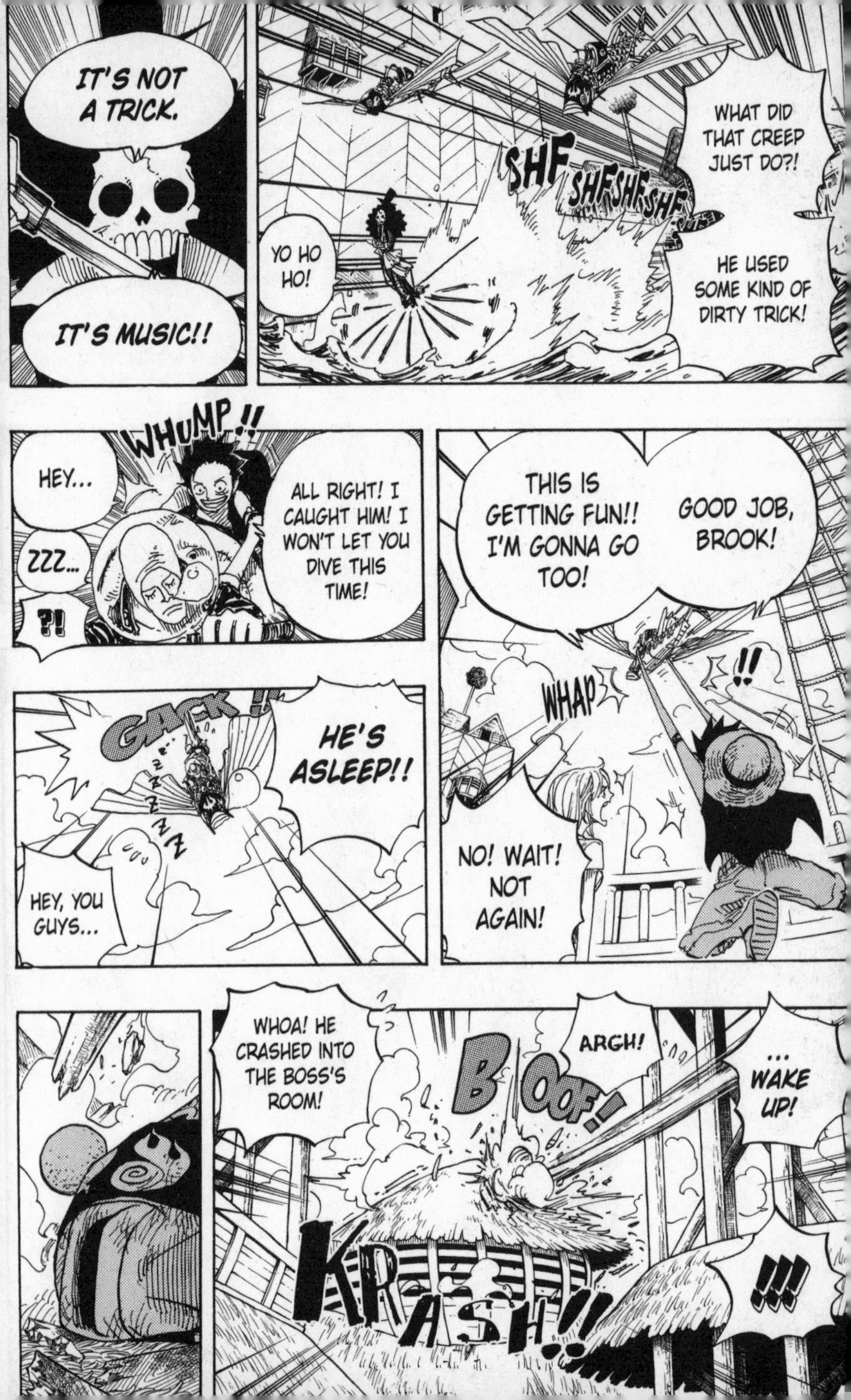
WHAT DID THAT CREEP JUST DO?!
HE USED SOME KIND OF DIRTY TRICK!
SHF SHFSHFSHF
YO HO HO!
IT'S NOT A TRICK.
IT'S MUSIC!!
GOOD JOB, BROOK!
THIS IS GETTING FUN!! I'M GONNA GO TOO!
!!
WHAP
NO! WAIT! NOT AGAIN!
WHUMP!!
ALL RIGHT! I CAUGHT HIM! I WON'T LET YOU DIVE THIS TIME!
HEY...
ZZZ...
?!
GACK
HE'S ASLEEP!!
ZZZZ
HEY, YOU GUYS...
... WAKE UP!
!!!
ARGH!
BOOF!
WHOA! HE CRASHED INTO THE BOSS'S ROOM!
KRASH!!

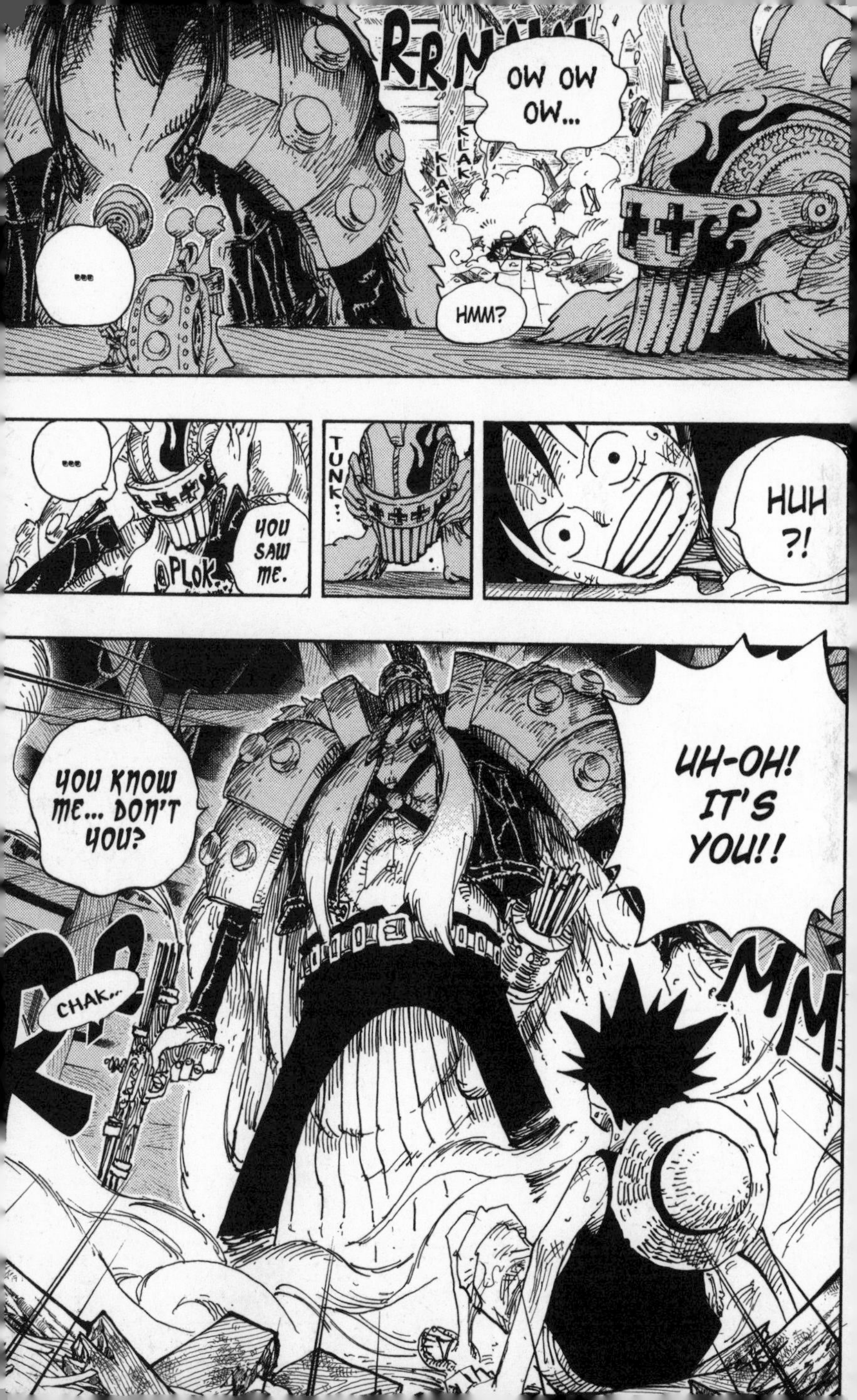
OW OW OW...
KLAK KLAK
HMM?
...
HUH ?!
TUNK...
...
YOU SAW ME.
PLOK
UH-OH! IT'S YOU!!
MM
YOU KNOW ME... DON'T YOU?
CHAK...

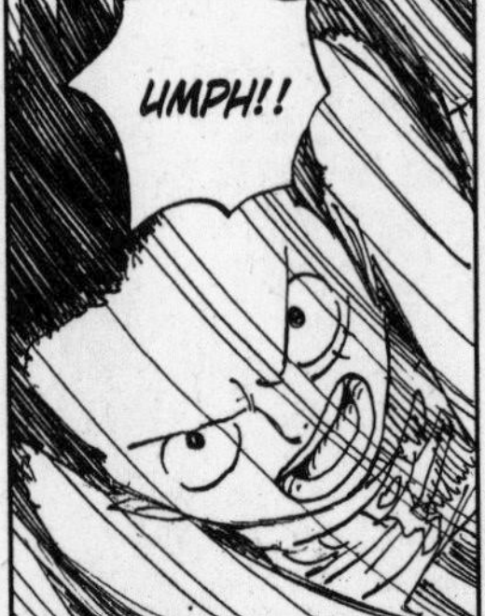
UMPH!!

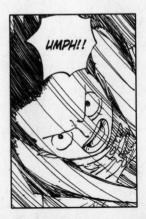

Chapter 494:
DUVAL'S TRAGEDY

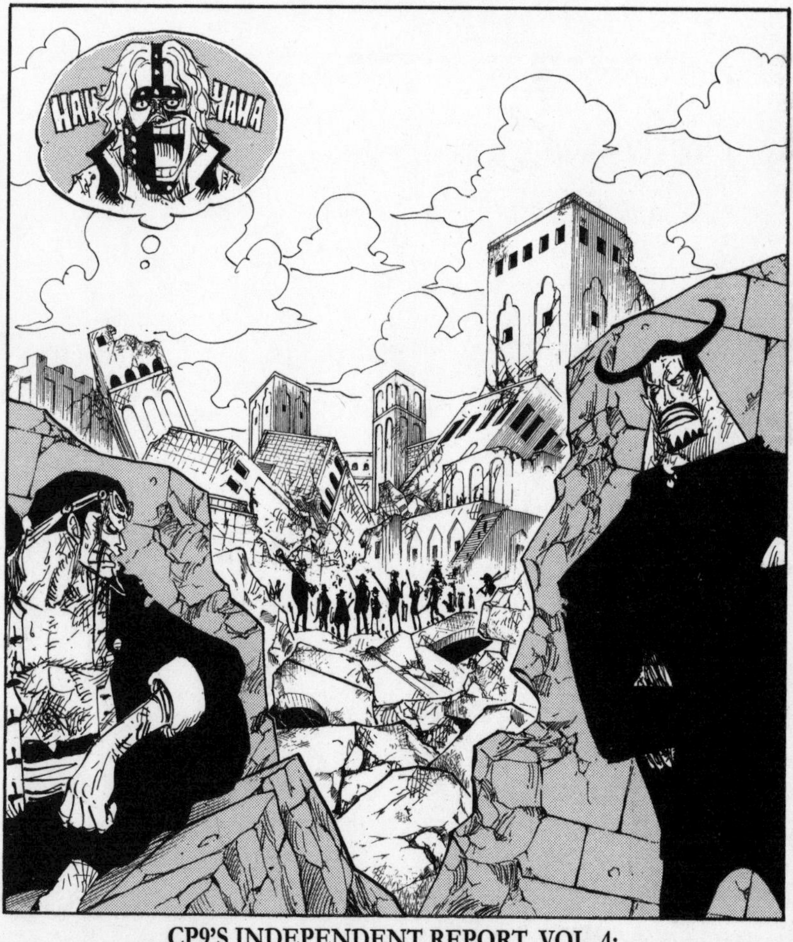
HAHA
HAHA

CP9'S INDEPENDENT REPORT, VOL. 4:
"FAILURE! PURSUED BY THE WORLD GOVERNMENT"

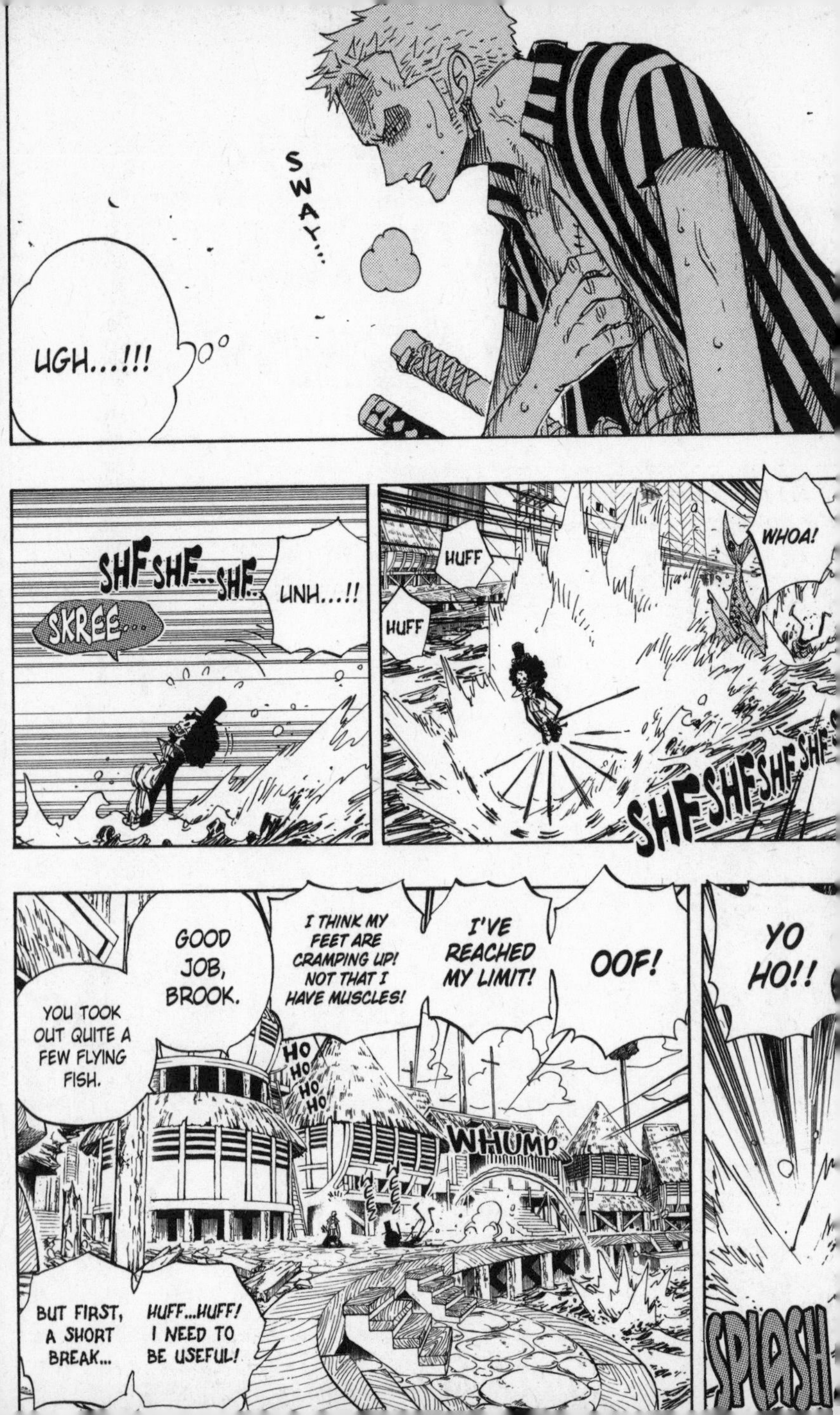
SWAY...
UGH...!!!
WHOA!
HUFF
HUFF
SHF SHF SHF SHF SHF
UNH...!!
SHF SHF... SHF...
SKREE...
YO HO!!
SPLASH
OOF!
I'VE REACHED MY LIMIT!
I THINK MY FEET ARE CRAMPING UP! NOT THAT I HAVE MUSCLES!
GOOD JOB, BROOK.
YOU TOOK OUT QUITE A FEW FLYING FISH.
HO HO HO HO HO
WHUMP
HUFF...HUFF! I NEED TO BE USEFUL!
BUT FIRST, A SHORT BREAK...

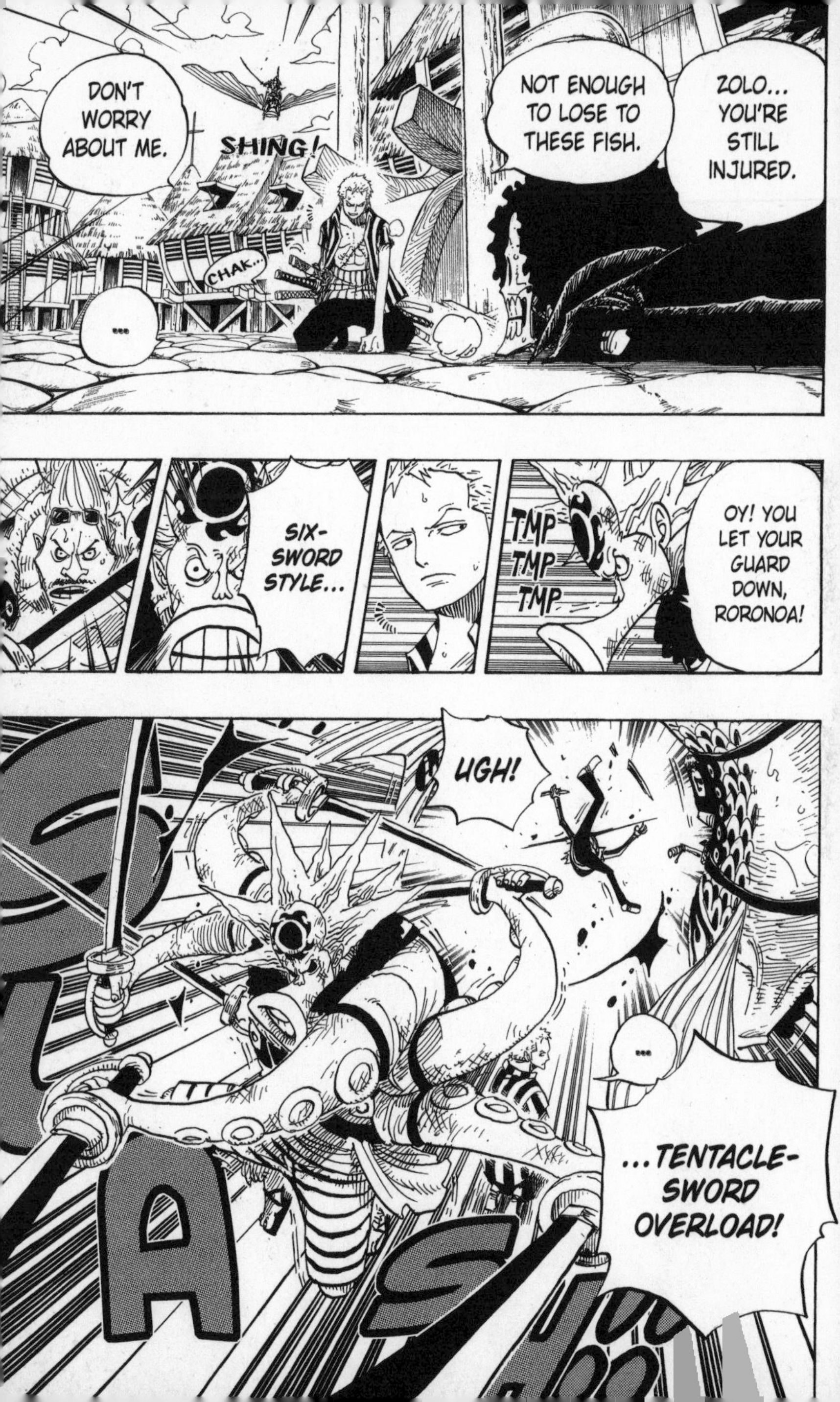
ZOLO... YOU'RE STILL INJURED.
NOT ENOUGH TO LOSE TO THESE FISH.
SHING!
DON'T WORRY ABOUT ME.
CHAK...
...
OY! YOU LET YOUR GUARD DOWN, RORONOA!
TMP TMP TMP
SIX-SWORD STYLE...
UGH!
...
...TENTACLE-SWORD OVERLOAD!

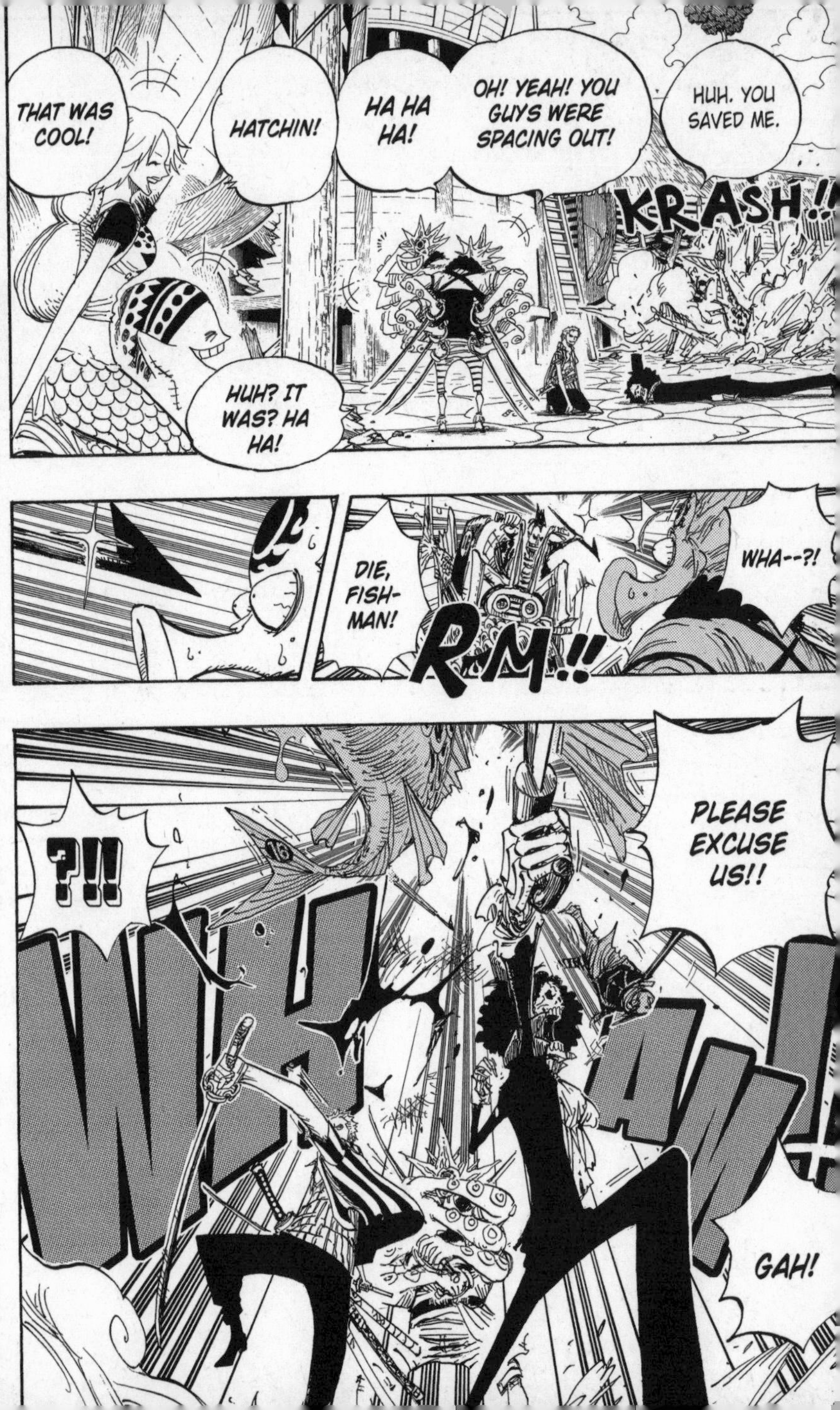
HUH. YOU SAVED ME.
KRASH!!
OH! YEAH! YOU GUYS WERE SPACING OUT!
HA HA HA!
HATCHIN!
THAT WAS COOL!
HUH? IT WAS? HA HA!
WHA--?!
DIE, FISH-MAN!
R-M!!
PLEASE EXCUSE US!!
GAH!
?!!

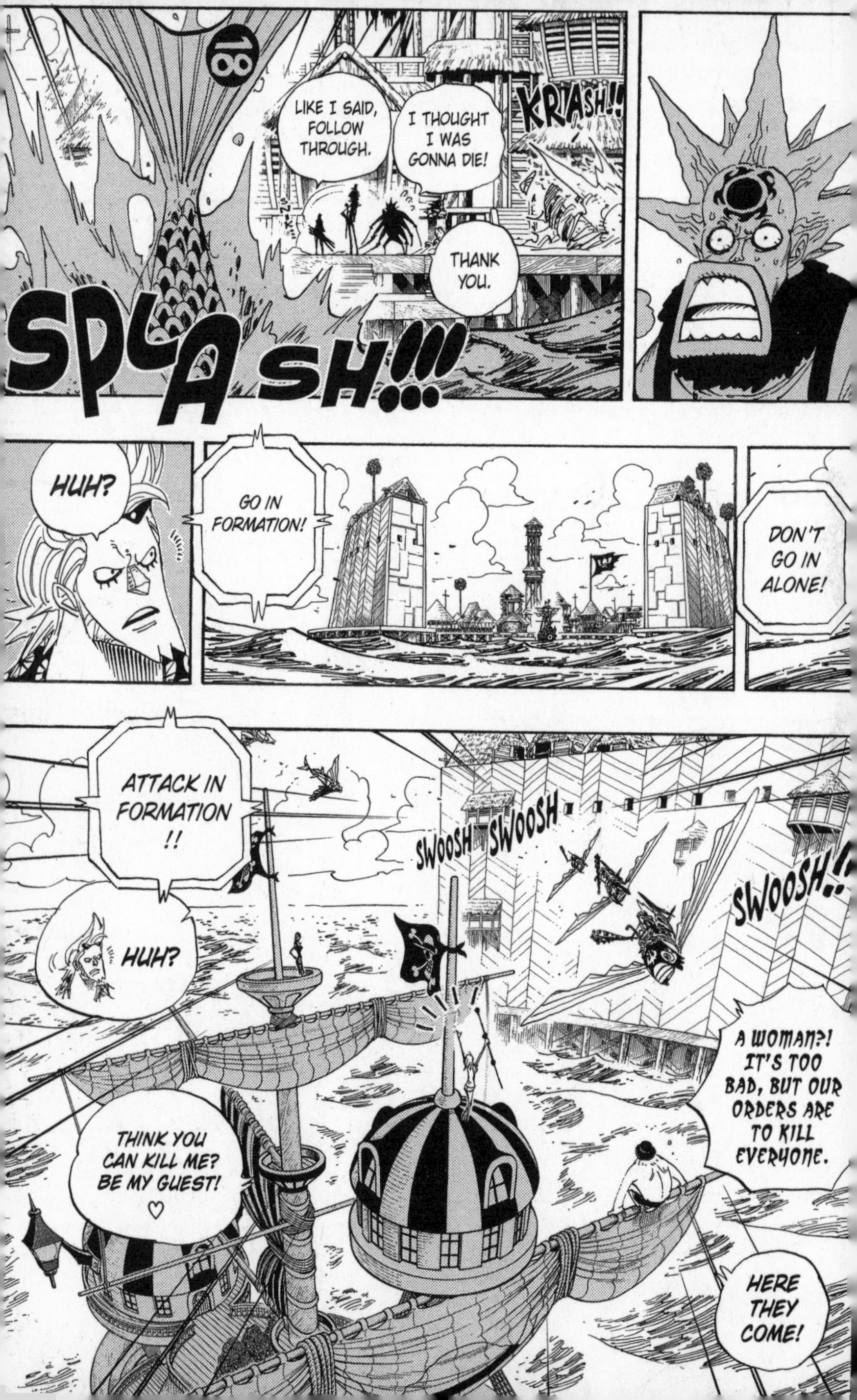
KRASH!!
I THOUGHT I WAS GONNA DIE!
LIKE I SAID, FOLLOW THROUGH.
THANK YOU.
SPLASH!!!
DON'T GO IN ALONE!
GO IN FORMATION!
HUH?
SWOOSH!!
SWOOSH SWOOSH
A WOMAN?! IT'S TOO BAD, BUT OUR ORDERS ARE TO KILL EVERYONE.
ATTACK IN FORMATION!!
HUH?
HERE THEY COME!
THINK YOU CAN KILL ME? BE MY GUEST! ♡

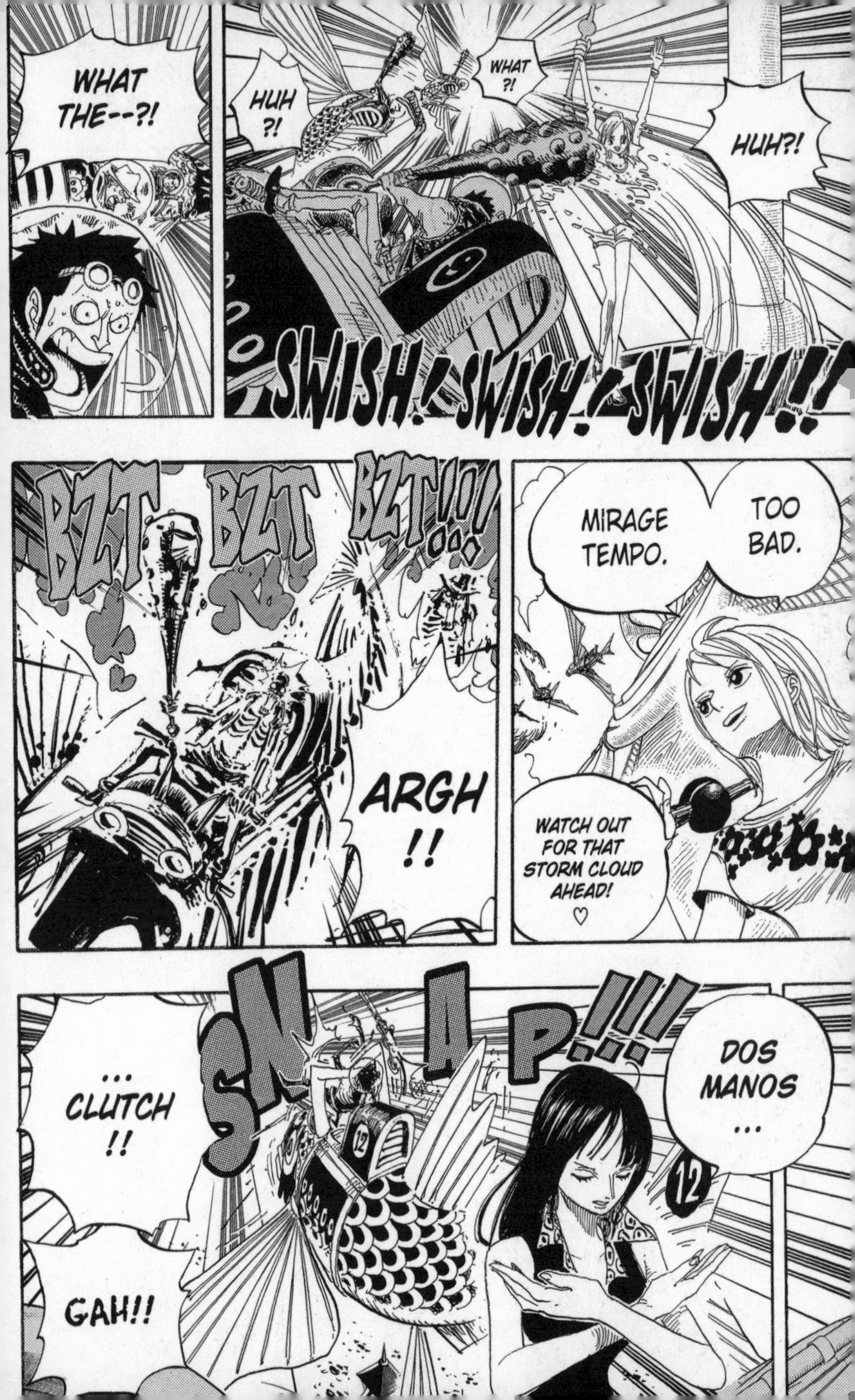
HUH?!
WHAT ?!
HUH ?!
SWISH! SWISH! SWISH!!
WHAT THE--?!
TOO BAD.
MIRAGE TEMPO.
WATCH OUT FOR THAT STORM CLOUD AHEAD! ♡
BZT BZT BZT!!!
ARGH !!
DOS MANOS ...
SNAP!!!
... CLUTCH !!
GAH!!

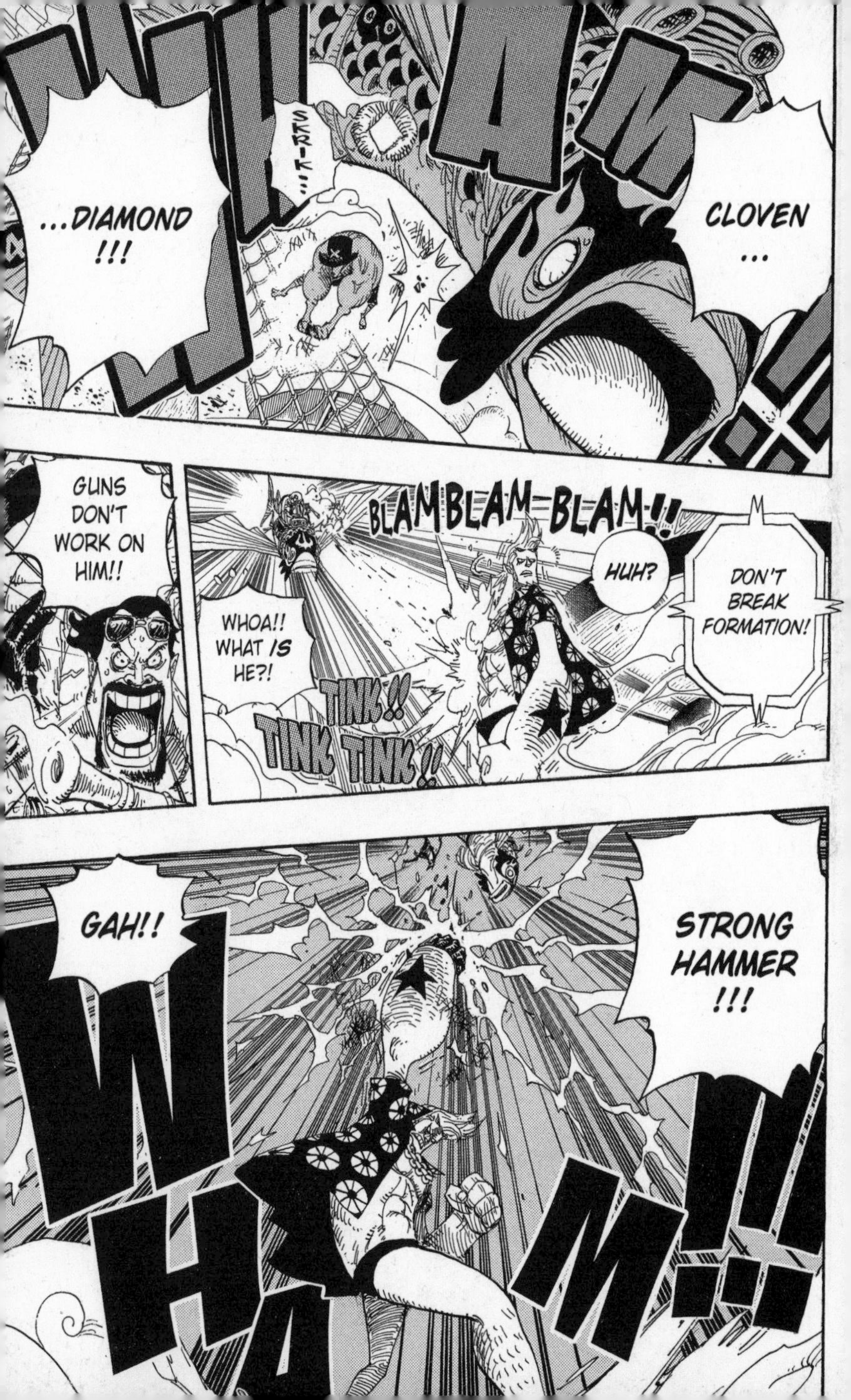
CLOVEN...
...DIAMOND!!!
SKRIK...
DON'T BREAK FORMATION!
HUH?
BLAMBLAM BLAM!!
WHOA!! WHAT IS HE?!
TINK!! TINK TINK!!
GUNS DON'T WORK ON HIM!!
STRONG HAMMER!!!
GAH!!

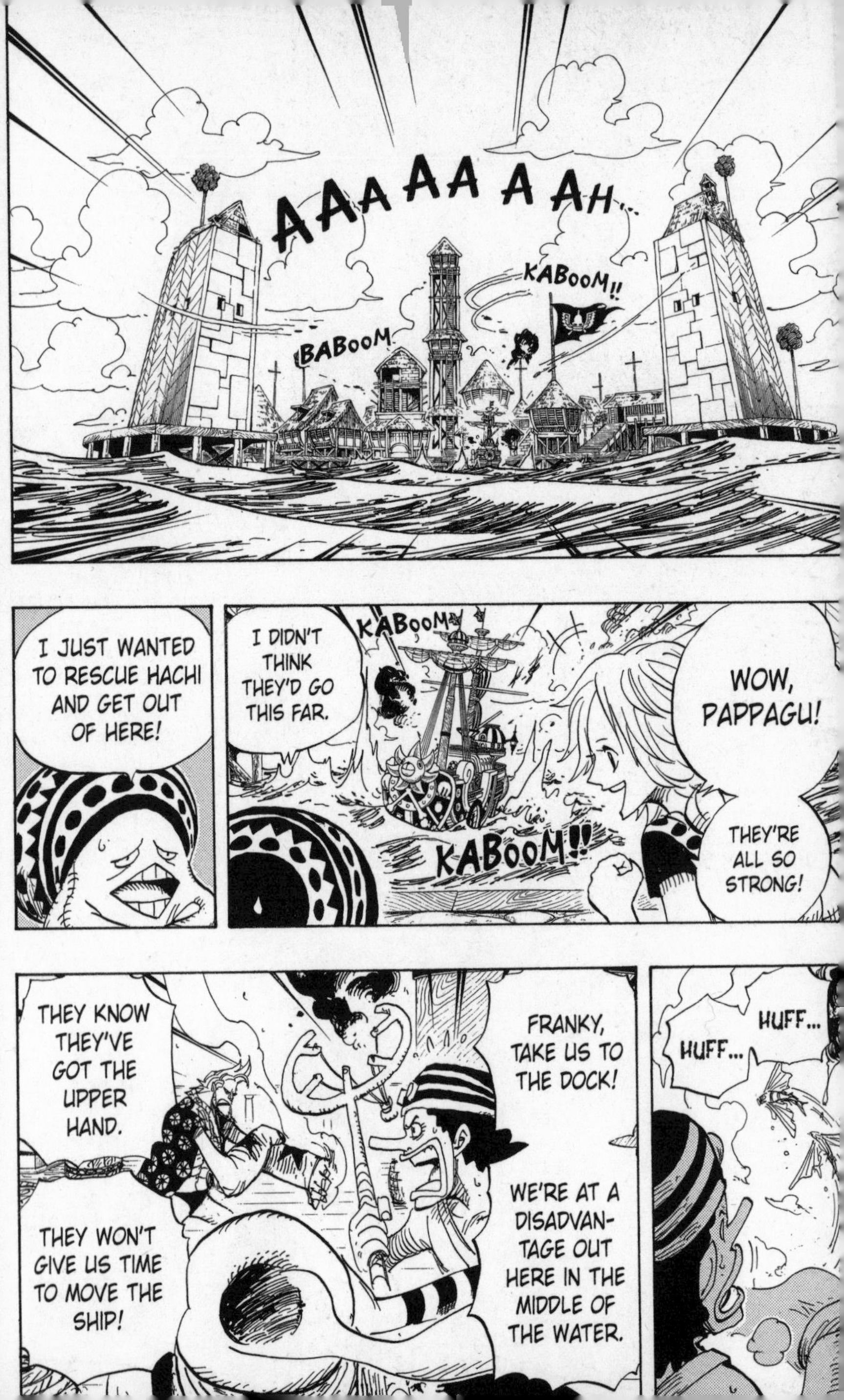
AAAAAAAAH...
KABOOM!!
BABOOM
WOW, PAPPAGU!
THEY'RE ALL SO STRONG!
KABOOM
I DIDN'T THINK THEY'D GO THIS FAR.
KABOOM!!
I JUST WANTED TO RESCUE HACHI AND GET OUT OF HERE!
HUFF...
HUFF...
FRANKY, TAKE US TO THE DOCK!
WE'RE AT A DISADVAN-TAGE OUT HERE IN THE MIDDLE OF THE WATER.
THEY KNOW THEY'VE GOT THE UPPER HAND.
THEY WON'T GIVE US TIME TO MOVE THE SHIP!

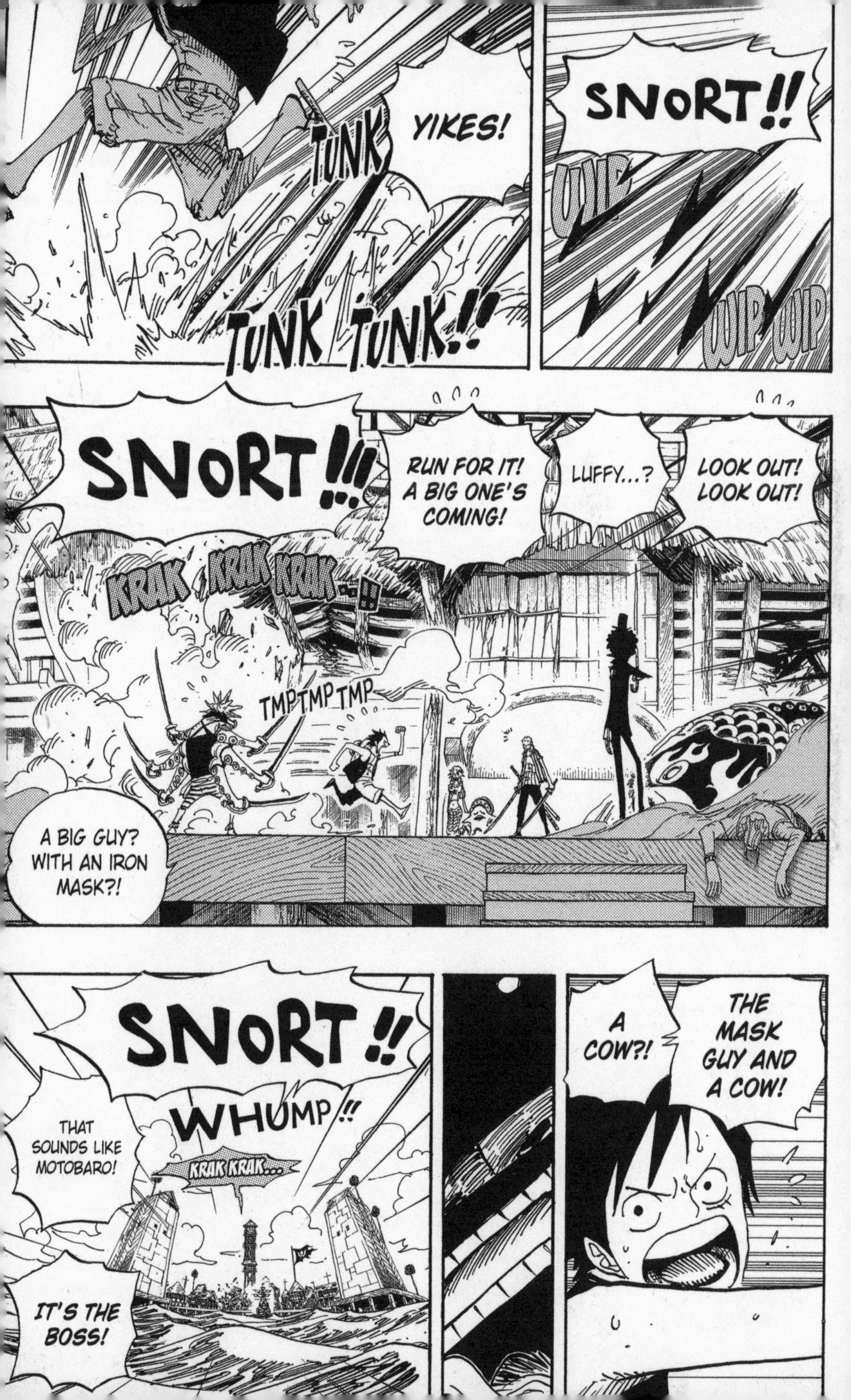
SNORT!!
WIP WIP
YIKES!
TUNK
TUNK TUNK!!
LOOK OUT! LOOK OUT!
LUFFY...?
RUN FOR IT! A BIG ONE'S COMING!
SNORT!!!
KRAK KRAK KRAK..!!
TMP TMP TMP
A BIG GUY? WITH AN IRON MASK?!
THE MASK GUY AND A COW!
A COW?!
SNORT!!
WHUMP!!
KRAK KRAK...
THAT SOUNDS LIKE MOTOBARO!
IT'S THE BOSS!

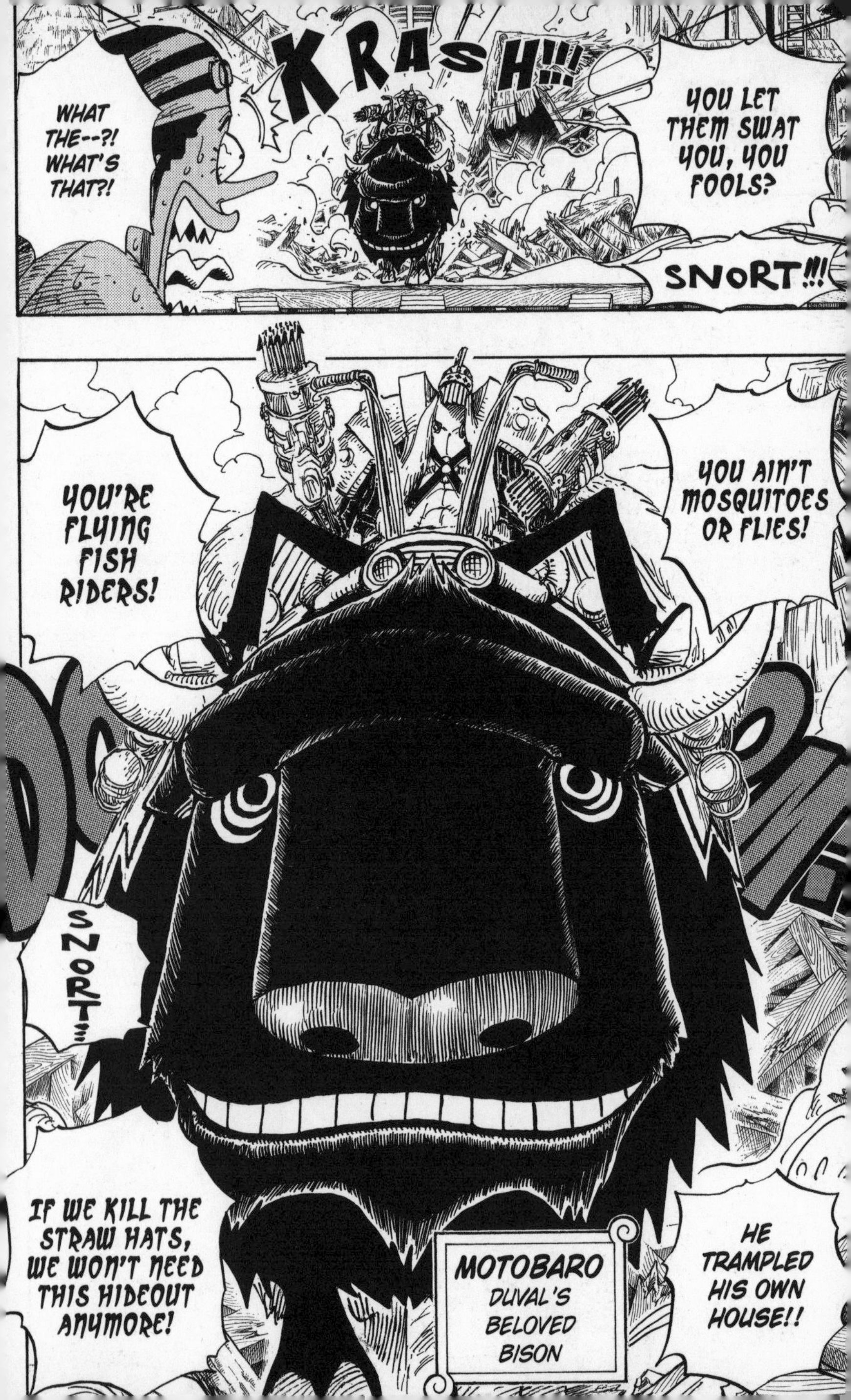
YOU LET THEM SWAT YOU, YOU FOOLS?
KRASH!!!
WHAT THE--?! WHAT'S THAT?!
SNORT!!!
YOU AIN'T MOSQUITOES OR FLIES!
YOU'RE FLYING FISH RIDERS!
SNORT!!!
HE TRAMPLED HIS OWN HOUSE!!
MOTOBARO
DUVAL'S BELOVED BISON
IF WE KILL THE STRAW HATS, WE WON'T NEED THIS HIDEOUT ANYMORE!

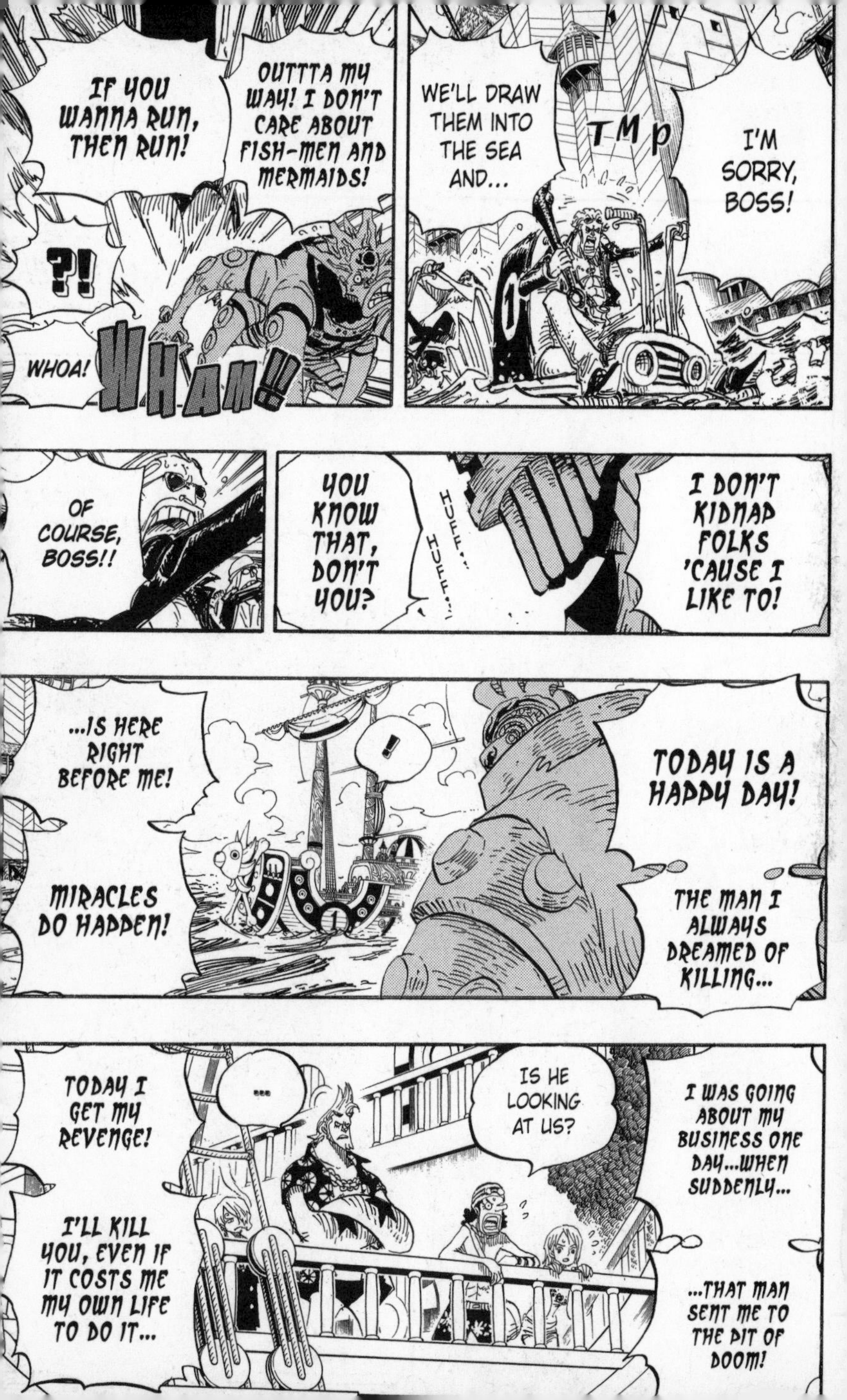

I'M SORRY, BOSS!
TMP
WE'LL DRAW THEM INTO THE SEA AND...
OUTTTA MY WAY! I DON'T CARE ABOUT FISH-MEN AND MERMAIDS!
IF YOU WANNA RUN, THEN RUN!
?!
WHAM!!
WHOA!
I DON'T KIDNAP FOLKS 'CAUSE I LIKE TO!
HUFF HUFF
YOU KNOW THAT, DON'T YOU?
OF COURSE, BOSS!!
TODAY IS A HAPPY DAY!
THE MAN I ALWAYS DREAMED OF KILLING...
!
...IS HERE RIGHT BEFORE ME!
MIRACLES DO HAPPEN!
I WAS GOING ABOUT MY BUSINESS ONE DAY...WHEN SUDDENLY...
...THAT MAN SENT ME TO THE PIT OF DOOM!
IS HE LOOKING AT US?
...
TODAY I GET MY REVENGE!
I'LL KILL YOU, EVEN IF IT COSTS ME MY OWN LIFE TO DO IT...

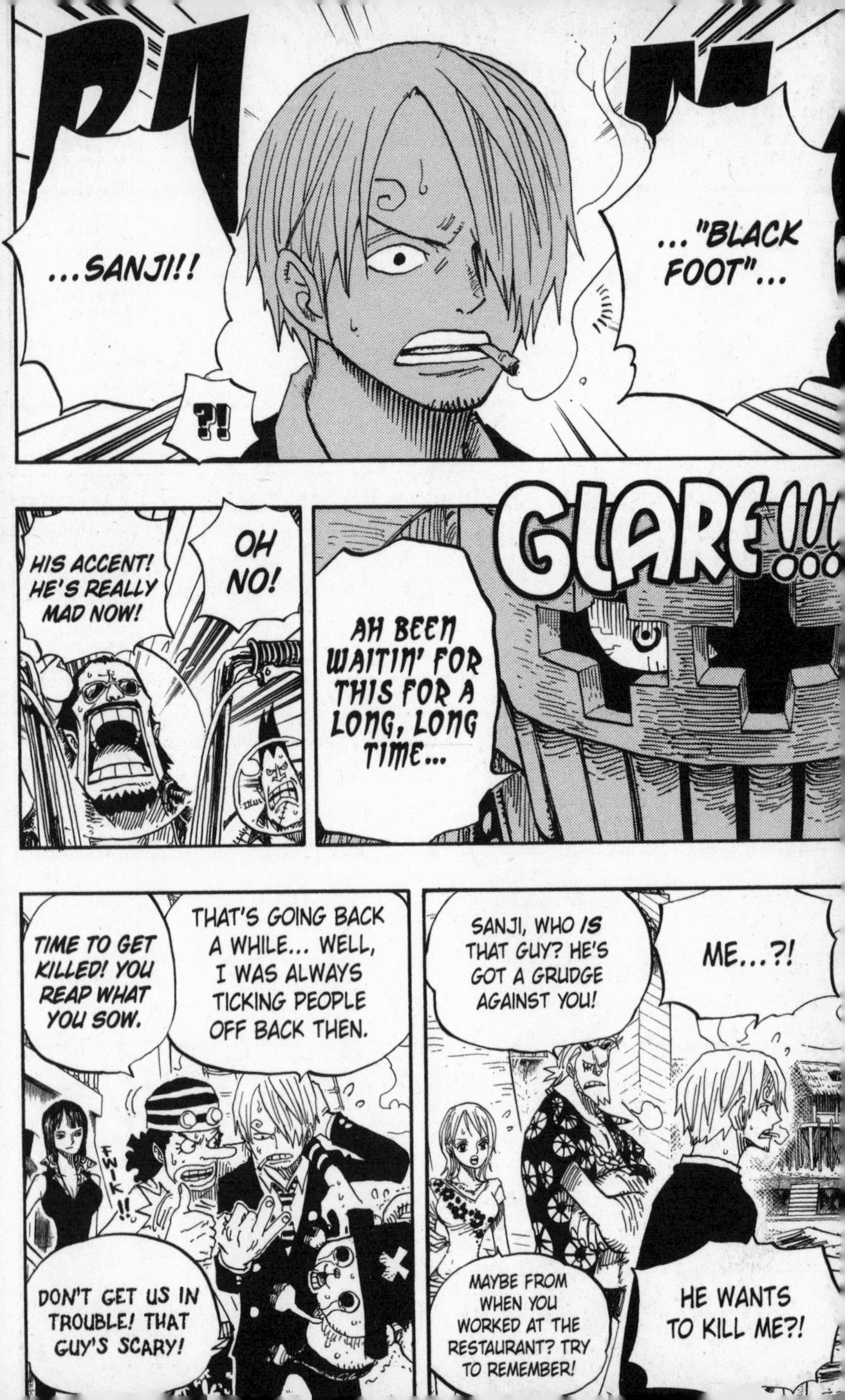
..."BLACK FOOT"...
...SANJI!!
?!
GLARE!!!
AH BEEN WAITIN' FOR THIS FOR A LONG, LONG TIME...
OH NO!
HIS ACCENT! HE'S REALLY MAD NOW!
ME...?!
SANJI, WHO *IS* THAT GUY? HE'S GOT A GRUDGE AGAINST YOU!
HE WANTS TO KILL ME?!
MAYBE FROM WHEN YOU WORKED AT THE RESTAURANT? TRY TO REMEMBER!
THAT'S GOING BACK A WHILE... WELL, I WAS ALWAYS TICKING PEOPLE OFF BACK THEN.
TIME TO GET KILLED! YOU REAP WHAT YOU SOW.
FWIK!!
DON'T GET US IN TROUBLE! THAT GUY'S SCARY!

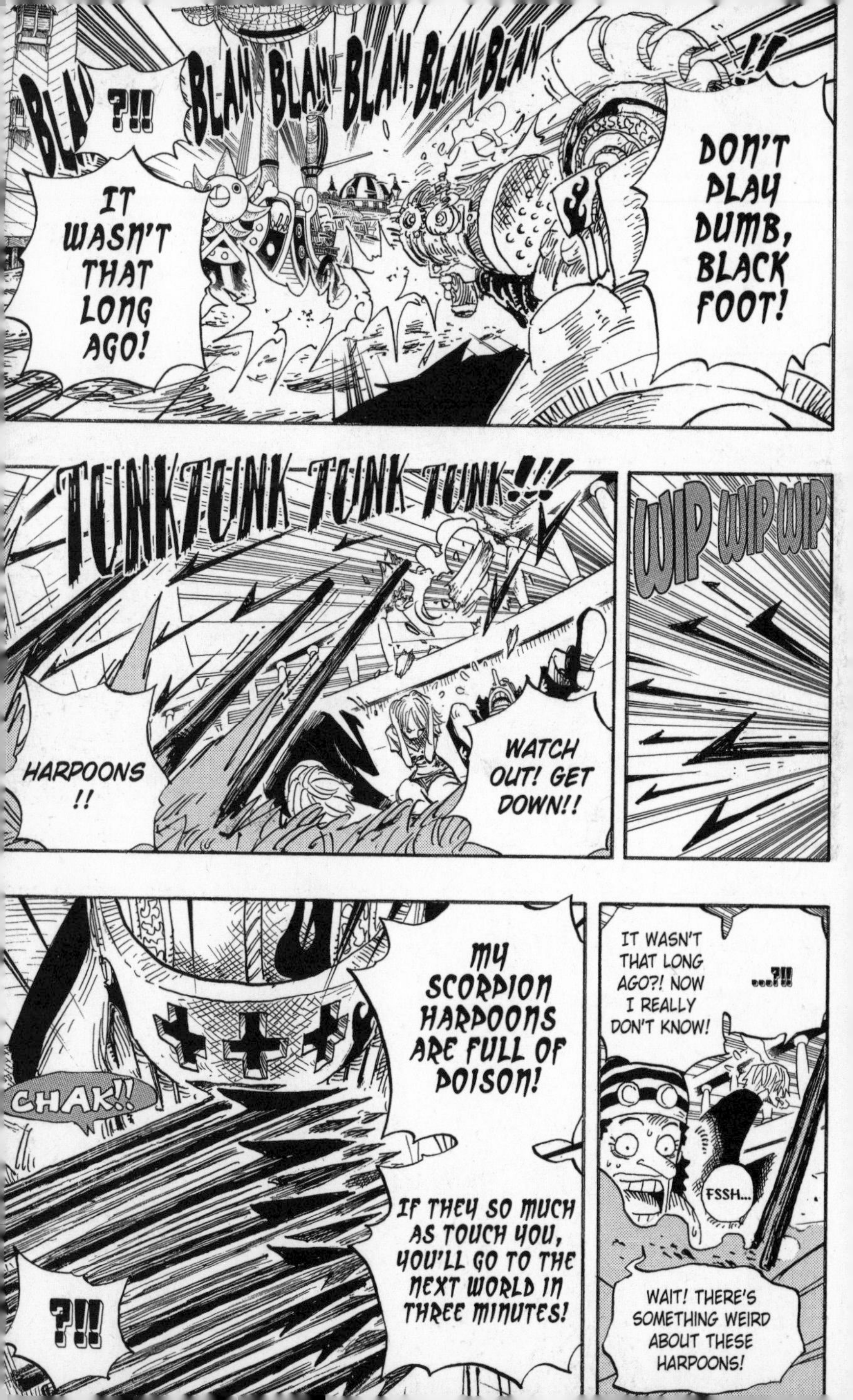
!!
DON'T PLAY DUMB, BLACK FOOT!
BLAM BLAM BLAM BLAM BLAM
?!!
BLA
IT WASN'T THAT LONG AGO!
WIP WIP WIP
TUNK TUNK TUNK TUNK!!!
WATCH OUT! GET DOWN!!
HARPOONS!!
...?!!
IT WASN'T THAT LONG AGO?! NOW I REALLY DON'T KNOW!
FSSH...
WAIT! THERE'S SOMETHING WEIRD ABOUT THESE HARPOONS!
MY SCORPION HARPOONS ARE FULL OF POISON!
CHAK!!
IF THEY SO MUCH AS TOUCH YOU, YOU'LL GO TO THE NEXT WORLD IN THREE MINUTES!
?!!

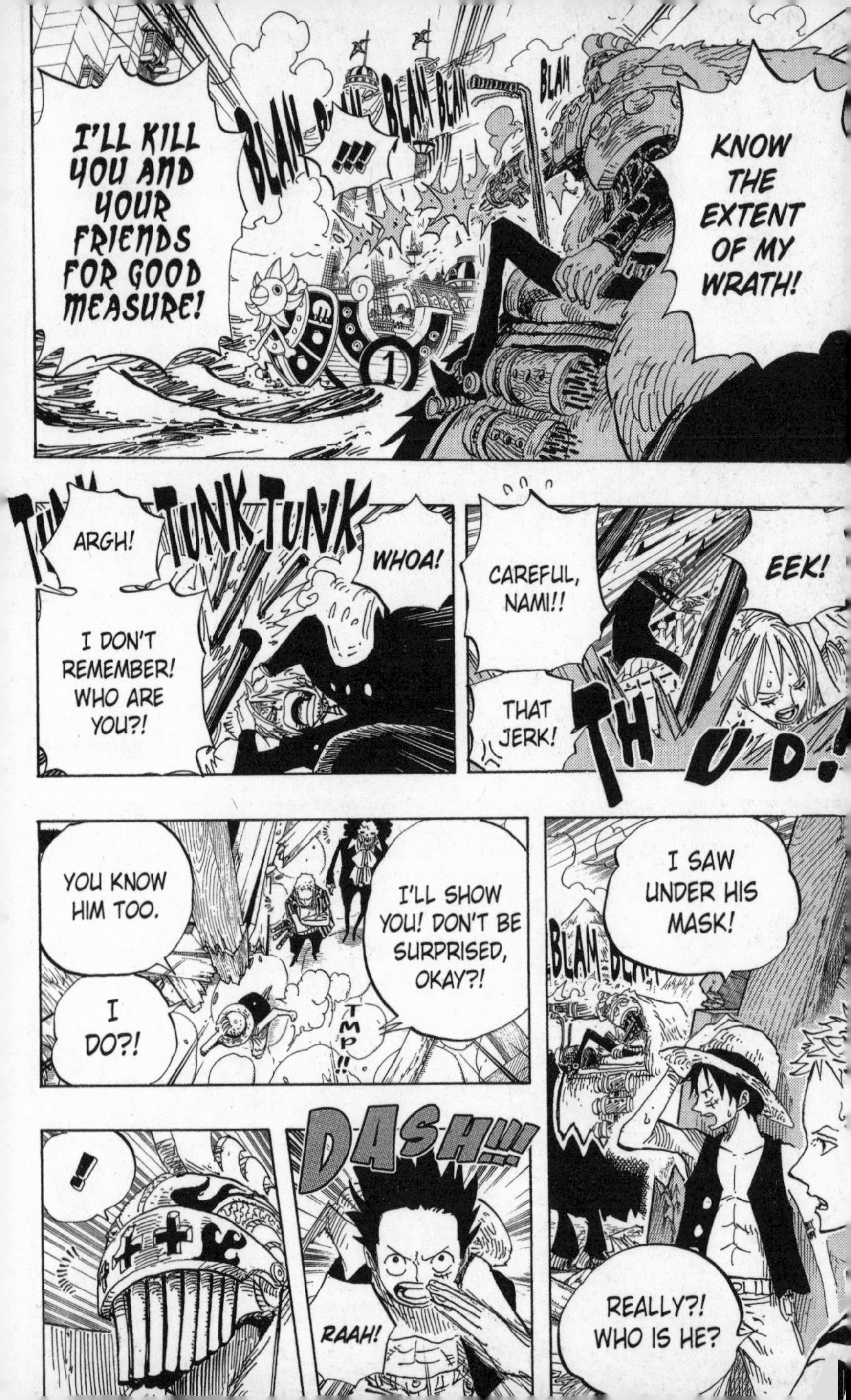
KNOW THE EXTENT OF MY WRATH!
BLAM
BLAM BLAM
!!!
I'LL KILL YOU AND YOUR FRIENDS FOR GOOD MEASURE!
EEK!
CAREFUL, NAMI!!
THAT JERK!
THUD!!
WHOA!
TUNK TUNK
ARGH!
I DON'T REMEMBER! WHO ARE YOU?!
I SAW UNDER HIS MASK!
BLAM
REALLY?! WHO IS HE?
I'LL SHOW YOU! DON'T BE SURPRISED, OKAY?!
TMP!!
YOU KNOW HIM TOO.
I DO?!
DASH!!!
RAAH!
!

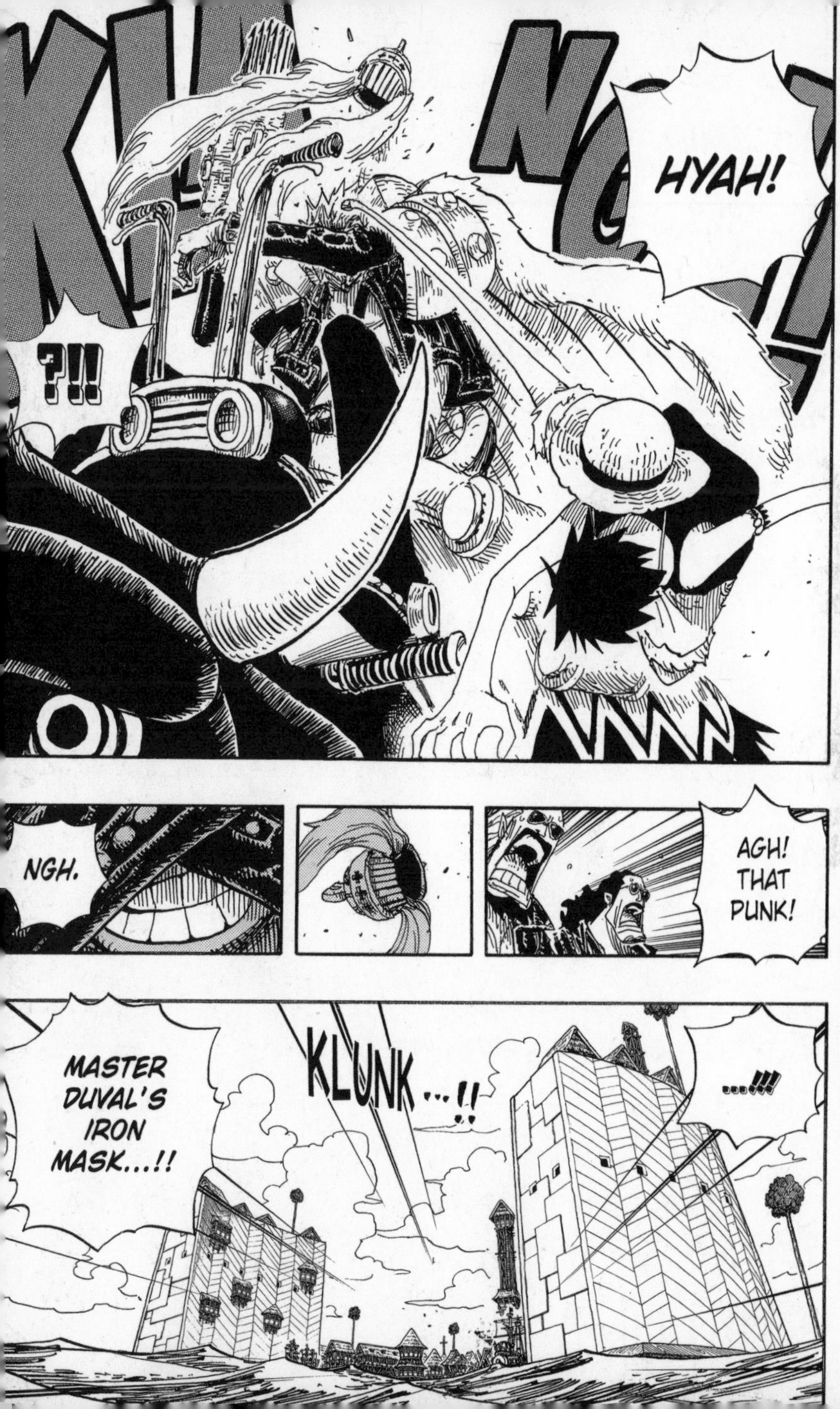
HYAH!
?!!
AGH! THAT PUNK!
NGH.
...!!!
KLUNK...!!
MASTER DUVAL'S IRON MASK...!!

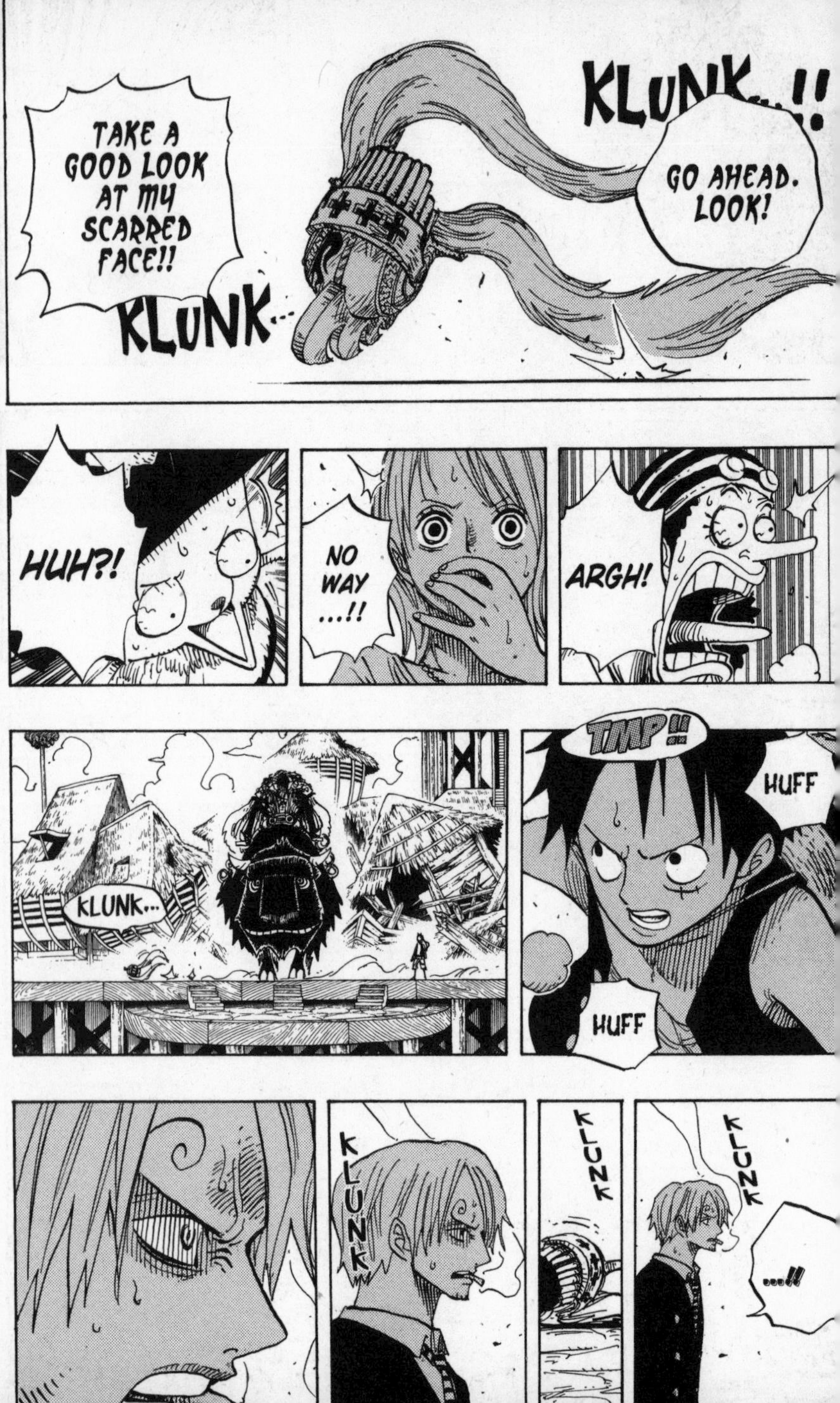
KLUNK...!!
GO AHEAD. LOOK!
TAKE A GOOD LOOK AT MY SCARRED FACE!!
KLUNK...
ARGH!
NO WAY ...!!
HUH?!
TMP!!
HUFF
HUFF
KLUNK...
KLUNK
...!!
KLUNK
KLUNK

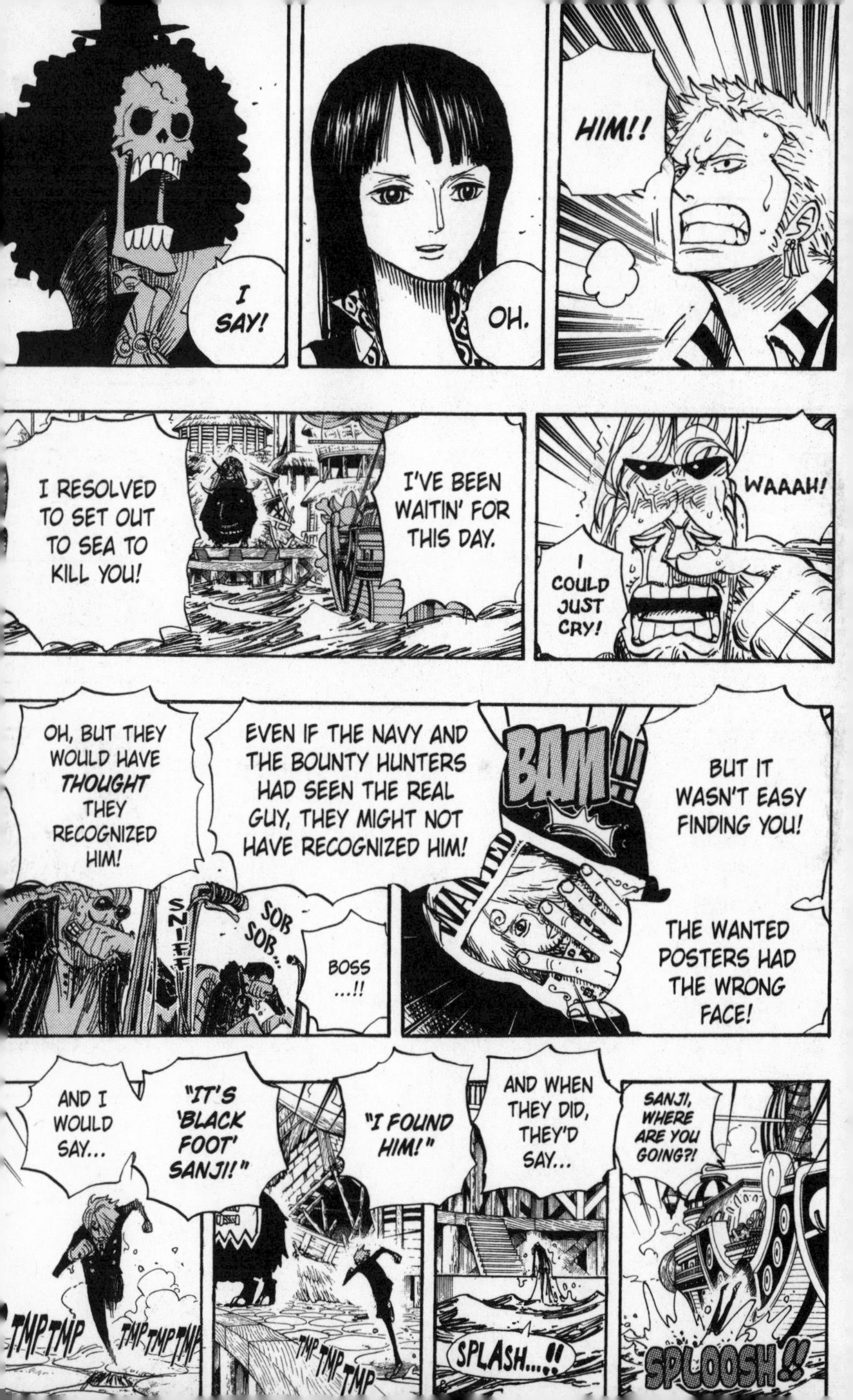
HIM!!
OH.
I SAY!
WAAAH!
I COULD JUST CRY!
I'VE BEEN WAITIN' FOR THIS DAY.
I RESOLVED TO SET OUT TO SEA TO KILL YOU!
BUT IT WASN'T EASY FINDING YOU!
BAM!!
WANTED
THE WANTED POSTERS HAD THE WRONG FACE!
EVEN IF THE NAVY AND THE BOUNTY HUNTERS HAD SEEN THE REAL GUY, THEY MIGHT NOT HAVE RECOGNIZED HIM!
OH, BUT THEY WOULD HAVE *THOUGHT* THEY RECOGNIZED HIM!
SOB SOB...
SNIFF
BOSS ...!!
SANJI, WHERE ARE YOU GOING?!
SPLOOSH!!
AND WHEN THEY DID, THEY'D SAY...
SPLASH...!!
"I FOUND HIM!"
TMP TMP TMP
"IT'S 'BLACK FOOT' SANJI!"
AND I WOULD SAY...
TMP TMP TMP
TMP TMP

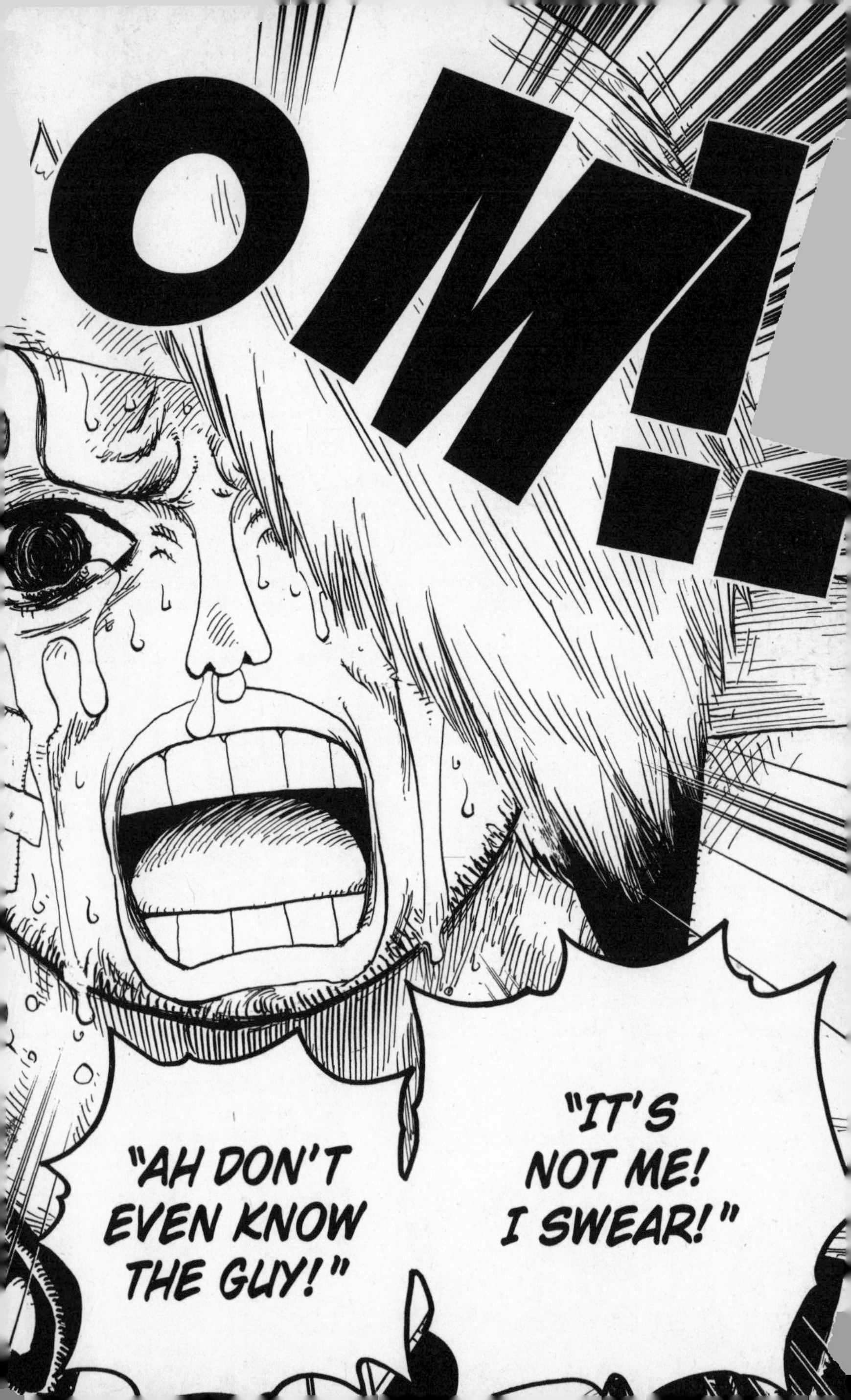
OW!!
"IT'S NOT ME! I SWEAR!"
"AH DON'T EVEN KNOW THE GUY!"

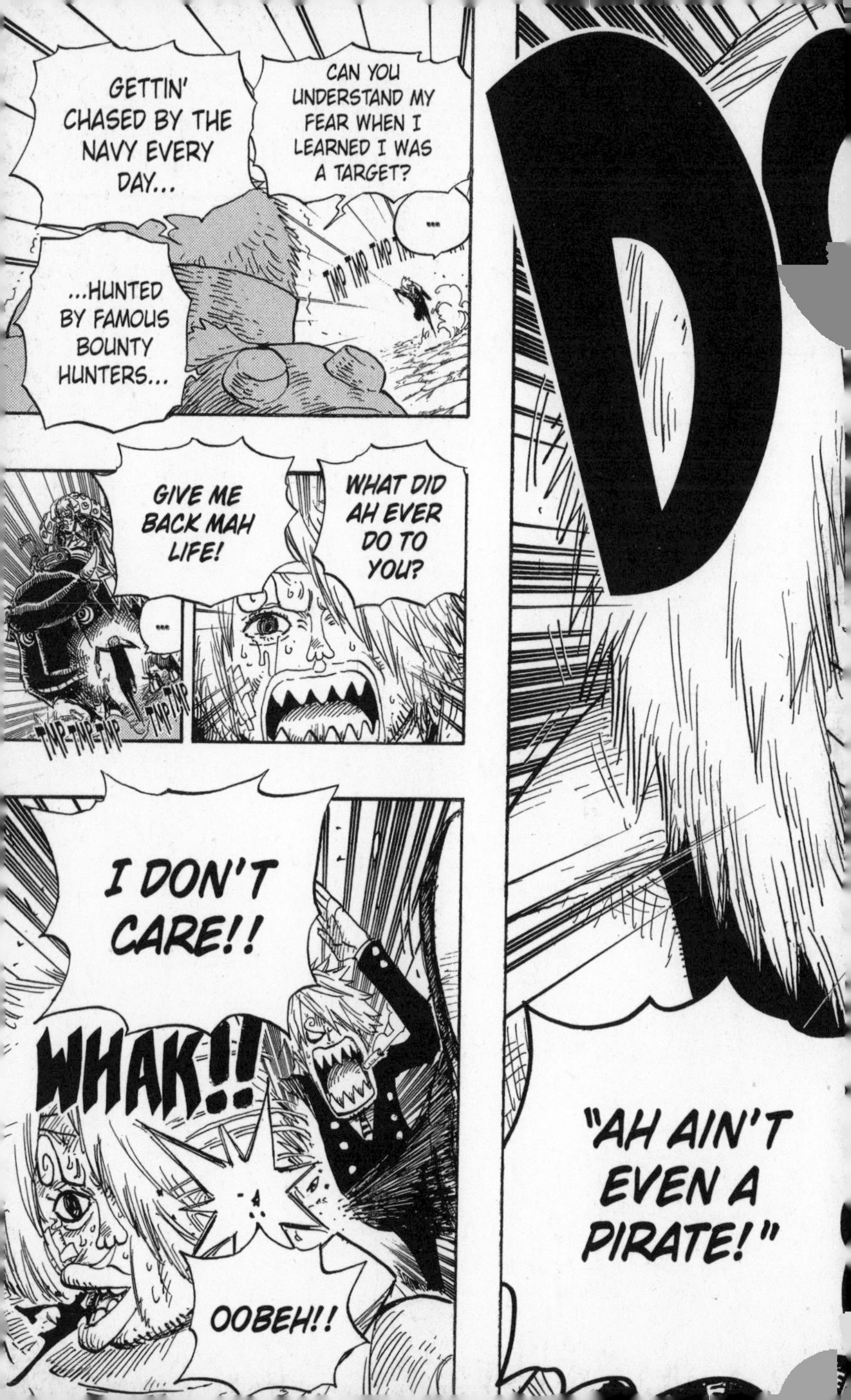

DO
"AH AIN'T EVEN A PIRATE!"
CAN YOU UNDERSTAND MY FEAR WHEN I LEARNED I WAS A TARGET?
GETTIN' CHASED BY THE NAVY EVERY DAY...
...
TMP TMP TMP
...HUNTED BY FAMOUS BOUNTY HUNTERS...
WHAT DID AH EVER DO TO YOU?
GIVE ME BACK MAH LIFE!
...
TMP TMP
TMP TMP TMP
I DON'T CARE!!
WHAK!!
OOBEH!!

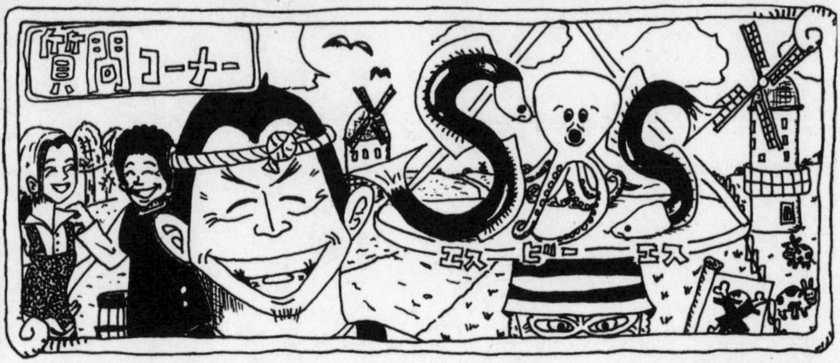
質問コーナー
SBS
エス ビー エス

(Mami Wako, Saitama)

Q: Nice to meet you, Odacchi! I've got a question. Somewhere around volume 46, Brook said, "If my tears had not already dried," but then in volume 50 he was crying tears like normal. Why?

--Kyo-chan

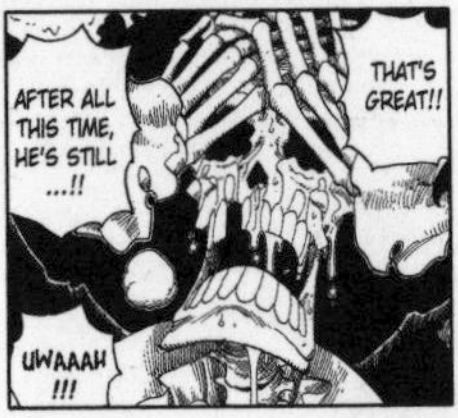
THAT'S GREAT!!
AFTER ALL THIS TIME, HE'S STILL ...!!
UWAAAH !!!

A: That's because even if your tears of sadness dry up, tears of happiness never dry up. Why? Because people...are kind.

All right, moving on (← Said in a low, dignified voice.)

Q: I'll be Moria's replacement!

--Small Onion

A: All right, moving on (← Said in a low, dignified voice.)

Q: Odacchi!! Hello! ☆ I'm a bright and healthy 14-year-old girl! ♡ I'd like to ask you—someone I greatly respect—a question! There are compound words made of four kanji, aren't there? (Did you know that?) If you were to describe the Straw Hats in a four-kanji compound word, what would it be?! *Ishinden-shin* (telepathy)? *Juunintoiro* (it takes all kinds)? Oh, I know!! *Yakiniku teishoku* (barbecue set lunch)?

--Gachapin's Cousin ♡

A: Do I know four-kanji compounds? Of course I do! My favorites include jakakuhakken (snake and crane arts of Shaolin), shorin soccer (Shaolin soccer) and kuro oolong cha (Black oolong tea)!* Oh, you want one that expresses the spirit of the Straw Hat crew? It's gotta be zendaimimon (unprecedented). They were called that during the events at Enies Lobby. I always want them to be unconventional.

**Snake and Crane Arts of Shaolin* and *Shaolin Soccer* are both movies.--Ed.

Q: Marry me!

--Man

A: No! (← Said in a low, dignified voice.)

Chapter 495:
GAON CANNON

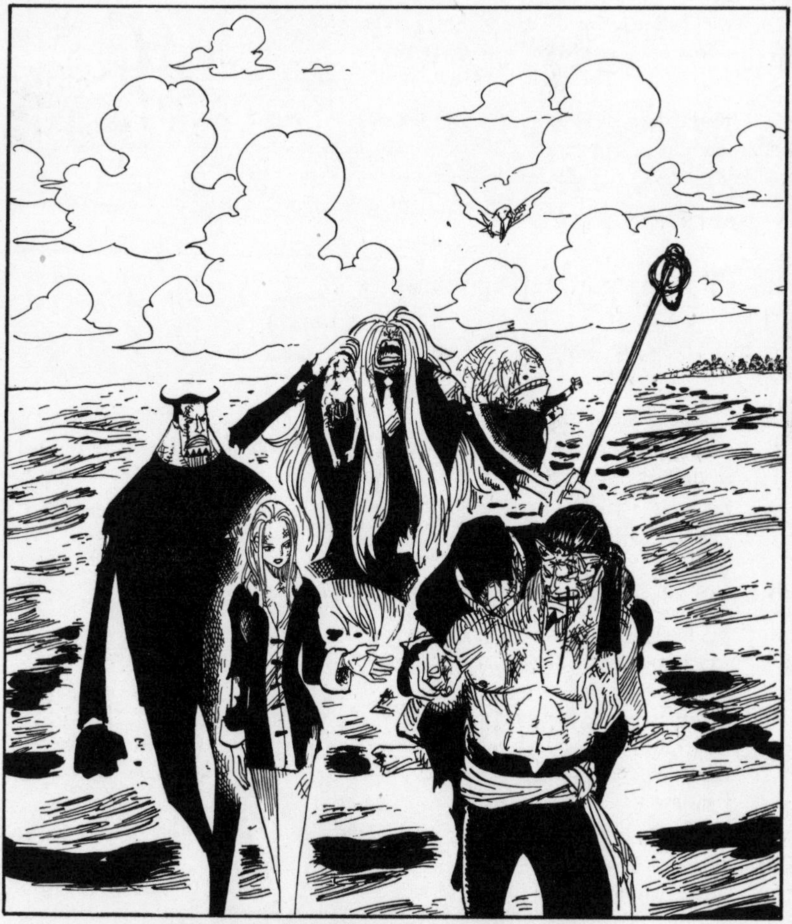

CP9'S INDEPENDENT REPORT, VOL. 5:
"THE PATH OF ESCAPE"

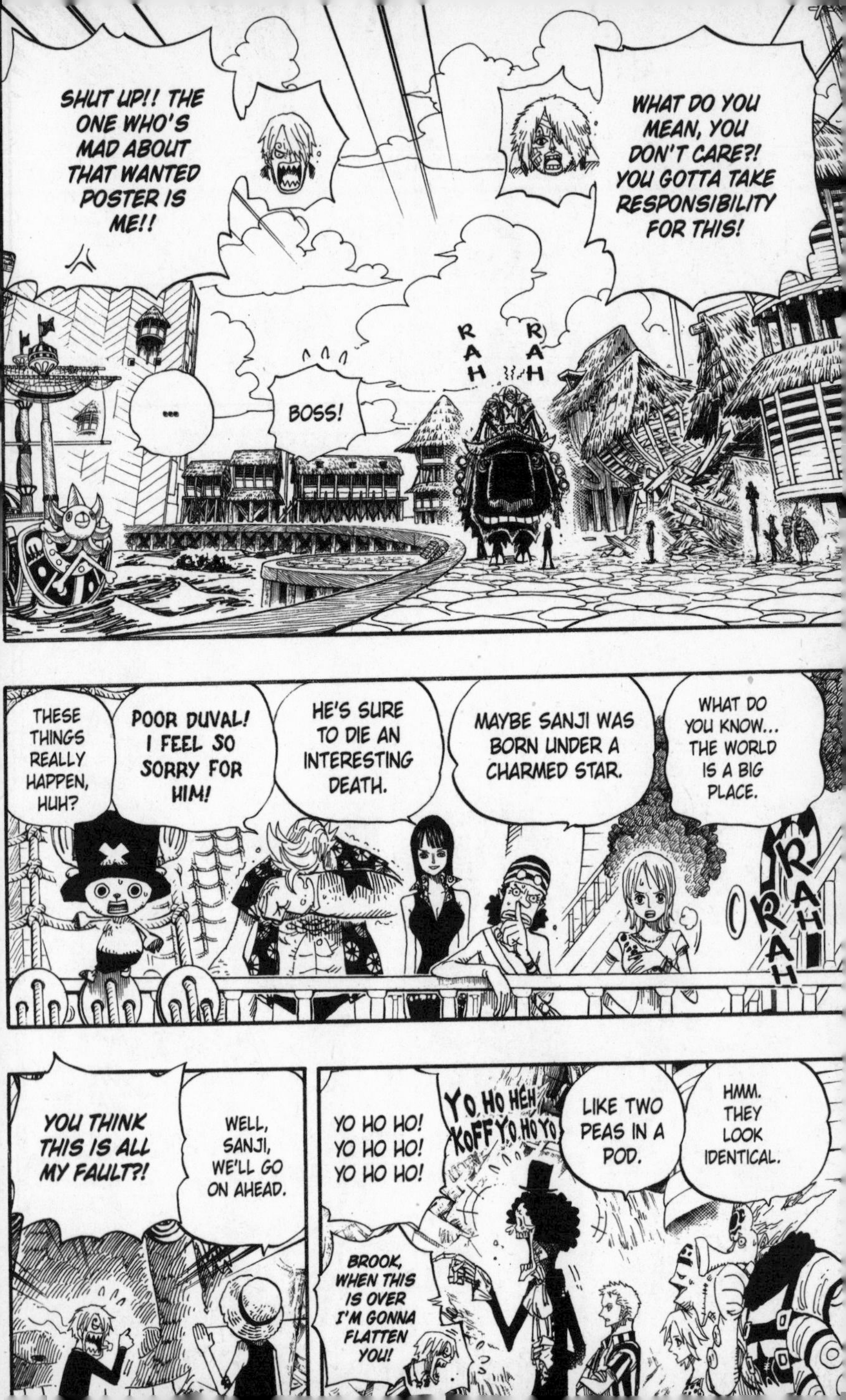
WHAT DO YOU MEAN, YOU DON'T CARE?! YOU GOTTA TAKE RESPONSIBILITY FOR THIS!
SHUT UP!! THE ONE WHO'S MAD ABOUT THAT WANTED POSTER IS ME!!
RAH RAH
RAH RAH
BOSS!
...
RAH RAH
RAH RAH
WHAT DO YOU KNOW... THE WORLD IS A BIG PLACE.
MAYBE SANJI WAS BORN UNDER A CHARMED STAR.
HE'S SURE TO DIE AN INTERESTING DEATH.
POOR DUVAL! I FEEL SO SORRY FOR HIM!
THESE THINGS REALLY HAPPEN, HUH?
HMM. THEY LOOK IDENTICAL.
LIKE TWO PEAS IN A POD.
YO HO HEH KOFF YO HO YO
YO HO HO! YO HO HO! YO HO HO!
BROOK, WHEN THIS IS OVER I'M GONNA FLATTEN YOU!
WELL, SANJI, WE'LL GO ON AHEAD.
YOU THINK THIS IS ALL MY FAULT?!

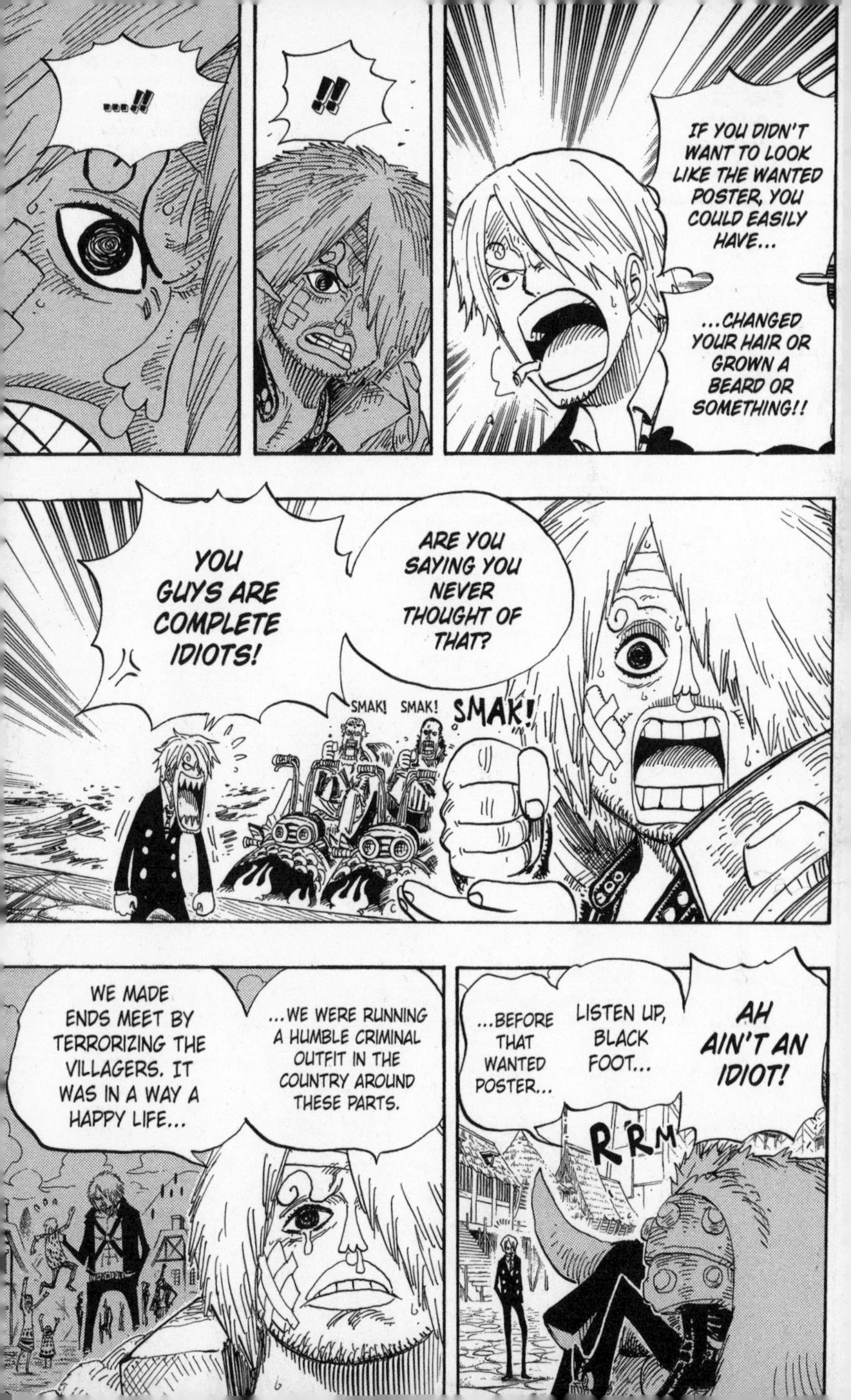
IF YOU DIDN'T WANT TO LOOK LIKE THE WANTED POSTER, YOU COULD EASILY HAVE...
...CHANGED YOUR HAIR OR GROWN A BEARD OR SOMETHING!!
!!
...!!
ARE YOU SAYING YOU NEVER THOUGHT OF THAT?
YOU GUYS ARE COMPLETE IDIOTS!
SMAK!
SMAK!
SMAK!
AH AIN'T AN IDIOT!
LISTEN UP, BLACK FOOT...
...BEFORE THAT WANTED POSTER...
RRM
...WE WERE RUNNING A HUMBLE CRIMINAL OUTFIT IN THE COUNTRY AROUND THESE PARTS.
WE MADE ENDS MEET BY TERRORIZING THE VILLAGERS. IT WAS IN A WAY A HAPPY LIFE...

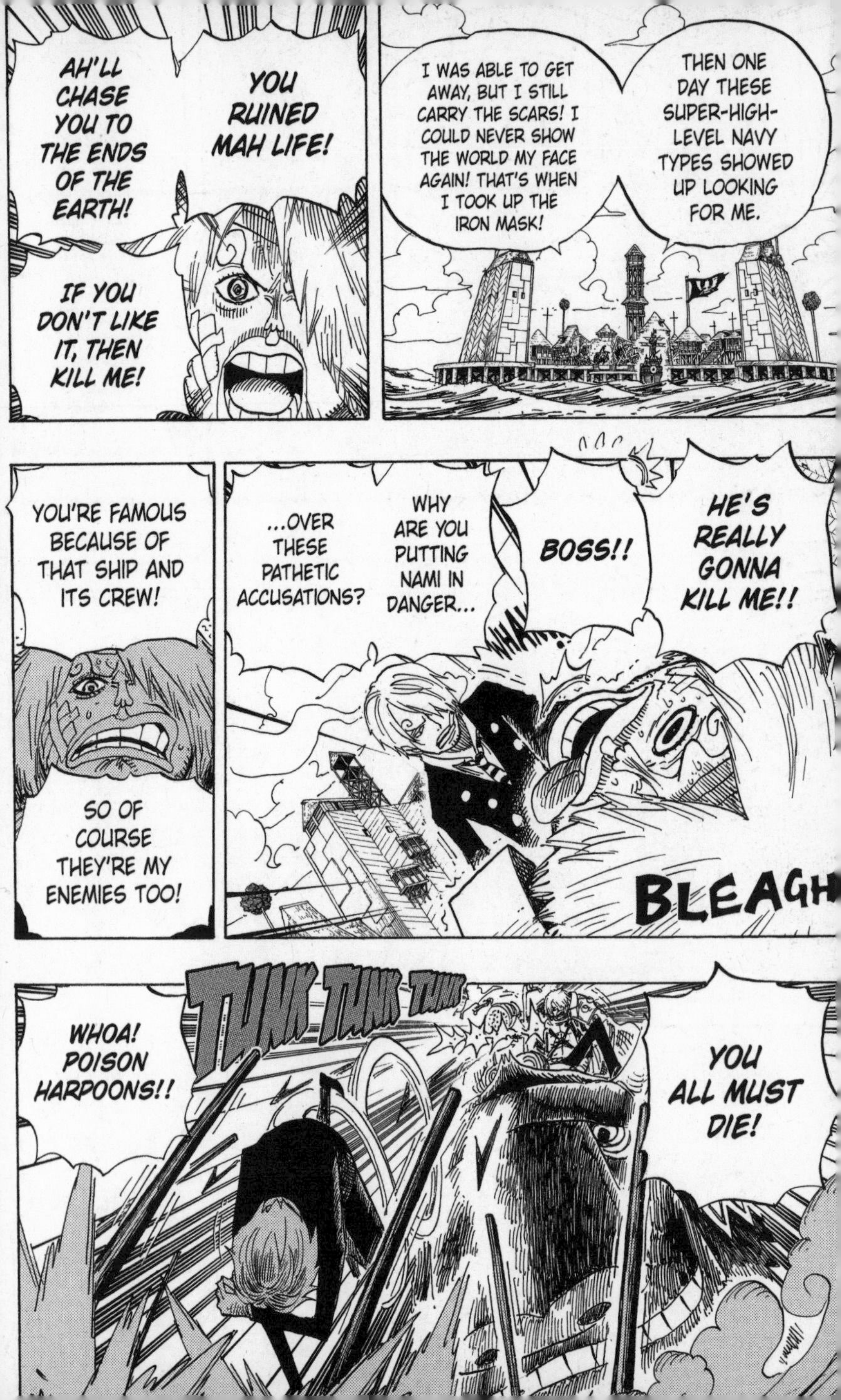
THEN ONE DAY THESE SUPER-HIGH-LEVEL NAVY TYPES SHOWED UP LOOKING FOR ME.
I WAS ABLE TO GET AWAY, BUT I STILL CARRY THE SCARS! I COULD NEVER SHOW THE WORLD MY FACE AGAIN! THAT'S WHEN I TOOK UP THE IRON MASK!
YOU RUINED MAH LIFE!
AH'LL CHASE YOU TO THE ENDS OF THE EARTH!
IF YOU DON'T LIKE IT, THEN KILL ME!
HE'S REALLY GONNA KILL ME!!
BOSS!!
WHY ARE YOU PUTTING NAMI IN DANGER...
...OVER THESE PATHETIC ACCUSATIONS?
BLEAGH
YOU'RE FAMOUS BECAUSE OF THAT SHIP AND ITS CREW!
SO OF COURSE THEY'RE MY ENEMIES TOO!
YOU ALL MUST DIE!
TUNK TUNK TUNK
WHOA! POISON HARPOONS!!

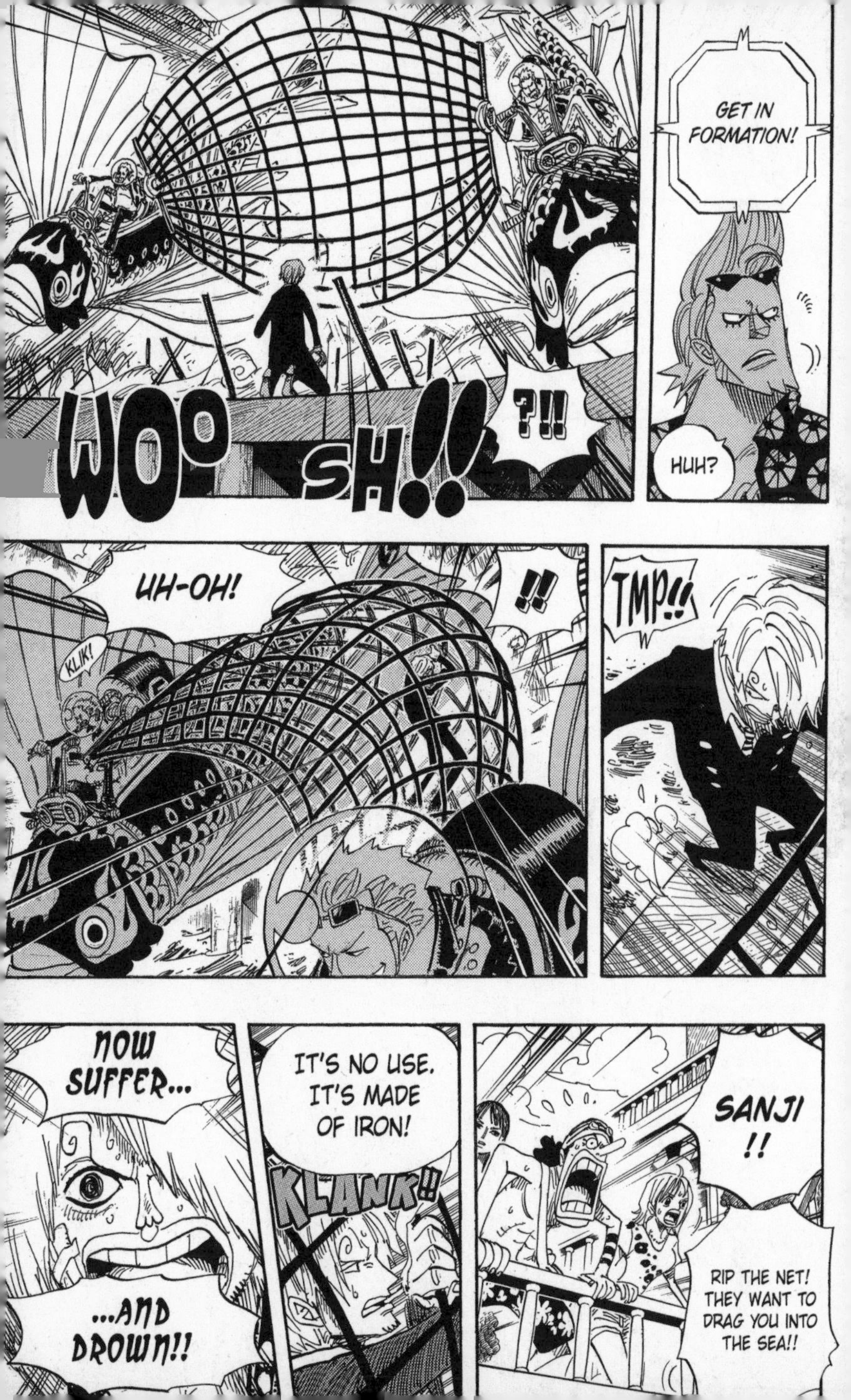
GET IN FORMATION!
HUH?
?!!
WOOOSH!!
TMP!!
!!
UH-OH!
KLIK!
SANJI !!
RIP THE NET! THEY WANT TO DRAG YOU INTO THE SEA!!
IT'S NO USE. IT'S MADE OF IRON!
KLANK!!
NOW SUFFER...
...AND DROWN!!

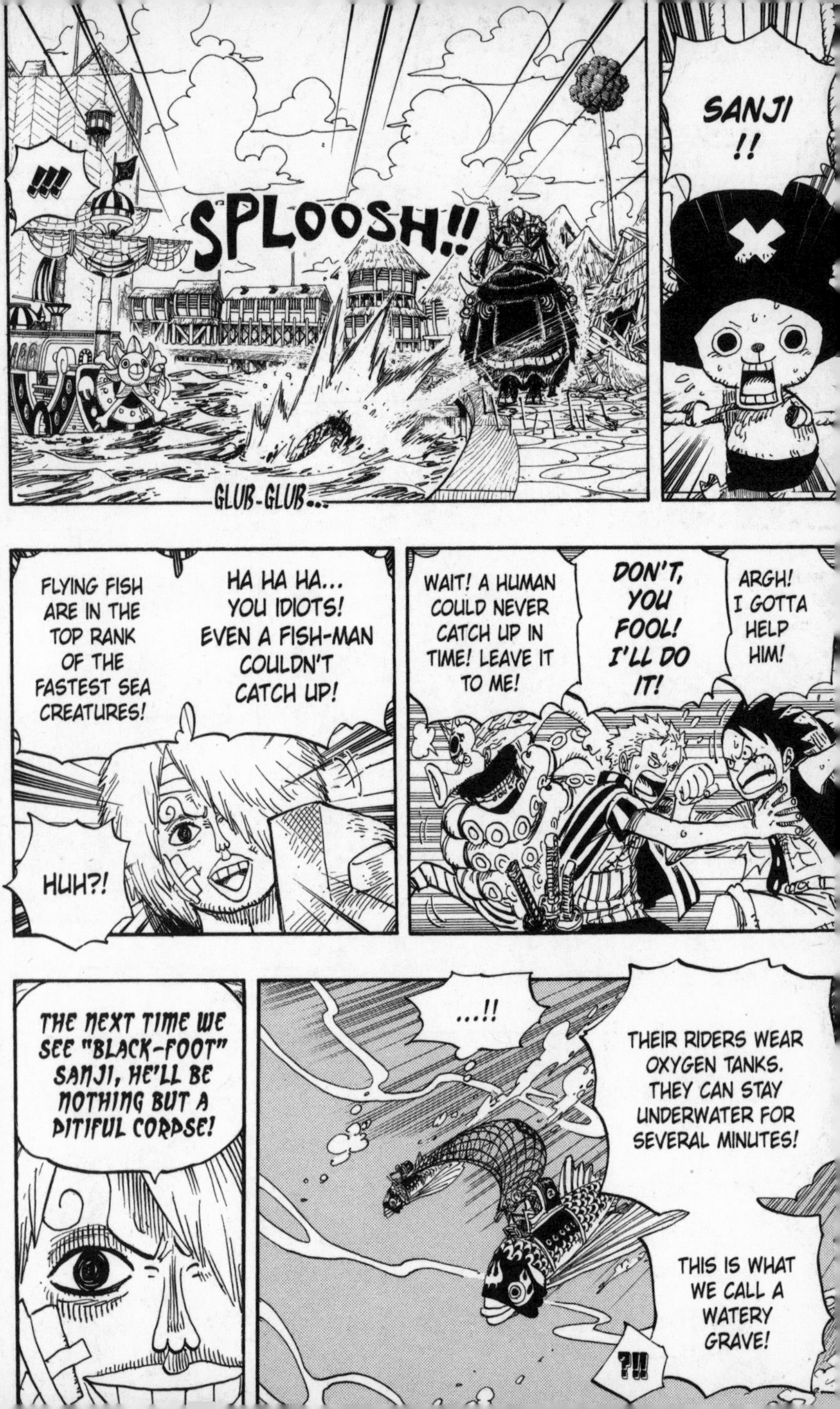
SANJI !!
!!!
SPLOOSH!!
GLUB-GLUB...
ARGH! I GOTTA HELP HIM!
DON'T, YOU FOOL! I'LL DO IT!
WAIT! A HUMAN COULD NEVER CATCH UP IN TIME! LEAVE IT TO ME!
HA HA HA... YOU IDIOTS! EVEN A FISH-MAN COULDN'T CATCH UP!
FLYING FISH ARE IN THE TOP RANK OF THE FASTEST SEA CREATURES!
HUH?!
...!!
THEIR RIDERS WEAR OXYGEN TANKS. THEY CAN STAY UNDERWATER FOR SEVERAL MINUTES!
THIS IS WHAT WE CALL A WATERY GRAVE!
?!!
THE NEXT TIME WE SEE "BLACK-FOOT" SANJI, HE'LL BE NOTHING BUT A PITIFUL CORPSE!

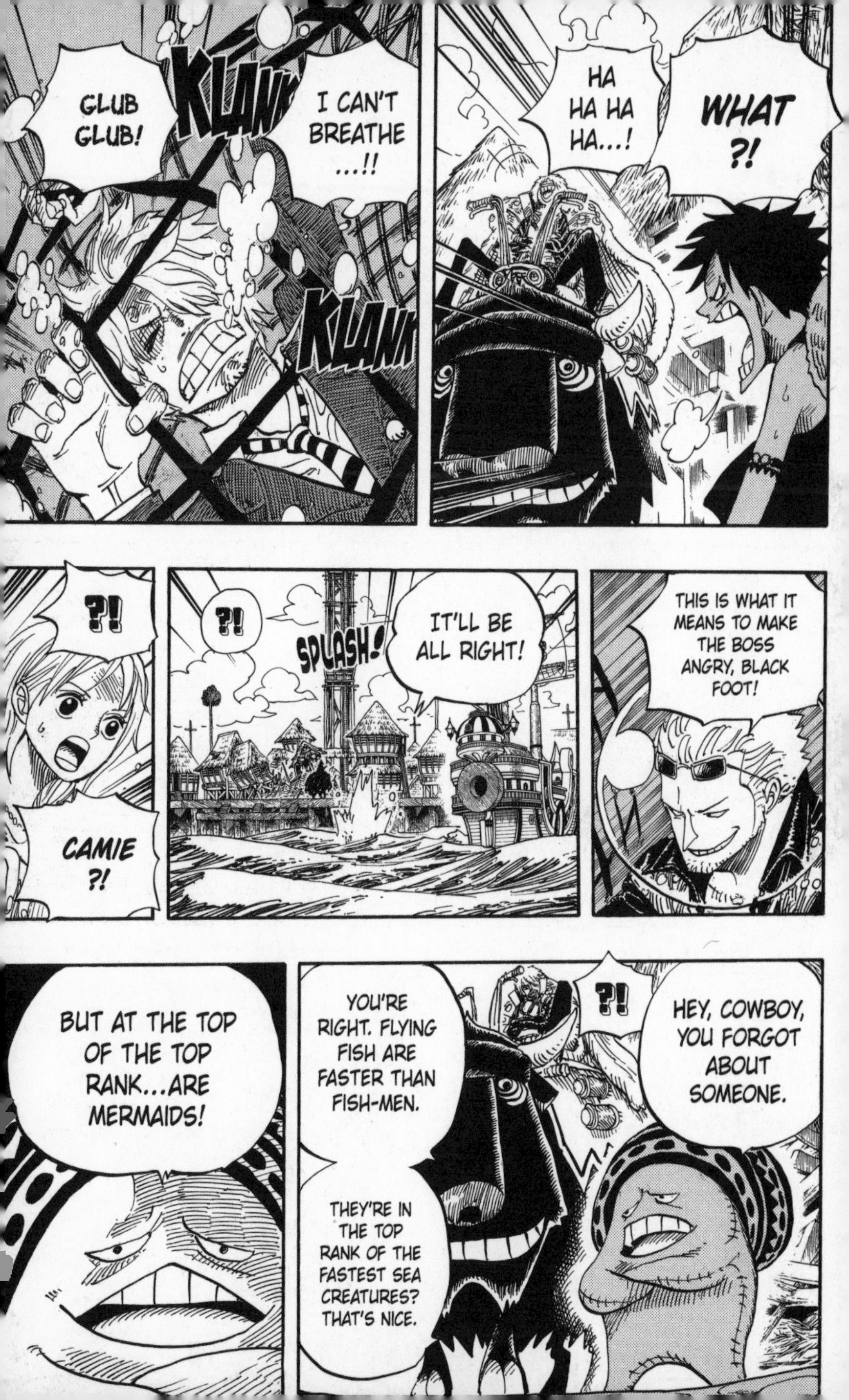
WHAT ?!
HA HA HA HA...!
I CAN'T BREATHE ...!!
GLUB GLUB!
THIS IS WHAT IT MEANS TO MAKE THE BOSS ANGRY, BLACK FOOT!
IT'LL BE ALL RIGHT!
SPLASH!
?!
?!
CAMIE ?!
HEY, COWBOY, YOU FORGOT ABOUT SOMEONE.
?!
YOU'RE RIGHT. FLYING FISH ARE FASTER THAN FISH-MEN.
THEY'RE IN THE TOP RANK OF THE FASTEST SEA CREATURES? THAT'S NICE.
BUT AT THE TOP OF THE TOP RANK...ARE MERMAIDS!

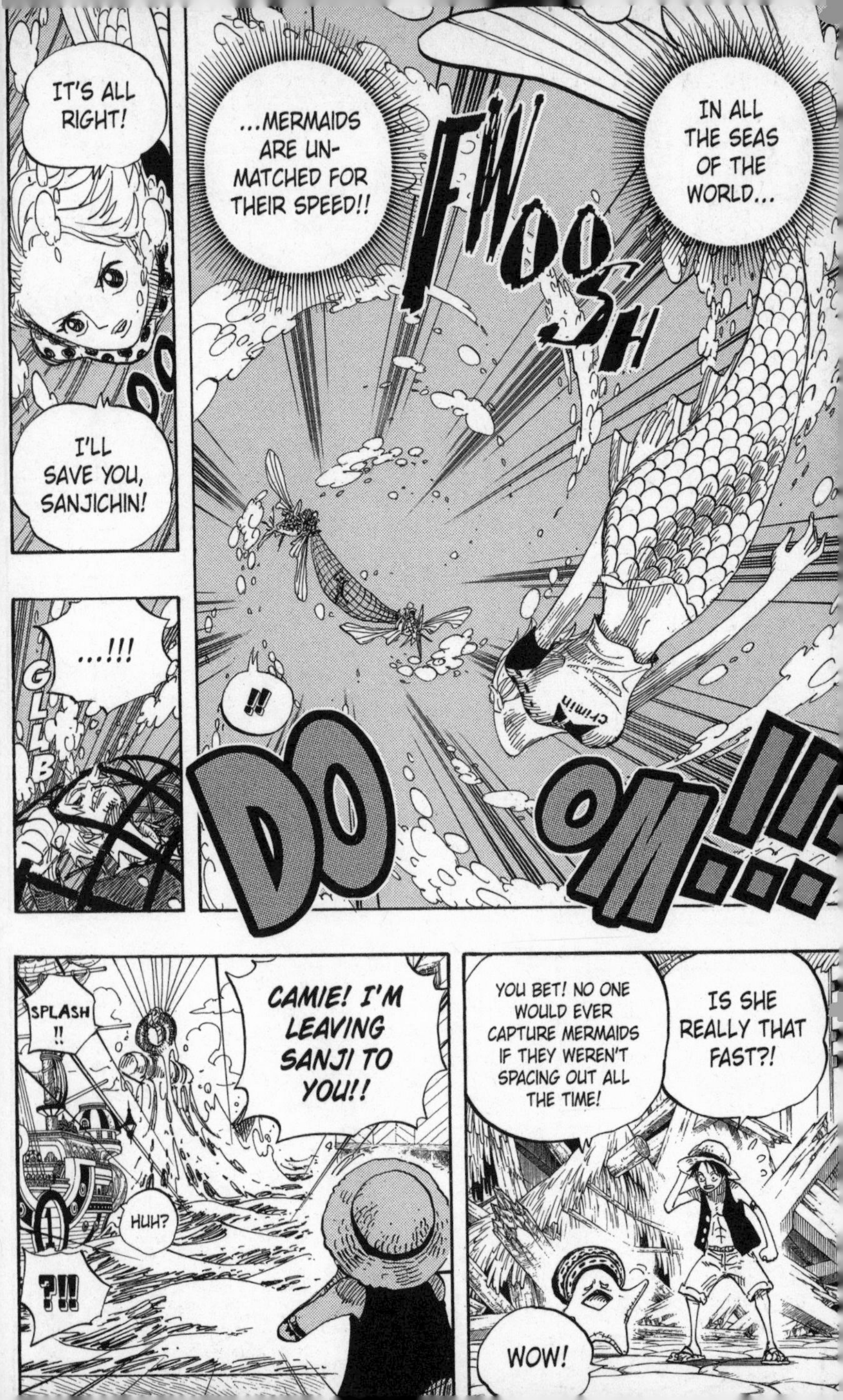
IN ALL THE SEAS OF THE WORLD...
...MERMAIDS ARE UN-MATCHED FOR THEIR SPEED!!
FWOOSH
!!
DOOM...!!!
IT'S ALL RIGHT!
I'LL SAVE YOU, SANJICHIN!
...!!!
GLLB
IS SHE REALLY THAT FAST?!
YOU BET! NO ONE WOULD EVER CAPTURE MERMAIDS IF THEY WEREN'T SPACING OUT ALL THE TIME!
WOW!
CAMIE! I'M LEAVING SANJI TO YOU!!
SPLASH !!
HUH?
?!!

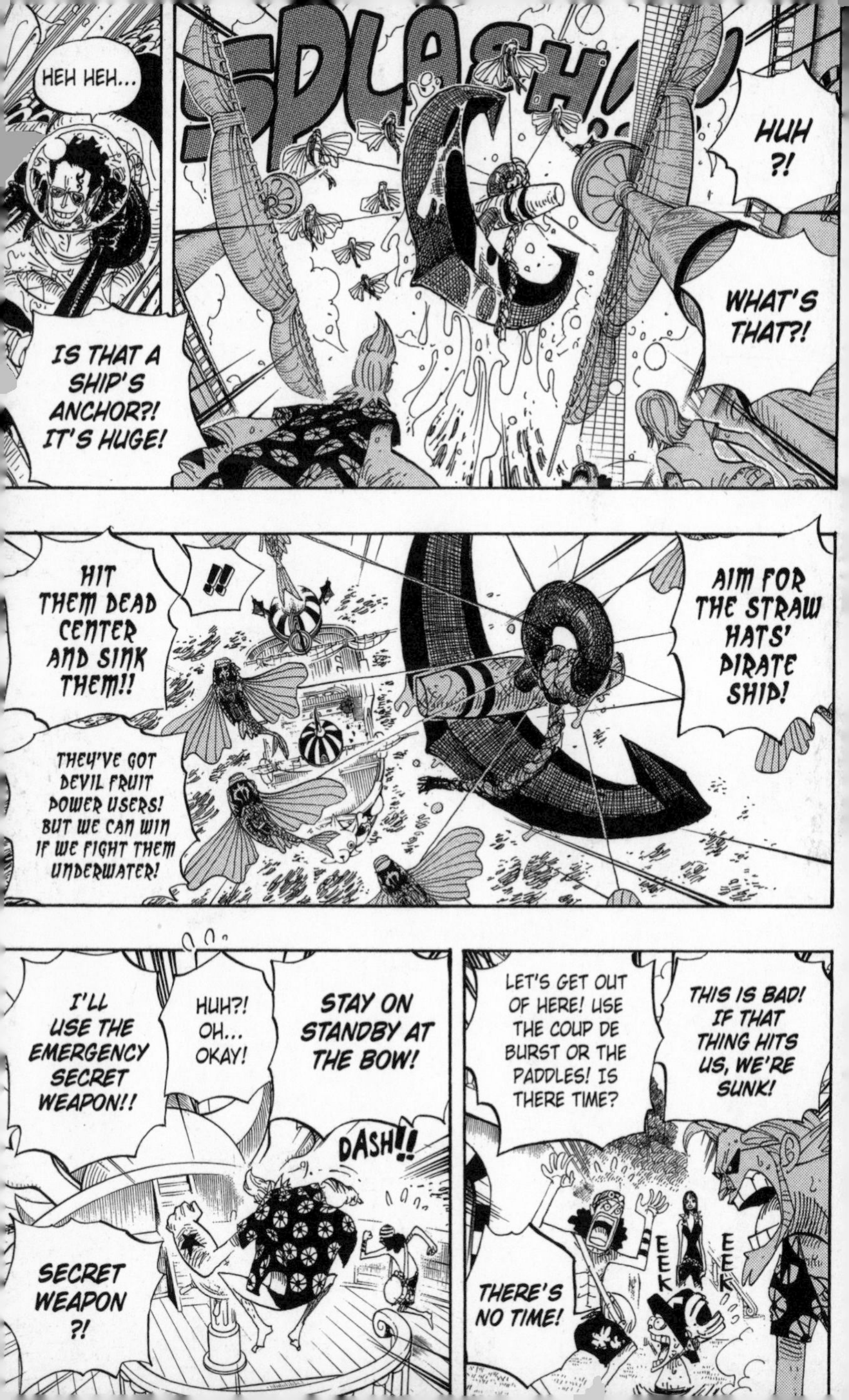
SPLASH!!
HUH ?!
WHAT'S THAT?!
HEH HEH...
IS THAT A SHIP'S ANCHOR?! IT'S HUGE!
AIM FOR THE STRAW HATS' PIRATE SHIP!
!!
HIT THEM DEAD CENTER AND SINK THEM!!
THEY'VE GOT DEVIL FRUIT POWER USERS! BUT WE CAN WIN IF WE FIGHT THEM UNDERWATER!
THIS IS BAD! IF THAT THING HITS US, WE'RE SUNK!
LET'S GET OUT OF HERE! USE THE COUP DE BURST OR THE PADDLES! IS THERE TIME?
EEK
EEK
THERE'S NO TIME!
STAY ON STANDBY AT THE BOW!
HUH?! OH... OKAY!
I'LL USE THE EMERGENCY SECRET WEAPON!!
DASH!!
SECRET WEAPON ?!

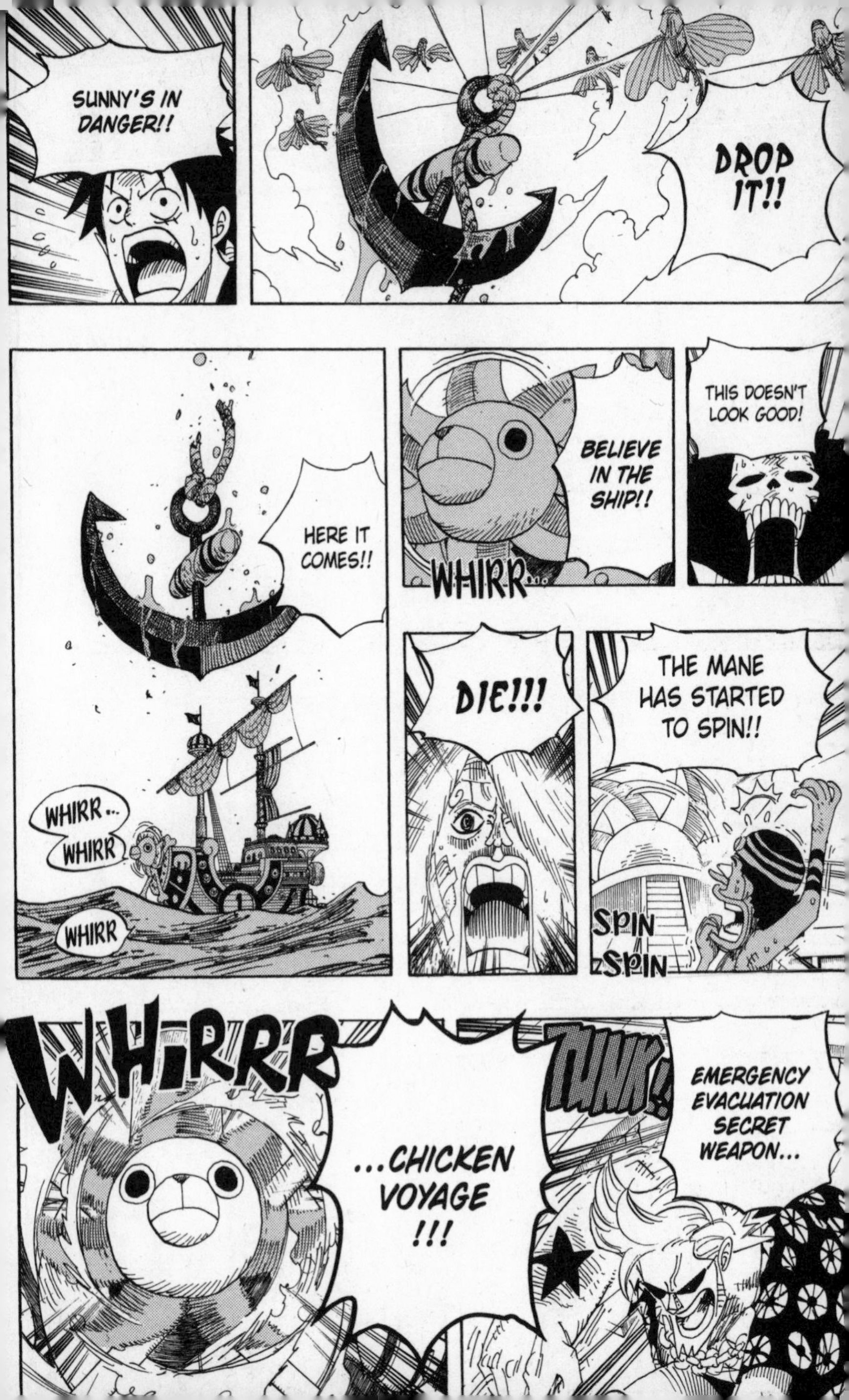
DROP IT!!
SUNNY'S IN DANGER!!
THIS DOESN'T LOOK GOOD!
BELIEVE IN THE SHIP!!
WHIRR
THE MANE HAS STARTED TO SPIN!!
SPIN SPIN
DIE!!!
HERE IT COMES!!
WHIRR... WHIRR
WHIRR
EMERGENCY EVACUATION SECRET WEAPON...
TUNK!
...CHICKEN VOYAGE !!!
WHIRRR

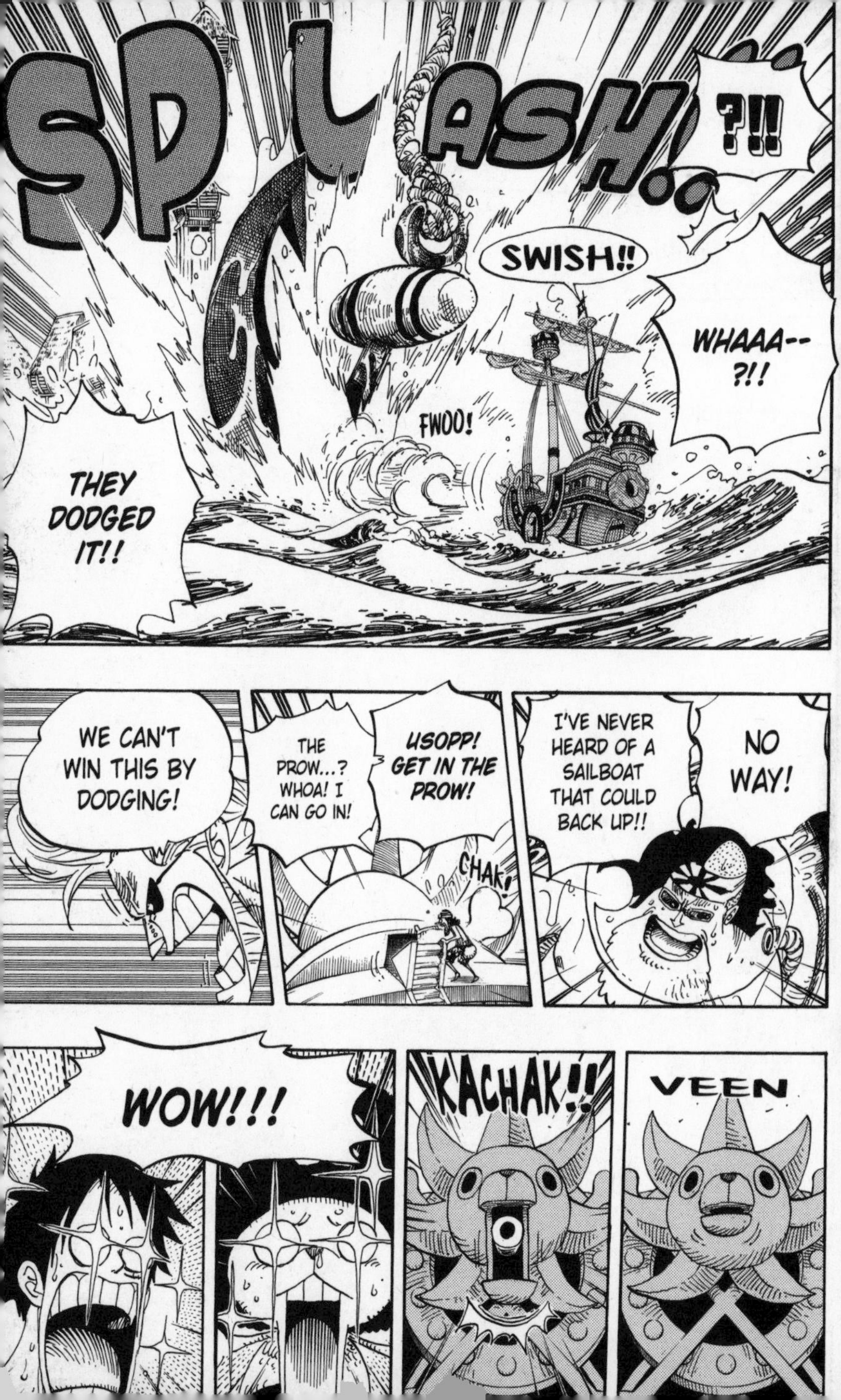
?!!
SPLASH...
SWISH!!
WHAAA-- ?!!
FWOO!
THEY DODGED IT!!
NO WAY!
I'VE NEVER HEARD OF A SAILBOAT THAT COULD BACK UP!!
USOPP! GET IN THE PROW!
THE PROW...? WHOA! I CAN GO IN!
CHAK!
WE CAN'T WIN THIS BY DODGING!
VEEN
KACHAK!!
WOW!!!

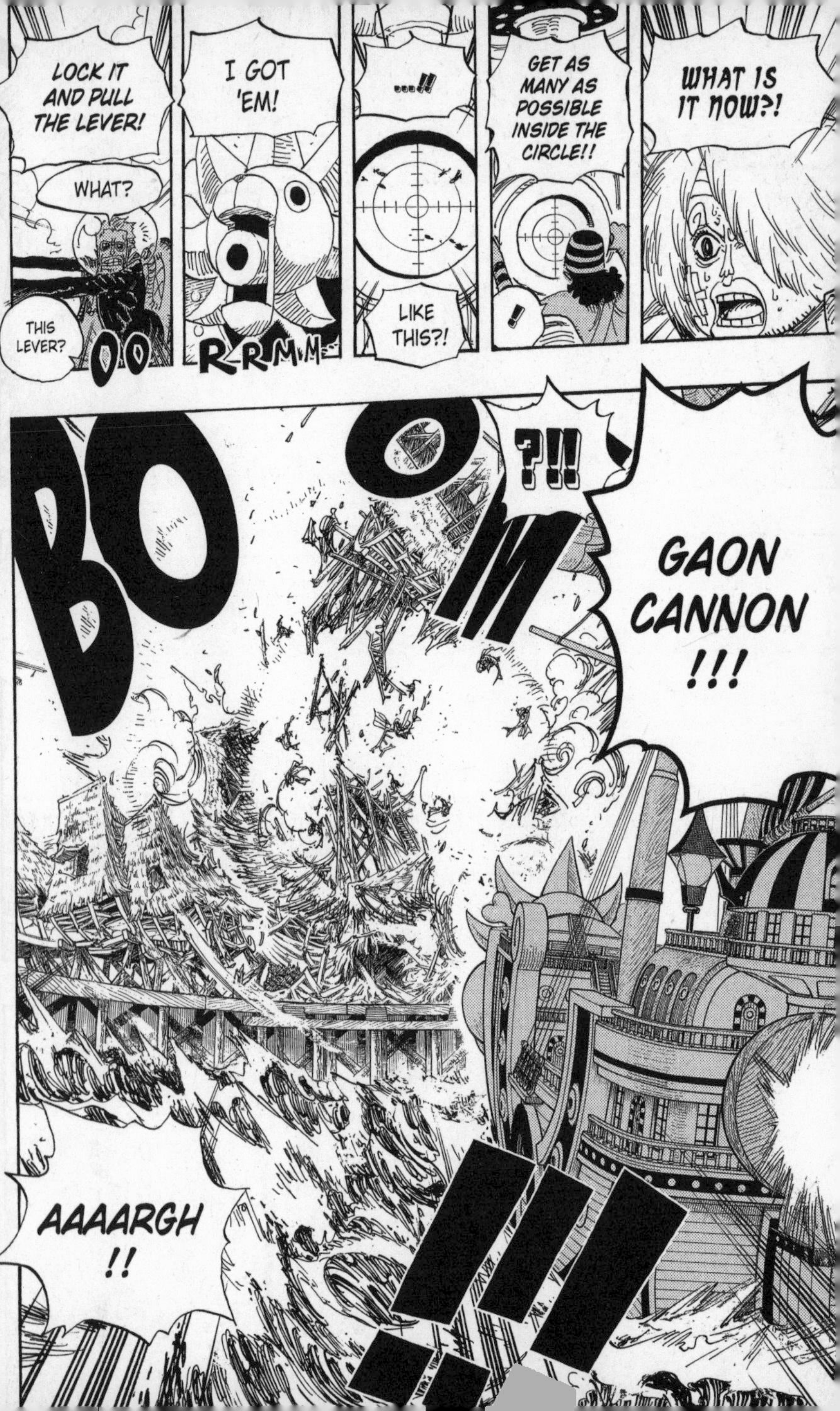
WHAT IS IT NOW?!
GET AS MANY AS POSSIBLE INSIDE THE CIRCLE!!
!
...!!
LIKE THIS?!
I GOT 'EM!
RRMM
LOCK IT AND PULL THE LEVER!
WHAT?
THIS LEVER?
OO
?!!
GAON CANNON!!!
BOOM
AAAARGH!!
!!

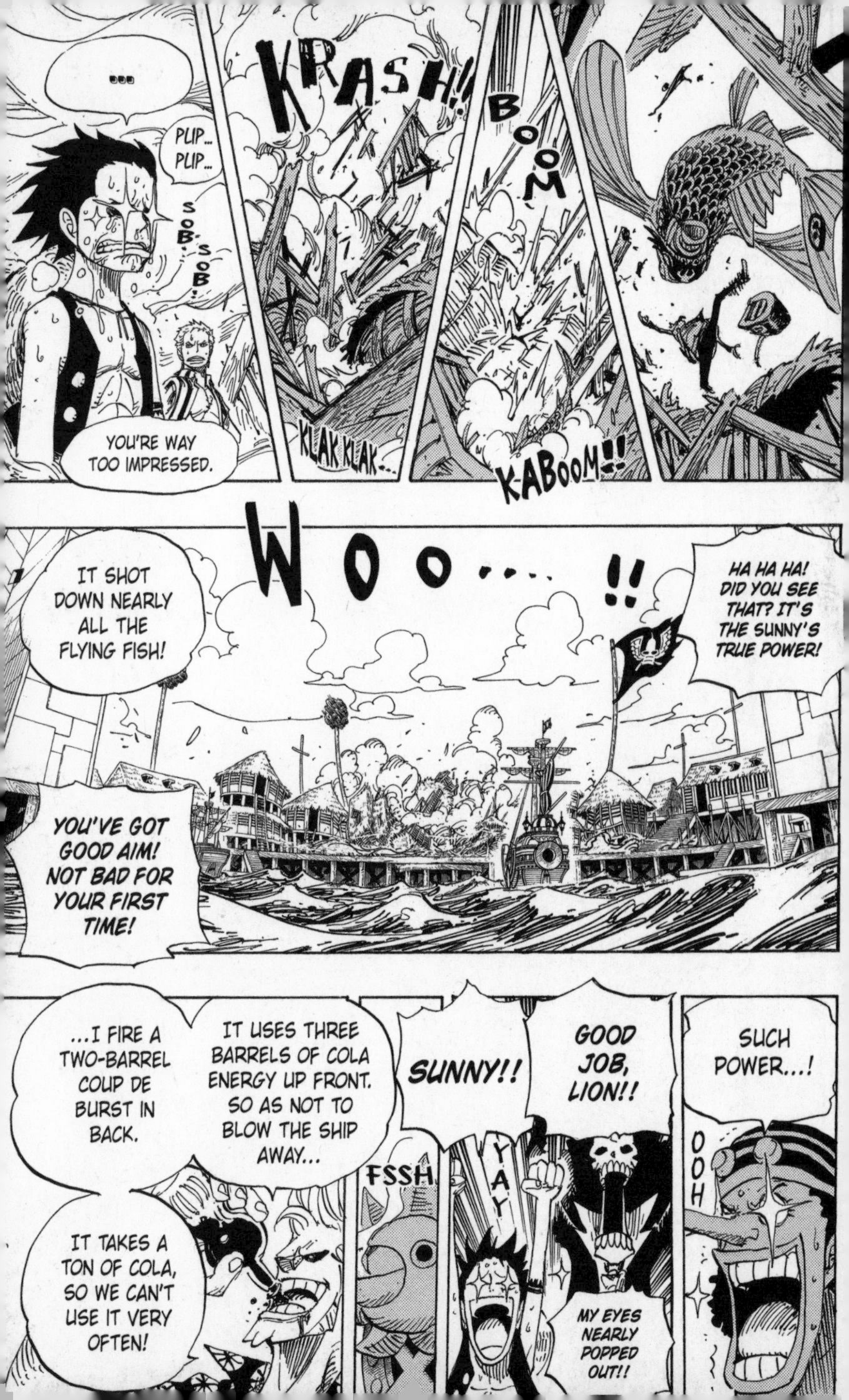

BOOM
K-ABOOM!!
KRASH!!
KLAK KLAK...
...
PLIP... PLIP...
SOB SOB
YOU'RE WAY TOO IMPRESSED.
WOO...!!
HA HA HA! DID YOU SEE THAT? IT'S THE SUNNY'S TRUE POWER!
IT SHOT DOWN NEARLY ALL THE FLYING FISH!
YOU'VE GOT GOOD AIM! NOT BAD FOR YOUR FIRST TIME!
SUCH POWER...!
OOH
GOOD JOB, LION!!
MY EYES NEARLY POPPED OUT!!
SUNNY!!
YAY
FSSH
IT USES THREE BARRELS OF COLA ENERGY UP FRONT. SO AS NOT TO BLOW THE SHIP AWAY...
...I FIRE A TWO-BARREL COUP DE BURST IN BACK.
IT TAKES A TON OF COLA, SO WE CAN'T USE IT VERY OFTEN!

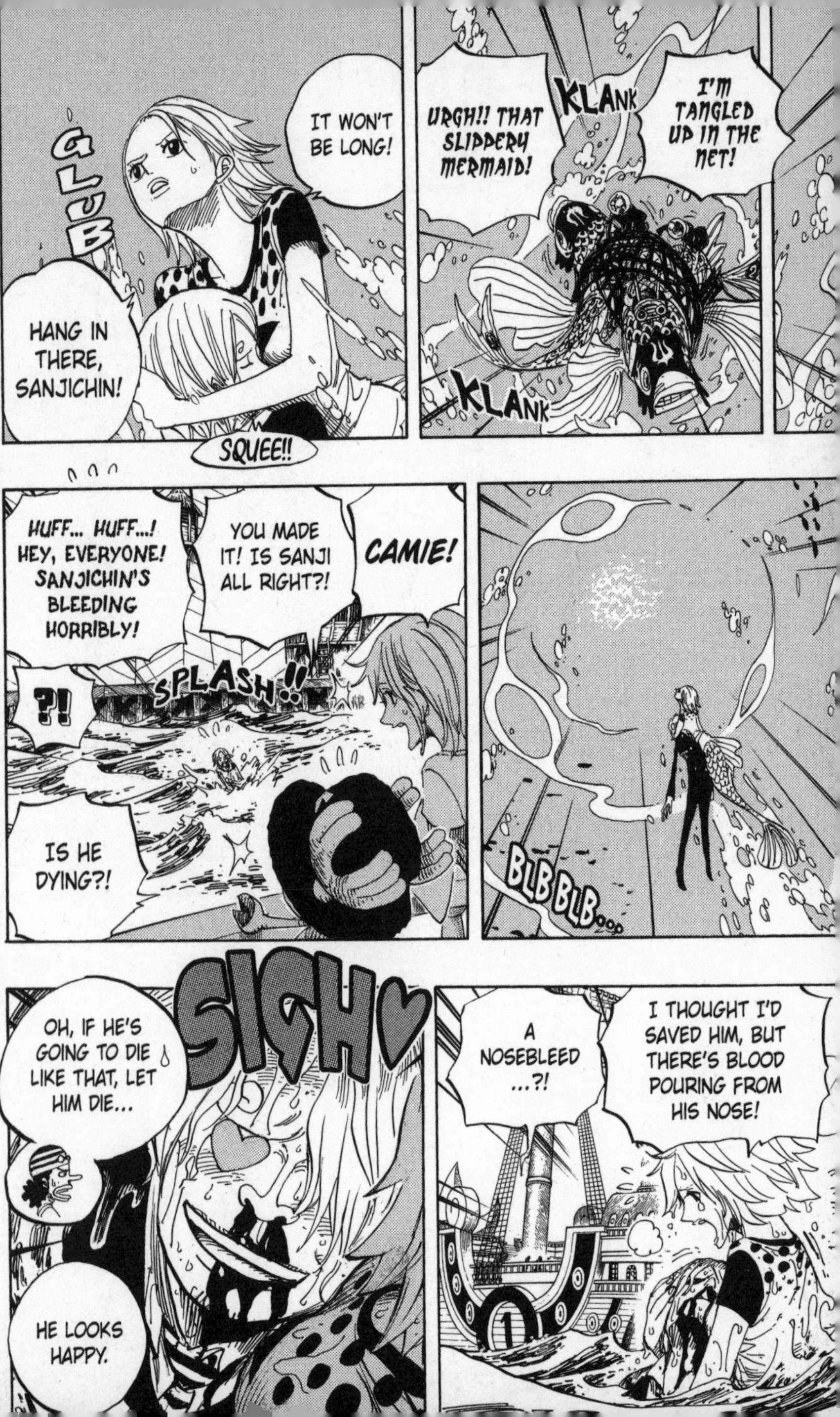
I'M TANGLED UP IN THE NET!
URGH!! THAT SLIPPERY MERMAID!
KLANK
KLANK
IT WON'T BE LONG!
GLUB
HANG IN THERE, SANJICHIN!
SQUEE!!
BLB BLB...
CAMIE!
YOU MADE IT! IS SANJI ALL RIGHT?!
HUFF... HUFF...! HEY, EVERYONE! SANJICHIN'S BLEEDING HORRIBLY!
SPLASH!!
?!
IS HE DYING?!
I THOUGHT I'D SAVED HIM, BUT THERE'S BLOOD POURING FROM HIS NOSE!
A NOSEBLEED ...?!
SIGH♥
OH, IF HE'S GOING TO DIE LIKE THAT, LET HIM DIE...
HE LOOKS HAPPY.

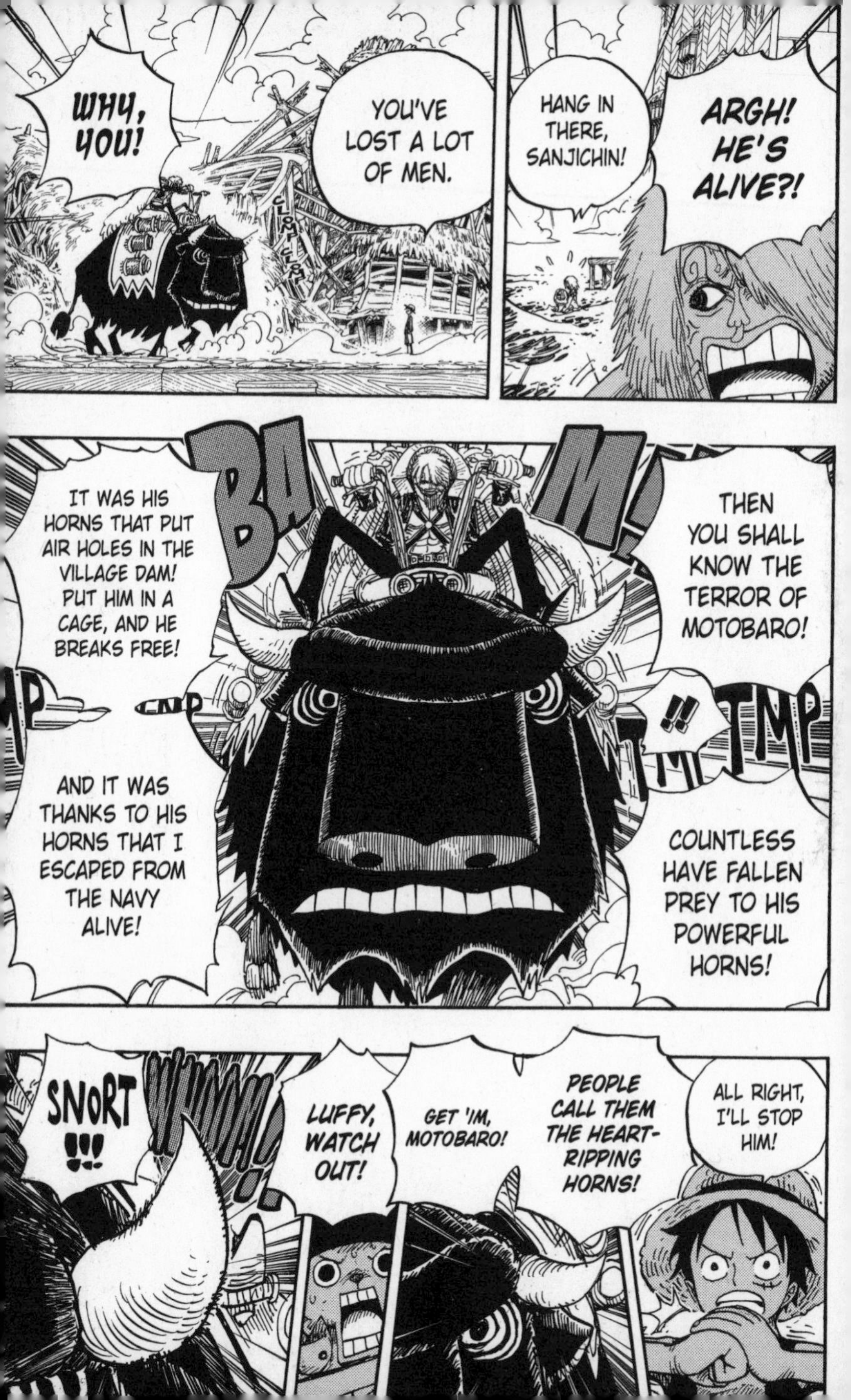
ARGH! HE'S ALIVE?!
HANG IN THERE, SANJICHIN!
YOU'VE LOST A LOT OF MEN.
CLOMP CLOMP
WHY, YOU!
THEN YOU SHALL KNOW THE TERROR OF MOTOBARO!
BAM!
IT WAS HIS HORNS THAT PUT AIR HOLES IN THE VILLAGE DAM! PUT HIM IN A CAGE, AND HE BREAKS FREE!
TMP TMP!!
COUNTLESS HAVE FALLEN PREY TO HIS POWERFUL HORNS!
AND IT WAS THANKS TO HIS HORNS THAT I ESCAPED FROM THE NAVY ALIVE!
ALL RIGHT, I'LL STOP HIM!
PEOPLE CALL THEM THE HEART-RIPPING HORNS!
GET 'IM, MOTOBARO!
LUFFY, WATCH OUT!
SNORT!!!

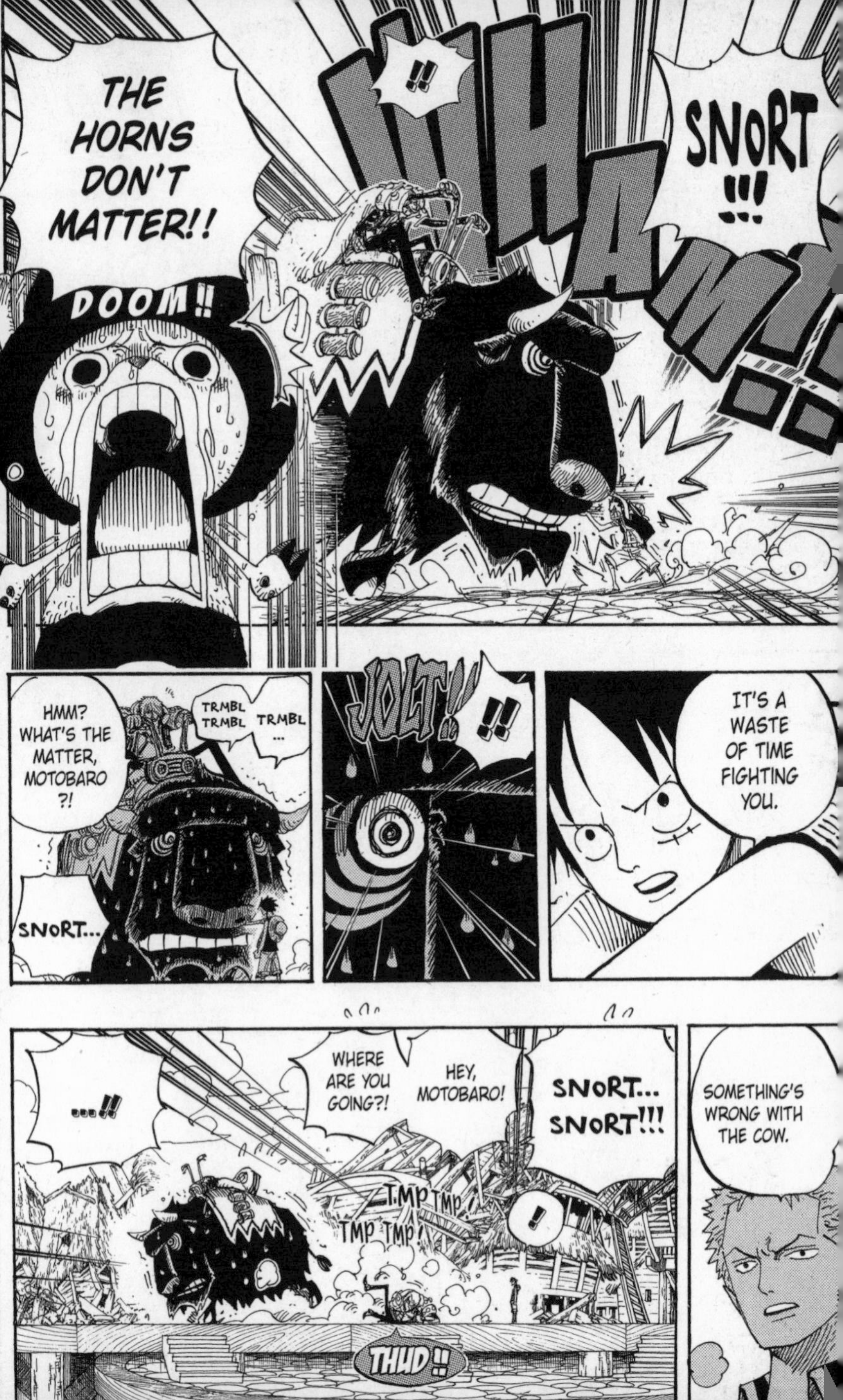
SNORT !!!
WHAM!!
!!
THE HORNS DON'T MATTER!!
DOOM!!
IT'S A WASTE OF TIME FIGHTING YOU.
JOLT!!
!!
HMM? WHAT'S THE MATTER, MOTOBARO ?!
TRMBL TRMBL TRMBL ...
SNORT...
SOMETHING'S WRONG WITH THE COW.
SNORT... SNORT!!!
HEY, MOTOBARO!
WHERE ARE YOU GOING?!
...!!
TMP TMP
TMP TMP
!
THUD!!

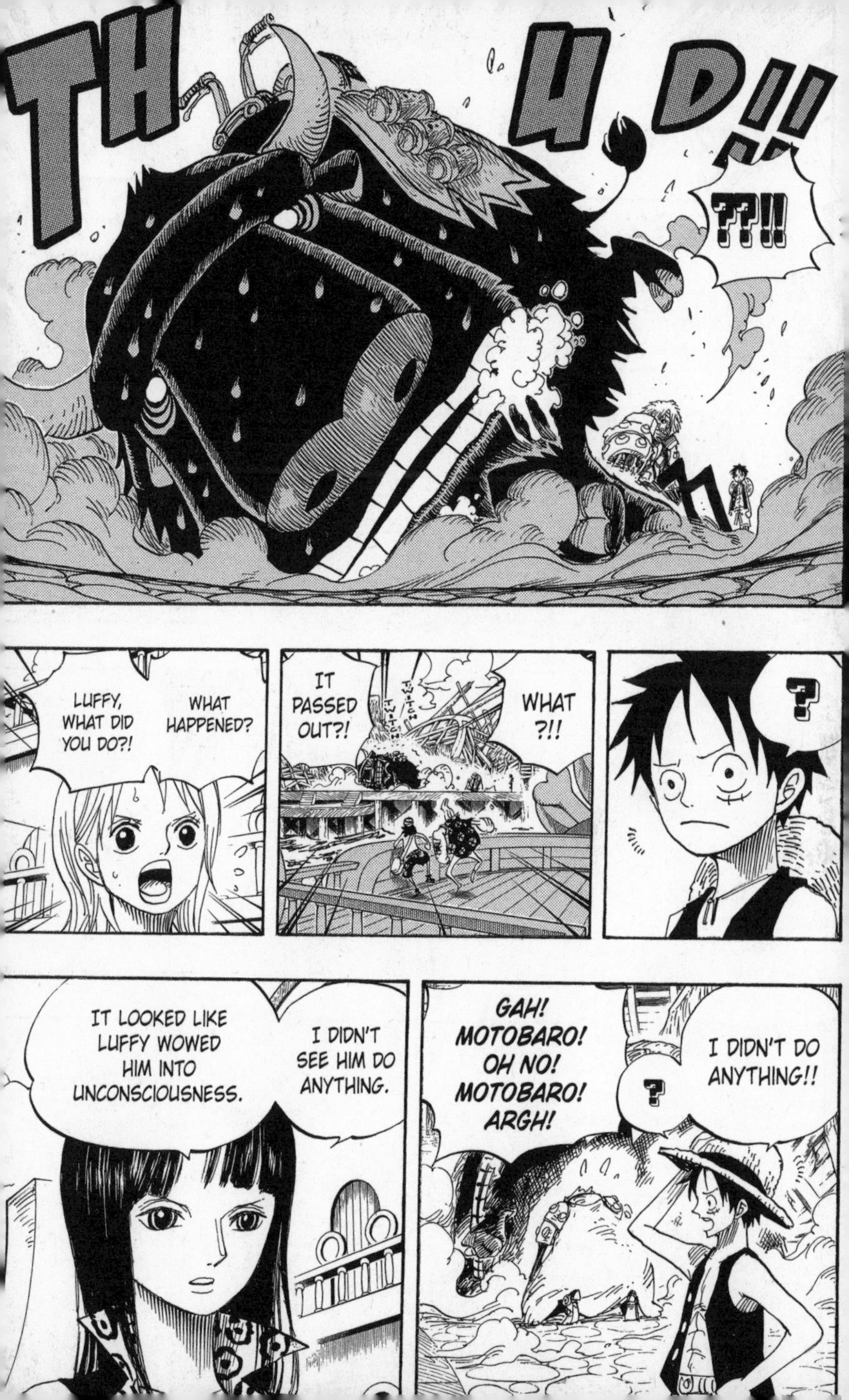
THUD!!
??!!
?
WHAT ?!!
IT PASSED OUT?!
TWITCH TWITCH
WHAT HAPPENED?
LUFFY, WHAT DID YOU DO?!
I DIDN'T DO ANYTHING!!
?
GAH! MOTOBARO! OH NO! MOTOBARO! ARGH!
I DIDN'T SEE HIM DO ANYTHING.
IT LOOKED LIKE LUFFY WOWED HIM INTO UNCONSCIOUSNESS.

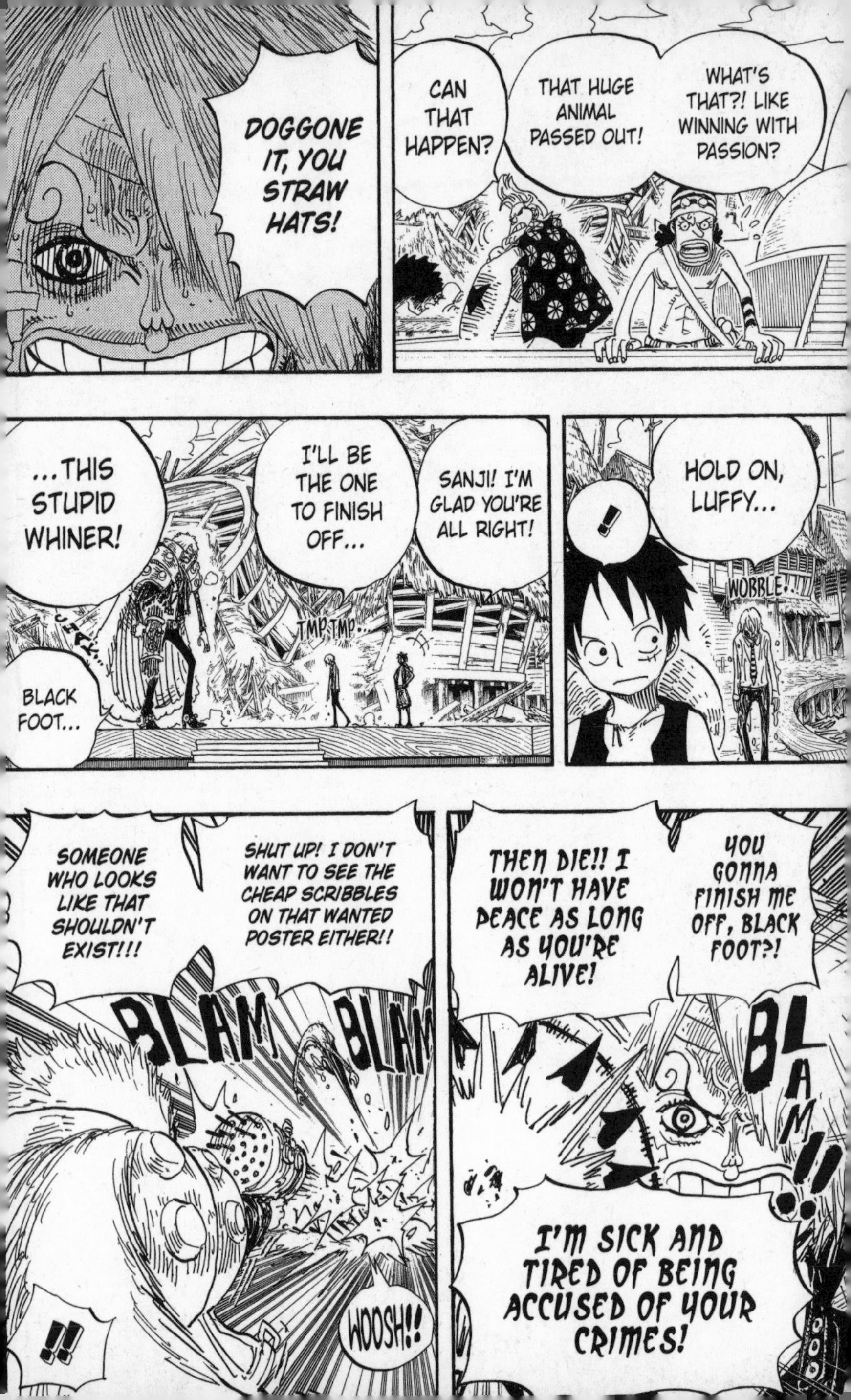
WHAT'S THAT?! LIKE WINNING WITH PASSION?
THAT HUGE ANIMAL PASSED OUT!
CAN THAT HAPPEN?
DOGGONE IT, YOU STRAW HATS!
HOLD ON, LUFFY...
!
WOBBLE
SANJI! I'M GLAD YOU'RE ALL RIGHT!
I'LL BE THE ONE TO FINISH OFF...
...THIS STUPID WHINER!
TMP TMP...
BLACK FOOT...
YOU GONNA FINISH ME OFF, BLACK FOOT?!
THEN DIE!! I WON'T HAVE PEACE AS LONG AS YOU'RE ALIVE!
BLAM!!
I'M SICK AND TIRED OF BEING ACCUSED OF YOUR CRIMES!
SHUT UP! I DON'T WANT TO SEE THE CHEAP SCRIBBLES ON THAT WANTED POSTER EITHER!!
SOMEONE WHO LOOKS LIKE THAT SHOULDN'T EXIST!!!
BLAM BLAM
WOOSH!!
!!

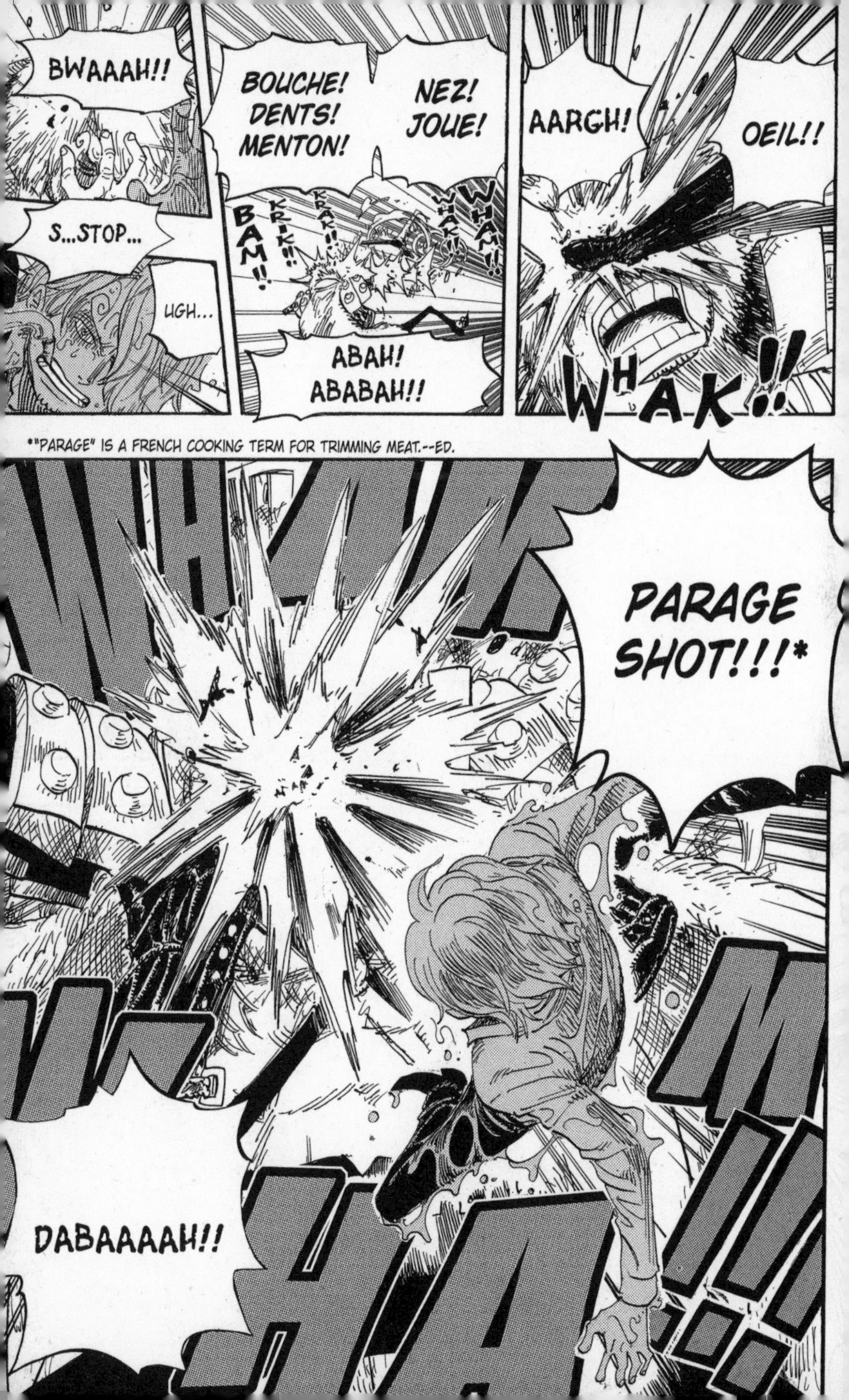
AARGH!
OEIL!!
WHAK!!
NEZ! JOUE!
BOUCHE! DENTS! MENTON!
BAM!!
KRIK!!
KRAK!!
WHAK!!
WHAM!!
ABAH! ABABAH!!
BWAAAH!!
S...STOP...
UGH...
PARAGE SHOT!!!*
DABAAAAH!!

*"PARAGE" IS A FRENCH COOKING TERM FOR TRIMMING MEAT.--ED.

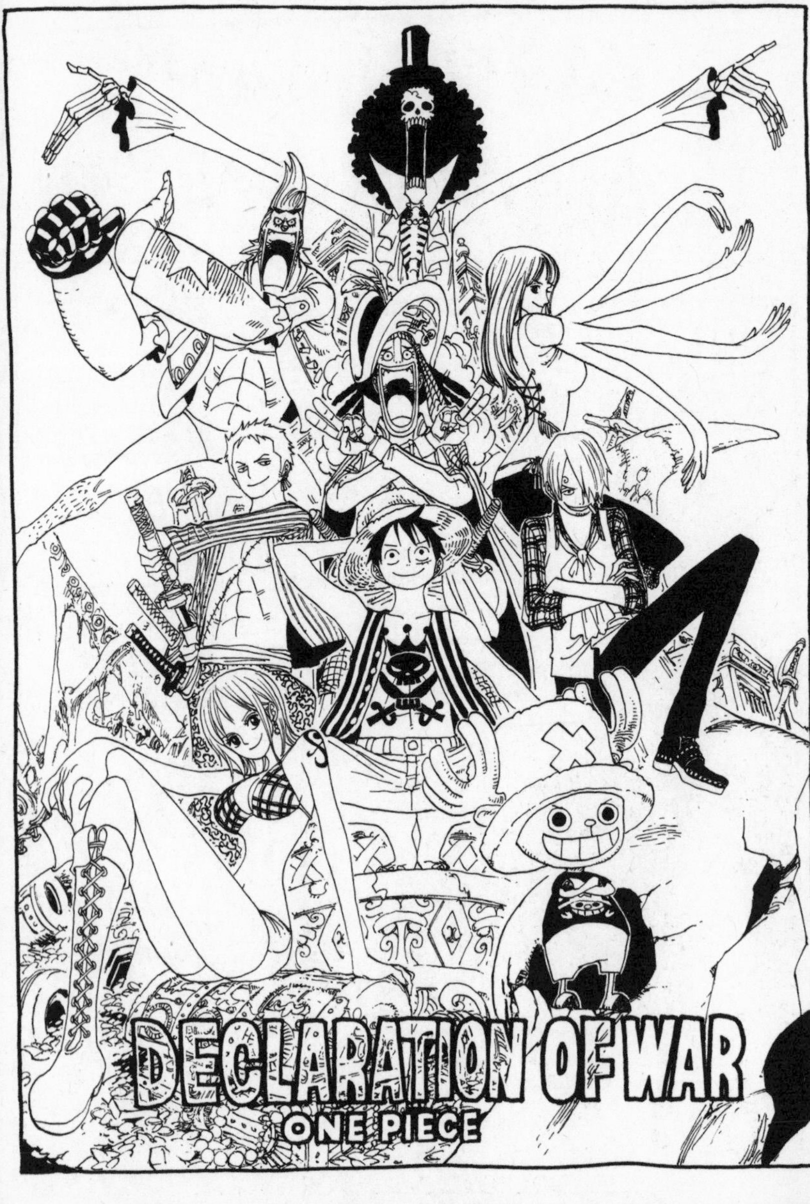
DECLARATION OF WAR
ONE PIECE

Chapter 496:
YARUKIMAN MANGROVE

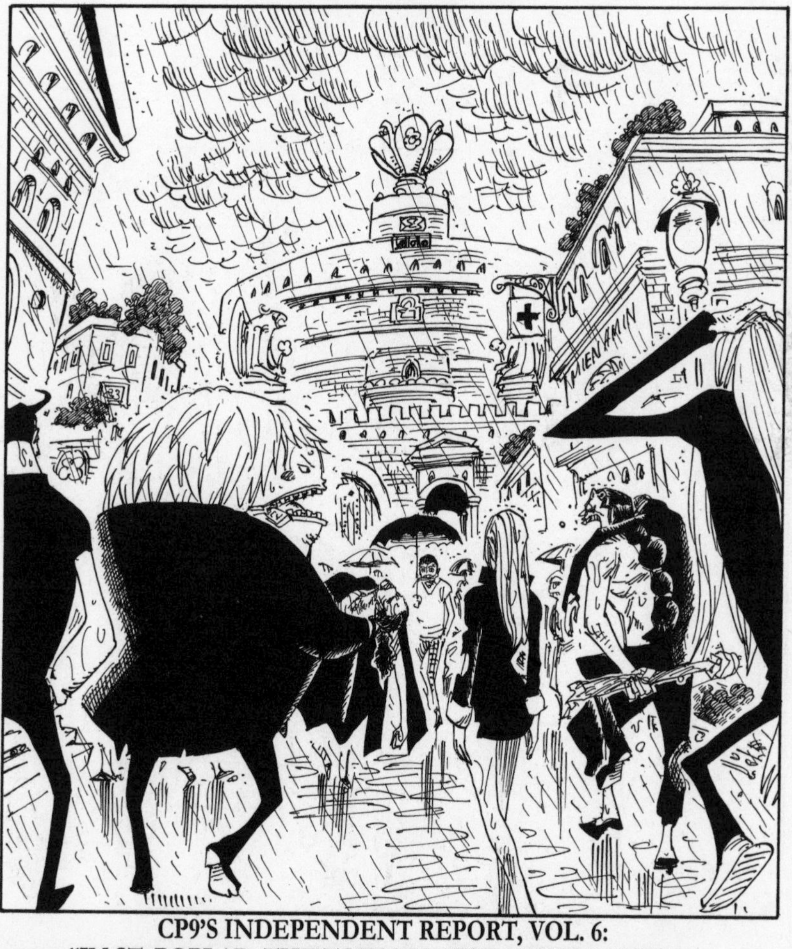

CP9'S INDEPENDENT REPORT, VOL. 6:
"IN ST. POPLAR, THE TOWN OF THE SPRING QUEEN, WITHOUT MONEY FOR MEDICAL CARE"

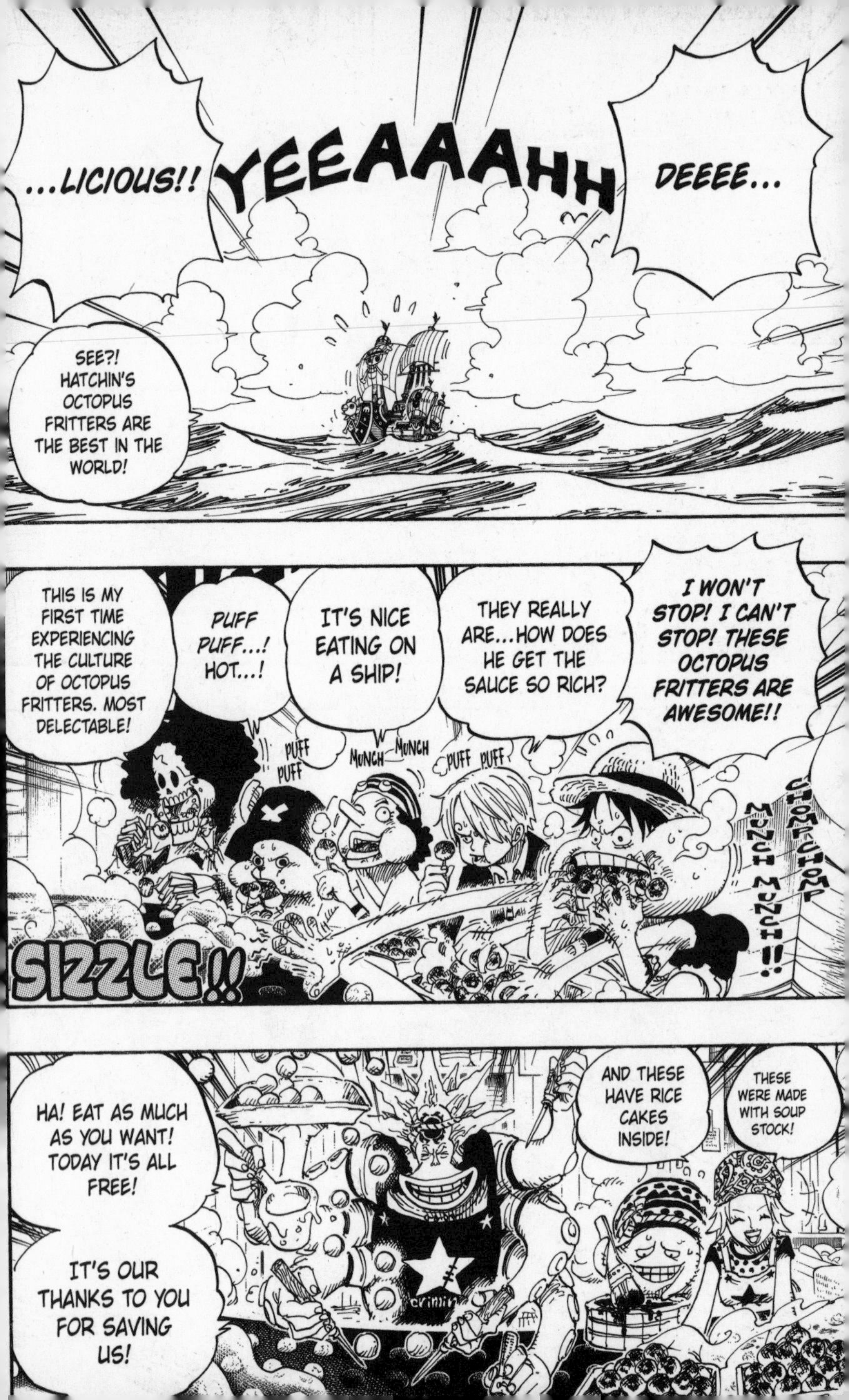
DEEEE...
YEEAAAHH
...LICIOUS!!
SEE?! HATCHIN'S OCTOPUS FRITTERS ARE THE BEST IN THE WORLD!
I WON'T STOP! I CAN'T STOP! THESE OCTOPUS FRITTERS ARE AWESOME!!
CHOMP CHOMP
MUNCH MUNCH MUNCH!!
THEY REALLY ARE...HOW DOES HE GET THE SAUCE SO RICH?
PUFF PUFF
IT'S NICE EATING ON A SHIP!
MUNCH MUNCH
PUFF PUFF...! HOT...!
PUFF PUFF
THIS IS MY FIRST TIME EXPERIENCING THE CULTURE OF OCTOPUS FRITTERS. MOST DELECTABLE!
SIZZLE!!
THESE WERE MADE WITH SOUP STOCK!
AND THESE HAVE RICE CAKES INSIDE!
HA! EAT AS MUCH AS YOU WANT! TODAY IT'S ALL FREE!
IT'S OUR THANKS TO YOU FOR SAVING US!

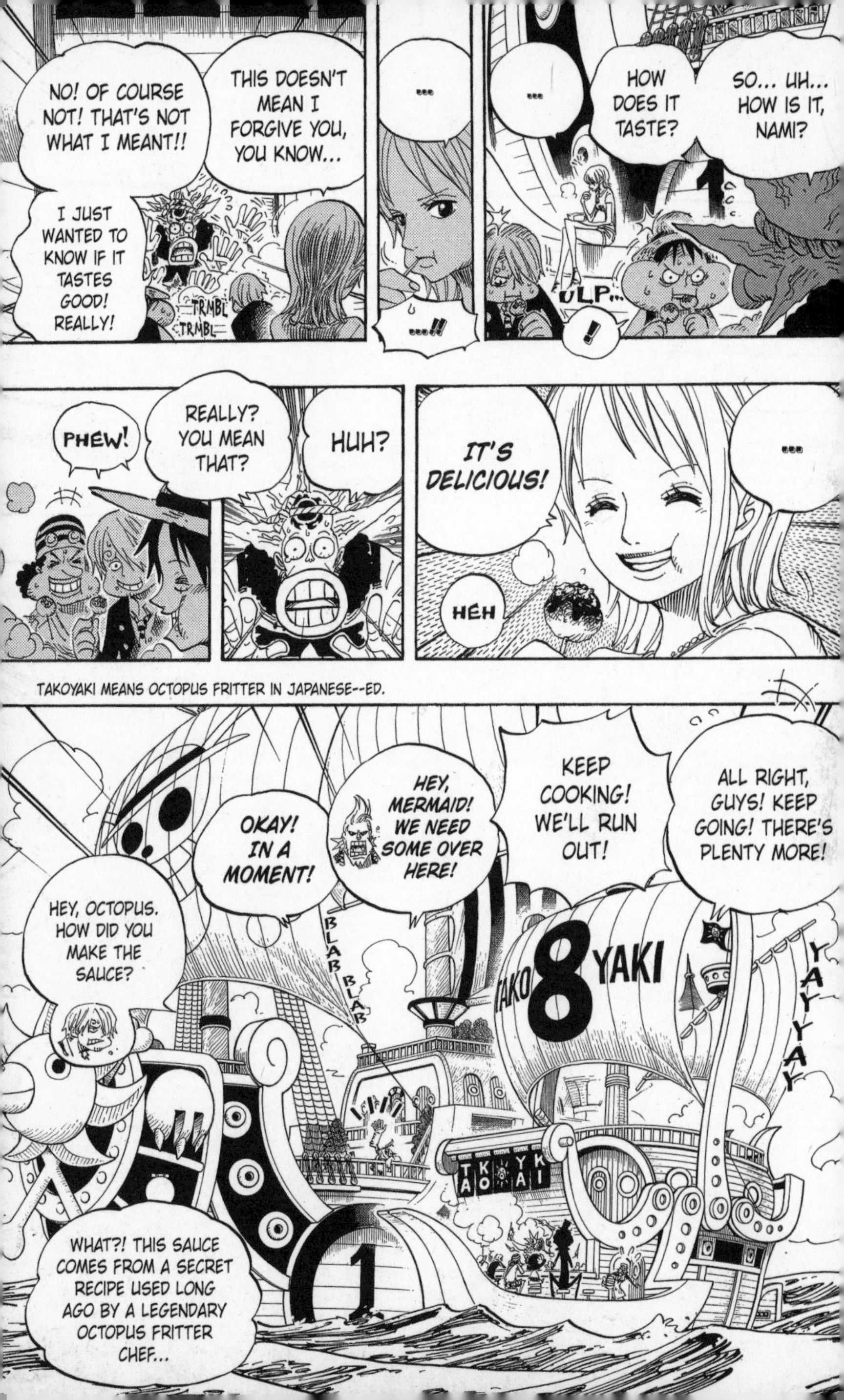
SO... UH... HOW IS IT, NAMI?
HOW DOES IT TASTE?
...
ULP...
!
...
...!!
THIS DOESN'T MEAN I FORGIVE YOU, YOU KNOW...
NO! OF COURSE NOT! THAT'S NOT WHAT I MEANT!!
I JUST WANTED TO KNOW IF IT TASTES GOOD! REALLY!
TRMBL TRMBL
...
IT'S DELICIOUS!
HEH
HUH?
REALLY? YOU MEAN THAT?
PHEW!
ALL RIGHT, GUYS! KEEP GOING! THERE'S PLENTY MORE!
KEEP COOKING! WE'LL RUN OUT!
HEY, MERMAID! WE NEED SOME OVER HERE!
OKAY! IN A MOMENT!
YAY YAY YAY
TAKO 8 YAKI
TAKOYAKI
BLAB BLAB
HEY, OCTOPUS. HOW DID YOU MAKE THE SAUCE?
WHAT?! THIS SAUCE COMES FROM A SECRET RECIPE USED LONG AGO BY A LEGENDARY OCTOPUS FRITTER CHEF...

TAKOYAKI MEANS OCTOPUS FRITTER IN JAPANESE--ED.

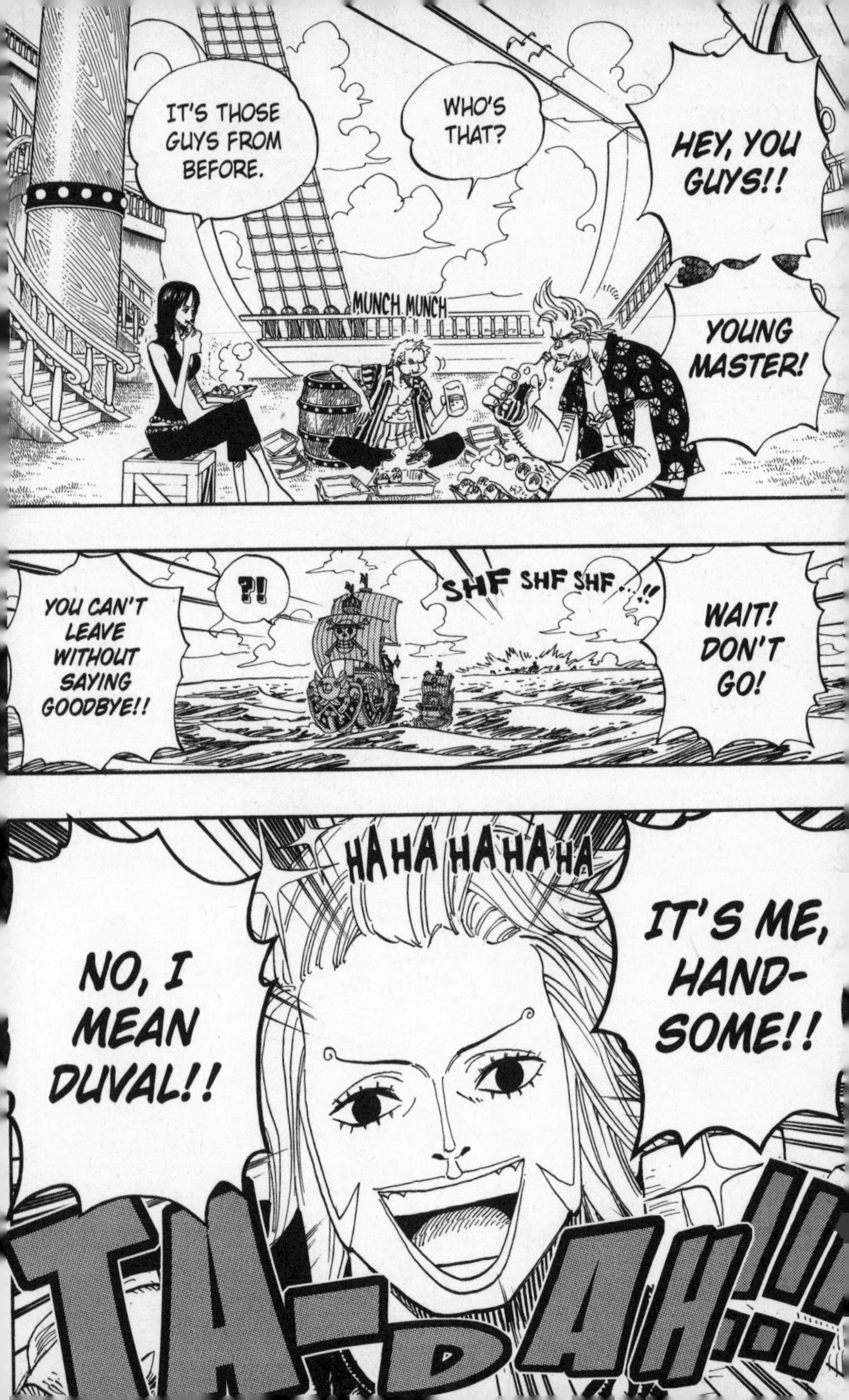
HEY, YOU GUYS!!
YOUNG MASTER!
WHO'S THAT?
IT'S THOSE GUYS FROM BEFORE.
MUNCH MUNCH
WAIT! DON'T GO!
SHF SHF SHF...!!
?!
YOU CAN'T LEAVE WITHOUT SAYING GOODBYE!!
IT'S ME, HAND-SOME!!
HAHA HAHAHAHA
NO, I MEAN DUVAL!!
TA-DAH...!!

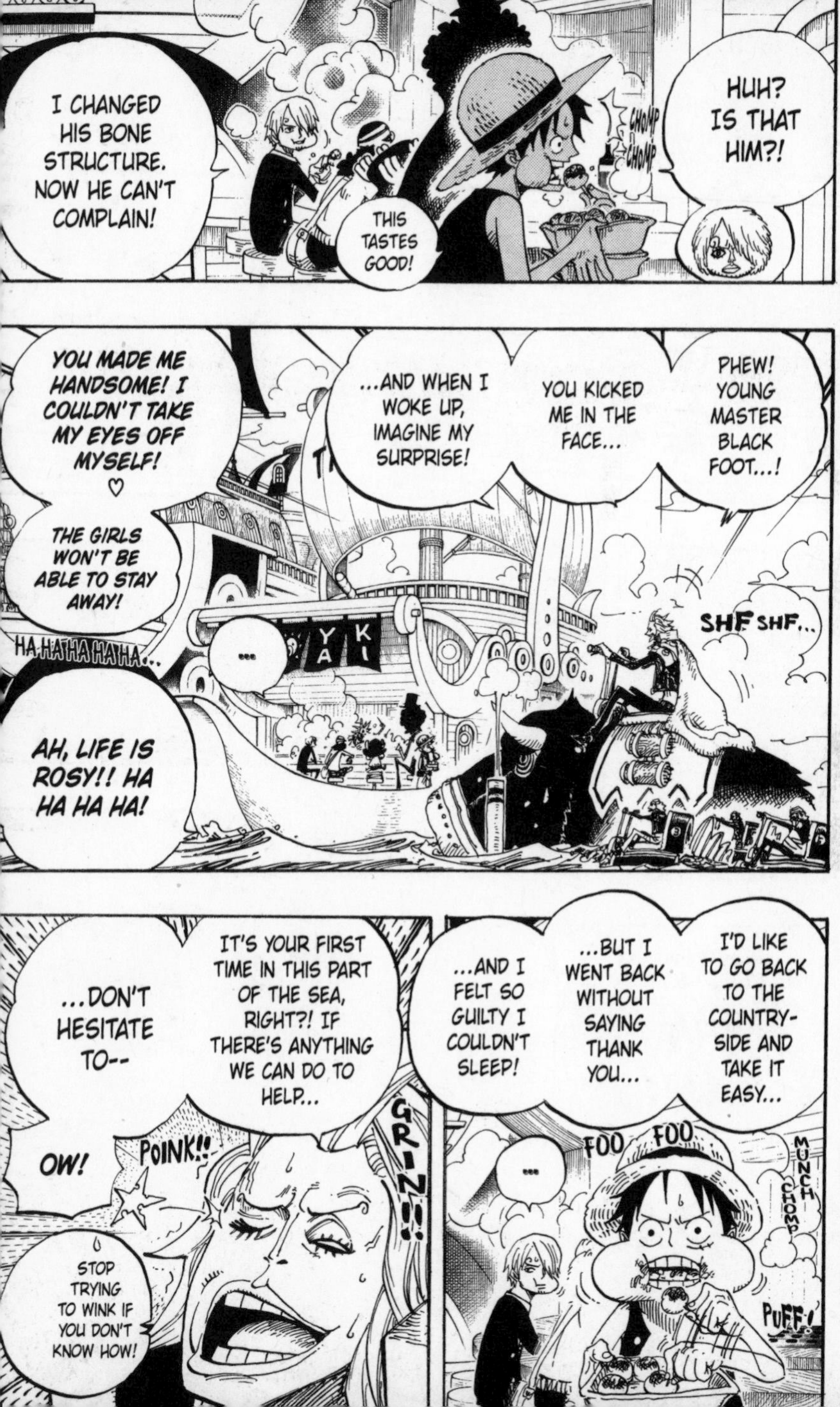

HUH? IS THAT HIM?!
CHOMP CHOMP
THIS TASTES GOOD!
I CHANGED HIS BONE STRUCTURE. NOW HE CAN'T COMPLAIN!
PHEW! YOUNG MASTER BLACK FOOT...!
YOU KICKED ME IN THE FACE...
...AND WHEN I WOKE UP, IMAGINE MY SURPRISE!
YOU MADE ME HANDSOME! I COULDN'T TAKE MY EYES OFF MYSELF! ♡
THE GIRLS WON'T BE ABLE TO STAY AWAY!
SHF SHF...
...
HA HA HA HA HA HA...
AH, LIFE IS ROSY!! HA HA HA HA!
I'D LIKE TO GO BACK TO THE COUNTRY-SIDE AND TAKE IT EASY...
...BUT I WENT BACK WITHOUT SAYING THANK YOU...
...AND I FELT SO GUILTY I COULDN'T SLEEP!
FOO FOO
MUNCH CHOMP
...
PUFF
IT'S YOUR FIRST TIME IN THIS PART OF THE SEA, RIGHT?! IF THERE'S ANYTHING WE CAN DO TO HELP...
...DON'T HESITATE TO--
GRIN!!
POINK!!
OW!
STOP TRYING TO WINK IF YOU DON'T KNOW HOW!

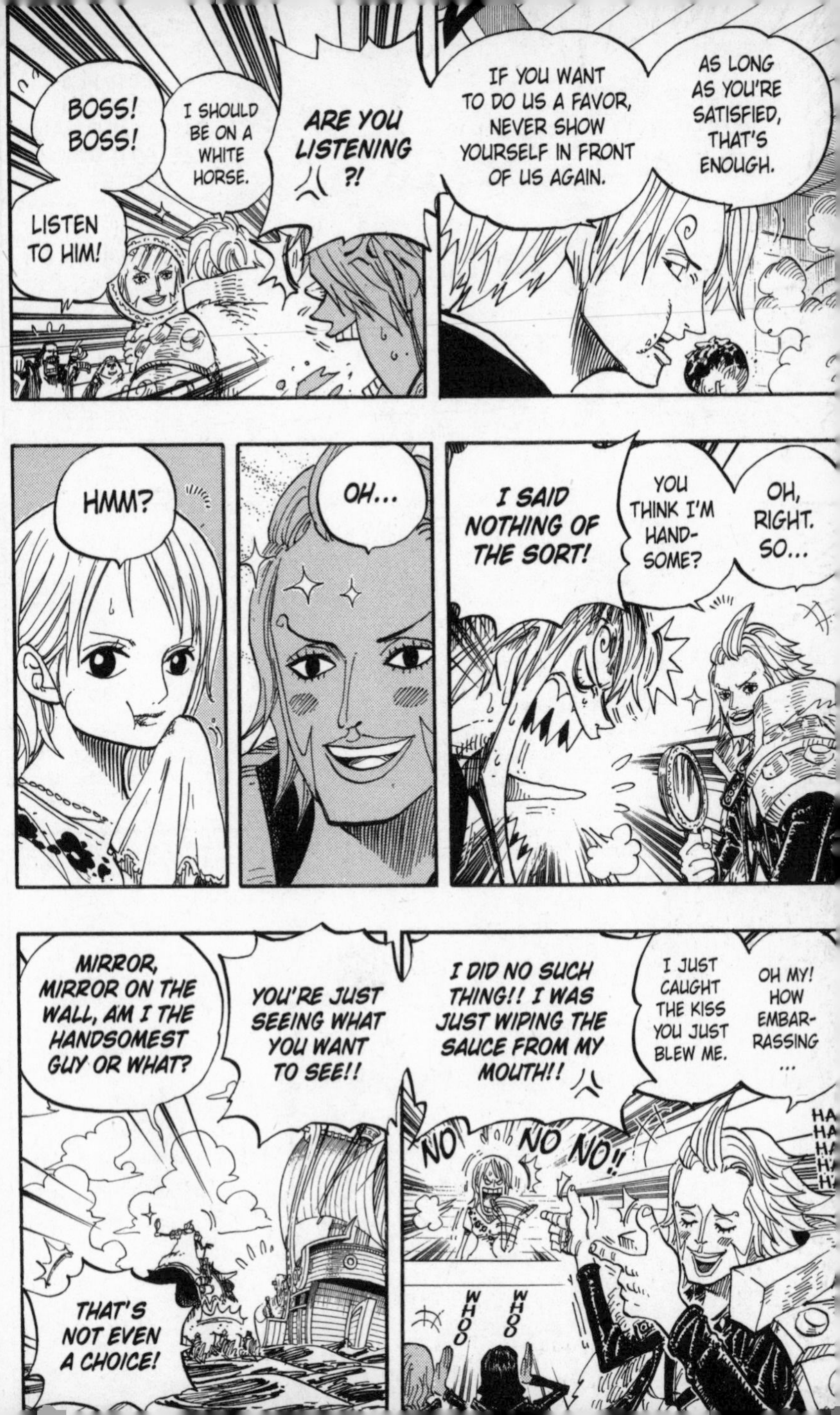
AS LONG AS YOU'RE SATISFIED, THAT'S ENOUGH.
IF YOU WANT TO DO US A FAVOR, NEVER SHOW YOURSELF IN FRONT OF US AGAIN.
ARE YOU LISTENING ?!
I SHOULD BE ON A WHITE HORSE.
BOSS! BOSS!
LISTEN TO HIM!
OH, RIGHT. SO...
YOU THINK I'M HAND-SOME?
I SAID NOTHING OF THE SORT!
OH...
HMM?
OH MY! HOW EMBAR-RASSING ...
I JUST CAUGHT THE KISS YOU JUST BLEW ME.
I DID NO SUCH THING!! I WAS JUST WIPING THE SAUCE FROM MY MOUTH!!
HA HA HA HA HA
NO NO NO!!
WHOO WHOO
YOU'RE JUST SEEING WHAT YOU WANT TO SEE!!
MIRROR, MIRROR ON THE WALL, AM I THE HANDSOMEST GUY OR WHAT?
THAT'S NOT EVEN A CHOICE!

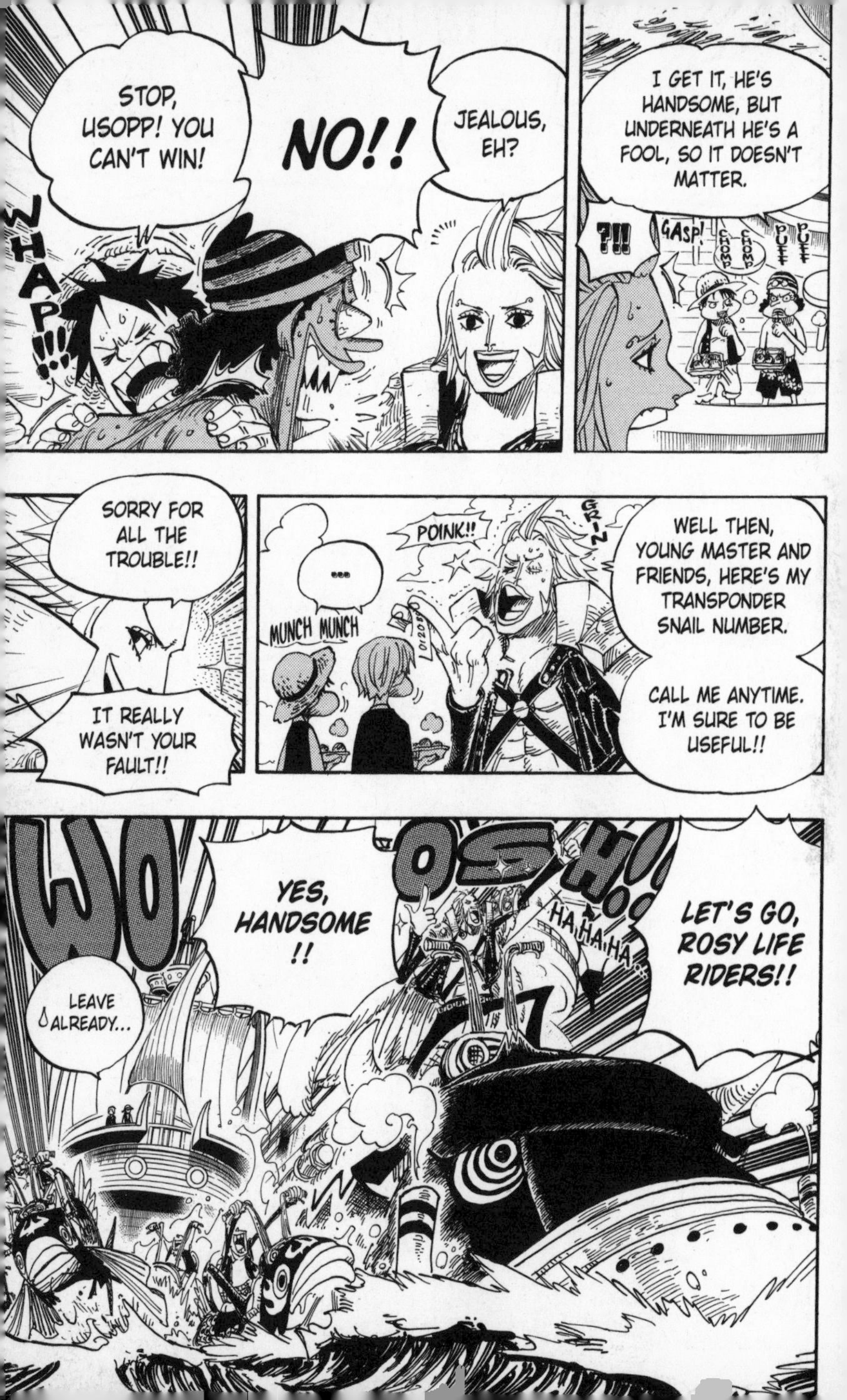
I GET IT, HE'S HANDSOME, BUT UNDERNEATH HE'S A FOOL, SO IT DOESN'T MATTER.
?!!
GASP!
CHOMP CHOMP
PUFF PUFF
JEALOUS, EH?
NO!!
STOP, USOPP! YOU CAN'T WIN!
WHAP!!!
GRIN
WELL THEN, YOUNG MASTER AND FRIENDS, HERE'S MY TRANSPONDER SNAIL NUMBER.
CALL ME ANYTIME. I'M SURE TO BE USEFUL!!
POINK!!
...
MUNCH MUNCH
SORRY FOR ALL THE TROUBLE!!
IT REALLY WASN'T YOUR FAULT!!
LET'S GO, ROSY LIFE RIDERS!!
HA HA HA
WOOSH!!
YES, HANDSOME!!
LEAVE ALREADY...

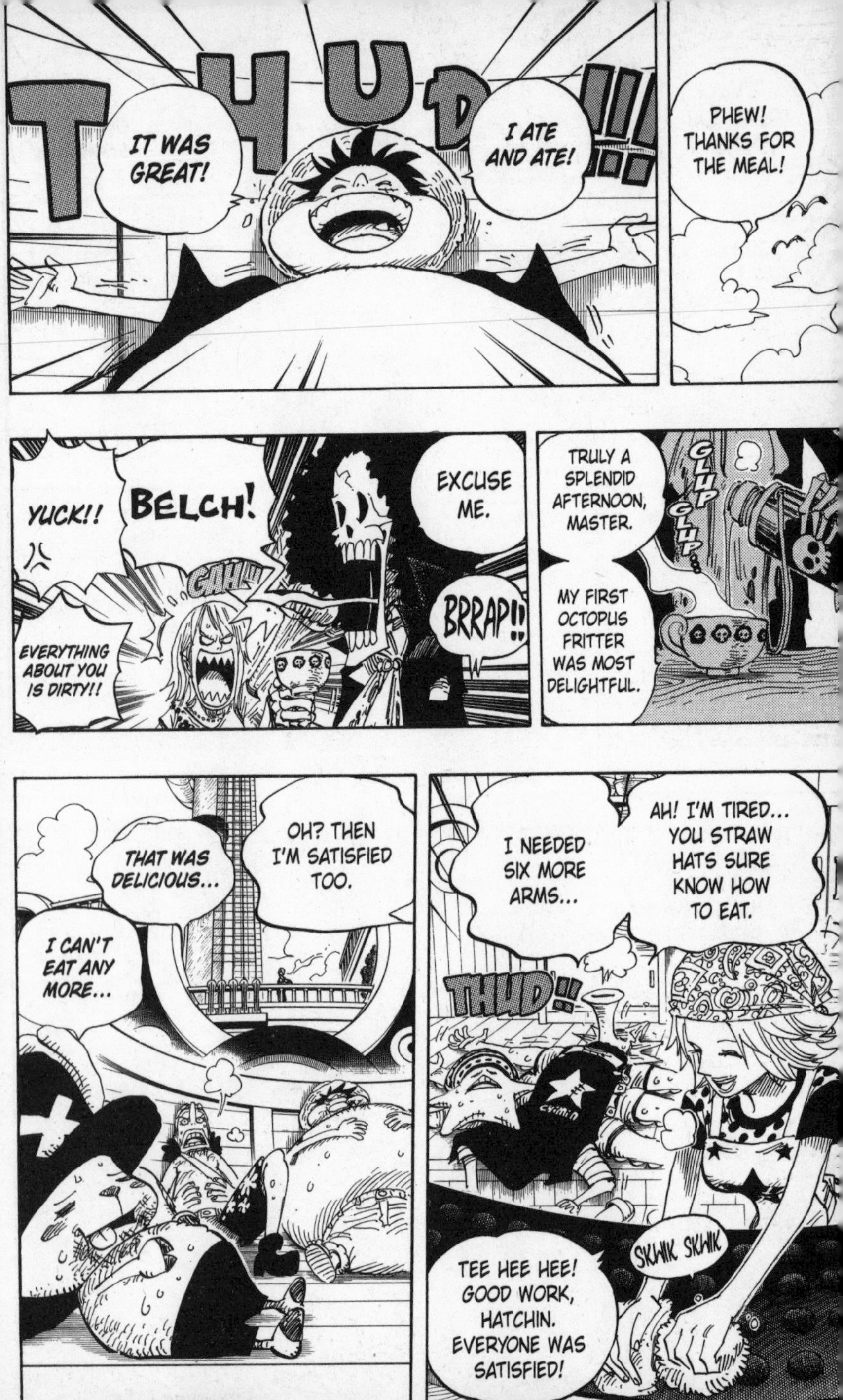
PHEW! THANKS FOR THE MEAL!
I ATE AND ATE!
THUD!!
IT WAS GREAT!
TRULY A SPLENDID AFTERNOON, MASTER.
MY FIRST OCTOPUS FRITTER WAS MOST DELIGHTFUL.
GLUP GLUP GLUP
EXCUSE ME.
BRRAP!!
BELCH!
GAH!!
YUCK!!
EVERYTHING ABOUT YOU IS DIRTY!!
AH! I'M TIRED... YOU STRAW HATS SURE KNOW HOW TO EAT.
I NEEDED SIX MORE ARMS...
THUD!!
SKWIK SKWIK
TEE HEE HEE! GOOD WORK, HATCHIN. EVERYONE WAS SATISFIED!
OH? THEN I'M SATISFIED TOO.
THAT WAS DELICIOUS...
I CAN'T EAT ANY MORE...

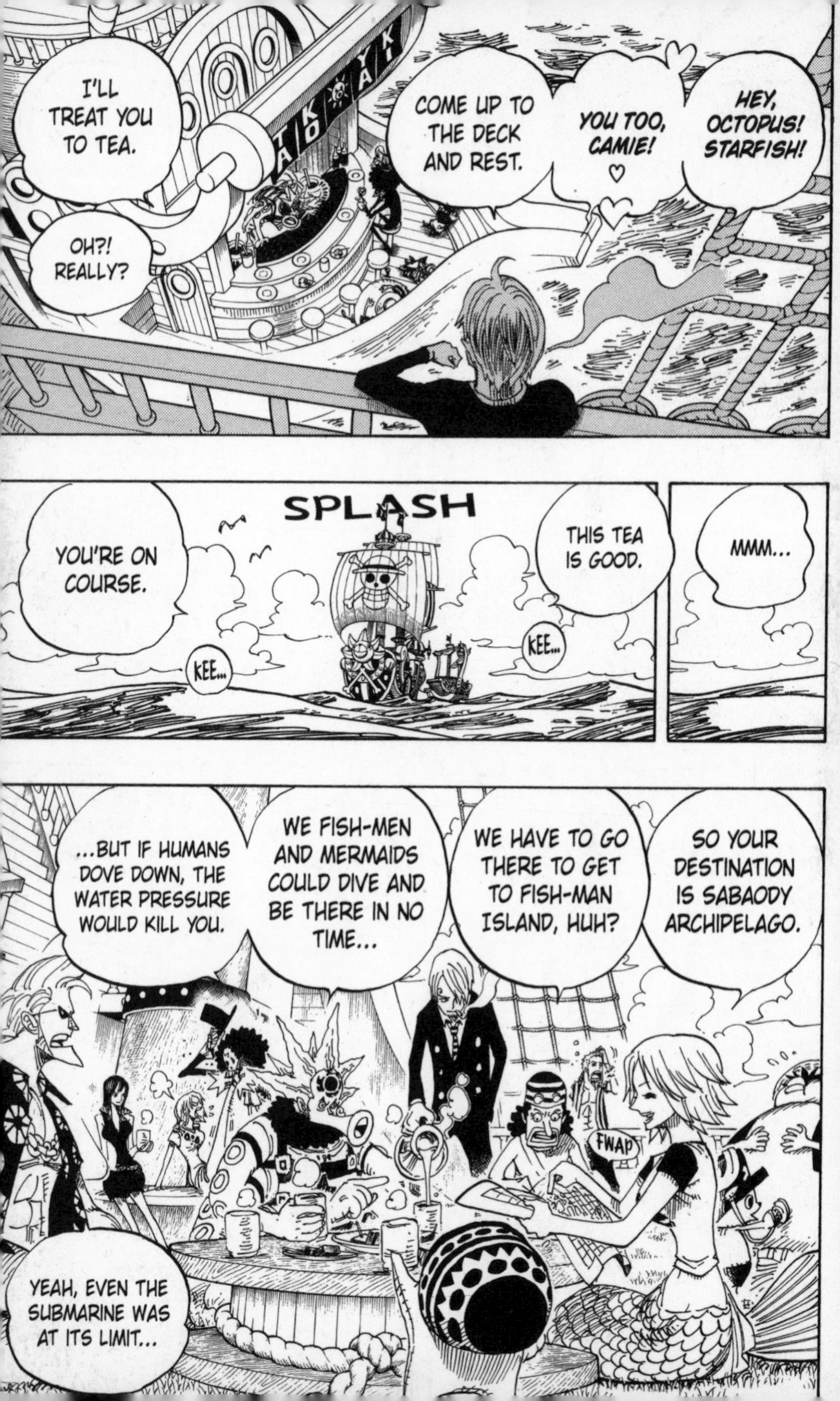
HEY, OCTOPUS! STARFISH!
YOU TOO, CAMIE! ♡
COME UP TO THE DECK AND REST.
I'LL TREAT YOU TO TEA.
OH?! REALLY?
MMM...
THIS TEA IS GOOD.
SPLASH
KEE...
YOU'RE ON COURSE.
KEE...
SO YOUR DESTINATION IS SABAODY ARCHIPELAGO.
WE HAVE TO GO THERE TO GET TO FISH-MAN ISLAND, HUH?
FWAP
WE FISH-MEN AND MERMAIDS COULD DIVE AND BE THERE IN NO TIME...
...BUT IF HUMANS DOVE DOWN, THE WATER PRESSURE WOULD KILL YOU.
YEAH, EVEN THE SUBMARINE WAS AT ITS LIMIT...

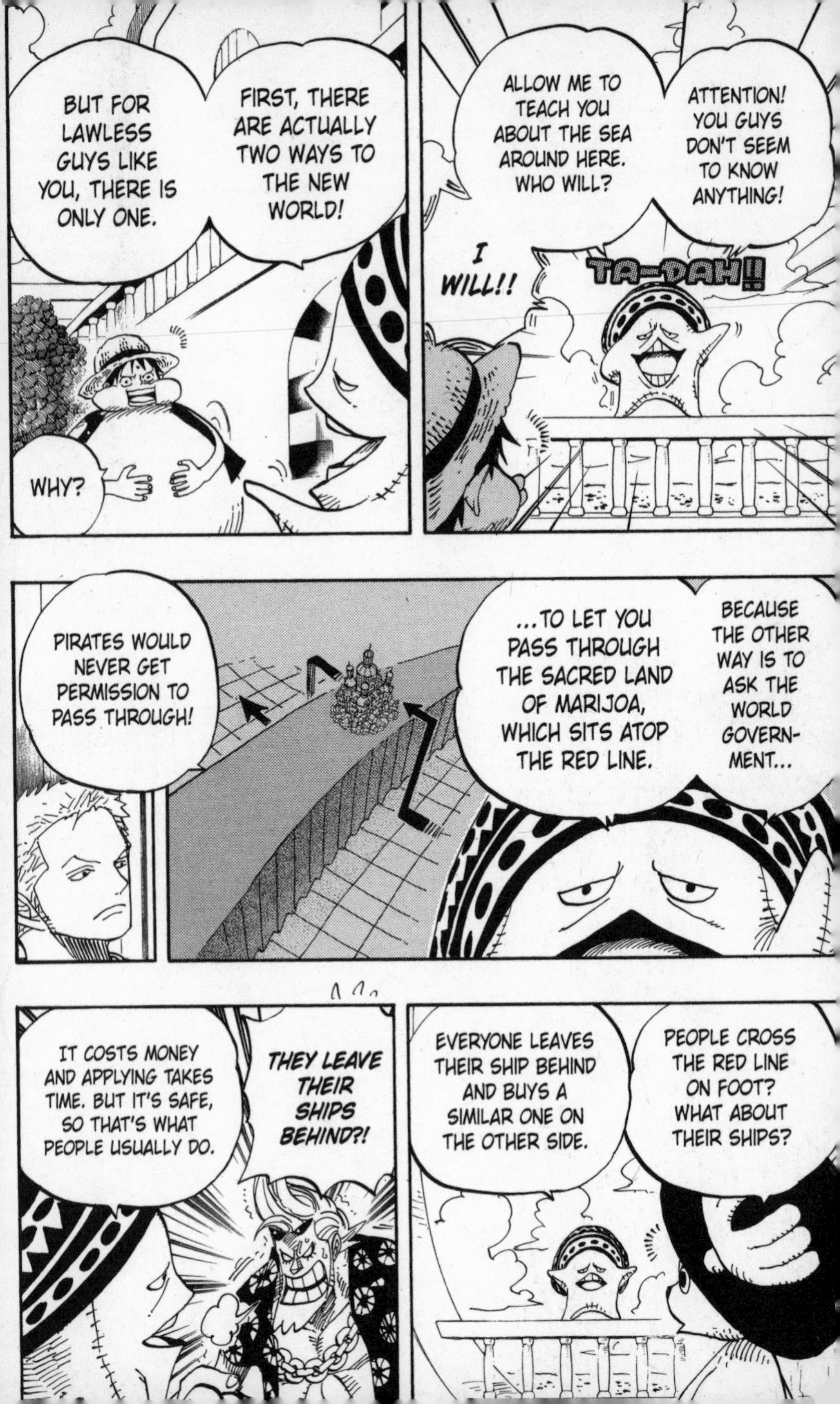
ATTENTION! YOU GUYS DON'T SEEM TO KNOW ANYTHING!
ALLOW ME TO TEACH YOU ABOUT THE SEA AROUND HERE. WHO WILL?
TA-DAH!!
I WILL!!
FIRST, THERE ARE ACTUALLY TWO WAYS TO THE NEW WORLD!
BUT FOR LAWLESS GUYS LIKE YOU, THERE IS ONLY ONE.
WHY?
BECAUSE THE OTHER WAY IS TO ASK THE WORLD GOVERN-MENT...
...TO LET YOU PASS THROUGH THE SACRED LAND OF MARIJOA, WHICH SITS ATOP THE RED LINE.
PIRATES WOULD NEVER GET PERMISSION TO PASS THROUGH!
PEOPLE CROSS THE RED LINE ON FOOT? WHAT ABOUT THEIR SHIPS?
EVERYONE LEAVES THEIR SHIP BEHIND AND BUYS A SIMILAR ONE ON THE OTHER SIDE.
THEY LEAVE THEIR SHIPS BEHIND?!
IT COSTS MONEY AND APPLYING TAKES TIME. BUT IT'S SAFE, SO THAT'S WHAT PEOPLE USUALLY DO.

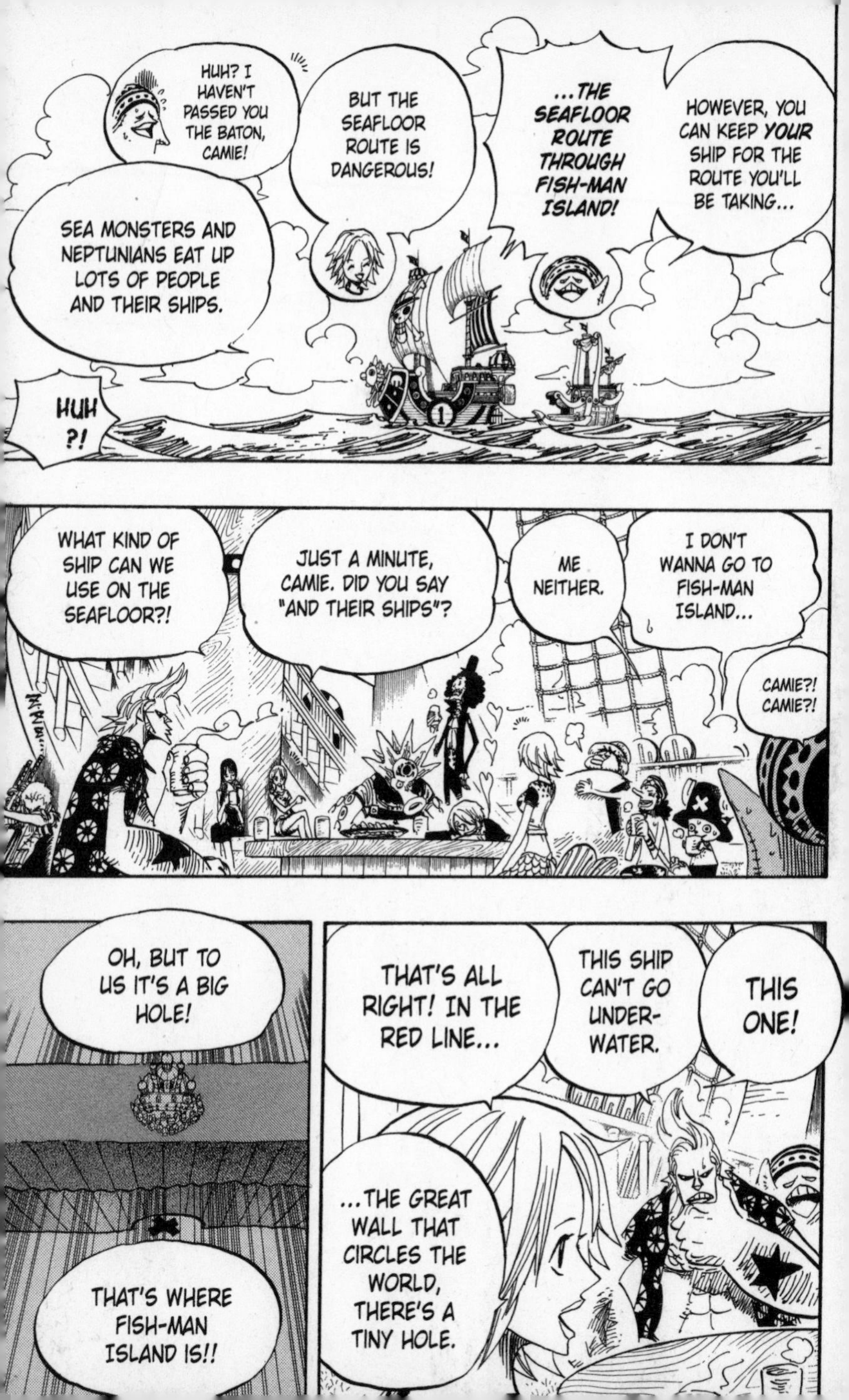
HOWEVER, YOU CAN KEEP YOUR SHIP FOR THE ROUTE YOU'LL BE TAKING...
...THE SEAFLOOR ROUTE THROUGH FISH-MAN ISLAND!
BUT THE SEAFLOOR ROUTE IS DANGEROUS!
HUH? I HAVEN'T PASSED YOU THE BATON, CAMIE!
SEA MONSTERS AND NEPTUNIANS EAT UP LOTS OF PEOPLE AND THEIR SHIPS.
HUH ?!
I DON'T WANNA GO TO FISH-MAN ISLAND...
ME NEITHER.
CAMIE?! CAMIE?!
JUST A MINUTE, CAMIE. DID YOU SAY "AND THEIR SHIPS"?
WHAT KIND OF SHIP CAN WE USE ON THE SEAFLOOR?!
THIS ONE!
THIS SHIP CAN'T GO UNDER-WATER.
THAT'S ALL RIGHT! IN THE RED LINE...
...THE GREAT WALL THAT CIRCLES THE WORLD, THERE'S A TINY HOLE.
OH, BUT TO US IT'S A BIG HOLE!
THAT'S WHERE FISH-MAN ISLAND IS!!

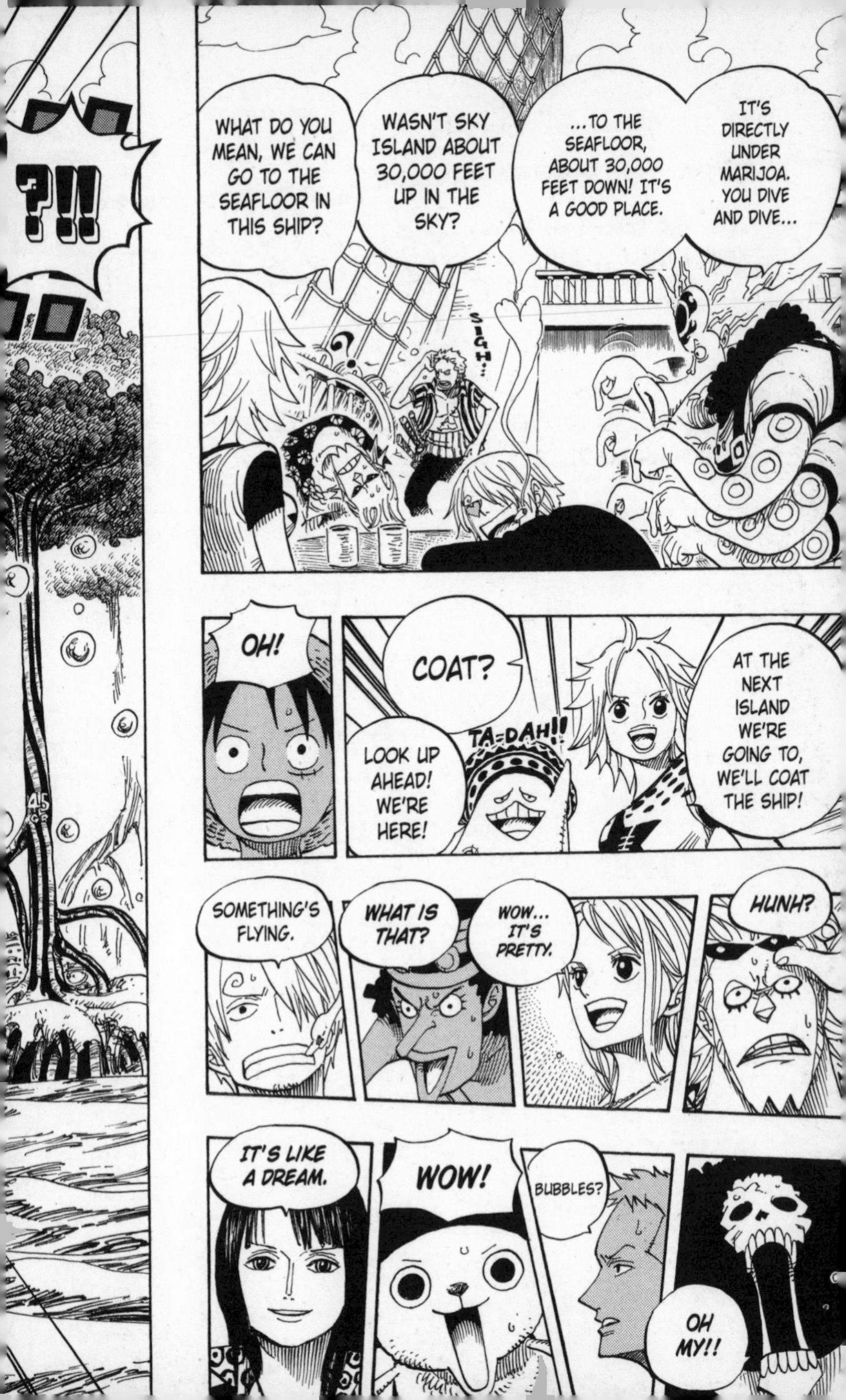
IT'S DIRECTLY UNDER MARIJOA. YOU DIVE AND DIVE...
...TO THE SEAFLOOR, ABOUT 30,000 FEET DOWN! IT'S A GOOD PLACE.
WASN'T SKY ISLAND ABOUT 30,000 FEET UP IN THE SKY?
WHAT DO YOU MEAN, WE CAN GO TO THE SEAFLOOR IN THIS SHIP?
SIGH..
AT THE NEXT ISLAND WE'RE GOING TO, WE'LL COAT THE SHIP!
TA-DAH!!
COAT?
LOOK UP AHEAD! WE'RE HERE!
OH!
HUNH?
WOW... IT'S PRETTY.
WHAT IS THAT?
SOMETHING'S FLYING.
OH MY!!
BUBBLES?
WOW!
IT'S LIKE A DREAM.
?!!

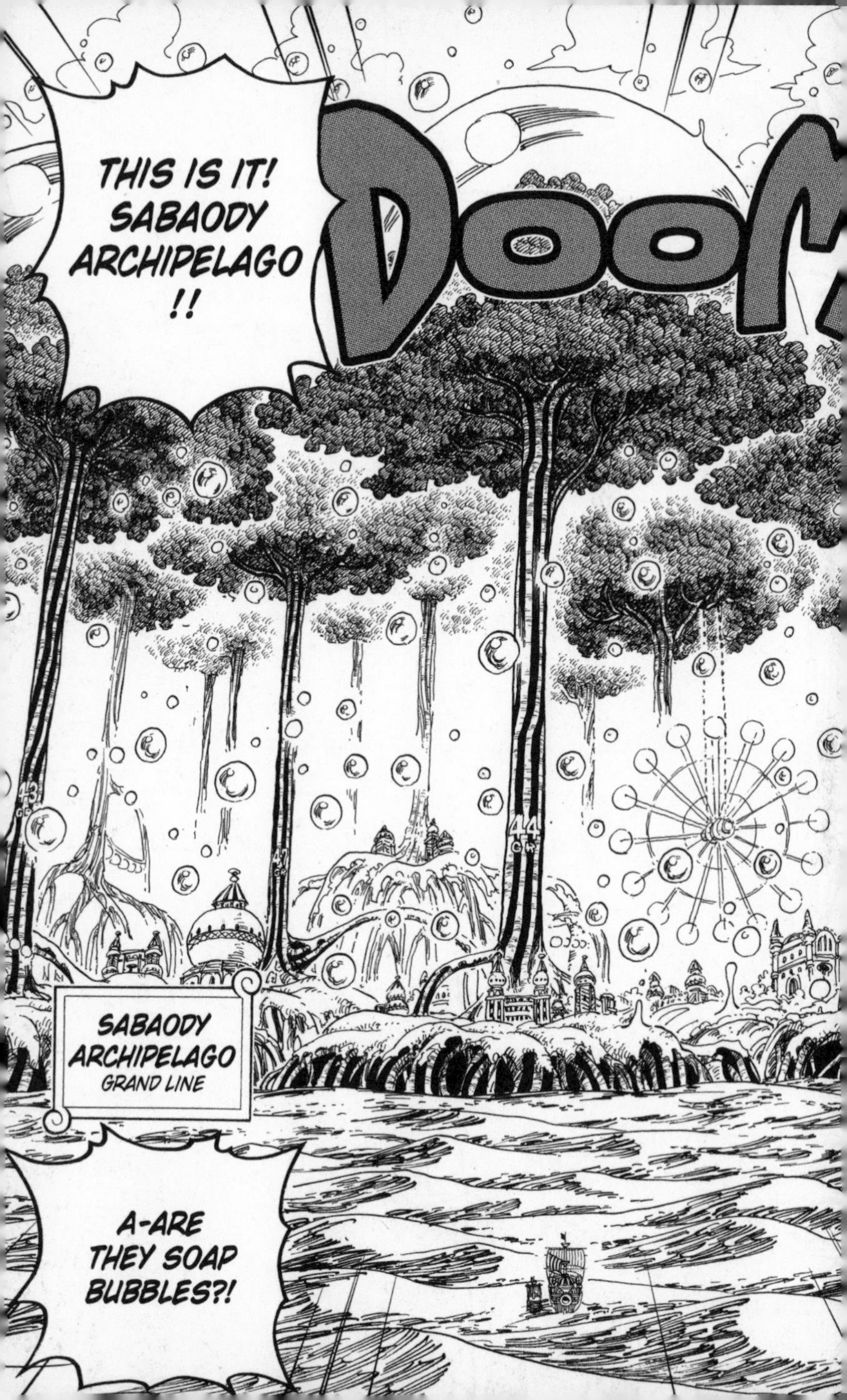
DOOM
THIS IS IT! SABAODY ARCHIPELAGO !!
SABAODY ARCHIPELAGO GRAND LINE
A-ARE THEY SOAP BUBBLES?!

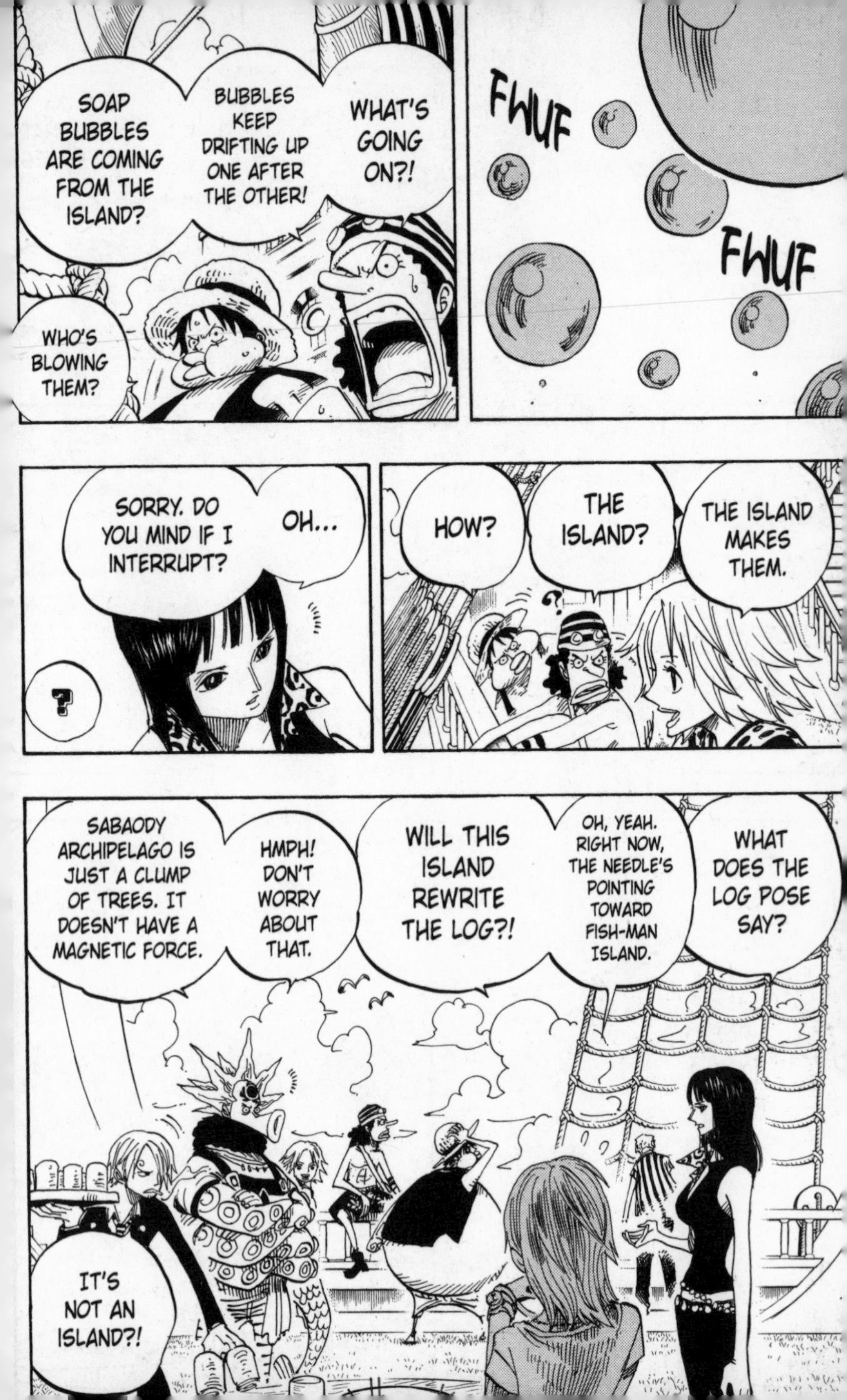
FWUF
FWUF
WHAT'S GOING ON?!
BUBBLES KEEP DRIFTING UP ONE AFTER THE OTHER!
SOAP BUBBLES ARE COMING FROM THE ISLAND?
WHO'S BLOWING THEM?
THE ISLAND MAKES THEM.
THE ISLAND?
HOW?
OH...
SORRY. DO YOU MIND IF I INTERRUPT?
?
WHAT DOES THE LOG POSE SAY?
OH, YEAH. RIGHT NOW, THE NEEDLE'S POINTING TOWARD FISH-MAN ISLAND.
WILL THIS ISLAND REWRITE THE LOG?!
HMPH! DON'T WORRY ABOUT THAT.
SABAODY ARCHIPELAGO IS JUST A CLUMP OF TREES. IT DOESN'T HAVE A MAGNETIC FORCE.
IT'S NOT AN ISLAND?!

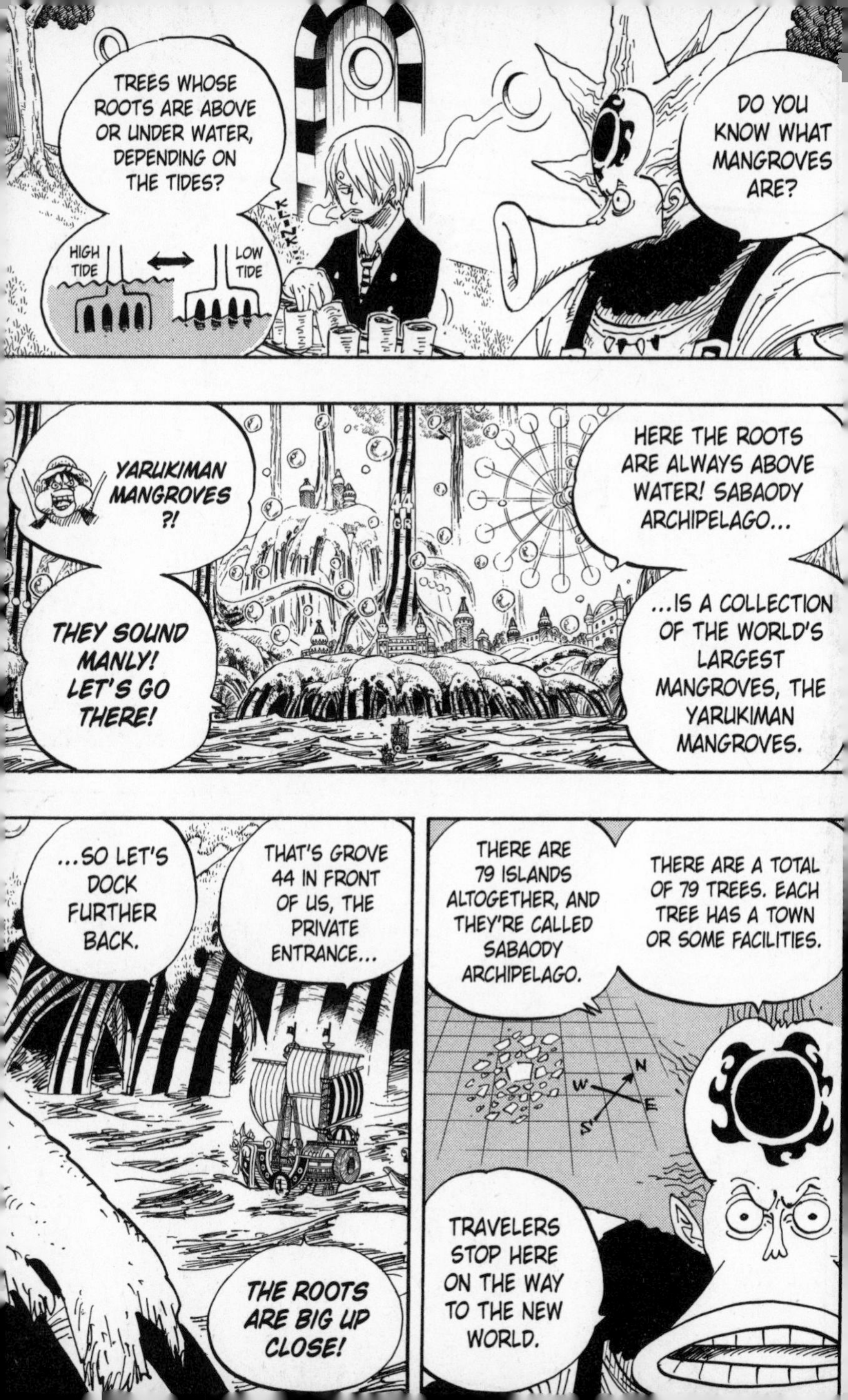
DO YOU KNOW WHAT MANGROVES ARE?
TREES WHOSE ROOTS ARE ABOVE OR UNDER WATER, DEPENDING ON THE TIDES?
HIGH TIDE
LOW TIDE
HERE THE ROOTS ARE ALWAYS ABOVE WATER! SABAODY ARCHIPELAGO...
...IS A COLLECTION OF THE WORLD'S LARGEST MANGROVES, THE YARUKIMAN MANGROVES.
44 GR
YARUKIMAN MANGROVES ?!
THEY SOUND MANLY! LET'S GO THERE!
THERE ARE A TOTAL OF 79 TREES. EACH TREE HAS A TOWN OR SOME FACILITIES.
THERE ARE 79 ISLANDS ALTOGETHER, AND THEY'RE CALLED SABAODY ARCHIPELAGO.
N
W
E
S
TRAVELERS STOP HERE ON THE WAY TO THE NEW WORLD.
THAT'S GROVE 44 IN FRONT OF US, THE PRIVATE ENTRANCE...
...SO LET'S DOCK FURTHER BACK.
THE ROOTS ARE BIG UP CLOSE!

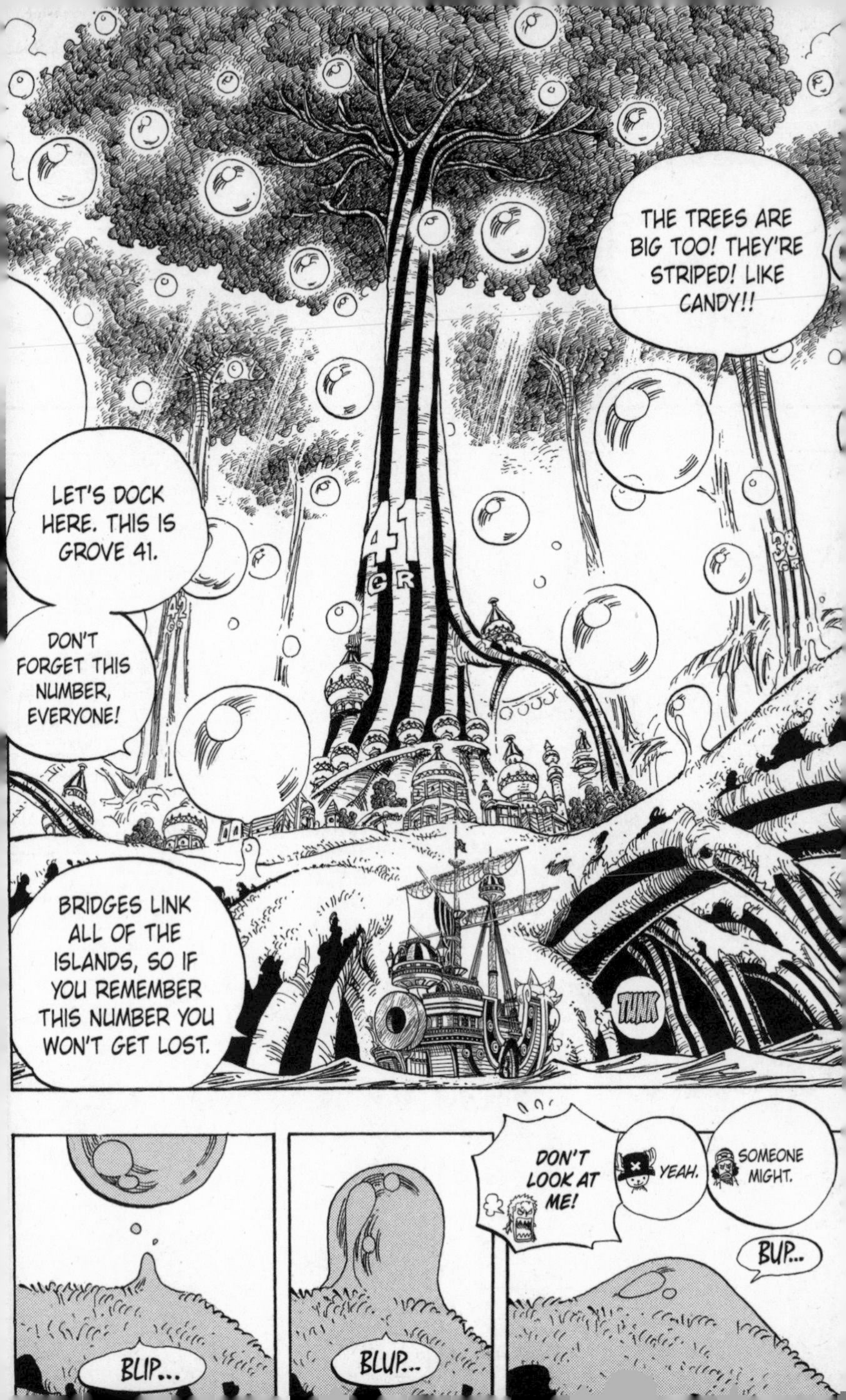
THE TREES ARE BIG TOO! THEY'RE STRIPED! LIKE CANDY!!
41 GR
LET'S DOCK HERE. THIS IS GROVE 41.
DON'T FORGET THIS NUMBER, EVERYONE!
BRIDGES LINK ALL OF THE ISLANDS, SO IF YOU REMEMBER THIS NUMBER YOU WON'T GET LOST.
THUNK
SOMEONE MIGHT.
YEAH.
DON'T LOOK AT ME!
BUP...
BLUP...
BLIP...

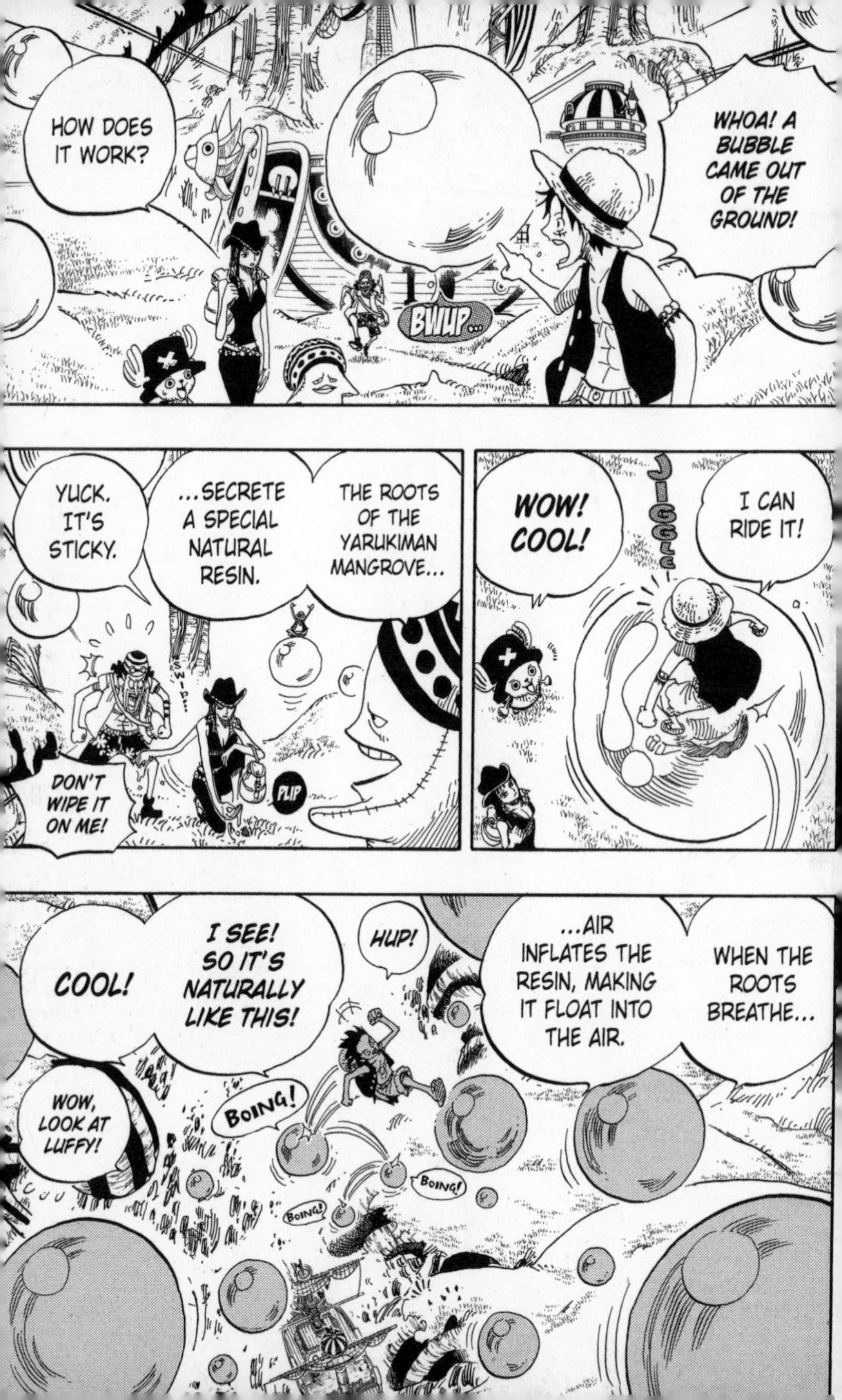
WHOA! A BUBBLE CAME OUT OF THE GROUND!
HOW DOES IT WORK?
BWUP...
I CAN RIDE IT!
JIGGLE
WOW! COOL!
THE ROOTS OF THE YARUKIMAN MANGROVE...
...SECRETE A SPECIAL NATURAL RESIN.
YUCK. IT'S STICKY.
SWIP...
PLIP
DON'T WIPE IT ON ME!
WHEN THE ROOTS BREATHE...
...AIR INFLATES THE RESIN, MAKING IT FLOAT INTO THE AIR.
HUP!
I SEE! SO IT'S NATURALLY LIKE THIS!
COOL!
BOING!
BOING!
BOING!
WOW, LOOK AT LUFFY!

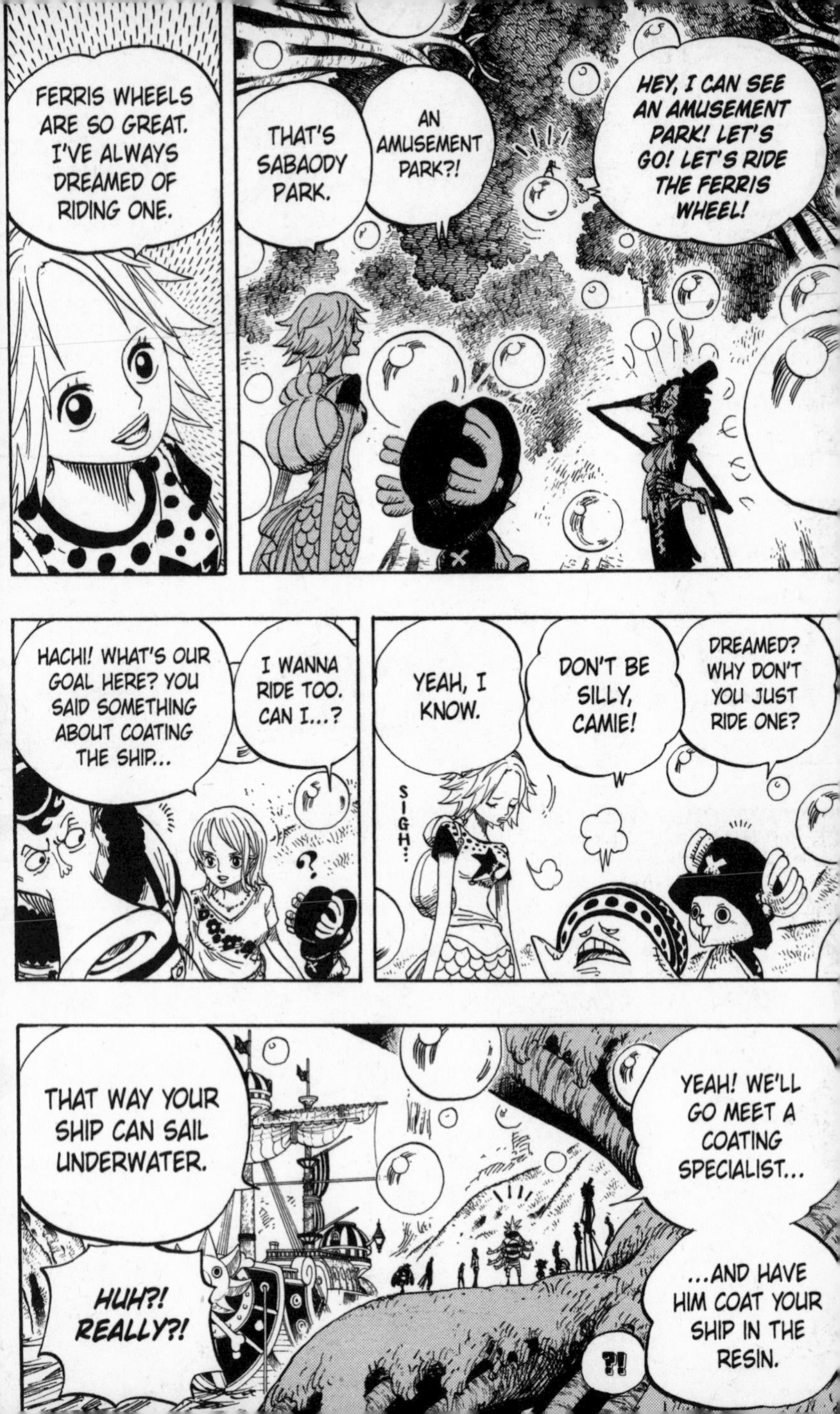
HEY, I CAN SEE AN AMUSEMENT PARK! LET'S GO! LET'S RIDE THE FERRIS WHEEL!
AN AMUSEMENT PARK?!
THAT'S SABAODY PARK.
FERRIS WHEELS ARE SO GREAT. I'VE ALWAYS DREAMED OF RIDING ONE.
DREAMED? WHY DON'T YOU JUST RIDE ONE?
DON'T BE SILLY, CAMIE!
YEAH, I KNOW.
SIGH...
I WANNA RIDE TOO. CAN I...?
HACHI! WHAT'S OUR GOAL HERE? YOU SAID SOMETHING ABOUT COATING THE SHIP...
YEAH! WE'LL GO MEET A COATING SPECIALIST...
...AND HAVE HIM COAT YOUR SHIP IN THE RESIN.
?!
THAT WAY YOUR SHIP CAN SAIL UNDERWATER.
HUH?! REALLY?!

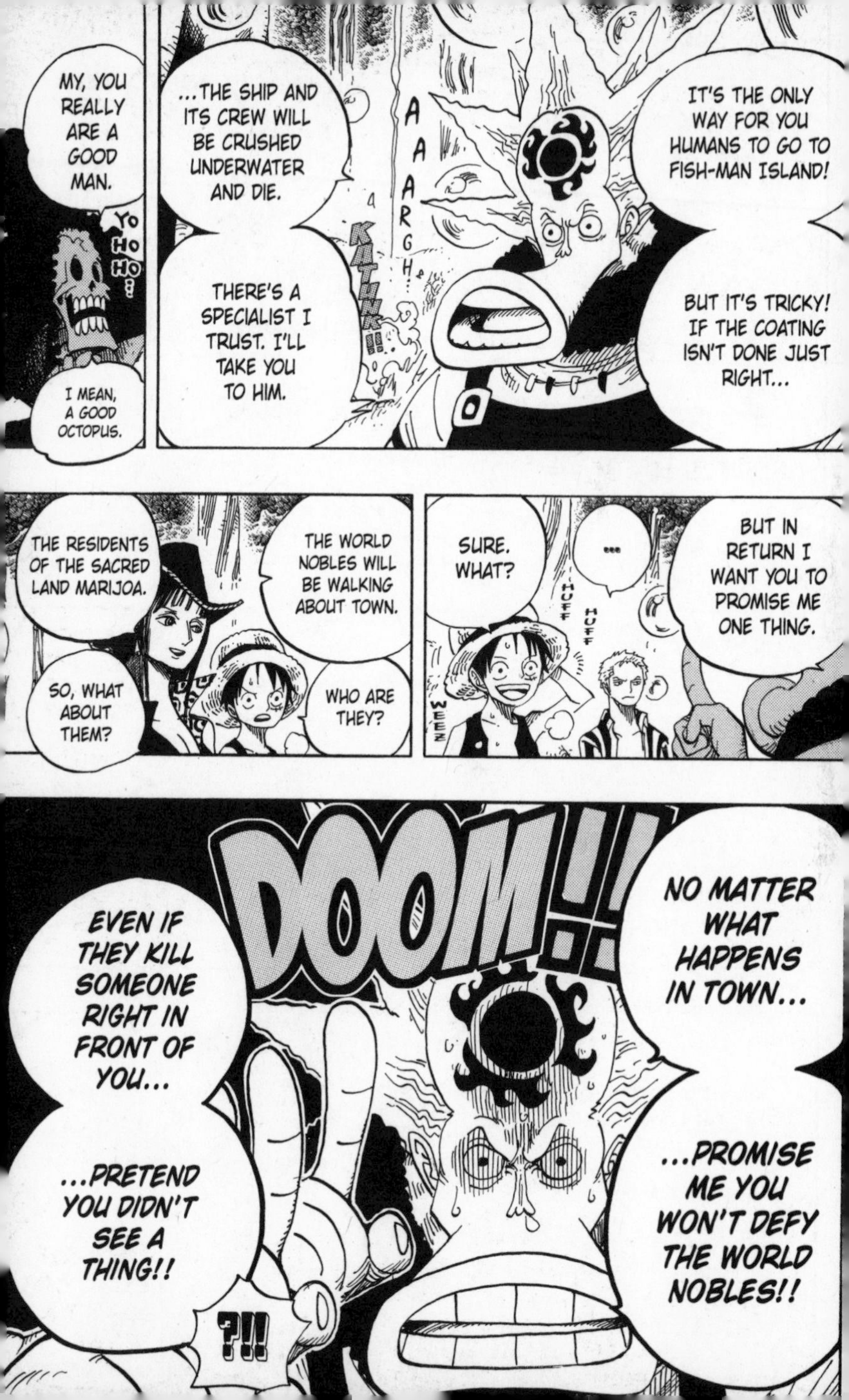
IT'S THE ONLY WAY FOR YOU HUMANS TO GO TO FISH-MAN ISLAND!
BUT IT'S TRICKY! IF THE COATING ISN'T DONE JUST RIGHT...
...THE SHIP AND ITS CREW WILL BE CRUSHED UNDERWATER AND DIE.
AAARGH
KATUNK!!
THERE'S A SPECIALIST I TRUST. I'LL TAKE YOU TO HIM.
MY, YOU REALLY ARE A GOOD MAN.
YOHOHO!
I MEAN, A GOOD OCTOPUS.
BUT IN RETURN I WANT YOU TO PROMISE ME ONE THING.
...
HUFF HUFF
SURE. WHAT?
WEEZ
THE WORLD NOBLES WILL BE WALKING ABOUT TOWN.
WHO ARE THEY?
THE RESIDENTS OF THE SACRED LAND MARIJOA.
SO, WHAT ABOUT THEM?
DOOM!!
NO MATTER WHAT HAPPENS IN TOWN...
...PROMISE ME YOU WON'T DEFY THE WORLD NOBLES!!
EVEN IF THEY KILL SOMEONE RIGHT IN FRONT OF YOU...
...PRETEND YOU DIDN'T SEE A THING!!
?!!

(Saki Kamikita, Osaka)

Q: Here's how to draw the Straw Hat crew in email! They've got spirit! DOOM!

--Rosy

ONE PIECE!!(·□´·‡)=≡⊃))

Zzz(-＿-)╱╱╱　　(· ε (((()y-°°°°

β ˇ(„· ∇ ·„)|||　　°~Y(·⊂⌋·§

ミ〈▼∧⌋▼〉　　ψ(·ω´·„ψ

.。·*·°X(μ＿μ *)　§●Ⅲ●§~♪

A: Whoa. This is interesting. You're pretty good. Yeah, I can see the resemblances.

ONE PIECE!!	Luffy
Zolo	Sanji
Nami	Usopp
Franky	Chopper
Robin	Brook

What power of representation! Chopper and Robin are brilliant. I applaud you!

Q: When the crew is at sea, who takes care of the laundry, which is almost as important as meals? Nami doesn't seem the type (sorry). And if Sanji did it, he would be distracted by the lingerie! Yow! ♡

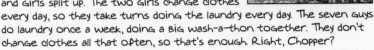

A: The laundry? As you can imagine, Sanji certainly wouldn't do it all himself, of course. The guys and girls split up. The two girls change clothes every day, so they take turns doing the laundry every day. The seven guys do laundry once a week, doing a big wash-a-thon together. They don't change clothes all that often, so that's enough. Right, Chopper?

Chopper: Yeah, they're really smelly!! Everyone's dirty!

Q: Odacchi, something good's gonna happen! Thumbs up.

--From Low-Ranking God of Happiness

A: Seriously?! I'm so happy! I wonder what it is. Will racy magazines fall from the sky? Ugh... (← depressed at how small I think)

Q: If Captain Lola is so cool, why have 4,444 of her engagements been broken off? Is there a reason?

--Akie Brand

A: Well, on top of her incredible presence...she tries too hard. Someday she'll find happiness. (Not that it's any of my business.)

Chapter 497: ADVENTURE ON THE ARCHIPELAGO OF DANCING SOAP BUBBLES

SCROLL SAYS "MEMORIES OF MY MOM"--ED.

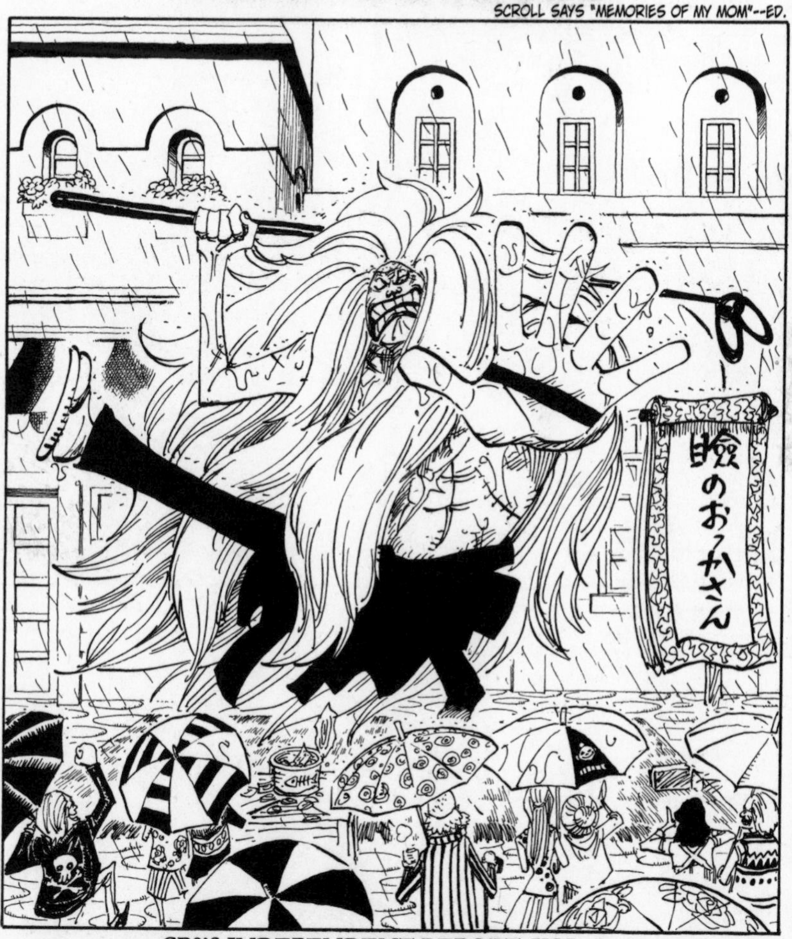
瞼のおっかさん

CP9'S INDEPENDENT REPORT, VOL. 7:
"SAVE ROB LUCCI: KUMADORI PERFORMS TO RAISE MONEY FOR MEDICAL EXPENSES"

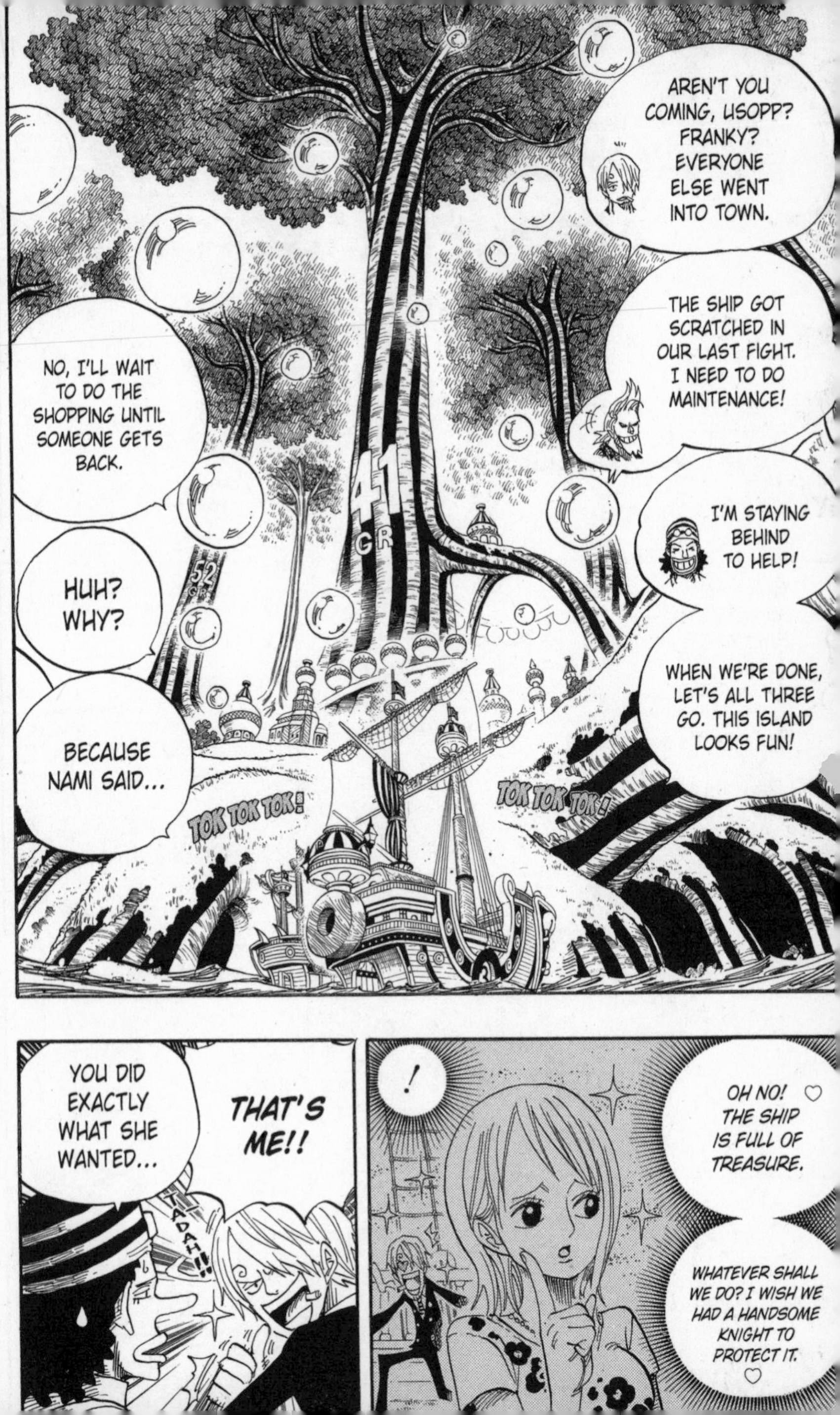
AREN'T YOU COMING, USOPP? FRANKY? EVERYONE ELSE WENT INTO TOWN.
THE SHIP GOT SCRATCHED IN OUR LAST FIGHT. I NEED TO DO MAINTENANCE!
I'M STAYING BEHIND TO HELP!
WHEN WE'RE DONE, LET'S ALL THREE GO. THIS ISLAND LOOKS FUN!
41 GR
NO, I'LL WAIT TO DO THE SHOPPING UNTIL SOMEONE GETS BACK.
52 GR
HUH? WHY?
TOK TOK TOK!
BECAUSE NAMI SAID...
TOK TOK TOK!
!
OH NO! ♡ THE SHIP IS FULL OF TREASURE.
WHATEVER SHALL WE DO? I WISH WE HAD A HANDSOME KNIGHT TO PROTECT IT. ♡
THAT'S ME!!
YOU DID EXACTLY WHAT SHE WANTED...
TADAH!!

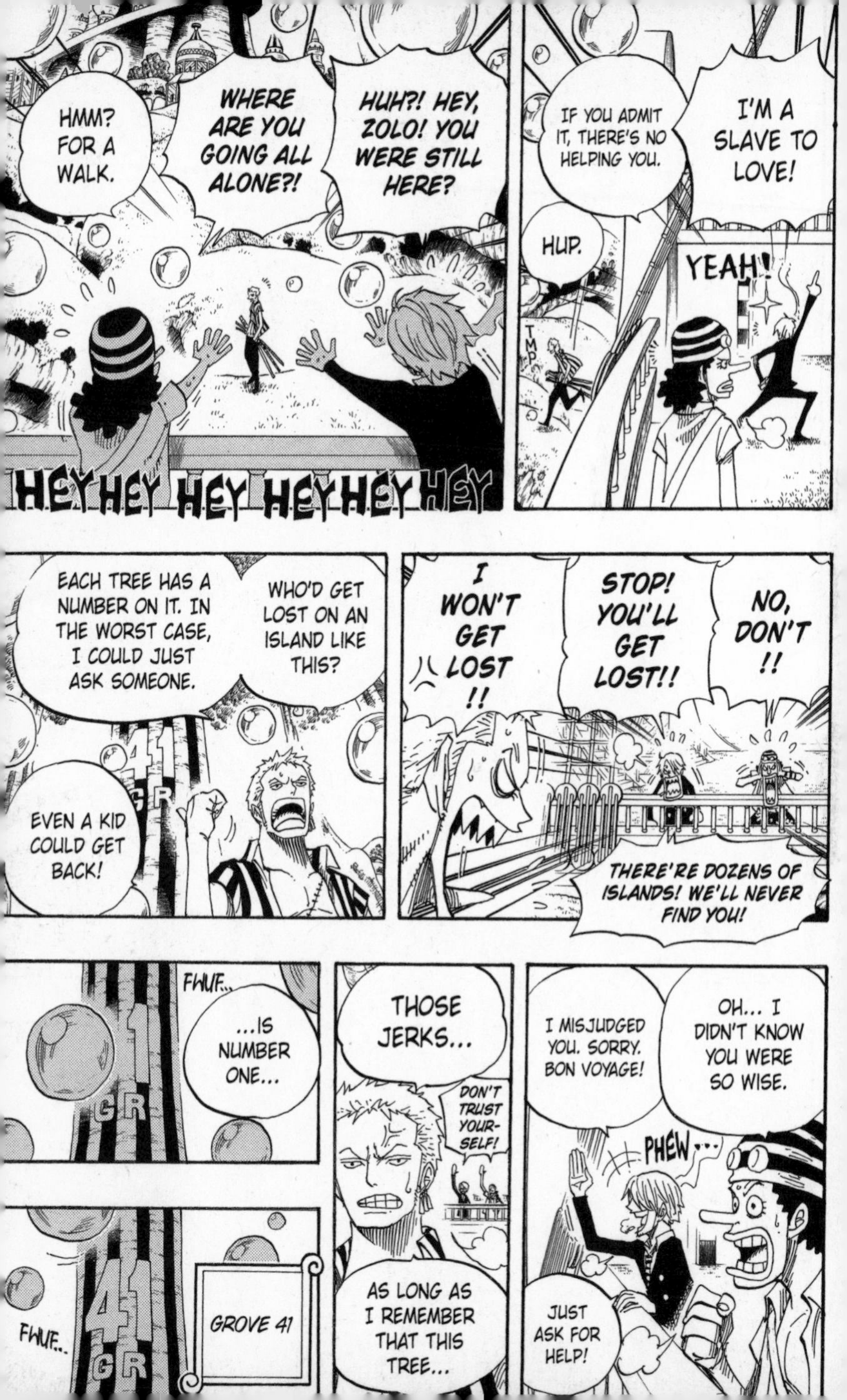
I'M A SLAVE TO LOVE!
IF YOU ADMIT IT, THERE'S NO HELPING YOU.
YEAH!
HUP.
TMP
HUH?! HEY, ZOLO! YOU WERE STILL HERE?
WHERE ARE YOU GOING ALL ALONE?!
HMM? FOR A WALK.
HEY HEY HEY HEY HEY HEY
NO, DON'T!!
STOP! YOU'LL GET LOST!!
I WON'T GET LOST!!
THERE'RE DOZENS OF ISLANDS! WE'LL NEVER FIND YOU!
WHO'D GET LOST ON AN ISLAND LIKE THIS?
EACH TREE HAS A NUMBER ON IT. IN THE WORST CASE, I COULD JUST ASK SOMEONE.
41 GR
EVEN A KID COULD GET BACK!
OH... I DIDN'T KNOW YOU WERE SO WISE.
I MISJUDGED YOU. SORRY. BON VOYAGE!
PHEW...
JUST ASK FOR HELP!
THOSE JERKS...
DON'T TRUST YOURSELF!
AS LONG AS I REMEMBER THAT THIS TREE...
FWUF...
...IS NUMBER ONE...
1 GR
GROVE 41
FWUF..
41 GR

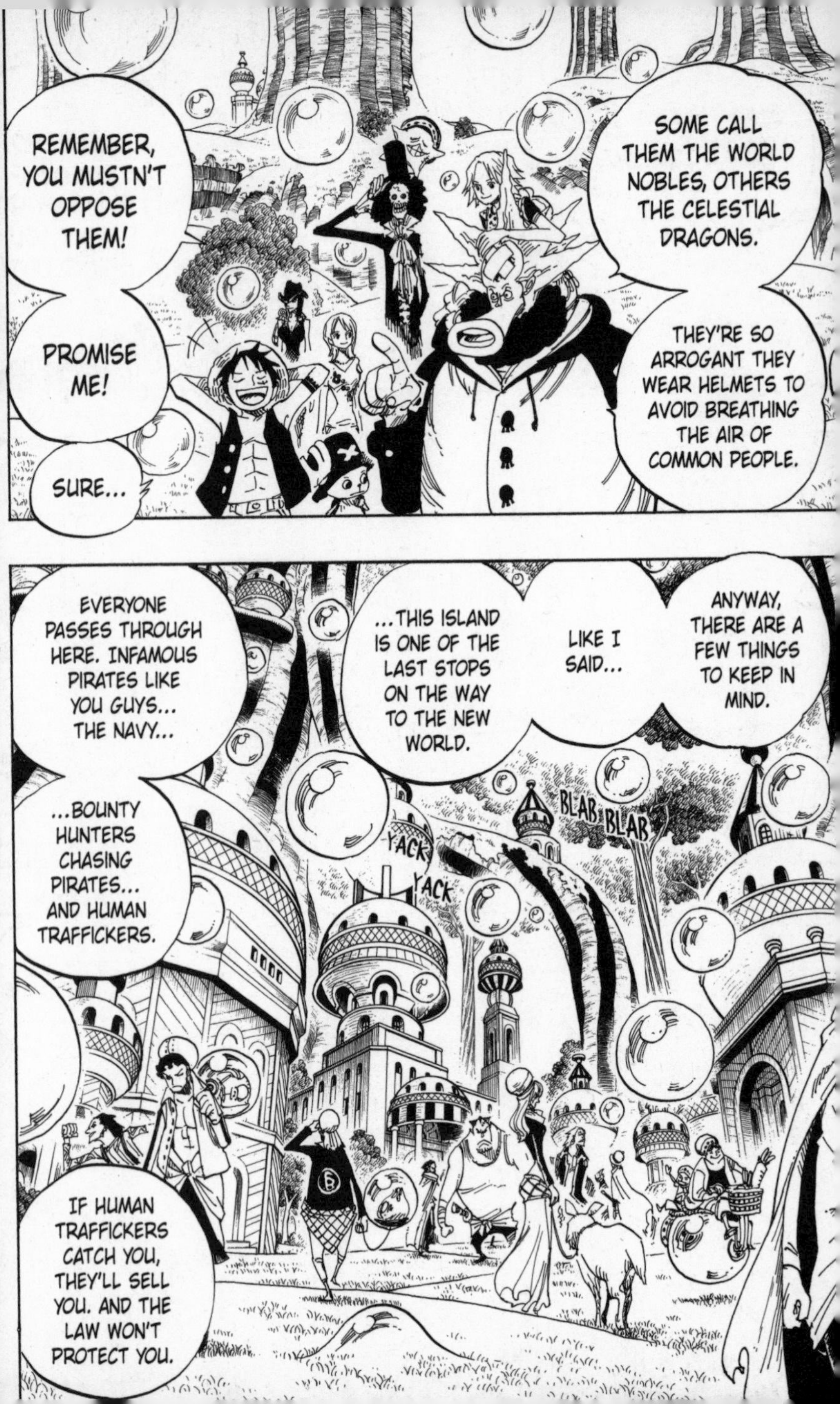
SOME CALL THEM THE WORLD NOBLES, OTHERS THE CELESTIAL DRAGONS.
THEY'RE SO ARROGANT THEY WEAR HELMETS TO AVOID BREATHING THE AIR OF COMMON PEOPLE.
REMEMBER, YOU MUSTN'T OPPOSE THEM!
PROMISE ME!
SURE...
ANYWAY, THERE ARE A FEW THINGS TO KEEP IN MIND.
LIKE I SAID...
...THIS ISLAND IS ONE OF THE LAST STOPS ON THE WAY TO THE NEW WORLD.
EVERYONE PASSES THROUGH HERE. INFAMOUS PIRATES LIKE YOU GUYS... THE NAVY...
...BOUNTY HUNTERS CHASING PIRATES... AND HUMAN TRAFFICKERS.
BLAB BLAB
YACK
YACK
IF HUMAN TRAFFICKERS CATCH YOU, THEY'LL SELL YOU. AND THE LAW WON'T PROTECT YOU.

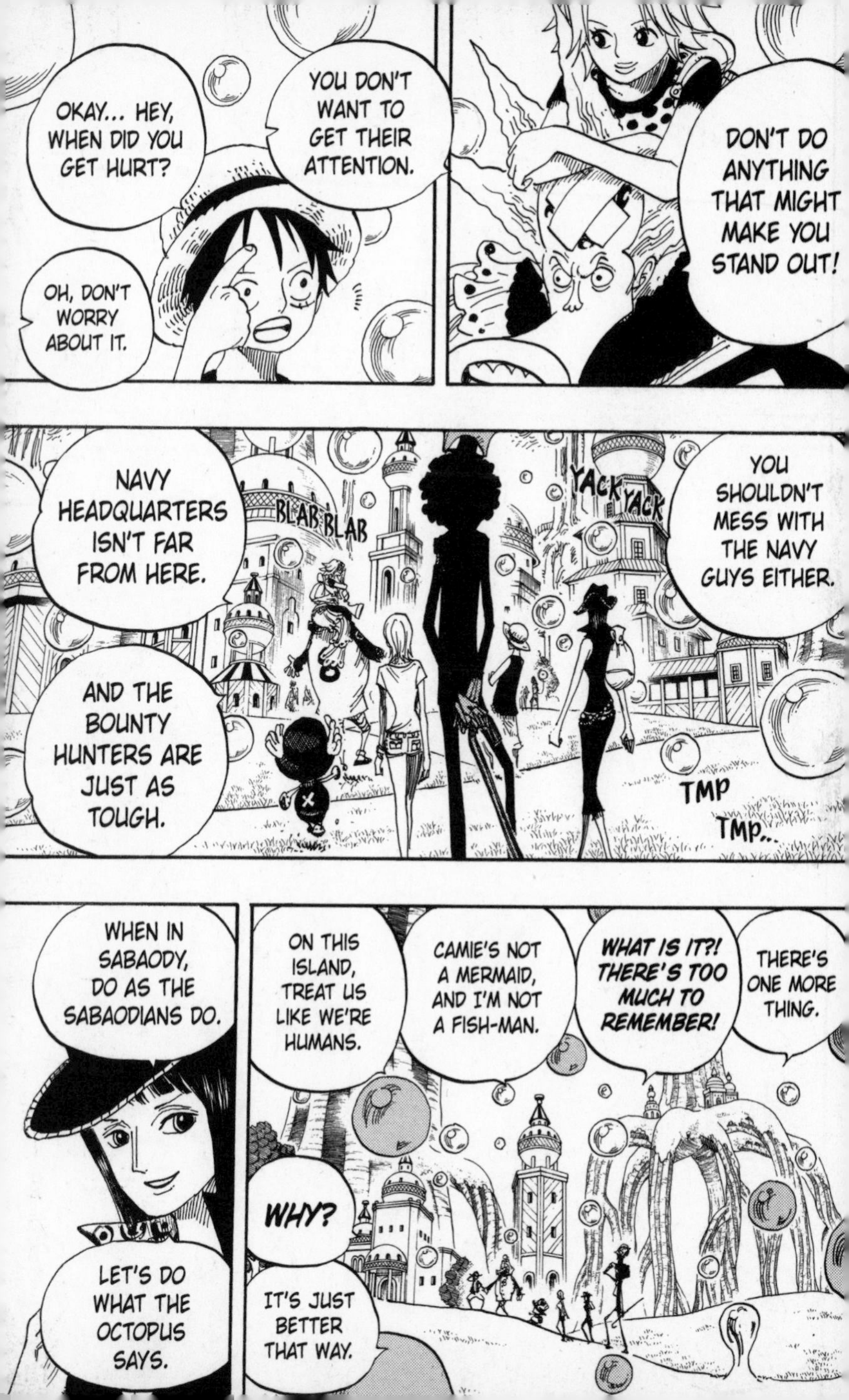
DON'T DO ANYTHING THAT MIGHT MAKE YOU STAND OUT!
YOU DON'T WANT TO GET THEIR ATTENTION.
OKAY... HEY, WHEN DID YOU GET HURT?
OH, DON'T WORRY ABOUT IT.
YOU SHOULDN'T MESS WITH THE NAVY GUYS EITHER.
YACK YACK
BLAB BLAB
NAVY HEADQUARTERS ISN'T FAR FROM HERE.
AND THE BOUNTY HUNTERS ARE JUST AS TOUGH.
TMP
TMP..
THERE'S ONE MORE THING.
WHAT IS IT?! THERE'S TOO MUCH TO REMEMBER!
CAMIE'S NOT A MERMAID, AND I'M NOT A FISH-MAN.
ON THIS ISLAND, TREAT US LIKE WE'RE HUMANS.
WHY?
IT'S JUST BETTER THAT WAY.
WHEN IN SABAODY, DO AS THE SABAODIANS DO.
LET'S DO WHAT THE OCTOPUS SAYS.

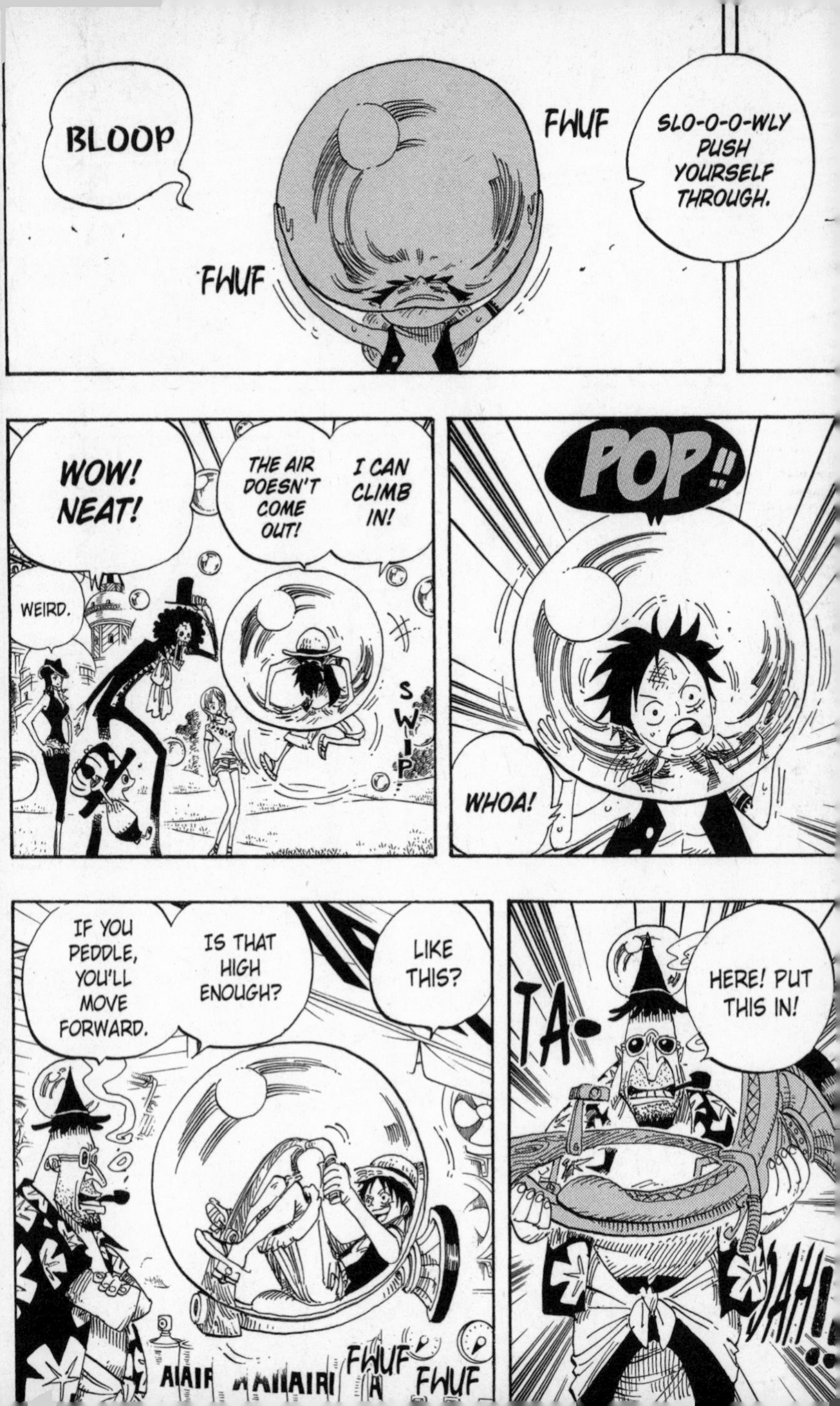
SLO-O-O-WLY PUSH YOURSELF THROUGH.
FWUF
BLOOP
FWUF
POP!!
WHOA!
I CAN CLIMB IN!
THE AIR DOESN'T COME OUT!
WOW! NEAT!
WEIRD.
SWIP
HERE! PUT THIS IN!
TA-
DAH!!
LIKE THIS?
IS THAT HIGH ENOUGH?
IF YOU PEDDLE, YOU'LL MOVE FORWARD.
FWUF
FWUF

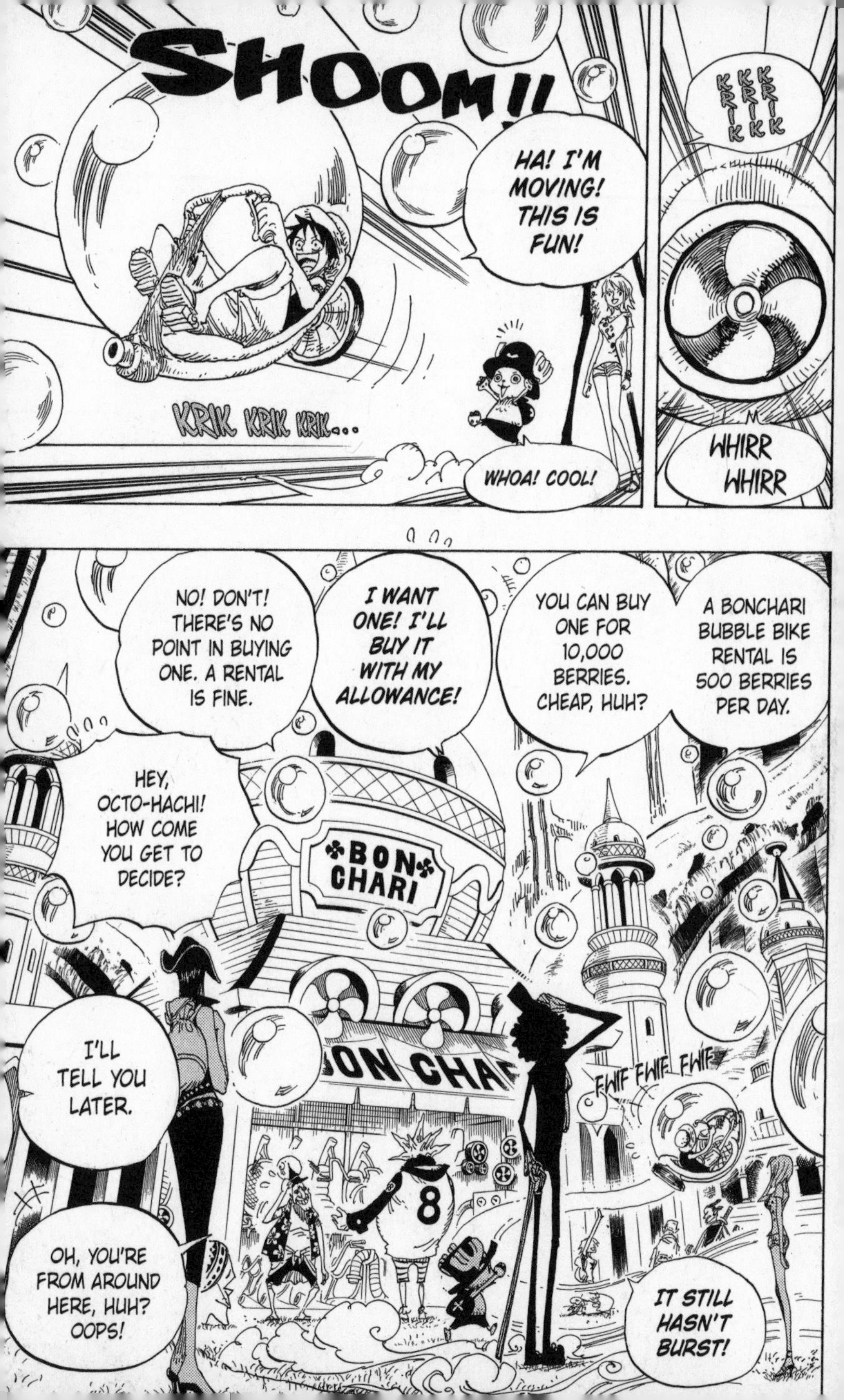
KRIK KRIK KRIK
WHIRR WHIRR
SHOOM!!
HA! I'M MOVING! THIS IS FUN!
WHOA! COOL!
KRIK KRIK KRIK...
A BONCHARI BUBBLE BIKE RENTAL IS 500 BERRIES PER DAY.
YOU CAN BUY ONE FOR 10,000 BERRIES. CHEAP, HUH?
I WANT ONE! I'LL BUY IT WITH MY ALLOWANCE!
NO! DON'T! THERE'S NO POINT IN BUYING ONE. A RENTAL IS FINE.
HEY, OCTO-HACHI! HOW COME YOU GET TO DECIDE?
BON CHARI
BON CHA
FWIF FWIF FWIF
I'LL TELL YOU LATER.
IT STILL HASN'T BURST!
OH, YOU'RE FROM AROUND HERE, HUH? OOPS!

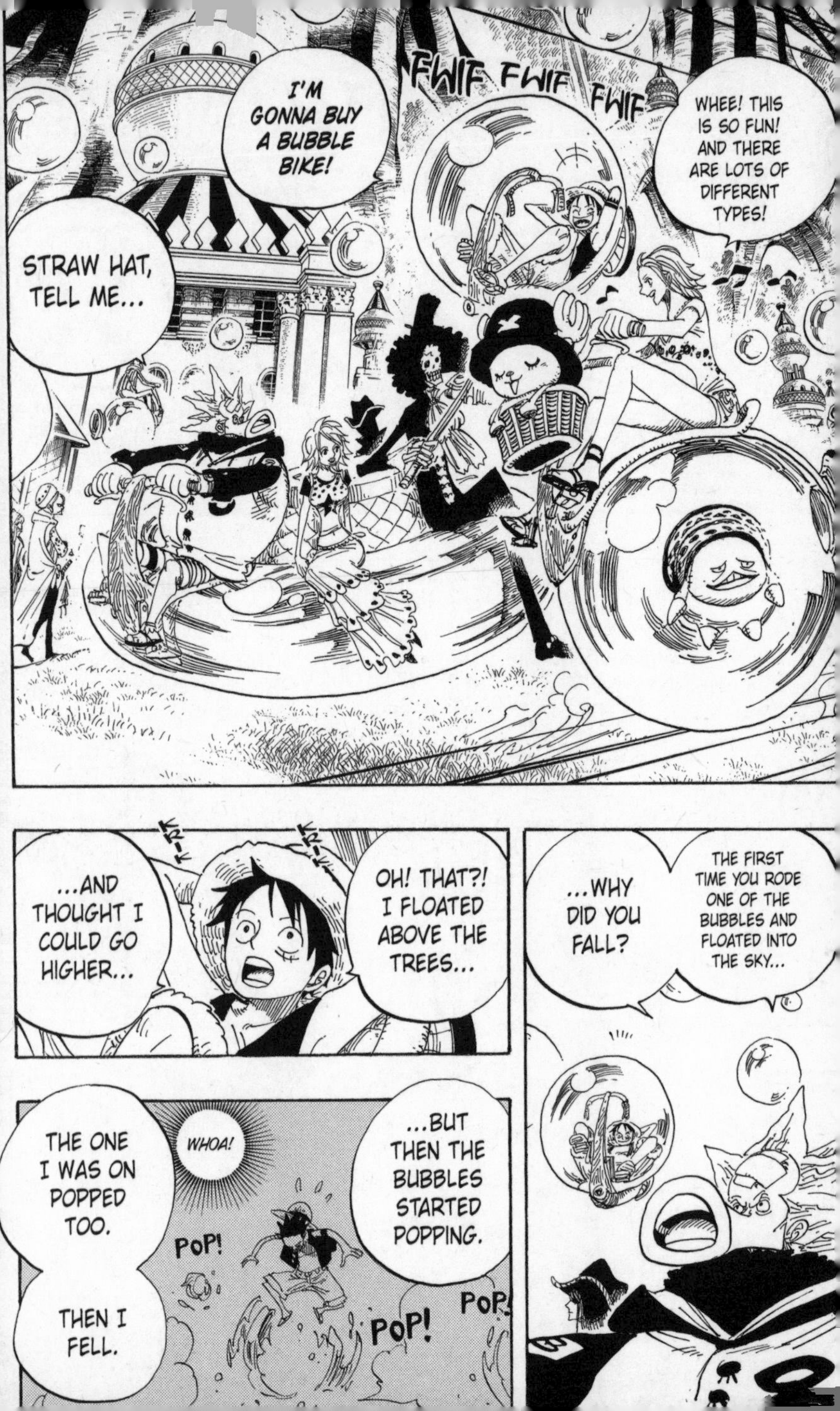
WHEE! THIS IS SO FUN! AND THERE ARE LOTS OF DIFFERENT TYPES!
FWIF FWIF FWIF
I'M GONNA BUY A BUBBLE BIKE!
STRAW HAT, TELL ME...
THE FIRST TIME YOU RODE ONE OF THE BUBBLES AND FLOATED INTO THE SKY...
...WHY DID YOU FALL?
KRIK
OH! THAT?! I FLOATED ABOVE THE TREES...
KRIK
...AND THOUGHT I COULD GO HIGHER...
...BUT THEN THE BUBBLES STARTED POPPING.
WHOA!
THE ONE I WAS ON POPPED TOO.
POP!
POP!
POP!
THEN I FELL.

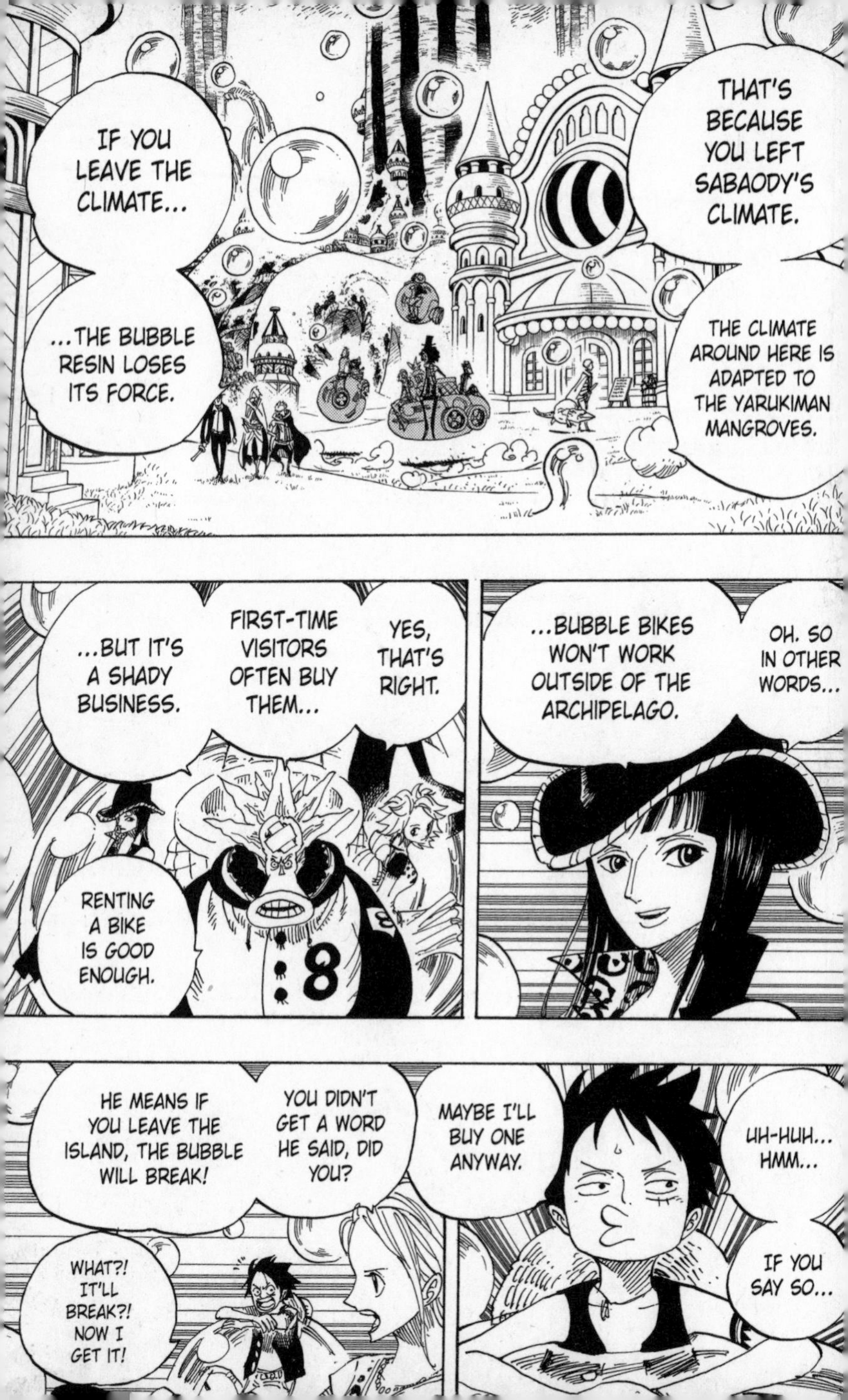
THAT'S BECAUSE YOU LEFT SABAODY'S CLIMATE.
THE CLIMATE AROUND HERE IS ADAPTED TO THE YARUKIMAN MANGROVES.
IF YOU LEAVE THE CLIMATE...
...THE BUBBLE RESIN LOSES ITS FORCE.
OH. SO IN OTHER WORDS...
...BUBBLE BIKES WON'T WORK OUTSIDE OF THE ARCHIPELAGO.
YES, THAT'S RIGHT.
FIRST-TIME VISITORS OFTEN BUY THEM...
...BUT IT'S A SHADY BUSINESS.
RENTING A BIKE IS GOOD ENOUGH.
UH-HUH... HMM...
MAYBE I'LL BUY ONE ANYWAY.
IF YOU SAY SO...
YOU DIDN'T GET A WORD HE SAID, DID YOU?
HE MEANS IF YOU LEAVE THE ISLAND, THE BUBBLE WILL BREAK!
WHAT?! IT'LL BREAK?! NOW I GET IT!

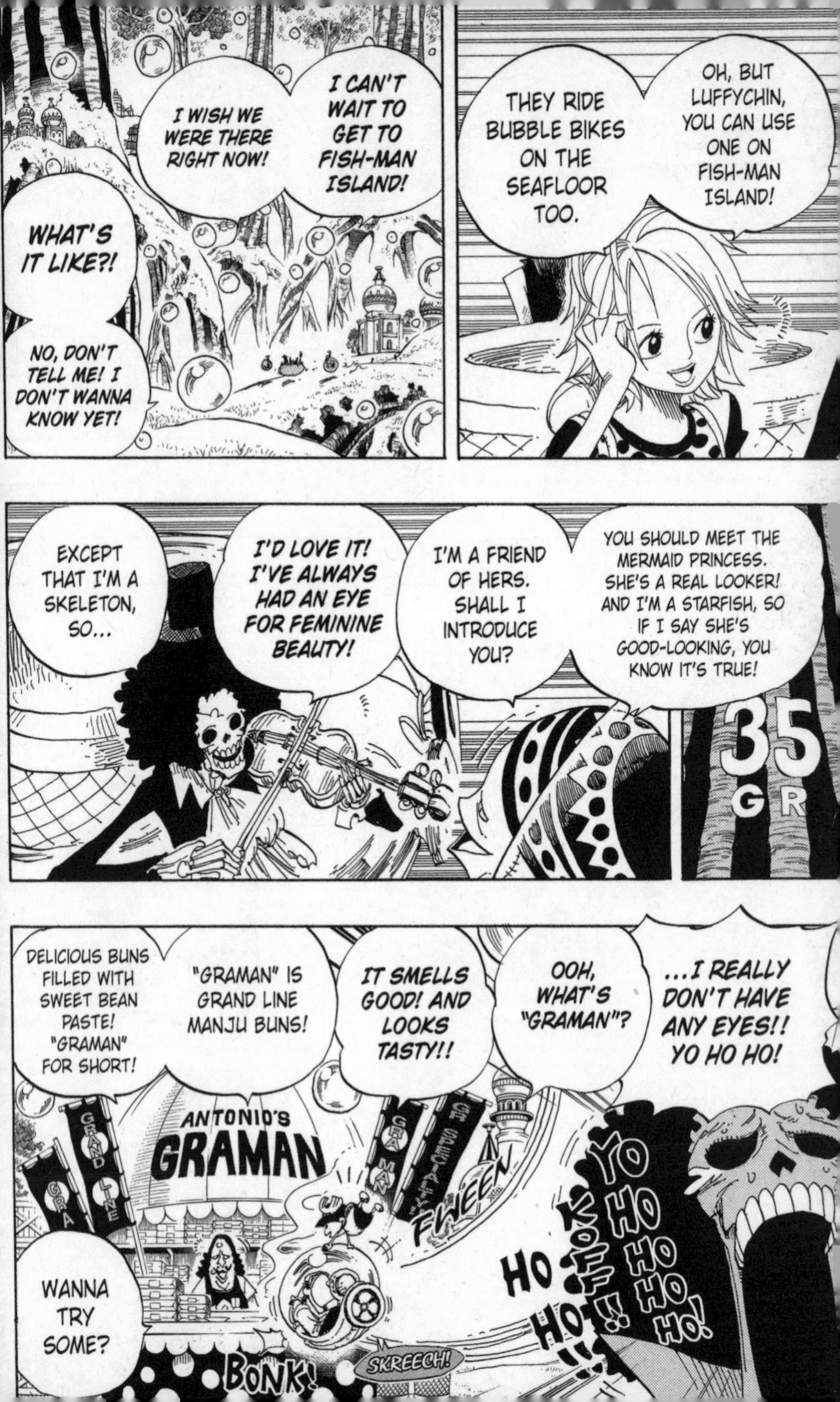
OH, BUT LUFFYCHIN, YOU CAN USE ONE ON FISH-MAN ISLAND!
THEY RIDE BUBBLE BIKES ON THE SEAFLOOR TOO.
I CAN'T WAIT TO GET TO FISH-MAN ISLAND!
I WISH WE WERE THERE RIGHT NOW!
WHAT'S IT LIKE?!
NO, DON'T TELL ME! I DON'T WANNA KNOW YET!
35 GR
YOU SHOULD MEET THE MERMAID PRINCESS. SHE'S A REAL LOOKER! AND I'M A STARFISH, SO IF I SAY SHE'S GOOD-LOOKING, YOU KNOW IT'S TRUE!
I'M A FRIEND OF HERS. SHALL I INTRODUCE YOU?
I'D LOVE IT! I'VE ALWAYS HAD AN EYE FOR FEMININE BEAUTY!
EXCEPT THAT I'M A SKELETON, SO...
...I REALLY DON'T HAVE ANY EYES!! YO HO HO!
YO HO HO HO HO HO HO HO!!
KOFF!!
OOH, WHAT'S "GRAMAN"?
IT SMELLS GOOD! AND LOOKS TASTY!!
"GRAMAN" IS GRAND LINE MANJU BUNS!
DELICIOUS BUNS FILLED WITH SWEET BEAN PASTE! "GRAMAN" FOR SHORT!
GR SPECIALTY
GRA MAN
FWEEN
ANTONIO'S GRAMAN
GRAND LINE
GRA
WANNA TRY SOME?
SKREECH!
BONK!

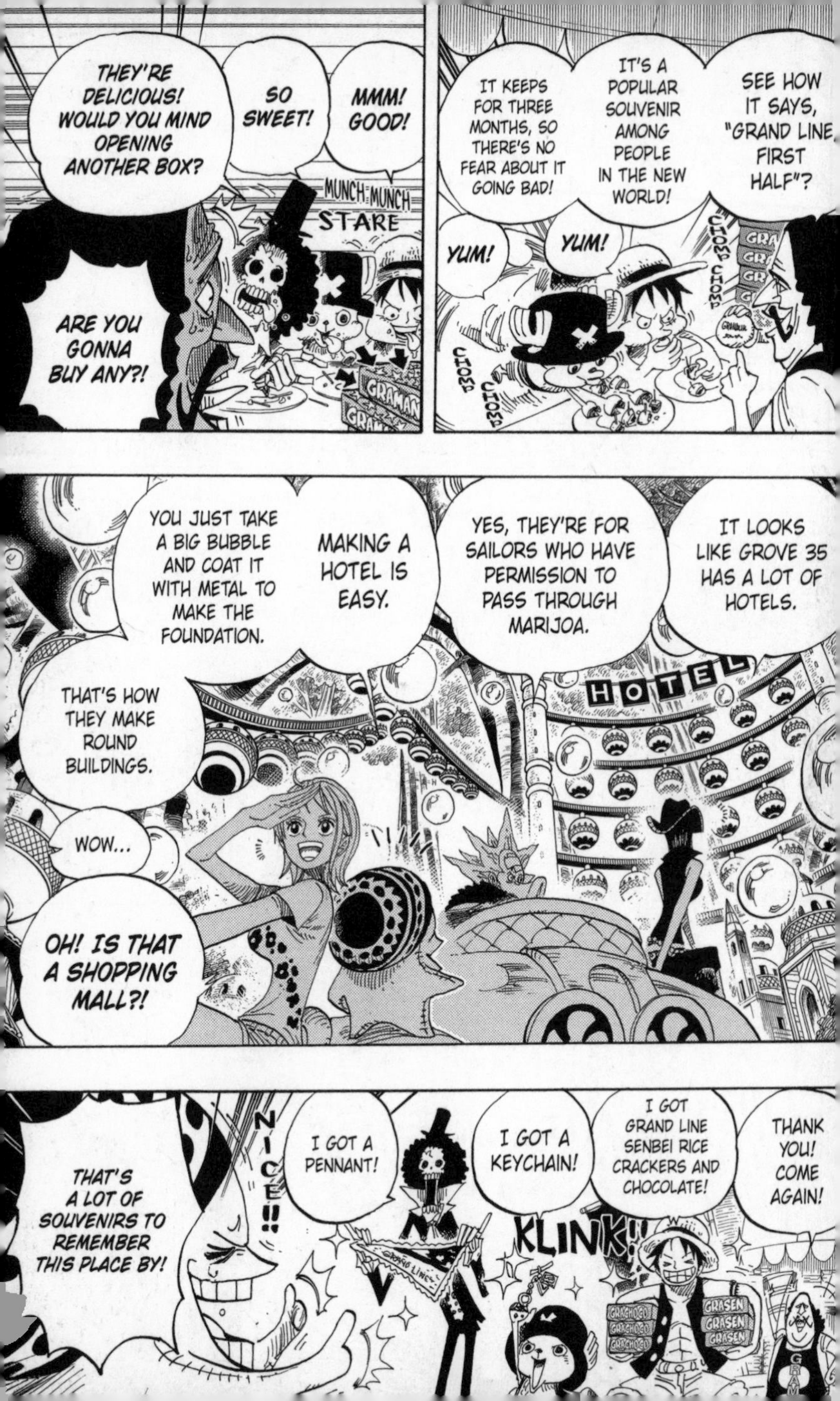
SEE HOW IT SAYS, "GRAND LINE FIRST HALF"?
IT'S A POPULAR SOUVENIR AMONG PEOPLE IN THE NEW WORLD!
IT KEEPS FOR THREE MONTHS, SO THERE'S NO FEAR ABOUT IT GOING BAD!
CHOMP CHOMP
YUM!
YUM!
CHOMP CHOMP
MMM! GOOD!
SO SWEET!
THEY'RE DELICIOUS! WOULD YOU MIND OPENING ANOTHER BOX?
MUNCH MUNCH
STARE
ARE YOU GONNA BUY ANY?!
IT LOOKS LIKE GROVE 35 HAS A LOT OF HOTELS.
YES, THEY'RE FOR SAILORS WHO HAVE PERMISSION TO PASS THROUGH MARIJOA.
MAKING A HOTEL IS EASY.
YOU JUST TAKE A BIG BUBBLE AND COAT IT WITH METAL TO MAKE THE FOUNDATION.
HOTEL
THAT'S HOW THEY MAKE ROUND BUILDINGS.
WOW...
OH! IS THAT A SHOPPING MALL?!
THANK YOU! COME AGAIN!
I GOT GRAND LINE SENBEI RICE CRACKERS AND CHOCOLATE!
I GOT A KEYCHAIN!
KLINK!!
I GOT A PENNANT!
NICE!!
THAT'S A LOT OF SOUVENIRS TO REMEMBER THIS PLACE BY!

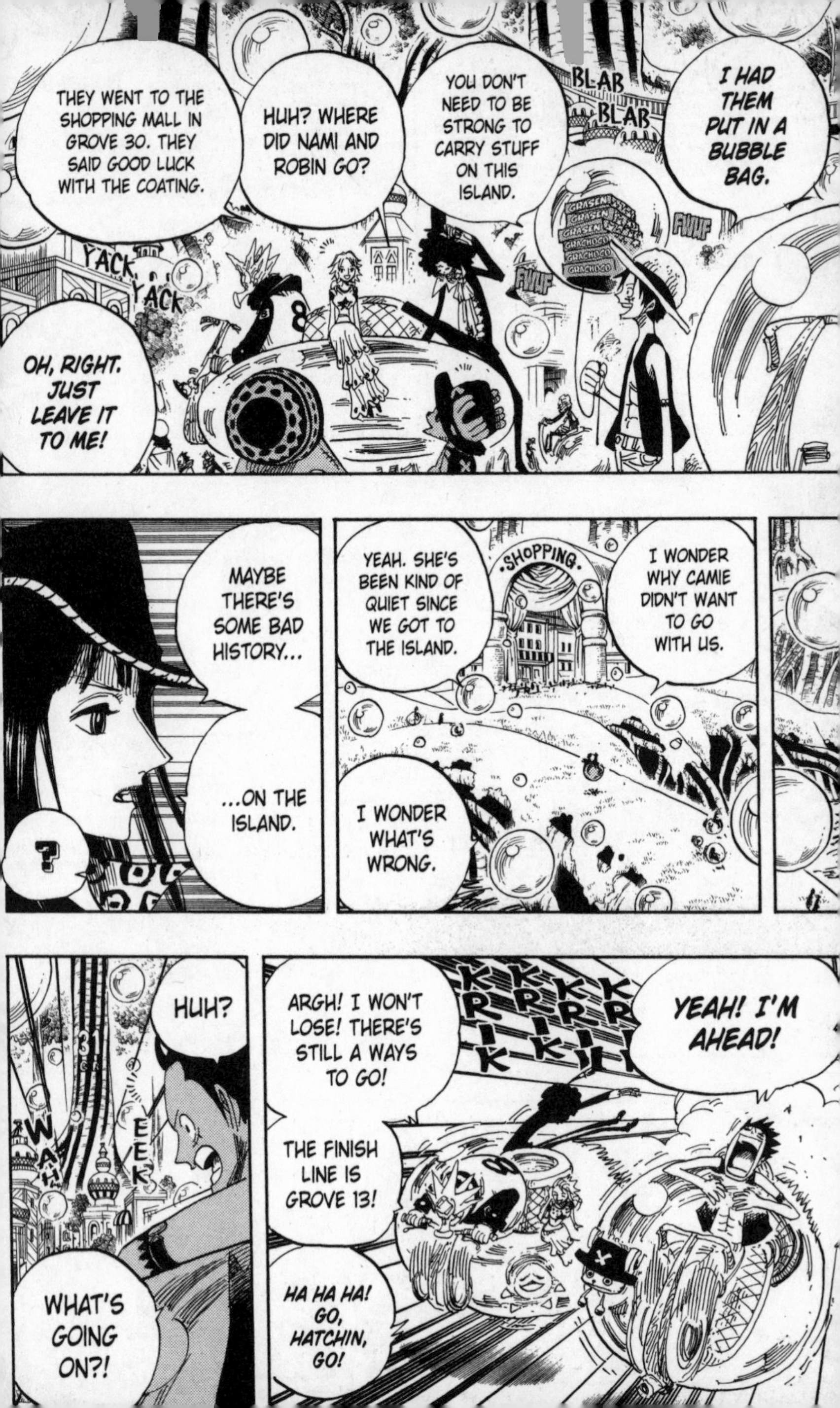
I HAD THEM PUT IN A BUBBLE BAG.
BLAB BLAB
FWUF
YOU DON'T NEED TO BE STRONG TO CARRY STUFF ON THIS ISLAND.
HUH? WHERE DID NAMI AND ROBIN GO?
THEY WENT TO THE SHOPPING MALL IN GROVE 30. THEY SAID GOOD LUCK WITH THE COATING.
FWUF
YACK YACK
OH, RIGHT. JUST LEAVE IT TO ME!
I WONDER WHY CAMIE DIDN'T WANT TO GO WITH US.
SHOPPING
YEAH. SHE'S BEEN KIND OF QUIET SINCE WE GOT TO THE ISLAND.
I WONDER WHAT'S WRONG.
MAYBE THERE'S SOME BAD HISTORY...
...ON THE ISLAND.
?
YEAH! I'M AHEAD!
KRIK KRIK KRIK KRIK KRIK
ARGH! I WON'T LOSE! THERE'S STILL A WAYS TO GO!
THE FINISH LINE IS GROVE 13!
HA HA HA! GO, HATCHIN, GO!
HUH?
EEK
WAH
WHAT'S GOING ON?!

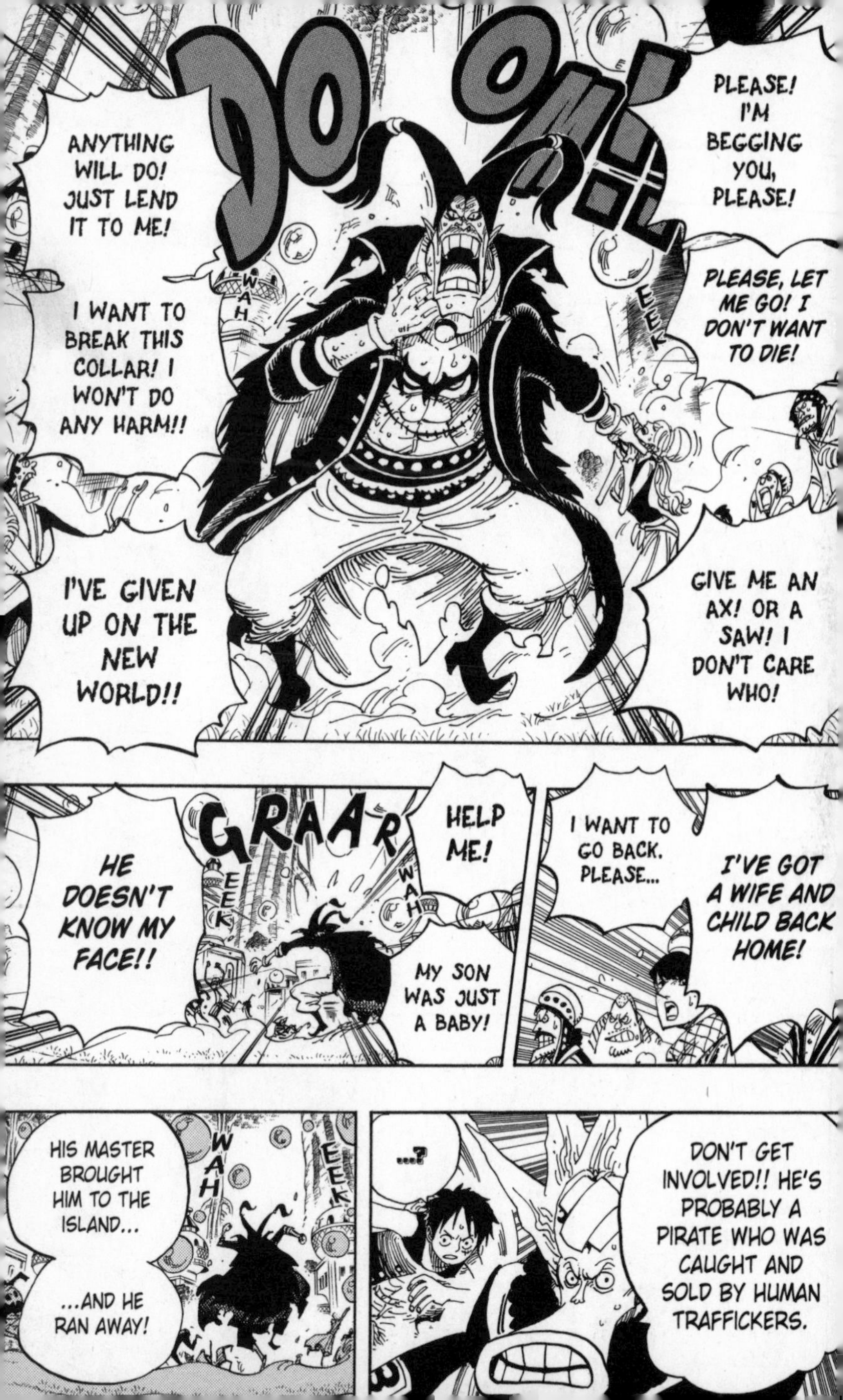
DOOM!
PLEASE! I'M BEGGING YOU, PLEASE!
ANYTHING WILL DO! JUST LEND IT TO ME!
WAH
EEK
PLEASE, LET ME GO! I DON'T WANT TO DIE!
I WANT TO BREAK THIS COLLAR! I WON'T DO ANY HARM!!
GIVE ME AN AX! OR A SAW! I DON'T CARE WHO!
I'VE GIVEN UP ON THE NEW WORLD!!
I'VE GOT A WIFE AND CHILD BACK HOME!
I WANT TO GO BACK. PLEASE...
HELP ME!
GRAAR
WAH
EEK
MY SON WAS JUST A BABY!
HE DOESN'T KNOW MY FACE!!
DON'T GET INVOLVED!! HE'S PROBABLY A PIRATE WHO WAS CAUGHT AND SOLD BY HUMAN TRAFFICKERS.
...?
EEK
WAH
HIS MASTER BROUGHT HIM TO THE ISLAND...
...AND HE RAN AWAY!

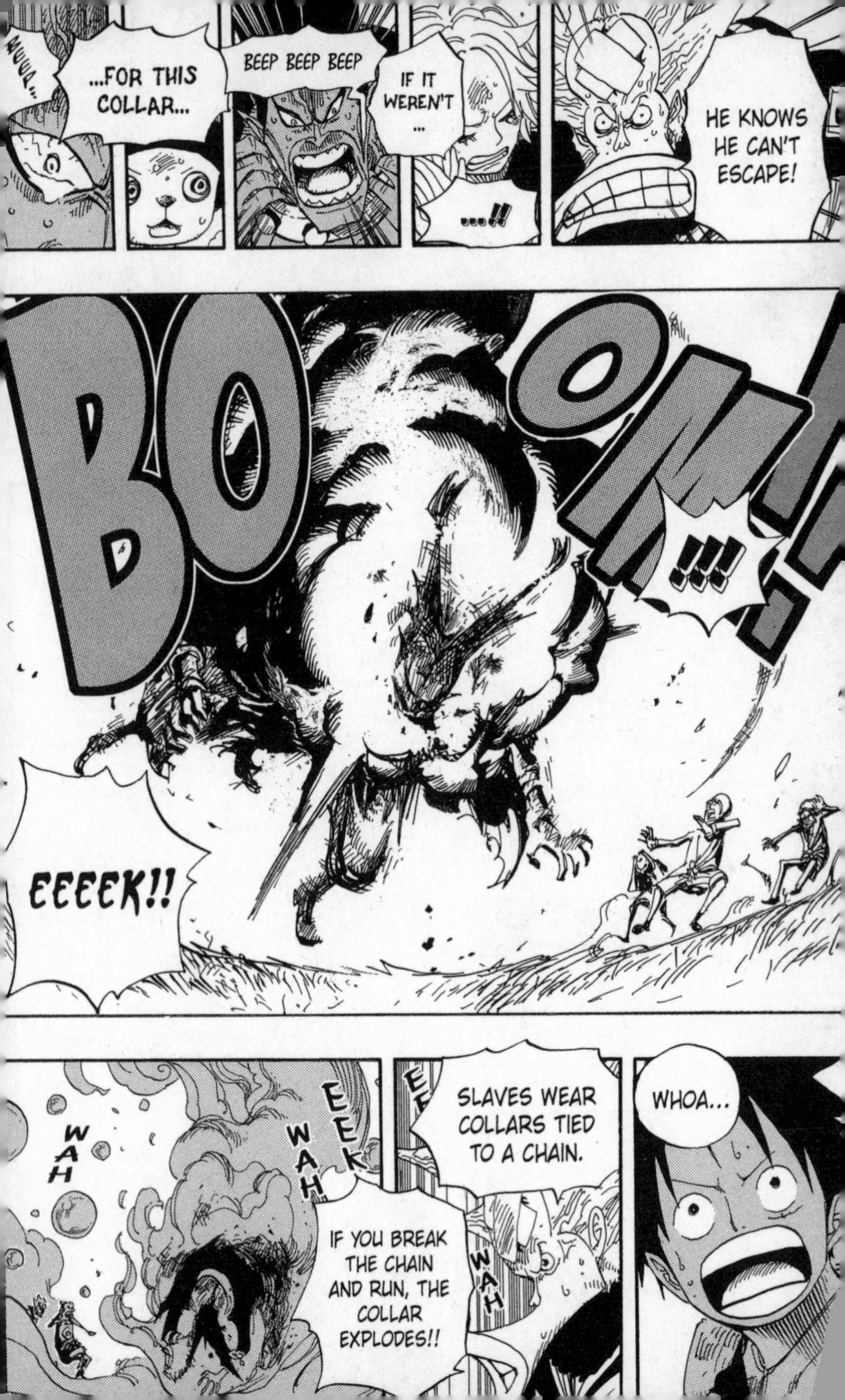
HE KNOWS HE CAN'T ESCAPE!
...!!
IF IT WEREN'T ...
BEEP BEEP BEEP
...FOR THIS COLLAR...
BOOM!!!
EEEEK!!
WHOA...
SLAVES WEAR COLLARS TIED TO A CHAIN.
WAH
IF YOU BREAK THE CHAIN AND RUN, THE COLLAR EXPLODES!!
EEEK
WAH
WAH

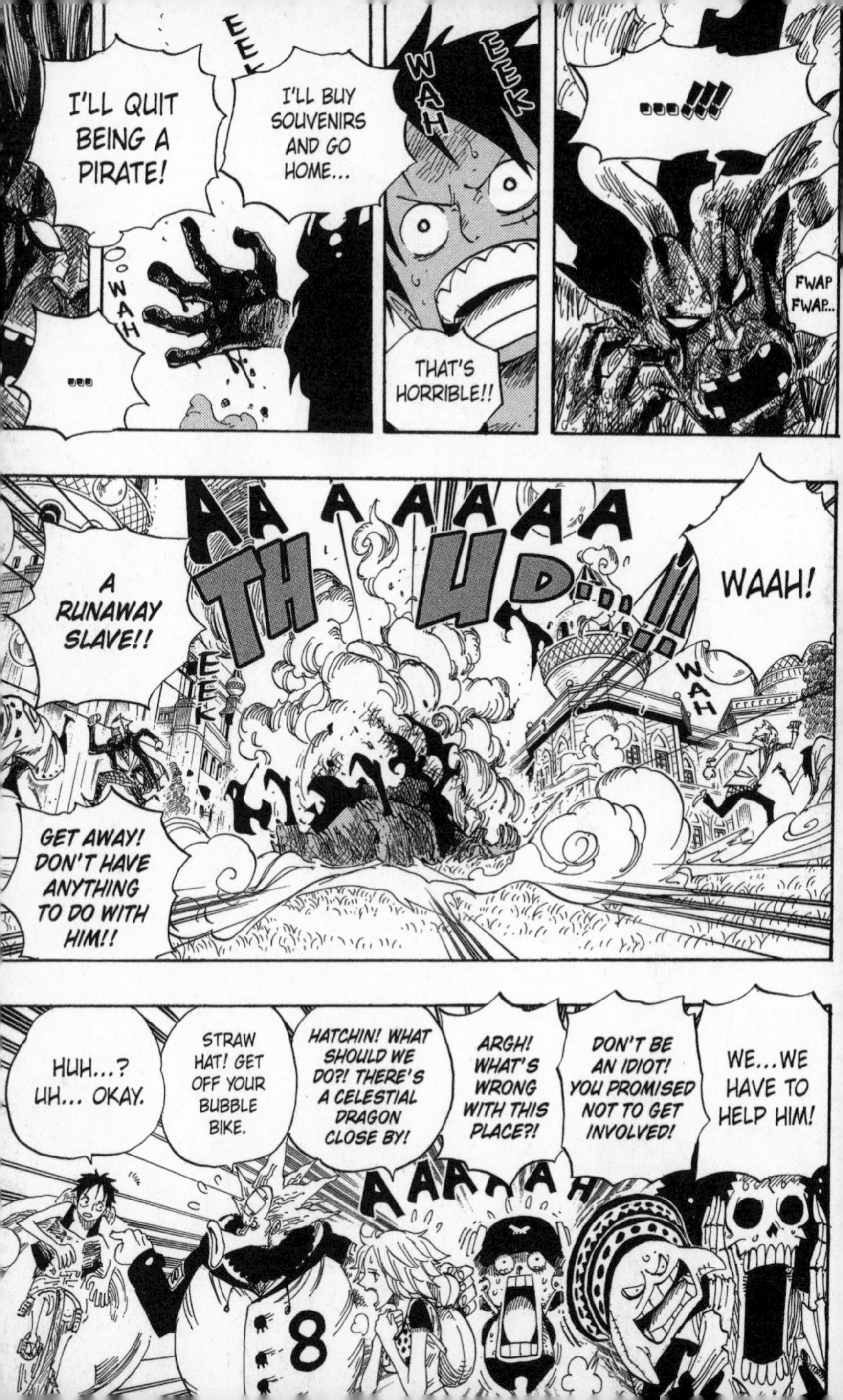

...!!!
FWAP FWAP...
EEK
WAH
THAT'S HORRIBLE!!
I'LL BUY SOUVENIRS AND GO HOME...
EEK
I'LL QUIT BEING A PIRATE!
WAH
...
WAAH!
WAH
AAAAAA
THUD
A RUNAWAY SLAVE!!
EEK
GET AWAY! DON'T HAVE ANYTHING TO DO WITH HIM!!
WE...WE HAVE TO HELP HIM!
DON'T BE AN IDIOT! YOU PROMISED NOT TO GET INVOLVED!
ARGH! WHAT'S WRONG WITH THIS PLACE?!
HATCHIN! WHAT SHOULD WE DO?! THERE'S A CELESTIAL DRAGON CLOSE BY!
STRAW HAT! GET OFF YOUR BUBBLE BIKE.
HUH...? UH... OKAY.
AAAAAH

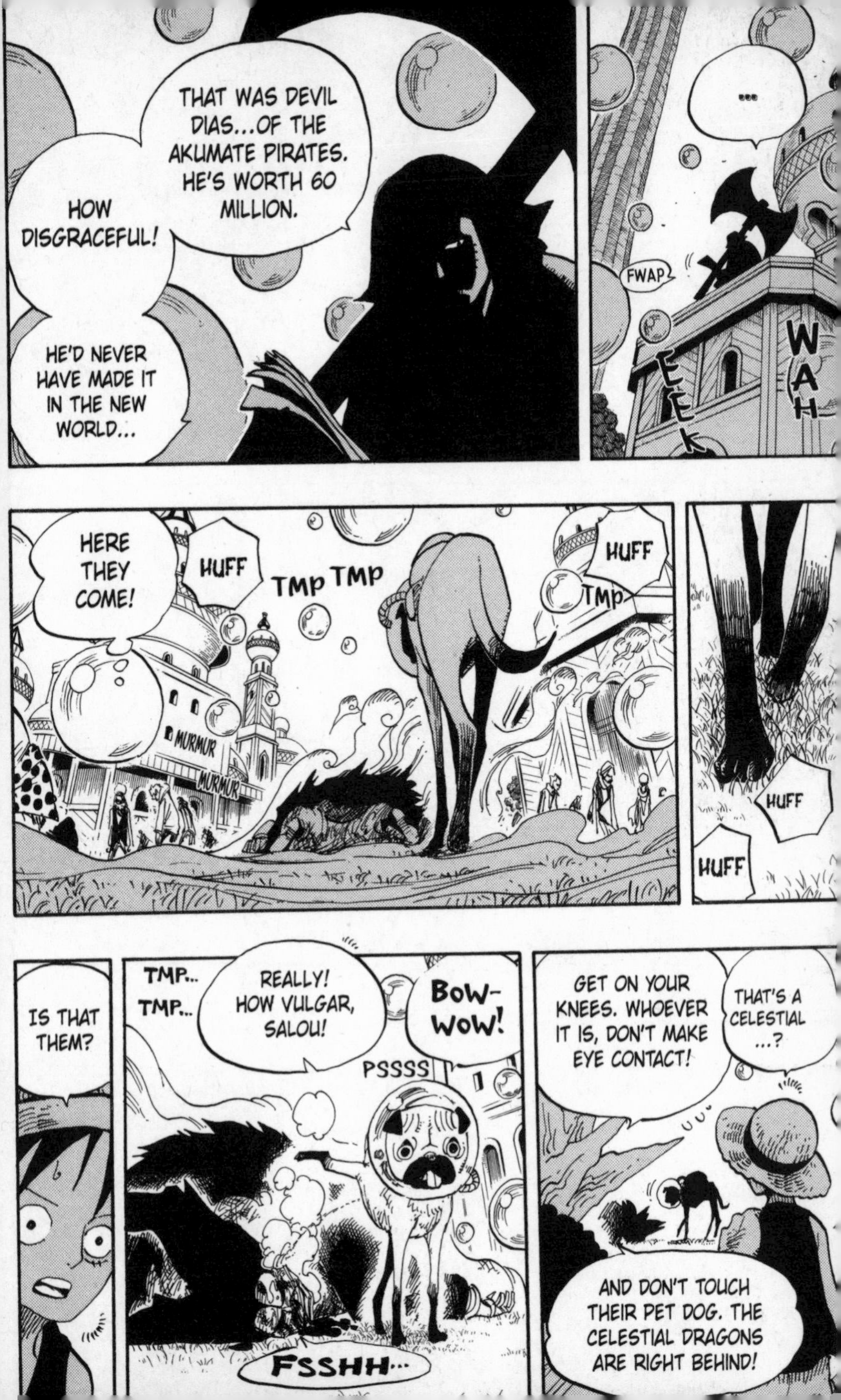
...
FWAP
EEK
WAH
THAT WAS DEVIL DIAS...OF THE AKUMATE PIRATES. HE'S WORTH 60 MILLION.
HOW DISGRACEFUL!
HE'D NEVER HAVE MADE IT IN THE NEW WORLD...
HUFF
HUFF
HUFF
TMp
TMp TMp
HUFF
HERE THEY COME!
MURMUR
MURMUR
THAT'S A CELESTIAL ...?
GET ON YOUR KNEES. WHOEVER IT IS, DON'T MAKE EYE CONTACT!
AND DON'T TOUCH THEIR PET DOG. THE CELESTIAL DRAGONS ARE RIGHT BEHIND!
BOW-WOW!
REALLY! HOW VULGAR, SALOU!
TMP...
TMP...
PSSSS
FSSHH...
IS THAT THEM?

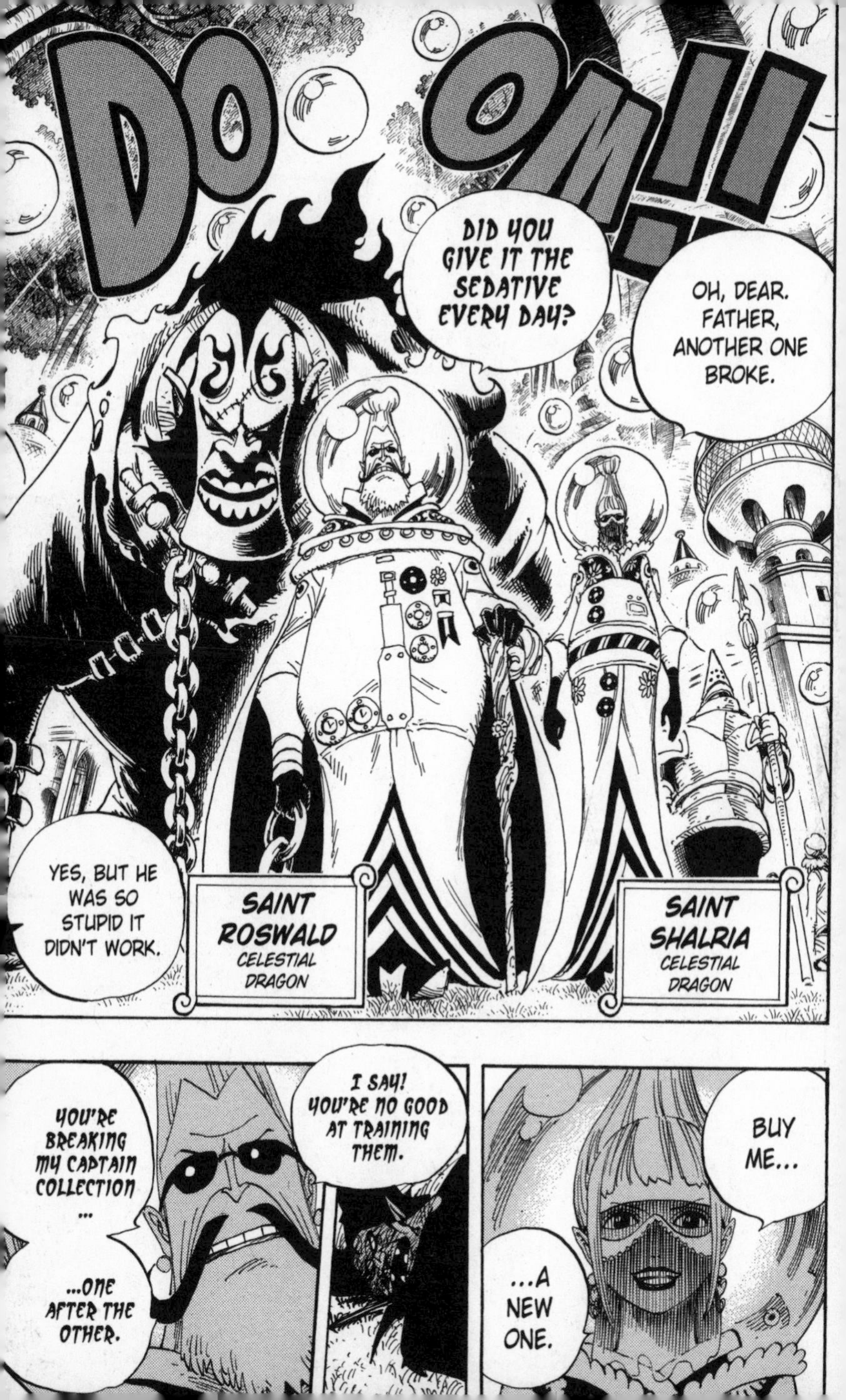
DOOM!!
OH, DEAR. FATHER, ANOTHER ONE BROKE.
DID YOU GIVE IT THE SEDATIVE EVERY DAY?
SAINT SHALRIA CELESTIAL DRAGON
YES, BUT HE WAS SO STUPID IT DIDN'T WORK.
SAINT ROSWALD CELESTIAL DRAGON
BUY ME...
...A NEW ONE.
I SAY! YOU'RE NO GOOD AT TRAINING THEM.
YOU'RE BREAKING MY CAPTAIN COLLECTION ...
...ONE AFTER THE OTHER.

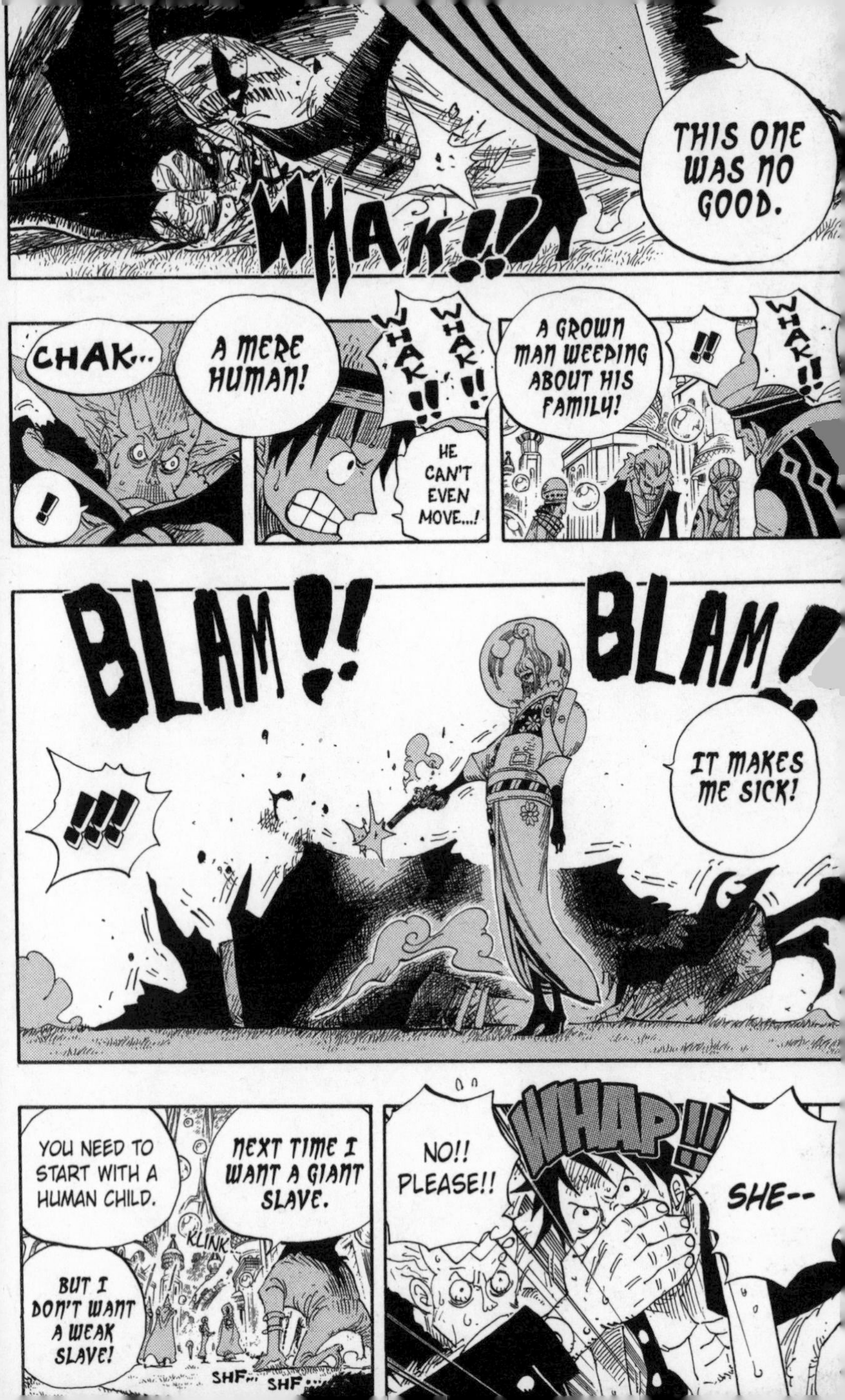
THIS ONE WAS NO GOOD.
WHAK!!
!!
WHAK!!
A GROWN MAN WEEPING ABOUT HIS FAMILY!
WHAK!!
WHAK!!
HE CAN'T EVEN MOVE...!
A MERE HUMAN!
CHAK...
!
BLAM!
IT MAKES ME SICK!
BLAM!!
!!!
SHE--
WHAP!!
NO!! PLEASE!!
NEXT TIME I WANT A GIANT SLAVE.
YOU NEED TO START WITH A HUMAN CHILD.
KLINK...
BUT I DON'T WANT A WEAK SLAVE!
SHF... SHF...

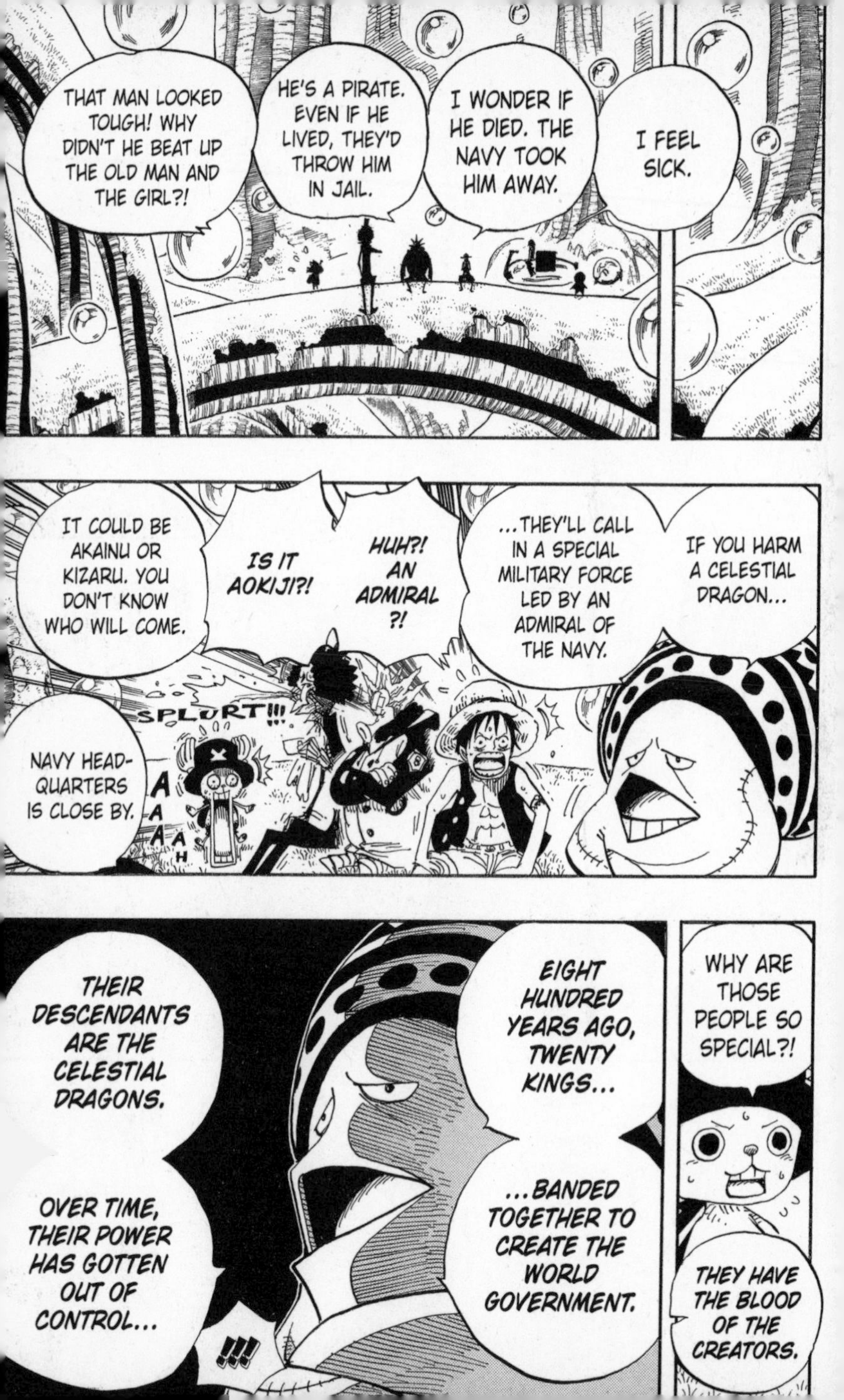
I FEEL SICK.
I WONDER IF HE DIED. THE NAVY TOOK HIM AWAY.
HE'S A PIRATE. EVEN IF HE LIVED, THEY'D THROW HIM IN JAIL.
THAT MAN LOOKED TOUGH! WHY DIDN'T HE BEAT UP THE OLD MAN AND THE GIRL?!
IF YOU HARM A CELESTIAL DRAGON...
...THEY'LL CALL IN A SPECIAL MILITARY FORCE LED BY AN ADMIRAL OF THE NAVY.
HUH?! AN ADMIRAL?!
IS IT AOKIJI?!
IT COULD BE AKAINU OR KIZARU. YOU DON'T KNOW WHO WILL COME.
SPLURT!!!
NAVY HEAD-QUARTERS IS CLOSE BY.
AAAAAH
WHY ARE THOSE PEOPLE SO SPECIAL?!
THEY HAVE THE BLOOD OF THE CREATORS.
EIGHT HUNDRED YEARS AGO, TWENTY KINGS...
...BANDED TOGETHER TO CREATE THE WORLD GOVERNMENT.
THEIR DESCENDANTS ARE THE CELESTIAL DRAGONS.
OVER TIME, THEIR POWER HAS GOTTEN OUT OF CONTROL...
!!!

Chapter 498:
THE ELEVEN SUPERNOVAS

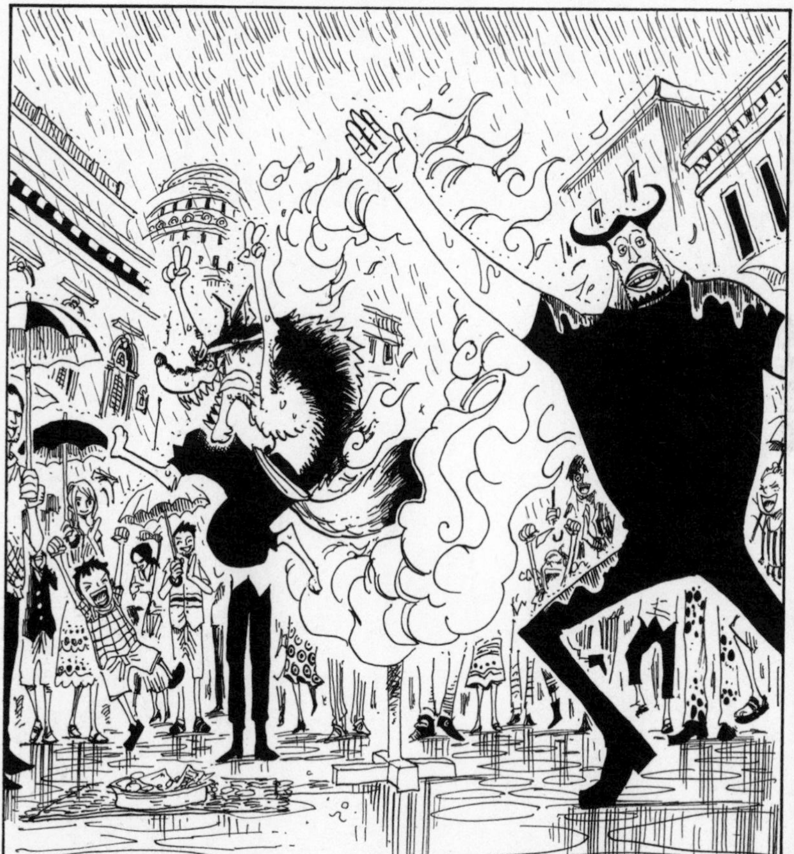

CP9'S INDEPENDENT REPORT, VOL. 8: "PERFORMING TO PAY MEDICAL EXPENSES: JABRA & BLUENO'S WILD ANIMAL SHOW"

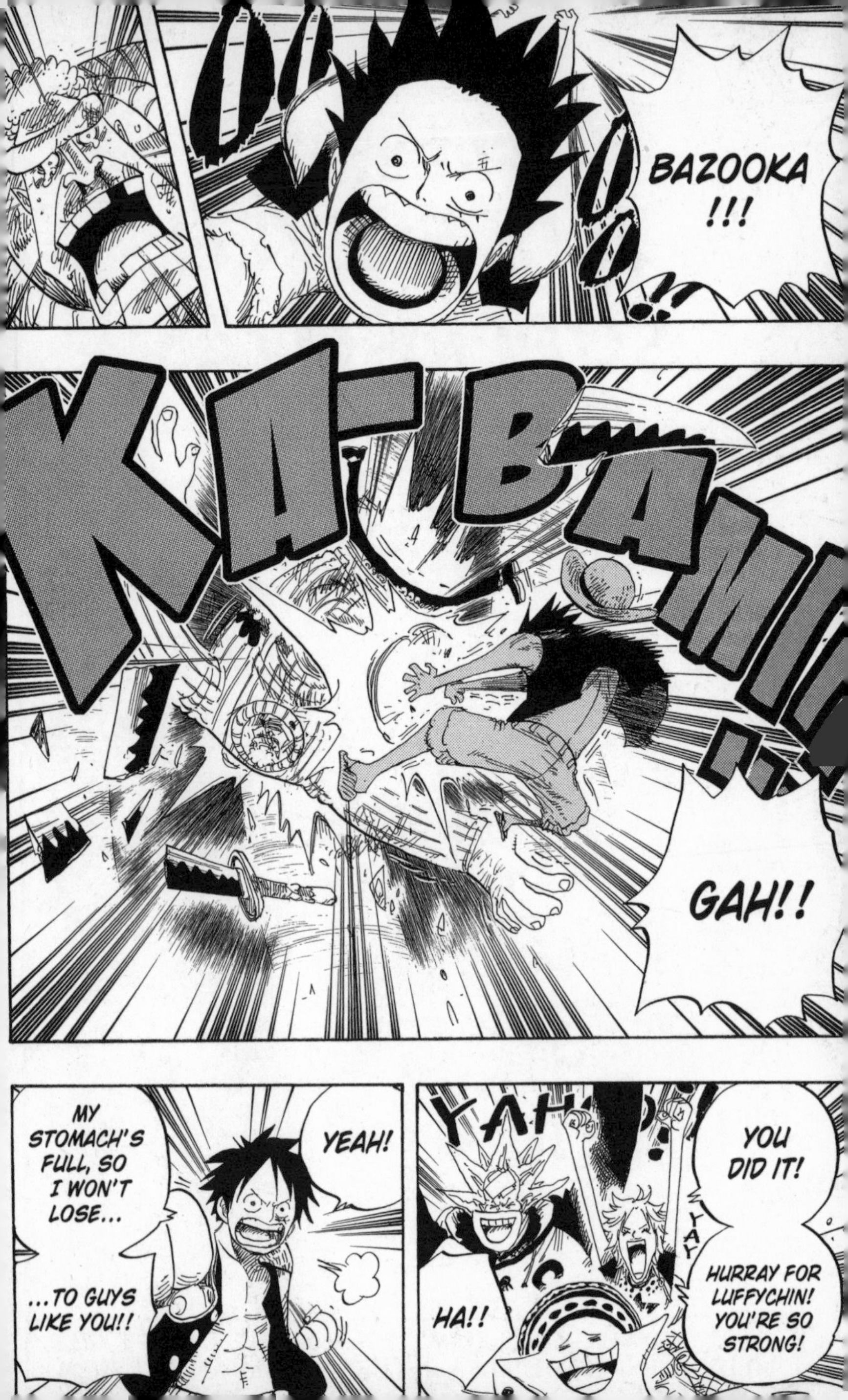
BAZOOKA !!!
KABAM!!
GAH!!
YAH
YOU DID IT!
YAY
HURRAY FOR LUFFYCHIN! YOU'RE SO STRONG!
HA!!
YEAH!
MY STOMACH'S FULL, SO I WON'T LOSE...
...TO GUYS LIKE YOU!!

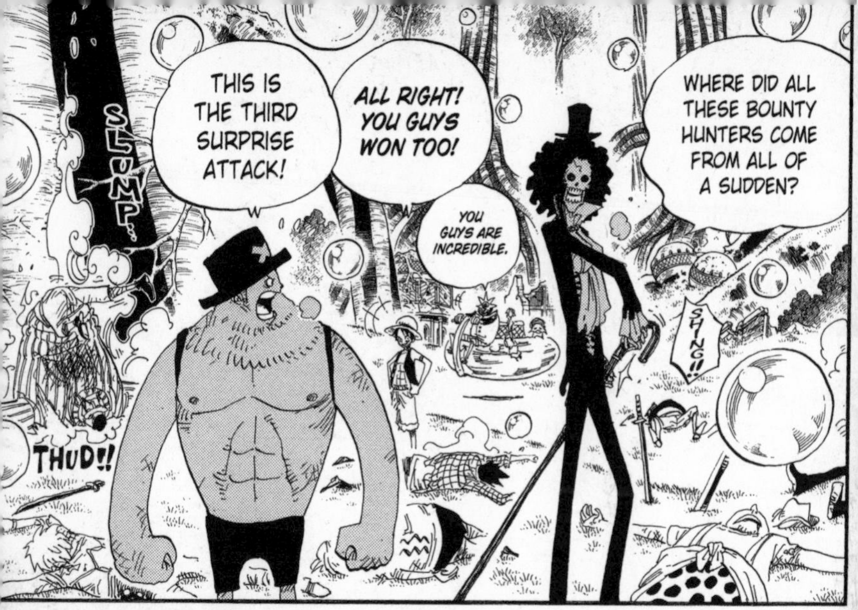
WHERE DID ALL THESE BOUNTY HUNTERS COME FROM ALL OF A SUDDEN?
SHING!!
YOU GUYS ARE INCREDIBLE.
ALL RIGHT! YOU GUYS WON TOO!
THIS IS THE THIRD SURPRISE ATTACK!
SLUMP..
THUD!!

SIGN SAYS "NAVY STAY OUT"--ED.

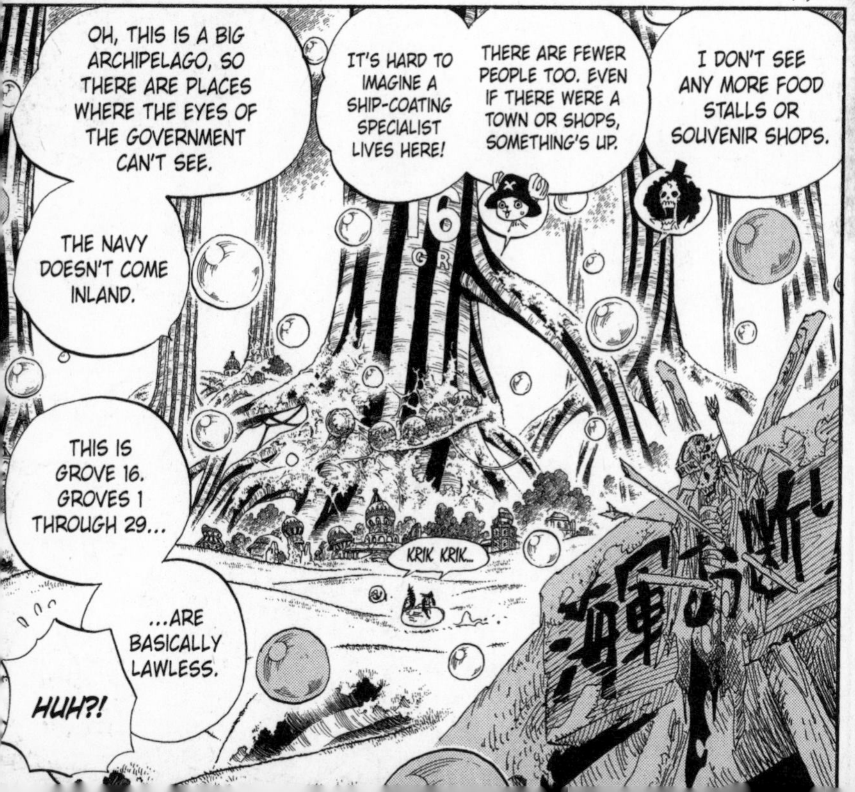
I DON'T SEE ANY MORE FOOD STALLS OR SOUVENIR SHOPS.
THERE ARE FEWER PEOPLE TOO. EVEN IF THERE WERE A TOWN OR SHOPS, SOMETHING'S UP.
IT'S HARD TO IMAGINE A SHIP-COATING SPECIALIST LIVES HERE!
OH, THIS IS A BIG ARCHIPELAGO, SO THERE ARE PLACES WHERE THE EYES OF THE GOVERNMENT CAN'T SEE.
16 GR
THE NAVY DOESN'T COME INLAND.
海軍お断り
THIS IS GROVE 16. GROVES 1 THROUGH 29...
KRIK KRIK...
...ARE BASICALLY LAWLESS.
HUH?!

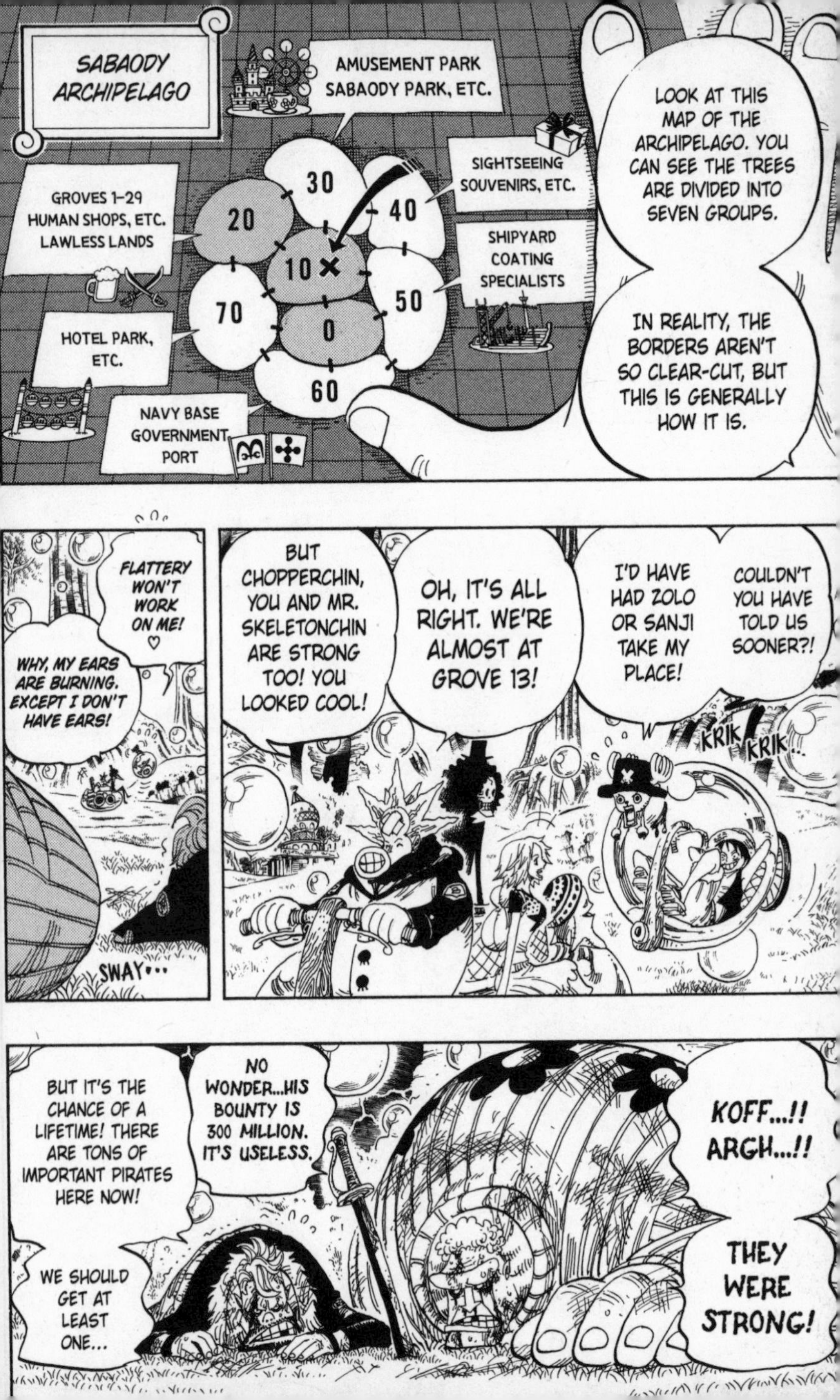
LOOK AT THIS MAP OF THE ARCHIPELAGO. YOU CAN SEE THE TREES ARE DIVIDED INTO SEVEN GROUPS.
IN REALITY, THE BORDERS AREN'T SO CLEAR-CUT, BUT THIS IS GENERALLY HOW IT IS.
SABAODY ARCHIPELAGO
AMUSEMENT PARK SABAODY PARK, ETC.
SIGHTSEEING SOUVENIRS, ETC.
SHIPYARD COATING SPECIALISTS
GROVES 1–29 HUMAN SHOPS, ETC. LAWLESS LANDS
HOTEL PARK, ETC.
NAVY BASE GOVERNMENT PORT
30
20
40
10 ×
70
50
0
60
COULDN'T YOU HAVE TOLD US SOONER?!
I'D HAVE HAD ZOLO OR SANJI TAKE MY PLACE!
OH, IT'S ALL RIGHT. WE'RE ALMOST AT GROVE 13!
BUT CHOPPERCHIN, YOU AND MR. SKELETONCHIN ARE STRONG TOO! YOU LOOKED COOL!
KRIK KRIK...
FLATTERY WON'T WORK ON ME! ♡
WHY, MY EARS ARE BURNING. EXCEPT I DON'T HAVE EARS!
SWAY...
KOFF...!! ARGH...!!
THEY WERE STRONG!
NO WONDER...HIS BOUNTY IS 300 MILLION. IT'S USELESS.
BUT IT'S THE CHANCE OF A LIFETIME! THERE ARE TONS OF IMPORTANT PIRATES HERE NOW!
WE SHOULD GET AT LEAST ONE...

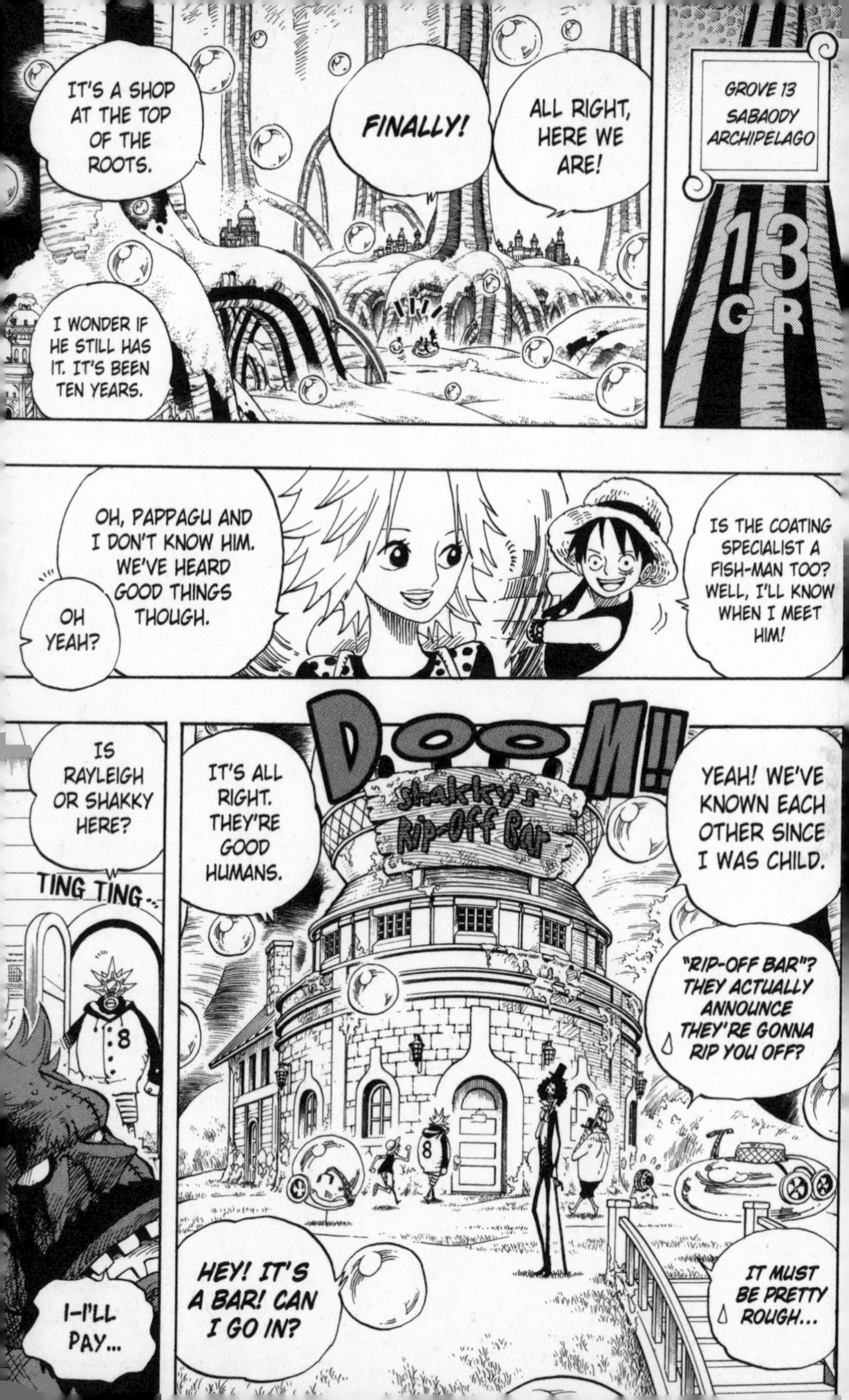
GROVE 13 SABAODY ARCHIPELAGO
13 GR
ALL RIGHT, HERE WE ARE!
FINALLY!
IT'S A SHOP AT THE TOP OF THE ROOTS.
I WONDER IF HE STILL HAS IT. IT'S BEEN TEN YEARS.
IS THE COATING SPECIALIST A FISH-MAN TOO? WELL, I'LL KNOW WHEN I MEET HIM!
OH, PAPPAGU AND I DON'T KNOW HIM. WE'VE HEARD GOOD THINGS THOUGH.
OH YEAH?
DOOM!!
Shakky's Rip-Off Bar
YEAH! WE'VE KNOWN EACH OTHER SINCE I WAS CHILD.
IT'S ALL RIGHT. THEY'RE GOOD HUMANS.
"RIP-OFF BAR"? THEY ACTUALLY ANNOUNCE THEY'RE GONNA RIP YOU OFF?
IT MUST BE PRETTY ROUGH...
HEY! IT'S A BAR! CAN I GO IN?
IS RAYLEIGH OR SHAKKY HERE?
TING TING...
I-I'LL PAY...

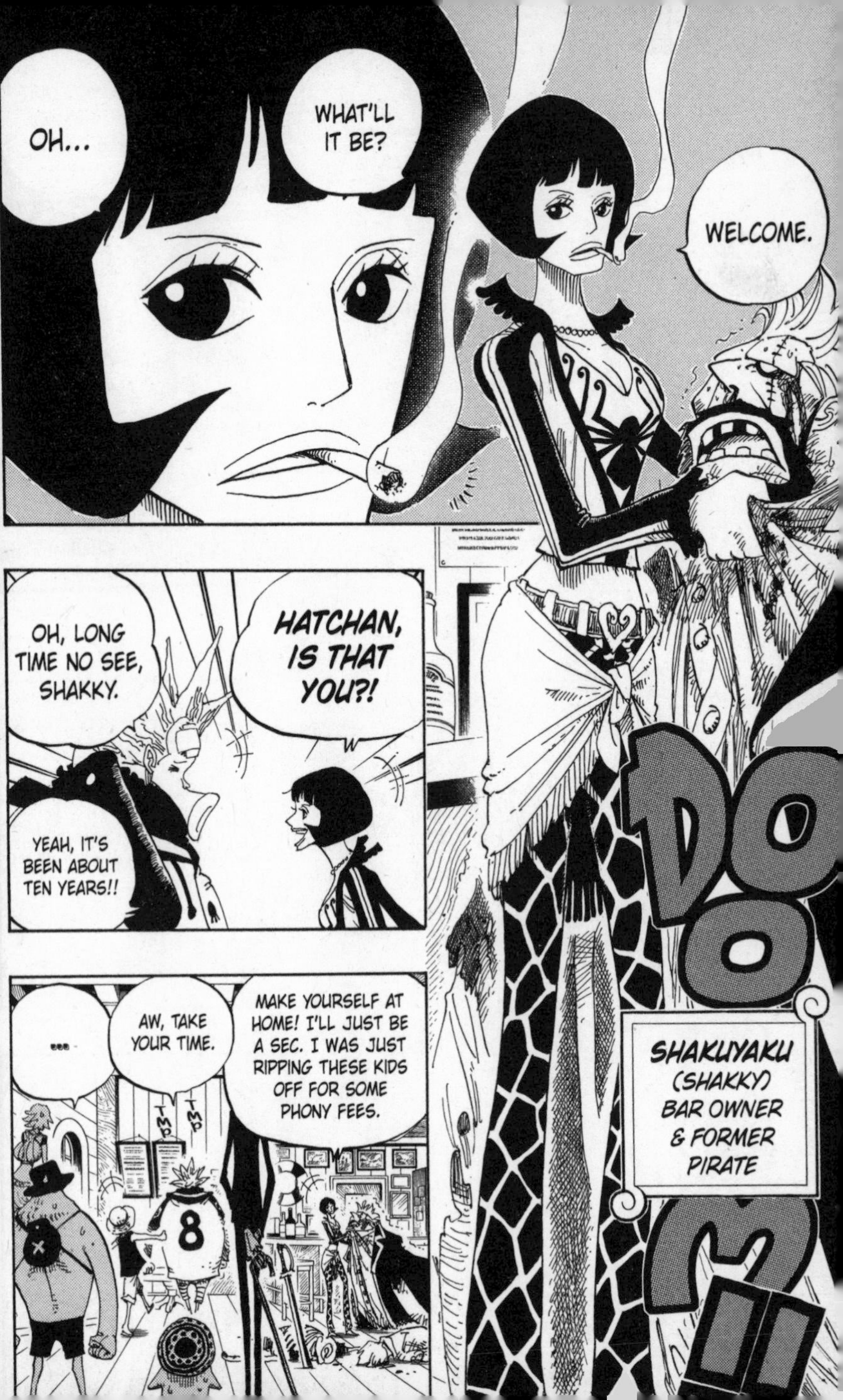
WELCOME.
DOOM
SHAKUYAKU (SHAKKY) BAR OWNER & FORMER PIRATE
WHAT'LL IT BE?
OH...
HATCHAN, IS THAT YOU?!
OH, LONG TIME NO SEE, SHAKKY.
YEAH, IT'S BEEN ABOUT TEN YEARS!!
MAKE YOURSELF AT HOME! I'LL JUST BE A SEC. I WAS JUST RIPPING THESE KIDS OFF FOR SOME PHONY FEES.
AW, TAKE YOUR TIME.
...
TMP TMP

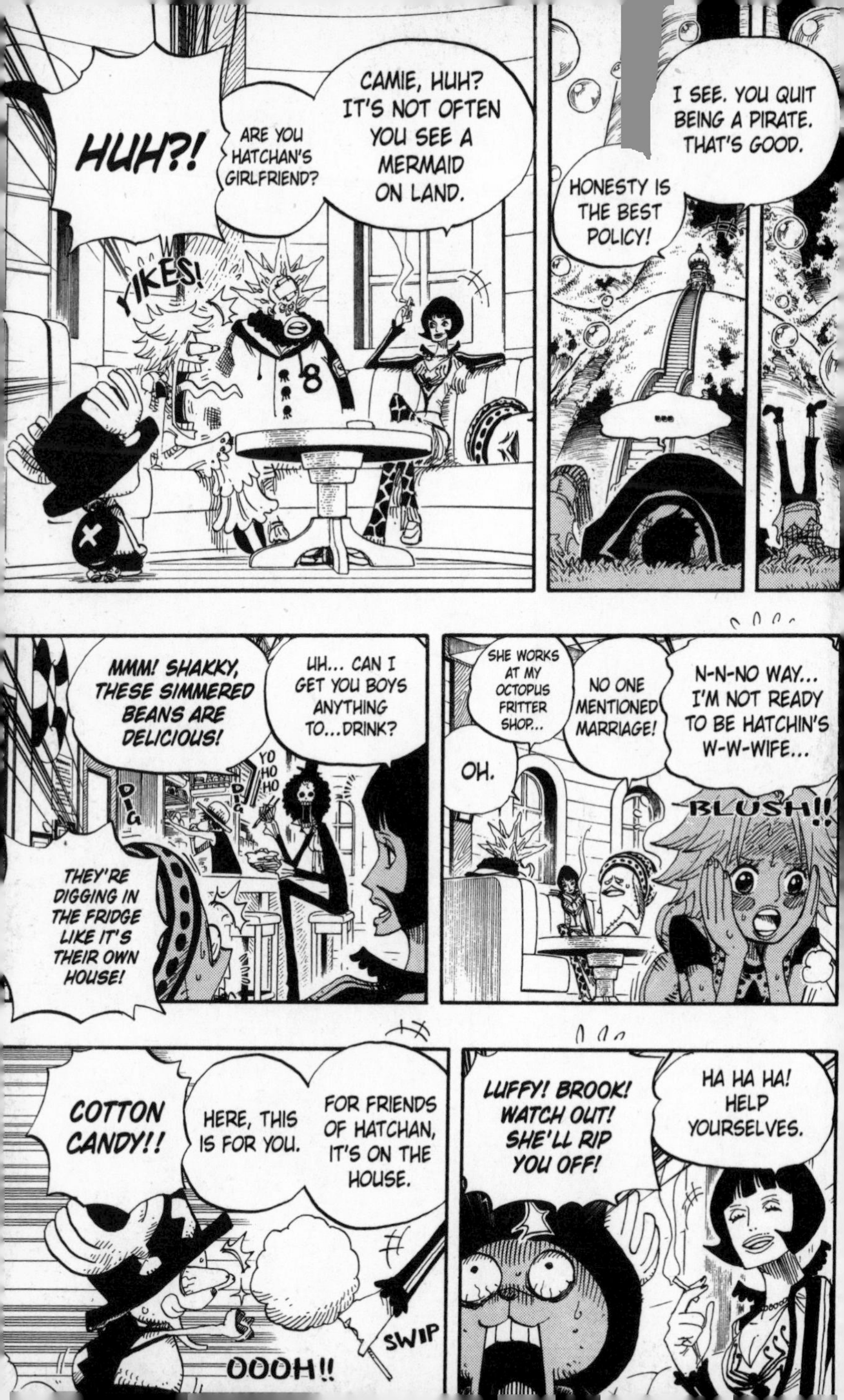
I SEE. YOU QUIT BEING A PIRATE. THAT'S GOOD.
HONESTY IS THE BEST POLICY!
...
CAMIE, HUH? IT'S NOT OFTEN YOU SEE A MERMAID ON LAND.
ARE YOU HATCHAN'S GIRLFRIEND?
HUH?!
YIKES!
N-N-NO WAY... I'M NOT READY TO BE HATCHIN'S W-W-WIFE...
NO ONE MENTIONED MARRIAGE!
SHE WORKS AT MY OCTOPUS FRITTER SHOP...
OH.
BLUSH!!
UH... CAN I GET YOU BOYS ANYTHING TO...DRINK?
MMM! SHAKKY, THESE SIMMERED BEANS ARE DELICIOUS!
YO HO HO
DIG
DIG
THEY'RE DIGGING IN THE FRIDGE LIKE IT'S THEIR OWN HOUSE!
HA HA HA! HELP YOURSELVES.
LUFFY! BROOK! WATCH OUT! SHE'LL RIP YOU OFF!
FOR FRIENDS OF HATCHAN, IT'S ON THE HOUSE.
HERE, THIS IS FOR YOU.
COTTON CANDY!!
SWIP
OOOH!!

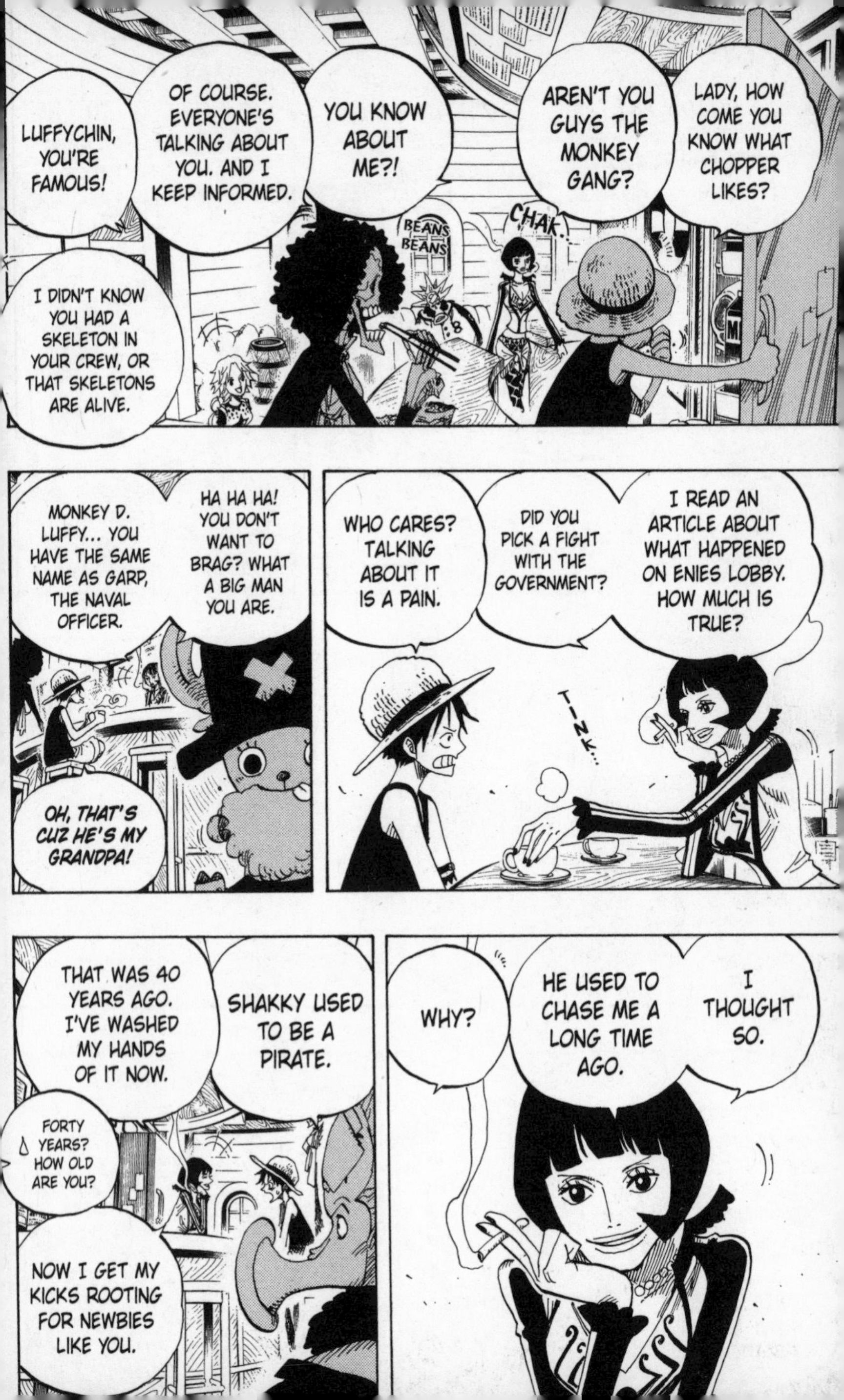
LADY, HOW COME YOU KNOW WHAT CHOPPER LIKES?
AREN'T YOU GUYS THE MONKEY GANG?
CHAK...
YOU KNOW ABOUT ME?!
OF COURSE. EVERYONE'S TALKING ABOUT YOU. AND I KEEP INFORMED.
LUFFYCHIN, YOU'RE FAMOUS!
BEANS BEANS
I DIDN'T KNOW YOU HAD A SKELETON IN YOUR CREW, OR THAT SKELETONS ARE ALIVE.
I READ AN ARTICLE ABOUT WHAT HAPPENED ON ENIES LOBBY. HOW MUCH IS TRUE?
DID YOU PICK A FIGHT WITH THE GOVERNMENT?
WHO CARES? TALKING ABOUT IT IS A PAIN.
TINK...
HA HA HA! YOU DON'T WANT TO BRAG? WHAT A BIG MAN YOU ARE.
MONKEY D. LUFFY... YOU HAVE THE SAME NAME AS GARP, THE NAVAL OFFICER.
OH, THAT'S CUZ HE'S MY GRANDPA!
I THOUGHT SO.
HE USED TO CHASE ME A LONG TIME AGO.
WHY?
SHAKKY USED TO BE A PIRATE.
THAT WAS 40 YEARS AGO. I'VE WASHED MY HANDS OF IT NOW.
FORTY YEARS? HOW OLD ARE YOU?
NOW I GET MY KICKS ROOTING FOR NEWBIES LIKE YOU.

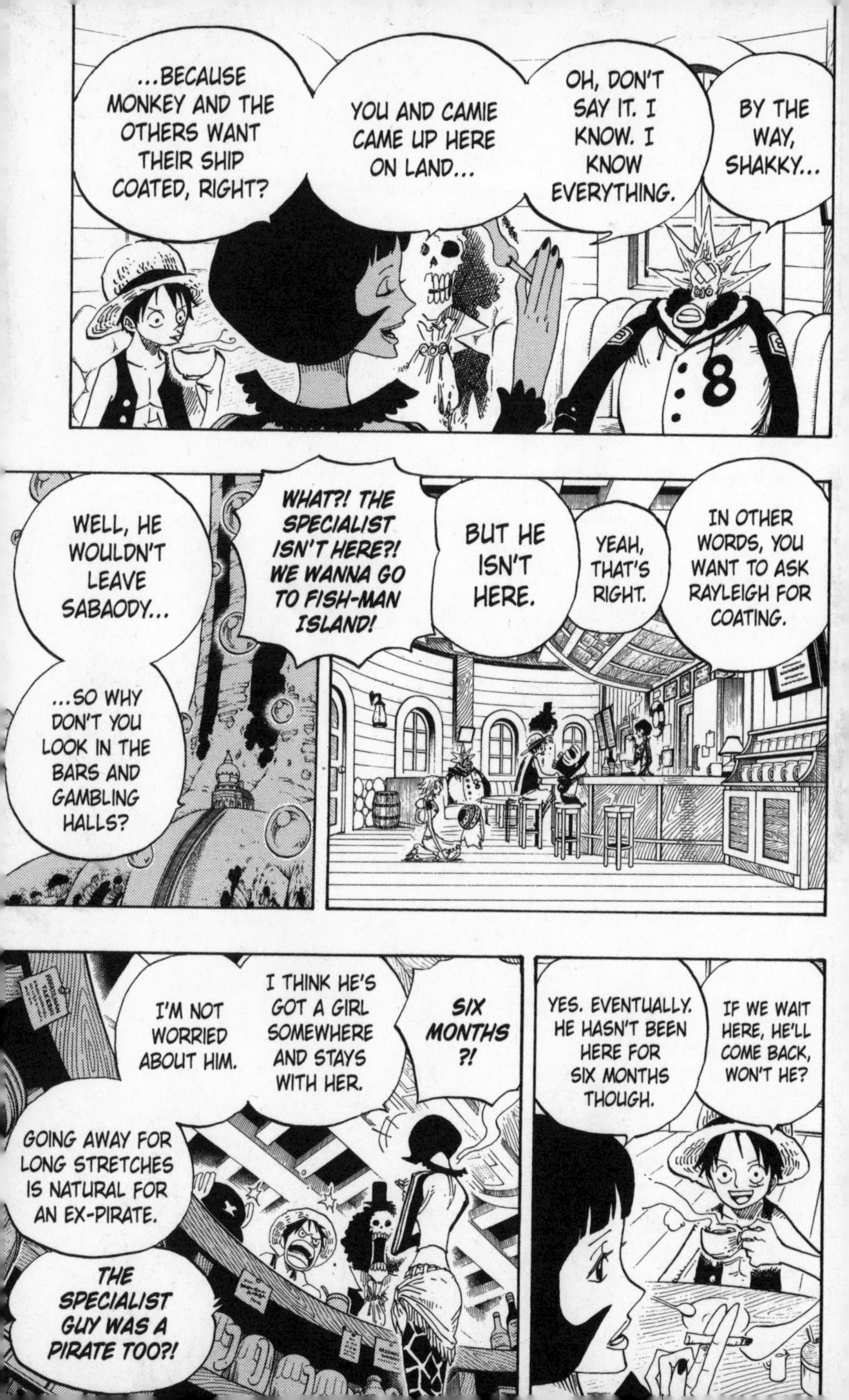
BY THE WAY, SHAKKY...
OH, DON'T SAY IT. I KNOW. I KNOW EVERYTHING.
YOU AND CAMIE CAME UP HERE ON LAND...
...BECAUSE MONKEY AND THE OTHERS WANT THEIR SHIP COATED, RIGHT?
IN OTHER WORDS, YOU WANT TO ASK RAYLEIGH FOR COATING.
YEAH, THAT'S RIGHT.
BUT HE ISN'T HERE.
WHAT?! THE SPECIALIST ISN'T HERE?! WE WANNA GO TO FISH-MAN ISLAND!
WELL, HE WOULDN'T LEAVE SABAODY...
...SO WHY DON'T YOU LOOK IN THE BARS AND GAMBLING HALLS?
IF WE WAIT HERE, HE'LL COME BACK, WON'T HE?
YES. EVENTUALLY. HE HASN'T BEEN HERE FOR SIX MONTHS THOUGH.
SIX MONTHS?!
I THINK HE'S GOT A GIRL SOMEWHERE AND STAYS WITH HER.
I'M NOT WORRIED ABOUT HIM.
GOING AWAY FOR LONG STRETCHES IS NATURAL FOR AN EX-PIRATE.
THE SPECIALIST GUY WAS A PIRATE TOO?!

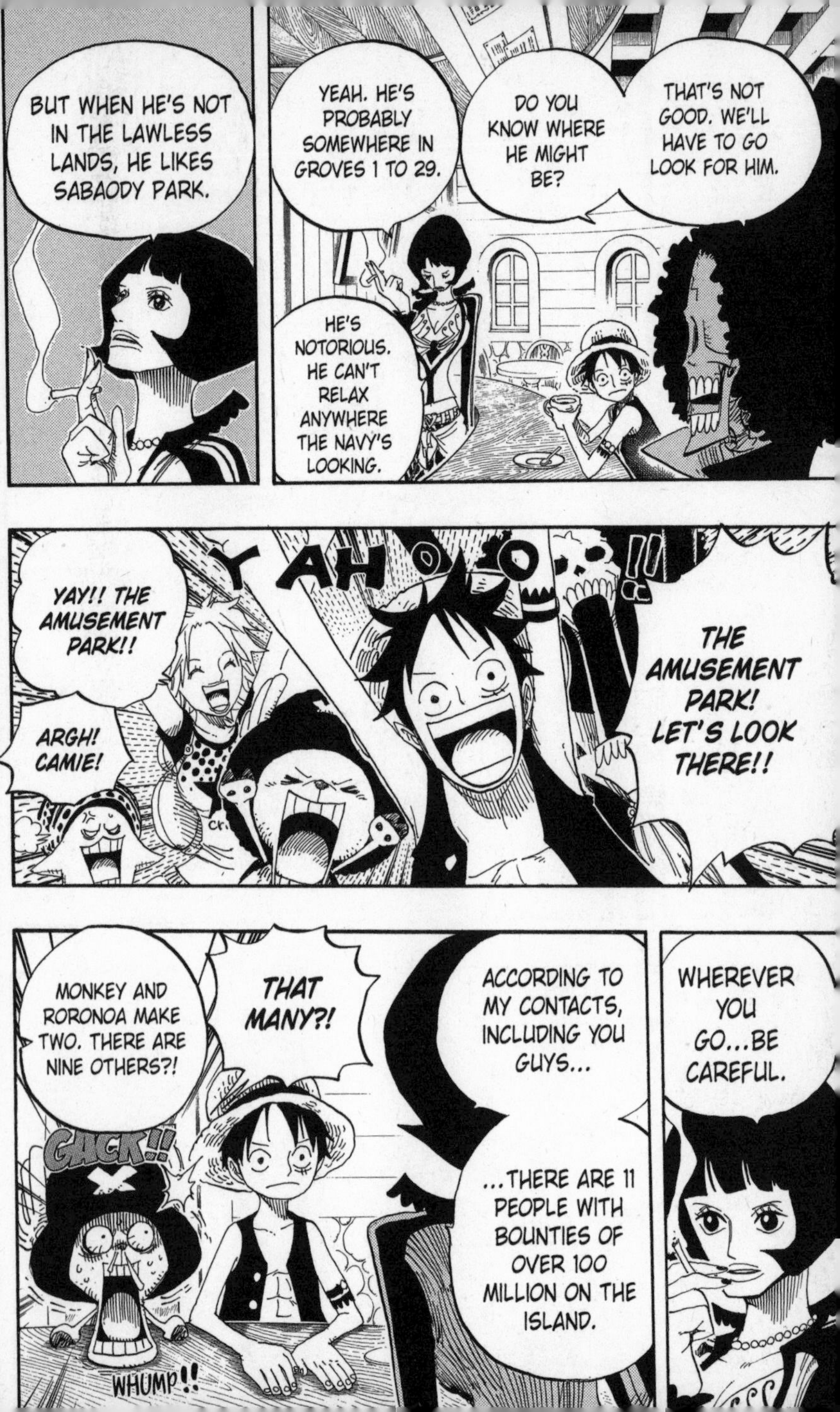
THAT'S NOT GOOD. WE'LL HAVE TO GO LOOK FOR HIM.
DO YOU KNOW WHERE HE MIGHT BE?
YEAH. HE'S PROBABLY SOMEWHERE IN GROVES 1 TO 29.
HE'S NOTORIOUS. HE CAN'T RELAX ANYWHERE THE NAVY'S LOOKING.
BUT WHEN HE'S NOT IN THE LAWLESS LANDS, HE LIKES SABAODY PARK.
THE AMUSEMENT PARK! LET'S LOOK THERE!!
YAHOOO!!
YAY!! THE AMUSEMENT PARK!!
ARGH! CAMIE!
WHEREVER YOU GO...BE CAREFUL.
ACCORDING TO MY CONTACTS, INCLUDING YOU GUYS...
...THERE ARE 11 PEOPLE WITH BOUNTIES OF OVER 100 MILLION ON THE ISLAND.
THAT MANY?!
MONKEY AND RORONOA MAKE TWO. THERE ARE NINE OTHERS?!
GACK!!
WHUMP!!

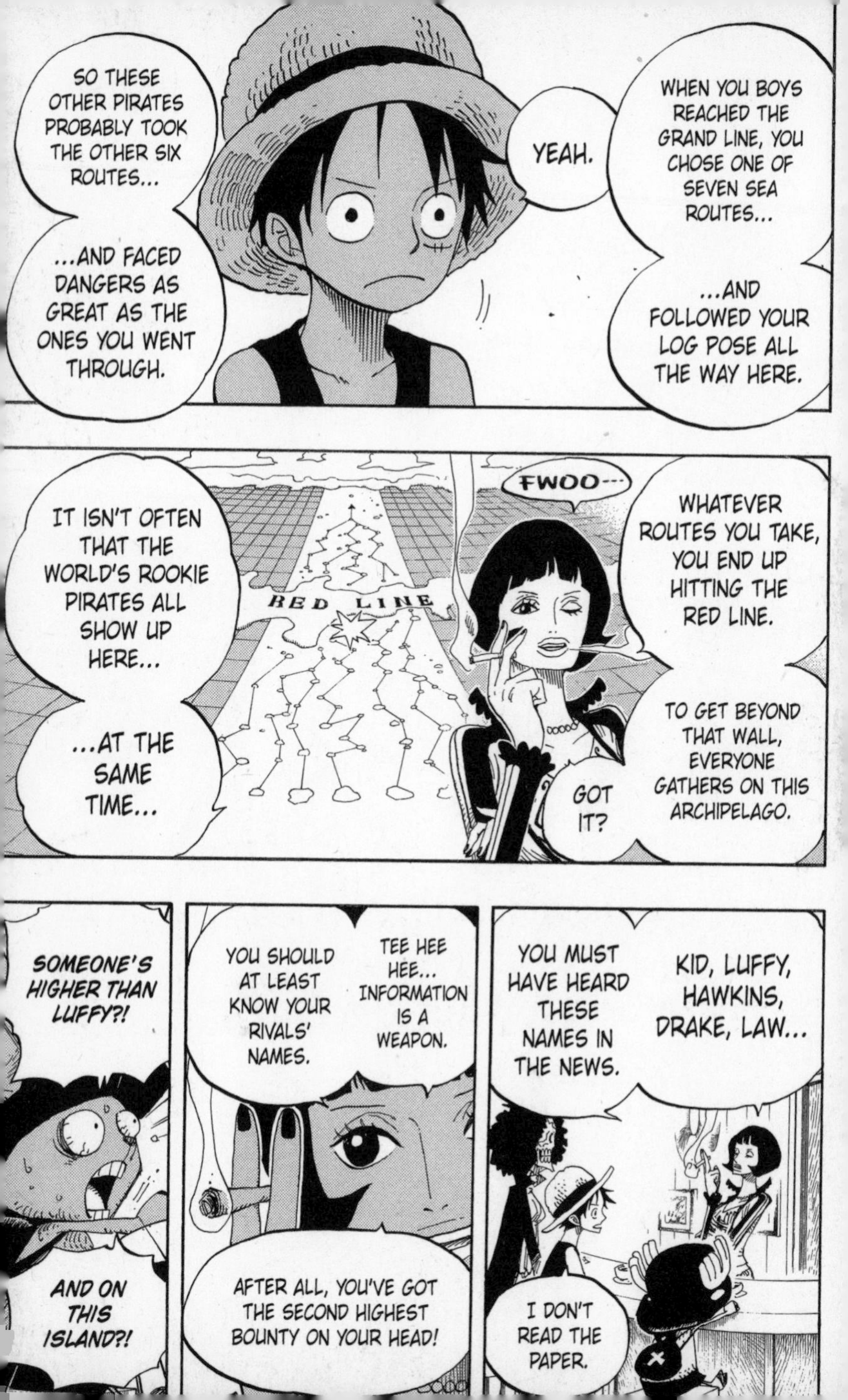
WHEN YOU BOYS REACHED THE GRAND LINE, YOU CHOSE ONE OF SEVEN SEA ROUTES...
...AND FOLLOWED YOUR LOG POSE ALL THE WAY HERE.
YEAH.
SO THESE OTHER PIRATES PROBABLY TOOK THE OTHER SIX ROUTES...
...AND FACED DANGERS AS GREAT AS THE ONES YOU WENT THROUGH.
FWOO---
WHATEVER ROUTES YOU TAKE, YOU END UP HITTING THE RED LINE.
TO GET BEYOND THAT WALL, EVERYONE GATHERS ON THIS ARCHIPELAGO.
GOT IT?
RED LINE
IT ISN'T OFTEN THAT THE WORLD'S ROOKIE PIRATES ALL SHOW UP HERE...
...AT THE SAME TIME...
KID, LUFFY, HAWKINS, DRAKE, LAW...
YOU MUST HAVE HEARD THESE NAMES IN THE NEWS.
I DON'T READ THE PAPER.
TEE HEE HEE... INFORMATION IS A WEAPON.
YOU SHOULD AT LEAST KNOW YOUR RIVALS' NAMES.
AFTER ALL, YOU'VE GOT THE SECOND HIGHEST BOUNTY ON YOUR HEAD!
SOMEONE'S HIGHER THAN LUFFY?!
AND ON THIS ISLAND?!

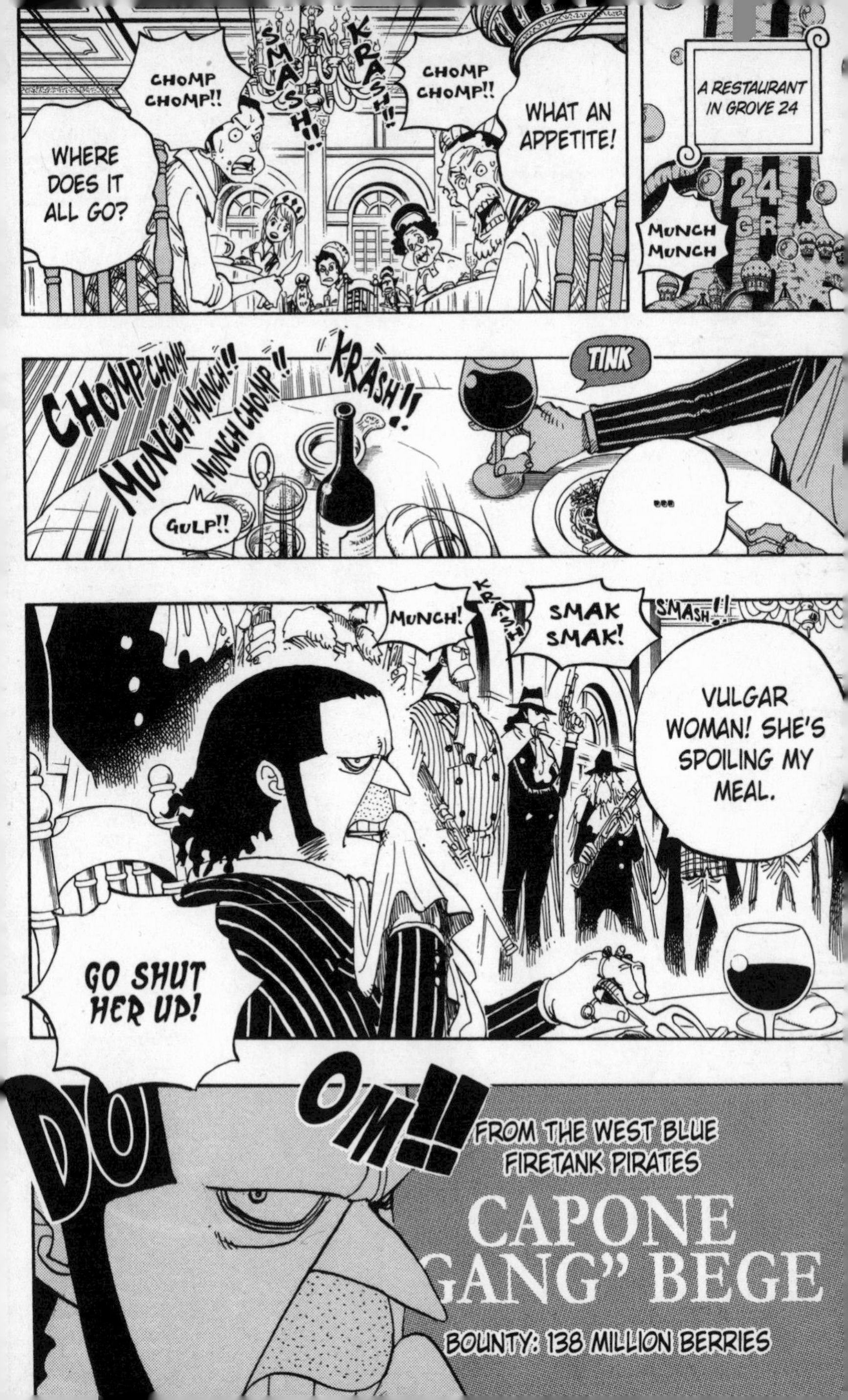
A RESTAURANT IN GROVE 24
24 GR
MUNCH MUNCH
WHAT AN APPETITE!
CHOMP CHOMP!!
KRASH!!
SMASH!!
CHOMP CHOMP!!
WHERE DOES IT ALL GO?
TINK
...
KRASH!!
MUNCH CHOMP!!
CHOMP CHOMP
MUNCH MUNCH!!
GULP!!
SMASH!!
VULGAR WOMAN! SHE'S SPOILING MY MEAL.
SMAK SMAK!
KRASH
MUNCH!
GO SHUT HER UP!
DOOM!!
FROM THE WEST BLUE
FIRETANK PIRATES
CAPONE
GANG” BEGE
BOUNTY: 138 MILLION BERRIES

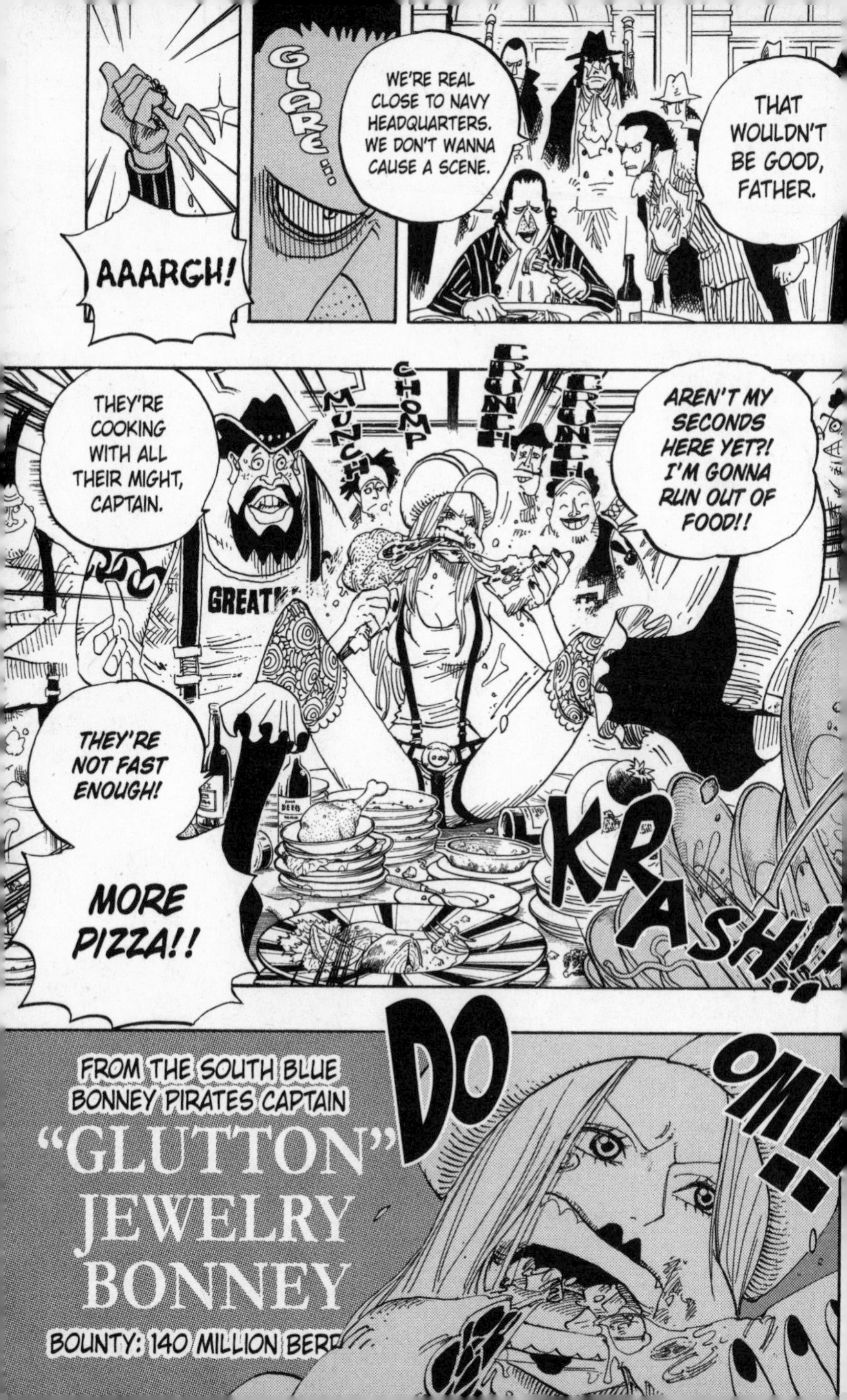
WE'RE REAL CLOSE TO NAVY HEADQUARTERS. WE DON'T WANNA CAUSE A SCENE.
THAT WOULDN'T BE GOOD, FATHER.
GLARE...
AAARGH!
AREN'T MY SECONDS HERE YET?! I'M GONNA RUN OUT OF FOOD!!
CRUNCH
CRUNCH
CHOMP
MUNCH
THEY'RE COOKING WITH ALL THEIR MIGHT, CAPTAIN.
KRASH!!
THEY'RE NOT FAST ENOUGH!
MORE PIZZA!!
DOOM!!
FROM THE SOUTH BLUE
BONNEY PIRATES CAPTAIN
"GLUTTON" JEWELRY BONNEY
BOUNTY: 140 MILLION BERI

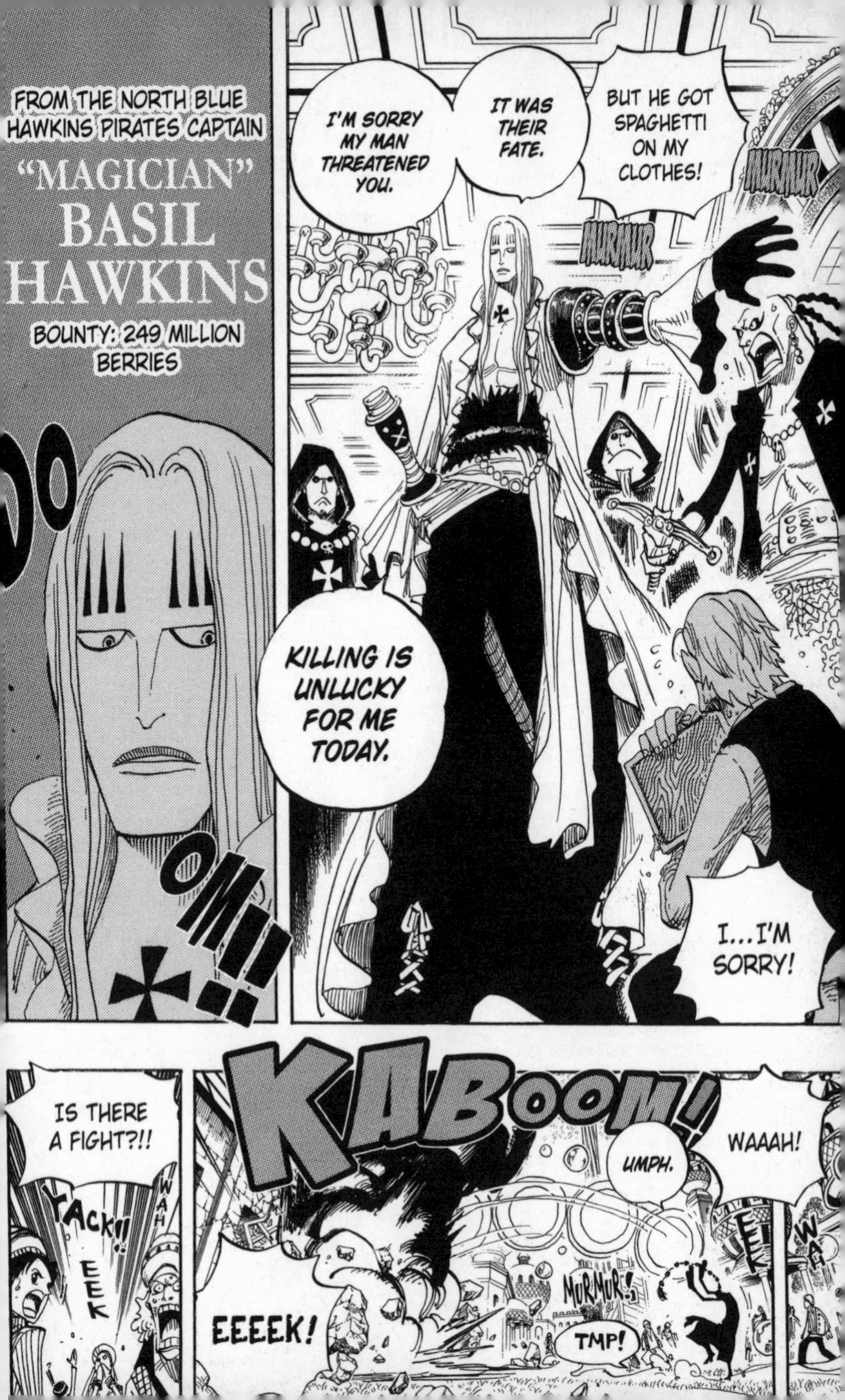
BUT HE GOT SPAGHETTI ON MY CLOTHES!
MURMUR
IT WAS THEIR FATE.
I'M SORRY MY MAN THREATENED YOU.
MURMUR
KILLING IS UNLUCKY FOR ME TODAY.
I...I'M SORRY!
FROM THE NORTH BLUE
HAWKINS PIRATES CAPTAIN
"MAGICIAN"
BASIL HAWKINS
BOUNTY: 249 MILLION BERRIES
WAH
KABOOM!
WAAAH!
UMPH.
EEK
MURMUR
TMP!
EEEEK!
IS THERE A FIGHT?!!
WAH
TACK!!
EEK

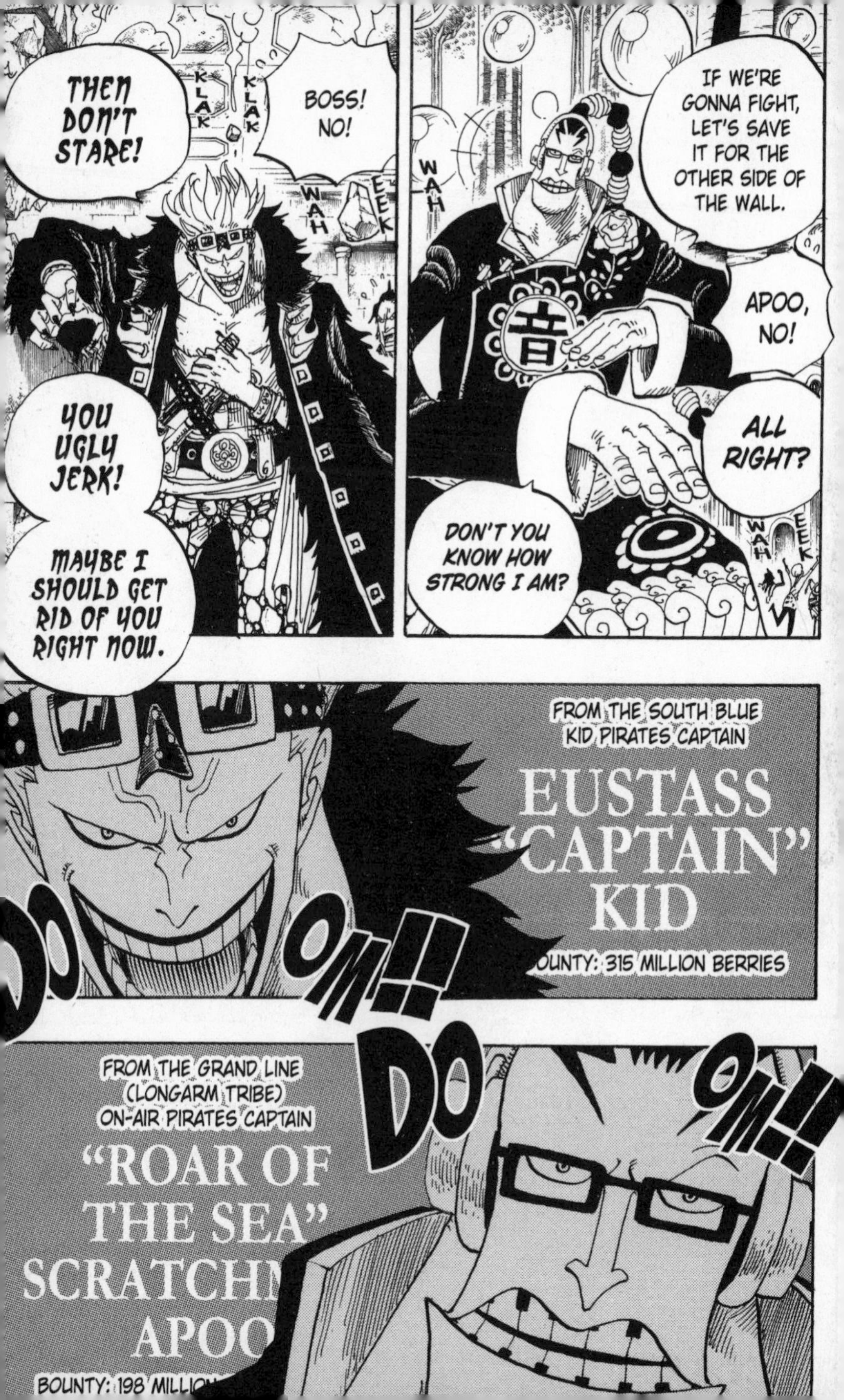
IF WE'RE GONNA FIGHT, LET'S SAVE IT FOR THE OTHER SIDE OF THE WALL.
APOO, NO!
ALL RIGHT?
WAH
EEK
DON'T YOU KNOW HOW STRONG I AM?
WAH
BOSS! NO!
KLAK
KLAK
EEK
WAH
THEN DON'T STARE!
YOU UGLY JERK!
MAYBE I SHOULD GET RID OF YOU RIGHT NOW.
FROM THE SOUTH BLUE
KID PIRATES CAPTAIN
EUSTASS "CAPTAIN" KID
OUNTY: 315 MILLION BERRIES
DOOM!!
DOOM!!
FROM THE GRAND LINE
(LONGARM TRIBE)
ON-AIR PIRATES CAPTAIN
"ROAR OF THE SEA" SCRATCHM
APOO
BOUNTY: 198 MILLIO

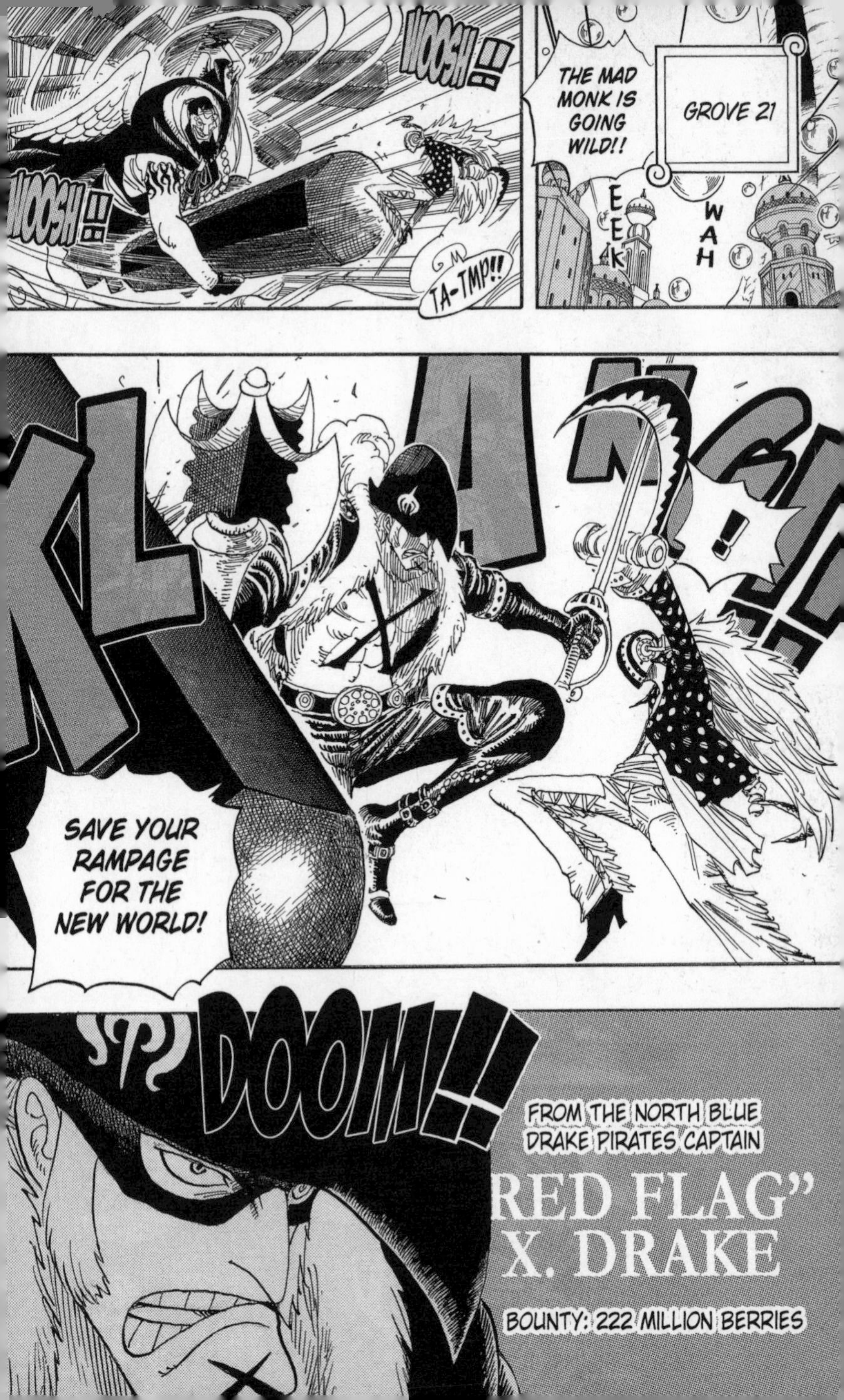
GROVE 21
THE MAD MONK IS GOING WILD!!
EEEK
WAH
WOOSH!!
WOOSH!!
TA-TMP!!
SAVE YOUR RAMPAGE FOR THE NEW WORLD!
DOOM!!
FROM THE NORTH BLUE
DRAKE PIRATES CAPTAIN
RED FLAG”
X. DRAKE
BOUNTY: 222 MILLION BERRIES

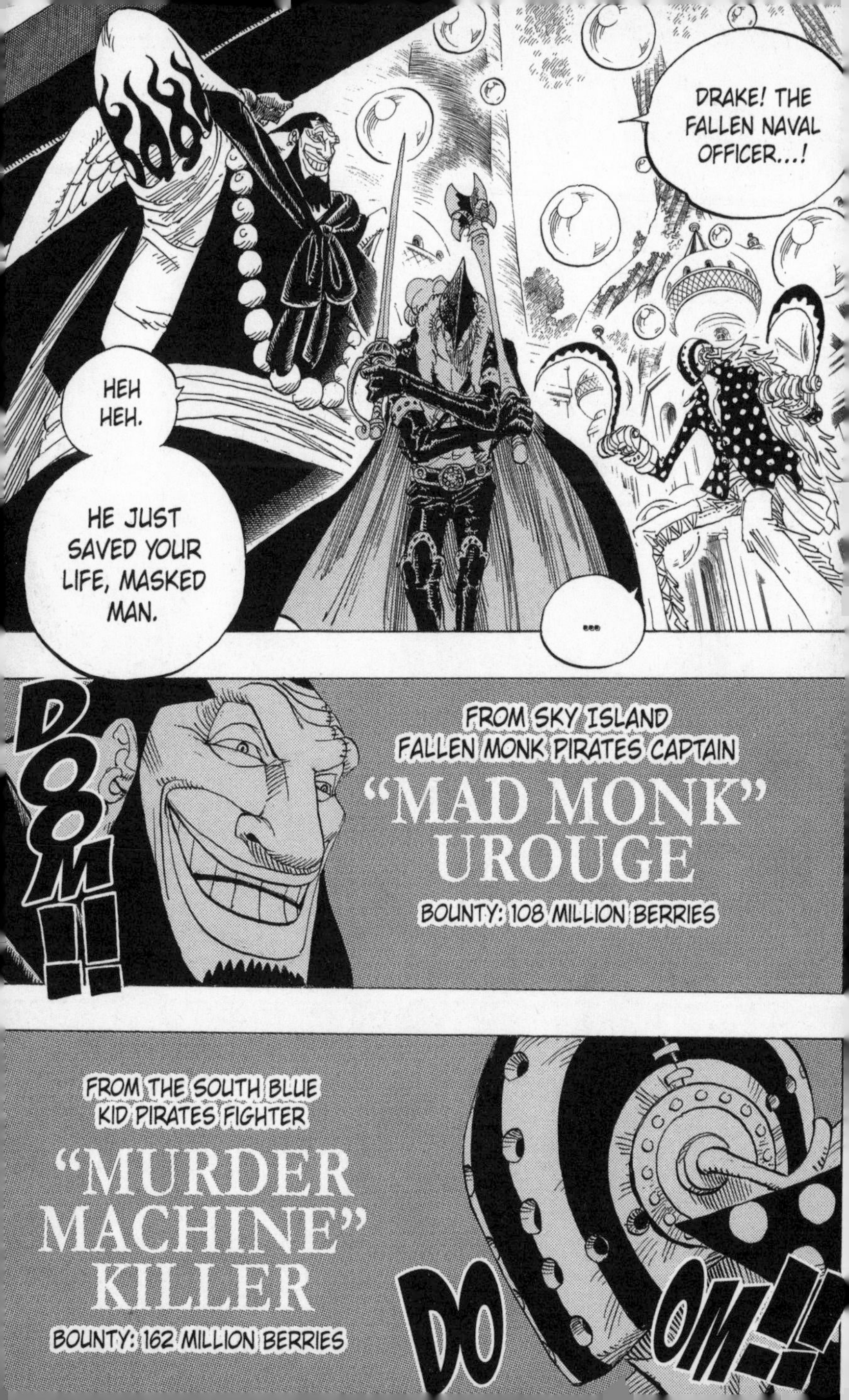
DRAKE! THE FALLEN NAVAL OFFICER...!
HEH HEH.
HE JUST SAVED YOUR LIFE, MASKED MAN.
...
FROM SKY ISLAND
FALLEN MONK PIRATES CAPTAIN
"MAD MONK" UROUGE
BOUNTY: 108 MILLION BERRIES
DOOM!!
DOOM!!
FROM THE SOUTH BLUE
KID PIRATES FIGHTER
"MURDER MACHINE" KILLER
BOUNTY: 162 MILLION BERRIES

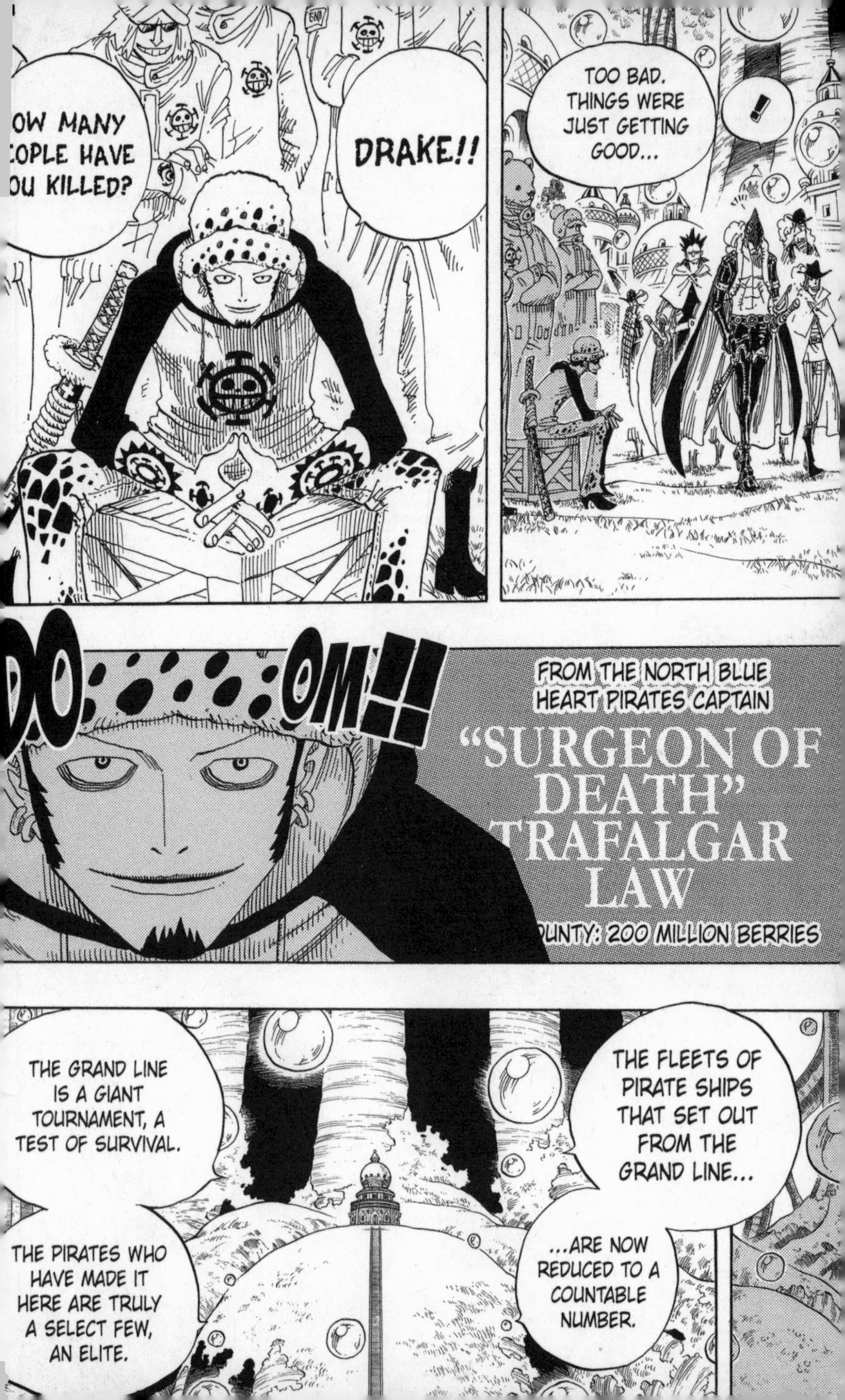
TOO BAD. THINGS WERE JUST GETTING GOOD...
!
DRAKE!!
OW MANY EOPLE HAVE OU KILLED?
DO OM!!
FROM THE NORTH BLUE HEART PIRATES CAPTAIN
"SURGEON OF DEATH" TRAFALGAR LAW
OUNTY: 200 MILLION BERRIES
THE FLEETS OF PIRATE SHIPS THAT SET OUT FROM THE GRAND LINE...
...ARE NOW REDUCED TO A COUNTABLE NUMBER.
THE GRAND LINE IS A GIANT TOURNAMENT, A TEST OF SURVIVAL.
THE PIRATES WHO HAVE MADE IT HERE ARE TRULY A SELECT FEW, AN ELITE.

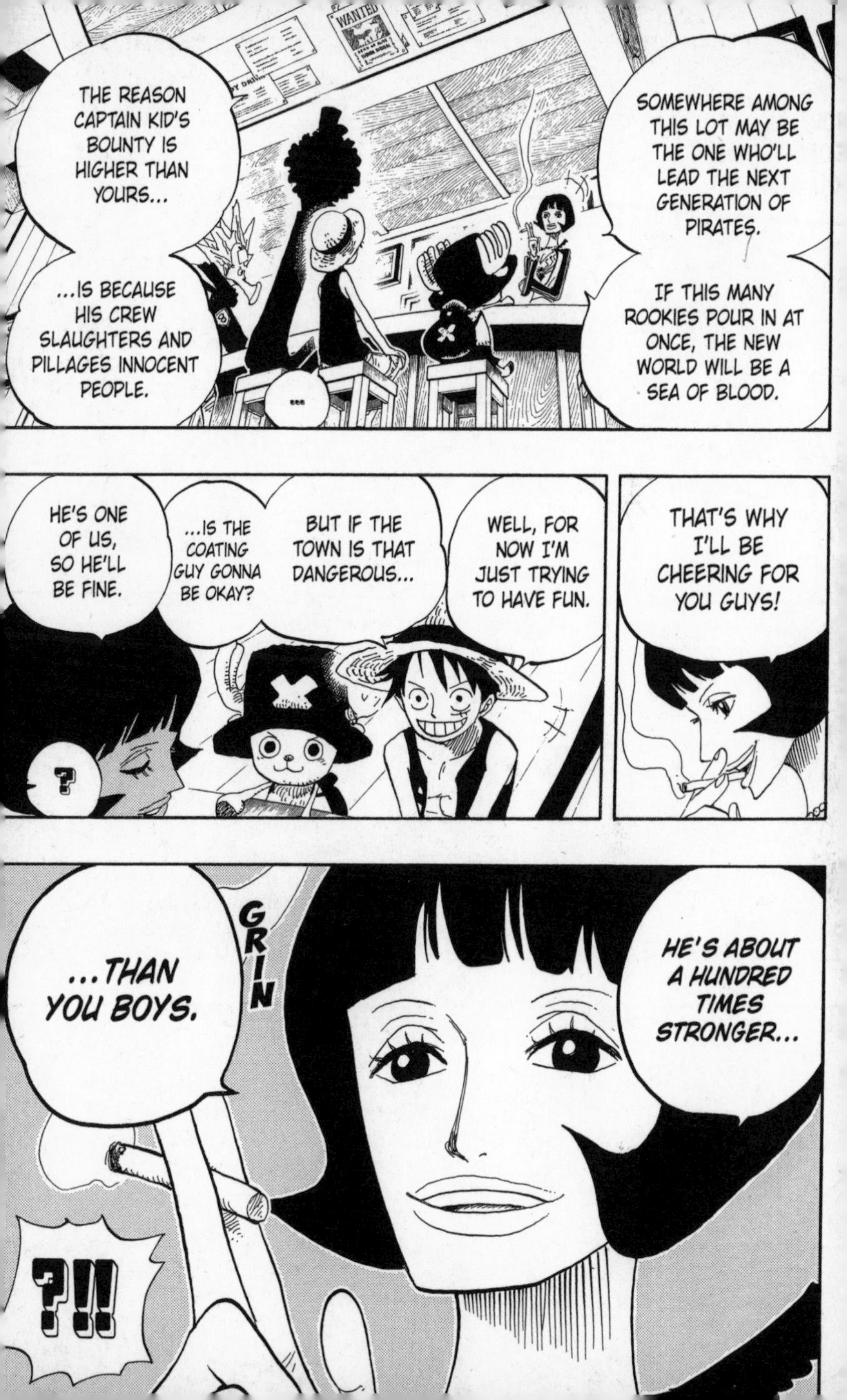
WANTED
SOMEWHERE AMONG THIS LOT MAY BE THE ONE WHO'LL LEAD THE NEXT GENERATION OF PIRATES.
IF THIS MANY ROOKIES POUR IN AT ONCE, THE NEW WORLD WILL BE A SEA OF BLOOD.
THE REASON CAPTAIN KID'S BOUNTY IS HIGHER THAN YOURS...
...IS BECAUSE HIS CREW SLAUGHTERS AND PILLAGES INNOCENT PEOPLE.
...
THAT'S WHY I'LL BE CHEERING FOR YOU GUYS!
WELL, FOR NOW I'M JUST TRYING TO HAVE FUN.
BUT IF THE TOWN IS THAT DANGEROUS...
...IS THE COATING GUY GONNA BE OKAY?
HE'S ONE OF US, SO HE'LL BE FINE.
?
HE'S ABOUT A HUNDRED TIMES STRONGER...
GRIN
...THAN YOU BOYS.
?!!

質問コーナー
SBS
エス ビー エス

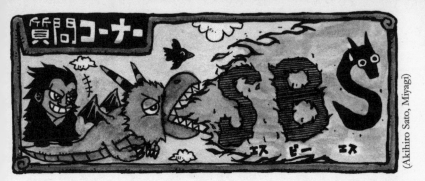

(Akihiro Sato, Miyagi)

Q: Hello, Oda Sensei. In volume 50, chapter 490, there was a circular rainbow. The other day I saw one in our school courtyard. How does that happen? Please show me brilliantly! Hee hee hee!

--Old Cloth

A ROUND RAINBOW!!
SHMMMMER
WOW!!!
'S SO
ETTY!!

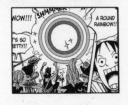

A: That's amazing. You can't see circular rainbows on the earth's surface except in the rarest of circumstances. But it's true, circular rainbows really do exist. I drew one in that panel. Actually, all rainbows are basically circular.

Fig. 1
What's a rainbow?
Curtain of water droplets
Sun
Angle of reflection: 42 degrees!

Fig. 2

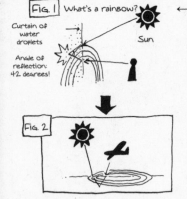

← This may be a little hard to understand, but rainbows occur when sunlight reflects off water droplets, and the light is broken down. A rainbow won't appear unless the sunlight, water droplets and the position of an observer appear as in the diagram on the left. It seems the angle of the reflection of light off the water droplets has to be 42 degrees, so for people on land, the bottom half of the circle falls below the horizon. Thus, the circular rainbow seen from the sea in the manga is not a common occurrence. I thought it might be all right, however, since the Straw Hats were on the Grand Line. I learned about this phenomenon when a manga colleague of mine saw a circular rainbow from inside an airplane. Theoretically, you can see them if you are in the air. But you can see them above a school courtyard too?! And what is this, a science textbook?! This is a broadcast of the stupid manga One Piece. Don't change the channel!

Chapter 499: SABAODY PARK

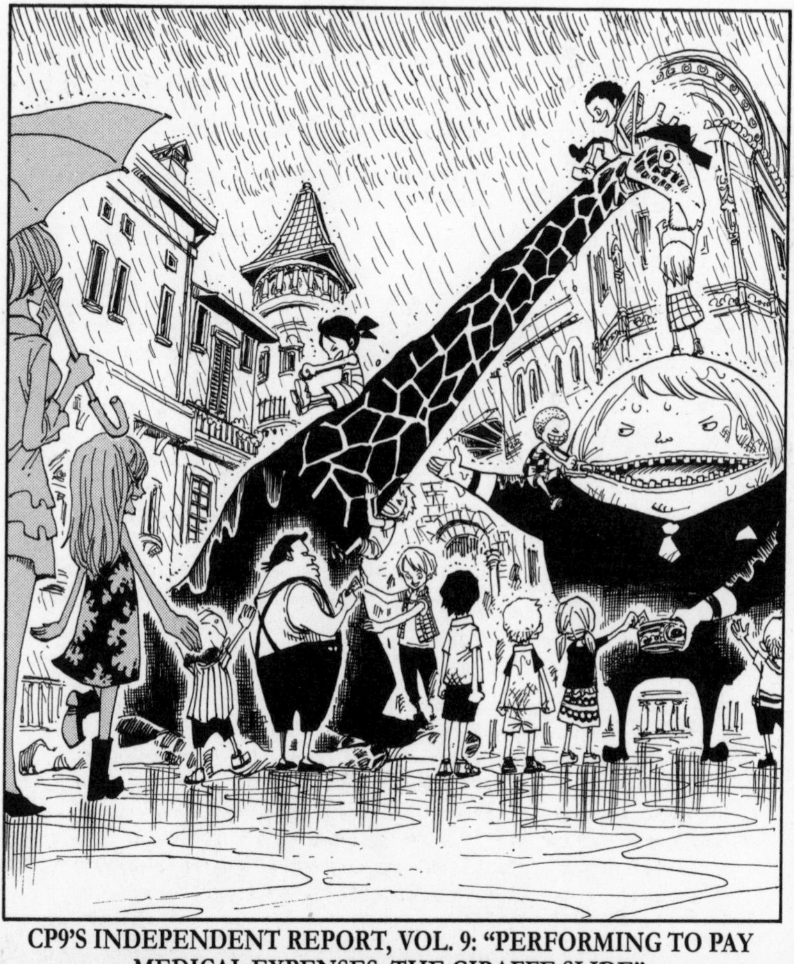

CP9'S INDEPENDENT REPORT, VOL. 9: "PERFORMING TO PAY MEDICAL EXPENSES: THE GIRAFFE SLIDE"

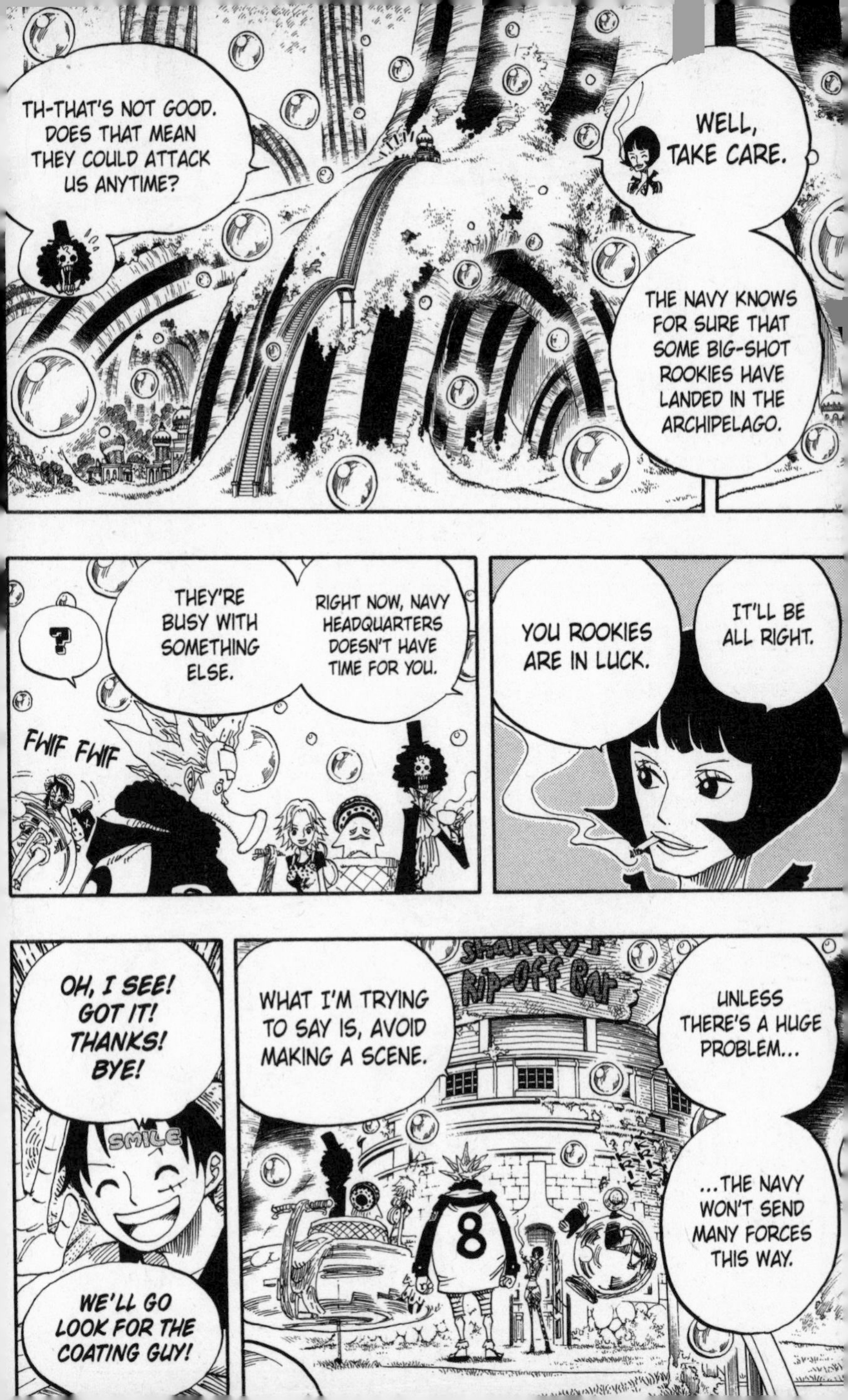
WELL, TAKE CARE.
THE NAVY KNOWS FOR SURE THAT SOME BIG-SHOT ROOKIES HAVE LANDED IN THE ARCHIPELAGO.
TH-THAT'S NOT GOOD. DOES THAT MEAN THEY COULD ATTACK US ANYTIME?
IT'LL BE ALL RIGHT.
YOU ROOKIES ARE IN LUCK.
RIGHT NOW, NAVY HEADQUARTERS DOESN'T HAVE TIME FOR YOU.
THEY'RE BUSY WITH SOMETHING ELSE.
?
FWIF FWIF
Rip-Off Bar
UNLESS THERE'S A HUGE PROBLEM...
...THE NAVY WON'T SEND MANY FORCES THIS WAY.
WHAT I'M TRYING TO SAY IS, AVOID MAKING A SCENE.
OH, I SEE! GOT IT! THANKS! BYE!
SMILE
WE'LL GO LOOK FOR THE COATING GUY!

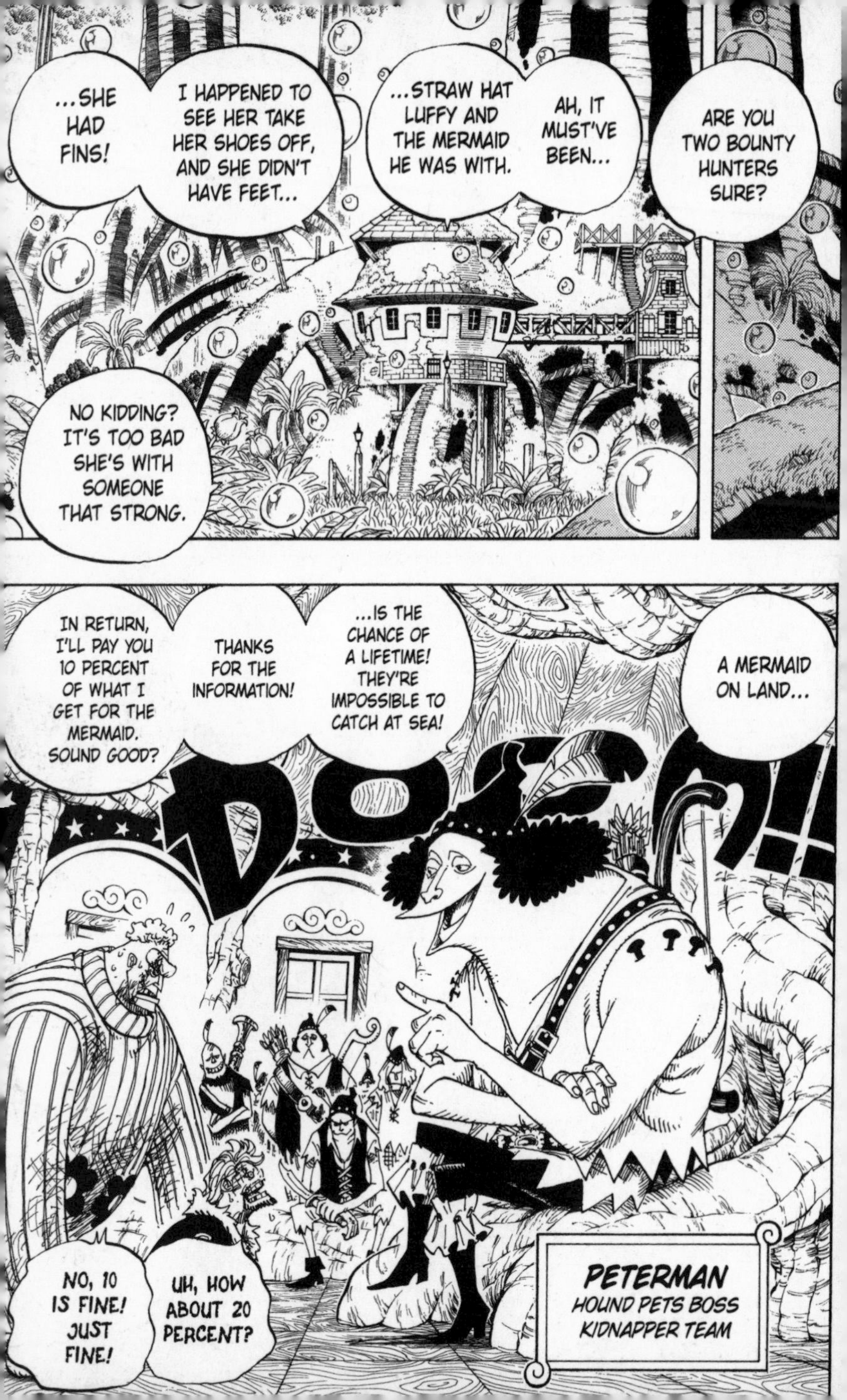

ARE YOU TWO BOUNTY HUNTERS SURE?
AH, IT MUST'VE BEEN...
...STRAW HAT LUFFY AND THE MERMAID HE WAS WITH.
I HAPPENED TO SEE HER TAKE HER SHOES OFF, AND SHE DIDN'T HAVE FEET...
...SHE HAD FINS!
NO KIDDING? IT'S TOO BAD SHE'S WITH SOMEONE THAT STRONG.
A MERMAID ON LAND...
...IS THE CHANCE OF A LIFETIME! THEY'RE IMPOSSIBLE TO CATCH AT SEA!
THANKS FOR THE INFORMATION!
IN RETURN, I'LL PAY YOU 10 PERCENT OF WHAT I GET FOR THE MERMAID. SOUND GOOD?
PETERMAN
HOUND PETS BOSS
KIDNAPPER TEAM
UH, HOW ABOUT 20 PERCENT?
NO, 10 IS FINE! JUST FINE!

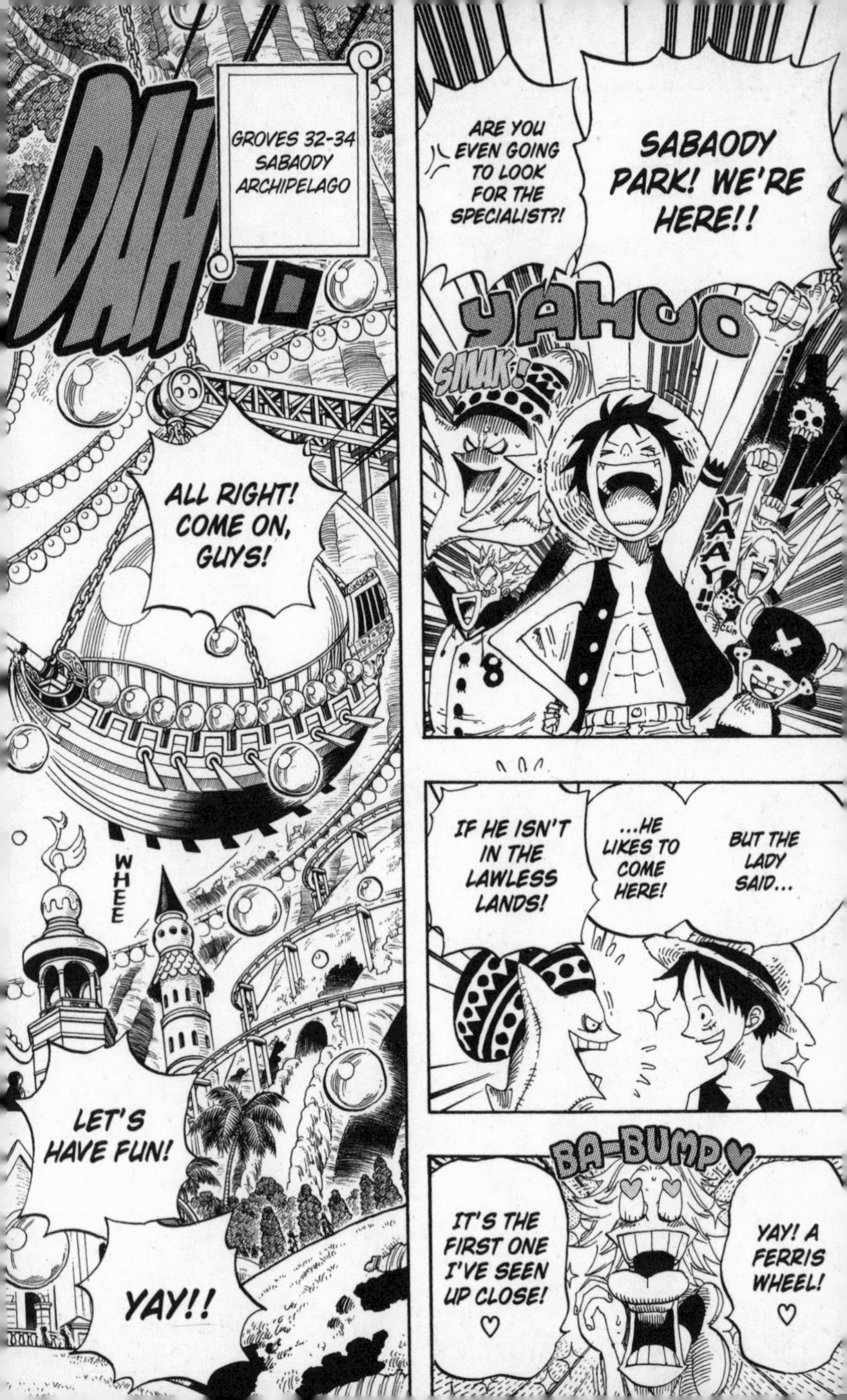
SABAODY PARK! WE'RE HERE!!
ARE YOU EVEN GOING TO LOOK FOR THE SPECIALIST?!
YAHOO
SMAK!
YAAY!!
BUT THE LADY SAID...
...HE LIKES TO COME HERE!
IF HE ISN'T IN THE LAWLESS LANDS!
BA-BUMP♥
YAY! A FERRIS WHEEL! ♡
IT'S THE FIRST ONE I'VE SEEN UP CLOSE! ♡
GROVES 32-34 SABAODY ARCHIPELAGO
ALL RIGHT! COME ON, GUYS!
WHEE
LET'S HAVE FUN!
YAY!!

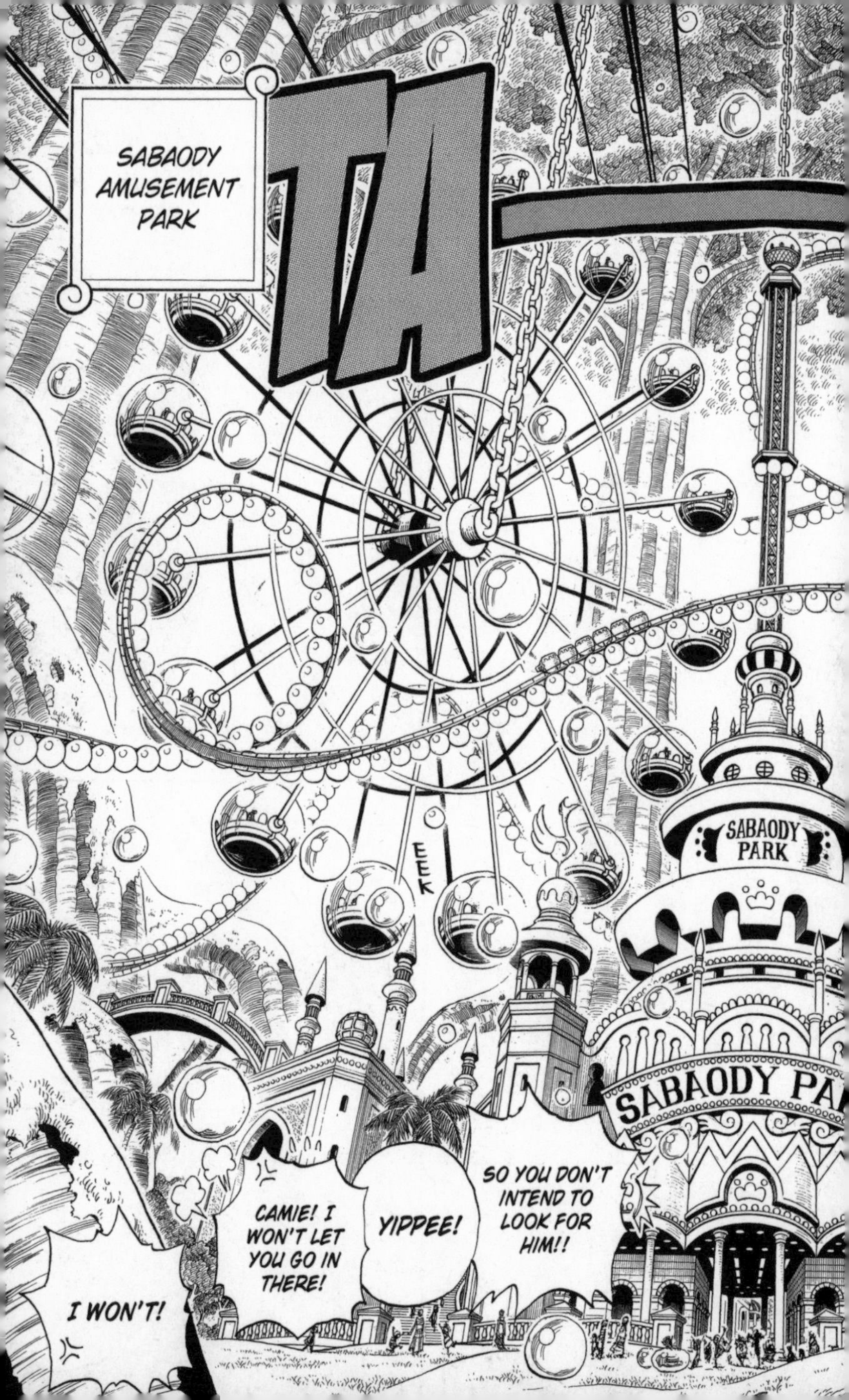
SABAODY AMUSEMENT PARK
TA—
SABAODY PARK
EEK
SO YOU DON'T INTEND TO LOOK FOR HIM!!
YIPPEE!
CAMIE! I WON'T LET YOU GO IN THERE!
I WON'T!

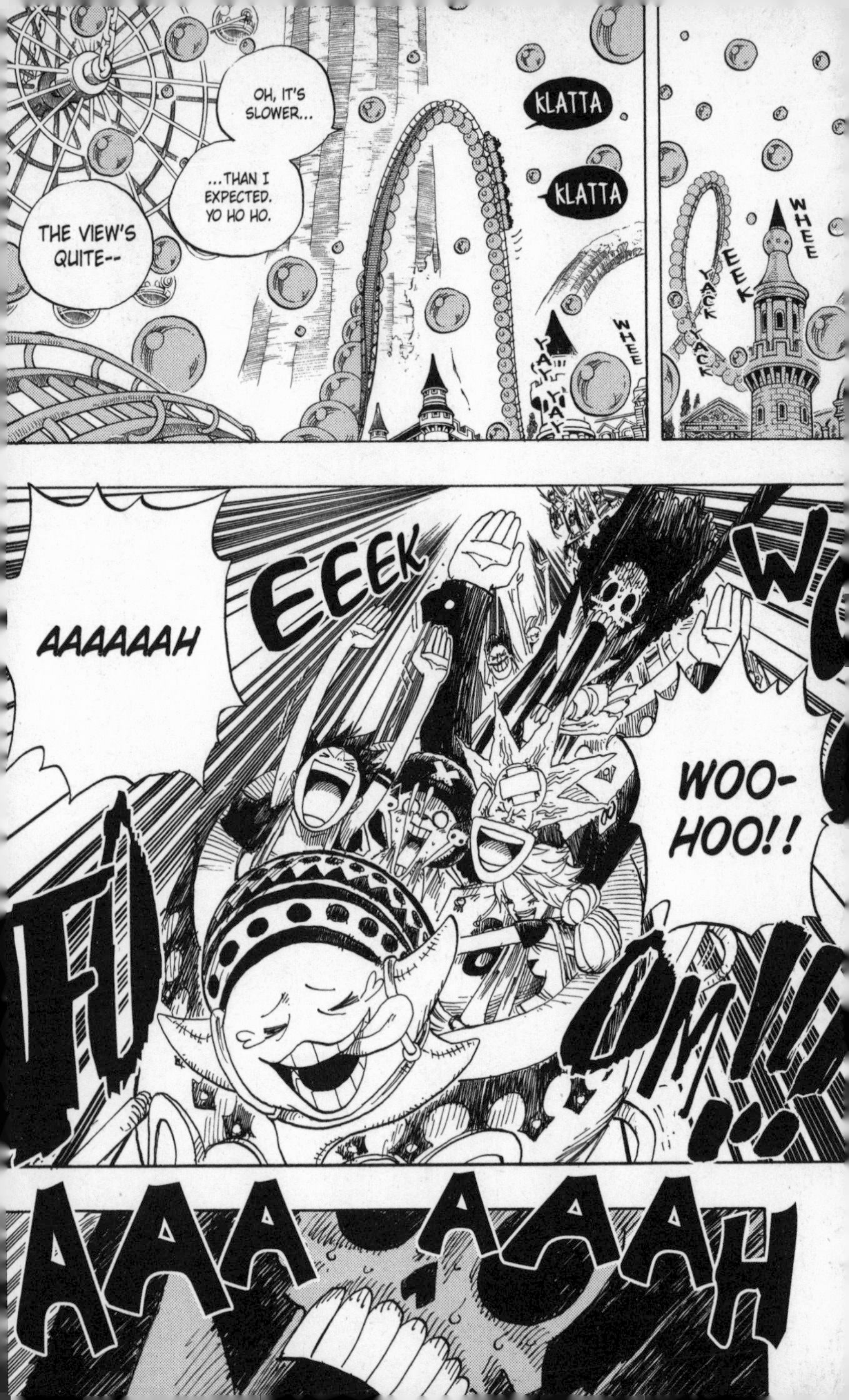
WHEE
EEK
YACK
YACK
KLATTA
KLATTA
WHEE
YAY YAY
OH, IT'S SLOWER...
...THAN I EXPECTED. YO HO HO.
THE VIEW'S QUITE--
WO
EEEK
WOO-HOO!!
AAAAAAH
OM!!
AAA-AAAAH

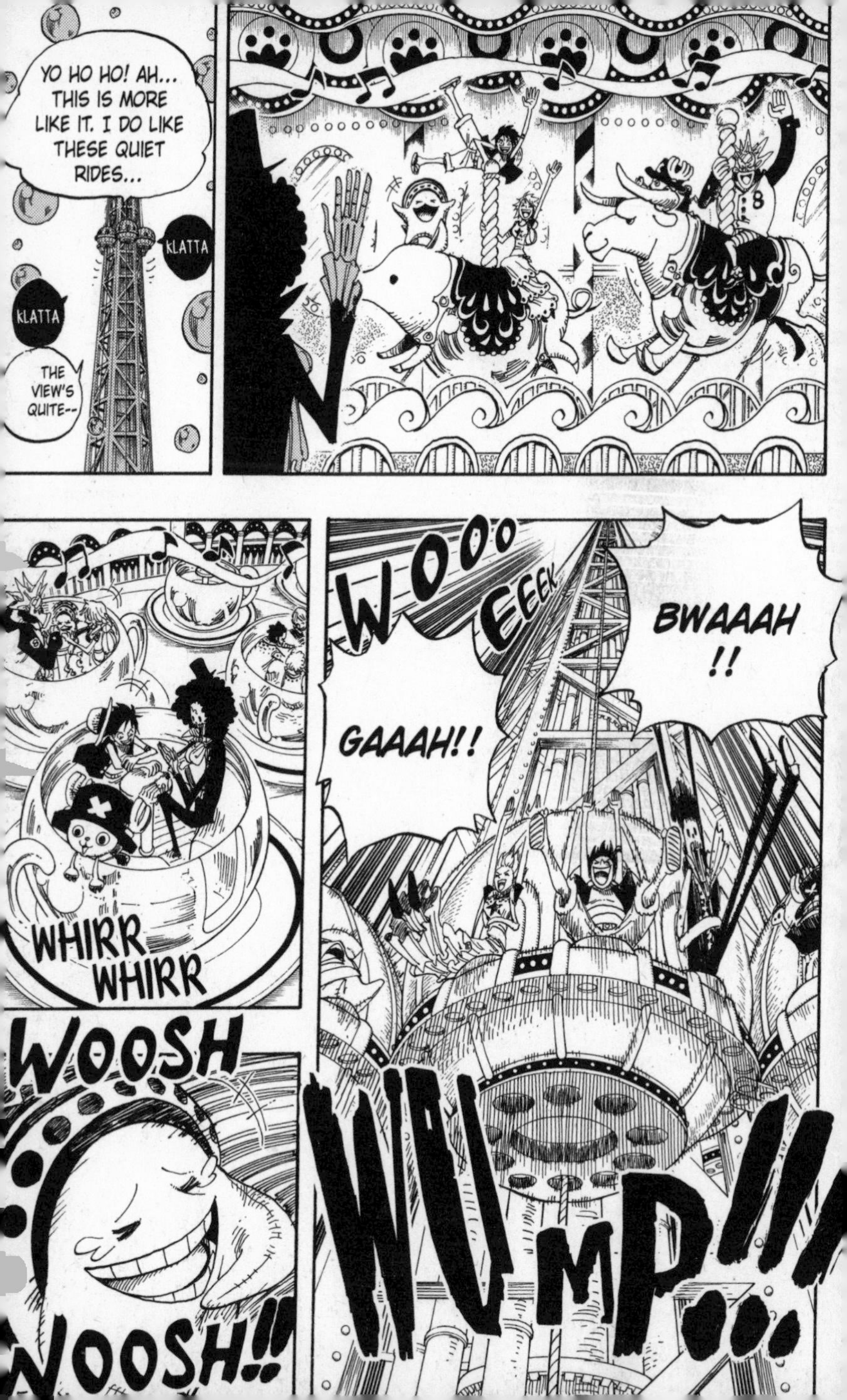
YO HO HO! AH... THIS IS MORE LIKE IT. I DO LIKE THESE QUIET RIDES...
KLATTA
KLATTA
THE VIEW'S QUITE--
WOOO
EEEK
BWAAAH!!
GAAAH!!
WUMP!!!
WHIRR WHIRR
WOOSH
WOOSH!!

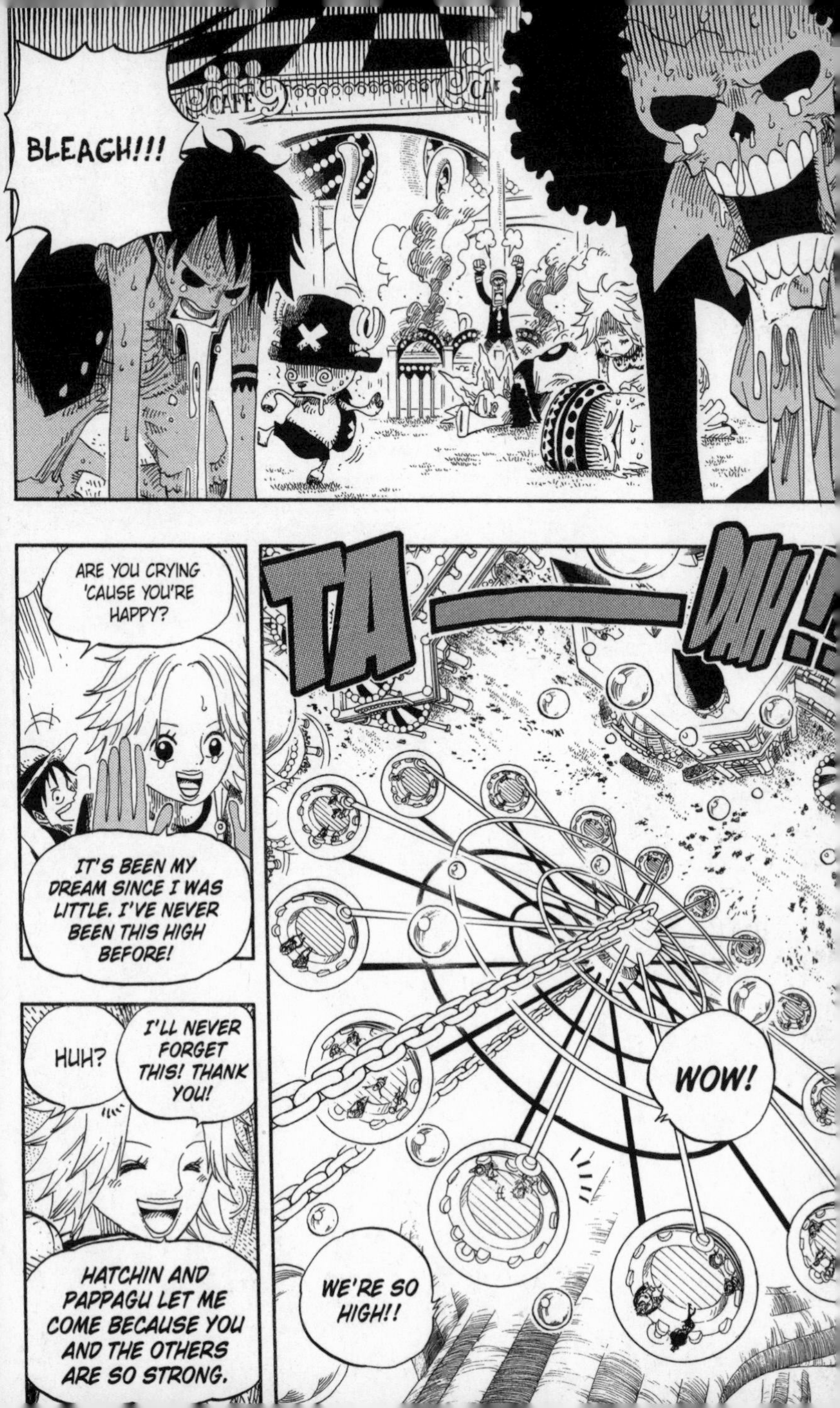
BLEACH!!!
TA—DAH!!
WOW!
WE'RE SO HIGH!!
ARE YOU CRYING 'CAUSE YOU'RE HAPPY?
IT'S BEEN MY DREAM SINCE I WAS LITTLE. I'VE NEVER BEEN THIS HIGH BEFORE!
I'LL NEVER FORGET THIS! THANK YOU!
HUH?
HATCHIN AND PAPPAGU LET ME COME BECAUSE YOU AND THE OTHERS ARE SO STRONG.

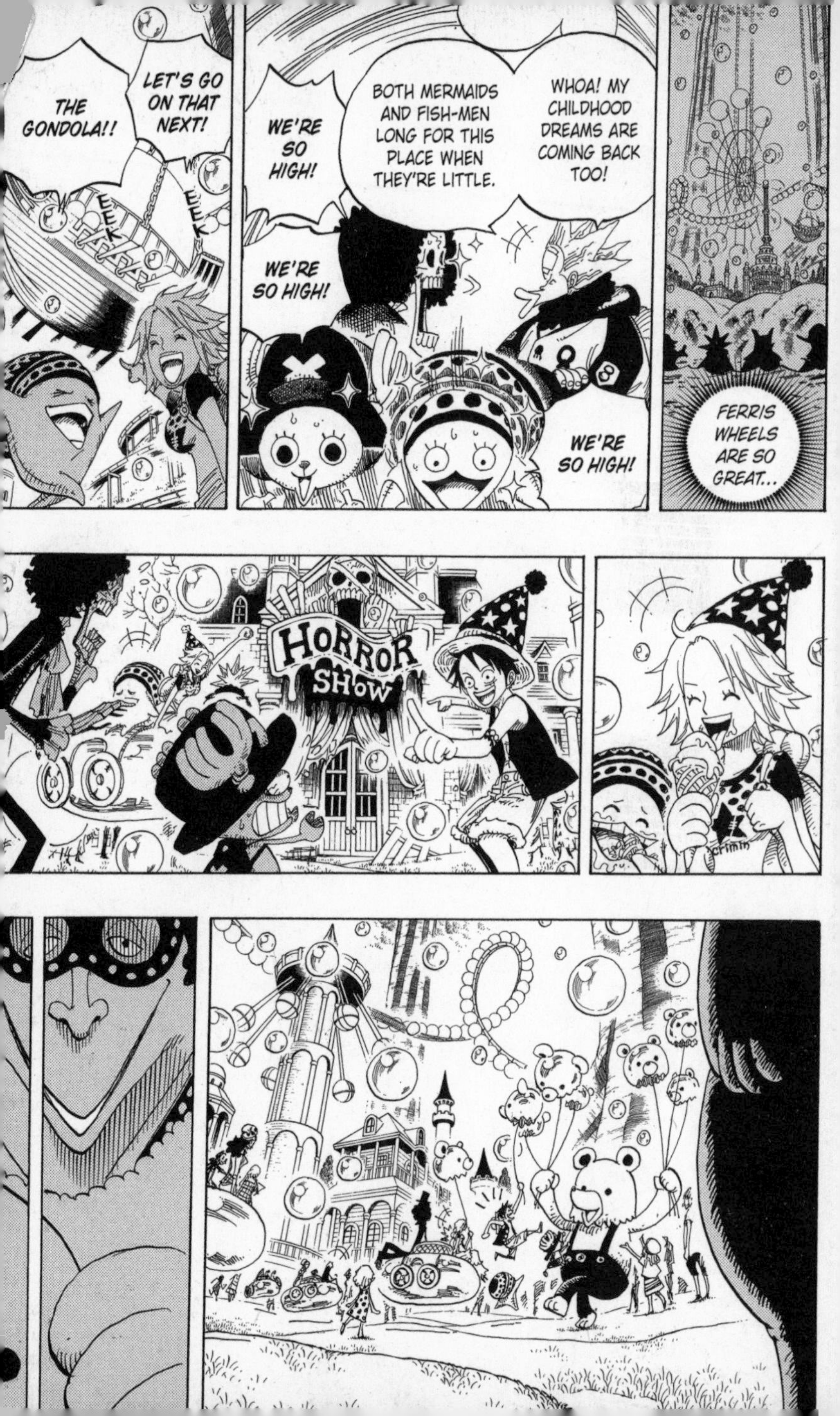
FERRIS WHEELS ARE SO GREAT...
WHOA! MY CHILDHOOD DREAMS ARE COMING BACK TOO!
BOTH MERMAIDS AND FISH-MEN LONG FOR THIS PLACE WHEN THEY'RE LITTLE.
WE'RE SO HIGH!
WE'RE SO HIGH!
WE'RE SO HIGH!
LET'S GO ON THAT NEXT!
THE GONDOLA!!
EEK
EEK
HORROR SHOW

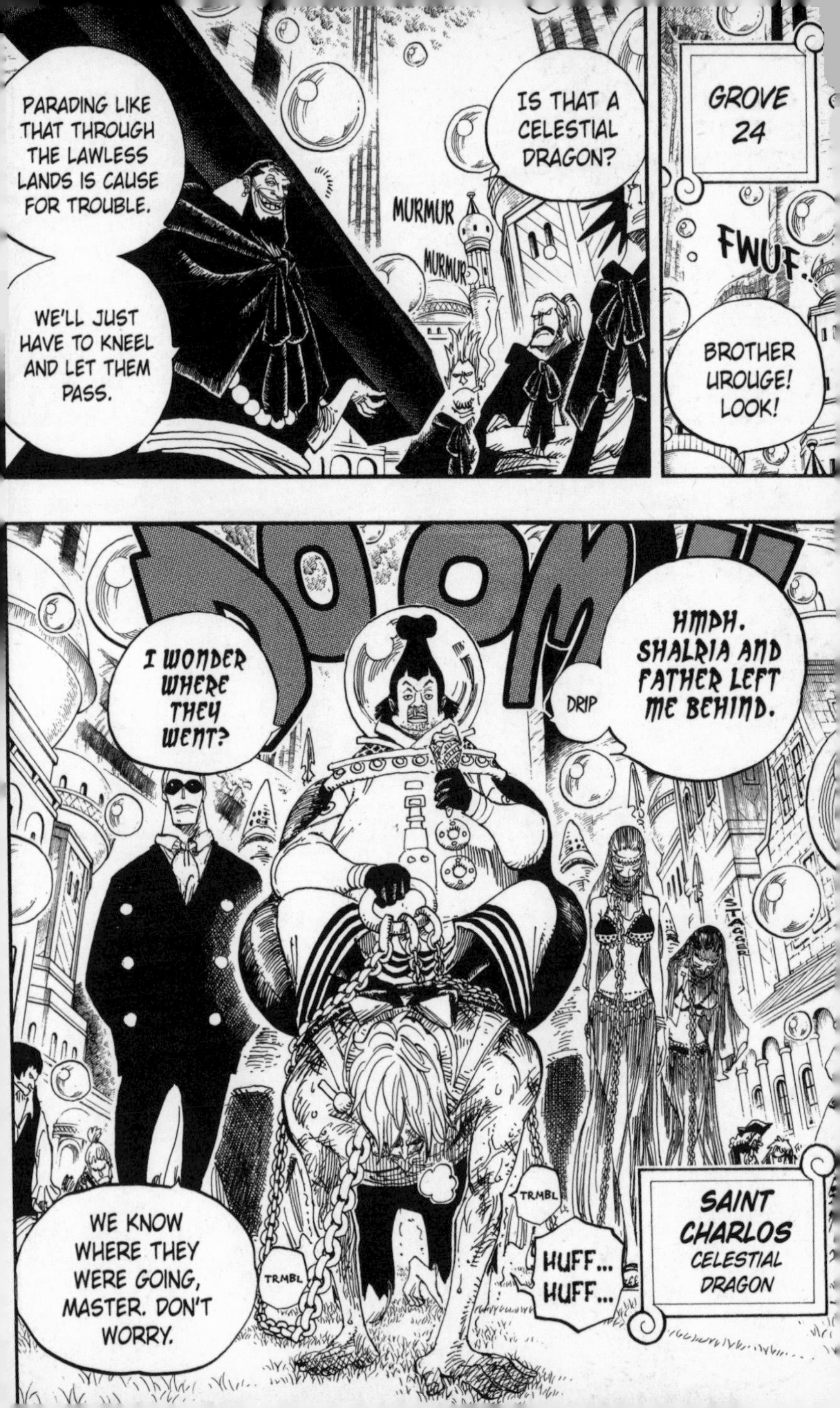

GROVE 24
FWUF...
BROTHER UROUGE! LOOK!
IS THAT A CELESTIAL DRAGON?
MURMUR
MURMUR
PARADING LIKE THAT THROUGH THE LAWLESS LANDS IS CAUSE FOR TROUBLE.
WE'LL JUST HAVE TO KNEEL AND LET THEM PASS.
HMPH. SHALRIA AND FATHER LEFT ME BEHIND.
DRIP
I WONDER WHERE THEY WENT?
STAGGER
SAINT CHARLOS
CELESTIAL DRAGON
TRMBL
HUFF... HUFF...
TRMBL
WE KNOW WHERE THEY WERE GOING, MASTER. DON'T WORRY.

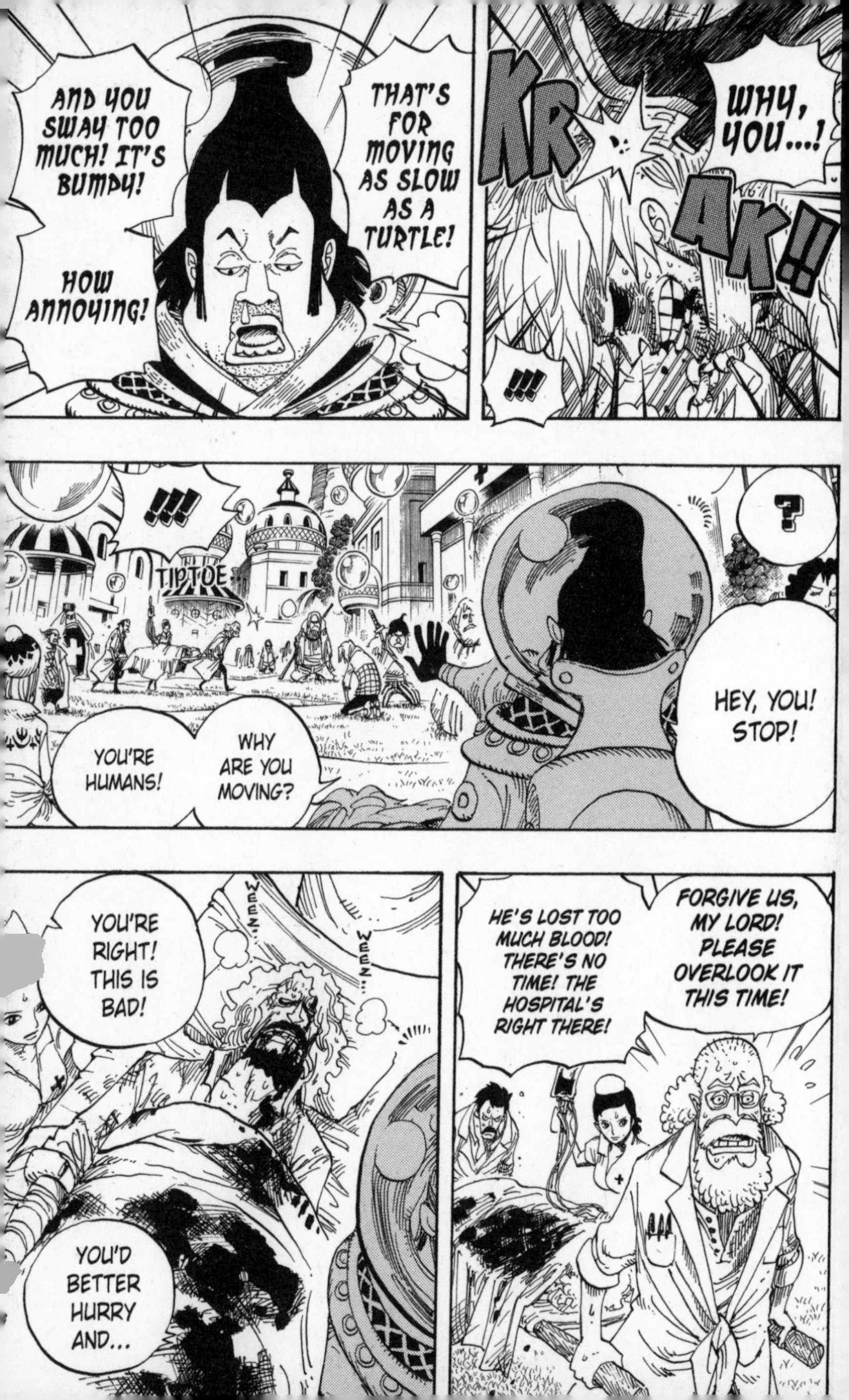
WHY, YOU...!
KRAK!!
!!!
THAT'S FOR MOVING AS SLOW AS A TURTLE!
AND YOU SWAY TOO MUCH! IT'S BUMPY!
HOW ANNOYING!
?
HEY, YOU! STOP!
!!!
TIPTOE
WHY ARE YOU MOVING?
YOU'RE HUMANS!
FORGIVE US, MY LORD! PLEASE OVERLOOK IT THIS TIME!
HE'S LOST TOO MUCH BLOOD! THERE'S NO TIME! THE HOSPITAL'S RIGHT THERE!
YOU'RE RIGHT! THIS IS BAD!
WEEZ...
WEEZ...
YOU'D BETTER HURRY AND...

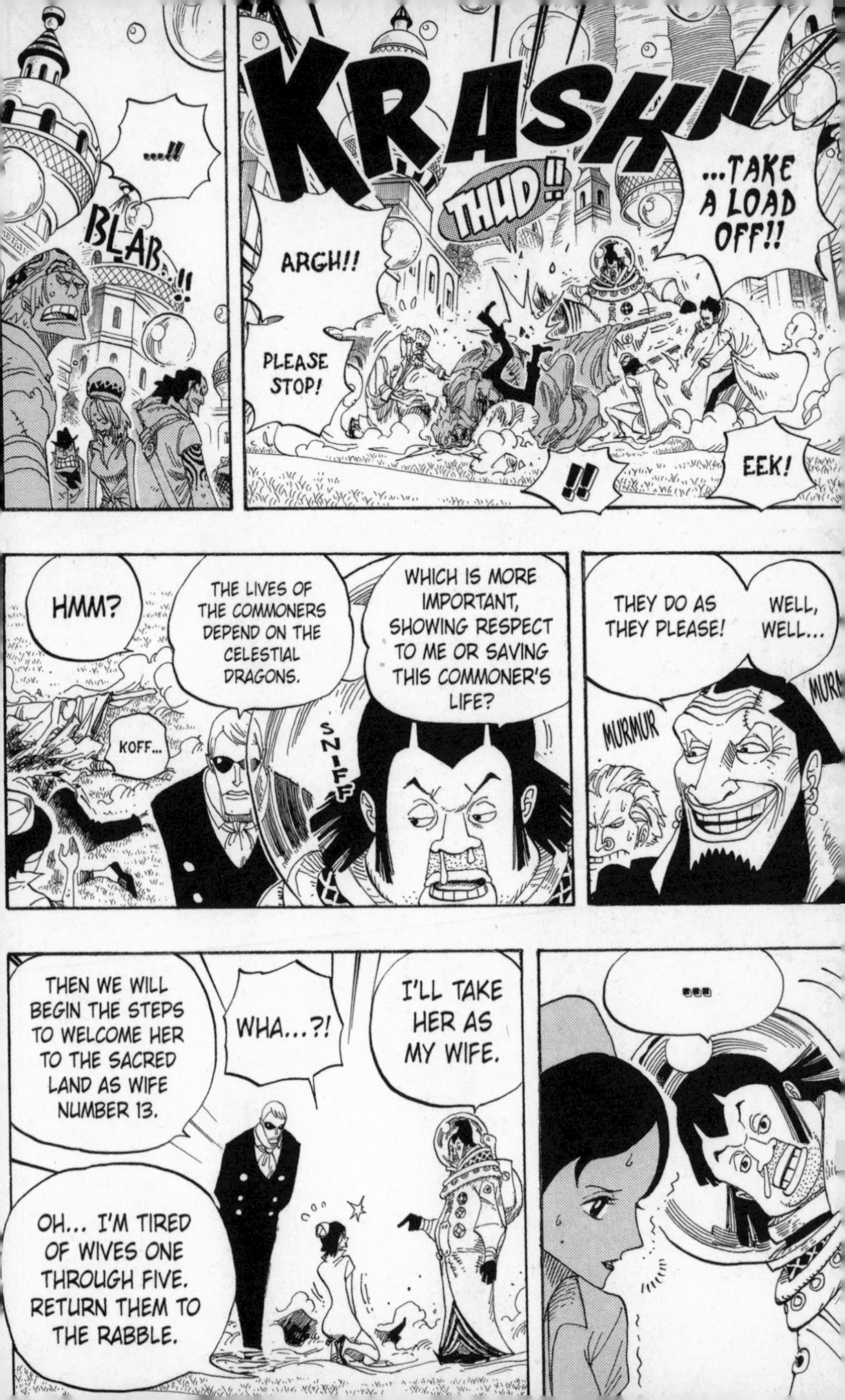
KRASH
...TAKE A LOAD OFF!!
THUD!!
ARGH!!
PLEASE STOP!
EEK!
!!
...!!
BLAB!!
WELL, WELL...
THEY DO AS THEY PLEASE!
MURMUR
WHICH IS MORE IMPORTANT, SHOWING RESPECT TO ME OR SAVING THIS COMMONER'S LIFE?
SNIFF
THE LIVES OF THE COMMONERS DEPEND ON THE CELESTIAL DRAGONS.
HMM?
KOFF...
...
I'LL TAKE HER AS MY WIFE.
WHA...?!
THEN WE WILL BEGIN THE STEPS TO WELCOME HER TO THE SACRED LAND AS WIFE NUMBER 13.
OH... I'M TIRED OF WIVES ONE THROUGH FIVE. RETURN THEM TO THE RABBLE.

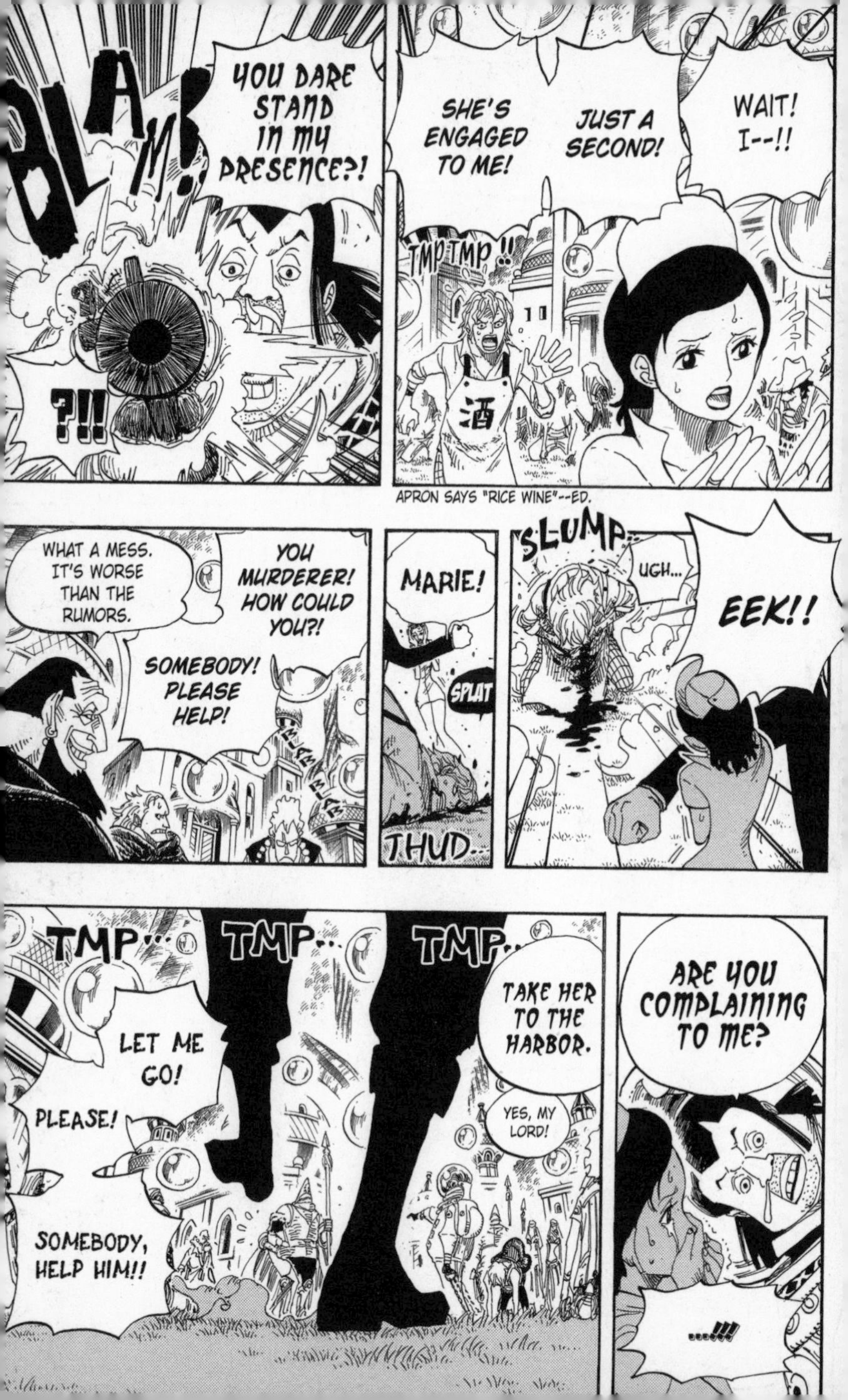
WAIT! I--!!
JUST A SECOND!
SHE'S ENGAGED TO ME!
TMP TMP !!
BLAM!
YOU DARE STAND IN MY PRESENCE?!
?!!
APRON SAYS "RICE WINE"--ED.
SLUMP...
UGH...
EEK!!
MARIE!
SPLAT
THUD..
YOU MURDERER! HOW COULD YOU?!
WHAT A MESS. IT'S WORSE THAN THE RUMORS.
SOMEBODY! PLEASE HELP!
ARE YOU COMPLAINING TO ME?
...!!!
TMP...
TMP...
TMP...
TAKE HER TO THE HARBOR.
YES, MY LORD!
LET ME GO!
PLEASE!
SOMEBODY, HELP HIM!!

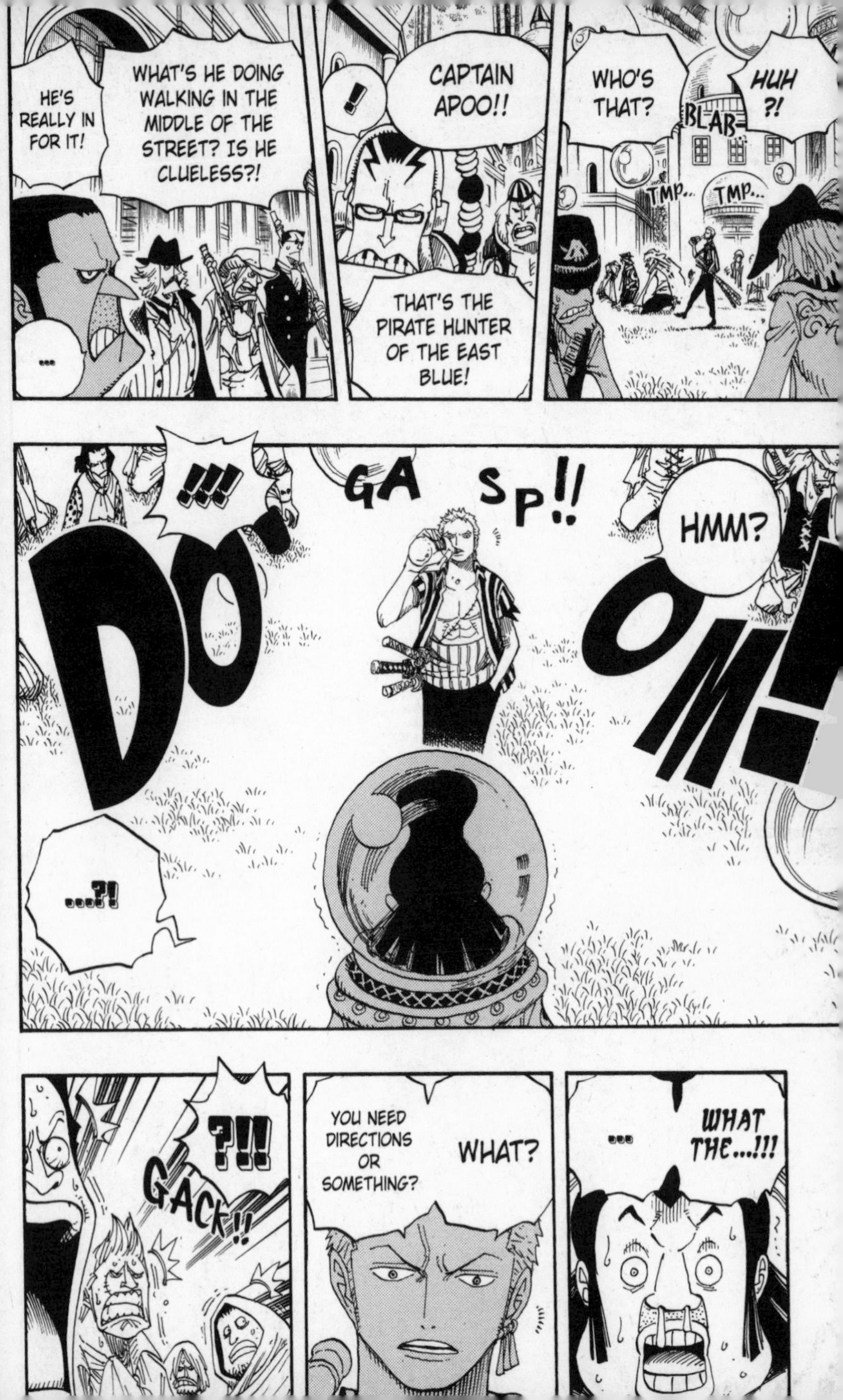
HUH ?!
WHO'S THAT?
BLAB
TMP...
TMP...
CAPTAIN APOO!!
!
THAT'S THE PIRATE HUNTER OF THE EAST BLUE!
WHAT'S HE DOING WALKING IN THE MIDDLE OF THE STREET? IS HE CLUELESS?!
HE'S REALLY IN FOR IT!
...
HMM?
GASP!!
!!!
DOOM!!
...?!
WHAT THE...!!!
...
WHAT?
YOU NEED DIRECTIONS OR SOMETHING?
?!!
GACK!!

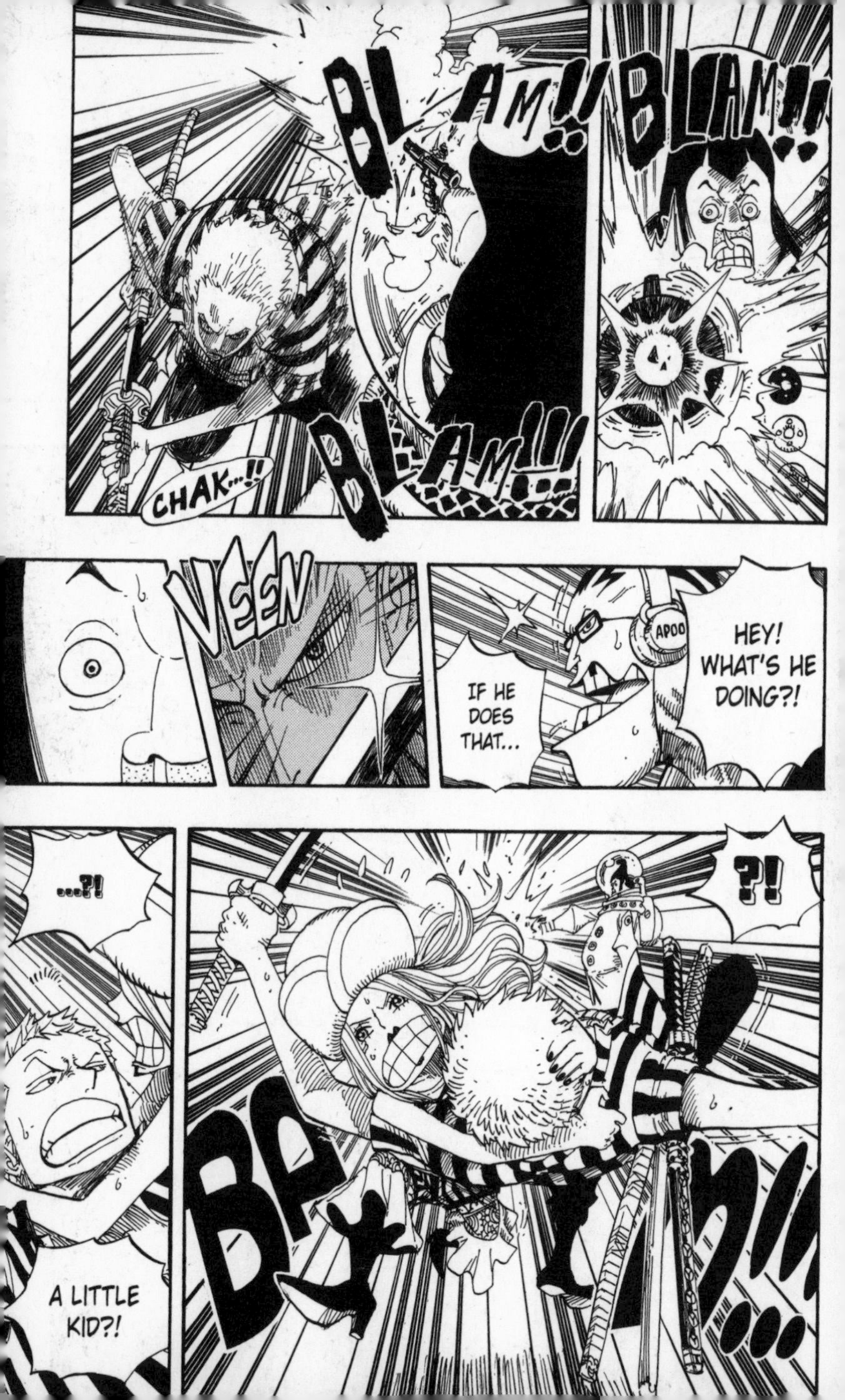
BLAM!!
BLAM!!
CHAK...!!
BLAM!!!
HEY! WHAT'S HE DOING?!
APOO
IF HE DOES THAT...
VEEN
?!
...?!
A LITTLE KID?!

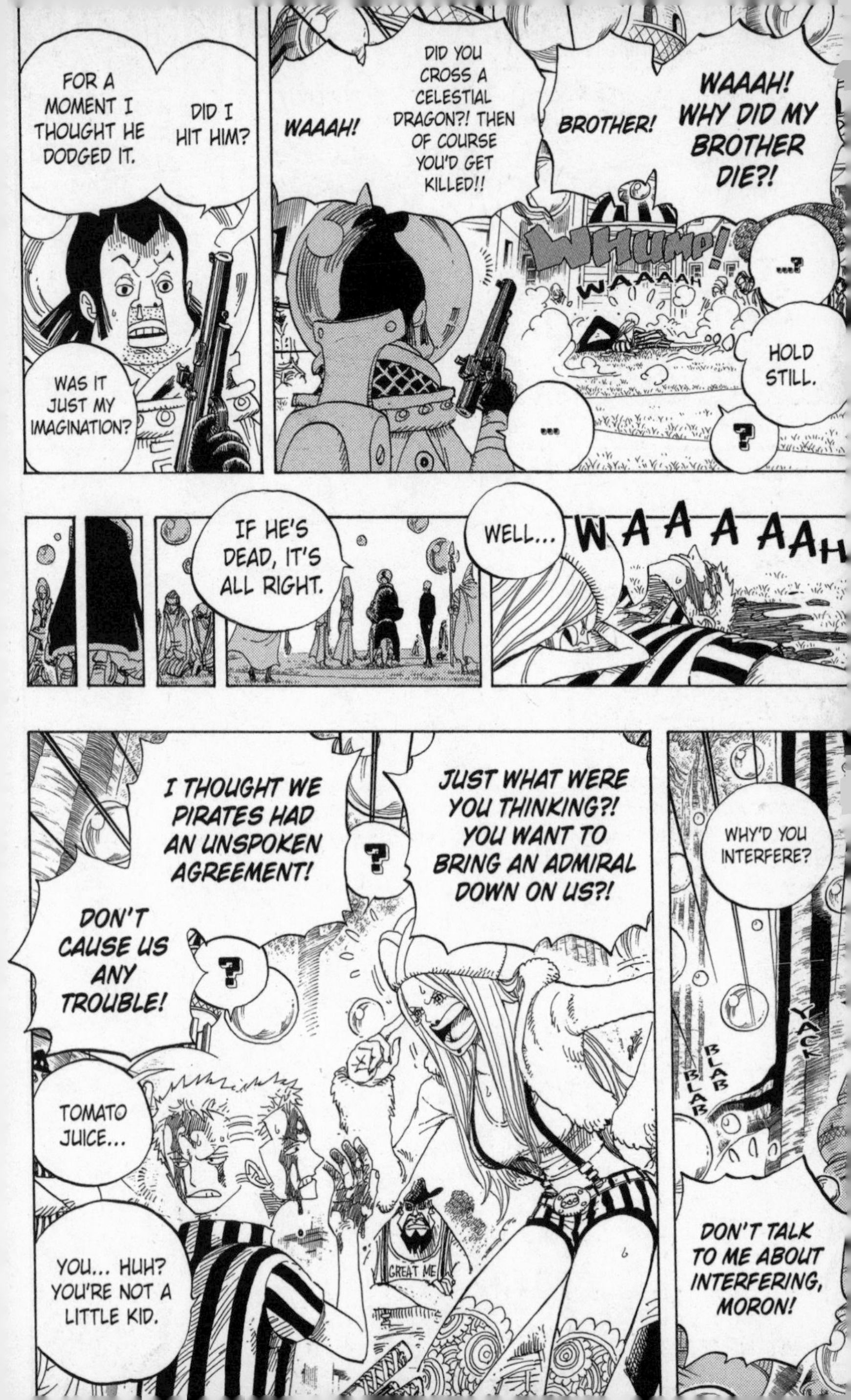
WAAAH! WHY DID MY BROTHER DIE?!
BROTHER!
DID YOU CROSS A CELESTIAL DRAGON?! THEN OF COURSE YOU'D GET KILLED!!
WAAAH!
...?
WHUMP!
WAAAAAH
HOLD STILL.
?
...
DID I HIT HIM?
FOR A MOMENT I THOUGHT HE DODGED IT.
WAS IT JUST MY IMAGINATION?
WAAAAAH
WELL...
IF HE'S DEAD, IT'S ALL RIGHT.
WHY'D YOU INTERFERE?
YACK
BLAB BLAB
DON'T TALK TO ME ABOUT INTERFERING, MORON!
JUST WHAT WERE YOU THINKING?! YOU WANT TO BRING AN ADMIRAL DOWN ON US?!
?
I THOUGHT WE PIRATES HAD AN UNSPOKEN AGREEMENT!
DON'T CAUSE US ANY TROUBLE!
?
TOMATO JUICE...
GREAT ME
YOU... HUH? YOU'RE NOT A LITTLE KID.

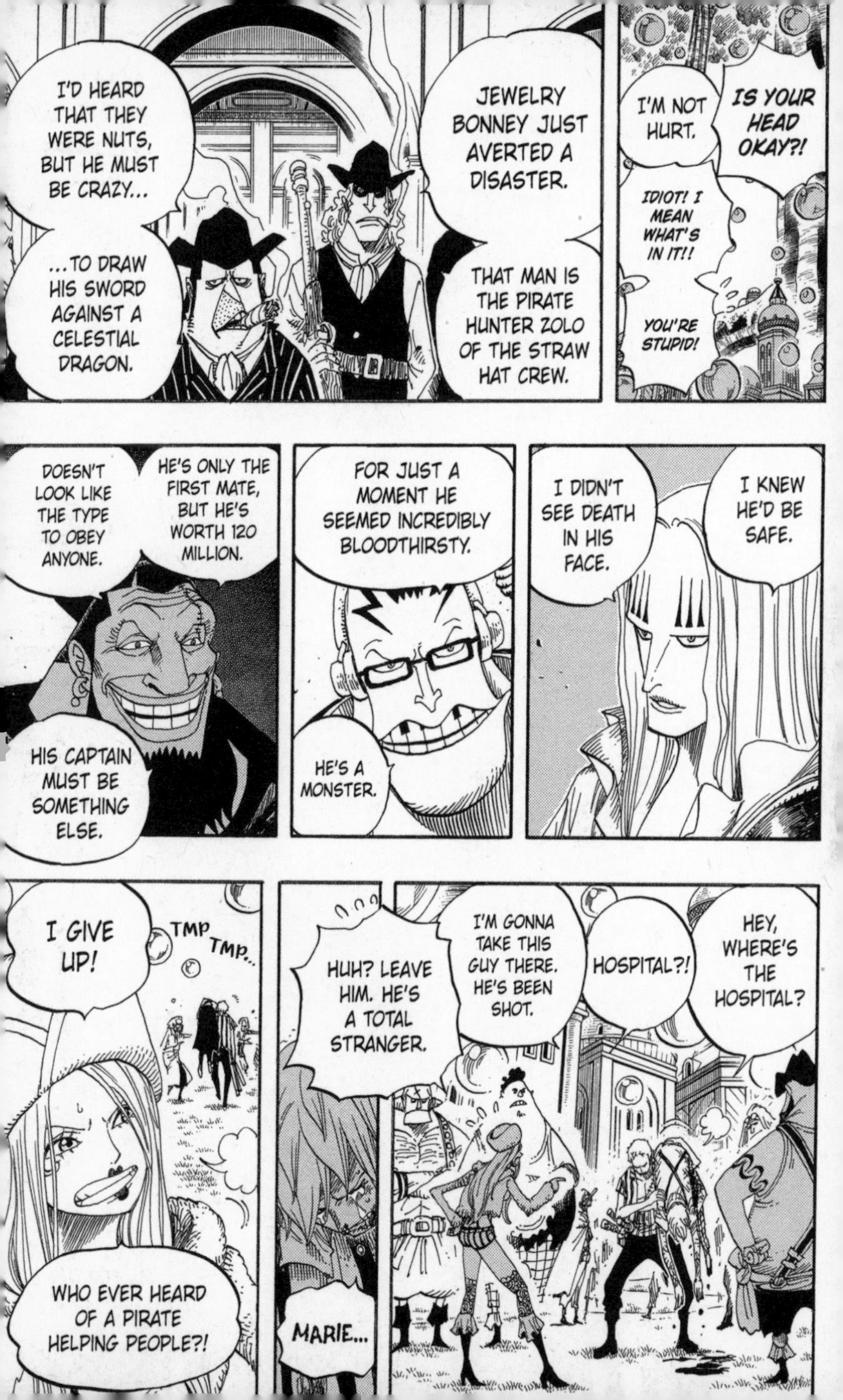
IS YOUR HEAD OKAY?!
I'M NOT HURT.
IDIOT! I MEAN WHAT'S IN IT!!
YOU'RE STUPID!
JEWELRY BONNEY JUST AVERTED A DISASTER.
THAT MAN IS THE PIRATE HUNTER ZOLO OF THE STRAW HAT CREW.
I'D HEARD THAT THEY WERE NUTS, BUT HE MUST BE CRAZY...
...TO DRAW HIS SWORD AGAINST A CELESTIAL DRAGON.
I KNEW HE'D BE SAFE.
I DIDN'T SEE DEATH IN HIS FACE.
FOR JUST A MOMENT HE SEEMED INCREDIBLY BLOODTHIRSTY.
HE'S A MONSTER.
HE'S ONLY THE FIRST MATE, BUT HE'S WORTH 120 MILLION.
DOESN'T LOOK LIKE THE TYPE TO OBEY ANYONE.
HIS CAPTAIN MUST BE SOMETHING ELSE.
HEY, WHERE'S THE HOSPITAL?
HOSPITAL?!
I'M GONNA TAKE THIS GUY THERE. HE'S BEEN SHOT.
HUH? LEAVE HIM. HE'S A TOTAL STRANGER.
MARIE...
I GIVE UP!
TMP TMP...
WHO EVER HEARD OF A PIRATE HELPING PEOPLE?!

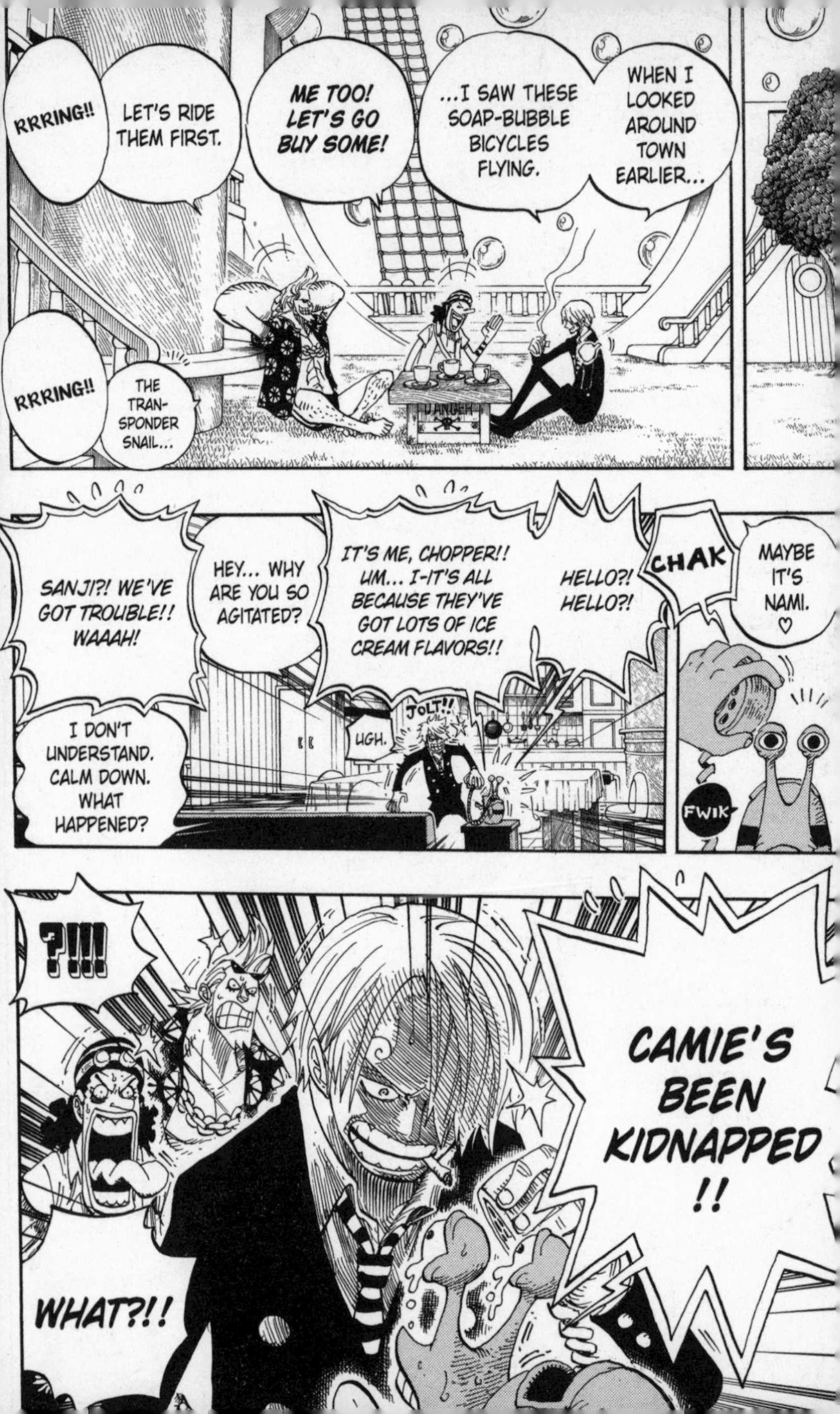
WHEN I LOOKED AROUND TOWN EARLIER...
...I SAW THESE SOAP-BUBBLE BICYCLES FLYING.
ME TOO! LET'S GO BUY SOME!
LET'S RIDE THEM FIRST.
RRRING!!
THE TRAN-SPONDER SNAIL...
RRRING!!
MAYBE IT'S NAMI. ♡
CHAK
FWIK
HELLO?! HELLO?!
IT'S ME, CHOPPER!! UM... I-IT'S ALL BECAUSE THEY'VE GOT LOTS OF ICE CREAM FLAVORS!!
HEY... WHY ARE YOU SO AGITATED?
SANJI?! WE'VE GOT TROUBLE!! WAAAH!
JOLT!!
UGH.
I DON'T UNDERSTAND. CALM DOWN. WHAT HAPPENED?
CAMIE'S BEEN KIDNAPPED!!
?!!!
WHAT?!!

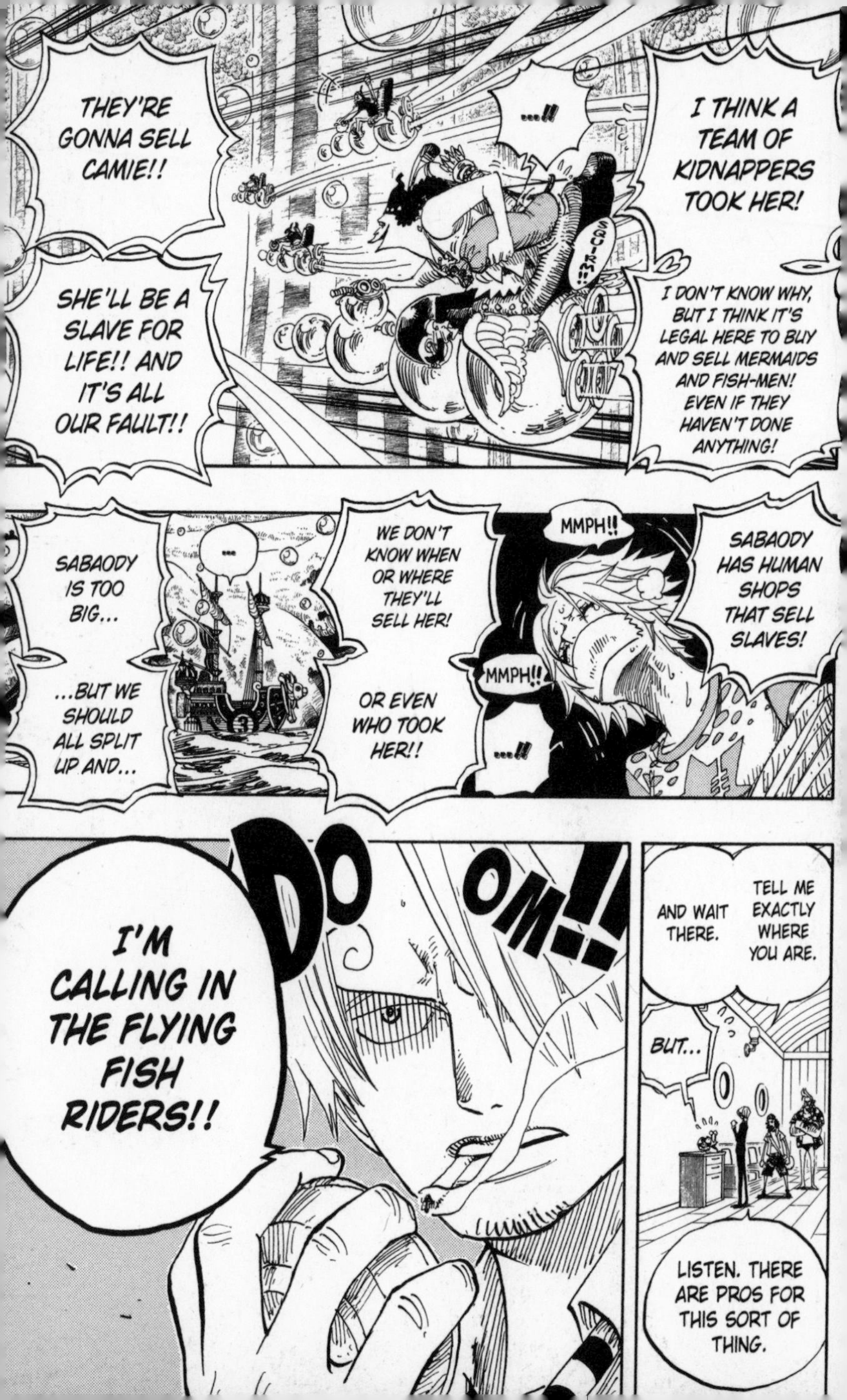
I THINK A TEAM OF KIDNAPPERS TOOK HER!
I DON'T KNOW WHY, BUT I THINK IT'S LEGAL HERE TO BUY AND SELL MERMAIDS AND FISH-MEN! EVEN IF THEY HAVEN'T DONE ANYTHING!
...!!
SQUIRM!!
THEY'RE GONNA SELL CAMIE!!
SHE'LL BE A SLAVE FOR LIFE!! AND IT'S ALL OUR FAULT!!
SABAODY HAS HUMAN SHOPS THAT SELL SLAVES!
MMPH!!
MMPH!!
...!!
WE DON'T KNOW WHEN OR WHERE THEY'LL SELL HER!
OR EVEN WHO TOOK HER!!
...
SABAODY IS TOO BIG...
...BUT WE SHOULD ALL SPLIT UP AND...
TELL ME EXACTLY WHERE YOU ARE.
AND WAIT THERE.
BUT...
LISTEN. THERE ARE PROS FOR THIS SORT OF THING.
DOOM!!
I'M CALLING IN THE FLYING FISH RIDERS!!

ONE PIECE **STORYBOARD PREVIEW!!** #25

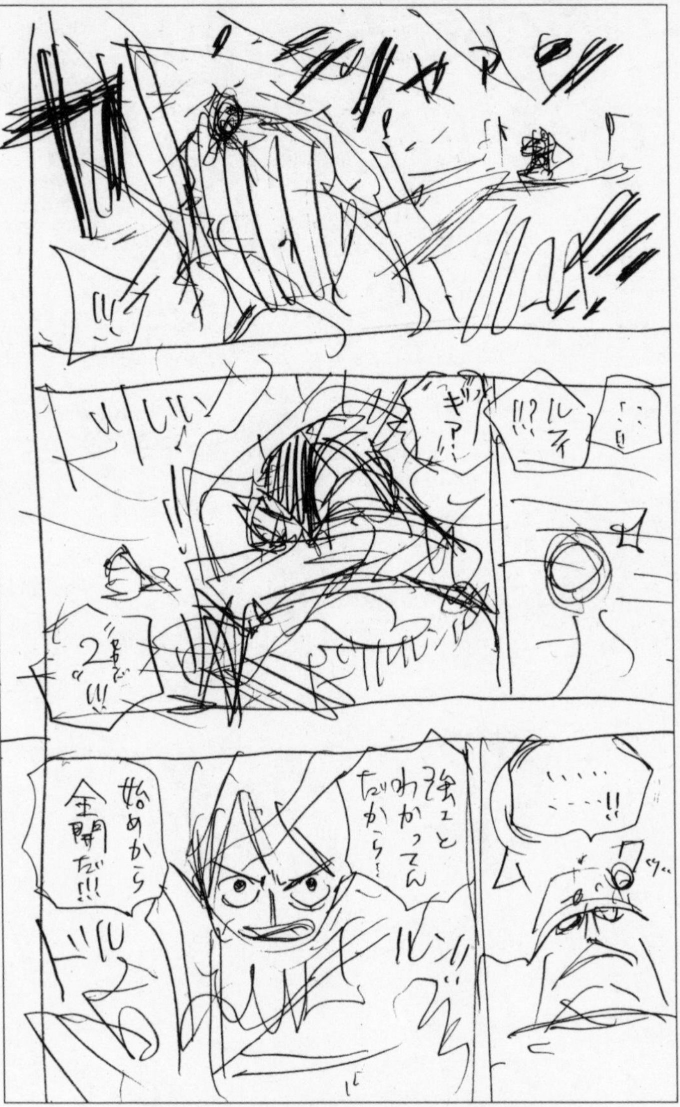
ルフィ!!?
ギア…
2
いご…!!
強ェとわかってんだから…
始めから全開だ!!!

SEE THE FINAL VERSION IN VOLUME 52, P. 126--ED.

Chapter 500:
THE EMBERS OF HISTORY

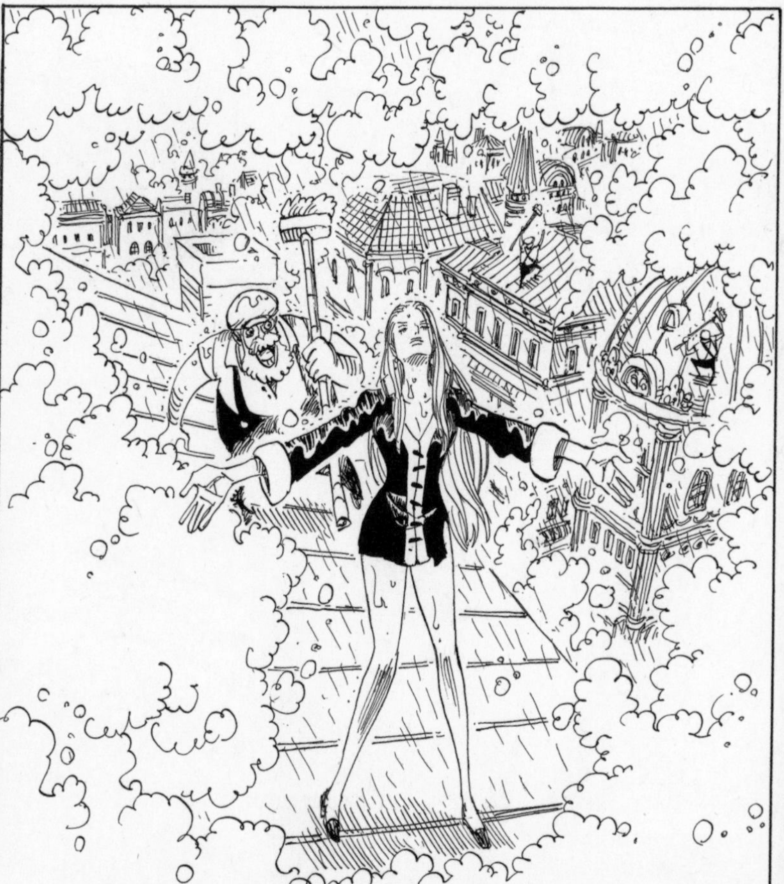

CP9'S INDEPENDENT REPORT, VOL. 10: "WORKING TO PAY MEDICAL EXPENSES: CLEANING UP THE TOWN"

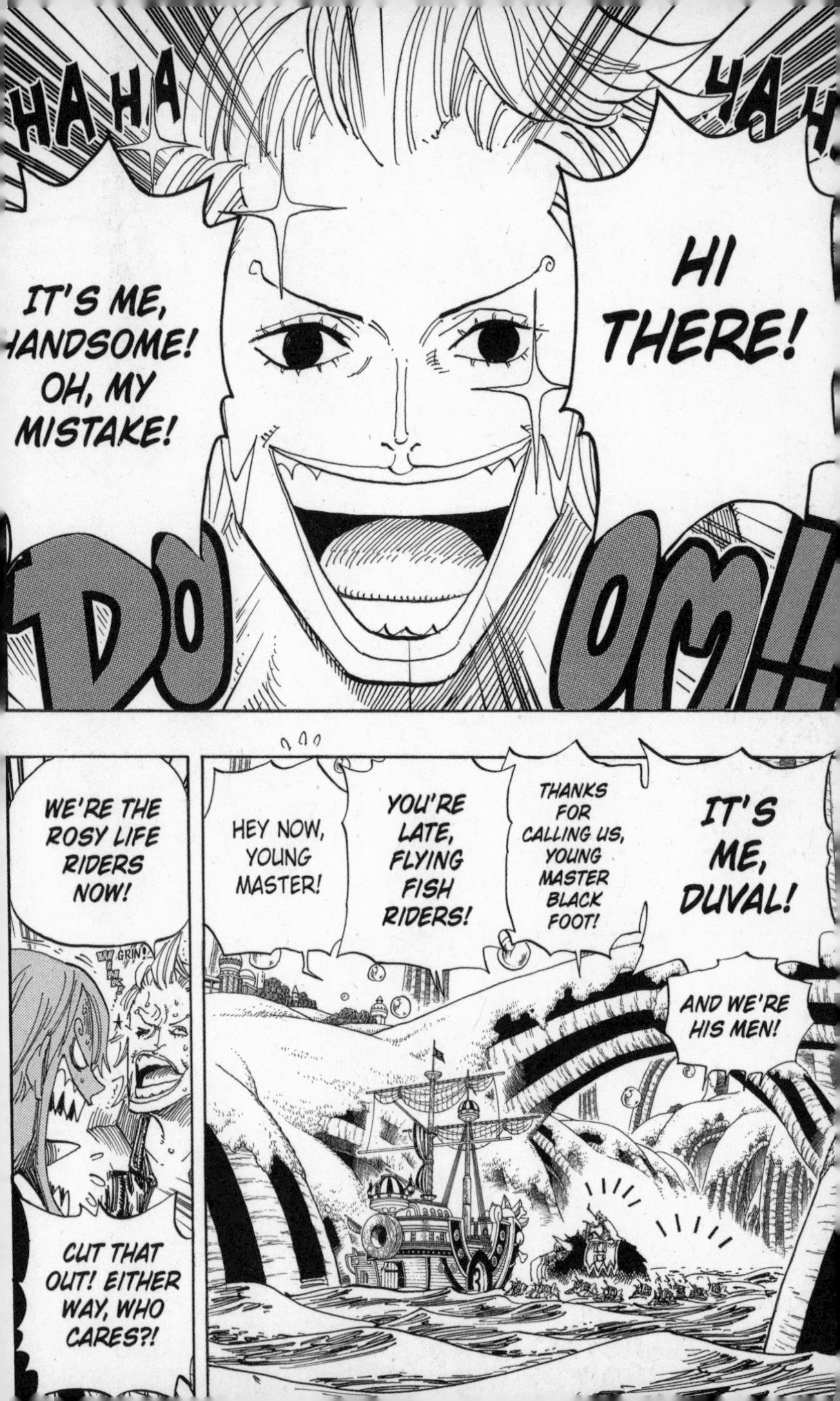
YAHA
HI THERE!
HAHAHA
IT'S ME, HANDSOME! OH, MY MISTAKE!
DOOM!!
IT'S ME, DUVAL!
THANKS FOR CALLING US, YOUNG MASTER BLACK FOOT!
YOU'RE LATE, FLYING FISH RIDERS!
HEY NOW, YOUNG MASTER!
AND WE'RE HIS MEN!
WE'RE THE ROSY LIFE RIDERS NOW!
GRIN
CUT THAT OUT! EITHER WAY, WHO CARES?!

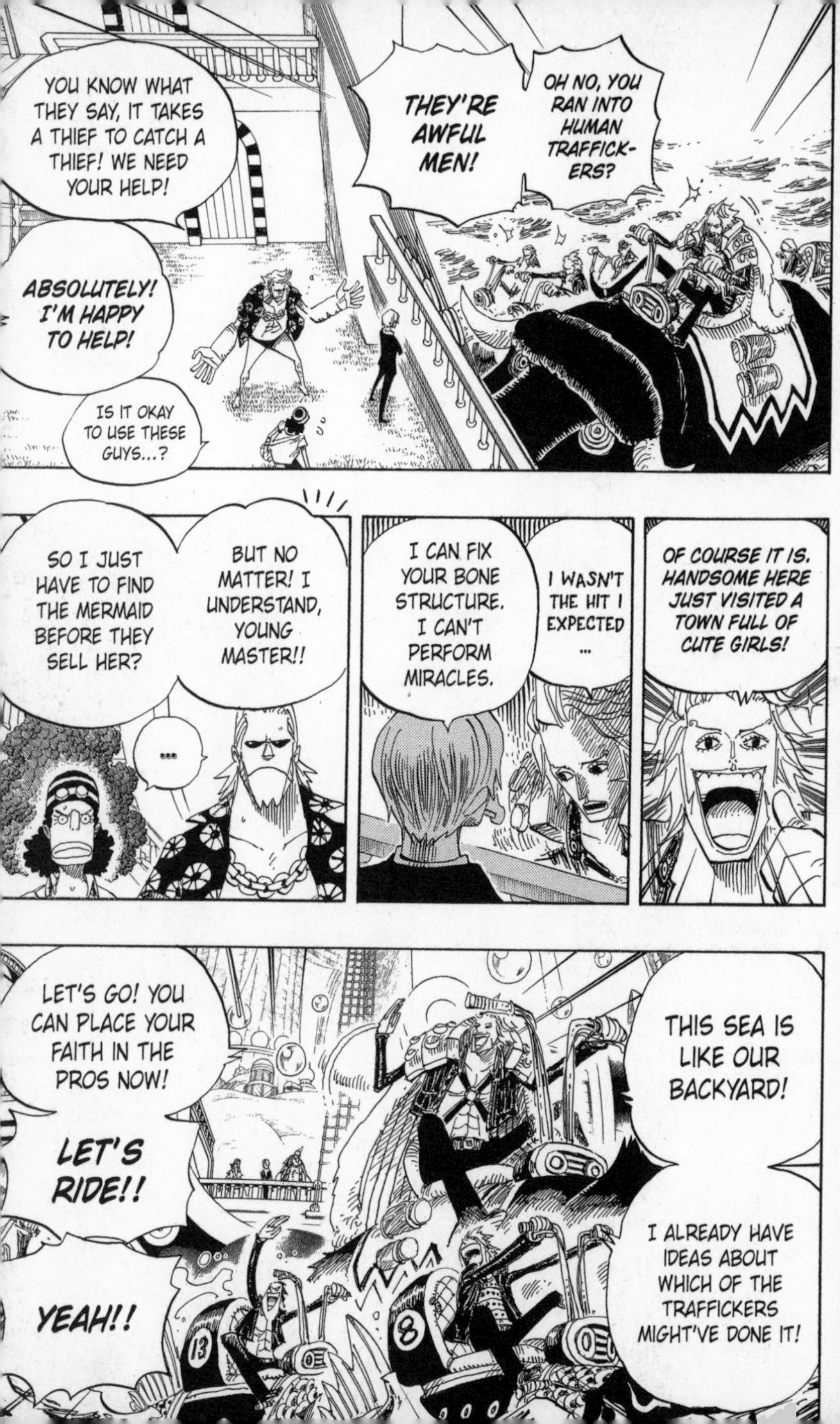
OH NO, YOU RAN INTO HUMAN TRAFFICK-ERS?
THEY'RE AWFUL MEN!
YOU KNOW WHAT THEY SAY, IT TAKES A THIEF TO CATCH A THIEF! WE NEED YOUR HELP!
ABSOLUTELY! I'M HAPPY TO HELP!
IS IT OKAY TO USE THESE GUYS...?
OF COURSE IT IS. HANDSOME HERE JUST VISITED A TOWN FULL OF CUTE GIRLS!
I WASN'T THE HIT I EXPECTED ...
I CAN FIX YOUR BONE STRUCTURE. I CAN'T PERFORM MIRACLES.
BUT NO MATTER! I UNDERSTAND, YOUNG MASTER!!
SO I JUST HAVE TO FIND THE MERMAID BEFORE THEY SELL HER?
...
THIS SEA IS LIKE OUR BACKYARD!
I ALREADY HAVE IDEAS ABOUT WHICH OF THE TRAFFICKERS MIGHT'VE DONE IT!
LET'S GO! YOU CAN PLACE YOUR FAITH IN THE PROS NOW!
LET'S RIDE!!
YEAH!!

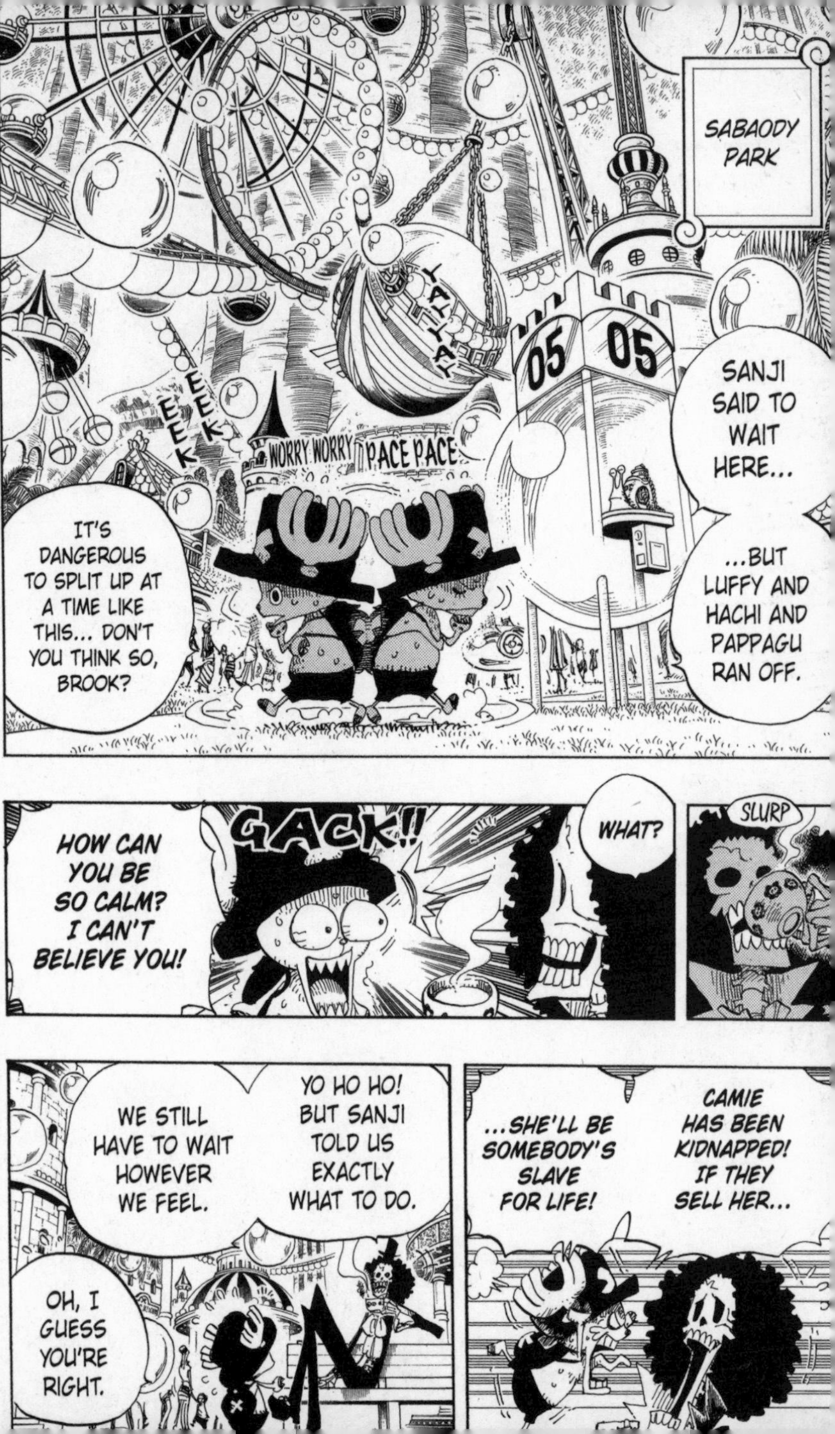
SABAODY PARK
SANJI SAID TO WAIT HERE...
...BUT LUFFY AND HACHI AND PAPPAGU RAN OFF.
05
05
PACE PACE
WORRY WORRY
EEK
EEK
IT'S DANGEROUS TO SPLIT UP AT A TIME LIKE THIS... DON'T YOU THINK SO, BROOK?
SLURP
WHAT?
GACK!!
HOW CAN YOU BE SO CALM? I CAN'T BELIEVE YOU!
CAMIE HAS BEEN KIDNAPPED! IF THEY SELL HER...
...SHE'LL BE SOMEBODY'S SLAVE FOR LIFE!
YO HO HO! BUT SANJI TOLD US EXACTLY WHAT TO DO.
WE STILL HAVE TO WAIT HOWEVER WE FEEL.
OH, I GUESS YOU'RE RIGHT.

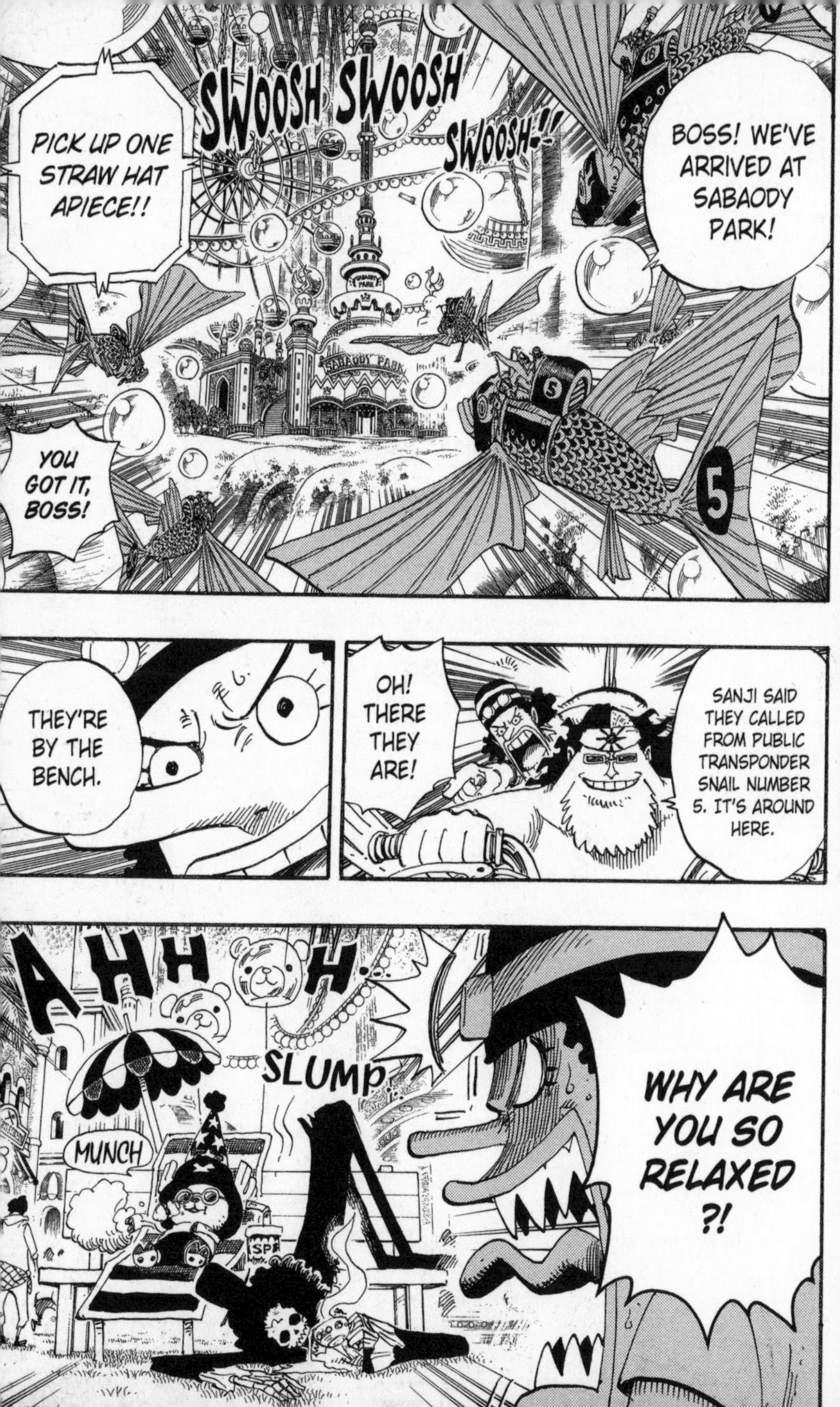
BOSS! WE'VE ARRIVED AT SABAODY PARK!
SWOOSH SWOOSH
SWOOSH!!
SABAODY PARK
PICK UP ONE STRAW HAT APIECE!!
YOU GOT IT, BOSS!
5
SANJI SAID THEY CALLED FROM PUBLIC TRANSPONDER SNAIL NUMBER 5. IT'S AROUND HERE.
OH! THERE THEY ARE!
THEY'RE BY THE BENCH.
WHY ARE YOU SO RELAXED?!
AHHH.
SLUMP
MUNCH

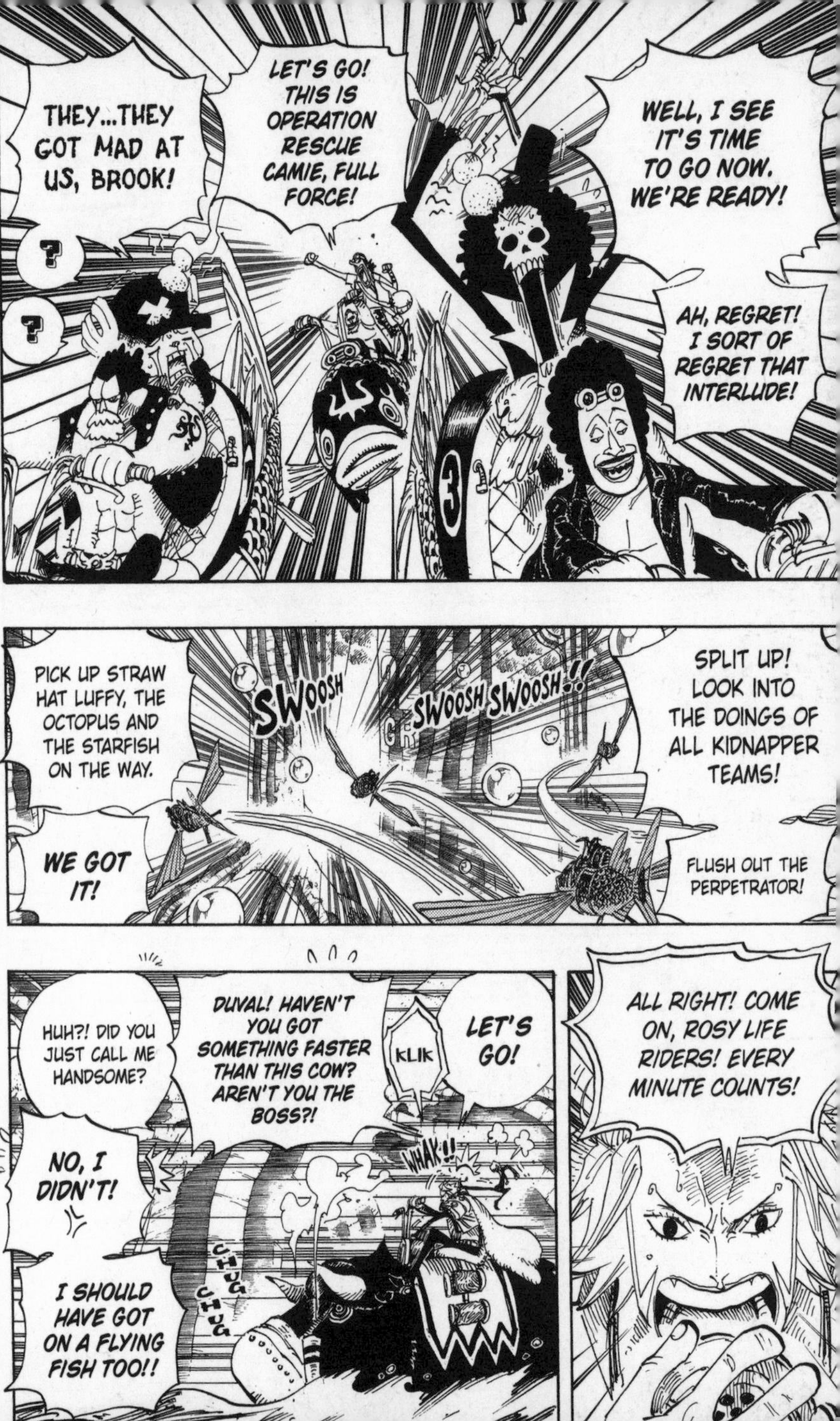

WELL, I SEE IT'S TIME TO GO NOW. WE'RE READY!
AH, REGRET! I SORT OF REGRET THAT INTERLUDE!
LET'S GO! THIS IS OPERATION RESCUE CAMIE, FULL FORCE!
THEY...THEY GOT MAD AT US, BROOK!
?
?
SPLIT UP! LOOK INTO THE DOINGS OF ALL KIDNAPPER TEAMS!
FLUSH OUT THE PERPETRATOR!
SWOOSH SWOOSH!!
SWOOSH
PICK UP STRAW HAT LUFFY, THE OCTOPUS AND THE STARFISH ON THE WAY.
WE GOT IT!
ALL RIGHT! COME ON, ROSY LIFE RIDERS! EVERY MINUTE COUNTS!
LET'S GO!
KLIK
DUVAL! HAVEN'T YOU GOT SOMETHING FASTER THAN THIS COW? AREN'T YOU THE BOSS?!
WHAK!!
HUH?! DID YOU JUST CALL ME HANDSOME?
NO, I DIDN'T!
CHUG CHUG
I SHOULD HAVE GOT ON A FLYING FISH TOO!!

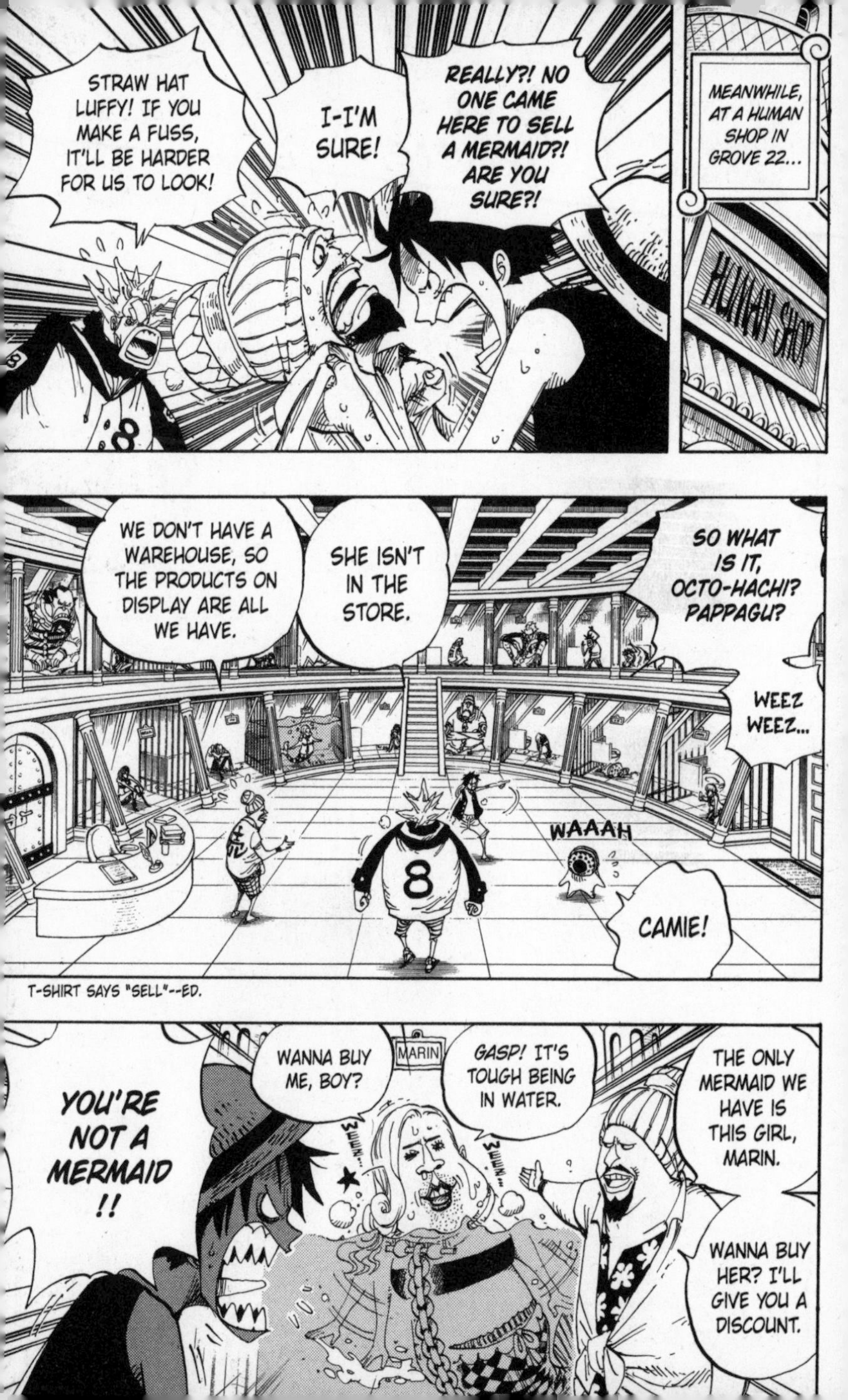
MEANWHILE, AT A HUMAN SHOP IN GROVE 22...
HUMAN SHOP
REALLY?! NO ONE CAME HERE TO SELL A MERMAID?! ARE YOU SURE?!
I-I'M SURE!
STRAW HAT LUFFY! IF YOU MAKE A FUSS, IT'LL BE HARDER FOR US TO LOOK!
SO WHAT IS IT, OCTO-HACHI? PAPPAGU?
WEEZ WEEZ...
SHE ISN'T IN THE STORE.
WE DON'T HAVE A WAREHOUSE, SO THE PRODUCTS ON DISPLAY ARE ALL WE HAVE.
WAAAH
CAMIE!
T-SHIRT SAYS "SELL"--ED.
THE ONLY MERMAID WE HAVE IS THIS GIRL, MARIN.
GASP! IT'S TOUGH BEING IN WATER.
MARIN
WANNA BUY ME, BOY?
WEEN...
WEEN...
WANNA BUY HER? I'LL GIVE YOU A DISCOUNT.
YOU'RE NOT A MERMAID !!

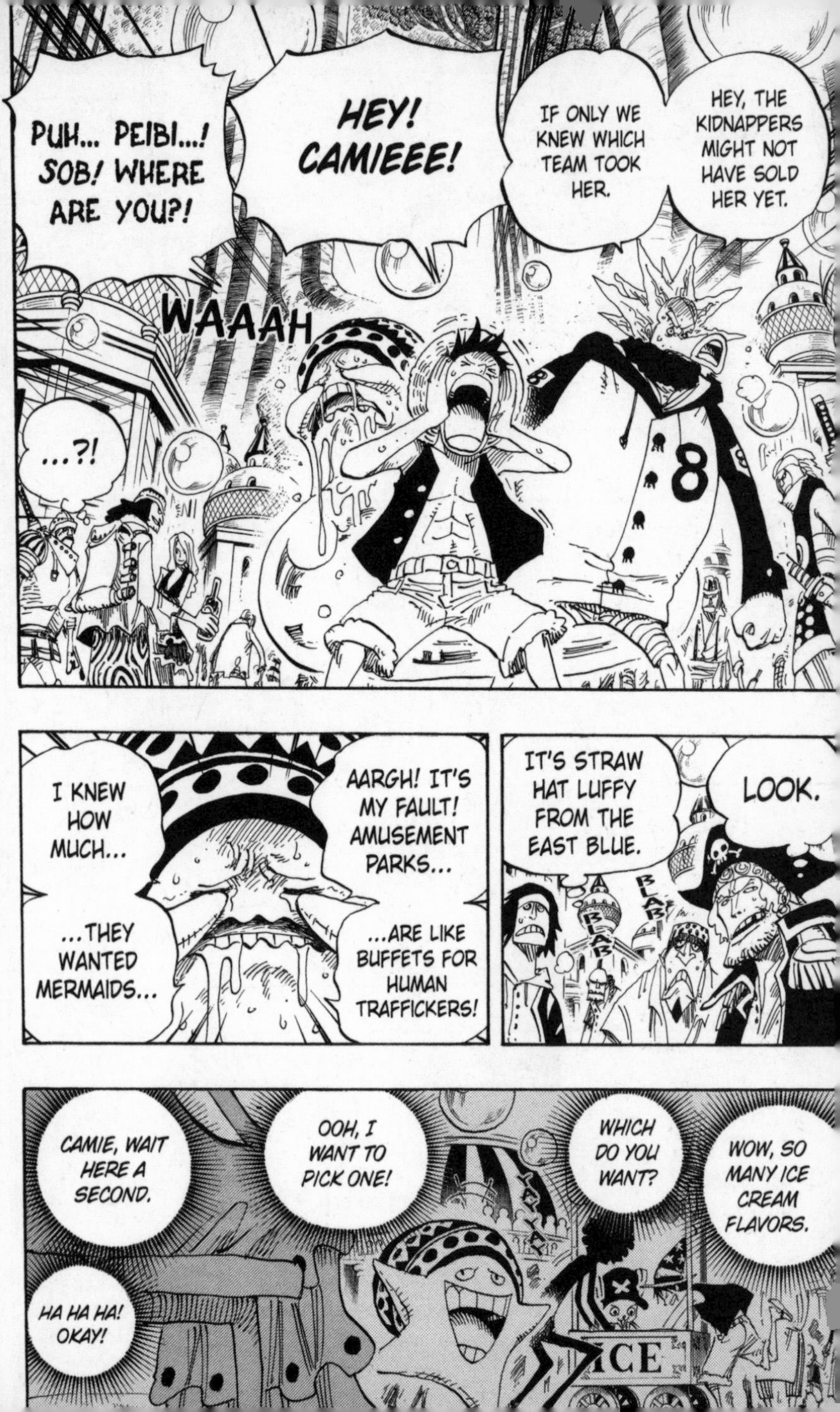
HEY, THE KIDNAPPERS MIGHT NOT HAVE SOLD HER YET.
IF ONLY WE KNEW WHICH TEAM TOOK HER.
HEY! CAMIEEE!
PUH... PEIBI...! SOB! WHERE ARE YOU?!
WAAAH
...?!
LOOK.
IT'S STRAW HAT LUFFY FROM THE EAST BLUE.
BLAB
BLAB
AARGH! IT'S MY FAULT! AMUSEMENT PARKS...
I KNEW HOW MUCH...
...ARE LIKE BUFFETS FOR HUMAN TRAFFICKERS!
...THEY WANTED MERMAIDS...
WOW, SO MANY ICE CREAM FLAVORS.
WHICH DO YOU WANT?
OOH, I WANT TO PICK ONE!
CAMIE, WAIT HERE A SECOND.
HA HA HA! OKAY!
ICE

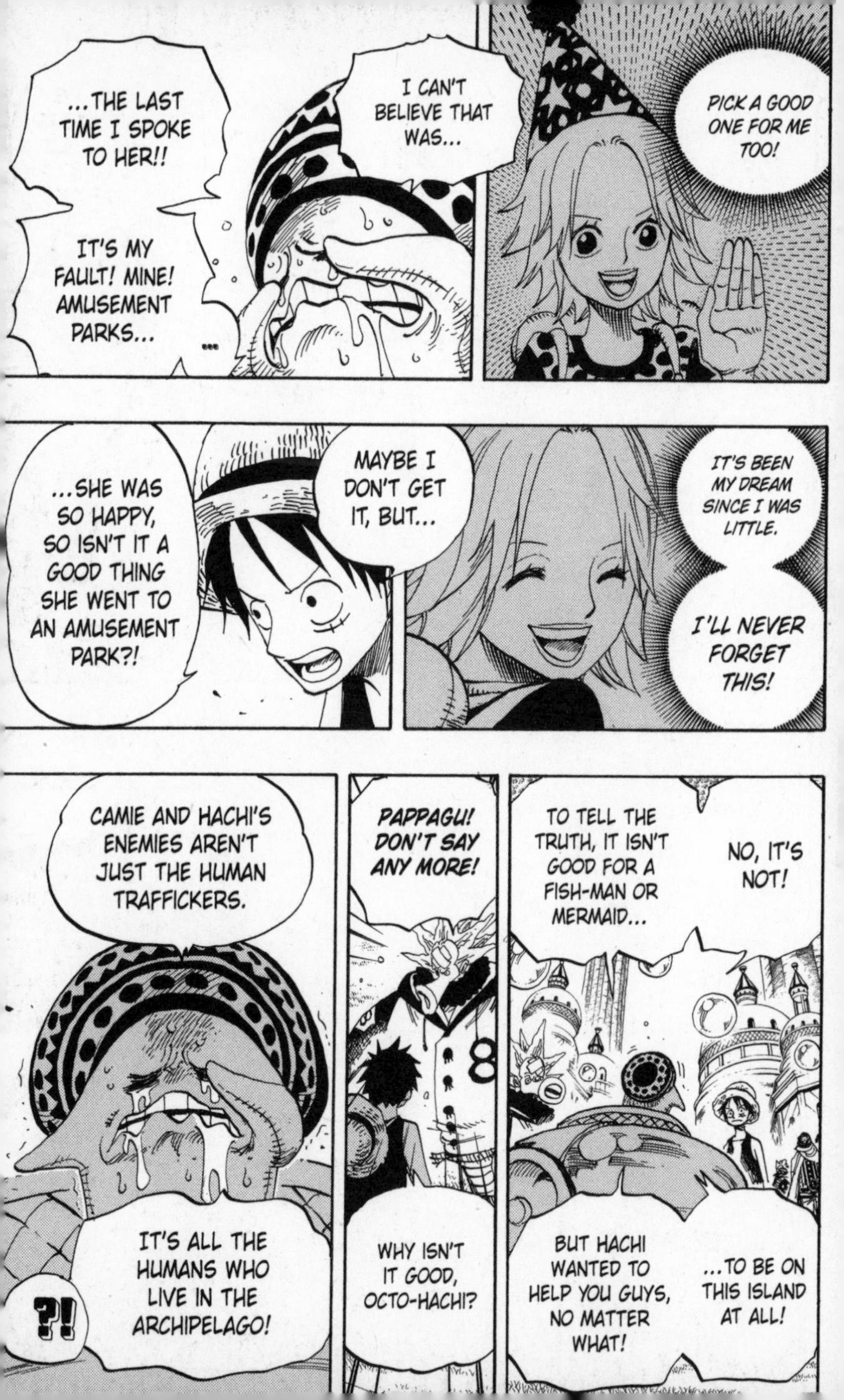
PICK A GOOD ONE FOR ME TOO!
I CAN'T BELIEVE THAT WAS...
...THE LAST TIME I SPOKE TO HER!!
IT'S MY FAULT! MINE! AMUSEMENT PARKS...
IT'S BEEN MY DREAM SINCE I WAS LITTLE.
I'LL NEVER FORGET THIS!
MAYBE I DON'T GET IT, BUT...
...SHE WAS SO HAPPY, SO ISN'T IT A GOOD THING SHE WENT TO AN AMUSEMENT PARK?!
NO, IT'S NOT!
TO TELL THE TRUTH, IT ISN'T GOOD FOR A FISH-MAN OR MERMAID...
...TO BE ON THIS ISLAND AT ALL!
BUT HACHI WANTED TO HELP YOU GUYS, NO MATTER WHAT!
PAPPAGU! DON'T SAY ANY MORE!
WHY ISN'T IT GOOD, OCTO-HACHI?
CAMIE AND HACHI'S ENEMIES AREN'T JUST THE HUMAN TRAFFICKERS.
IT'S ALL THE HUMANS WHO LIVE IN THE ARCHIPELAGO!
?!

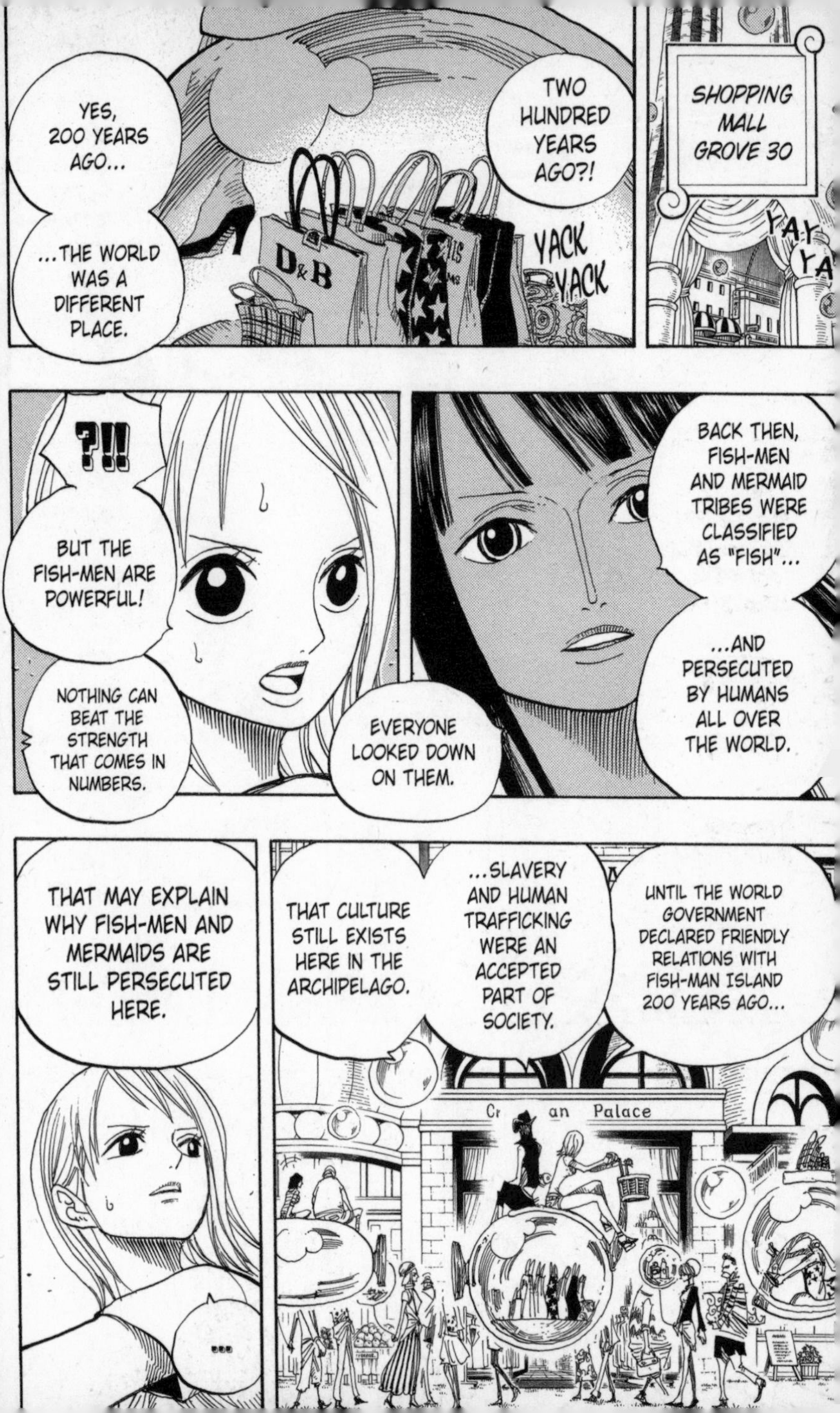
SHOPPING MALL GROVE 30
YAY YA
TWO HUNDRED YEARS AGO?!
YACK YACK
YES, 200 YEARS AGO...
...THE WORLD WAS A DIFFERENT PLACE.
BACK THEN, FISH-MEN AND MERMAID TRIBES WERE CLASSIFIED AS "FISH"...
...AND PERSECUTED BY HUMANS ALL OVER THE WORLD.
EVERYONE LOOKED DOWN ON THEM.
?!!
BUT THE FISH-MEN ARE POWERFUL!
NOTHING CAN BEAT THE STRENGTH THAT COMES IN NUMBERS.
UNTIL THE WORLD GOVERNMENT DECLARED FRIENDLY RELATIONS WITH FISH-MAN ISLAND 200 YEARS AGO...
...SLAVERY AND HUMAN TRAFFICKING WERE AN ACCEPTED PART OF SOCIETY.
THAT CULTURE STILL EXISTS HERE IN THE ARCHIPELAGO.
Cr an Palace
THAT MAY EXPLAIN WHY FISH-MEN AND MERMAIDS ARE STILL PERSECUTED HERE.
...

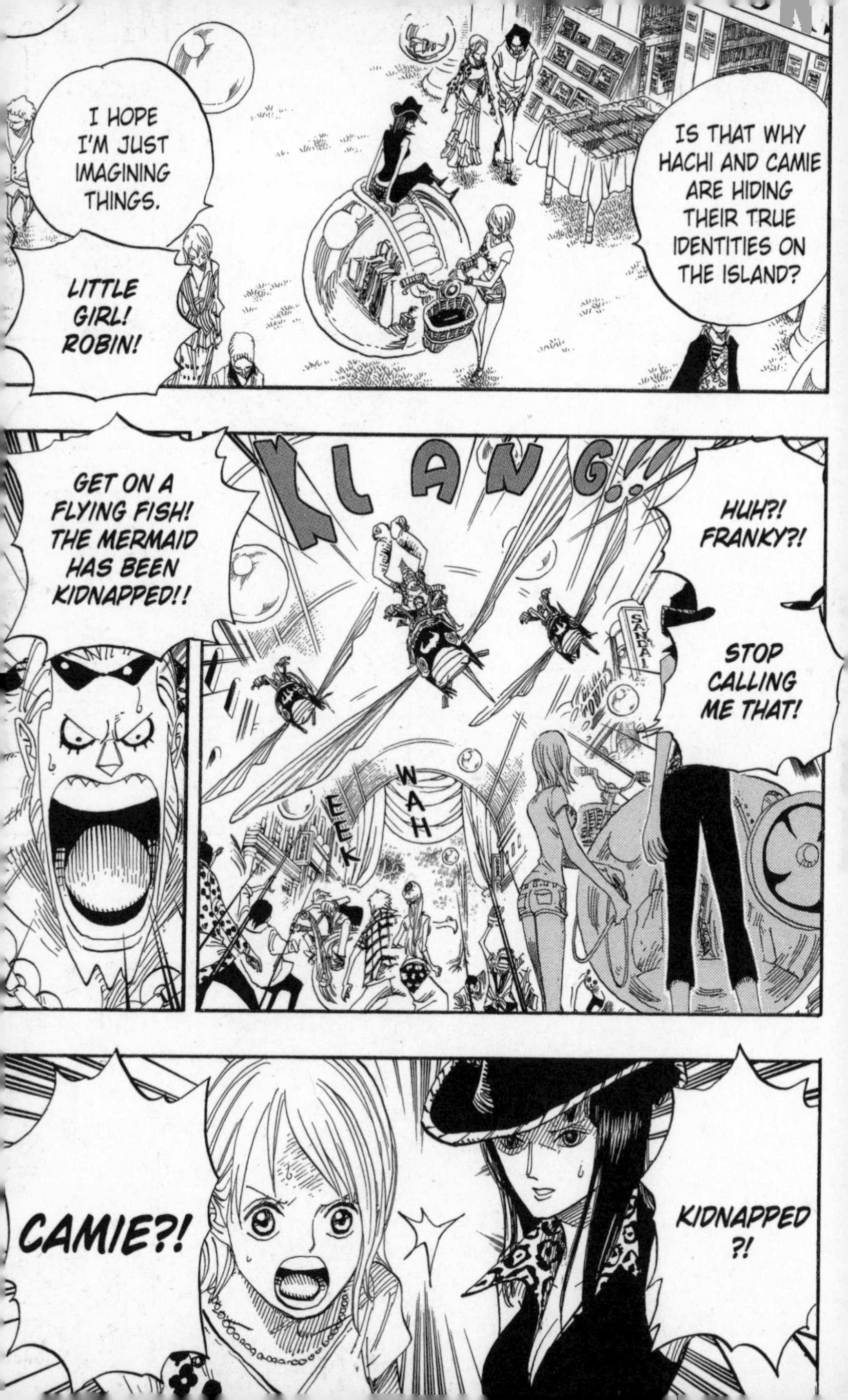
IS THAT WHY HACHI AND CAMIE ARE HIDING THEIR TRUE IDENTITIES ON THE ISLAND?
I HOPE I'M JUST IMAGINING THINGS.
LITTLE GIRL! ROBIN!
KLANG!!
HUH?! FRANKY?!
STOP CALLING ME THAT!
WAH
EEK
GET ON A FLYING FISH! THE MERMAID HAS BEEN KIDNAPPED!!
KIDNAPPED?!
CAMIE?!

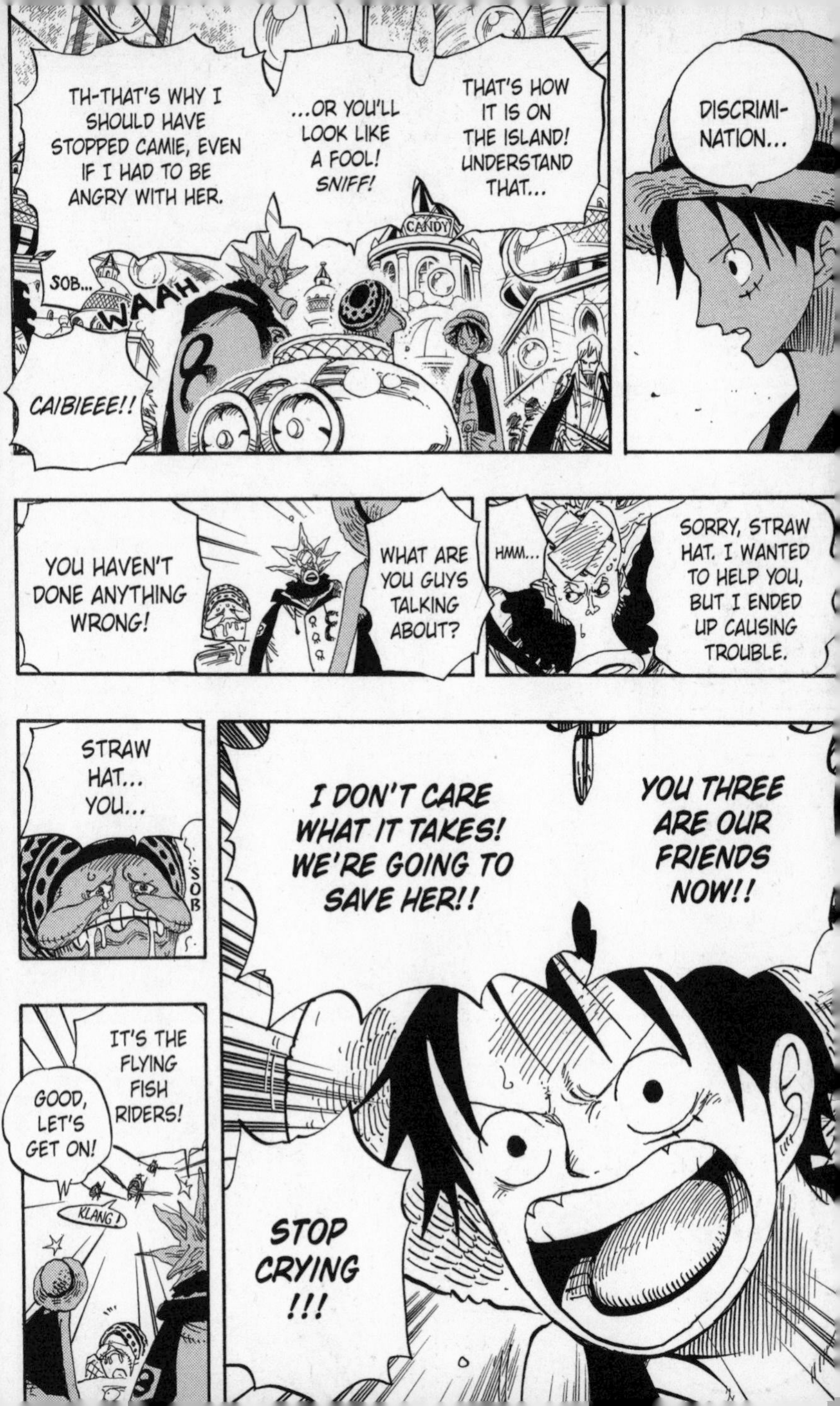
DISCRIMI-NATION...
THAT'S HOW IT IS ON THE ISLAND! UNDERSTAND THAT...
...OR YOU'LL LOOK LIKE A FOOL! SNIFF!
TH-THAT'S WHY I SHOULD HAVE STOPPED CAMIE, EVEN IF I HAD TO BE ANGRY WITH HER.
CANDY
SOB...
WAAH
CAIBIEEE!!
SORRY, STRAW HAT. I WANTED TO HELP YOU, BUT I ENDED UP CAUSING TROUBLE.
HMM...
WHAT ARE YOU GUYS TALKING ABOUT?
YOU HAVEN'T DONE ANYTHING WRONG!
YOU THREE ARE OUR FRIENDS NOW!!
I DON'T CARE WHAT IT TAKES! WE'RE GOING TO SAVE HER!!
STOP CRYING!!!
STRAW HAT... YOU...
SOB
IT'S THE FLYING FISH RIDERS!
GOOD, LET'S GET ON!
KLANG!

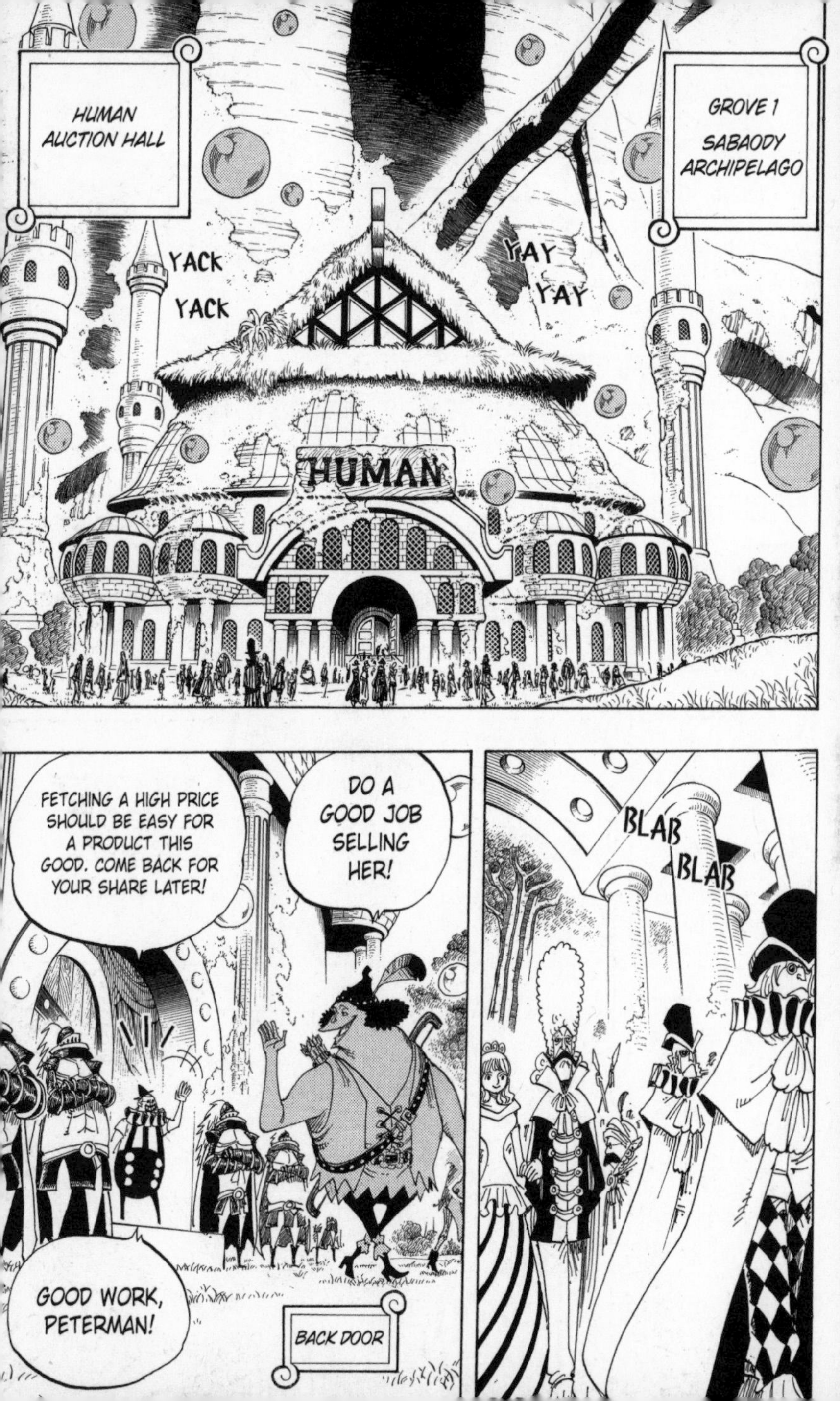
GROVE 1
SABAODY ARCHIPELAGO
YAY YAY
HUMAN AUCTION HALL
YACK YACK
HUMAN
BLAB BLAB
DO A GOOD JOB SELLING HER!
FETCHING A HIGH PRICE SHOULD BE EASY FOR A PRODUCT THIS GOOD. COME BACK FOR YOUR SHARE LATER!
GOOD WORK, PETERMAN!
BACK DOOR

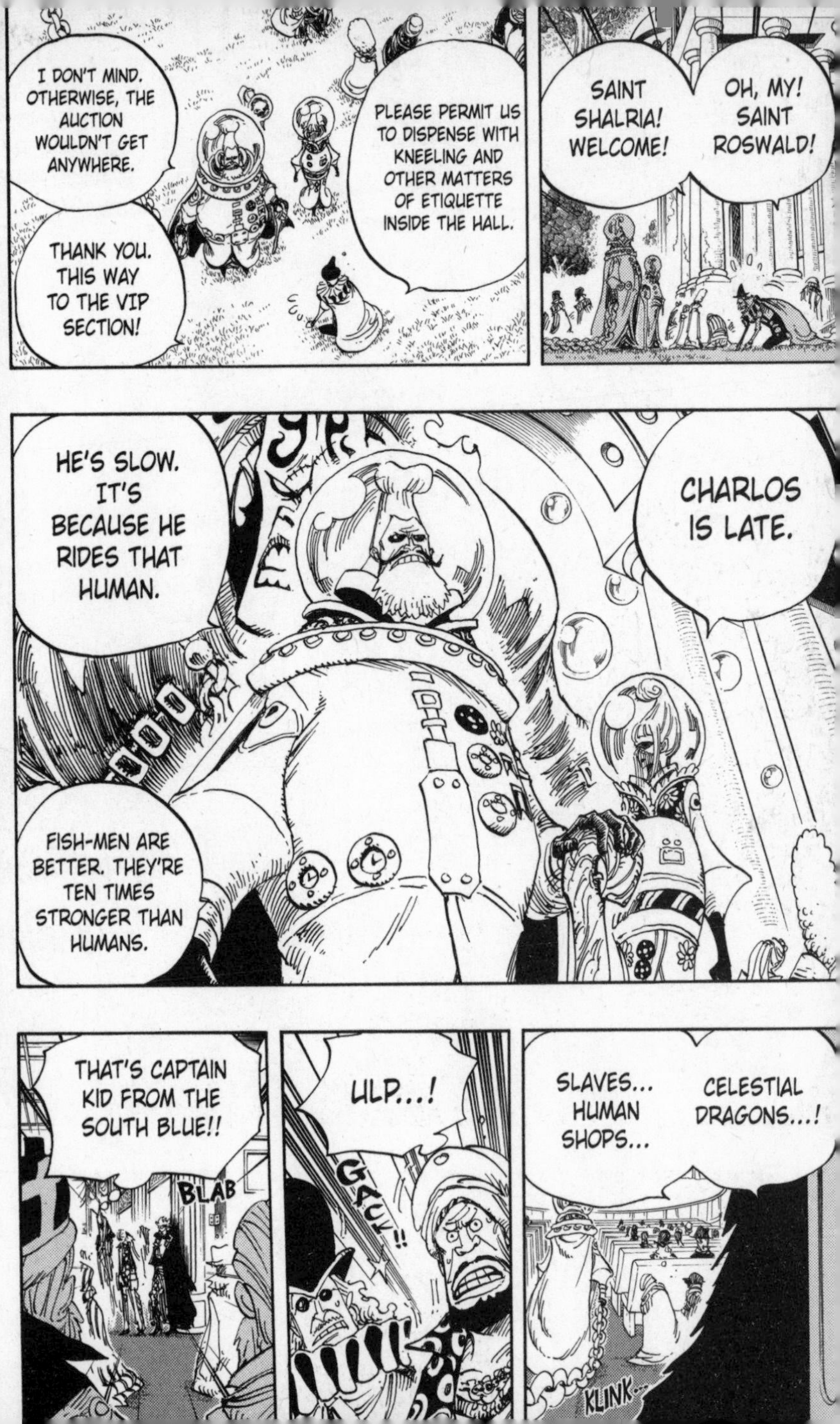
OH, MY! SAINT ROSWALD!
SAINT SHALRIA! WELCOME!
PLEASE PERMIT US TO DISPENSE WITH KNEELING AND OTHER MATTERS OF ETIQUETTE INSIDE THE HALL.
I DON'T MIND. OTHERWISE, THE AUCTION WOULDN'T GET ANYWHERE.
THANK YOU. THIS WAY TO THE VIP SECTION!
CHARLOS IS LATE.
HE'S SLOW. IT'S BECAUSE HE RIDES THAT HUMAN.
FISH-MEN ARE BETTER. THEY'RE TEN TIMES STRONGER THAN HUMANS.
CELESTIAL DRAGONS...!
SLAVES... HUMAN SHOPS...
KLINK...
ULP...!
GACK!!
THAT'S CAPTAIN KID FROM THE SOUTH BLUE!!
BLAB

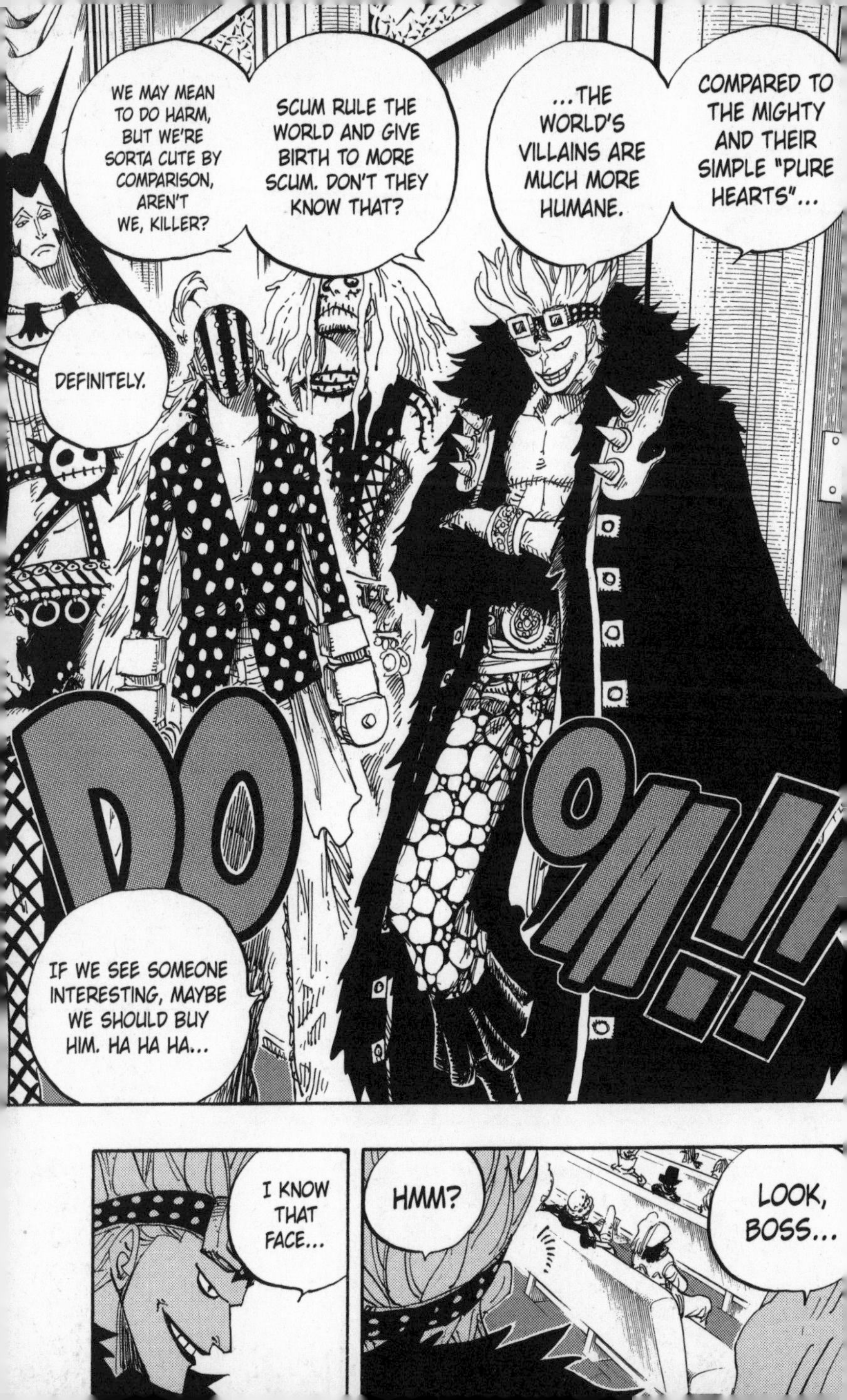
COMPARED TO THE MIGHTY AND THEIR SIMPLE "PURE HEARTS"...
...THE WORLD'S VILLAINS ARE MUCH MORE HUMANE.
SCUM RULE THE WORLD AND GIVE BIRTH TO MORE SCUM. DON'T THEY KNOW THAT?
WE MAY MEAN TO DO HARM, BUT WE'RE SORTA CUTE BY COMPARISON, AREN'T WE, KILLER?
DEFINITELY.
DOOM!!
IF WE SEE SOMEONE INTERESTING, MAYBE WE SHOULD BUY HIM. HA HA HA...
LOOK, BOSS...
HMM?
I KNOW THAT FACE...

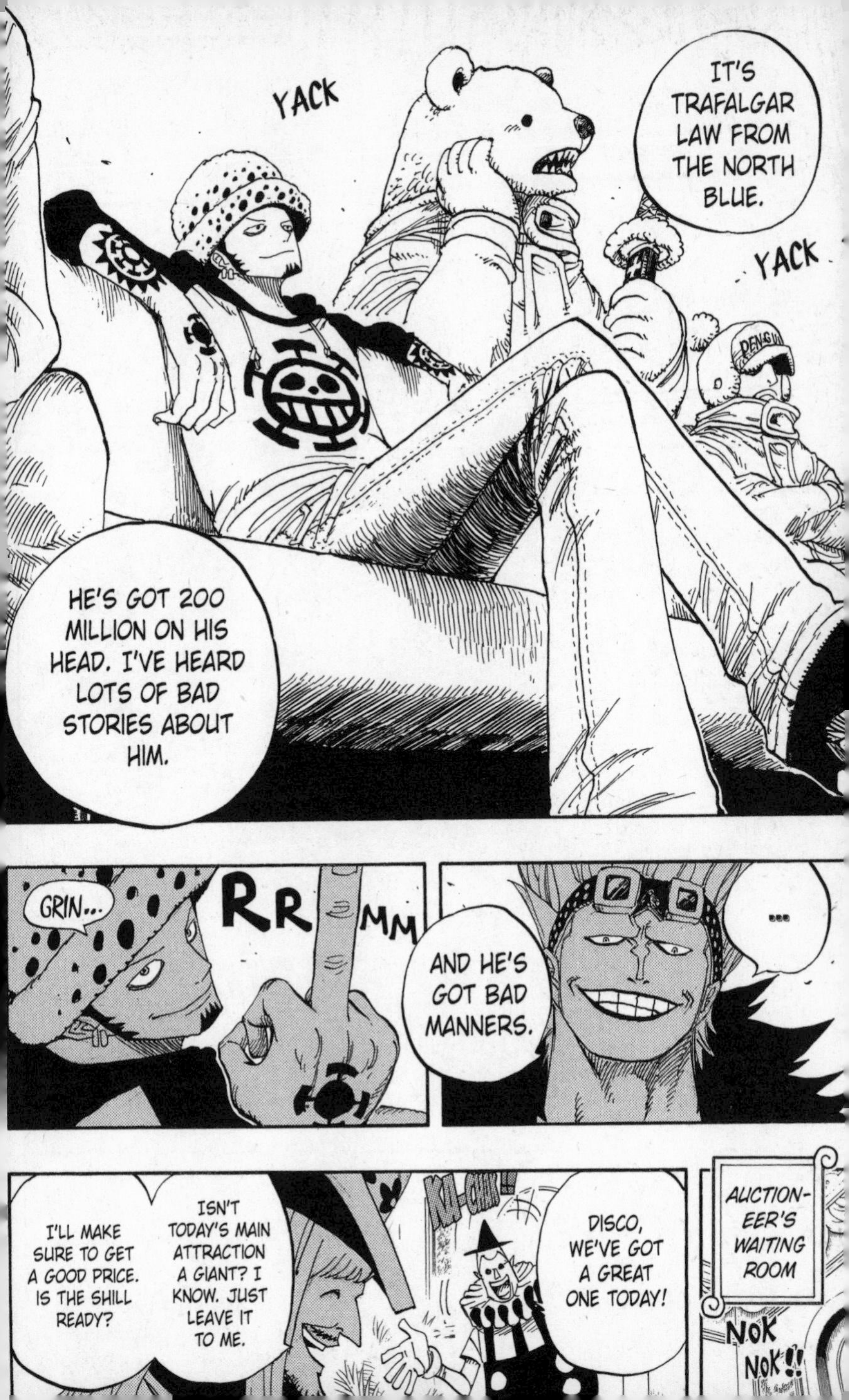
IT'S TRAFALGAR LAW FROM THE NORTH BLUE.
YACK
YACK
HE'S GOT 200 MILLION ON HIS HEAD. I'VE HEARD LOTS OF BAD STORIES ABOUT HIM.
...
AND HE'S GOT BAD MANNERS.
RR
MM
GRIN...
AUCTIONEER'S WAITING ROOM
NOK
NOK!!
DISCO, WE'VE GOT A GREAT ONE TODAY!
ISN'T TODAY'S MAIN ATTRACTION A GIANT? I KNOW. JUST LEAVE IT TO ME.
I'LL MAKE SURE TO GET A GOOD PRICE. IS THE SHILL READY?

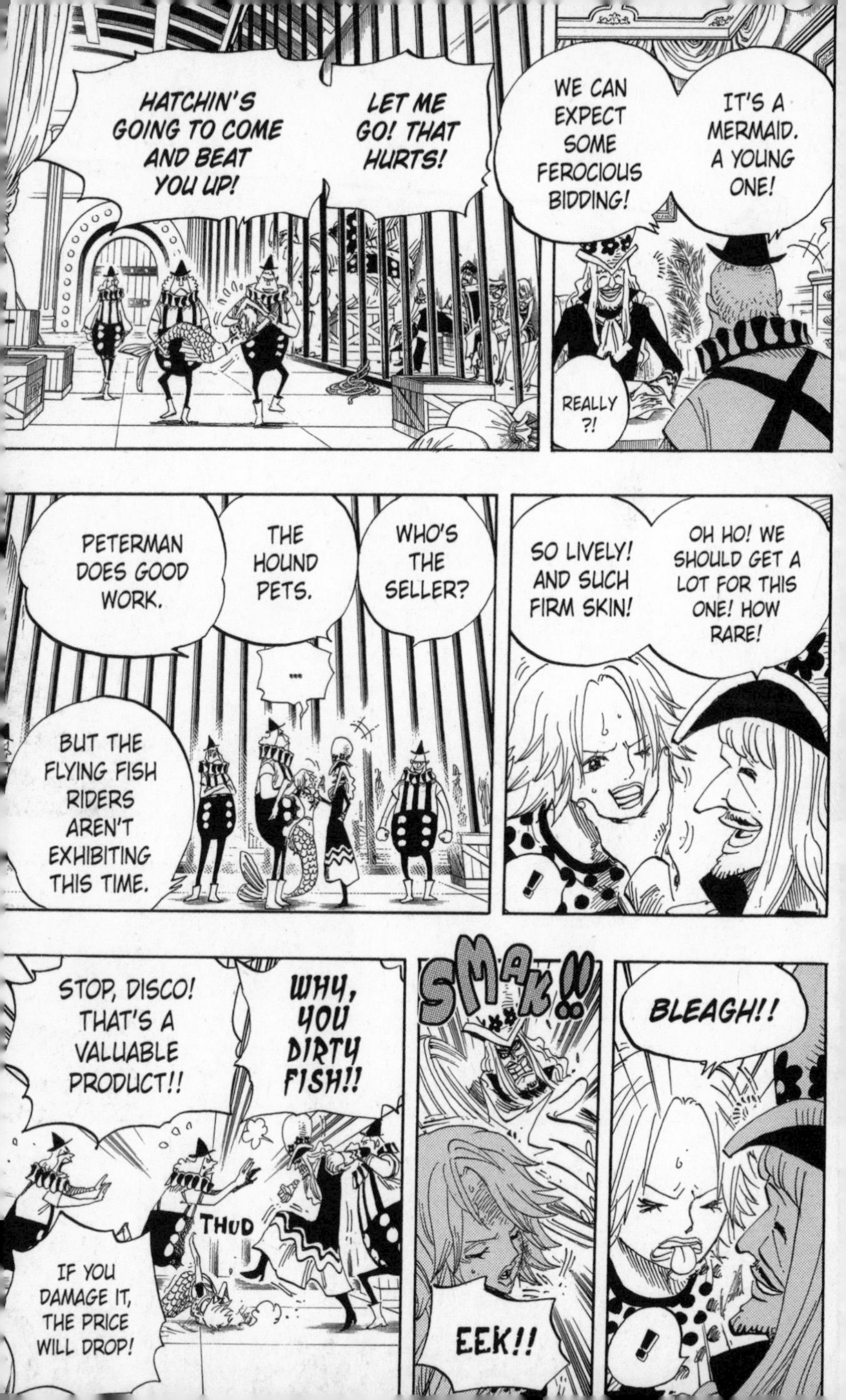
IT'S A MERMAID. A YOUNG ONE!
WE CAN EXPECT SOME FEROCIOUS BIDDING!
REALLY?!
LET ME GO! THAT HURTS!
HATCHIN'S GOING TO COME AND BEAT YOU UP!
OH HO! WE SHOULD GET A LOT FOR THIS ONE! HOW RARE!
SO LIVELY! AND SUCH FIRM SKIN!
!
WHO'S THE SELLER?
THE HOUND PETS.
PETERMAN DOES GOOD WORK.
...
BUT THE FLYING FISH RIDERS AREN'T EXHIBITING THIS TIME.
BLEAGH!!
!
SMAK!!
EEK!!
WHY, YOU DIRTY FISH!!
STOP, DISCO! THAT'S A VALUABLE PRODUCT!!
THUD
IF YOU DAMAGE IT, THE PRICE WILL DROP!

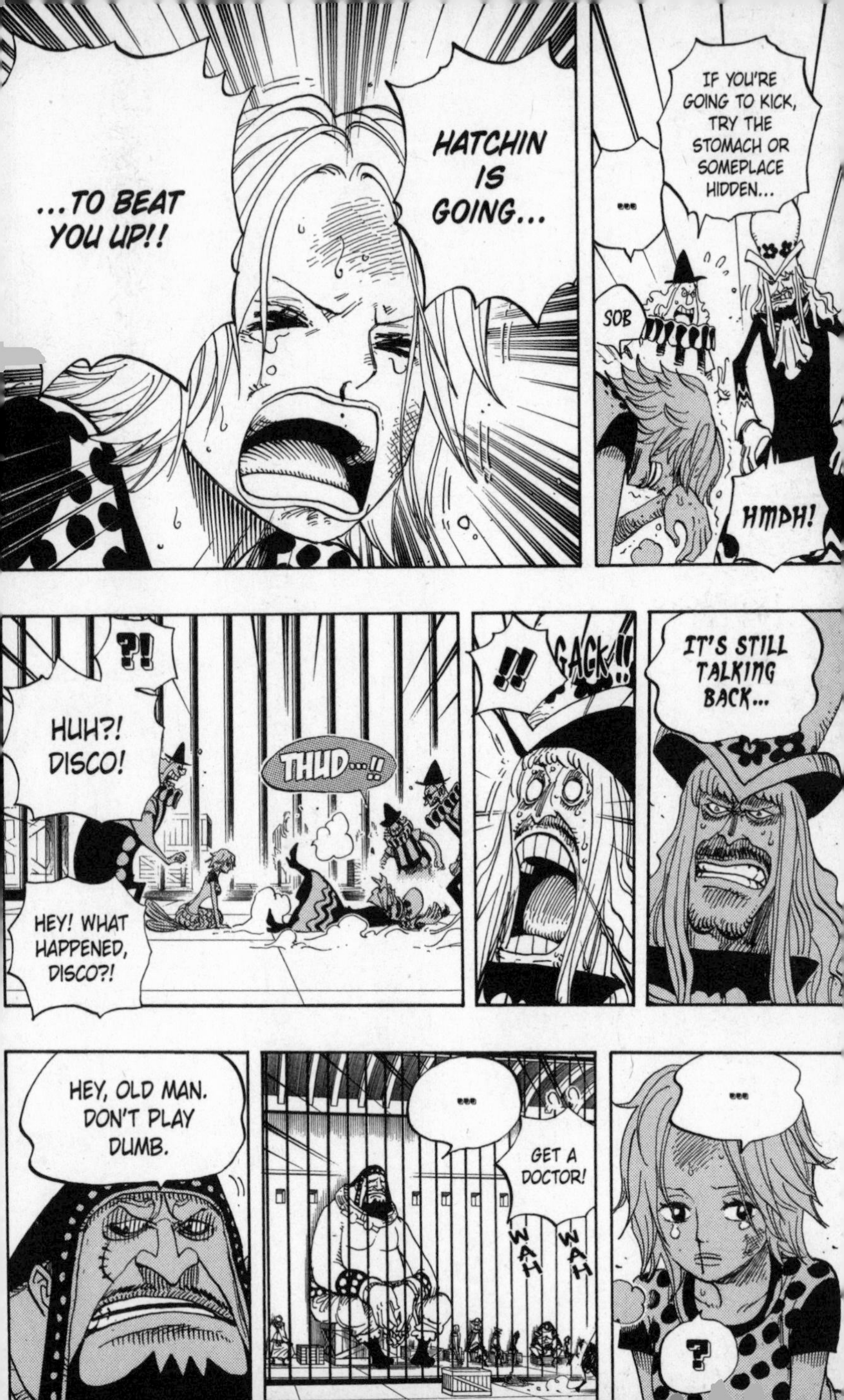

IF YOU'RE GOING TO KICK, TRY THE STOMACH OR SOMEPLACE HIDDEN...
...
SOB
HMPH!
HATCHIN IS GOING...
...TO BEAT YOU UP!!
IT'S STILL TALKING BACK...
GACK!!
!!
?!
HUH?! DISCO!
THUD...!!
HEY! WHAT HAPPENED, DISCO?!
...
?
...
GET A DOCTOR!
WAH
WAH
HEY, OLD MAN. DON'T PLAY DUMB.

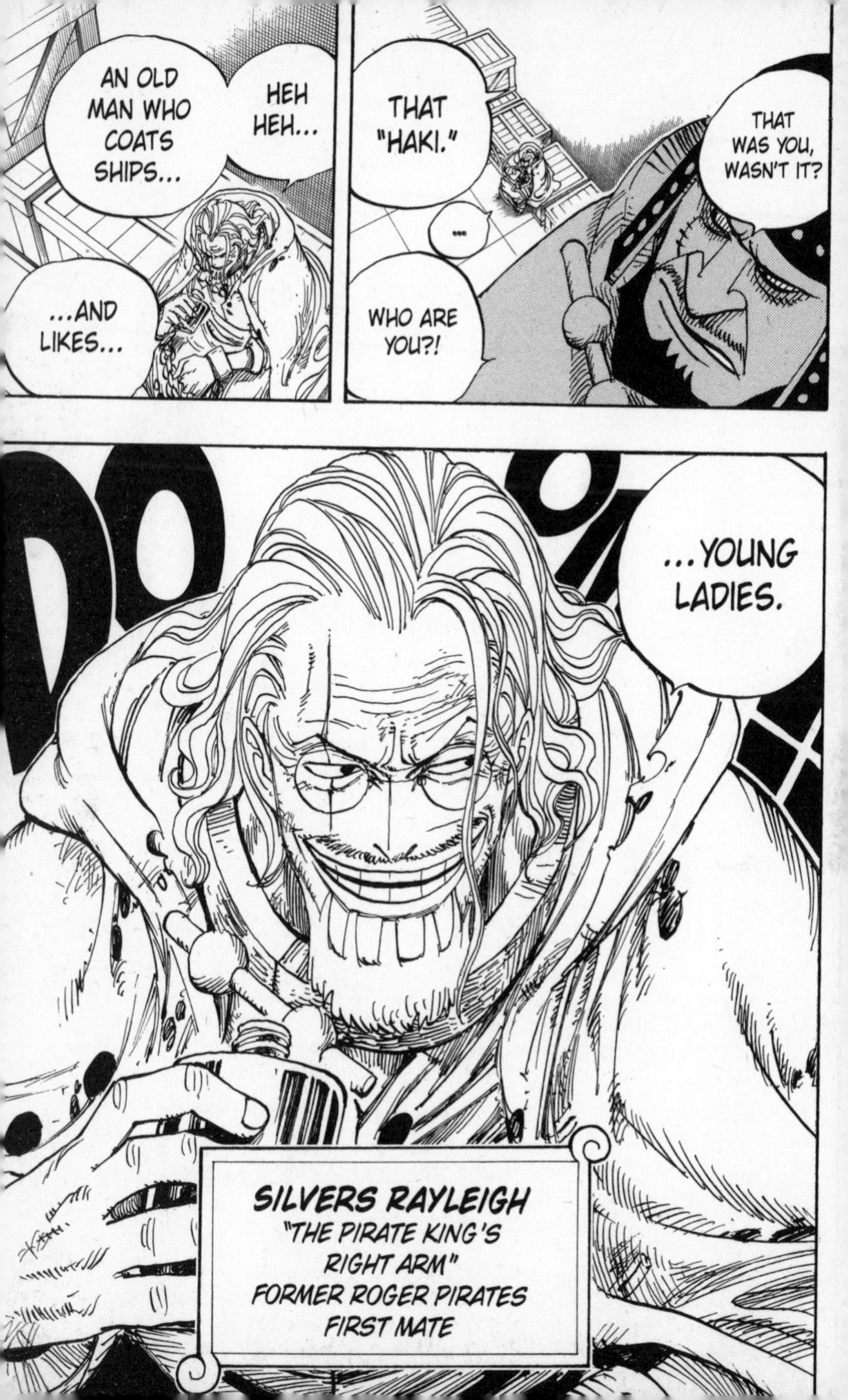
THAT WAS YOU, WASN'T IT?
THAT "HAKI."
...
WHO ARE YOU?!
HEH HEH...
AN OLD MAN WHO COATS SHIPS...
...AND LIKES...
...YOUNG LADIES.
DO
SILVERS RAYLEIGH
"THE PIRATE KING'S RIGHT ARM"
FORMER ROGER PIRATES FIRST MATE

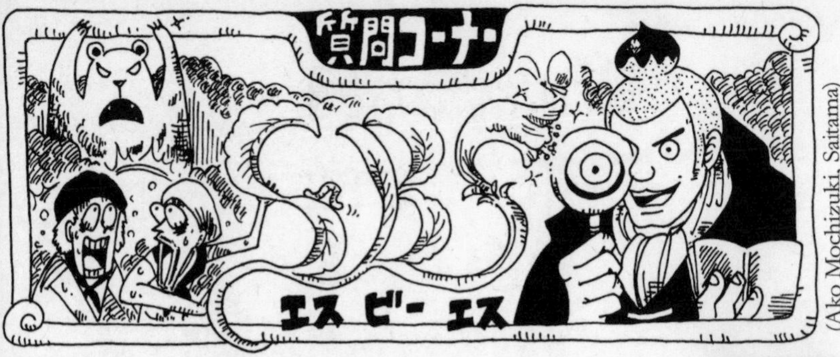
質問コーナー
SBS
エス ビー エス

(Ako Mochizuki, Saitama)

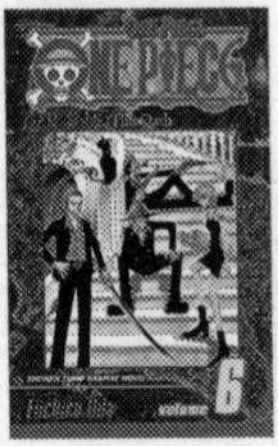
ONE PIECE
6

Q: Odacchi! Odacchi! Is your uncle a taxi driver? When I went to Kyoto, this man gave me a *One Piece* poster and a copy of the cover of volume 6! I've been wondering about him so much I can't study for my entrance exams! ♡

--Jana

A: Oh, that was most likely my uncle. He said he was doing that: "Ei-chan, I always promote your manga." The company had to ask him to tone it down, but he's still cruising around Kyoto somewhere. If you end up in the taxi with tell him I said hi.

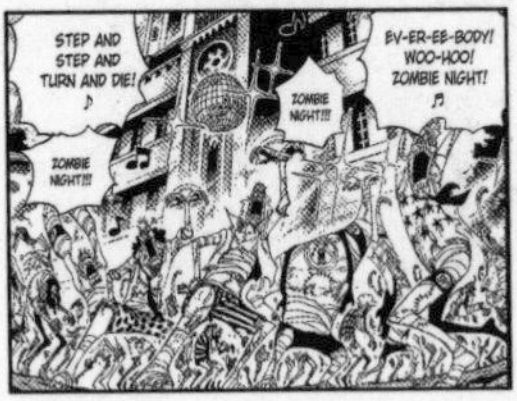
EV-ER-EE-BODY! WOO-HOO! ZOMBIE NIGHT! ♪
ZOMBIE NIGHT!!!
STEP AND STEP AND TURN AND DIE! ♪
ZOMBIE NIGHT!!!

Q: Did you have *The Addams Family* and *The Nightmare Before Christmas* in mind when you wrote the Thriller Bark arc? I like that kind of atmosphere.

--Cindry, Who Likes Plates

A: You mean the movies, don't you? I like movies like that too. I had to force myself to watch a lot of zombie movies. I basically don't like anything scary. Even though I used more black than usual to get the right atmosphere in the drawings, I was aiming for bright, fun zombies. Whenever manga creators write on topics that might bring bad luck, like ghosts and dead people, they go to a shrine to be blessed--and I did the same! I'm super scared of curses.

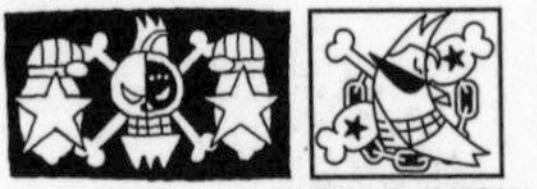

Q: Oda Sensei, I have something to tell you! The design for Franky's skull and crossbones on page 166 in volume 47 was different than in the pamphlet for the movie *Episode of Chopper*.

--Cola with Lemon

A: You noticed...? I noticed after the fact. Before I drew the manga, someone from Toei Animation had submitted a design for Franky's symbol for my approval. I completely forgot that I had okayed it and ended up making another design. Well, they're both Franky's symbols. It's all right if he has two!

Chapter 501:
THE WORLD BEGINS TO SWELL

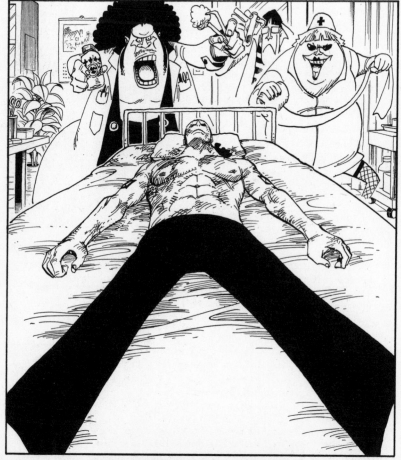

CP9'S INDEPENDENT REPORT, VOL. 11:
"SOAKING-WET MONEY RECEIVED"

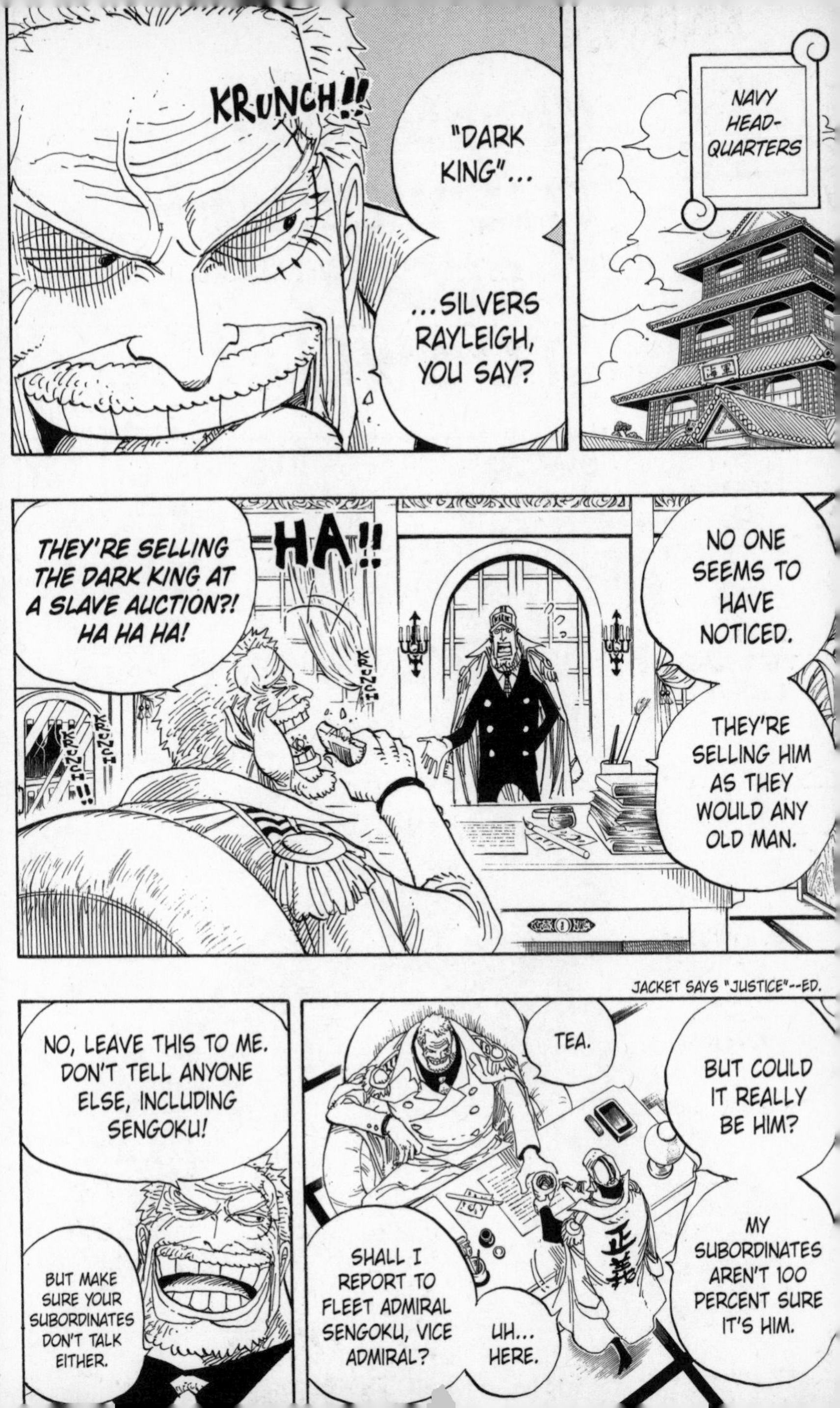
NAVY HEADQUARTERS
KRUNCH!!
"DARK KING"...
...SILVERS RAYLEIGH, YOU SAY?
NO ONE SEEMS TO HAVE NOTICED.
THEY'RE SELLING HIM AS THEY WOULD ANY OLD MAN.
HA!!
THEY'RE SELLING THE DARK KING AT A SLAVE AUCTION?! HA HA HA!
KRUNCH
KRUNCH KRUNCH!!
JACKET SAYS "JUSTICE"--ED.
BUT COULD IT REALLY BE HIM?
MY SUBORDINATES AREN'T 100 PERCENT SURE IT'S HIM.
TEA.
UH... HERE.
SHALL I REPORT TO FLEET ADMIRAL SENGOKU, VICE ADMIRAL?
NO, LEAVE THIS TO ME. DON'T TELL ANYONE ELSE, INCLUDING SENGOKU!
BUT MAKE SURE YOUR SUBORDINATES DON'T TALK EITHER.

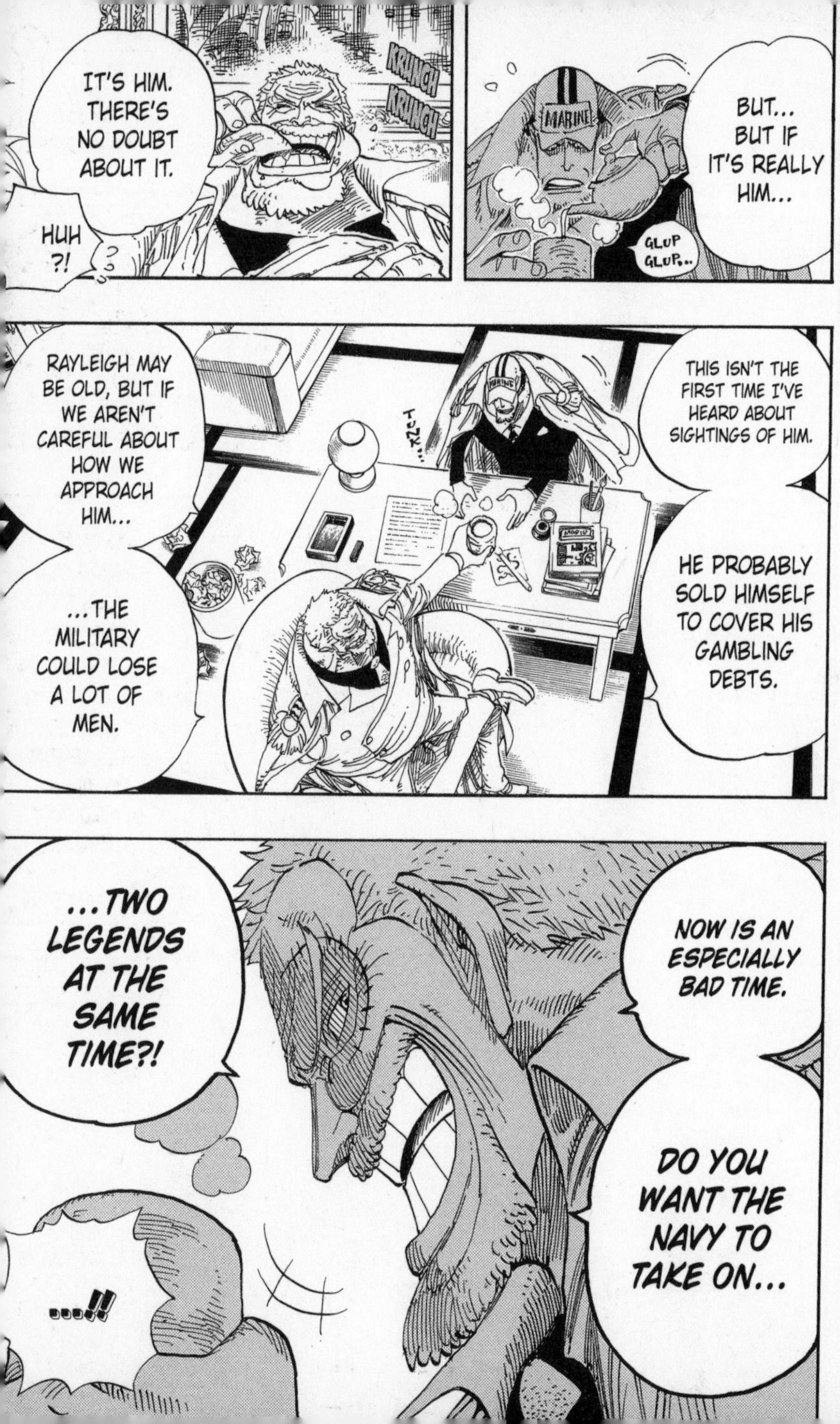
BUT... BUT IF IT'S REALLY HIM...
GLUP GLUP...
KRUNCH
KRUNCH
IT'S HIM. THERE'S NO DOUBT ABOUT IT.
HUH ?!
THIS ISN'T THE FIRST TIME I'VE HEARD ABOUT SIGHTINGS OF HIM.
HE PROBABLY SOLD HIMSELF TO COVER HIS GAMBLING DEBTS.
TUNK...
RAYLEIGH MAY BE OLD, BUT IF WE AREN'T CAREFUL ABOUT HOW WE APPROACH HIM...
...THE MILITARY COULD LOSE A LOT OF MEN.
NOW IS AN ESPECIALLY BAD TIME.
DO YOU WANT THE NAVY TO TAKE ON...
...TWO LEGENDS AT THE SAME TIME?!
...!!

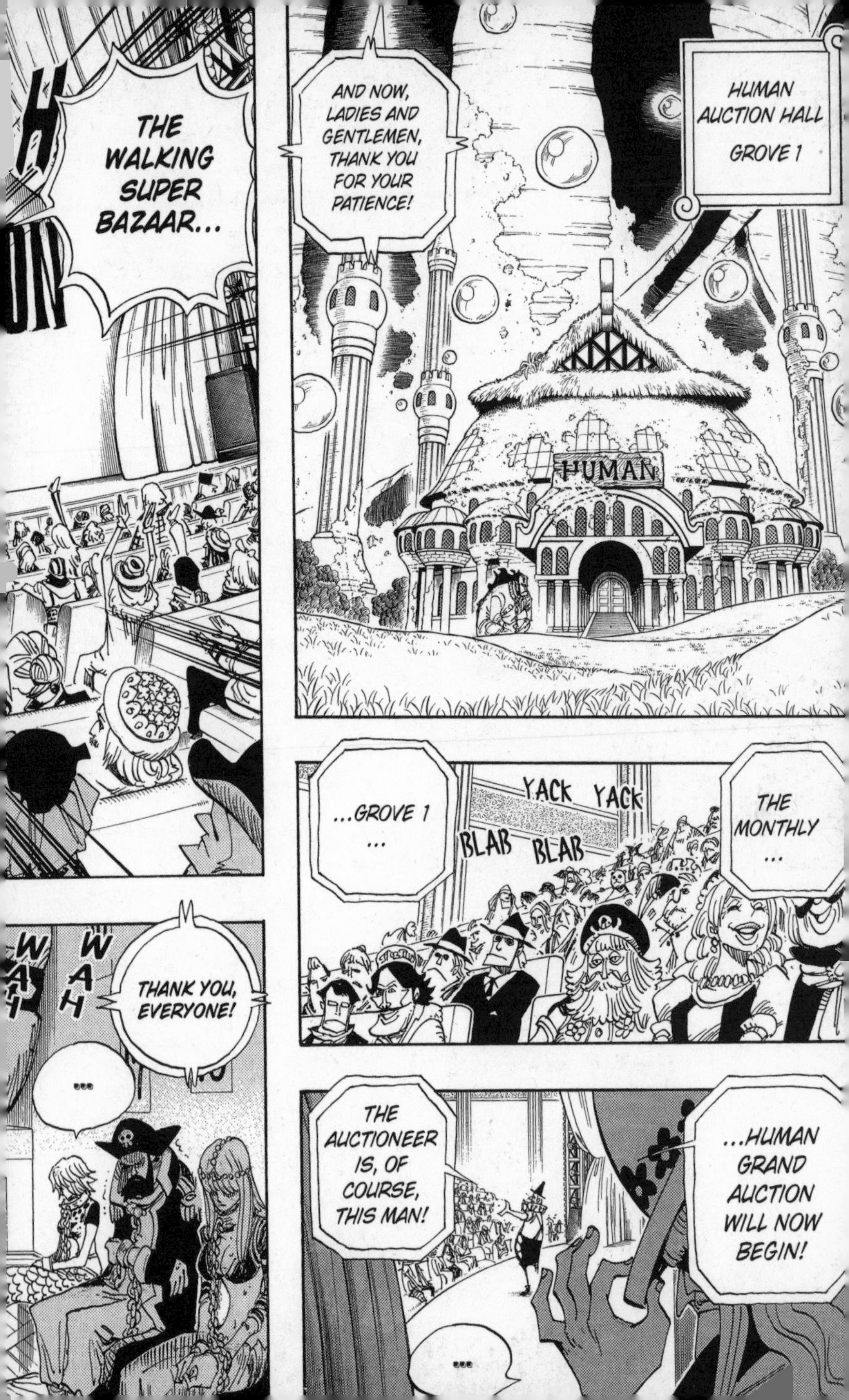
HUMAN AUCTION HALL GROVE 1
AND NOW, LADIES AND GENTLEMEN, THANK YOU FOR YOUR PATIENCE!
HUMAN
THE MONTHLY ...
YACK YACK
BLAB BLAB
...GROVE 1 ...
...HUMAN GRAND AUCTION WILL NOW BEGIN!
THE AUCTIONEER IS, OF COURSE, THIS MAN!
...
THE WALKING SUPER BAZAAR...
WAH WAH
THANK YOU, EVERYONE!
...

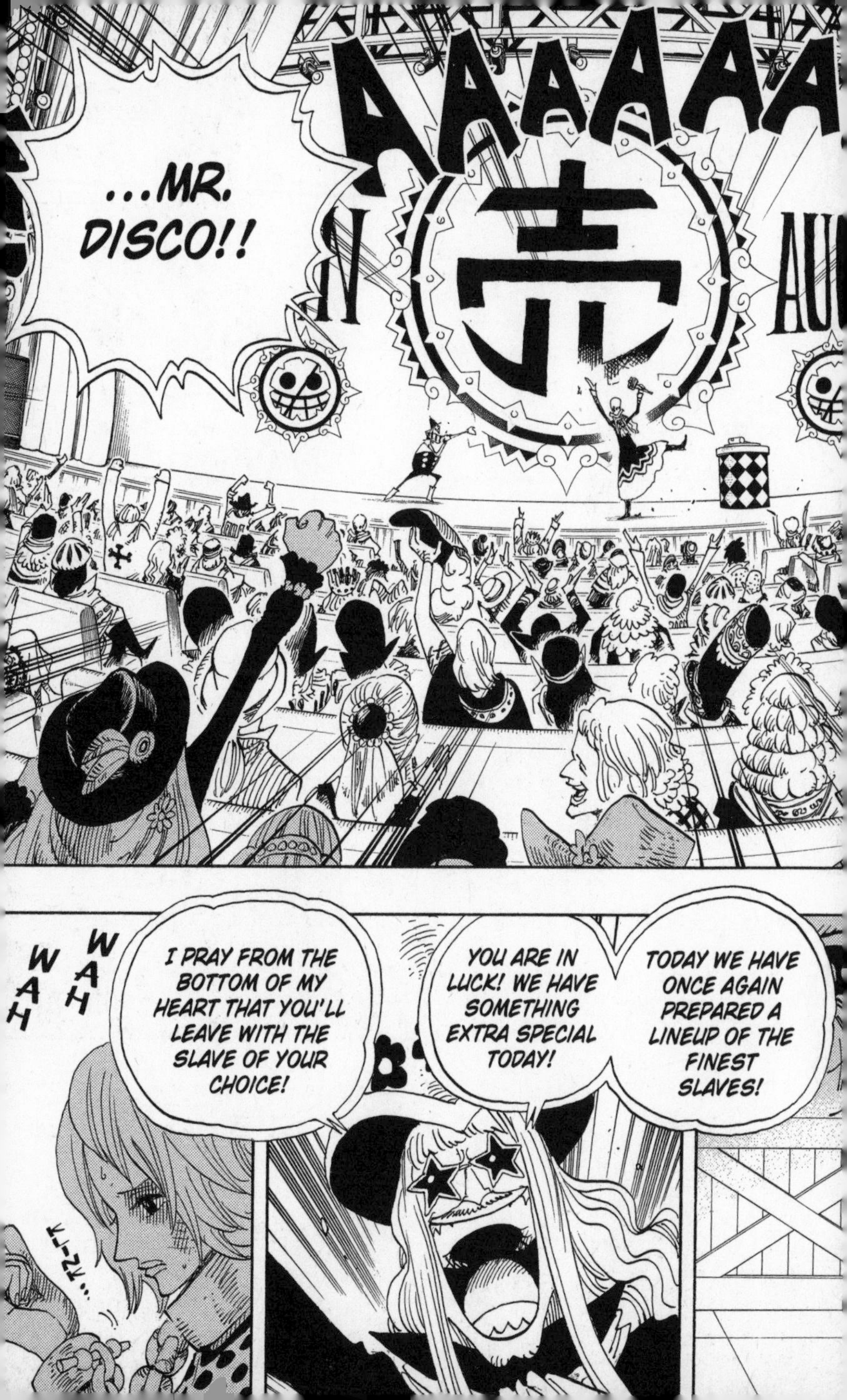

AAAAA
...MR. DISCO!!
TODAY WE HAVE ONCE AGAIN PREPARED A LINEUP OF THE FINEST SLAVES!
YOU ARE IN LUCK! WE HAVE SOMETHING EXTRA SPECIAL TODAY!
I PRAY FROM THE BOTTOM OF MY HEART THAT YOU'LL LEAVE WITH THE SLAVE OF YOUR CHOICE!
WAH WAH
KLINK...

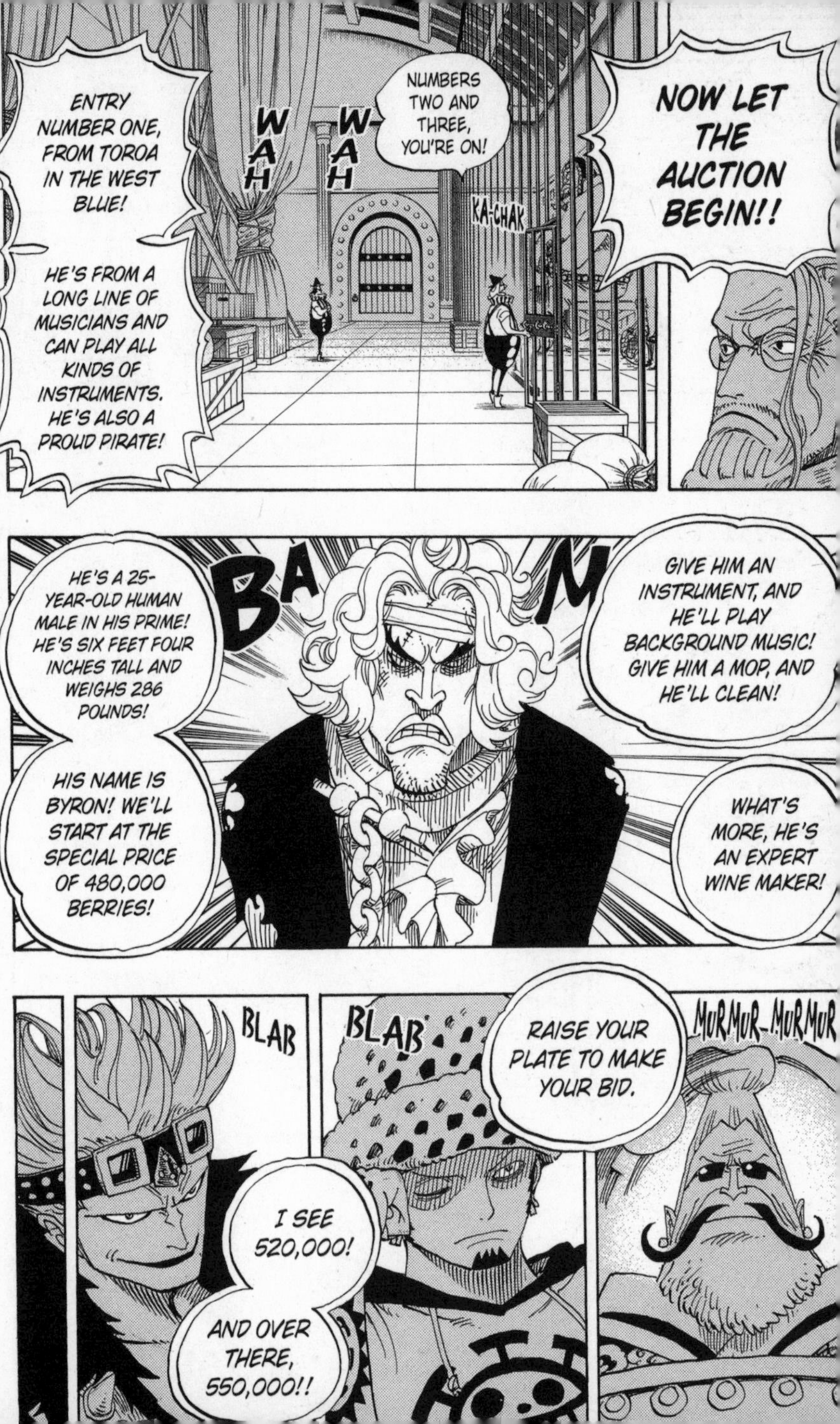
NOW LET THE AUCTION BEGIN!!
NUMBERS TWO AND THREE, YOU'RE ON!
KA-CHAK
WAH WAH
ENTRY NUMBER ONE, FROM TOROA IN THE WEST BLUE!
HE'S FROM A LONG LINE OF MUSICIANS AND CAN PLAY ALL KINDS OF INSTRUMENTS. HE'S ALSO A PROUD PIRATE!
GIVE HIM AN INSTRUMENT, AND HE'LL PLAY BACKGROUND MUSIC! GIVE HIM A MOP, AND HE'LL CLEAN!
WHAT'S MORE, HE'S AN EXPERT WINE MAKER!
BAM
HE'S A 25-YEAR-OLD HUMAN MALE IN HIS PRIME! HE'S SIX FEET FOUR INCHES TALL AND WEIGHS 286 POUNDS!
HIS NAME IS BYRON! WE'LL START AT THE SPECIAL PRICE OF 480,000 BERRIES!
MURMUR MURMUR
RAISE YOUR PLATE TO MAKE YOUR BID.
BLAB
I SEE 520,000!
AND OVER THERE, 550,000!!
BLAB

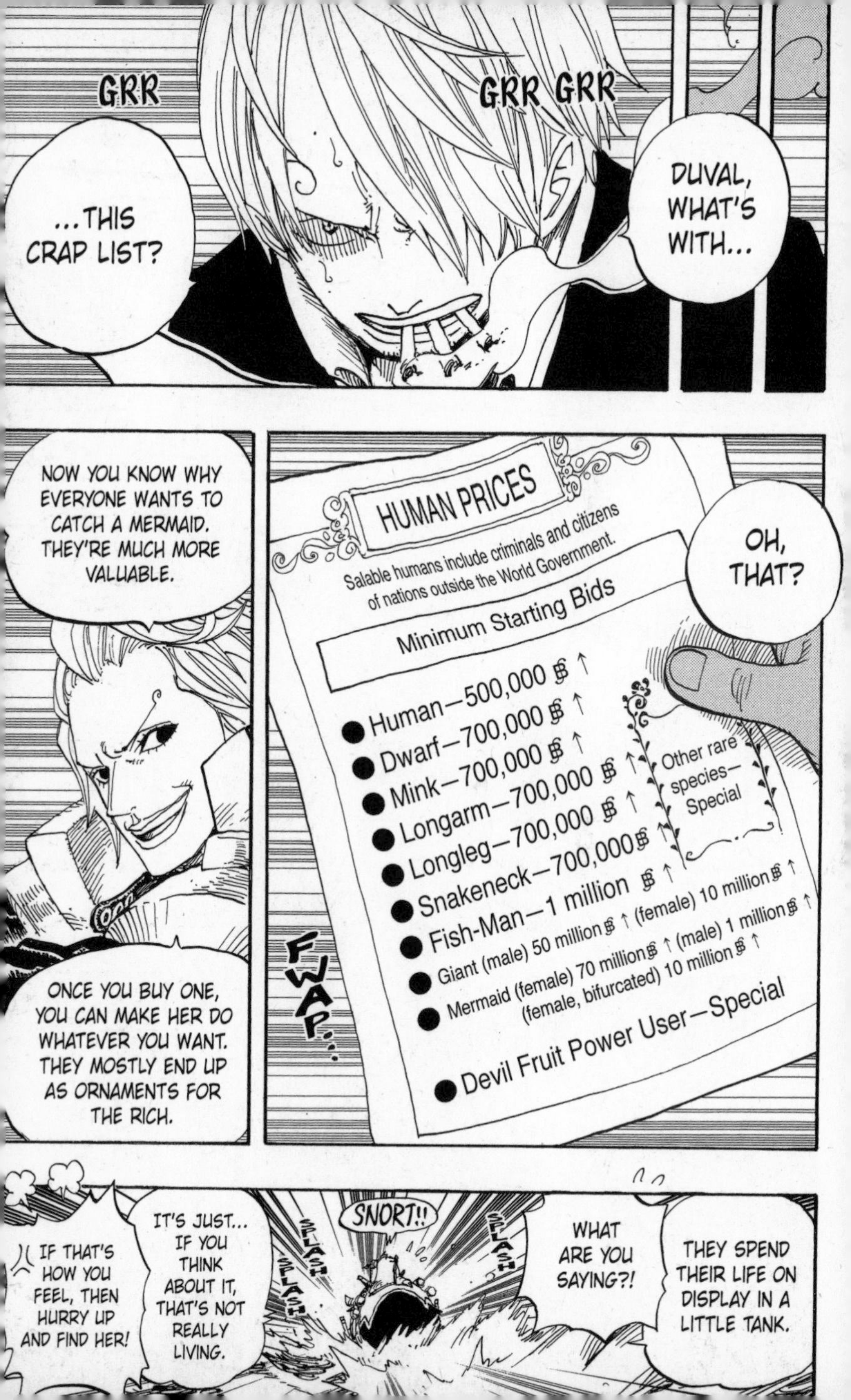
GRR GRR
DUVAL, WHAT'S WITH...
GRR
...THIS CRAP LIST?
OH, THAT?
HUMAN PRICES
Salable humans include criminals and citizens of nations outside the World Government.
Minimum Starting Bids
Human—500,000 ฿ ↑
Dwarf—700,000 ฿ ↑
Mink—700,000 ฿ ↑
Longarm—700,000 ฿ ↑
Longleg—700,000 ฿ ↑
Snakeneck—700,000 ฿ ↑
Fish-Man—1 million ฿ ↑ (female) 10 million ฿ ↑
Giant (male) 50 million ฿ ↑ (female) 1 million ฿ ↑
Mermaid (female) 70 million ฿ ↑ (male) 1 million ฿ ↑
(female, bifurcated) 10 million ฿ ↑
Devil Fruit Power User—Special
Other rare species—Special
FWAP...
NOW YOU KNOW WHY EVERYONE WANTS TO CATCH A MERMAID. THEY'RE MUCH MORE VALUABLE.
ONCE YOU BUY ONE, YOU CAN MAKE HER DO WHATEVER YOU WANT. THEY MOSTLY END UP AS ORNAMENTS FOR THE RICH.
THEY SPEND THEIR LIFE ON DISPLAY IN A LITTLE TANK.
WHAT ARE YOU SAYING?!
SPLASH
SNORT!!
SPLASH
SPLASH
IT'S JUST... IF YOU THINK ABOUT IT, THAT'S NOT REALLY LIVING.
IF THAT'S HOW YOU FEEL, THEN HURRY UP AND FIND HER!

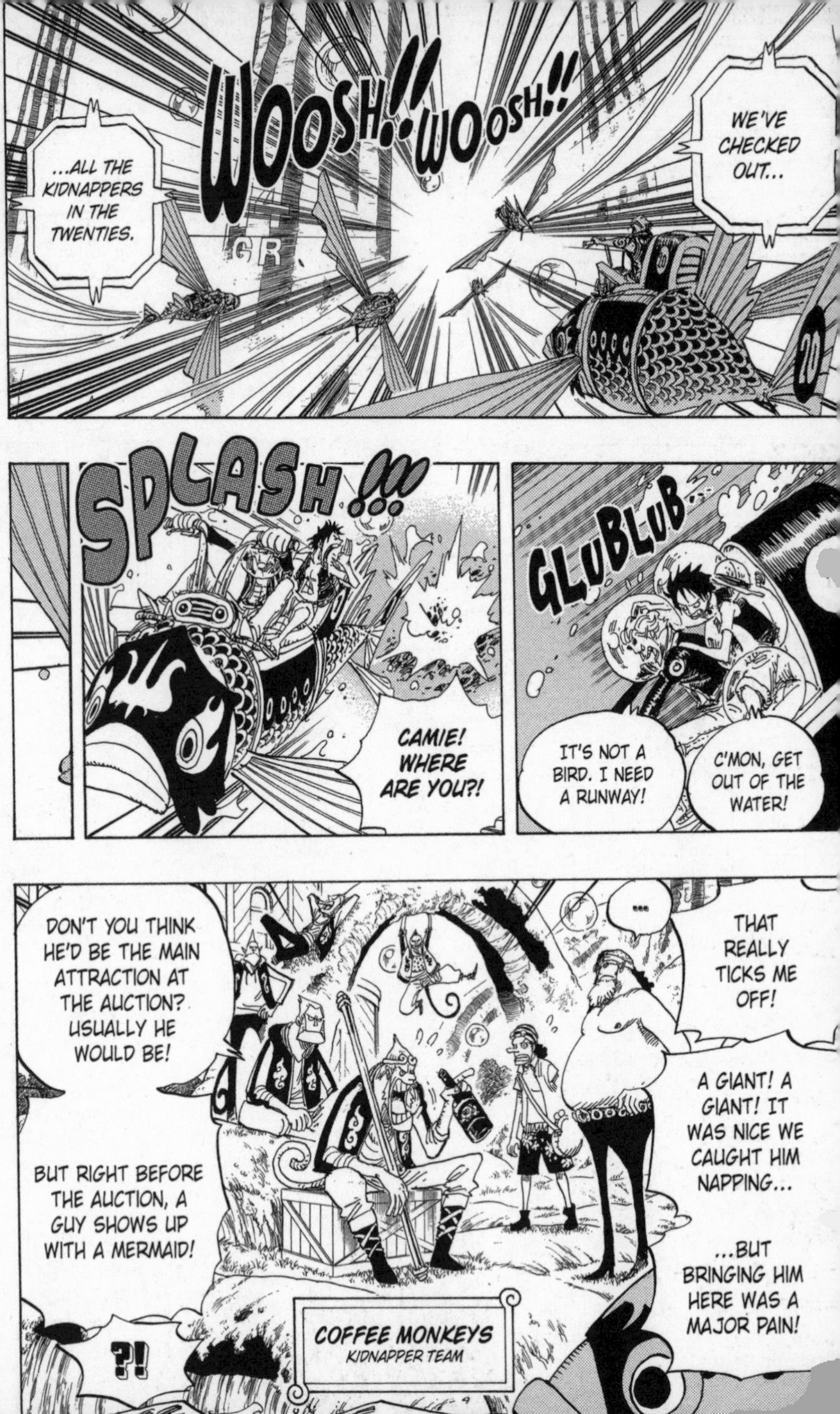
WE'VE CHECKED OUT...
WOOSH!! WOOSH!!
GR
...ALL THE KIDNAPPERS IN THE TWENTIES.
GLUBLUB
C'MON, GET OUT OF THE WATER!
IT'S NOT A BIRD. I NEED A RUNWAY!
SPLASH!!!
CAMIE! WHERE ARE YOU?!
...
THAT REALLY TICKS ME OFF!
A GIANT! A GIANT! IT WAS NICE WE CAUGHT HIM NAPPING...
...BUT BRINGING HIM HERE WAS A MAJOR PAIN!
DON'T YOU THINK HE'D BE THE MAIN ATTRACTION AT THE AUCTION? USUALLY HE WOULD BE!
BUT RIGHT BEFORE THE AUCTION, A GUY SHOWS UP WITH A MERMAID!
COFFEE MONKEYS
KIDNAPPER TEAM
?!

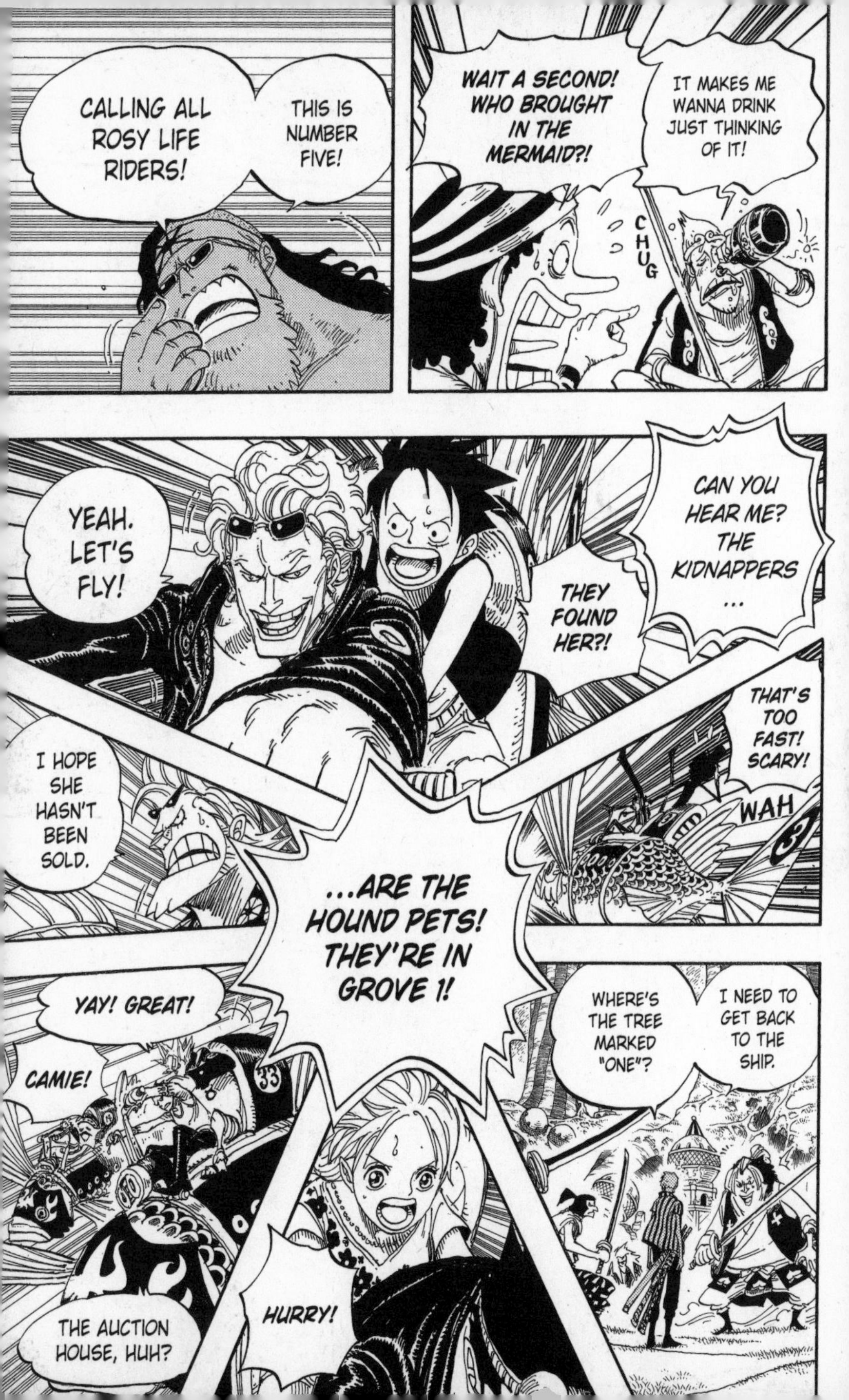
IT MAKES ME WANNA DRINK JUST THINKING OF IT!
WAIT A SECOND! WHO BROUGHT IN THE MERMAID?!
CHUG
THIS IS NUMBER FIVE!
CALLING ALL ROSY LIFE RIDERS!
CAN YOU HEAR ME? THE KIDNAPPERS ...
THEY FOUND HER?!
YEAH. LET'S FLY!
THAT'S TOO FAST! SCARY!
WAH
I HOPE SHE HASN'T BEEN SOLD.
...ARE THE HOUND PETS! THEY'RE IN GROVE 1!
I NEED TO GET BACK TO THE SHIP.
WHERE'S THE TREE MARKED "ONE"?
HURRY!
YAY! GREAT!
CAMIE!
THE AUCTION HOUSE, HUH?

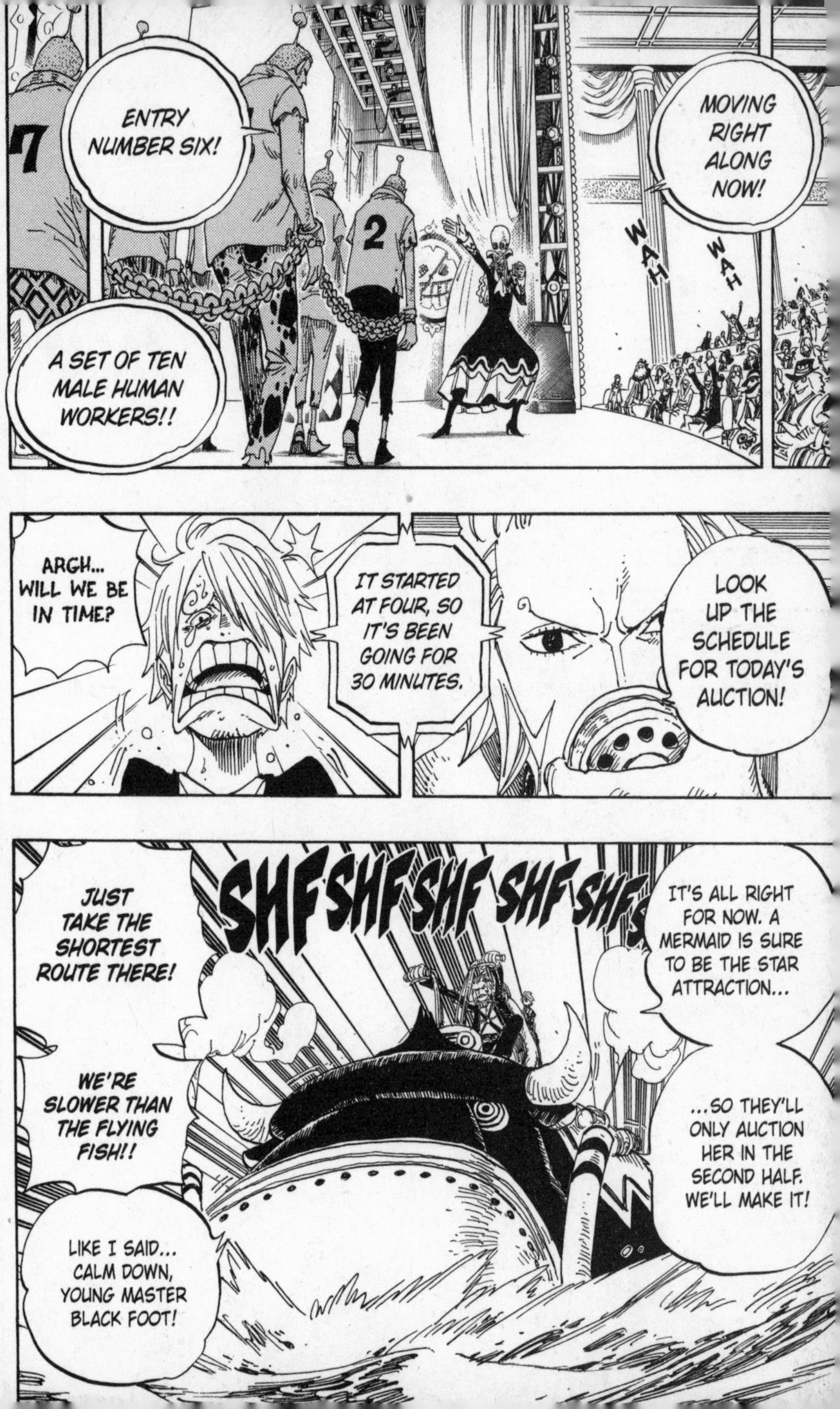
MOVING RIGHT ALONG NOW!
WAH
WAH
ENTRY NUMBER SIX!
A SET OF TEN MALE HUMAN WORKERS!!
LOOK UP THE SCHEDULE FOR TODAY'S AUCTION!
IT STARTED AT FOUR, SO IT'S BEEN GOING FOR 30 MINUTES.
ARGH... WILL WE BE IN TIME?
SHF SHF SHF SHF SHF
IT'S ALL RIGHT FOR NOW. A MERMAID IS SURE TO BE THE STAR ATTRACTION...
...SO THEY'LL ONLY AUCTION HER IN THE SECOND HALF. WE'LL MAKE IT!
JUST TAKE THE SHORTEST ROUTE THERE!
WE'RE SLOWER THAN THE FLYING FISH!!
LIKE I SAID... CALM DOWN, YOUNG MASTER BLACK FOOT!

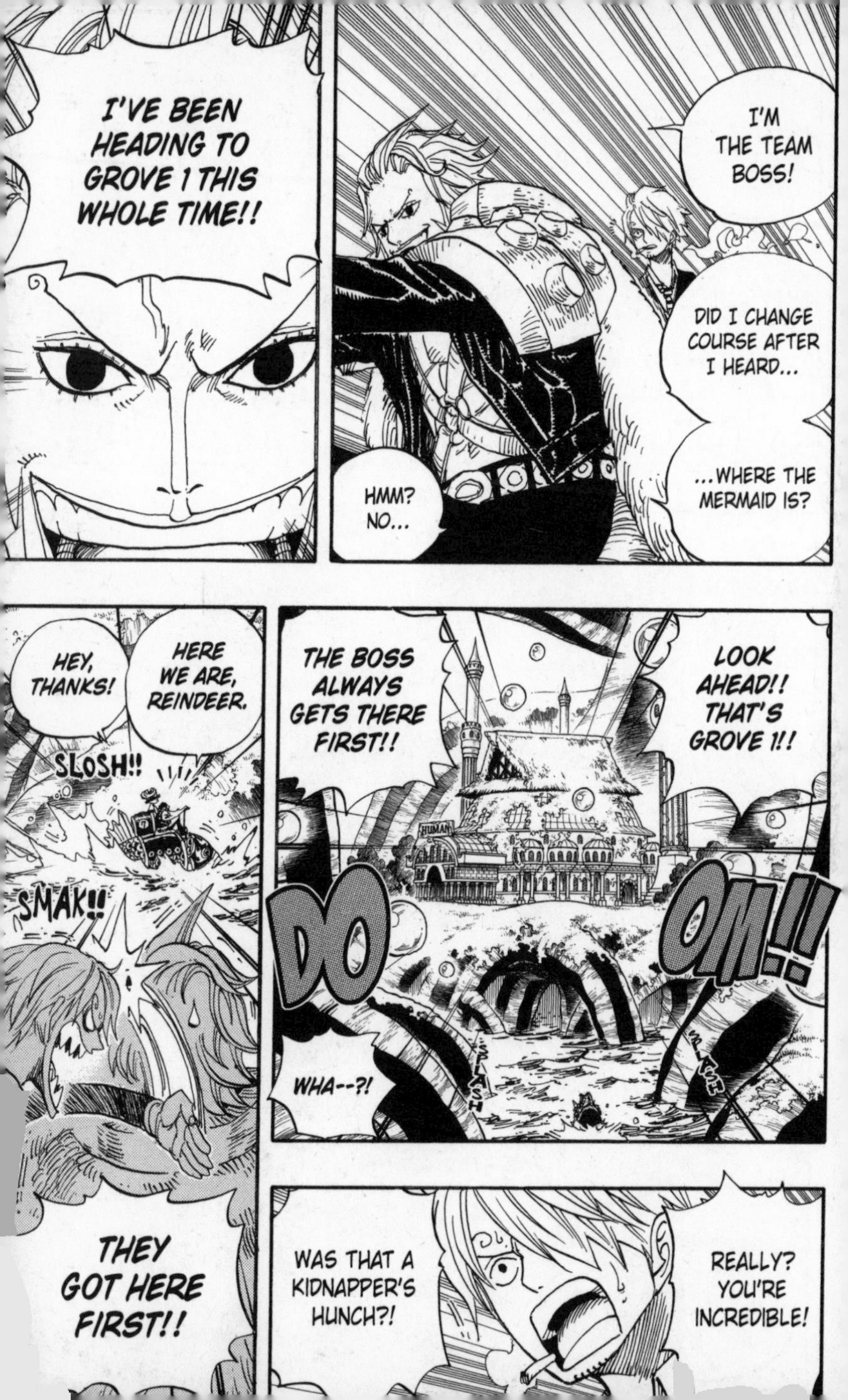
I'M THE TEAM BOSS!
DID I CHANGE COURSE AFTER I HEARD...
...WHERE THE MERMAID IS?
HMM? NO...
I'VE BEEN HEADING TO GROVE 1 THIS WHOLE TIME!!
LOOK AHEAD!! THAT'S GROVE 1!!
THE BOSS ALWAYS GETS THERE FIRST!!
HUMAN
DOOM!!
SPLASH
SPLASH
WHA--?!
REALLY? YOU'RE INCREDIBLE!
WAS THAT A KIDNAPPER'S HUNCH?!
HERE WE ARE, REINDEER.
HEY, THANKS!
SLOSH!!
SMAK!!
THEY GOT HERE FIRST!!

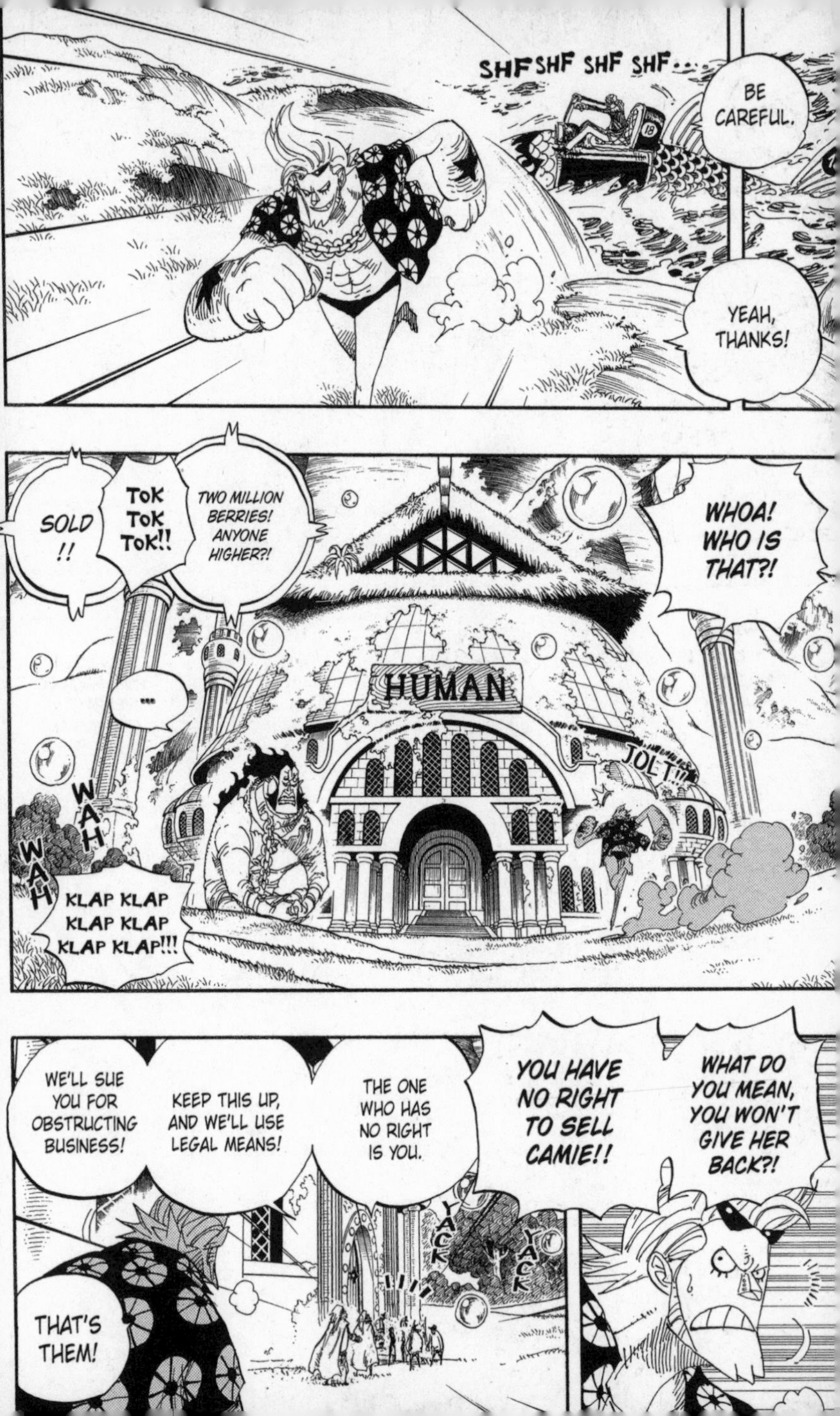
BE CAREFUL.
SHF SHF SHF SHF...
YEAH, THANKS!
WHOA! WHO IS THAT?!
TWO MILLION BERRIES! ANYONE HIGHER?!
TOK TOK TOK!!
SOLD!!
HUMAN
JOLT!!
...
WAH WAH
KLAP KLAP KLAP KLAP KLAP KLAP!!!
WHAT DO YOU MEAN, YOU WON'T GIVE HER BACK?!
YOU HAVE NO RIGHT TO SELL CAMIE!!
THE ONE WHO HAS NO RIGHT IS YOU.
KEEP THIS UP, AND WE'LL USE LEGAL MEANS!
WE'LL SUE YOU FOR OBSTRUCTING BUSINESS!
YACK YACK
THAT'S THEM!

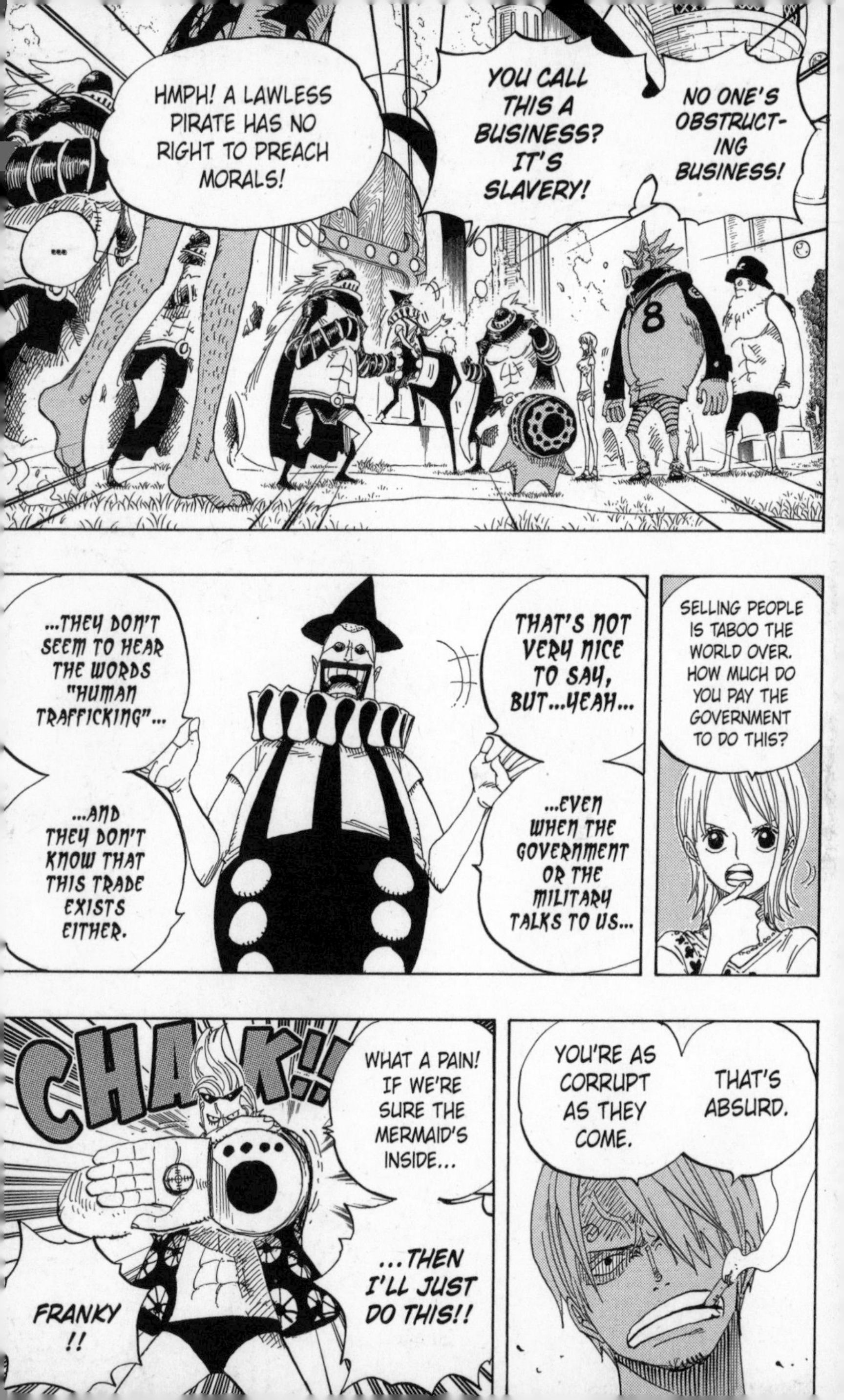
NO ONE'S OBSTRUCTING BUSINESS!
YOU CALL THIS A BUSINESS? IT'S SLAVERY!
HMPH! A LAWLESS PIRATE HAS NO RIGHT TO PREACH MORALS!
...
SELLING PEOPLE IS TABOO THE WORLD OVER. HOW MUCH DO YOU PAY THE GOVERNMENT TO DO THIS?
THAT'S NOT VERY NICE TO SAY, BUT...YEAH...
...EVEN WHEN THE GOVERNMENT OR THE MILITARY TALKS TO US...
...THEY DON'T SEEM TO HEAR THE WORDS "HUMAN TRAFFICKING"...
...AND THEY DON'T KNOW THAT THIS TRADE EXISTS EITHER.
THAT'S ABSURD.
YOU'RE AS CORRUPT AS THEY COME.
CHAK!!
WHAT A PAIN! IF WE'RE SURE THE MERMAID'S INSIDE...
...THEN I'LL JUST DO THIS!!
FRANKY !!

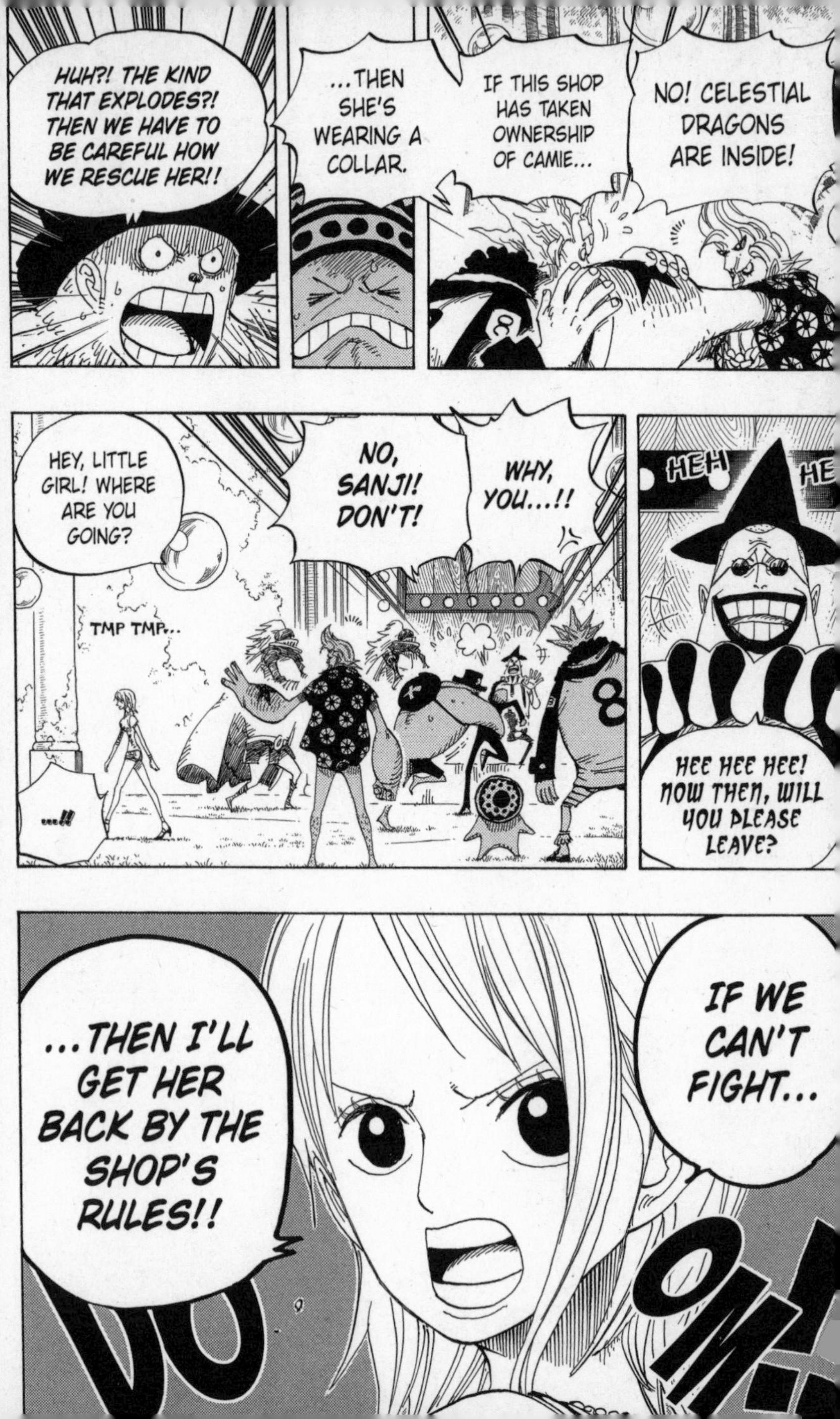
NO! CELESTIAL DRAGONS ARE INSIDE!
IF THIS SHOP HAS TAKEN OWNERSHIP OF CAMIE...
...THEN SHE'S WEARING A COLLAR.
HUH?! THE KIND THAT EXPLODES?! THEN WE HAVE TO BE CAREFUL HOW WE RESCUE HER!!
HEH HE
HEE HEE HEE! NOW THEN, WILL YOU PLEASE LEAVE?
WHY, YOU...!!
NO, SANJI! DON'T!
HEY, LITTLE GIRL! WHERE ARE YOU GOING?
TMP TMP...
...!!
IF WE CAN'T FIGHT...
...THEN I'LL GET HER BACK BY THE SHOP'S RULES!!

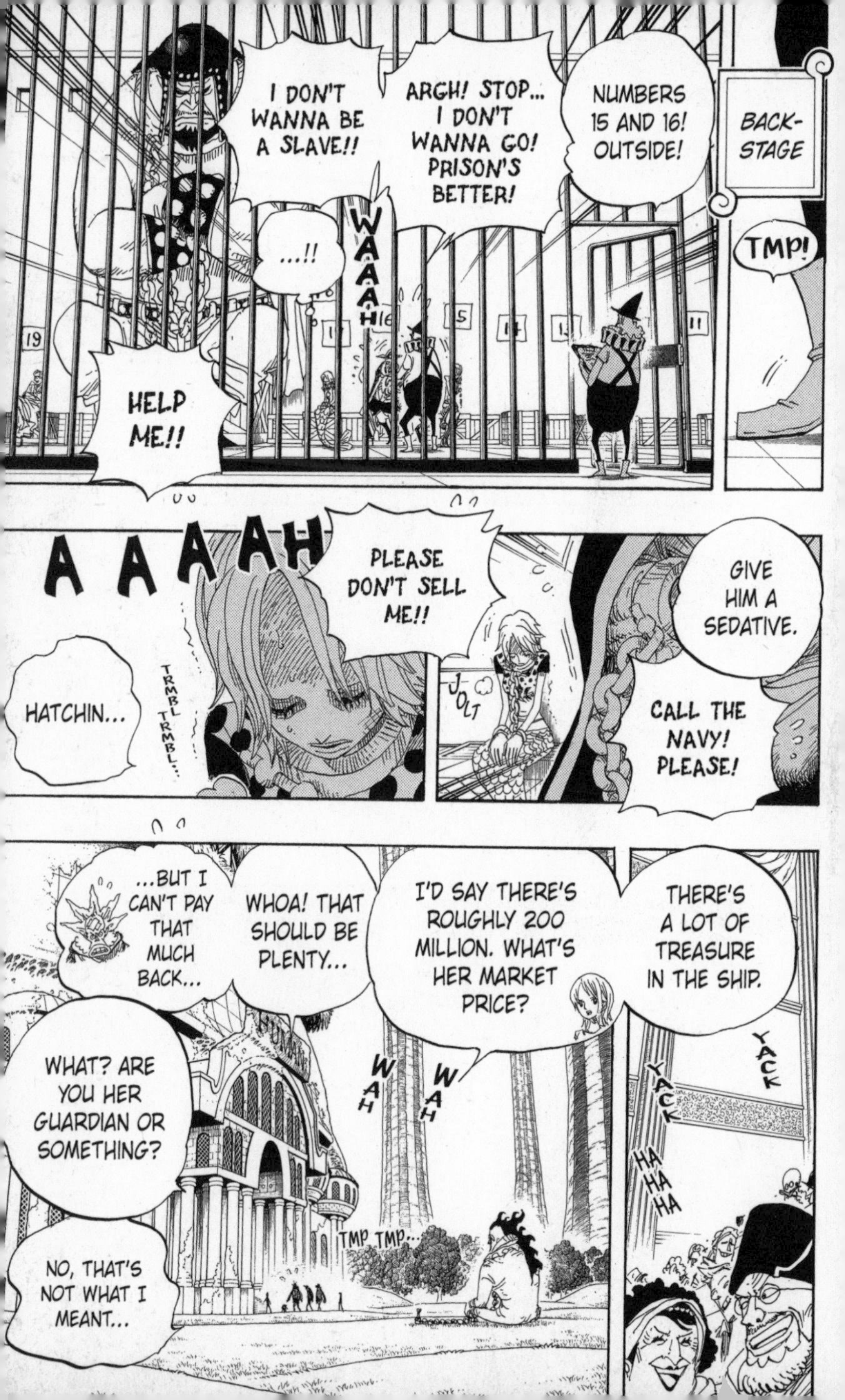
BACK-STAGE
TMP!
NUMBERS 15 AND 16! OUTSIDE!
ARGH! STOP... I DON'T WANNA GO! PRISON'S BETTER!
I DON'T WANNA BE A SLAVE!!
...!!
WAAAAH
HELP ME!!
GIVE HIM A SEDATIVE.
CALL THE NAVY! PLEASE!
JOLT
PLEASE DON'T SELL ME!!
AAAAH
HATCHIN...
TRMBL TRMBL...
THERE'S A LOT OF TREASURE IN THE SHIP.
YACK YACK
HA HA HA
I'D SAY THERE'S ROUGHLY 200 MILLION. WHAT'S HER MARKET PRICE?
WHOA! THAT SHOULD BE PLENTY...
...BUT I CAN'T PAY THAT MUCH BACK...
WAH WAH
WHAT? ARE YOU HER GUARDIAN OR SOMETHING?
TMP TMP...
NO, THAT'S NOT WHAT I MEANT...

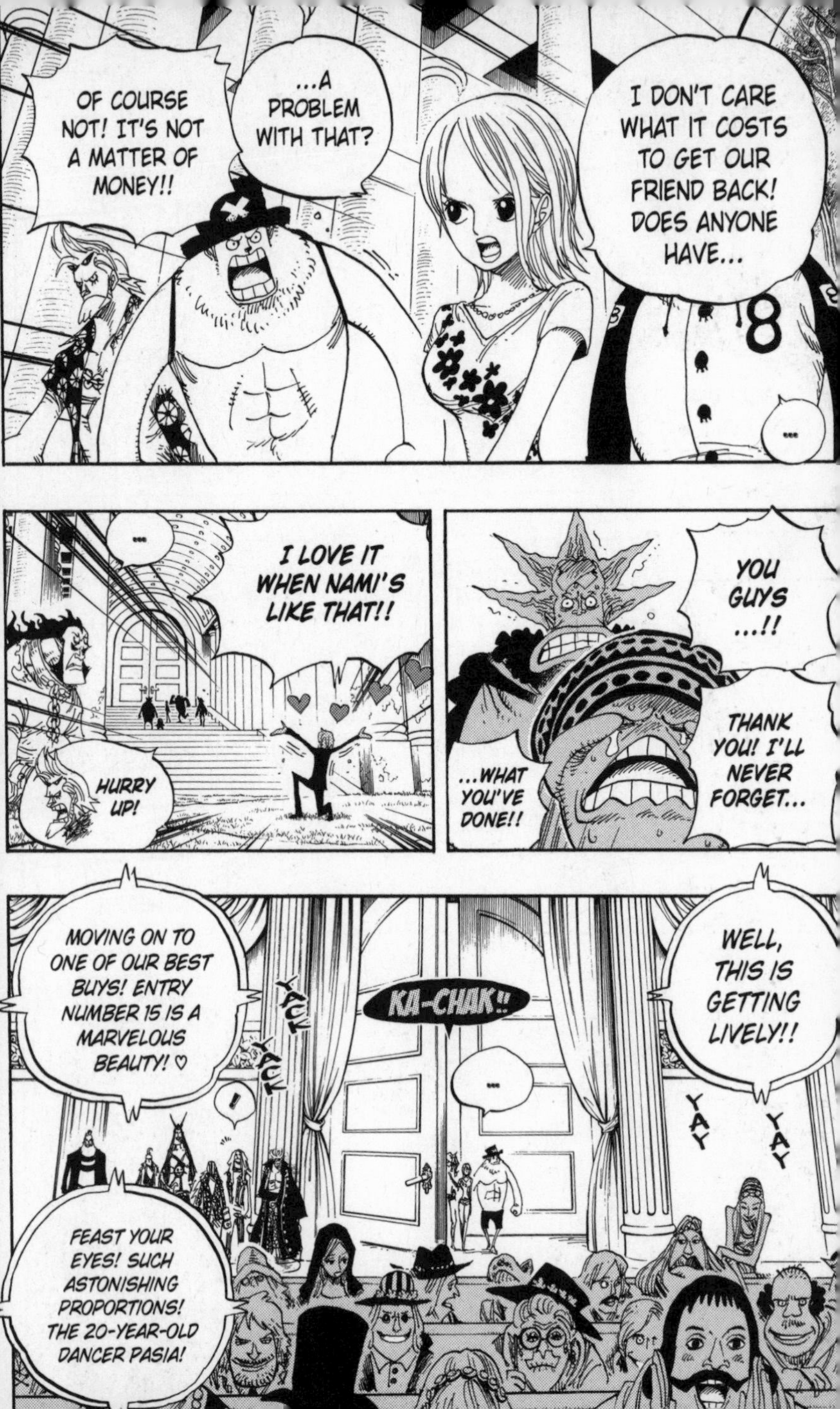
I DON'T CARE WHAT IT COSTS TO GET OUR FRIEND BACK! DOES ANYONE HAVE...
...A PROBLEM WITH THAT?
OF COURSE NOT! IT'S NOT A MATTER OF MONEY!!
...
YOU GUYS ...!!
THANK YOU! I'LL NEVER FORGET...
...WHAT YOU'VE DONE!!
I LOVE IT WHEN NAMI'S LIKE THAT!!
...
HURRY UP!
WELL, THIS IS GETTING LIVELY!!
YAY YAY
KA-CHAK!!
...
MOVING ON TO ONE OF OUR BEST BUYS! ENTRY NUMBER 15 IS A MARVELOUS BEAUTY! ♡
YACK YACK
!
FEAST YOUR EYES! SUCH ASTONISHING PROPORTIONS! THE 20-YEAR-OLD DANCER PASIA!

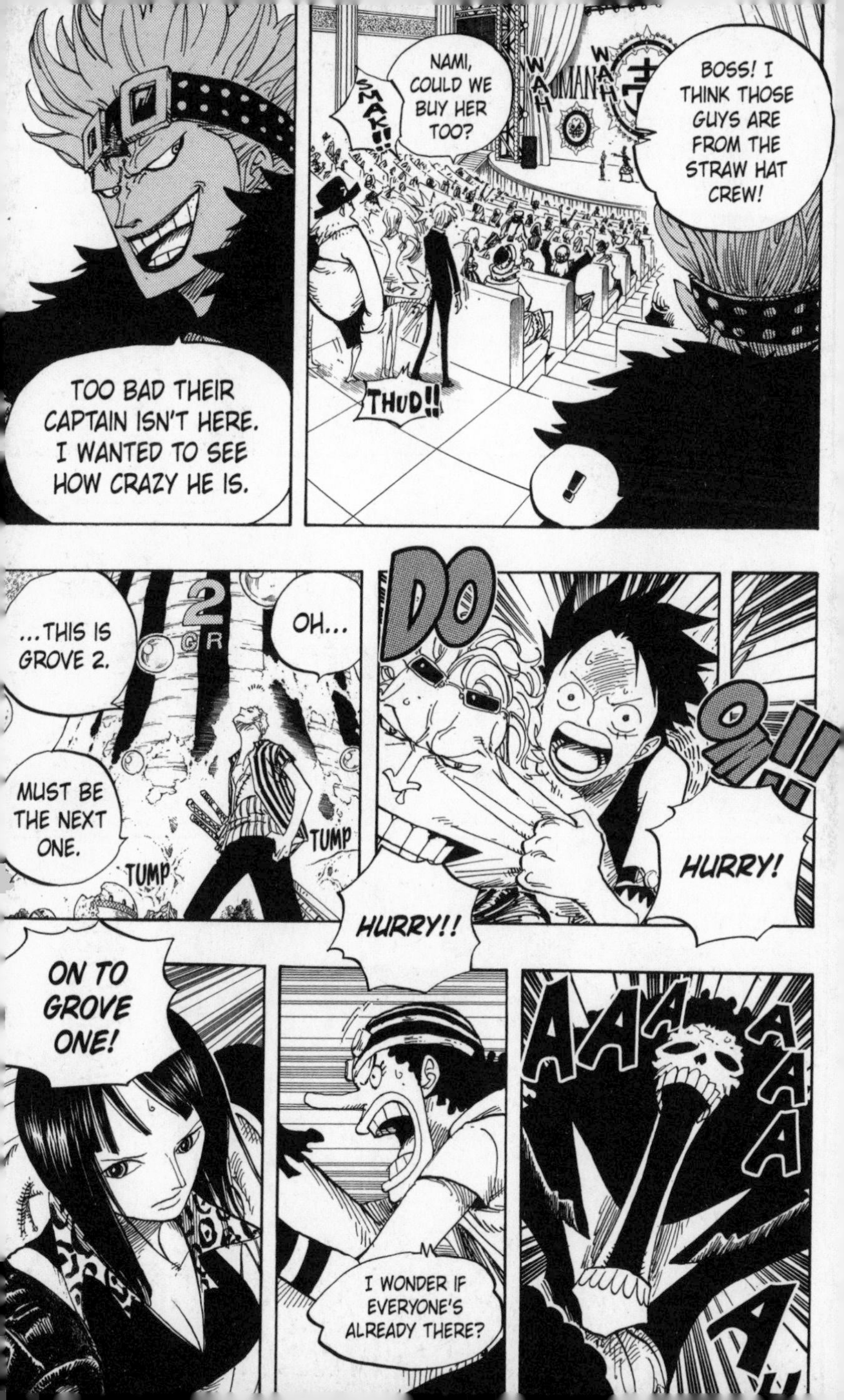
BOSS! I THINK THOSE GUYS ARE FROM THE STRAW HAT CREW!
WAH WAH
NAMI, COULD WE BUY HER TOO?
SMAK!!
THUD!!
!
TOO BAD THEIR CAPTAIN ISN'T HERE. I WANTED TO SEE HOW CRAZY HE IS.
DO
OH!!
HURRY!
HURRY!!
OH...
...THIS IS GROVE 2.
2 GR
MUST BE THE NEXT ONE.
TUMP
TUMP
AAAAAAAA
I WONDER IF EVERYONE'S ALREADY THERE?
ON TO GROVE ONE!

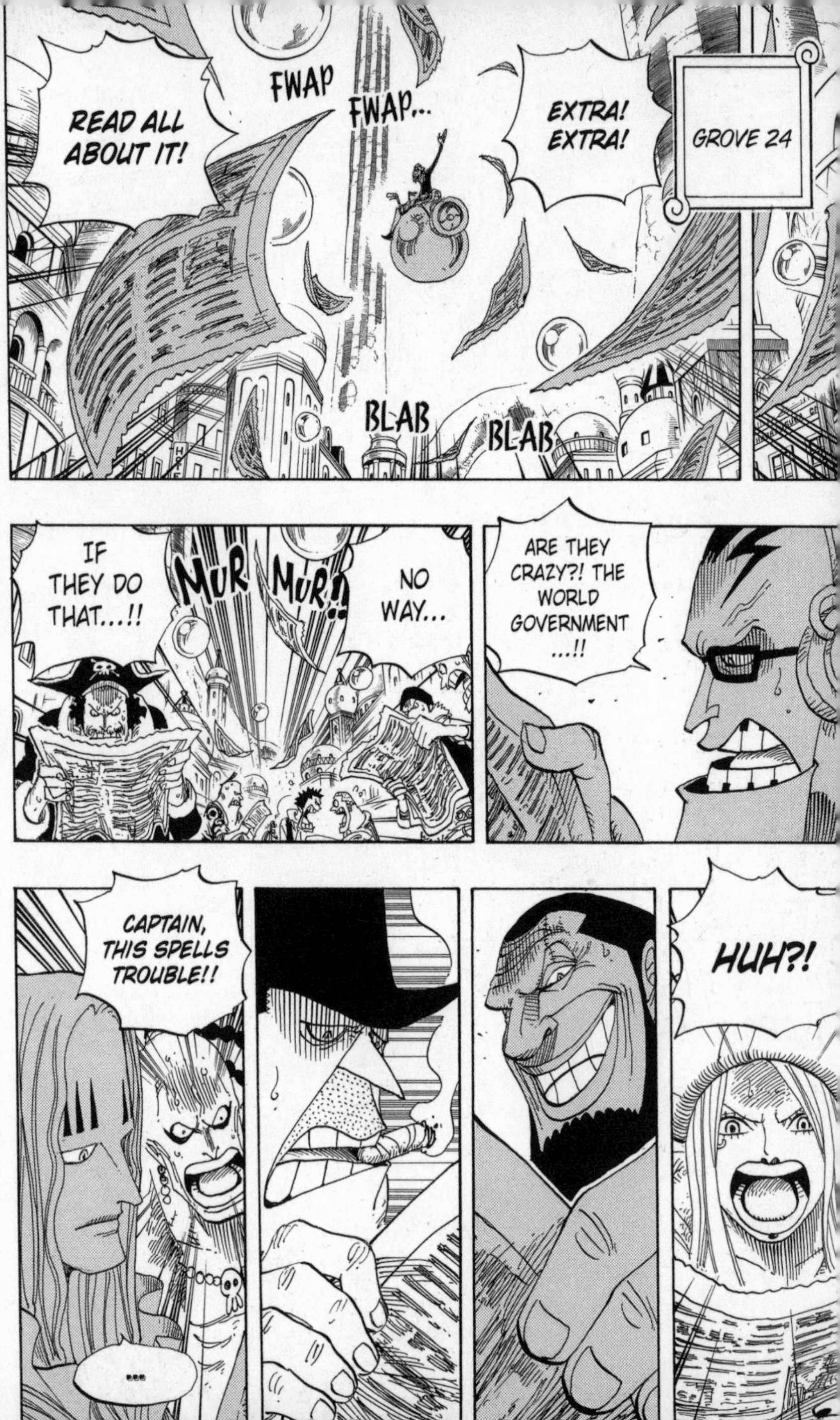
GROVE 24
EXTRA! EXTRA!
FWAP
FWAP...
READ ALL ABOUT IT!
BLAB
BLAB
ARE THEY CRAZY?! THE WORLD GOVERNMENT ...!!
NO WAY...
MUR MUR!!
IF THEY DO THAT...!!
HUH?!
CAPTAIN, THIS SPELLS TROUBLE!!
...

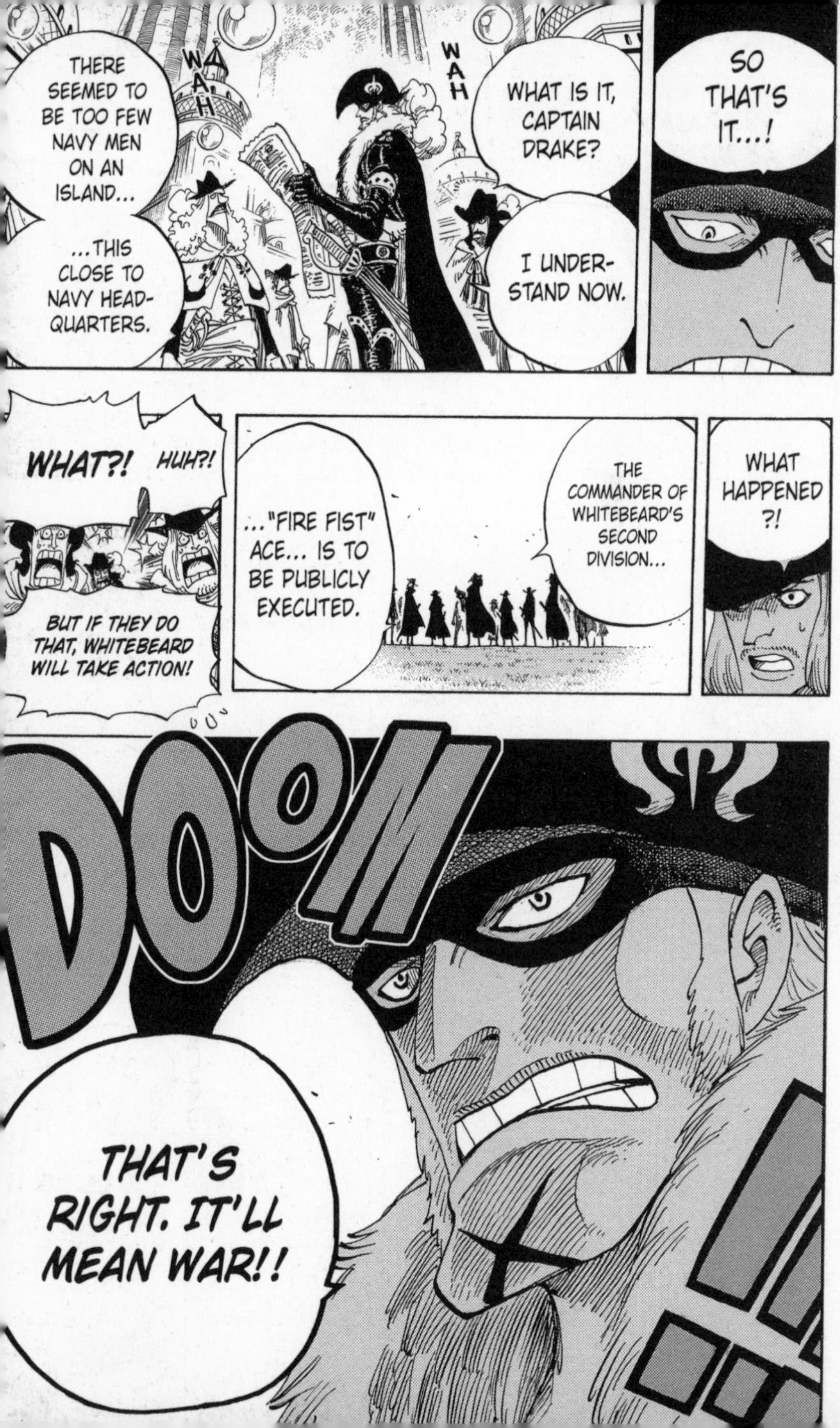
SO THAT'S IT...!
WAH
WHAT IS IT, CAPTAIN DRAKE?
I UNDER-STAND NOW.
WAH
THERE SEEMED TO BE TOO FEW NAVY MEN ON AN ISLAND...
...THIS CLOSE TO NAVY HEAD-QUARTERS.
WHAT HAPPENED ?!
THE COMMANDER OF WHITEBEARD'S SECOND DIVISION...
..."FIRE FIST" ACE... IS TO BE PUBLICLY EXECUTED.
HUH?!
WHAT?!
BUT IF THEY DO THAT, WHITEBEARD WILL TAKE ACTION!
DOOM
THAT'S RIGHT. IT'LL MEAN WAR!!

DUVAL IS SAYING, "OOPS! I MEAN SBS QUESTION CORNER!"

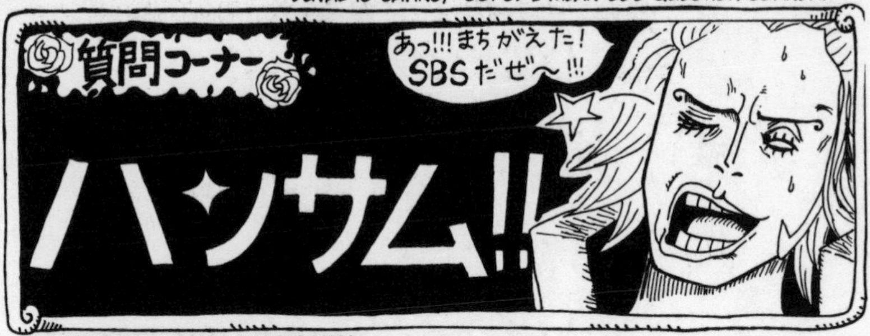
質問コーナー
あっ!!!まちがえた!
SBSだぜ〜!!!
ハンサム!!

(A★S, Kanagawa)

BACKGROUND READS "HANDSOME."

Q: Hello, Oda Sensei! For more than ten years you've kept me on the edge of my seat, biting my fingernails, and now I've got a question for you. In Chapter 501: The World Begins to Swell, at the bottom of the price list, where it lists mermaids, it says "bifurcated." Does that mean a mermaid who dates two different guys at the same time? I'm so worried about it, I can't get a girlfriend.

--Kinta

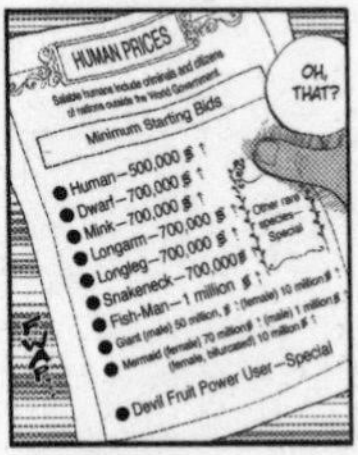
HUMAN PRICES
OH, THAT?
Minimum Starting Bids
Human—500,000 ฿↑
Dwarf—700,000 ฿↑
Mink—700,000 ฿↑
Longarm—700,000 ฿↑
Longleg—700,000 ฿↑
Snakeneck—700,000 ฿↑
Fish-Man—1 million ฿↑
Devil Fruit Power User—Special

A: Yes, that's right. A two-timing mermaid who plays around with two different men sells for a lower price! Or so it seems. That's the way it goes. Not! In volume 44, chapter 424, Kokoro explains it, saying "At thirty, the prime of a mermaid's life, her tailfin splits in two so she can live on land." That's all there is to it. Young mermaids like Camie sell for a higher price. Maybe I should devote some space in the manga to explaining the biology of mermaids in greater detail.

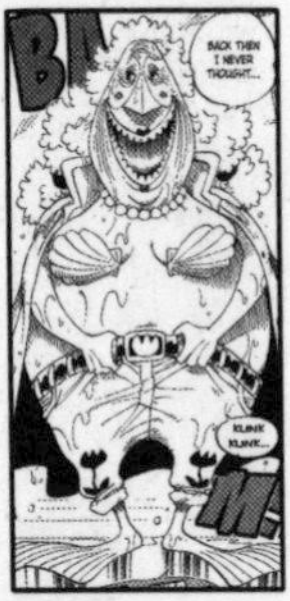
BACK THEN I NEVER THOUGHT...

Q: Sometimes Kuma has trouble saying he is a Paw-Paw Man who ate the Paw-Paw Fruit. He does, doesn't he?*

--Tomo-san

*In Japanese, "Paw-Paw" is "Nikyu-Nikyu." In other words, a real tongue-twister!--Ed.

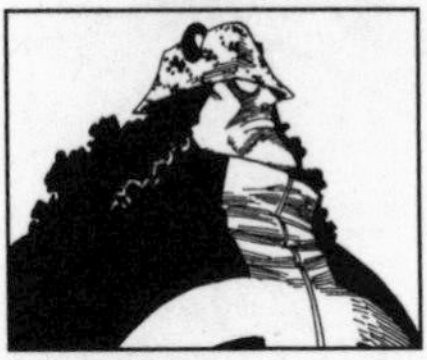

A: No, he doesn't! He's one of the Seven Warlords of the Sea! Right, Kuma? All right, let's have the man himself say it three times fast! Take it away!

Kuma: **Pah-paw...**

A: The Question Corner...is now...over. See you next volume...

Kuma: **Poppah...**

A: Forget it!!

Chapter 502:
THE INCIDENT OF THE CELESTIAL DRAGONS

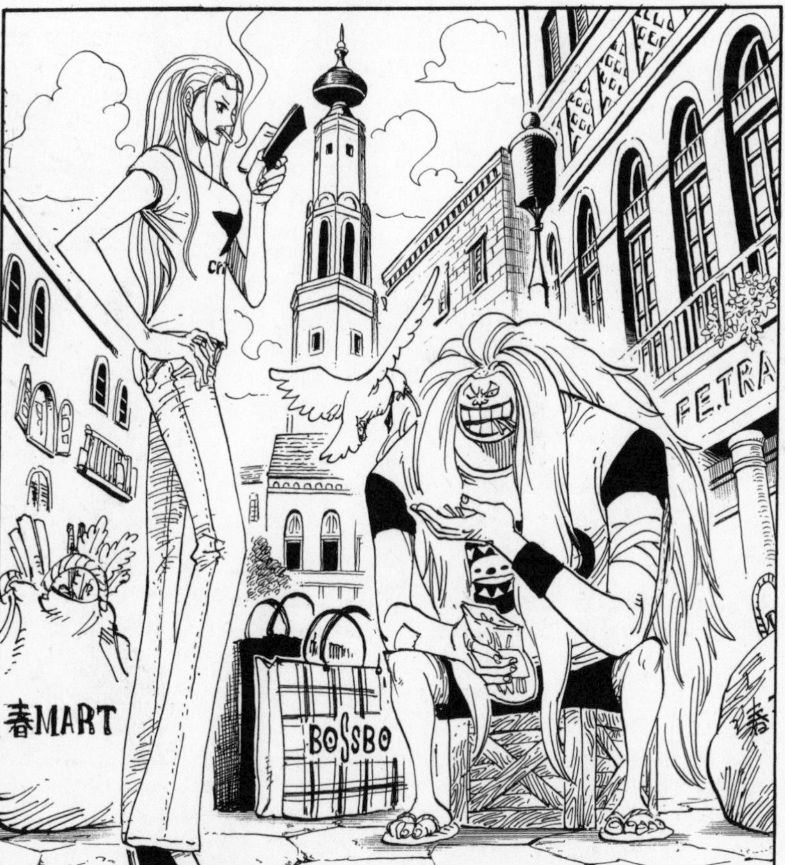

FE.TRA
春MART
BOSSBO

CP9'S INDEPENDENT REPORT, VOL. 12:
"SHOPPING AND A SHORT BREAK"

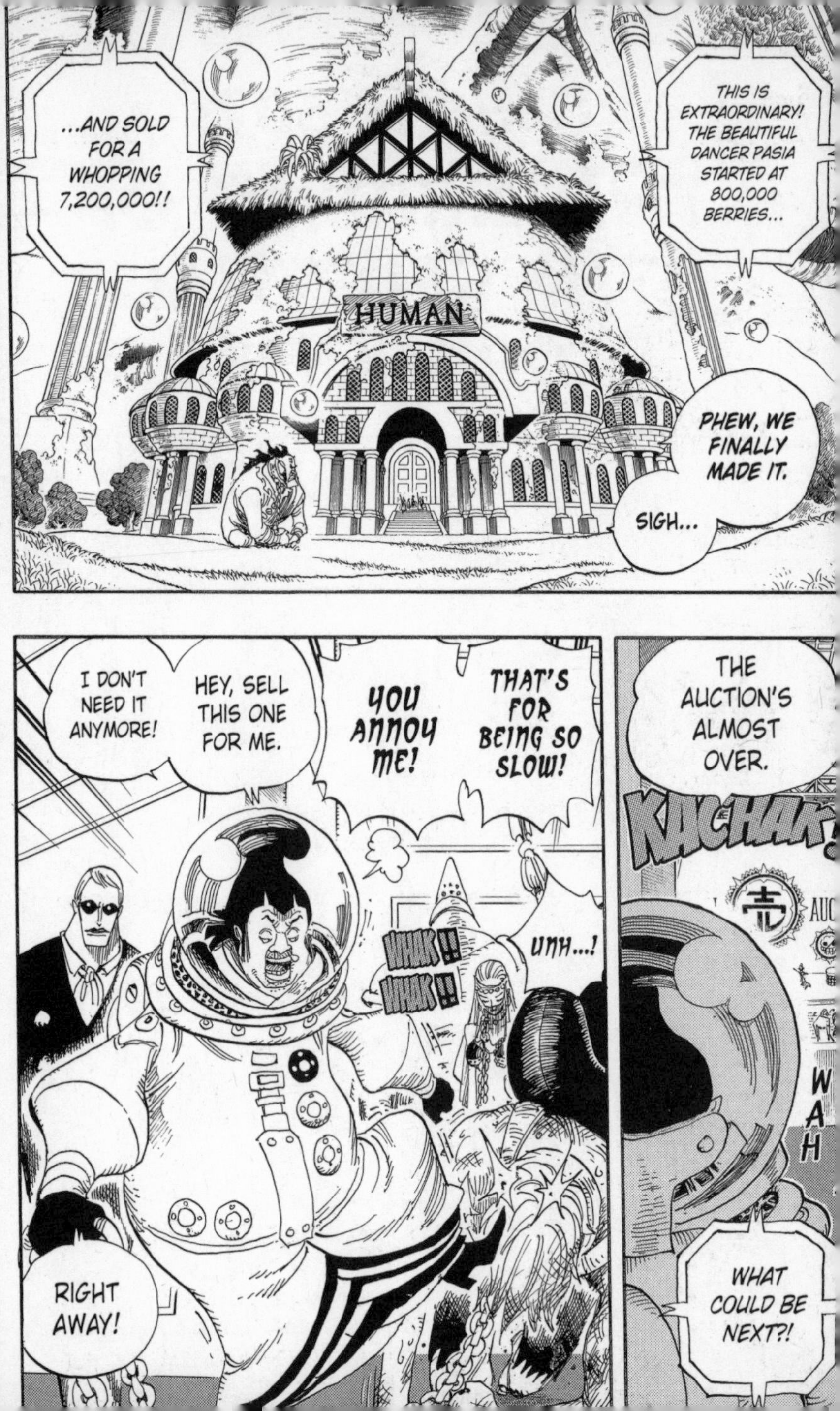
THIS IS EXTRAORDINARY! THE BEAUTIFUL DANCER PASIA STARTED AT 800,000 BERRIES...
...AND SOLD FOR A WHOPPING 7,200,000!!
HUMAN
PHEW, WE FINALLY MADE IT.
SIGH...
THE AUCTION'S ALMOST OVER.
KACHAK!
WAH
WHAT COULD BE NEXT?!
THAT'S FOR BEING SO SLOW!
YOU ANNOY ME!
HEY, SELL THIS ONE FOR ME.
I DON'T NEED IT ANYMORE!
WHAK!!
WHAK!!
UNH...!
RIGHT AWAY!

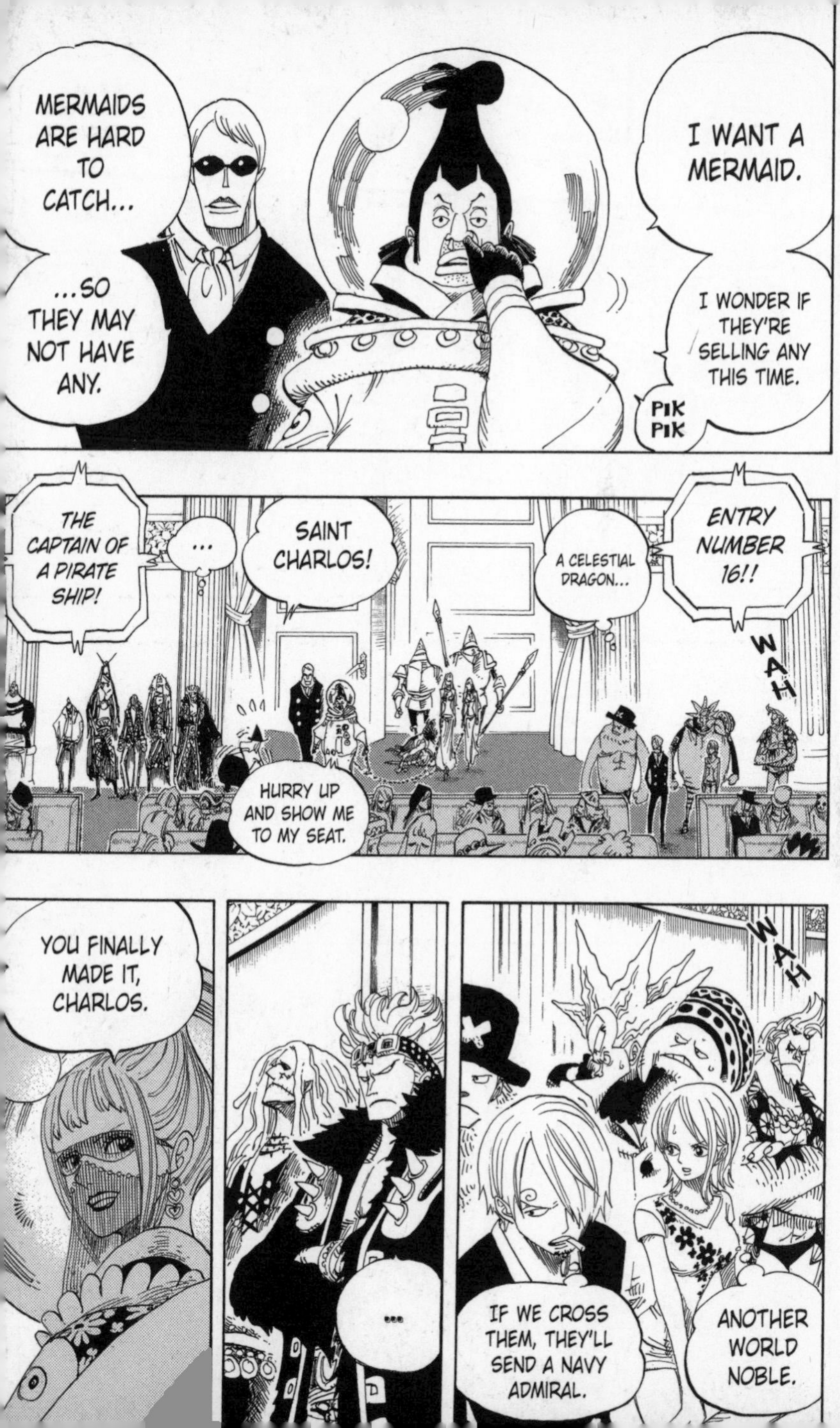
I WANT A MERMAID.
I WONDER IF THEY'RE SELLING ANY THIS TIME.
PIK PIK
MERMAIDS ARE HARD TO CATCH...
...SO THEY MAY NOT HAVE ANY.
ENTRY NUMBER 16!!
WAH
A CELESTIAL DRAGON...
SAINT CHARLOS!
...
THE CAPTAIN OF A PIRATE SHIP!
HURRY UP AND SHOW ME TO MY SEAT.
WAH
ANOTHER WORLD NOBLE.
IF WE CROSS THEM, THEY'LL SEND A NAVY ADMIRAL.
...
YOU FINALLY MADE IT, CHARLOS.

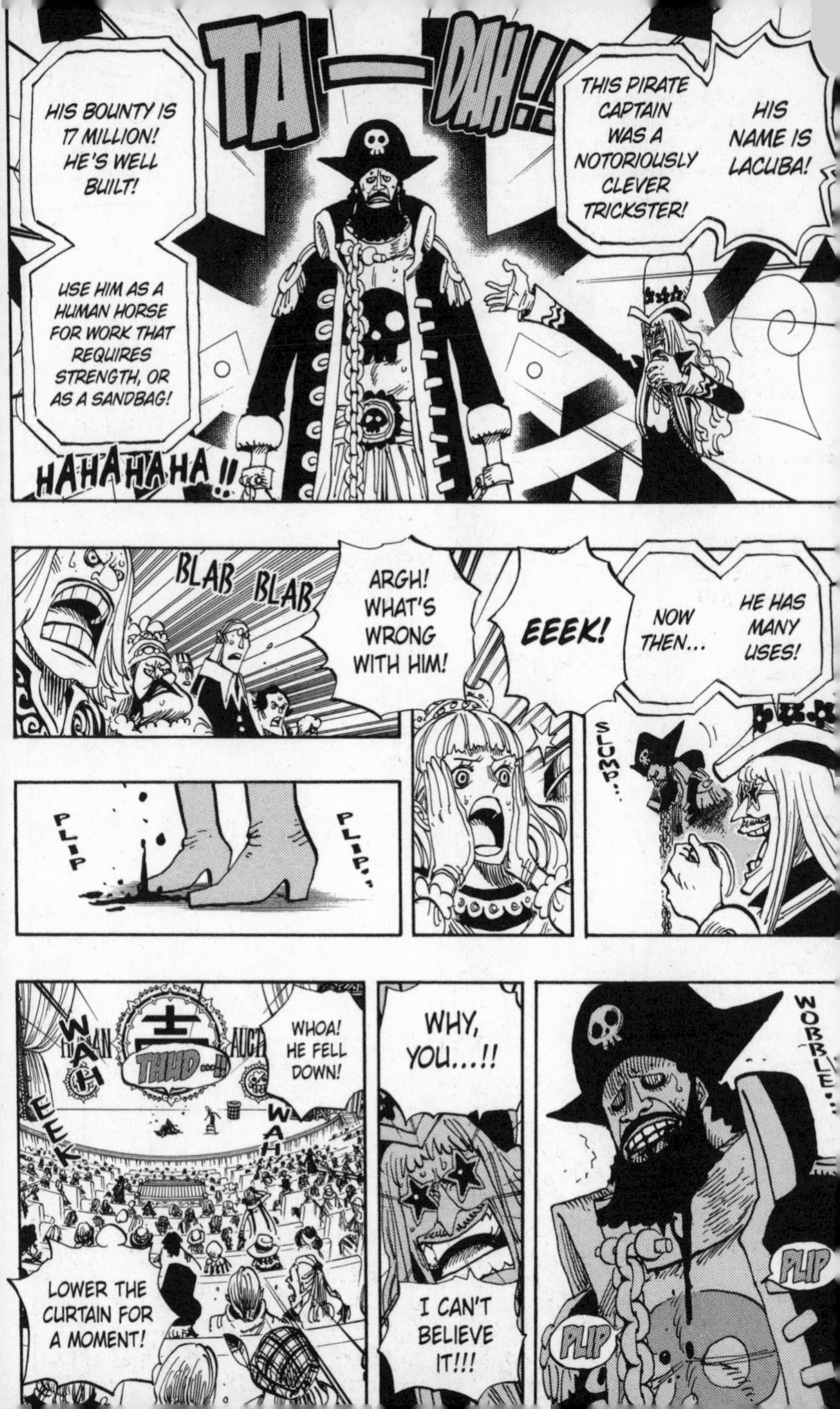
HIS NAME IS LACUBA!
THIS PIRATE CAPTAIN WAS A NOTORIOUSLY CLEVER TRICKSTER!
TA—DAH!!
HIS BOUNTY IS 17 MILLION! HE'S WELL BUILT!
USE HIM AS A HUMAN HORSE FOR WORK THAT REQUIRES STRENGTH, OR AS A SANDBAG!
HAHAHAHA!!
HE HAS MANY USES!
NOW THEN...
SLUMP...
EEEK!
BLAB BLAB
ARGH! WHAT'S WRONG WITH HIM!
PLIP
PLIP...
WOBBLE...
PLIP
PLIP
WHY, YOU...!!
I CAN'T BELIEVE IT!!!
WHOA! HE FELL DOWN!
THUD...!!
WAH
WAH
EEEK
LOWER THE CURTAIN FOR A MOMENT!

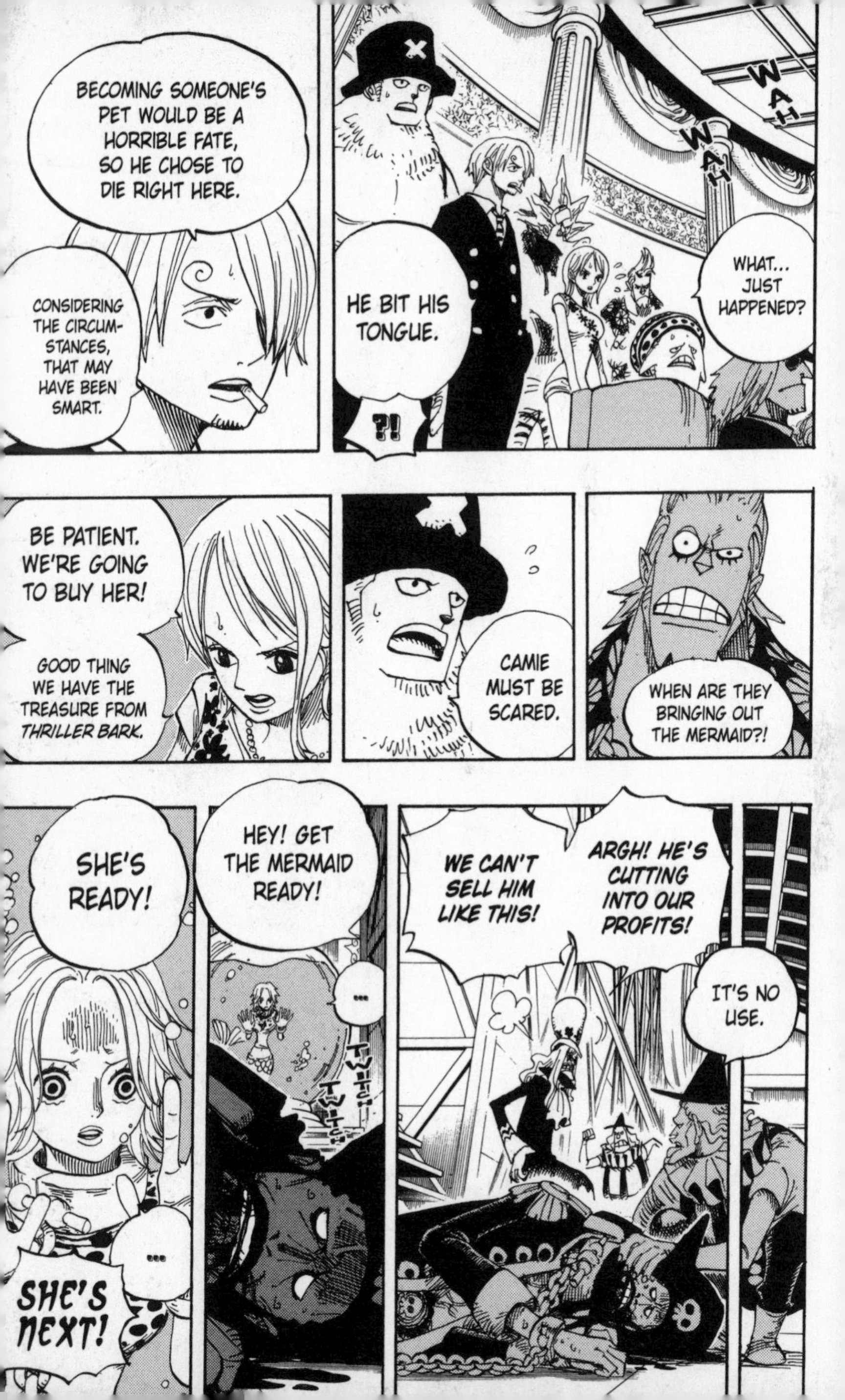
WAH
WAH
WHAT... JUST HAPPENED?
HE BIT HIS TONGUE.
?!
BECOMING SOMEONE'S PET WOULD BE A HORRIBLE FATE, SO HE CHOSE TO DIE RIGHT HERE.
CONSIDERING THE CIRCUM-STANCES, THAT MAY HAVE BEEN SMART.
WHEN ARE THEY BRINGING OUT THE MERMAID?!
CAMIE MUST BE SCARED.
BE PATIENT. WE'RE GOING TO BUY HER!
GOOD THING WE HAVE THE TREASURE FROM *THRILLER BARK*.
ARGH! HE'S CUTTING INTO OUR PROFITS!
WE CAN'T SELL HIM LIKE THIS!
IT'S NO USE.
HEY! GET THE MERMAID READY!
...
TWITCH
TWITCH
SHE'S READY!
...
SHE'S NEXT!

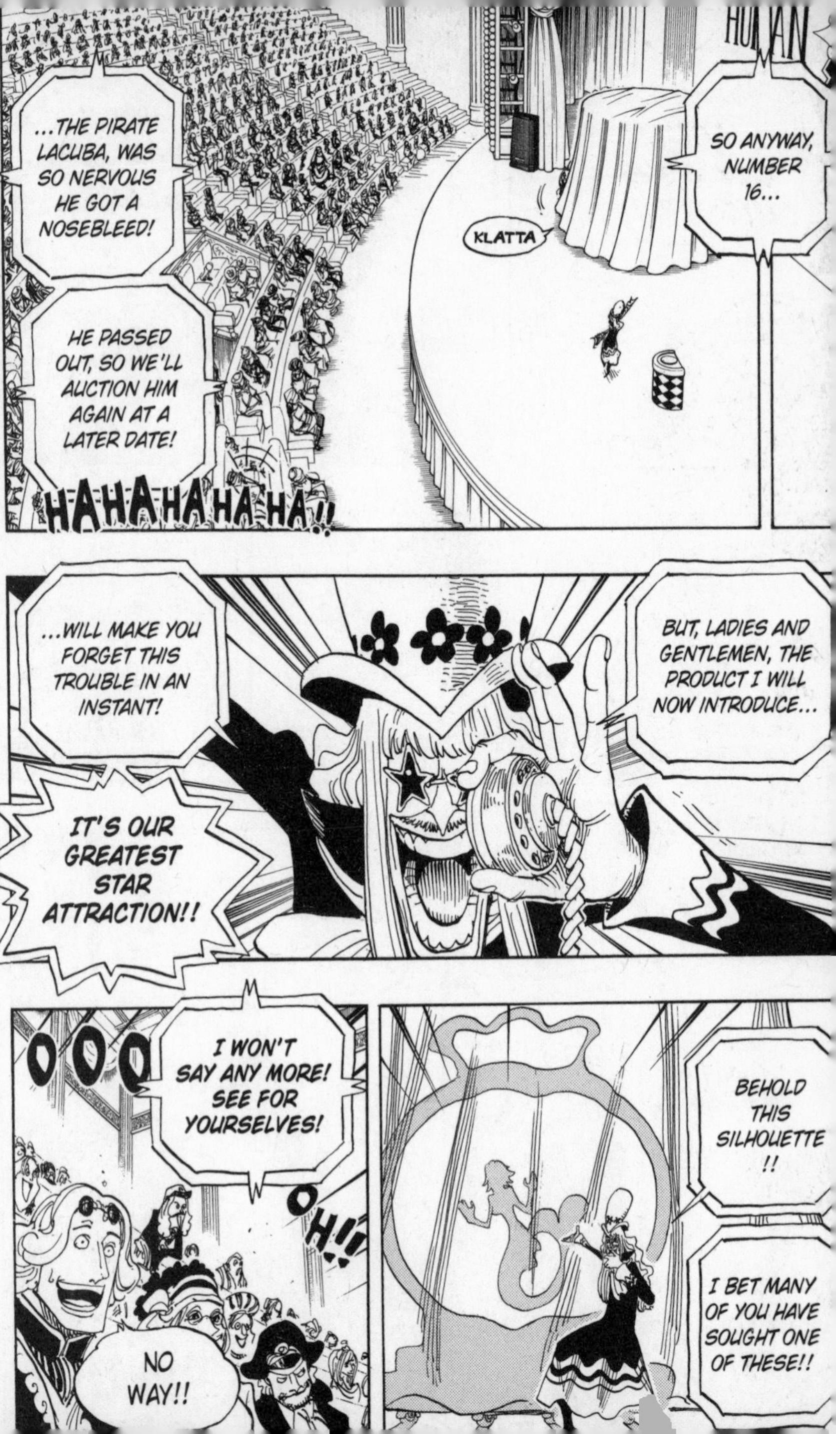
HUMAN
SO ANYWAY, NUMBER 16...
KLATTA
...THE PIRATE LACUBA, WAS SO NERVOUS HE GOT A NOSEBLEED!
HE PASSED OUT, SO WE'LL AUCTION HIM AGAIN AT A LATER DATE!
HAHAHAHAHAHA!!
BUT, LADIES AND GENTLEMEN, THE PRODUCT I WILL NOW INTRODUCE...
...WILL MAKE YOU FORGET THIS TROUBLE IN AN INSTANT!
IT'S OUR GREATEST STAR ATTRACTION!!
BEHOLD THIS SILHOUETTE!!
I BET MANY OF YOU HAVE SOUGHT ONE OF THESE!!
I WON'T SAY ANY MORE! SEE FOR YOURSELVES!
OOO
OH!!
NO WAY!!

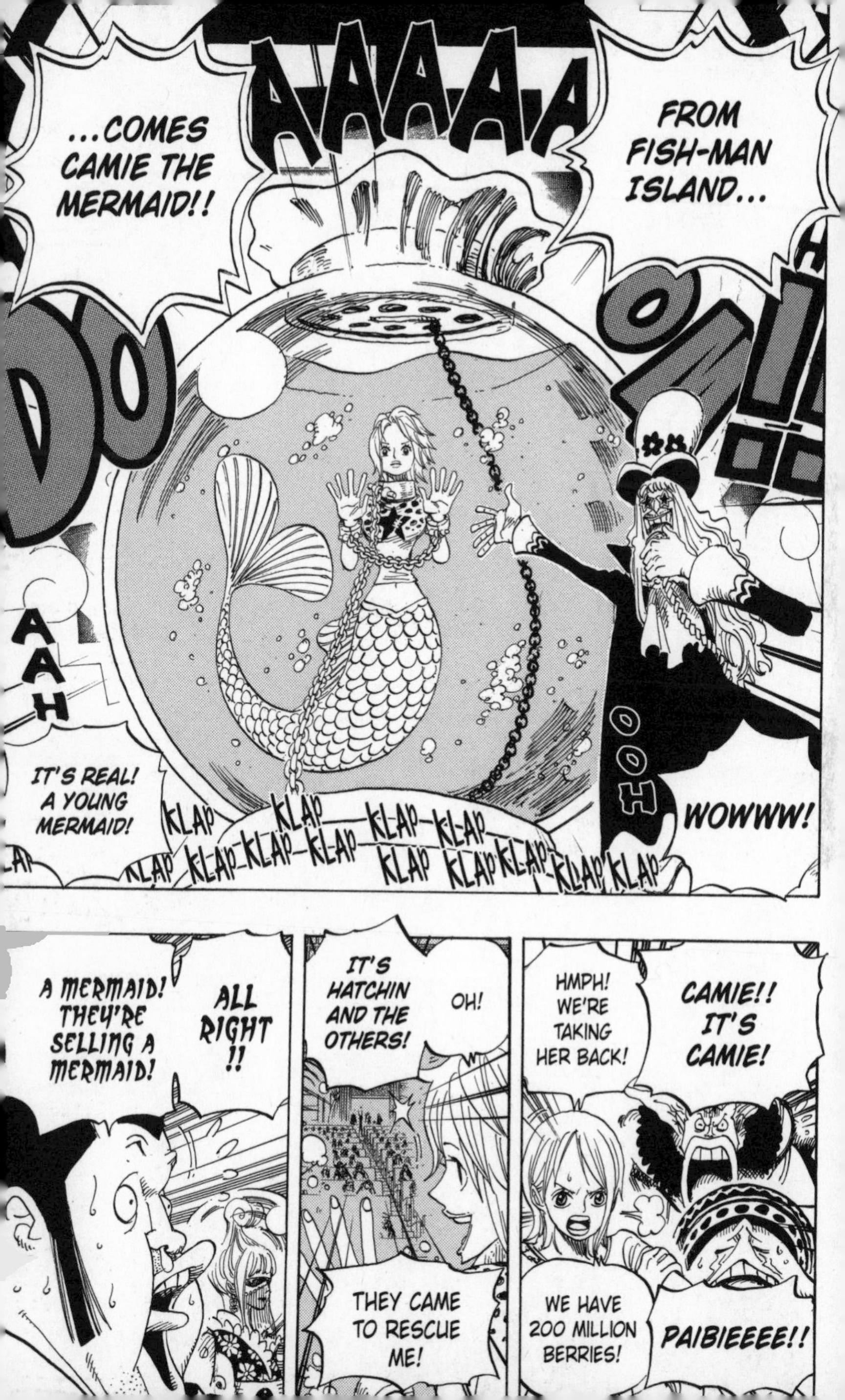
FROM FISH-MAN ISLAND...
AAAAA
...COMES CAMIE THE MERMAID!!
OOH
WOWWW!
AAH
IT'S REAL! A YOUNG MERMAID!
KLAP KLAP KLAP KLAP KLAP KLAP KLAP KLAP KLAP KLAP KLAP KLAP KLAP
CAMIE!! IT'S CAMIE!
HMPH! WE'RE TAKING HER BACK!
PAIBIEEEE!!
WE HAVE 200 MILLION BERRIES!
OH!
IT'S HATCHIN AND THE OTHERS!
THEY CAME TO RESCUE ME!
ALL RIGHT!!
A MERMAID! THEY'RE SELLING A MERMAID!

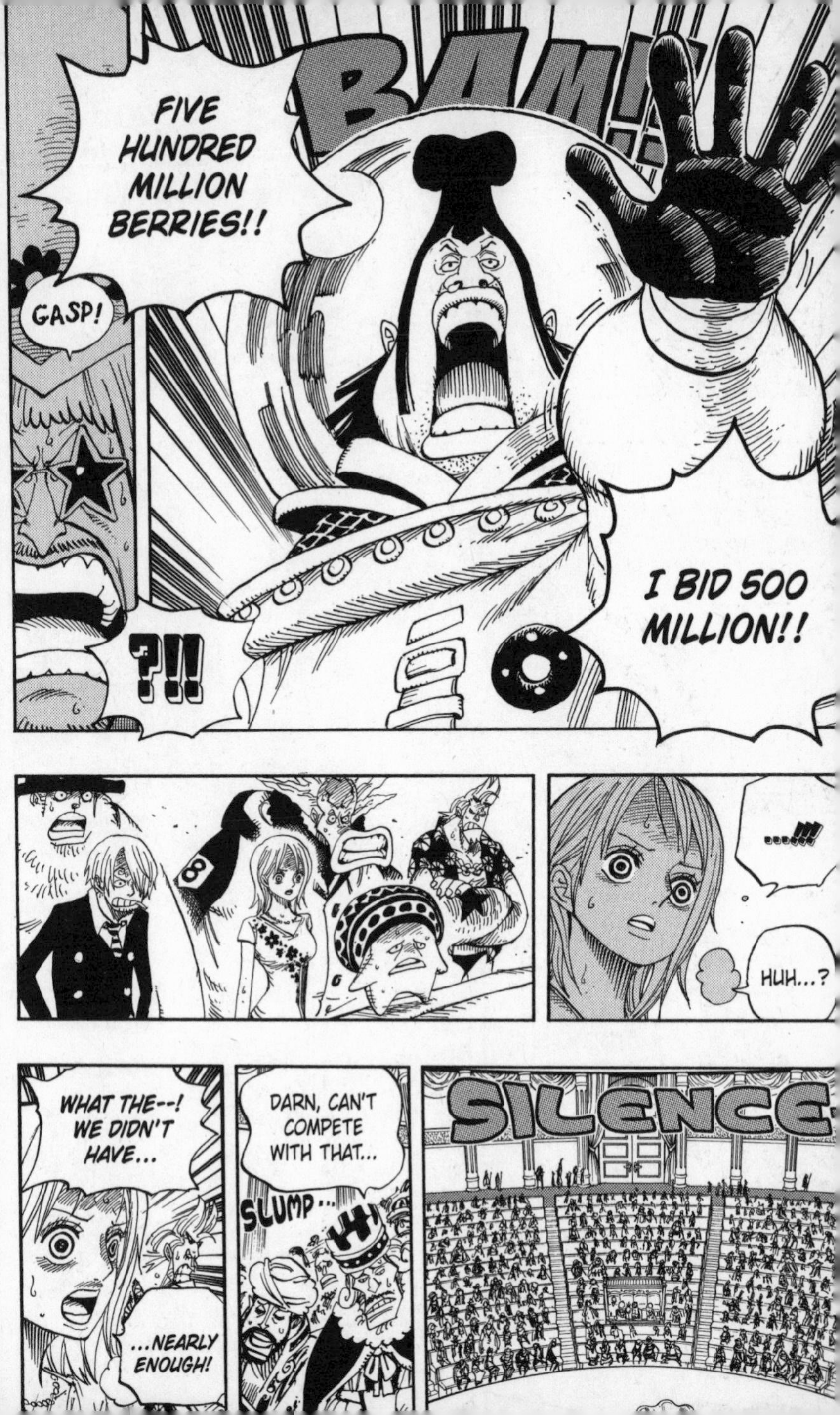
BAM!!
FIVE HUNDRED MILLION BERRIES!!
I BID 500 MILLION!!
GASP!
?!!
...!!!
HUH...?
SILENCE
DARN, CAN'T COMPETE WITH THAT...
SLUMP...
WHAT THE--! WE DIDN'T HAVE...
...NEARLY ENOUGH!

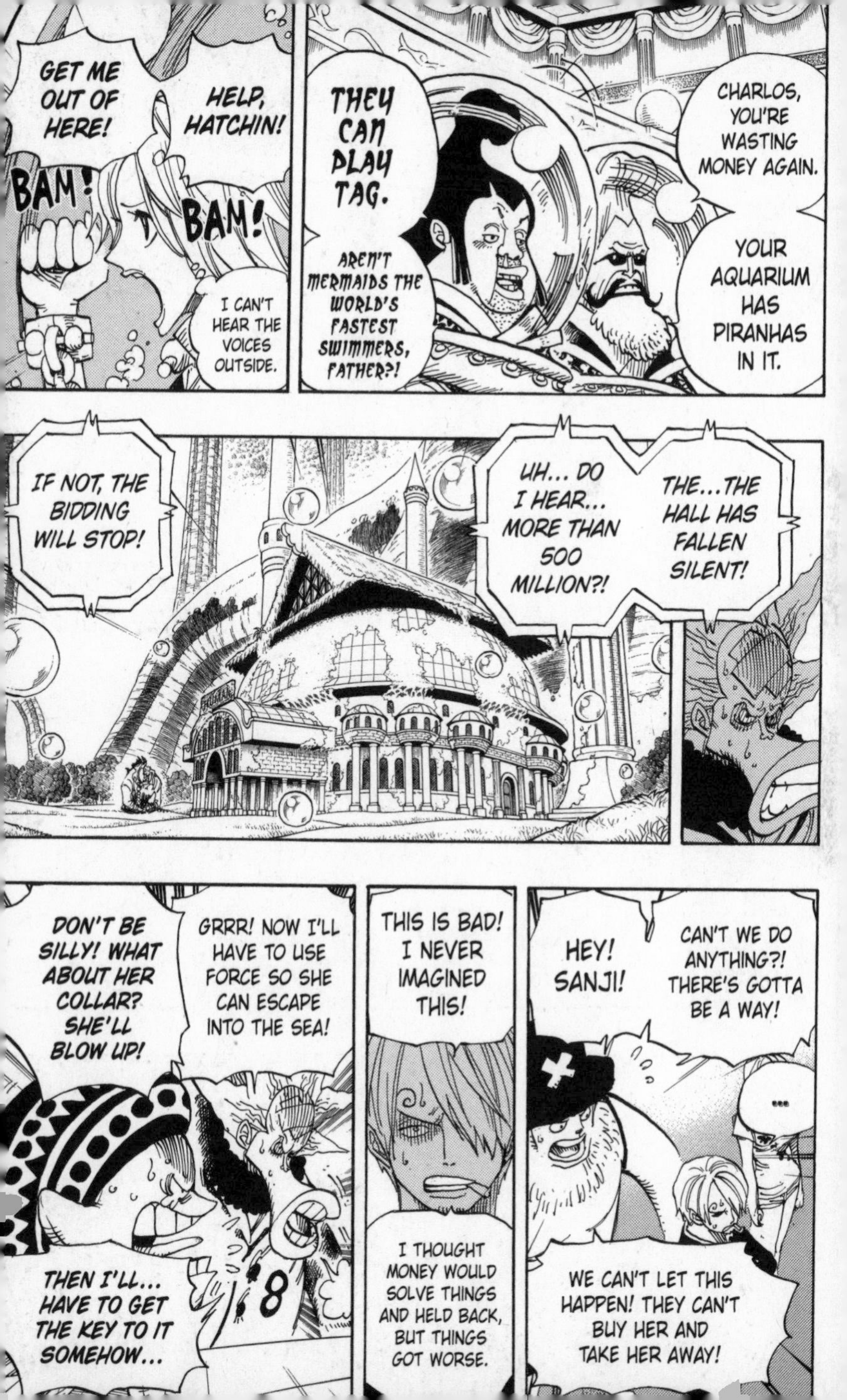
CHARLOS, YOU'RE WASTING MONEY AGAIN.
YOUR AQUARIUM HAS PIRANHAS IN IT.
THEY CAN PLAY TAG.
AREN'T MERMAIDS THE WORLD'S FASTEST SWIMMERS, FATHER?!
HELP, HATCHIN!
GET ME OUT OF HERE!
BAM!
BAM!
I CAN'T HEAR THE VOICES OUTSIDE.
THE...THE HALL HAS FALLEN SILENT!
UH... DO I HEAR... MORE THAN 500 MILLION?!
IF NOT, THE BIDDING WILL STOP!
CAN'T WE DO ANYTHING?! THERE'S GOTTA BE A WAY!
HEY! SANJI!
...
WE CAN'T LET THIS HAPPEN! THEY CAN'T BUY HER AND TAKE HER AWAY!
THIS IS BAD! I NEVER IMAGINED THIS!
I THOUGHT MONEY WOULD SOLVE THINGS AND HELD BACK, BUT THINGS GOT WORSE.
GRRR! NOW I'LL HAVE TO USE FORCE SO SHE CAN ESCAPE INTO THE SEA!
DON'T BE SILLY! WHAT ABOUT HER COLLAR? SHE'LL BLOW UP!
THEN I'LL... HAVE TO GET THE KEY TO IT SOMEHOW...

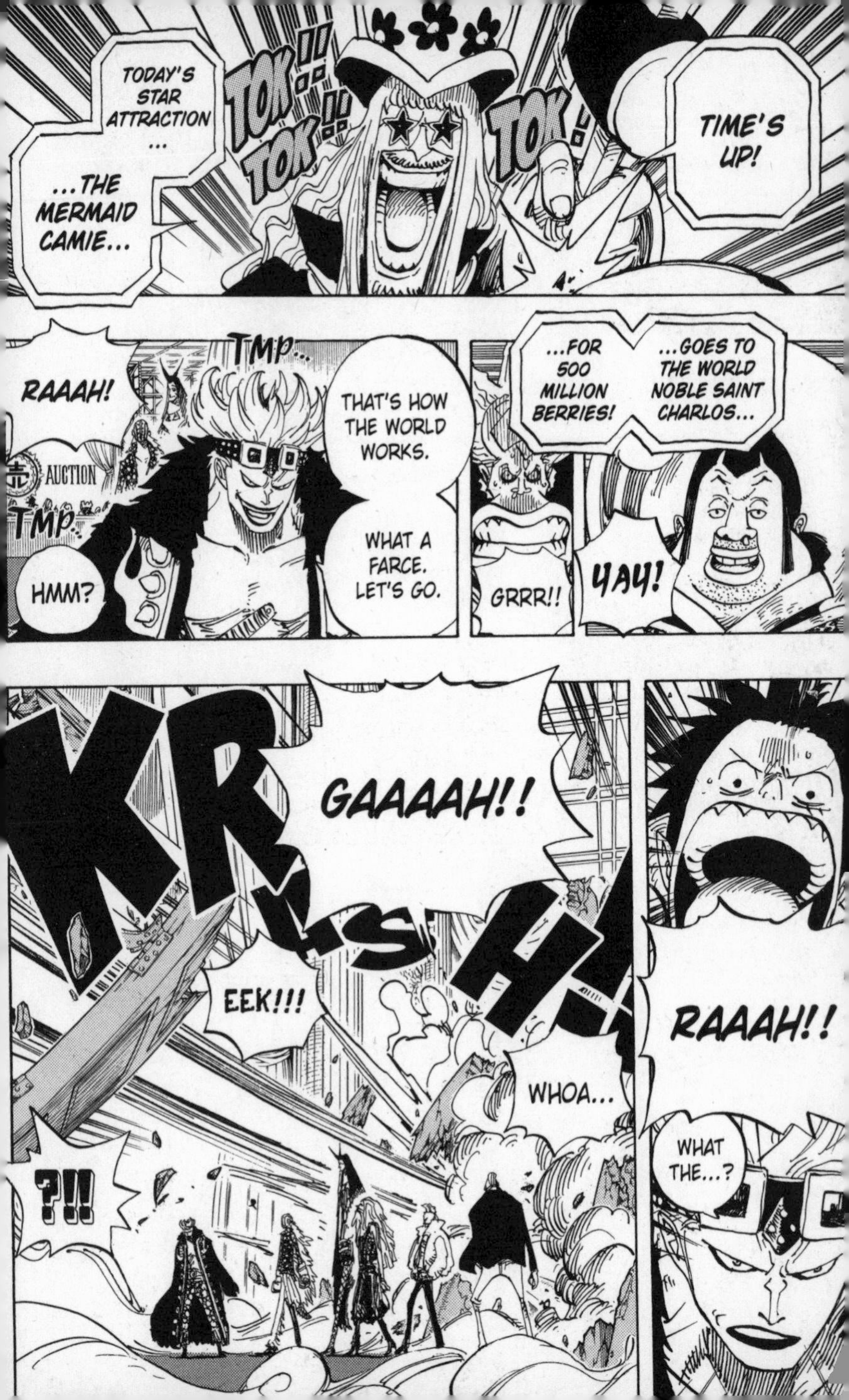
TIME'S UP!
TOK!!
TOK!!
TOK!!
TODAY'S STAR ATTRACTION...
...THE MERMAID CAMIE...
...GOES TO THE WORLD NOBLE SAINT CHARLOS...
...FOR 500 MILLION BERRIES!
YAY!
GRRR!!
TMP...
THAT'S HOW THE WORLD WORKS.
WHAT A FARCE. LET'S GO.
RAAAH!
AUCTION
TMP...
HMM?
RAAAH!!
WHAT THE...?
GAAAAH!!
KRASH
EEK!!!
WHOA...
?!!

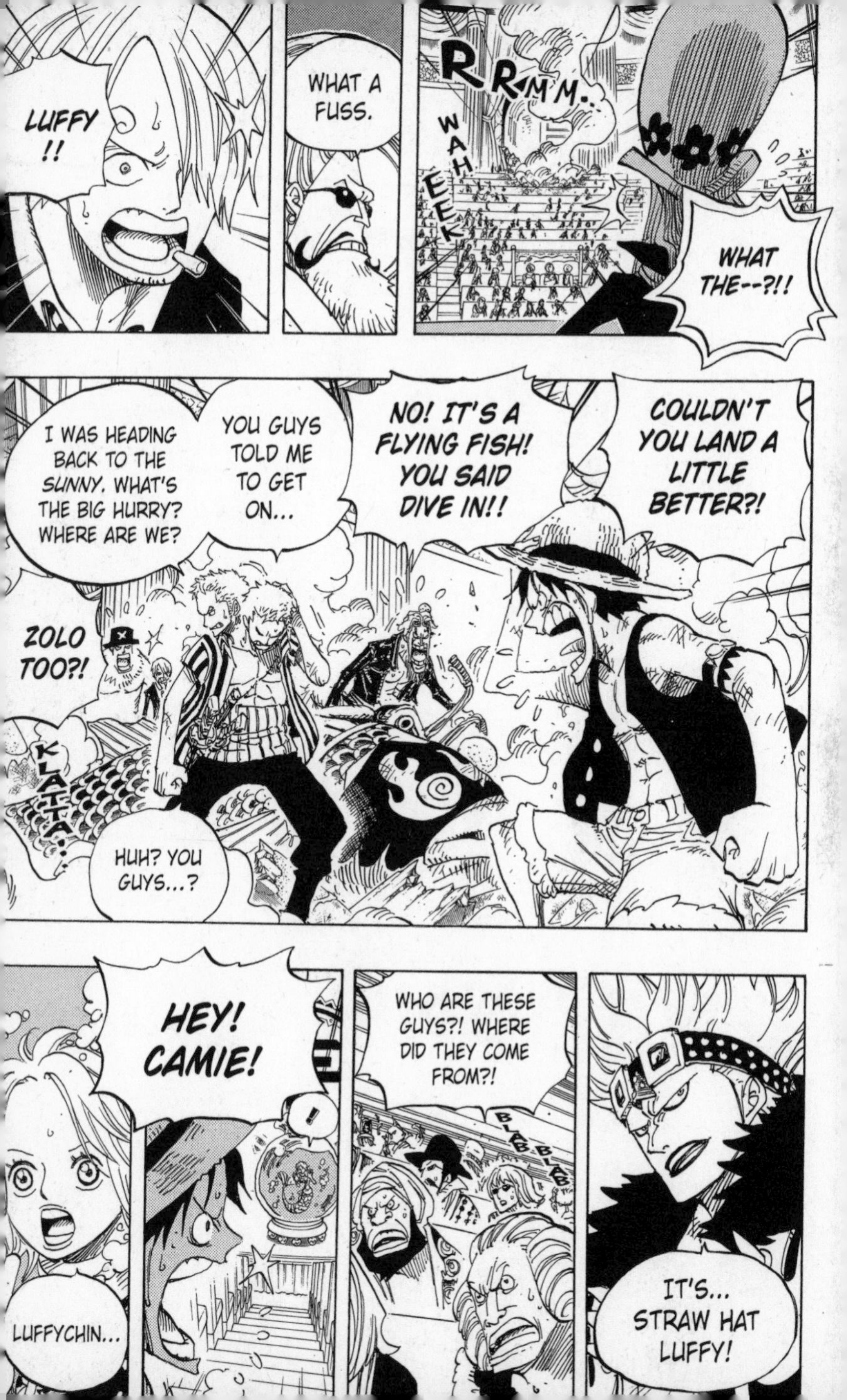
RRMM...
WAH
EEK
WHAT THE--?!!
WHAT A FUSS.
LUFFY!!
COULDN'T YOU LAND A LITTLE BETTER?!
NO! IT'S A FLYING FISH! YOU SAID DIVE IN!!
YOU GUYS TOLD ME TO GET ON...
I WAS HEADING BACK TO THE SUNNY. WHAT'S THE BIG HURRY? WHERE ARE WE?
ZOLO TOO?!
KLATTA!
HUH? YOU GUYS...?
IT'S... STRAW HAT LUFFY!
WHO ARE THESE GUYS?! WHERE DID THEY COME FROM?!
BLAB BLAB
HEY! CAMIE!
!
LUFFYCHIN...

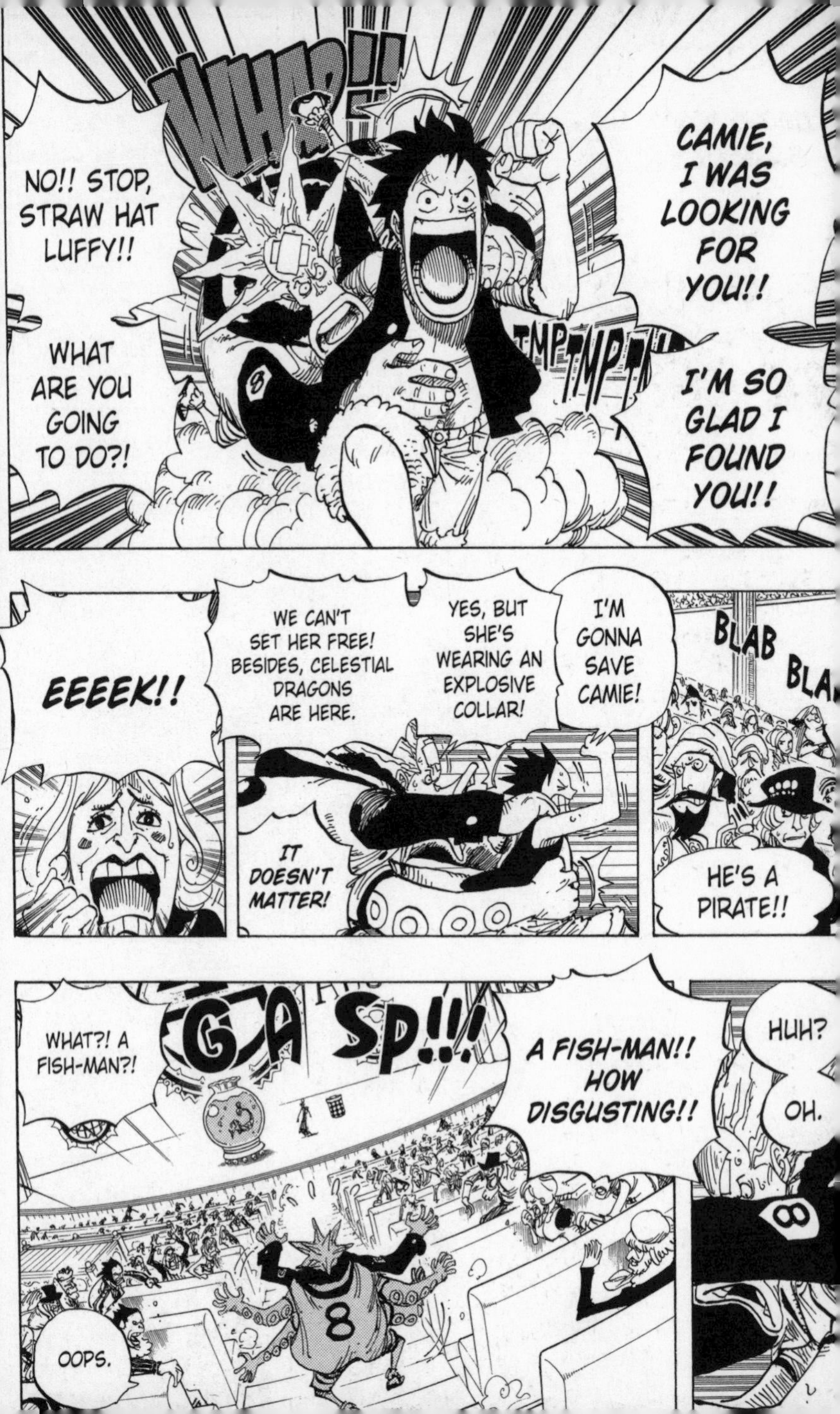
CAMIE, I WAS LOOKING FOR YOU!!
I'M SO GLAD I FOUND YOU!!
WHAP!!
TMP TMP
NO!! STOP, STRAW HAT LUFFY!!
WHAT ARE YOU GOING TO DO?!
BLAB
HE'S A PIRATE!!
I'M GONNA SAVE CAMIE!
YES, BUT SHE'S WEARING AN EXPLOSIVE COLLAR!
WE CAN'T SET HER FREE! BESIDES, CELESTIAL DRAGONS ARE HERE.
IT DOESN'T MATTER!
EEEEK!!
HUH?
OH.
A FISH-MAN!! HOW DISGUSTING!!
GASP!!!
WHAT?! A FISH-MAN?!
OOPS.

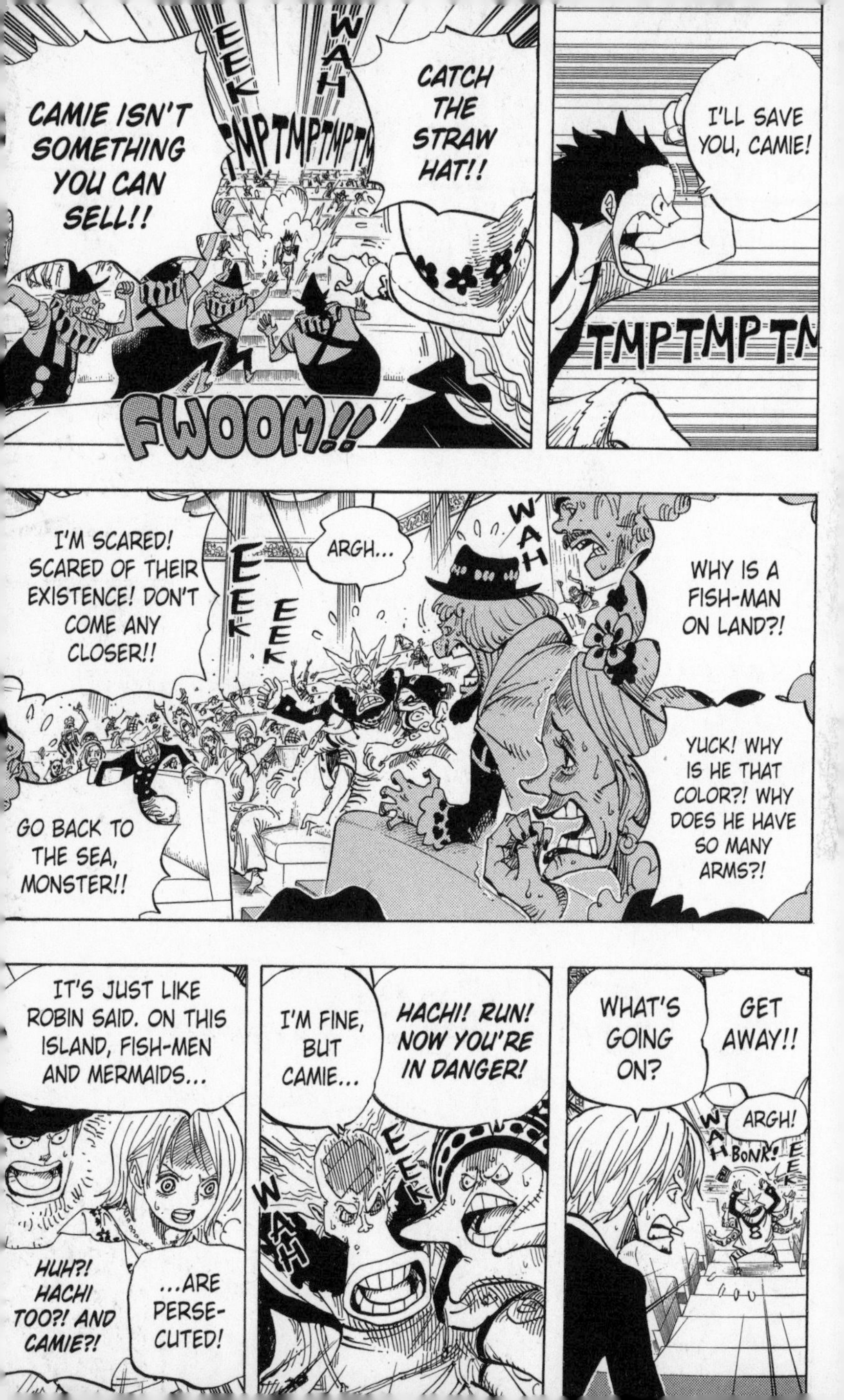

I'LL SAVE YOU, CAMIE!
TMPTMPTM
CATCH THE STRAW HAT!!
WAH
EEK
TMPTMPTMPTM
CAMIE ISN'T SOMETHING YOU CAN SELL!!
FWOOM!!
WAH
WHY IS A FISH-MAN ON LAND?!
YUCK! WHY IS HE THAT COLOR?! WHY DOES HE HAVE SO MANY ARMS?!
ARGH...
EEK
EEK
I'M SCARED! SCARED OF THEIR EXISTENCE! DON'T COME ANY CLOSER!!
GO BACK TO THE SEA, MONSTER!!
GET AWAY!!
WHAT'S GOING ON?
ARGH!
WAH
BONK!
EEK
HACHI! RUN! NOW YOU'RE IN DANGER!
I'M FINE, BUT CAMIE...
EEK
WAH
IT'S JUST LIKE ROBIN SAID. ON THIS ISLAND, FISH-MEN AND MERMAIDS...
...ARE PERSECUTED!
HUH?! HACHI TOO?! AND CAMIE?!

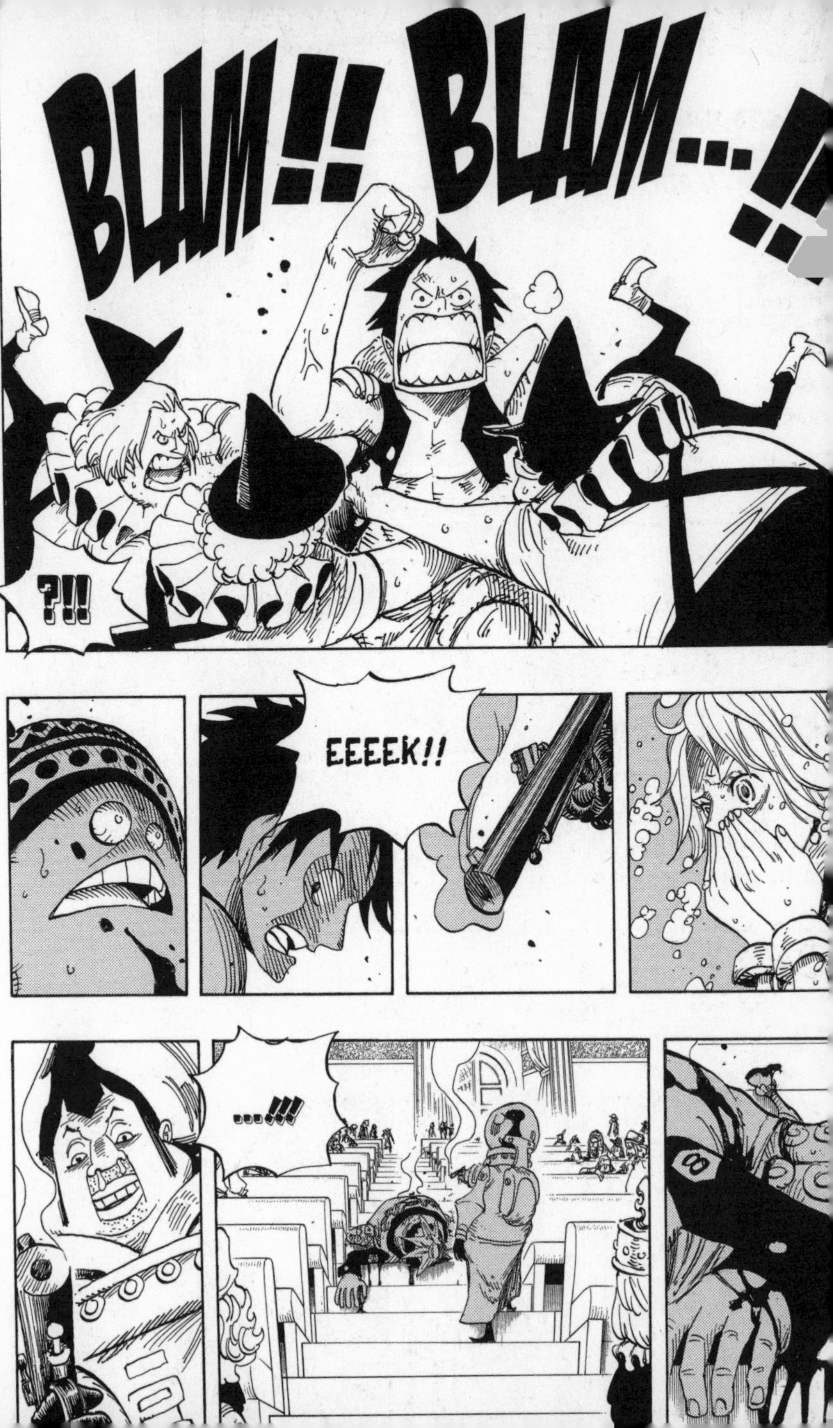
BLAM!! BLAM...!!
?!!
EEEEK!!
...!!!

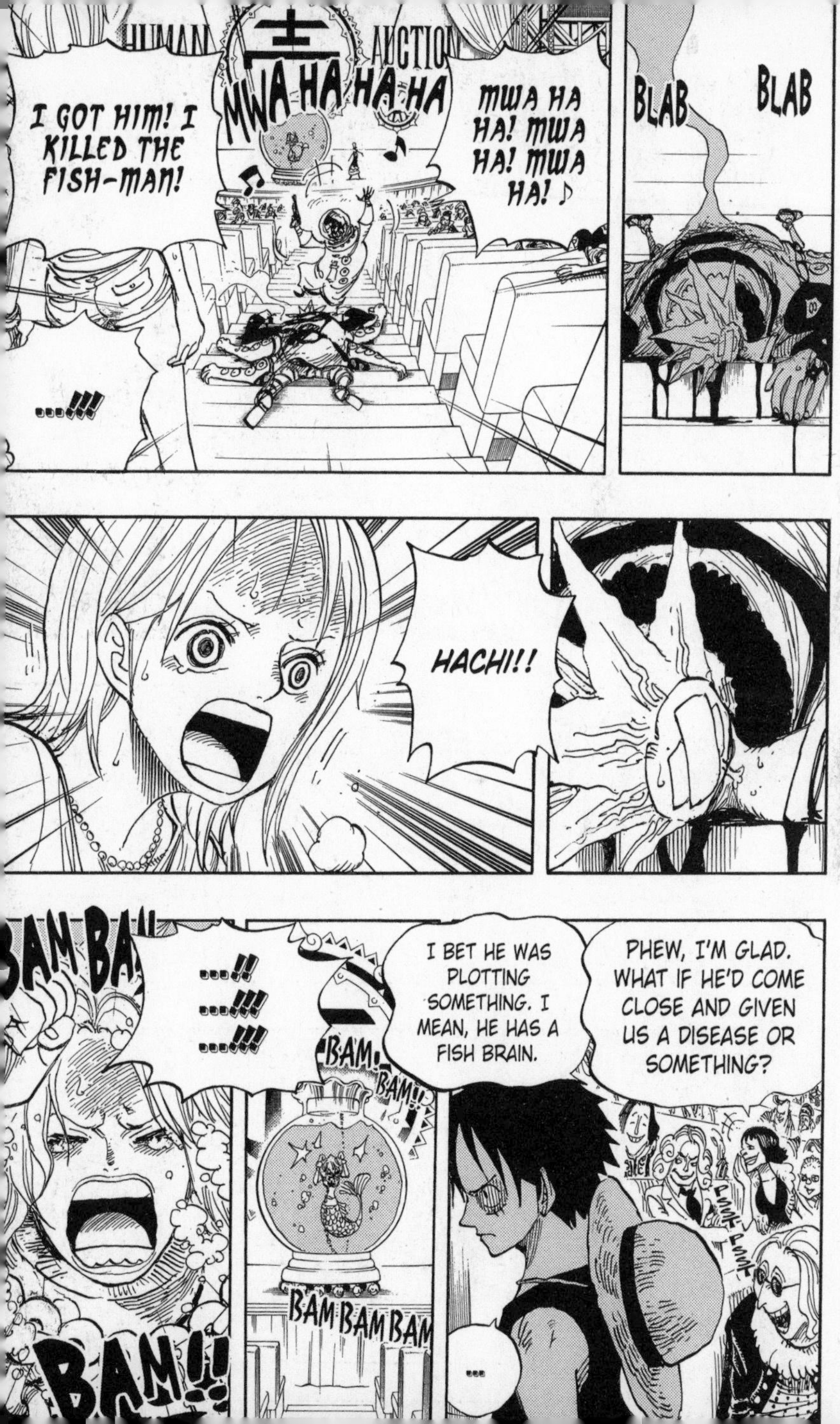
BLAB BLAB
HUMAN AUCTION
MWA HA HA! MWA HA! MWA HA! ♪
MWA HA HA HA
I GOT HIM! I KILLED THE FISH-MAN!
...!!!
HACHI!!
PHEW, I'M GLAD. WHAT IF HE'D COME CLOSE AND GIVEN US A DISEASE OR SOMETHING?
I BET HE WAS PLOTTING SOMETHING. I MEAN, HE HAS A FISH BRAIN.
PSST PSST
...
BAM BAM!!
BAM BAM BAM
...!!
...!!!
...!!!
BAM!!

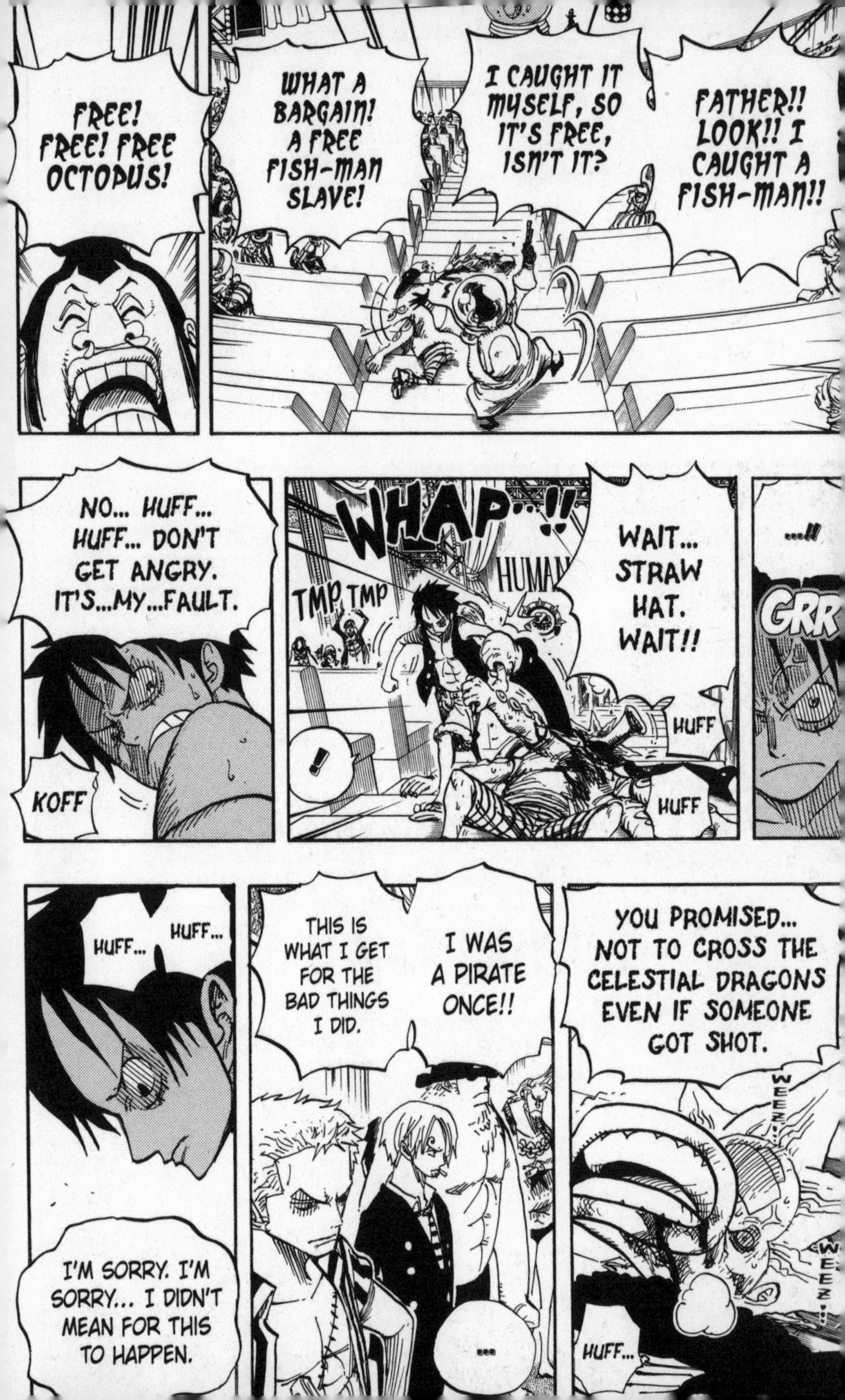
FATHER!! LOOK!! I CAUGHT A FISH-MAN!!
I CAUGHT IT MYSELF, SO IT'S FREE, ISN'T IT?
WHAT A BARGAIN! A FREE FISH-MAN SLAVE!
FREE! FREE! FREE OCTOPUS!
...!!
GRR
WAIT... STRAW HAT. WAIT!!
WHAP...!!
TMP TMP
!
HUFF
HUFF
NO... HUFF... HUFF... DON'T GET ANGRY. IT'S...MY...FAULT.
KOFF
YOU PROMISED... NOT TO CROSS THE CELESTIAL DRAGONS EVEN IF SOMEONE GOT SHOT.
WEEZ...
WEEZ...
HUFF...
I WAS A PIRATE ONCE!!
THIS IS WHAT I GET FOR THE BAD THINGS I DID.
...
HUFF... HUFF...
I'M SORRY. I'M SORRY... I DIDN'T MEAN FOR THIS TO HAPPEN.

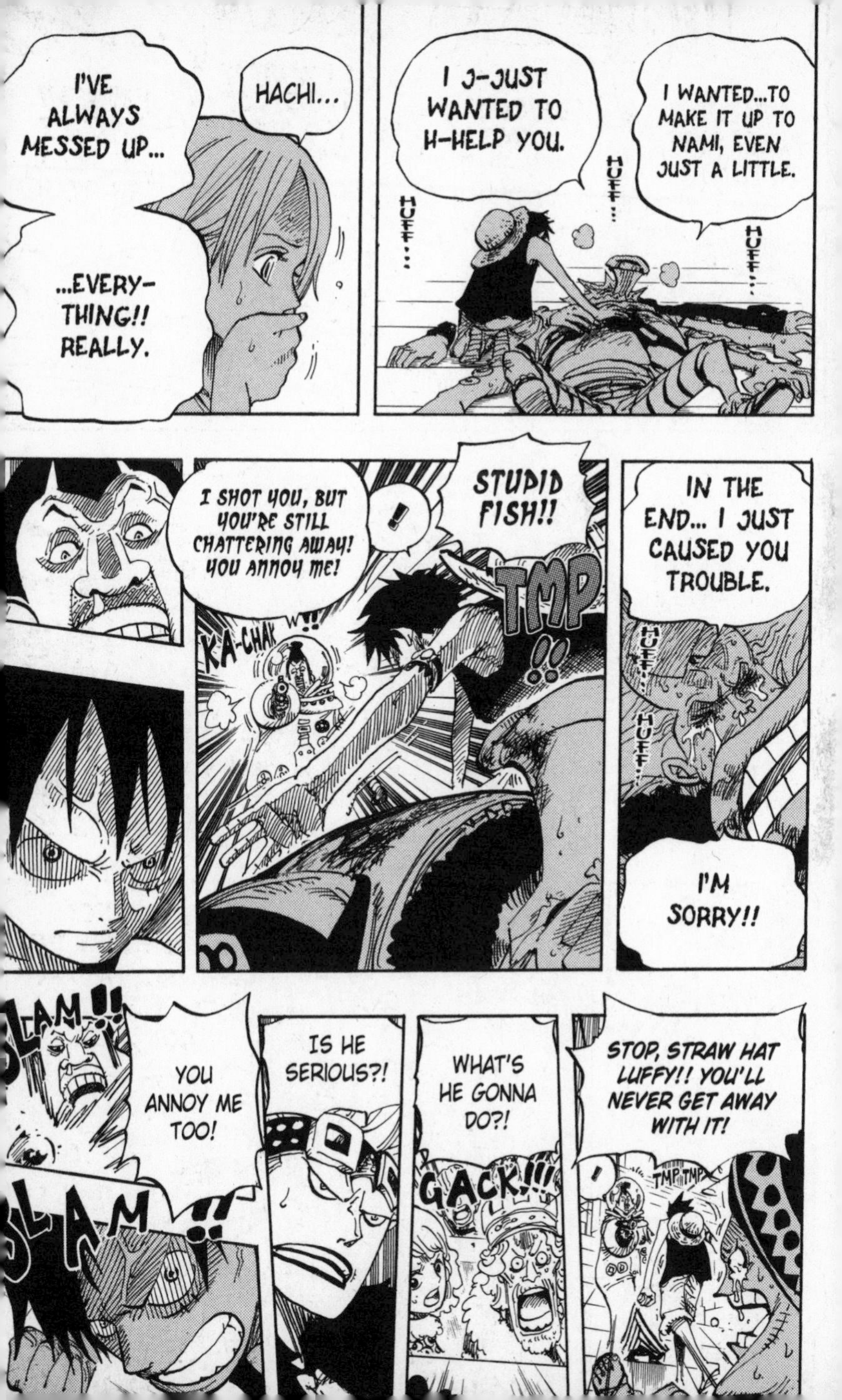
I WANTED...TO MAKE IT UP TO NAMI, EVEN JUST A LITTLE.
HUFF...
I J-JUST WANTED TO H-HELP YOU.
HUFF...
HUFF...
HACHI...
I'VE ALWAYS MESSED UP...
...EVERY-THING!! REALLY.
IN THE END... I JUST CAUSED YOU TROUBLE.
HUFF...
HUFF...
I'M SORRY!!
STUPID FISH!!
!
I SHOT YOU, BUT YOU'RE STILL CHATTERING AWAY! YOU ANNOY ME!
TMP!!
KA-CHAK!!
STOP, STRAW HAT LUFFY!! YOU'LL NEVER GET AWAY WITH IT!
!
TMP TMP
WHAT'S HE GONNA DO?!
GACK!!!
IS HE SERIOUS?!
YOU ANNOY ME TOO!
SLAM!!
SLAM!!

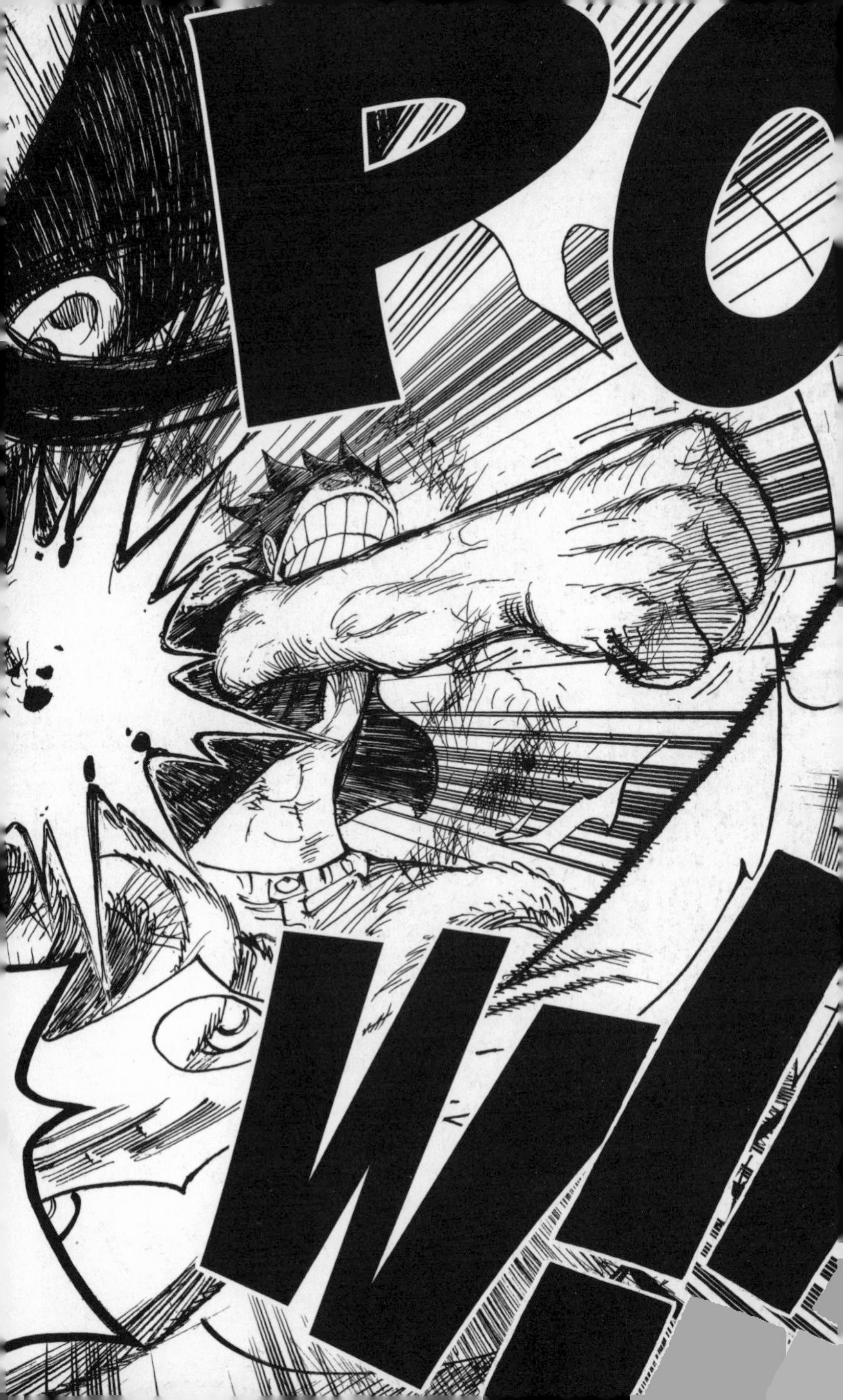
PO
W!!

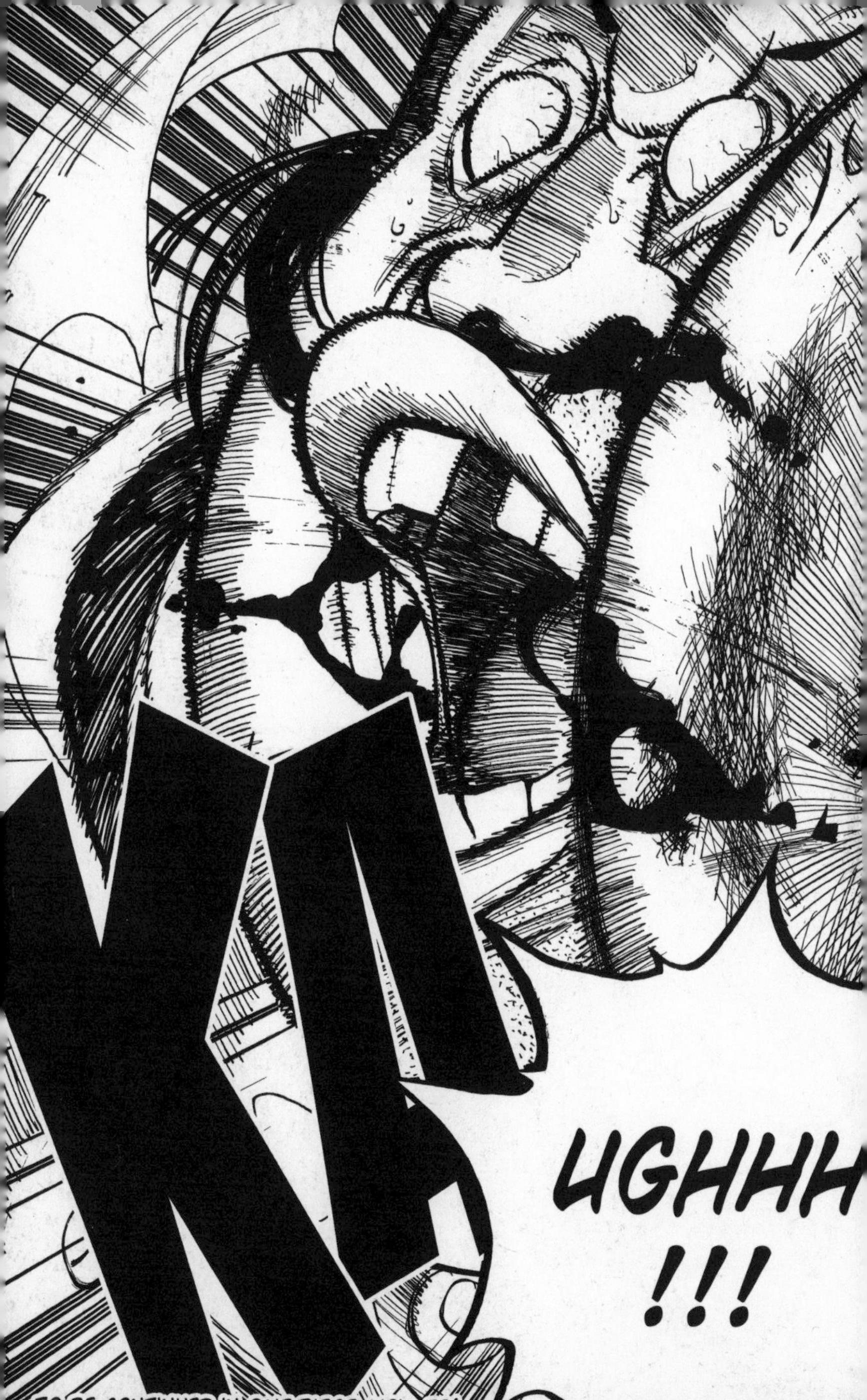
UGHHH
!!!

TO BE CONTINUED IN ONE PIECE, VOL. 52!

COMING NEXT VOLUME:

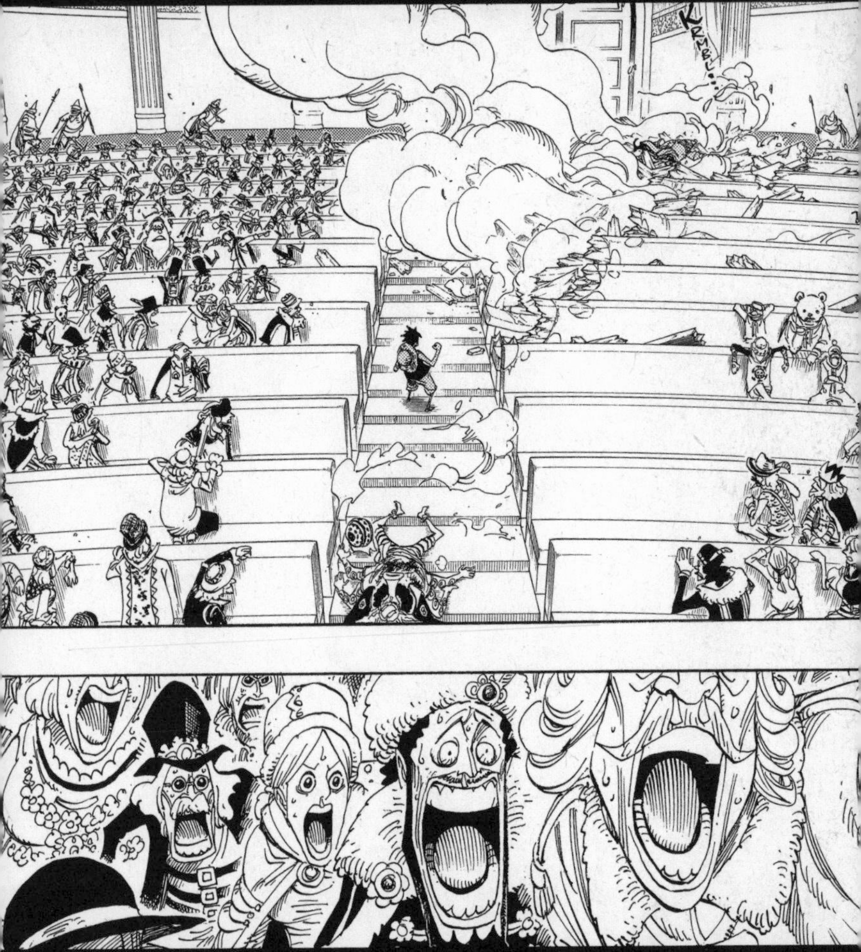
KRMBL...

Luffy tries to save Camie from being sold to the highest bidder and attacks an exalted Celestial Dragon, giving the Navy an excuse to send the admirals after him. But the Straw Hats get help from an unexpected source!

ON SALE NOW!

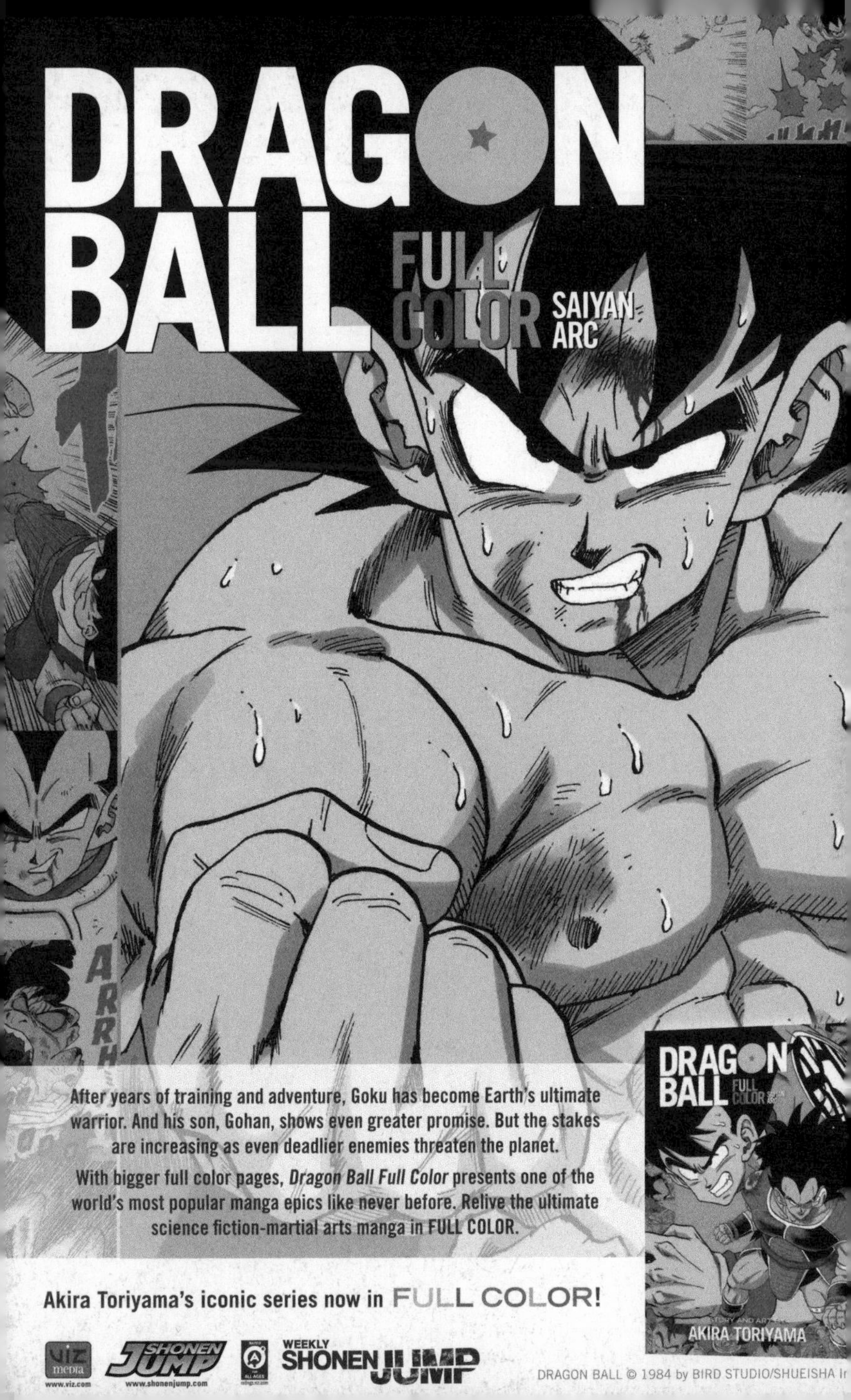
DRAGON BALL
FULL COLOR
SAIYAN ARC
ARRH
After years of training and adventure, Goku has become Earth's ultimate warrior. And his son, Gohan, shows even greater promise. But the stakes are increasing as even deadlier enemies threaten the planet.
With bigger full color pages, *Dragon Ball Full Color* presents one of the world's most popular manga epics like never before. Relive the ultimate science fiction-martial arts manga in FULL COLOR.
Akira Toriyama's iconic series now in FULL COLOR!
DRAGON BALL FULL COLOR
AKIRA TORIYAMA
VIZ media
www.viz.com
SHONEN JUMP
www.shonenjump.com
WEEKLY SHONEN JUMP
DRAGON BALL © 1984 by BIRD STUDIO/SHUEISHA Ir

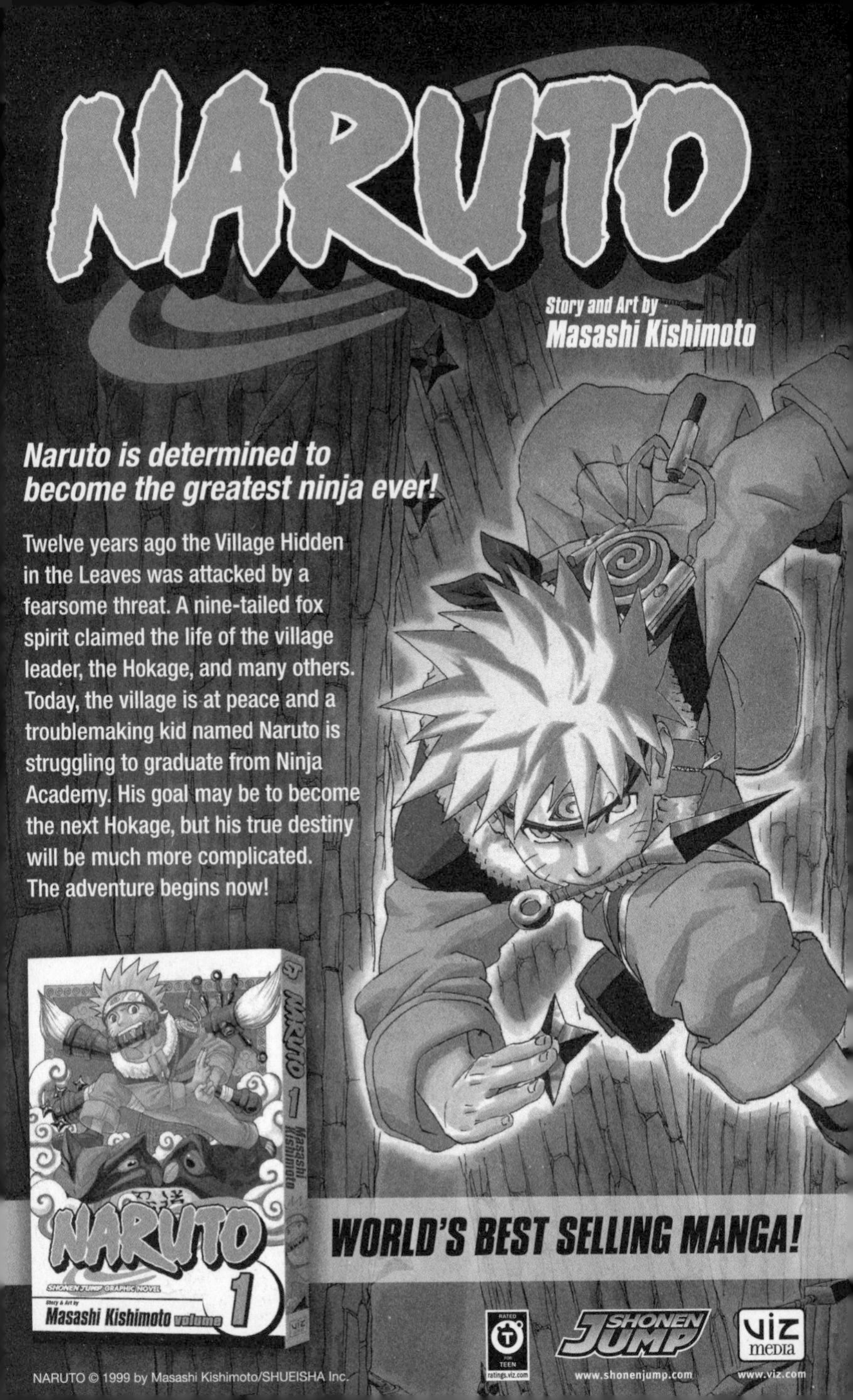
NARUTO
Story and Art by
Masashi Kishimoto
Naruto is determined to become the greatest ninja ever!
Twelve years ago the Village Hidden in the Leaves was attacked by a fearsome threat. A nine-tailed fox spirit claimed the life of the village leader, the Hokage, and many others. Today, the village is at peace and a troublemaking kid named Naruto is struggling to graduate from Ninja Academy. His goal may be to become the next Hokage, but his true destiny will be much more complicated. The adventure begins now!
NARUTO
SHONEN JUMP GRAPHIC NOVEL
Story & Art by
Masashi Kishimoto volume 1
WORLD'S BEST SELLING MANGA!
RATED T TEEN
ratings.viz.com
SHONEN JUMP
www.shonenjump.com
VIZ media
www.viz.com
NARUTO © 1999 by Masashi Kishimoto/SHUEISHA Inc.

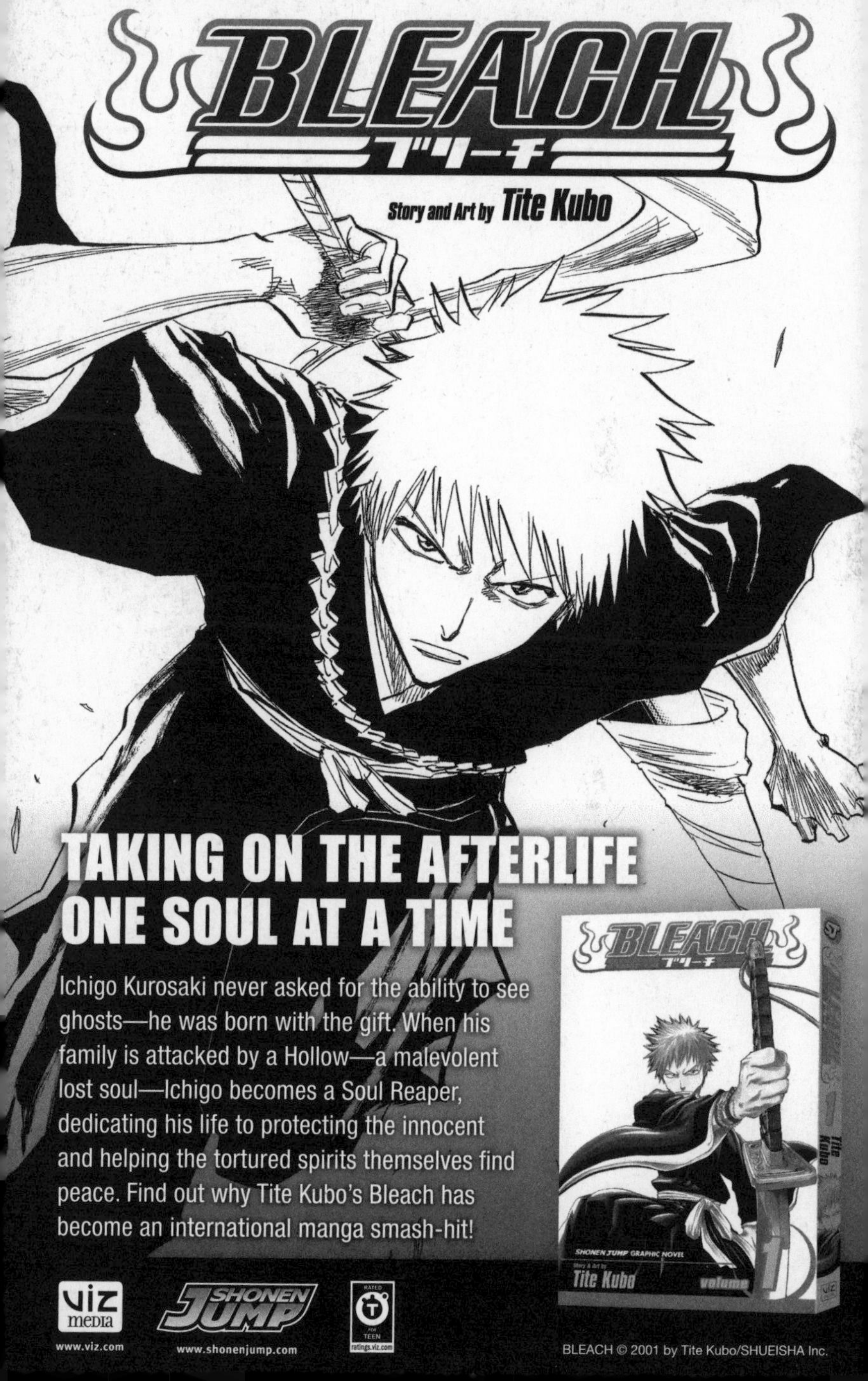
BLEACH
ブリーチ
Story and Art by Tite Kubo
TAKING ON THE AFTERLIFE ONE SOUL AT A TIME
Ichigo Kurosaki never asked for the ability to see ghosts—he was born with the gift. When his family is attacked by a Hollow—a malevolent lost soul—Ichigo becomes a Soul Reaper, dedicating his life to protecting the innocent and helping the tortured spirits themselves find peace. Find out why Tite Kubo's Bleach has become an international manga smash-hit!
BLEACH
ブリーチ
SHONEN JUMP GRAPHIC NOVEL
Story & Art by
Tite Kubo
volume 1
viz media
SHONEN JUMP
RATED T FOR TEEN
ratings.viz.com
www.viz.com
www.shonenjump.com
BLEACH © 2001 by Tite Kubo/SHUEISHA Inc.

IN A SAVAGE WORLD RULED BY THE PURSUIT OF THE MOST DELICIOUS FOODS, IT'S EITHER EAT OR BE EATEN!

"The most bizarrely entertaining manga out there on comic shelves. *Toriko* is a great series. If you're looking for a weirdly fun book or a fighting manga with a bizarre take, this is the story for you to read."

—ComicAttack.com

TORIKO

Story and Art by Mitsutoshi Shimabukuro

In an era where the world's gone crazy for increasingly bizarre gourmet foods, only Gourmet Hunter Toriko can hunt down the ferocious ingredients that supply the world's best restaurants. Join Toriko as he tracks and defeats the tastiest and most dangerous animals with his bare hands.

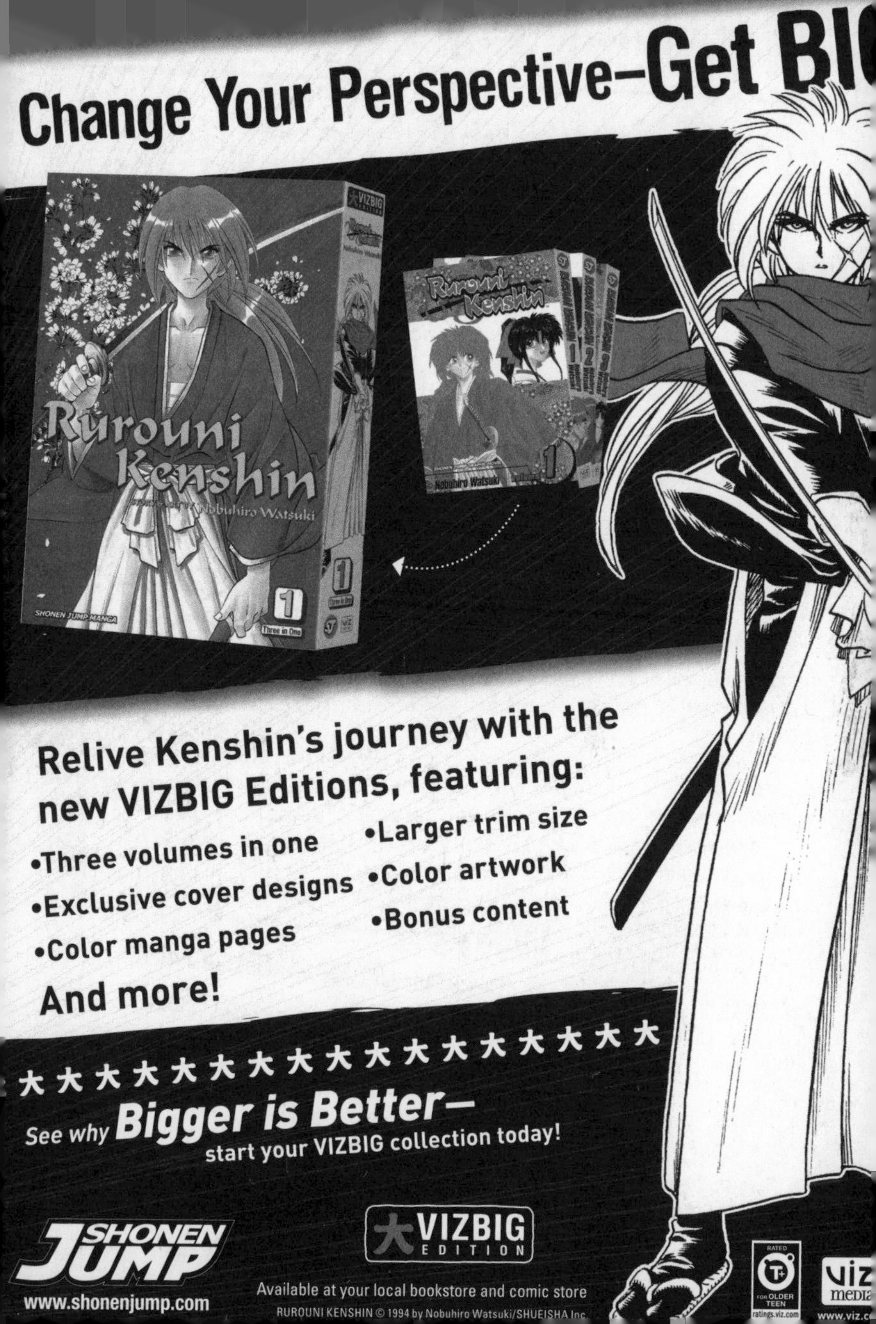
Change Your Perspective–Get BI
Relive Kenshin's journey with the new VIZBIG Editions, featuring:
•Three volumes in one
•Exclusive cover designs
•Color manga pages
•Larger trim size
•Color artwork
•Bonus content
And more!
See why Bigger is Better—
start your VIZBIG collection today!
SHONEN JUMP
www.shonenjump.com
VIZBIG EDITION
Available at your local bookstore and comic store
RUROUNI KENSHIN © 1994 by Nobuhiro Watsuki/SHUEISHA Inc.
RATED T+ FOR OLDER TEEN
ratings.viz.com

You're Reading in the Wrong Direction!!

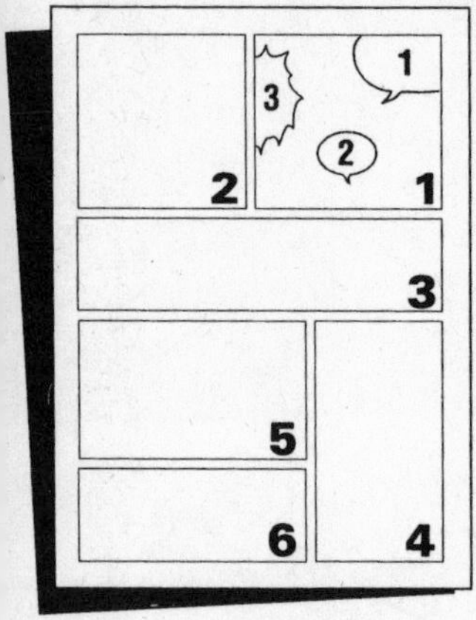
1
2
3
1
2
3
4
5
6

Whoops! Guess what? You're starting at the wrong end of the comic!

...It's true! In keeping with the original Japanese format, **One Piece** is meant to be read from right to left, starting in the upper-right corner.

Unlike English, which is read from left to right, Japanese is read from right to left, meaning that action, sound effects and word-balloon order are completely reversed...something which can make readers unfamiliar with Japanese feel pretty backwards themselves. For this reason, manga or Japanese comics published in the U.S. in English have sometimes been published "flopped"—that is, printed in exact reverse order, as though seen from the other side of a mirror.

By flopping pages, U.S. publishers can avoid confusing readers, but the compromise is not without its downside. For one thing, a character in a flopped manga series who once wore in the original Japanese version a T-shirt emblazoned with "M A Y" (as in "the merry month of") now wears one which reads "Y A M"! Additionally, many manga creators in Japan are themselves unhappy with the process, as some feel the mirror-imaging of their art skews their original intentions.

We are proud to bring you Eiichiro Oda's **One Piece** in the original unflopped format. For now, though, turn to the other side of the book and let the journey begin...!

–Editor

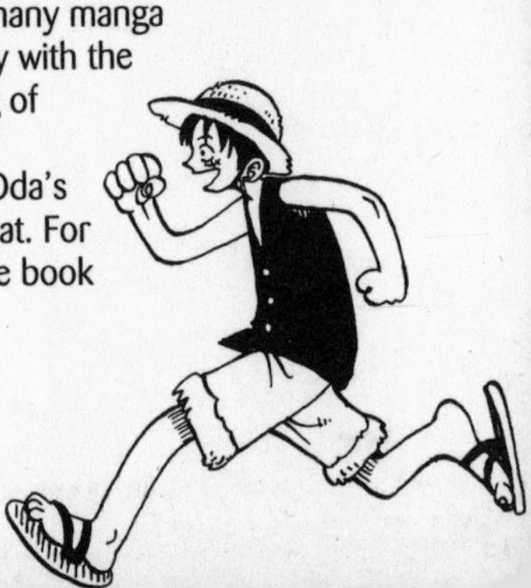